Sustainable Urban Development

Sustainable Urban Development Volume 2: The Environmental Assessment Methods offers contributions from leading authorities on the methodology of environmental assessment, providing a unique insight into questions of critical importance to sustainable urban development. Using the framework and protocols set out in Volume 1 as its point of departure, Volume 2 examines how well the environmental assessment methods evaluate the ecological integrity of urban development and equity of the resulting resource distribution. The examination focuses on:

- the instruments of environmental assessment
- approaches to environmental assessment based in systems-thinking
- methods for environmental, economic and social assessments
- their use in evaluating the sustainability of urban development.

This is the second of three volumes in the research and debate of the BEQUEST (Building, Environmental Quality Evaluation for Sustainability) network funded by the European Commission. Together the books provide a framework, set of protocols, environmental assessment methods and toolkit for policy-makers, academics, professionals and advanced-level students in Urban Planning, Urban Property Development, Urban Design, Architecture, Construction and related areas of the Built Environment.

Mark Deakin is Senior Lecturer and Teaching Fellow at the School of the Built Environment, Napier University. **Gordon Mitchell** is Lecturer at the School of Geography and Institute for Transport Studies, Leeds University. **Peter Nijkamp** is Professor in Regional and Urban Economics and Economic Geography at the VU University, Amsterdam. **Ron Vreeker** is Lecturer and Researcher at the Department of Spatial Economics, VU University, Amsterdam.

Sustainable Urban Development
Editors:
Steven Curwell, Salford University, UK
Mark Deakin, Napier University, UK
Martin Symes, University of the West of England, UK

Sustainable Urban Development Volume 1
The Framework and Protocols for Environmental Assessment
Steven Curwell, Mark Deakin and Martin Symes (eds)

Sustainable Urban Development Volume 2
The Environmental Assessment Methods
Mark Deakin, Gordon Mitchell, Peter Nijkamp and Ron Vreeker (eds)

Sustainable Urban Development Volume 3   Publishing 2007
A Toolkit for Assessment
Ron Vreeker, Mark Deakin and Steven Curwell (eds)

These volumes are based on the research and debate of the European BEQUEST network (**B**uilding **E**nvironmental **QU**ality **E**valuation for **S**us**T**ainability). Together the books provide a toolkit of interest and value to policy-makers, professionals and advanced-level students in a variety of disciplines.

Sustainable Urban Development

Volume 2: The Environmental Assessment Methods

Edited by Mark Deakin, Gordon Mitchell,
Peter Nijkamp and Ron Vreeker

Routledge
Taylor & Francis Group

LONDON AND NEW YORK

First published 2007
by Routledge
2 Park Square, Milton Park, Abingdon, Oxon OX14 4RN

Simultaneously published in the USA and Canada
by Routledge
270 Madison Ave, New York, NY 10016

Routledge is an imprint of the Taylor & Francis Group, an informa business

© 2007 Mark Deakin, Gordon Mitchell, Peter Nijkamp and Ron Vreeker for
selection and editorial material; individual chapters, the contributors

Typeset in Akzidenz Grotesk by
Integra Software Services Pvt. Ltd., Pondicherry, India
Printed and bound in Great Britain by
The Cromwell Press, Trowbridge, Wiltshire

British Library Cataloguing in Publication Data
A catalogue record for this book is available from the British Library

Library of Congress Cataloging in Publication Data
Sustainable urban development / edited by Stephen Curwell, Mark Deakin and
Martin Symes.-- 1 st ed.
p. cm.
Includes bibliographical references and index.
ISBN 0-415-32214-6 (hb : alk. paper) -- ISBN 0-415-32215-4 (pb : alk. paper) --
ISBN 0-203-29991-4
1. City planning.   2. Sustainable development.   I. Curwell, S. R.,
1950-   II. Deakin, Mark.   III. Symes, Martin.
HT166.S9134 2005
307.1'216--dc22
2004030447

ISBN10: 0-415-32216-2 (hbk)
ISBN10: 0-415-32217-0 (pbk)
ISBN10: 0-203-41703-8 (ebk)

ISBN13: 978-0-415-32216-4 (hbk)
ISBN13: 978-0-415-32217-1 (pbk)
ISBN13: 978-0-203-41703-4 (ebk)

Contents

Contributors

Tüzin Baycan-Levent, Technical University of Istanbul

Andreas Blum, Leibniz-Institute of Ecological and Regional Development, Dresden

Peter Brandon, School of Construction and Property Management, University of Salford

Frank Bruinsma, Department of Spatial Economics, Vrije Universiteit, Amsterdam

Maria Cerreta, University of Naples 'Federico II'

Steven Curwell, School of Construction and Property Management, Salford University

Katherine A. Daniell, Australian National University

Mark Deakin, School of the Built Environment, Napier University, Edinburgh

Bernadette A. Foley, School of Civil and Environmental Engineering, University of Adelaide, Australia

Fabiana Forte, Second University of Naples

Luigi Fusco Girard, University of Naples 'Federico II'

Simon Guy, School of Environment and Development, University of Manchester

Pekka Huovila, VTT Consultants, Helsinki

Ashley B. Kingsborough, KBR Adelaide, Australia

Niklaus Kohler, IFIB, University of Karlsruhe

René van der Kruk, Department of Spatial Economics, Vrije Universiteit, Amsterdam

Eveline van Leeuwen, Department of Spatial Economics, Vrije Universiteit, Amsterdam

Patrizia Lombardi, Casa-Citta Department, Polytechnic of Turin

Holger R. Maier, School of Civil and Environmental Engineering, University of Adelaide, Australia

David J. Malovka, KBR Adelaide, Australia

Simon Marvin, Sustainable Urban and Regional Futures (SURF), University of Salford

Gordon Mitchell, School of Geography, Leeds University

Giulio Mondini, Casa-Citta Department, Polytechnic of Turin

Andrea De Montis, Department of Engineering, University of Sassari

Giuseppe Munda, Department of Economics and Economic History, Universitat Autonoma de Barcelona

Peter Nijkamp, Department of Spatial Economics, Vrije Universiteit, Amsterdam

Paulo Nunes, John Hopkins University, Bologna

Caroline Rodenburg, Real Estate Advisory Services and International Location Advisory Services, Ernst & Young, Utrecht, The Netherlands

Craig Simmons, Best Foot Forward Co., Oxford

Heath C. Sommerville, SKM Melbourne, Australia

Klaus Spiekermann, Urban and Regional Research, Dortmund

Pasquale De Toro, University of Naples 'Federico II'

Marco Valle, Casa-Citta Department, Polytechnic of Turin

Ron Vreeker, Department of Spatial Economics, Vrije Universiteit, Amsterdam

Gordon Walker, Department of Geography, Lancaster University, Lancaster

Michael Wegener, Urban and Regional Research, Dortmund

Introduction

Mark Deakin, Gordon Mitchell, Peter Nijkamp and Ron Vreeker

Volume 1 of this book series began by outlining the principles, underlying concepts, model, vision and methodology of an integrated sustainable urban development (SUD) (Curwell et al., 2005). This drew attention to the framework BEQUEST has developed for such an understanding of SUD and went on to set out the protocol(s) the network argues should be followed for carrying out an environmental assessment. In this regard, Volume 1 argued:

- SUD's goal is to improve the quality of life for an increasingly urban population;
- actions aiming to improve the quality of life need a simple, clear framework for analysing the sustainability of urban development;
- this framework for analysis requires to provide a vision and methodology capable of bringing such concerns into the scope of actions targeting improvements in the quality of life;
- within this vision and methodology, protocol(s) provide a middle ground between the environmental assessment methods available to evaluate SUD and bring about improvements in the quality of life;
- such evaluations of SUD must transcend purely environmental factors and embed themselves securely in more comprehensive and integrated environmental, social and economic assessments;
- a community of academic and professional advisers is emerging, willing and able to use new information technology as a means of supporting such assessments and making the evaluations they produce available to local, regional, national and international agencies.

Having set out the BEQUEST framework, Volume 1 went on to develop the protocol for environmental assessment. This protocol was then presented as a set of guidelines to follow in assessing the environmental impact of urban development and as procedures for:

- 'screening' urban development activities;
- 'scoping' key sustainable development issues;
- 'clarifying' what activities – environmental, economic and social issues – need to be addressed;

- carrying out the required 'consultations' with affected parties;
- 'procuring' environmental assessments of urban development plans, programmes and projects;
- 'assessing' whether the said urban development plans, programmes and projects build the capacity which cities need to carry their cultural heritage and produce forms of human settlement that are sustainable;
- 'reporting' on the ecological integrity and equity of the resulting resource distribution and ability of the public to participate in decisions taken about the future of the city, its cultural heritage and forms of human settlement;
- 'monitoring' the sustainability of urban development.

The said protocol has its origins in the European Commission's (1997 and 2001) Directives on Environmental Impact Assessment (EIA) and Strategic Environmental Assessment (SEA) and points at the procedures to follow in assessing whether or not urban development plans, programmes and projects provide the capacity that cities need to support their cultural heritage and produce forms of human settlement which are sustainable. However, as Volume 1 went some length to point out, while such a representation of the protocol is valuable for the generic description of the environmental assessment process it advances, the procedures set out are currently not detailed enough to overcome the risk and uncertainty stakeholders face in trying to use them as methods for evaluating the sustainability of urban development.

As Volume 1 made clear, this is because the legal instruments surrounding environmental assessment are themselves insufficiently developed, too generic and not specific enough for stakeholders as diverse as planners, property developers, designers and construction contractors to follow in evaluating the sustainability of urban development. In response to this, Volume 1 went on to set out the 'soft' and 'hard' gates of environmental assessment and develop the five (planning, property development, design, construction, operation and use) protocols for evaluating the sustainability of urban development. Having done this, Volume 1 went on to outline the directory of environmental assessment methods available for such evaluations and reported on how they are currently being used to evaluate the sustainability of urban development. While this drew attention to the legal instruments of environmental assessment and tense relationship emerging between the 'hard' certainties of the bio-physical sciences and the more uncertain and risky sphere of economic and social relations, it did not provide a detailed account of the assessment methods, or examination of how those listed in the directory are currently being used to evaluate the sustainability of urban development. This is the object of Volume 2 in this series on *Sustainable Urban Development*.

VOLUME 2

Volume 2 on SUD takes the BEQUEST framework and protocols as its point of departure and brings together a number of contributions from recognized experts in environmental and SUD assessment and leading authorities in the use of such methods. The contributions provide a unique insight into environmental assessment and methodological questions of critical Importance to SUD. Volume 2 offers 23 contributions from leading authorities on the methodology of environmental assessment and are presented under the following headings:

- environmental assessment instruments;
- systems thinking-based approaches to assessment;
- environmental assessment methods;
- methods for environmental, economic and social assessments;
- evaluations of the ecological integrity, equity of resource distribution and participation of the public in matters concerning the future of urban development and sustainability of cities.

Part 1 of Volume 2 sets out the statutory instruments put in place by the European Commission (EC) to assess the environmental impact of urban development proposals. Focusing on the EU's 97/11/CE and 2001/42/CE Directives, it examines the development and use of strategic environmental assessment and environmental impact assessment to evaluate the sustainability of the development programme for the 2006 Winter Games. Part 2 uses these statutory instruments of environmental assessment as a platform to examine the systems thinking lying behind the methods, their approach to SUD and the role evaluation plays in this. Using this examination as a stage to account for further developments in environmental assessment, Part 3 sets out the methods that can be used to evaluate the sustainability of urban development. This section accounts for recent developments in the use of cost–benefit analysis (CBA) and multi-criteria analysis (MCA), contingent valuation method (CVM) and the hedonic price method used in environmental assessments. Part 4 examines the assessment methods that have recently emerged to meet the particular economic and social challenge SUD poses. Here attention is drawn to the environmental, economic and social assessments that have recently developed to evaluate SUD.

Parts 3 and 4 of the book are taken from BEQUEST's survey of the environmental assessment methods currently available for evaluating SUD. So far the survey has identified that 60 such methods are available to assess the environmental impact of urban development and sustainability of cities. It has also identified the methods that have been applied to the planning, property development, design, construction, operational and use activities of the urban development process and used by cities to evaluate the sustainability issues this raises at the various scales of assessment. The survey can be accessed via the website address for the BEQUEST project: http://www.surveying.salford.ac.uk/bq/extra. The website provides a list of the methods surveyed and in a number of cases offers hypertext links to the case-studies they have been drawn from. This provides the opportunity for the reader to explore the implications of applying the method in further detail and satisfying themselves as to whether the technique is appropriate for the matter under consideration.

The list of methods is drawn from a survey of the scientific literature and unpublished technical reports, written by professional members of the community. They have been drawn from textbooks, scientific journals and professional reports on the methodology of environmental assessment. The master list provides a survey of the assessment methods it is possible for cities in Europe, North America and Canada to use and case-study reviews of how they have been applied to evaluate the sustainability of urban development. In certain cases they represent assessment methods the partner and extranet members of BEQUEST have been engaged in developing, or have a detailed knowledge of (see Deakin et al., 2001, 2002a,b, 2004; Deakin and Lombardi, 2005a,b for further details of the survey).

Part 5 takes the evaluation of SUD full circle. This is achieved by reviewing how well the environmental assessment methods evaluate the ecological integrity of urban development and equity of the resulting resource distribution. Furthermore, this is done by evaluating whether or not this distribution of resources is based on decisions taken by the public participating in matters concerning the future of urban development and sustainability of cities.

THE ASSESSMENT METHODOLOGY

The assessment methodology Volume 2 adopts is based upon an understanding that the growing international and increasingly global nature of the relationship which exists between the environment and economy of civil society is uncertain, resulting in as yet incalculable degrees of risk and this in turn means standard 'tried and tested' methods of assessment are of limited help in evaluating SUD. Volume 2 argues the limitations of such standard measures can only be overcome by adopting a 'co-evolutionary approach' to environmental assessment and turning attention towards methods able to evaluate the ecology of resource consumption.

Volume 2 argues the value of this position lies in the opportunity that assessments of this kind provide to develop methods which apply the so-called 'hard' certainties of bio-physical science to the more uncertain, risky social relations of SUD – the relations that are 'softer' and which are by nature more difficult to predict. As shall be seen, this much-needed methodological development is achieved by emphasizing the co-evolutionary nature of the bio-physical and social in a framework of analysis with protocols that are cross-cutting and integrative and which in turn provide the assessments cities require for evaluating the sustainability of urban development. What is significant about this methodological development is the capacity it has not only to transcend the limitations of existing valuation techniques, but transform them into particular forms of assessment capable of evaluating SUD.

Taking this form, Volume 2 provides a detailed account of the environmental assessment methods key to this transformation. This provides the opportunity to highlight those assessment methods that are key to this transformation and building the environmental capacity which is needed to not only qualify the ecological integrity of urban development, but also provide the techniques of analysis required to evaluate whether this brings about an equitable distribution of resources. Evaluate whether the techniques of analysis bring about a distribution of resources which is equitable in the sense that it allows the public to participate in decisions affecting the economic and social future of cities. As such, Volume 2 provides the opportunity to provide a detailed account of those assessment methods that are key in **B**uilding the **E**nvironmental capacity which is needed to **QU**alify the ecological integrity of urban development and **E**valuate the equity of the public's participation in decisions affecting the future economic and social **S**us**T**ainability of cities.

A POST-BRUNDTLAND DIRECTORY OF ENVIRONMENTAL ASSESSMENT

Volume 2 on SUD presents what is referred to as a 'post-Brundtland directory of environmental assessment methods'. The objective of the said directory is fourfold. First, to direct decision-makers towards the master list of environmental assessment methods that are currently in existence and which it is possible for stakeholders to use in evaluating the sustainability of urban development. Secondly, to provide a standard description for each of the environmental assessment methods under consideration. Thirdly, to illustrate the classes of assessment the methods represent. Fourthly, to classify the assessment methods based on the complexity of the evaluations they advance. Here the stakeholders are represented as urban planners, property developers, designers (architects and engineers), construction contractors, operators and users. As each group offers expertise at various stages of the urban development process, it is recognized that each decision-maker requires to be directed towards a method of assessment which provides a detailed description of what each evaluation contributes to the sustainability of cities.

This is what the standard description of the assessment methods does. In providing a standard description of the assessment methods, it allows stakeholders to source the information of interest to them and to direct decision-makers towards the nature of the evaluation the techniques of analysis offers. Given the number of stakeholders in the urban development process and interests they represent, it is important to provide such a description because it is not always clear which sector of the community the assessment method is directed towards and what stage of the urban development process it relates to. The standard description aims to clarify these matters and avoid any such confusion over the use of the assessment methods. Ultimately, of course, the effects of the decisions taken on SUD are assumed to be fed back to the community so they can inform further research into the sustainability of cities.

The reason for this stakeholder approach is fourfold. First, it focuses attention on the agents of change (urban planners, architects, engineers, surveyors, construction contractors, etc.) Secondly, the attention paid to the agents of change and activities they undertake means the analysis is not limited to statutory urban planning instruments, but is more systematic. Thirdly, in taking this approach, it becomes possible to also take the property development, design, construction and operational interests of urban development into account. Fourthly, it allows the analysis to concentrate on the built environment and relationship this has to the economic and social sustainability of cities.

In taking on this form, the stakeholder analysis might be seen as an Agenda 21 'grass roots' approach by activists responsible for making urban development sustainable and supported by a growing body of professional knowledge and deepening academic understanding of this as a city-wide process. The benefits of this approach are seen to lie in the capacity the assessment methodology has to unify, rather than further fragment our knowledge and understanding of SUD. For rather than dividing the subject into sectional interests, professional fields and academic disciplines, the assessment methodology makes it possible to circumvent such divisions, something which it achieves by recognizing the inter-disciplinary, cross-sectional and inter-professional nature of what are trans-disciplinary issues.

STANDARD DESCRIPTION OF THE ASSESSMENTS

Given the diverse range and spread of methods currently in existence, the survey has sought to provide a standard description of the assessments in terms of the following characteristics:

- name of method;
- description;
- data required;
- status (well established or experimental);
- activity (planning, design, construction and operation);
- environmental and societal (environmental, economic, social and institutional) issues;
- scale of assessment (spatial level and time frame);
- references.

THE CLASSIFICATION

The classification BEQUEST has undertaken reveals that the said methods can be divided into two: those used for the purposes of carrying out 'environmental valuations' and those which augment into particular forms of 'sustainability assessments'. The classification shows that the environmental valuations provide assessments which focus on the ecological integrity and equity of SUD. It also shows that those methods which augment into particular forms of sustainability assessment tend to focus on building the environmental capacity needed to not only qualify the ecological integrity of urban development, but evaluate the equity of the resources this distributes and the degree to which the public are able to participate in decisions taken about the economic and social future of cities.

Examples of the 'environmental valuation' class include: contingent valuation, cost–benefit analysis, hedonic analysis and multi-criteria analysis. The forms of sustainability assessment have been sub-classified as simple base-line qualifications, complex and advanced and very advanced types of evaluation. The simple base-line qualifications include: the AHP (analytical hierarchy analysis), compatibility matrix and eco-profiling measures carried out to support ecological footprinting exercises. It also includes the environmental auditing techniques required for such purposes. These exercises are also supported by the flag method and spider analysis. The complex, advanced and very advanced methods include: BEES, BREEAM, Eco-points and the Green Building Challenge. They also include the MASTER framework, the pentagon model, the quantifiable city model, SPARTACUS, the sustainable city model, sustainable community, transit-orientated settlement models.

Table 1.1 provides an alpha list of the said classes, the assessment methods appearing under their respective headings and related evaluations.

Table 1.1 The classes of environmental assessment

Environmental valuations	Environmental, economic and social assessments	
	Simple	Complex, advanced and very advanced
Contingent valuation	AHP	*Complex*
Cost–benefit	Compatibility matrix	Regime analysis
analysis	Ecological foot-printing	
Hedonic analysis	Eco-profiling	*Advanced*
Multi-criteria analysis	Environmental auditing	BEES
Travel cost theory	Flag method	BREEAM
	Spider analysis	Eco-points
		Eco-prop
		Green Building Code
		LCA
		Meta-analysis (Pentagon Method)
		NAR model
		Very Advanced
		ASSIPAC
		AQM
		MASTER Framework
		Neighbourhood model
		Quantitative City model
		SPARTACUS
		Sustainable city
		Sustainable communities
		Transit-oriented settlement

WHAT THE METHODS ASSESS

What these methods assess is the environmental capacity – ecological integrity and equity of urban development plans, programmes and projects captured in terms of the built stock, transport, safety, security, health and well-being needed for cities to institute a quality of life. The built stock, transport, safety, security, health and well-being that are needed for cities to institute a quality of life in the districts, neighbourhoods, estates and buildings which the urban plans, programmes and projects develop as sustainable communities.

However, while the aforesaid marks a significant achievement in the development of environmental assessment, it is also evident that most of the methods still fail to address the institutional issues which underlie the evaluation of SUD. It is clear that in their current form, the methods find it difficult to address issues relating to the governance, morality and ethics of the SUD. The reasons for this are not currently known and require further investigation. It may be because most attention has been focused on environmental, economic and social issues and this has resulted in relative under-development of the institutional considerations. So it appears that if the assessment methods are to provide an appropriate basis for such evaluations, the governance, morality and ethics of urban development also need to be integrated into assessments concerning the sustainability of cities. This is important because without an evaluation of the institutional basis of SUD it will not be possible to throw light on the collaboration, consensus building, and commitment and leadership issues surrounding the actions taken to augment environmental capacity. Those actions and augmentations not only needed to build environmental capacity, but required to meet the ecological integrity and equity requirements of SUD. The ecological integrity and equity requirements that are of particular concern to the public and which have culminated in a call for greater participation in decisions taken about the economic and social future of cities. This shall be the object of Volume 3.

Table 1.2 sets out the statutory instruments, systems, classes of environmental assessment and scales for evaluating SUD. This shows SEA as an urban planning protocol for environmental assessment. By comparison EIA is represented as an urban planning, property development, design and construction protocol for assessing land uses at the building, estate, neighbourhood, district and city scales of evaluation. This indicates the following: that SEAs offer simple, complex and advanced assessments of environmental sustainability in terms of the ecological integrity and equity of urban planning, whereas the EIA protocol (the advanced and very advanced methods) offers detailed assessments of environmental, economic and social sustainability. Environmental, economic and social assessments which are set out in terms of what the urban planning, property development, design and construction sectors contribute to the ecological integrity and equity of the decisions taken by members of the public about the economic and social future of cities.

TYPES OF ASSESSMENT

Table 1.3 cross-references the BEQUEST framework and protocol(s) set out in Volume 1 against the statutory instruments, systems, classes and scales of environmental assessment for evaluating SUD. This shows the wide range of methods that exist for the assessment of SUD can be divided into five types. In terms of the complexity and completeness of the overall evaluation they provide:

- Environmental valuations in the form of contingent valuation, cost–benefit analysis, travel cost, hedonic and multi-criteria analysis, to assess the environmental sustainability (in this instance, ecological integrity) of urban development.
- Simple base-line or benchmarking methods to assess the environmental, economic and social issues underlying the policy commitment to SUD.

Table 1.2 The statutory instruments, systems, classes and scales of environmental assessment

Statutory Instruments	Systems	Environmental valuations	Environmental, economic and social assessments			
			Simple	Complex	Advanced	Very advanced
SEA	Multi-modal Human Cosmonomic Modelling	Contingent valuation Cost–benefit analysis Multi-criteria analysis Travel cost theory Hedonic analysis	AHP Compatibility matrix Eco-profiling Ecological footprint Environmental auditing Flag method Spider analysis	Regime analysis	Meta-analysis (Pentagon Method)	ASSIPAC MASTER Framework SPARTACUS
EIA		Contingent valuation Cost–benefit analysis	Compatibility matrix Eco-profiling Environmental auditing		BEES BREEAM Eco-points Green Building Code Life cycle analysis NAR model	Quantitative City model Sustainable City model Sustainable communities Transit-oriented settlement

Table 1.3 The framework, protocol(s) statutory instruments, systems, classes and scales of environmental assessment

BEQUEST framework	Protocol(s)	Statutory instruments	Systems	Environmental valuations	Environmental, economic and social assessments					Evaluating SUD
					Simple	Complex	Advanced	Very advanced	Scale	
Natural resources, land use, pollution and bio-diversity	Planning	SEA	Multi-model Human Sustainable Cosmonomic	Contingent valuation Cost–benefit analysis Multi-criteria analysis Travel cost theory Hedonic analysis	AHP Compatibility matrix Eco-profiling Ecological footprint Environmental auditing Flag method Spider analysis	Regime analysis	Meta-analysis (Pentagon method)	ASSIPAC MASTER Framework SARTACUS	Land-use	Ecological integrity and equity
Natural resources, land use, pollution and bio-diversity, build stock, transport, safety, security, health and well-being	Planning, property development design, construction stages	EIA		Contingent valuation Cost–benefit analysis Multi-criteria analysis	Compatibility matrix Eco-profiling				Land-use	Ecological integrity, equity, participation and futurity
							BEES BREEAM Eco-points Green Building Code NAR model		Building	
								Sustainable communities Quantifiable City model Sustainable City model Transit-oriented settlement	Estate neighbourhood and district City	

Examples of such methods include the use of compatibility, eco-profiling and ecological foot-printing exercises. They also include the use of environmental auditing techniques such as the flag method, or spider analysis.

- More complex methods to assess whether the planning, property development, design and construction of infrastructure projects (servicing energy, water and drainage, and transport) provide the environmental capacity (in this instance ecological integrity and equity) that is needed for urban development to carry the economic and social future of cities.

- Advanced methods that assess the contribution of construction to SUD, i.e. how particular construction projects and installations – e.g. energy systems, waste management provisions, repair and maintenance technologies – operate and what effect they have upon the environmental sustainability of cities. This includes an assessment of whether they have levels of energy consumption and emissions that have an adverse effect, or an impact which is more environmentally-friendly. Have an impact that is more environmentally friendly in the sense which the construction and operation of such installations augments, rather than diminishes, the environmental capacity (ecological integrity and equity) urban development has to carry the economic and social future of cities. These evaluations include BREEAM (Building Research Establishment Environmental Assessment Method), Eco-points, the Green Building Code and the NAR (net annual return) and Pentagon model.

- Very advanced models that assess the ecological integrity and equity of the alternative developments which it is possible for the public to participate in. The alternatives that it is possible for the public to participate in and select as those designs, constructions and operations which augment, rather than diminish, the environmental capacity of urban development to carry the economic and social future of cities. These methods include ASSIPAC, the MASTER Framework, the quantitative city model, SPARTACUS, the sustainable city and sustainable community model. They evaluate the environmental, economic and social sustainability of cities.

Irrespective of whether the environmental valuations are applied to urban planning policy, property development programmes, infrastructure designs, construction projects or the installation of operations, the object of the 'environmental valuations' is to assess the ecological integrity of the sustainable development issues (natural resources, land use, pollution and bio-diversity) under consideration. With this class of assessment, it is also noticeable that any economic analysis is confined to the urban planning, property development and design stage of the policy, programme and infrastructure provision and does not extend into the construction of projects, or installation of operations. This is also the case for any social issues that surface from the application of such assessment methods. With the 'environmental, economic and social assessments' the situation is different. This is because these methods address activities that run from planning through to property development and design and evaluate the ecological integrity, equity and participation of the public in decisions taken about the construction, operation and use of buildings and surrounding the future economic and social sustainability of cities. These environmental, economic and social assessments take SUD to include environmental sustainability, in terms of the ecological integrity, equity and participation of the public in decisions taken about the futurity of the building stock, transport, safety, security, health and well-being surrounding the economic and social sustainability of cities. This is a key point because it is here the assessment of SUD begins to become integrated – in the sense that the environment is evaluated in terms of the economic and social sustainability of cities.

It is evident that forms of environmental valuation – those assessing ecological integrity – have commonly provided the foundation for the other class of assess-ments which are carried out – in this instance, the environmental, economic and social assessments. This is common irrespective of whether the assessment is of the simple, complex, advanced or very advanced type. Examples of this can be seen with the use of contingent valuation and CBA. Another example of this is the transformation of multi-criteria assessments. This is also evident in the use of the multiple-regression component of the hedonic technique. There is also some evidence to suggest this transformation of environmental valuation is mediated through other methods. Examples of this include the use of:

- contingent valuation in the compatibility matrix and eco-profiling analysis;
- CBA in LCA (life cycle analysis) and the NAR (net annual return) model;
- MCA as the basis for AHP (the analytical hierarchy process), the flag method, spider and regime analysis.

Another observation that can be drawn from this type of transformation relates to the way in which the 'hard' (environmental) and 'soft' (economic and social) issues of SUD form part of the assessment methodology. With BEES (Building for Environ-mental and Economic Sustainability) and the quantifiable city model, the bio-physical aspects of the eco-system are the main issues. Here the sustainable development issues under assessment are those of energy consumption, material flows, waste and pollution. This is also the case for the quantifiable city model. Assessment methods integrating the bio-physical and social (environmental, economic and social) include BREEAM and the sustainable city models. It should also be recognized that such assessment methods are trans-disciplinary, cutting across traditional disciplines in the interests of advancing a methodology capable of providing evaluations which are more integrated in nature.

THE CONTRIBUTION(S)

Table 1.4 cross-references these classes and scales of assessment against the contributions contained in this volume. It shows that the environmental valuations are used for both strategic and detailed impact assessments. From Table 1.4 it is also noticeable that most of the assessment methods appear under the environmental, economic and social classification and as either simple base-line, benchmarking methods, complex, advanced or very advanced models for evaluating the sustainability of urban development.

Table 1.4 also illustrates what each class of assessment methods contributes to SUD. As can be seen, environmental valuations provide a pathway to SUD in terms of the ecological integrity and equity of urban planning. Whereas the environmental, economic and social assessments provide a pathway that reaches SUD by way of the ecological integrity, equity and ability of the public to participate in decisions taken about the future of cities. Decisions taken about the future of cities and in that sense the urban planning, property development, design and construction of the buildings, estates, neighbourhoods and districts upon which their economic and social sustainability rests.

EVALUATING SUD

From what has been said, it is evident that irrespective of whatever assessment is under consideration, the method in question can be seen as contributing something to the evaluation of SUD. For as the pathology of the assessment methods shows, irrespective of whether an environmental valuation acts as a foundation for a environmental, economic and social assessment, both classes contribute something to SUD. It is for this reason that having set out the statutory instruments of environmental assessment (SEA and EIA) and systems-based thinking on SUD, this volume goes on to provide case-study examples of the way in which both classes of environmental assessment are used as methods to evaluate the sustainability of urban development. Each case study is offered as an example of best practice in the use of an environmental assessment method for evaluating the sustainability of SUD. The examples of best practice are also set out to illustrate the standards which environmental assessment need to meet in order to evaluate the sustainability of urban development and ensure that any actions required to build environmental

Table 1.4 What each class of assessment methods contributes to SUD

Environmental valuations	Environmental, economic and social assessments				Scale	Evaluating SUD
	Simple	Complex	Advanced	Very advanced		
Cost–benefit analysis Multi-criteria analysis Contingent value analysis Hedonic analysis	AHP Compatibility matrix Eco-profiling Ecological footprint Environmental auditing Flag method Spider analysis	Regime analysis	Meta-analysis (Pentagon method)	ASSIPAC MASTER Framework SPARTACUS	City landscapes	Ecological integrity and equity
Cost–benefit analysis Multi-criteria analysis	Compatibility matrix Eco-profiling Ecological footprint	Community impact analysis Multi-functional analysis PROPOLIS			Land-use	Ecological integrity, (intra-generational) equity
			BEES, BREEAM Building passport, Eco-points, Eco-prop, Eco-quantity, ENVEST, Green Building Code, LCA, PIMWAQ		Building	Ecological integrity, (inter-generational) equity
				AUSTIME, H2OR, Quantifiable City model, Sustainable communities, Sustainable city model, Transit-oriented settlement	Estate, neighbourhood, district and city	Ecological integrity, (inter-generational) equity, participation and futurity

N.B. The environmental assessment methods highlighted are those reported on in this volume

capacity are able to carry the public's concerns about the economic and social futures of cities. In taking this form the case studies also provide the opportunity to:

- study environmental assessment in light of the challenge SUD poses;
- examine the response to this challenge in terms of the vision and methodology of an integrated SUD and scoping of the environmental assessment methods able to meet the call for such evaluations;
- organize the assessment methods by class and analyse their contribution to SUD;
- provide an up-to-date examination of the environmental assessments in question, setting out their rational, underlying methodology and scope;
- set out the techniques of analysis each assessment draws upon for screening SUD and detail the evaluations undertaken at various scales of assessment (building-to-city-wide);
- identify what they contribute to SUD and what each particular evaluation adds to our knowledge of environmental assessment;
- get an insight into the scope that exists for environmental assessment methods to enrich our understanding of urban development and provide us with a deeper insight into economic and social future of cities;
- show what each class of environmental assessment reveals about the ongoing transformation and track the direction which environmental assessment is travelling in terms of the pathways this provides towards SUD;
- reflect the technical and scientific challenges the transformation poses for the assessment community and what actions need to be taken in order to meet the standards of its emerging methodology;
- outline where further research and development is needed for the transformation to go full circle and provide the methods needed to bridge the gap between the building and city scale of assessment.

The contributions that make up Parts 3 and 4 of the book will address the first seven bullet points under the headings of environmental valuations and environmental, economic and social assessments. Part 5 will tackle the remaining points by reflecting on the contribution the evaluation makes to SUD respectively.

Organized by statutory instruments and classes of assessment, it is possible to identify what the contributions add to SUD and how they build the environmental capacity needed for the urban planning, property development, design and construction of cities to sustain the quality of life. Having set out the environmental valuations, it becomes possible to identify what the assessments contribute to the planning of SUD. This is done by showing how the methods have been transformed by urban planners, property developers, designers, building contractors and operators into simple, complex, advanced and very advanced environmental, economic and social assessments of land use at the building, estate, neighbourhood, district and city scales of assessment. The simple, complex, advanced and very advanced methods that provide the means by which to transcend environmental valuations and provide urban planners, property developers, designers, contractors, operators and users with the environmental, economic and social assessments needed to evaluate the sustainability of urban development at the required land use, building, estate, neighbourhood, district and city scale.

REFERENCES

Curwell, S., Deakin, M. and Symes, M. (eds) (2005) *Sustainable Urban Development: The Framework and Protocols for Environmental Assessment*, Routledge, Oxford.

Deakin, M. and Curwell, S. (2004) 'Sustainable urban development: the framework and directory of assessment methods', in M. Deakin, R. Mansburger and R. Dixon-Gough (eds) *Models and Instruments for Rural and Urban Development*, Ashgate Press, Aldershot.

Deakin, M. and Lombardi, P. (2005a) 'The directory of environmental assessment methods', in S. Curwell, M. Deakin and M. Symes (eds) *Sustainable Urban Development: The Framework and Protocols for Environmental Assessment*, Routledge, Oxford.

Deakin, M. and Lombardi, P. (2005b) 'Assessing the sustainability of urban development', in S. Curwell, M. Deakin and M. Symes (eds) *Sustainable Urban Development: The Framework and Protocols for Environmental Assessment*, Routledge, Oxford.

Deakin, M., Curwell, S. and Lombardi, P. (2001) 'BEQUEST: the framework and directory of assessment methods', *International Journal of Life Cycle Assessment*, 6(6): 373–383.

Deakin, M., Curwell, S. and Lombardi, P. (2002a) 'Sustainable urban development: the framework and directory of assessment methods', *Journal of Environmental Assessment Policy and Management*, 4(2): 171–197.

Deakin, M., Huovila, P., Rao, S., Sunikka, M. and Vreeker, R. (2002b) 'The assessment of sustainable urban development', *Building Research and Information*, 30(2): 95–108.

European Commission (EC) (1997) Council Directive 97/11/EC on the Assessment of Certain Public and Private Projects on the Environment, reported on in *Official Journal No. L073, 14/03/1997 P.0005*, EC, Brussels.

European Commission (2001) Council Directive 2001/42/EC (Article 13(3)) on the Assessment of the Effects of Certain Plans and Programmes on the Environment, EC, Brussels.

Part 1

Environmental Assessment

2

Environmental Assessments
within the EU
Giulio Mondini and Marco Valle

INTRODUCTION

It is undeniable that attention towards the quality of the environment has increased
in recent years, so much so as to become one of the most important points of
European politics. This interest can be seen in both the legislation that is in force and
in the search for new evaluation methodologies directed towards defining social and
environmental externalities as integrated parts of the overall judgement of feasibility
and compatibility.

The reflections presented here arose out of a critical comment made on
the present EU directives and from presentation of evaluation of some important
territorial experiences of development plans and projects. The procedural aspects
that are considered by the environmental assessments, which are the core of the
problem, will in particular be studied in detail.

EVALUATION OF THE ENVIRONMENT WITHIN THE EU

Far too often the objectives of protection of the environment and economic development have been considered to be in competition and an aggravation of the pressures
that exist between the environment and development of territory has occurred. This
has resulted in a very irregular distribution over the years of wealth, with an obvious
deterioration of the environment, which has led to a critical revision of the relationship
between the environment, territorial planning and economic development.

This interest, which has been more obvious in Europe since the 1970s, has
led to a very active comparison of these competing objectives, and has produced
a renewed legislative situation, including the introduction of Strategic Environmental
Assessment (SEA). However, it is difficult to establish the current status of experience in SEA; this depends to a great extent on the difficulty of establishing whether
an environmental assessment should be catalogued as a SEA or as an introduction
of evaluation elements within a determined decision process. In reality the impossibility of establishing the exact contents and limits of SEA, to define methodologies that are universally repeatable and formalised, seems to be positive. The great
amount of experience that has been gained at an international level in the last 15 years,

above all in experimental terms, has shown that there are extremely heterogeneous approaches and it is only in a few cases that the application of formalised and clearly structured models and procedures can be seen.

Among the evaluation processes connected to SEA is Environmental Impact Assessment (EIA), a procedure that has the purpose of considering the effects that could occur in the environment following a determined intervention and transformation of the territorial initiative (i.e. at a project level). This procedure, which is of an administrative nature (directive 85/337/CE, amended by directive 97/11/CE), allows information to be collected by the client and judgements to be made by the authority in charge, on the suitability of carrying out an EIA.

Whilst EIA addresses the evaluation of projects, SEA is already effective at the planning stage where the framework for future projects is set. Directive 2001/42/CE, inherent to SEA, originated in the European Economic Community in relation to interventions that could be financed with structural funds. The fourth paragraph of article 8, regulation EU 2081/93, the eighth paragraph of article 9 and the fifth paragraph of article 11b foresee that regional economic and social conversion plans presented by member countries should include an environmental assessment; on this basis, within the context of Agenda 2000, the DG XI European Commission 'Environment, nuclear safety and civil protection' proposed a series of modifications to the regulations on Structural Funds. In short, the Environmental Resources Management manual was drawn up with the purpose of illustrating how it is possible to include environmental problems in the elaboration of the regional plans stage in the most systematic way.

The SEA procedure was thus introduced which was aimed at being a structural procedure to anticipate development proposals and not to get around them. This formulation was then fully confirmed by Directive 42/2001, which is made up of 15 articles. The main innovations that were introduced by this directive concern the moment the evaluation itself is carried out which 'shall be carried out during the preparation of a plan or programme and before its adoption or submission to the legislative procedure' (article 4). SEA is therefore seen as a procedure that accompanies either the planning or programmatic procedure that is able to guarantee an accurate choice between the alternatives, where 'the objectives and the geographical scope of the plan or programme are identified, described and evaluated' (article 5).

The application fields of SEA are fixed by article 3 (part 2). Furthermore, in article 3 (parts 3, 4 and 5) the member countries can determine other types of plans or programmes with significant effects on the environment. A predominant characteristic of this procedure is the participation and protection of legitimate interests; anybody has the right to participate; the directive does not foresee a limit of interest connected to potential damage of rights. Article 2 clarifies the definition of the public, which should be understood as one or more physical or juridical bodies and their associations, organisations or groups. There are therefore significant differences between EIA and SEA; these are briefly summarised in Table 2.1.

The evaluation of regional or sectoral plans is expressed at a strategic level; it does not attempt to quantify impacts in detail but concentrates on the problems of the system. In other words, SEA is a systematic process that aims to evaluate the consequences of the proposed actions on the environment in order to guarantee that these consequences are included and dealt with in an adequate way from the beginning of the decision process (Deakin *et al.*, 2002). This is to guarantee that the obtained results offer an advantage to the subsequent planning levels, thus reducing the continuous conflicts that traditionally exist between the economic, social and environmental objectives.

This formulation recognises the environment as one of the main factors that determines the development of a region. The natural components (water, air, ground and physical agents) are the fundamental elements supporting ecosystems and

Table 2.1 Main differences between EIA and SEA

	SEA (plans)	EIA (projects)
Purpose	Programming and verification of the correspondence of development plans and of operative programmes with the objectives of sustainable development	Verification of the interferences of the projects with environmental factors
Procedure	A systematic process with the purpose of evaluating the consequences of a development policy on the environmental field	A scientific-administrative technique with the purpose of identifying the effects that a determined project, action or work would have on the environment
Data	Of various types (qualitative and quantified)	Mainly quantified
Evaluation scale	Regional	Local
Level of the impact	Global, national and regional	Mainly local
Impact forecasting methods	Simple, characterised by high uncertainties	Complex (and usually based on quantified data)
Public participation	There are no standardised procedures. The participation of the public is one of the fundamental elements of the concept of sustainability itself; SEA should therefore verify whether there has been participation in the formulation of the plan	Limited formal procedure. EIA is found at the proposed organisation and is available to anyone for possible observation. The publication of the project is through announcements in the press and indications of public assemblies
Results	General and qualitative	Detailed and quantitative

human beings, but they do not have an unlimited duration and cannot be exploited indefinitely without running out or deteriorating; it is therefore necessary to change from an approach that is based on economic efficiency to a wider one that is based on the concepts of sustainable development (Selman, 1996). The task remains to put into practice this concept – How do you carry out an evaluation of the environment at a regional level? How do you evaluate the impact on the environment? To do all this it is necessary to make recourse to the idea of resilience (Figure 2.1).

The term 'resilience' indicates the 'capacity of a system to maintain its own structure and its models of behaviour in the face of external disturbances, that is, its capacity to adapt to changes'. This capacity should be intended as an intrinsic quality of the system itself, thanks to which its dynamic functions are guaranteed. Speaking of resilience when referring to the environment means placing attention on the functioning of the systems that make it up, a functioning that is necessary to maintain equilibrium following pressure or external shocks (Smit and Spaling, 1995).

The concept of resilience leads to the definition of environmental assessment, which has the objective of verifying the cumulative effects of several pressures in order to determine pressure on the carrying capacity of the receiving body and to define compatibility criteria for territorial planning.

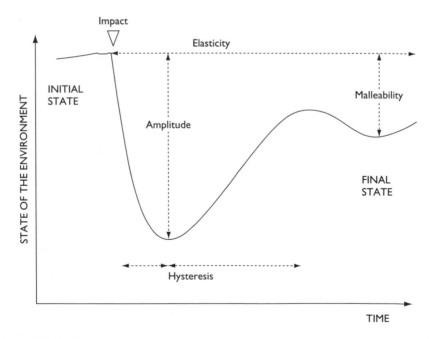

Figure 2.1 Resilience

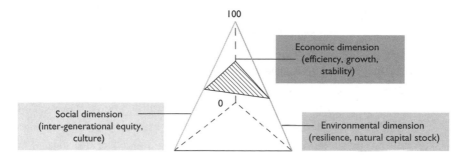

Figure 2.2 Sustainable development representation

Sustainable development-based studies attempt to solve the relationships between environment, development and economic growth by superseding the specific approaches in assessment activity with more integrated methods. The concept of sustainable development, in fact, allows one to consider both the quality and the efficiency of land transformations according to its three main dimensions: economic, social and environmental (Bartelmus, 1994). A representation of the concept of sustainable development is given in Figure 2.2.

The pyramid has a triangular base with vertices in the three main dimensions (economy, society and environment) and an apex in the ideal point of best sustainability. The percentage level of the corresponding sustainability that is reached can be identified along the three sides of the pyramid. Three points are determined, one for each side, by giving a score to each dimension. The connection of the points provides a triangular area that measures the sustainability that can be achieved: the smaller the area, the higher the sustainability level. Looking for sustainable development means moving along the three pyramid sides in order to find a balance between ecosystem integrity, economic efficiency and social equity.

This representation is particularly interesting in a complex reality such as the European one. The three dimensions that have been mentioned in fact do not have an equal weight in all the countries of the EU and, even on the inside of a country, there are very often areas in which the social and economic dimensions are more predominant than the environmental dimension. It is also necessary to underline that in Europe there are two opposing trends with respect to the interaction of society and territory: on one hand we can see the growth of globalisation processes, especially at an economic level, while on the other there is an increase in requests to regionalise policies and for local participation in planning. The first trend, connected to the concept of the 'global village', interprets territorial sustainability with a functionalist approach. Unambiguous responses are searched for that can be applied universally and which are efficient. This view approaches the problem of sustainable development with a top–down type of decision model, characterised by policies that are proposed/implemented by high-level authorities (EU, national government, etc.). The second approach believes that there are no responses to the problem of sustainability that can be generalised, and that solutions should be found by taking into consideration local realities. The decisional model is therefore a bottom–up type that is founded on the basic community and the local administrations. The search for new styles of life is exploited, as is the search for new ways of living and producing that are able to satisfy the requirements of the population within the limits of the productive capacity of the local ecosystems.

The reference model is that of a self-reliant territory that is able to make use of the local resources and use them in an integrated way. The concept of carrying capacity is important for both approaches in the definition of the limits within which the transformation is sustainable, even though it may be interpreted in different ways. In the first case, the practice of misappropriating the carrying capacity of other regions, often beyond national or continental boundaries (a practice which is still today very common and not always according to the law), would not be a problem. For those regions that 'export' carrying capacity, compensation mechanisms could be devised that would be able to re-balance the distribution of the riches. However, the actual situation teaches us that unequal exchange conditions between different economic realities tend to make the gap grow between the territories rather than decrease it. The second formulation closely follows the model of traditional cities that founded their preservation on the area close to the settlement. The main problem of this type of auto-centred development model (or eco-development) is that of closing the cycles (energy, waste, water, etc.) within the territory itself.

These considerations lead to the problem of the existence of criteria that are the same for all of Europe, criteria that could become reference points for each environmental evaluation. The EU has expressed 10 sustainability criteria in its Environmental Resources Management manual, prepared for DG XI of the European Commission with the cooperation and assistance of DG XVI 'Regional policies and cohesion' and DG VI 'Agriculture' of the European Union. These criteria, though expressing a common sustainability standard, are sufficiently general to be interpreted in the light of the different national situations (Table 2.2). They were identified as general reference points for objectives concerning the environment and sustainable development of plan programmes and projects.

These criteria involve the monitoring of plans, an indispensable step for the management and transformation of the territory in the period in which the plan is operational. Monitoring has the role of a strategic control and not of a simple balance between proposed and performed actions and it is developed according

Table 2.2 Ten European criteria for sustainable development

Sectors	Ten SEA criteria for sustainable development
Energy, Transport, Industry	1. Minimize use of non-renewable resources
Energy, Agriculture, Forestry, Tourism, Hydro resources, Environment, Transport, Industry	2. Use non-renewable resources within their regeneration capacity
Industry, Energy, Agriculture, Hydro resources, Environment	3. Use and management of dangerous and polluting wastes must be suitable from the environmental point of view (e.g. with assimilative capacities of sinks)
Industry, Energy, Agriculture, Hydro resources, Environment	4. The conservation and improvement of wild flora and fauna, habitats and landscape
Agriculture, Silviculture, Hydro resources, Environment, Industry, Tourism, Cultural resources	5. The conservation and improvement of the quality of soils and hydro resources
Tourism, Environment, Industry, Transport, Cultural resources	6. The conservation and improvement of the quality of historical and cultural resources
Urban environment, Industry, Tourism, Transport, Energy, Hydro resources, Cultural resources	7. The conservation and improvement of the quality of local environment
Transport, Energy, Industry	8. Atmospheric protection (global warming)
Research, Environment, Tourism, Cultural resources	9. Making people aware of environmental problems, and developing education programmes in the field of environment
All	10. Promoting the participation of people in decisions connected to sustainable development

to *in itinere* and *ex post* evaluations (Bentivegna *et al.*, 1999). The *in intinere* evaluations (or intermediate) are foreseen by article 25 of the EU coordination regulation no. 4253/88 and they contain a preliminary critical analysis of the collected data. They evaluate the objectives of the plan, and forecast the outcomes of the operation. The *ex post* (or final) evaluation is the concluding document of the monitoring which, together with the information obtained from the intermediate evaluations, furnishes the guidelines to establish new objectives of protection and evaluation of the resources in the territory.

The national legislation in Italy essentially refers to directive 85/337/CE, while at a regional level the situation differs greatly going from regional laws that, though fulfilling national laws, also refer to the latest European directives; to regions in which an applicative legislation has not yet been developed. It is in this situation, without precise standards, that the two evaluation procedures presented in the following sections were developed.

THE OLYMPIC PROGRAMME FOR TURIN 2006 WINTER GAMES

The first case study considers the evaluation of the development programme for the Olympic winter games held in Turin during 2006 (the Olympic Programme). Although many sports complexes already existed, work was needed to integrate and complete them (for a total amount of 1000 million Euro). These developments have a potential impact on the environment and the land in Turin and its mountains. The purpose of the SEA was to control all the effects that the Olympic Programme would have on the environment, the social-economic conditions and the cultural heritage, in order to minimise the negative impacts and to maximise positive interactions. It is important to underline the systemic character of the SEA. The procedure was not a sort of 'macro-EIA' of the sum of the works for the winter games but an assessment of several integrated operations. Considering the particular nature of the Olympic Programme and the lack of explanatory legislation in Italy, it was considered indispensable to supply a layout of the intervention. First of all it is necessary to differentiate between the objectives of the Olympic Programme and those of SEA.

1   The main objectives of the Olympic Programme were:

- rescue and transformation operations (the rescue of urban areas in Turin and transformation of existing sports complexes);
- operations on road networks and transport (re-organisation of the transport network also considering the post-winter games situation);
- operations on tourist and accommodating operations.

2   The main objectives of SEA can be described as:

- mitigation objectives: to minimise the environmental damage caused by the operations and to mitigate their negative impact;
- rationalisation objectives: to make the transformation processes compatible with the surrounding land and environment;
- sustainability objectives: to improve the environmental quality with the operations.

These objectives were applied to the five sectors that were considered to be of priority for the case under examination: energy, water and soil, biodiversity and landscape, transport and local sustainable development. The objectives addressed are given in Table 2.3 and their interconnections are represented in Figure 2.3.

Table 2.3 The plan objectives

Integrated objectives	Mitigation	Rationalization	Sustainability
1. *Energy*: energetic balance improvement	1.1. reduction of resource wastes 1.4. technological improvement	1.2. containment of the energy demand 1.5. cycles closing 1.6. refuse reuse	1.3. use of renewable source
2. *Water and soil*: improvement of the stability and of water and soil management	2.1. elimination of landslide 2.4. elimination of pollution 2.7. elimination of dangerous wells	2.2. reduction of landslide risk 2.5. reduction of flood risk 2.8. rationalization of wells	2.3. improvement of stability 2.6. improvement of the environmental quality
3. *Biodiversity and landscape*: biodiversity protection and functional improvement	3.1. elimination of pollution 3.4. reduction of visual damage	3.2. impacts minimization 3.5. landscape diversity protection	3.3. improvement of the connectivity 3.6. creation of protected areas 3.7. enhancement of the tourist landscape
4. *Transport*: cost/benefit improvement	4.1. reduction of infrastructure impacts 4.4. road network safety 4.7. traffic restriction	4.2. inter-modality displacement 4.5. network functional adaptation	4.3. integrated transport organization 4.6. logistic planning
5. *Local sustainable development*: internal development activation of processes	5.1. containment of the development of sport complexes	5.2. redistribution of supplies 5.4. better use of the social capital	5.3. exploitation of the natural heritage 5.5. exploitation of traditional activities

The SEA procedure adopted for the Olympic Programme 'Turin 2006' was structured in six stages:

1   *Environmental assessment*: The evaluation considered the environment and the future scenarios with reference to the physical environment, the social economic state, the urban state and infrastructure.
2   *Objectives definition*: The objectives of the Olympic Programme were related to the creation of internal local development processes and to the improvement of the quality of the environment. These objectives are placed in the 10 SEA criteria (Table 2.2) for sustainable development, supplied by the European Community.

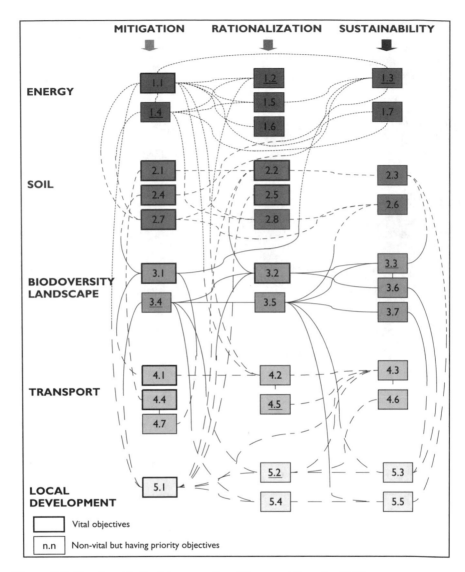

Figure 2.3 The plan objective interconnections (Peano and Brunetta, 2003)

3   *Draft of the plan and alternatives considered*: The main strategies considered
     in the Olympic Programme are related to: (a) development and improvement
     of the supply of sports complexes and tourist structures; and (b) improvement
     of the accessibility to the sports complex and of the general transport condi-
     tions. The identification of the strategies involves several alternatives being

considered (e.g. different sites or technologies), including the 'do nothing' option.

4   *Environmental assessment*: After having examined the Olympic Programme strategies and the considered operations, it is necessary to develop: (a) an evaluation of the whole system (Turin and the mountains); and (b) an evaluation of each single project and operation.

5   *Indicators*: The DPSR (driving forces, pressures, state, responses) model was applied to control the natural resources affected by the Olympic Programme. The indicator system that was developed gives information about both the impacts on the environment caused by new operations and the actions in the industry, energy, tourism and transport sectors.

6   *Integration of the evaluation*: The evaluation carried out was considered and integrated at many levels in the decision-making processes, from the initial projects to the final tests. Furthermore, the results of the evaluation were shared with all the subjects involved (Municipalities, Mountain Communities, sector operators, etc.). This procedure acts *ex ante, in itinere* and *ex post* as far as the Olympic Programme is concerned and it is schematically represented in Figure 2.4.

The SEA identified several types of operation which affect the environment in different ways:

•   *strictly functional operations* for the Winter Games: competition sports complexes and their service plants (e.g. hydro field for artificial snow, accommodation structures, road network operations);

•   *integrating operations* dedicated to improving the supply of future sport and the local development;

•   *leaded operations* to integrate the sports complexes into the environment and to improve the environmental quality of the areas.

In general, the Olympic Programme had no relevant or negative effects that could be mitigated as far as the previous objectives are concerned. The main effects can be summarised as given in Table 2.4.

In this context, it was therefore possible to plan and organise the Winter Olympic Games with particular attention being directed to the inheritance that will be left to the territory, taking care that this inheritance can be perceived and recognised as a positive legacy for the environment in the mountain and urban areas that will be involved.

Table 2.4 Main effects

Sector	Effects
Energy	It was necessary to carry out mitigation operations for the effects that are related to the increase in the energy demand.
Water and soils	New operations would contribute to increased pressure on water and soils and the subsequent effects needed to be mitigated, with: • displacement of some hydro fields for artificial snow; • project caution as far as landslide risks are concerned.
Biodiversity and landscape	There were some negative impacts that needed to be eliminated (e.g. it was compulsory to avoid natural pools for artificial snow) and others that were possible to mitigate (visual impact).
Transport	The foreseen operations would have contributed to an improved general environmental quality by decreasing atmospheric emissions via the development of a more suitable railway system.
Local Development	The operations of the Olympic Programme improved the local economy by changing the actual structure which was based on large sports complexes and constant building expansion to the detriment of the environment.

THE APPLICATION OF THE TERRITORIAL PERFORMANCE INDEX

In a more recent study on the establishment of indicator models for the evaluation of environmental compatibility, an attempt is made to synthesise the high number of indicators evident in such cases as the Winter Olympics development. A process has been developed, demonstrated here with respect to the Asti territorial are Italy (Bottero et al., 2002).

An indicator is a measure that reveals a theme for which some data are available; it is an observed value that is representative of a phenomenon that has to be studied and its role is to provide significant information in order to obtain the most essential aspects of the event that has to be evaluated. An indicator on its own is not very useful but it has to be part of a system of indicators that are coordinated from the logical and functional point of view. The aggregation of the indicators that belong to a system provides an index, which contains the final information of the phenomenon that is being analysed.

The analytical approach using indicators and an index is quite common in the field of sustainable development assessment methods, as sustainability is a multi-dimension concept that involves a great deal of problems and topics that need to be taken into account in the evaluation (Mondini and Valle, 2001). A very useful tool to investigate all the aspects that are involved in the policies and operations is the Political Performance Index (PPI). The PPI tries to integrate the common indicators (e.g. Net National Product, employment rate, inflation rate) used

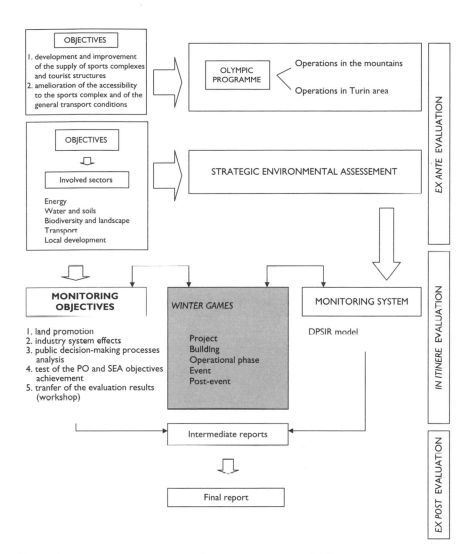

Figure 2.4 Relationships between the Olympic Programme and SEA

to appraise the success or failure of a policy, programme or plan (Giovanelli *et al.*, 2000). A representation of the method is given in Figure 2.5. The final index is obtained by aggregating the indicators as shown in Figure 2.6.

The aggregation considers three different levels that contain the final PPI in the middle circle, three partial indexes in the intermediate circle and several indicators in the external circle (NPP, inflation rate, employment level, poverty, air pollution, produced wastes, etc.). The dimension of each circular sector provides the weight of the corresponding index and the

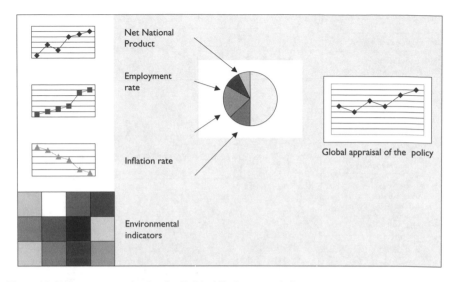

Figure 2.5 Data aggregation for the Political Performance Index

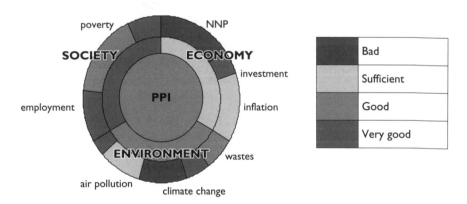

Figure 2.6 The Political Performance Index

shades reflect its level (from bad to very good). This procedure is illustrated here using an application that was carried out on an Italian regional structure plan in order to give an intermediate evaluation of the regulations that make up the plan itself. The process of creating the PPI is structured in four stages:

1   *Analysis of the objectives and the outcomes of the plan*: The performance index has been used to test the environmental compatibility of the Territorial Plan regulations, as indicated by regional legislation on the subject of environment impact assessment.

2 *Definition of partial indicators on which the aggregation is founded*: In order to obtain the declared objective, each article of the regulations corresponds to an indicator.

3 *Diagramming of the relationships between the indicators in order to arrange the data*: The Territorial Plan is divided into several systems:

- Environmental system;
- Infrastructures and connection system;
- Economic and settlement system;
- Hydro-geological system;
- Agriculture and forest system;
- Cultural, historical and landscape system.

The planning regulation set has been divided into 'land use regulations' and 'land protection regulations'; this division corresponds to planning levels of the Regional Territorial Plan, which can be considered as the 'obligation' levels (landscape, environmental themes and cultural-historical values) and the 'opportunity' levels (development strategies for activities and settlement).

4 *Weights and mathematical relations for the index definition*: The systems represent different aspects of one situation, the Territorial Plan, and for this reason they have been given the same weight in the final aggregation. The system of the assigned scores is represented in Table 2.5. Two different criteria have been used to analyse how each system contributes to obtain the environmental compatibility goal.

The evaluation of 'land protection regulations' (Table 2.6) considers the compatibility between plan objectives and national and international criteria. The assessment method is based on a matrix which has the rows that correspond to the regulations and the columns that correspond to the 'sustainability criteria' according to the European Commission, and which represent the environmental policy trends in the European context. As not all the intersections in the matrix can be considered

Table 2.5 Scoring system for compatibility assessment

The regulations contribute both directly and indirectly to protect the component or to reach the objective	+++
The regulations contribute directly to protect the component or to reach the objective	++
The regulations contribute indirectly to protect the component or to reach the objective	+
The regulations do not refer to the component or the objective	−

Table 2.6 Land protection systems

System	Components	Sustainability criteria (see Table 2.2)									
		I	II	III	IV	V	VI	VII	VIII	IX	X
Environmental System	Air	+++	+++	++				++	+++	++	++
	Surface hydro resources	++	+++	++	++	++				++	−
	Wastes	+	+	+	+	+		++		−	−
	Mining activities	+		+	+	+		+		−	−
	Contaminated sites				−	+		−		−	−
	Accident risks	+	+	+	+	+		+		−	−
	Noise							+++		++	+
	Electromagnetic emissions		++			++				−	−
	Connection elements	++	+++		+++			++	+	−	−
Hydro geological system	Flooding areas	++			−	+++	++			+	−
	Landslides	++			−	+++	++			+	++
	Underground hydro resources	+++	+++	++	−	+++				−	−
Agriculture and forest system	Forests	++	+++		+++	+++			+	++	+++
	Protected areas	−	+++		++	+++			+	++	+++
	Biological corridors and safeguard bands		+++		++	+++		++	−	−	−
	Agricultural areas	++	++		+++	+++	+++			−	+
	Plain productive lands	++	++		+++	++				−	+
Landscape system	Landscape sites	−			+++		+++	++		−	+
	High environment and landscape quality areas	++			−			+++	++	++	++
	Historical centres	+			−			+++	++	+	+
	Architectural monuments	++			++			+++	++	++	+
	Landscape values	+			+		+	+		−	+
	Tourist functions				−			+	−	−	+

significant and some relations can be excluded at a first glance, an identification of the possible relations has been carried out and the corresponding intersections have been shaded. Each shaded cell has been given a score with reference to the role of the regulation in the sustainability objectives: the greater the contribution to the criteria, the higher the score.

The evaluation of 'land use regulations' (Table 2.7) has been carried out by creating a matrix with rows that correspond to land protection systems and columns

Table 2.8 Compatibility of the systems

System	Component	Score	Max	Contribution	%	Compatibility %	Graph
Infrastructure system	Roads	18	39	0.462	46.2	32.1	
	Railways	11	33	0.333	33.3		
	Intermodal centres	2	12	0.167	16.7		
Economic and settlement system	Services	14	33	0.424	42.4	62.2	
	Productive activities	38	57	0.667	66.7		
	Trading activities	28	48	0.583	58.3		
	Houses	44	54	0.815	81.5		
Hydro geological system	Flooding areas	8	18	0.444	44.4	50.8	
	Landslides	10	18	0.556	55.6		
	Underground hydro resources	11	21	0.524	52.4		
Agriculture and forest system	Forests	17	21	0.810	81.0	63.5	
	Protected areas	14	21	0.667	66.7		
	Biological corridors	10	21	0.476	47.6		
	Agricultural areas	14	21	0.667	66.7		
	Plain production land	10	18	0.556	55.6		
Cultural, historical and landscape system	Landscape sites	9	18	0.500	50.0	43.9	
	Environmental and landscape quality areas	11	18	0.611	61.1		
	Historical centres	8	18	0.444	44.4		
	Architectural monuments	14	18	0.667	66.7		
	Landscape values	5	18	0.278	27.8		
	Tourist function	2	18	0.133	13.3		
Environmental system	Air	17	21	0.810	81.0	46.0	
	Surface hydro resources	13	21	0.619	61.9		
	Noise	6	9	0.667	66.7		
	Electromagnetic emissions	4	12	0.333	33.3		
	Connection elements	6	18	0.333	33.3		
	Soil				16.9		

Score (%)	Compatibility	
0–25 %	Not sufficient	
25–50 %	Low	
50–75 %	Good	
75–100 %	Very good	

Table 2.7 Land use systems

		Land use						
		Infrastructural system			Economic and settlement system			
Land protection		Roads	Railways	Intermodal centres	Services	Productive activities	Trading activities	Houses
Environmental system	Air	+++		+	+	++	−	++
	Surface hydro resources	−				++	++	++
	Wastes	+	+	−	++	++	++	++
	Mining activities				++	++	++	++
	Contaminated sites							
	Accident risk plants					+		
	Noise						++	
	Electromagnetic emissions	+++	++	−		+	−	++
	Connection elements	+	+			+	++	++
Hydro geological system	Flooding areas					+++	+	+++
	Landslides	+	−			+++	+	+++
	Underground hydro resources					+	+	+
Agriculture and forest system	Forests	++	++		−	+	+	+
	Protected areas and biological corridors	++	++			+	+++	+++
	Agricultural areas	++	++		++	+++	+++	+++
	Plain production lands				−	+	+	+++
Cultural, historical and landscape system	Landscape sites	+	−		++	+++	+++	+++
	High environment and landscape quality areas	+	−		++	+++	+++	+++
	Historical centres							+++
	Architectural monuments							+++
	Landscape values	−	−		++	+++	+++	+++
	Tourist functions	+	+	+	+	+++		

that correspond to land use systems. The assessment is directed towards testing how each article of the land use regulations is able to defend the components of the land protection systems. As not all the crossings can be considered significant, the environmental components that can be affected by land operations have been highlighted and the corresponding spaces have been shaded. The score reflects the suitability of the regulations to protect natural components: the stricter the protection imposed by the regulations, the higher the score.

Each indicator was evaluated by summing the obtained scores and comparing the quantity to the highest obtainable score: the percentage value provides the compatibility level of the analysed indicator. The environmental compatibility of each system is the average score that is obtained by the respective indicators, as shown in equation (1).

$$\text{compatibility\_system} = \frac{\text{compatibility\_indicators}}{n\_\text{indicators}} \quad (1)$$

The compatibility was assessed for single systems and then the results were aggregated to provide the final Territorial Performance Index (TPI), that is the average score of the compatibility of the systems. The mathematic expression of the final index is provided by equation (2). A representation of the working method is given in Tables 2.8 and 2.9.

$$\text{TPI} = \frac{\text{compatibility\_systems}}{n\_\text{systems}} \quad (2)$$

It is possible to make some observations from the results. First of all, among all the 'land use systems', the infrastructure system has the lowest compatibility because of the poor agreement of the inter-modal centres with the established objectives; secondly, among all the 'land protection systems' the landscape system is the worst from the point of view of compatibility with the sustainability criteria; finally, in the environmental system the soil has been disadvantaged as it has not been considered as a real resource.

CONCLUSIONS AND POSSIBLE DEVELOPMENTS

One point that should be considered by all those who are involved in experimenting with environmental evaluation procedures is the question of the reasonableness of the knowledge and of the evaluation methods that are used in decision procedures in order to define the degree of compatibility between the actions and the environmental reference system. In short, is it possible to

Table 2.9 The Territorial Performance Index

System	Environmental Compatibility %	TPI	Graph
Infrastructural system	32.1		
Economic and settlement system	62.2		
Hydrogeological system	50.8	49.8	
Agriculture and forest system	63.5		
Historical, cultural and landscape system	43.9		
Environmental system	46		

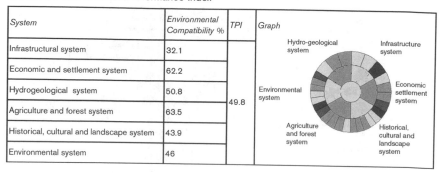

supply an answer to the 'relevant questions' that were asked at the beginning of this reflection? Among the many questions that were asked, two problems seem to be particularly interesting, in light of recent scientific debates and observations at an international level and from research programmes that are still under way: (a) What characteristics should instruments adopted in environmental evaluation have?; and (b) What is the potential of the performance indicators?

First, planning with respect to problems of the natural and built environment, the objective of sustainability analysis and the decisional processes is particularly complex (Bell and Morse, 1999). The supplied information is often insufficient as far as the real requirements are concerned; the impacts are uncertain and difficult to foresee in quantitative terms; the number of subjects that are involved (public, private, mixed, etc.) is very high; each of these is characterised by specific objectives that vary in time and priority; and the range of alternative scenarios is destined to change under the pressure of the interests at play. In cases like these it is necessary to use flexible procedures that, together with the most objective quantitative indications possible, can supply useful strategic results.

The usefulness of these evaluation methods rests not only in the fact that they improve the procedural rationality and therefore the quality of the planning process, but in that they are able to contribute to the design and implementation of new solutions. It is therefore necessary to develop methodologies that integrate qualitative and quantitative aspects. There are few examples of 'integrated' analysis in Europe to refer to and it might be useful to reflect on the present methodological procedures in light of recent international regulations pertaining to environmental problems. In order to face this uncertainty, it is necessary that the strategic evaluation should be able to identify, in adequate terms, some essential parameters that allow the relationship that exists between actions, pressure factors and environmental impact to be described. These parameters represent the same number of elements of strategic choice, which are accessible to the decision-maker in some way.

Secondly, the PPI, apart from respecting the aforementioned characteristics, can be used during the entire decisional process: starting data, objectives and regulation body, and monitoring system. These different functions should have an internal coherence that facilitates the comprehension of the planning strategies and which allows a monitoring system, based on parameters that represent the choices that have been made, to be developed. It is necessary to use the most flexible systems of indicators or indexes possible which, though being able to represent the specificity of the plan being analysed, should be shared and experimented at a large scale. From this point of view an index does not exist that would allow a universally valid reading of the territory, and it would be interesting to define specific systems of indicators and indexes sub-divided according to spatial scales and to type of plan, that could be representative both of the territory under analysis and of competences of the used instrument.

Finally, it is felt that the reflections that have been made are part of a European institutional and regulative picture that is in full evolution, and which is characterised by the development of innovative procedures and management hypotheses that aim to involve stakeholders in the preliminary and decisional stages of the planning process.

REFERENCES

Bartelmus, P. (1994). *Environment, Growth and Development. The Concepts and Strategies of Sustainability*, Routledge, London.

Bell, S. and Morse, S. (1999). *Sustainability Indicators: Measuring the Immeasurable?* Earthscan, London.

Bentivegna, V., Franchini, D. and Mondini, G. (1999). Manuale per l'applicazione delle valutazioni. Procedure e tecniche per la valutazione degli atti di programmazione e di pianificazione territoriale di competenza degli enti locali ai sensi della LR 5/1995, Edizioni Regione Toscana, Firenze.

Bottero, M., Mondini, G. and Valle, M. (2002). Problemi di valutazione nella relazione di compatibilità ambientale: il caso dei Piani Territoriali di Coordinamento, in Estimo e Territorio, Ed agricole, Bologna, no. 2.

Deakin, M., Mitchell, G. and Lombardi, P. (2002). Valutazione della sostenibilità: una verifica delle tecniche disponibili, *Urbanistica*, no. 118.

Giovanelli, F., Di Bella, I. and Coizet, R. (2000). La natura nel conto, Milano, Edizioni Ambiente.

Mondini, G. and Valle, M. (2001). Modellizzazione di un sistema di indicatori per la valutazione della qualità ambientale in un contesto urbano, in Genio Rurale, no. 1, Ed agricole, Bologna.

Peano, A. and Brunetta, G. (2003). *Valutazione Ambientale Strategica*, Il Sole 24 Ore, Milano.

Selman, P. (1996). *Local Sustainability*, Paul Chapman, London.

Smit, B. and Spaling, H. (1995). 'Methods for Cumulative Effects Assessment'. *Environmental Impact Assessment Review*, 15(1): 81–106.

INTERNET SITES

The following Internet sites provide further material to support integrated evaluation.

The environmental field

* http://www.un.org by the United Nations gives news, documents and publications in various fields including that of the environment.
* http://www.unece.org by the United Nations Economic Commission for Europe deals with energy, economic and environmental themes in the European environment.
* http://www.oecd.org by the Organisation for Economic Cooperation and Development presents documents and statistics pertaining to environmental development and economy.
* http://www.minambiente.it by the Italian Ministry of the Environment manages various databanks dealing with environmental material.
* http://www.c3ed.uvsq.fr/RESEAN by the Ministére francais de l'Aménagement du Territorie et de l'Environmen deals with international documents pertaining to sustainable development.

For indexes and indicator systems

* http://iisd.ca/measure/compendium.asp (International Institute for Sustainable Development, IISD) deals with environmental and sustainable indicator projects paying particular attention to projects that aim at integrate.
* The ONU site http://www.un.org/esa/sustdev/worklist.htm gives examples of environmental indicators that can be used in a study on sustainable development.
* The documents produced by the State of the Environment division of OCSE (http://www.ocse.it) gives examples of the DPSR model.
* The work by EUROSTAT (http://europa.eu.int/comm/eurostat) which follows the indications of European Community Commission document, Orientation

for the EU in the matter of environmental indicators and national green accountancy – Integration of environmental and economic information systems, Communication of the European Community Commission at the Council and at the European Parliament (COM(94) 670), 1994, which has recently presented a report on 60 indicators (http://esl.jrc.it/envind/index.htm).

- The http://iisd.ca/measure/compendium.asp site deals with projects of environmental and sustainability indicators with particular attention being paid to projects aimed at integrative analysis.

Institutions concerned with evaluation of plans, programmes and projects

- The European Agency for the Environment http://www.cea.eu.int/
- European Commission – Environmental Assessment http://europa.eu.int/comm/environment/eia/home.htm
- Environmental Protection Agency http://www.epa.gov/
- United Nations Environment Programme http://www.unep.org/
- Ministry of the Environment – Evaluation of Environmental Impact Service http://www.minambiente.it/Sito/settori azione/via/Home VIA.asp
- Ministry of the Environment – Sustainable Development Service http://www.minambiente.it/SVS.

Part 2

Systems Thinking-based Approaches

3

The Multimodal System Approach to Sustainability Planning Evaluation

Patrizia Lombardi and Peter Brandon

BACKGROUND

The systemic paradigm arose in the middle 1970s as an integration between cybernetic and structuralist paradigms. The latter is complementary to constructivism and, as Piaget (1968) expressed, is a method for describing an object in its totality, functioning and evolving, by taking a global perspective. This recognises a structure as formed by elements whose laws are distinct from those of the structure as a whole.

The theory of general systems which integrates the previous two paradigms is based on the work of L. von Bertalanffy (1968) who proposed an open system theory, i.e. an object possessing functions, structure and evolving. This work was later developed by Le Moigne (1994). Although this approach has the relevant feature of recognising the importance of information and organisation in making social sciences intelligible, as Eriksson (1996) noted, the approach may fall into relativism because the function of cognition is adaptive and does not tell us what kind of knowledge is constructed.

A second school of system thinking is the Multimodal System (MS) by de Raadt (1991, 1994, 1997). This aims to make complex systems intelligible by escaping the traditional Cartesian approach on the basis of comprehensive philosophical studies of multi-level perspectives.

Compared with the previous system school, the MS approach maps systems according to two axes, a multimodal one (vertical) and a systemic one (horizontal). Specifically, this approach is founded on the Cosmonomic philosophy of Herman Dooyeweerd (1958) and cybernetics as developed by Beer (1967, 1981) and Ashby (1978). Adapting and modifying these two foundations, MS has shifted focus of systems design and usage onto a number of levels of functioning (named modalities) in which systems operate instead of the systems themselves.

The main similarities and differences between the two systemic schools of le Moigne and de Raadt are shown as in Table 3.1.

A deeper explanation of this theory underlying this approach is provided in the following section, with the aim of showing the benefits that it is able to

Table 3.1 Le Moigne and de Raadt

Common ground	Systemic approach (Le Moigne)	Multi-modal system (de Raadt)
Both promote a re-conception of science in a personal relation denying the objective, independent notion.	Emphasis on the inadequacy of the analytical paradigm in understanding complexity.	Emphasis on the inadequacy of isolation of normative and determinative orders.
Both consider the quaint loop of information and organisation as fundamental in making social sciences intelligible as distinct from the traditional energetic notion of natural sciences.	Constructivism makes how we construct knowledge intelligent. This is received neither through senses nor by way of communication but is actively built up by a cognisant subject. The function of cognition is adaptive and serves the subjects' organisation of the experimental world, not the discovery of an objective ontological reality. This does not tell us what kind of knowledge is constructed. It may fall into relativism.	The assumption is that there is an absolute truth and ordered reality independent of human beings. It escapes relativism by focusing on a priori knowledge which is justified by faith. Our knowledge is limited. However it uses the cybernetic paradigm as an attempt to make social systems intelligible.
Both oppose the popular notion that social science is less exact or more fuzzy.		
Both try to find alternatives to the cybernetic paradigm which is considered to be insufficient. Both admit that ultimately faith is the last criterion of choice, or the last station on a multimodal stair.		

Source: Brandon and Lombardi (2005, p. 176)

offer to the problem of decision-making for sustainability. In particular, the Section 'Dooyeweerd's theory' introduces the philosophical framework, 'The Cosmonomic Idea of Reality' theory, and clarifies the importance of the concept of modality for analysing a complex system. Based on this theory, the Section 'A multimodal framework for evaluation in planning and design' illustrates the analytical framework which has been recently developed by the authors of this chapter for supporting decisions towards sustainability in planning and some main case studies (Brandon and Lombardi, 2005), while the Section 'Limitations and future directions of research' discusses the main limitations of this framework and the future steps of this research.

DOOYEWEERD'S THEORY: THE COSMONOMIC IDEA OF REALITY

The groundwork of the MS approach is the science methodology of Herman Dooyeweerd, a Dutch philosopher (1894–1975). This is known as the 'Cosmonomic Idea of Reality' which acknowledges an external reality which is independent of the acting and knowing subject (hence the term 'Cosmonomic'). We are affected by it but also affect it and have views and desires concerning it. It is based on the fundamental notion that nothing, not even theoretical thought, is absolute, but all is relative to the Creator God, who, by the act of creation, gave everything Meaning.

In the words of Basden (2001), 'the main motivation behind Dooyeweerd's work was to form a philosophical framework that did not make God-avoiding assumptions right from the start, and one that was self-consistent. He wanted it to account for the unity and diversity that we experience. Dooyeweerd was troubled by the fact that Biblical ideas do not seem to fit "comfortably" with most theoretical thinking, yet he was not satisfied with the explanation given by both secularists and fundamentalists that religion has nothing to do with this world of science, technology, business and, in particular, thinking.

The results of his work are included in three main volumes (1953–55). For a general description, see Clouser (1991) and Kalsbeek (1975), and for full theoretical treatment, see Dooyeweerd (1958) and Hart (1984). The present illustration makes copious references to the expositions made by de Raadt (1991, 1994, 1997) and Basden (1994, 1996, 2001).

The Cosmonomic theory of Reality claims there are two 'sides' to reality as we know it: a Law Side and an Entity Side. The Entity Side concerns things, systems, and in fact anything that does something: e.g. a person, a flower, a house, a government, a symphony, a town. The Law Side concerns modalities in which entities operate: e.g. physical, social, biotic, ethical, technical.

The two sides can be seen as orthogonal: an entity crosses several modalities. In everyday living the entities stand to the fore, as it were, and the Law Side recedes into the background, but in science the Law Side comes to the fore while the entities recede. That is, when we analyse reality we should study the Law Side, not the behaviour of entities. It is the Law Side that expresses the fundamental meaning, and it is the Law Side that enables entities to 'exist'. However, existence is not denied. Rather, it is seen as essentially dependent and meaning-bound.

A modality can be defined as an irreducible area of the functioning of a system. It is characterised by a nucleus of meaning which provides it with an internal order, named 'sphere sovereignty', and has its own order, or set of laws, by which it is governed (hence the alternative name Law-sphere given by Dooyeweerd), e.g. the laws of arithmetic, the laws of physics, the laws of aesthetics, the laws of ethics, etc. – which not only guide but enable entities (people, animals, etc.) to function in a variety of ways.

Modal laws – or orders – are fulfilled in two different ways. In the earlier (or lower or hard) modalities, such as numerical and spatial, and their equivalence in scientific disciplines, mathematics and geometry, the orders, or set of laws, that govern these modalities, are more determinative, i.e. 'the law always exerts its own fulfilment'. For example, within the physical modality, the law of gravity is always obeyed; it is a law of spatial aspect that nothing can be both round and square. However, in the later (or higher or soft) modalities, such as ethical and juridical, the laws are more normative since their fulfilment is contingent to people's inclination to follow these laws and they cannot be described through the harder modalities' determinative rules. In particular, the laws of the earlier aspects are more determinative while those of later aspects are more normative.

The laws are unique and irreducible, differing from modality to modality, so that it is not possible to entirely understand the behaviour of one modality on the basis of the laws of another modality (sphere sovereignty). However, there are definite relationships between them (sphere universality), which allow an entity to function in a coherent rather than fragmented manner.

An entity, such as a sheep or a person, acts as a subject in a number of these aspects and as object in others. While human beings can act as subject in all aspects, animals have a more limited range in which they function as subject. A sheep might act as an economic object, for instance, but not an economic subject.

There is an interrelation between the modalities which define their position. The economic modality is in fact dependent on the social, the social on the lingual, the lingual on the historical, and so on. Thus the Philosophy of the Cosmonomic Idea has not placed the 15 modalities in an arbitrary order, but the earlier aspects serve as foundations for the later (Dooyeweerd calls it 'the cosmic order of time').

The correspondence between the orders of different modalities allows one modality (named source) to be used as a metaphoric representation of another or several other modalities (named idioms). For example, social scientists often express aspects of social behaviour (operating in the social modality) in terms of quantitative measures (operating in the numeric modality). They can then use the laws of mathematics to manipulate aspects of behaviour in the social modality and derive conclusions which have been difficult to arrive at without the aid of these laws. In the words of de Raadt (1991), it is important to note that 'these conclusions rest upon the laws of the numeric modality and not on the basis of the social modality. Therefore, while they may be mathematically valid, they need not be necessarily valid in the social sphere'.

Although every modality can be an 'idiom' for another, its effectiveness as an idiom varies and the degree of correspondence declines as the distance between one modality and another increases. For example, the numeric modality is not a very suitable idiom for the juridical modality and it would be better to use a closer modality such as the ethical modality. In the words of de Raadt (1991), the softness of the normative order is not due to any indefiniteness, but due to the lower homomorphism that exists between the soft modalities and the logical and numerical modalities (these latter being the idioms employed by much of the hardest sciences) when compared with the homomorphism that exists between the hard modalities themselves.

Dooyeweerd illustrates a 'working' list of 15 modalities whose properties are exhibited by the objects of people's experience. These 15 aspects and their meaning-nuclei (in brackets) are the following: Quantitative (Quantity); Spatial (Continuous extension); Kinematics (Movement); Physical (Energy, mass); Biological (Life function); Sensitive (Senses, feeling); Analytic (Discerning of entities, logic); Historical (Formative power); Communicative (Informatory, symbolic representation); Social (Social intercourse, social exchange); Economic (Frugality, handling limited resources); Aesthetic (Harmony, beauty); Juridical (Retribution, fairness, rights); Ethical (Love, moral); Credal (Faith, commitment, trustworthiness). They were derived by taking every large-scale kind of property which has been distinguished in the history of philosophy and science.

In identifying the modalities and their order, however, not all authors are in accord. Hart (1984) identifies only 14 modalities, as he does not include aesthetic. In addition, he places analytic between historical and communicative, as a foundation for the informatory function. de Raadt (1997) adds two new aspects, epistemic (whose essence is wisdom) and operational (whose essence is production). These are placed, respectively, next to the communicative modality and to the social modality. Kalsbeek (1975) discusses the meaningfulness of including kinematics within physical as part of it.

A MULTIMODAL FRAMEWORK FOR EVALUATION IN PLANNING AND DESIGN

The 15 meaning-nuclei of the modalities are suggested to provide decision-makers with a qualification system to classify relevant sustainability issues in an urban design or planning situation. Specific attention has been paid to a definition of each modal aspect with headings which may be more familiar to a larger number of stakeholders, and, more specifically, to technical decision-makers.

A literature review on sustainable development and its understanding by various members of the community was at the basis of the development of this new vocabulary. This also takes into account the results of an assessment on the comprehension of the modalities by the non-expert users, which was undertaken at different stages of development of this framework (Lombardi, 2000). Table 3.2 illustrates the modalities and their suggested name.

As the definition of a sustainability aspect is a process which also includes non-technical aspects, the process must be guided by a scientific tool. In developing this framework, the PICABUE approach (Mitchell et al., 1995), whose benefits in

Table 3.2 Modalities, nuclei of meaning and sustainability aspects

Modalities	Nuclei of meaning	Redefined modalities to reflect sustainability
Numerical	'How much' of things	Numerical accounting
Spatial	Continuous extension	Spaces, shape and extension
Kinematics	Movement	Transport and mobility
Physical	Energy, mass	Physical environment, mass and energy
Biological	Life function	Health, bio-diversity, eco-protection
Sensitive	Senses, feeling	People's perceptions towards environment
Analytic	Discerning of entities	Analysis and formal knowledge
Historical	Formative power	Creativity and cultural development
Communicative	Informatory	Communications and the Media
Social	Social intercourse	Social climate and social cohesion
Economic	Frugality	Efficiency and Economic appraisal
Aesthetic	Harmony, beauty	Visual appeal and architectonic style
Juridical	Retribution, fairness	Rights and responsibilities
Ethical	Love, moral	Ethical issues
Credal	Faith, trustworthiness	Commitment, interest and vision

gauging the degree of common commitment of societal actors and representatives of different disciplines towards sustainable development have already been highlighted by several recent studies (Palmer *et al.*, 1997; Curwell *et al.*, 1998), were used for identifying appropriate questions under each sustainability aspect, linking them to the four recognised principles underlying sustainable development:

1   Futurity – a concern for future generations, not cheating on our children.
2   Social Equity – a concern for today's poor and disadvantaged, equal access to resources.
3   Environment – preserving the eco-system, ensuring that human activities do not threaten the integrity of ecological systems.
4   Public participation – a concern that individuals should have an opportunity to participate in decisions that affect them; ability to influence decisions.

Although other schemes exist which aim at understanding and classifying sustainability issues (Bentivegna *et al.*, 2002), PICABUE seems more appropriate in the context of this study. First, it is not scoped and limited to renewable energy policies or other sectorial and compartmentalised policy making as, for example, in the Pentagon model (Nijkamp and Pepping, 1998); rather, it is general and holistic. Secondly, it is founded on the sustainable principles that underlie official reports on Agenda 21, and therefore it is not too general or broad as is SLEPT (Social, Legal,

Economic, Political and Technical) system. PICABUE has often been used to classify quality issues and sustainability indicators within the context of a sustainability IT model for cities (May *et al.*, 1997). Thirdly, it is very simple and easy to understand by people, as revealed by the studies on stakeholders' concern about sustainability in planning and construction (Cooper and Curwell, 1998).

In parallel to activity of populating the framework with questions for guiding decision-makers, a number of current assessment methods and tools have been specified for each sustainability aspect. These evaluation methods belong to various different technical fields and scientific disciplines such as economics, different branches of engineering, structural technology, architecture, town planning, etc.

The final evaluation framework is illustrated in Table 3.3. It involves all the following: a technical and ecologically oriented assessment of the construction under development (a 'green design') that illustrates the environmental compatibility

Table 3.3 Examples related to the (re)development of an urban area

Modal aspects	Sustainability aspects	Key questions	Evaluation tools
Credal	Commitment, Interest and Vision It identifies the motivation for human actions and choices, reasons and goals underpinning urban policies and political strategies, the political point of view, the peoples' vision of a community development, etc.	Futurity: Is the political situation stable? Equity: Does the (re)development scheme meet with regional–national plans? Environment: Has a Strategic Environmental Assessment been undertaken? Will finance be available for environmental protection? Participation: Has the (re)development scheme been agreed on by stakeholders?	Strategic regional plan Focus groups Consultation
Ethical	Ethical issues It refers to a particular attitude towards the others, both living creatures or inanimate ones, which is governed by altruistic motives. It suggests that stakeholders go beyond mere duty in consideration of ownership and responsibility allowing collaboration and co-operation	Futurity: Does the development scheme provide the same or improved opportunities for people in the future as in the present? Equity: Does the development scheme reduce social inequalities? Does it support the action of voluntary groups? Environment: Does the scheme provide a protection of biosphere, ecosystem and animal species? Participation: Have the stakeholders been involved in the development of the scheme?	Community Impact Evaluation Environmental impact analysis

Table 3.3 (Continued)

Modal aspects	Sustainability aspects	Key questions	Evaluation tools
Juridical	Rights and responsibilities It expresses the human need for justice, usually institutionalised and formalised in a body of laws, regulating social justice. It also deals with property and planning laws, legal institutions and political structure, land titles regulations and other policy	Futurity: What are the modifications in current property structure? Have the rights and the responsibilities of all developers, land and building owners and users, been accounted for in the long term? Equity: Does the scheme provide an identification of those who benefit and those who pay for the development? Does it include some possibilities for the reimbursement of damage and a payment for the rights received? Environment: Is there compliance with the technical-planning standards related to the protection of the environment? Participation: What is the degree to which people can change their environment either directly or through elected representatives? What citizen groups are entitled to participate in the decision-making process?	Public Committees Public advisory boards Public Planning Councils European, National and Local Planning Laws and Regulations
Aesthetic	Visual appeal and architectonic style of buildings and settings It means beauty and harmony within the settlement In design it also means aesthetic quality related to architectonic style and decoration	Futurity: Does the development scheme improve the artistic character and significance of buildings and settlements in the short and long term? Does the condition of the built environment enhance the visual appeal? Equity: Are the planned interventions aesthetically satisfying to all the stakeholders? Environment: Is the development in harmony with the context, the surroundings and the eco-system? Does the scheme improve the visual appeal of natural settings? Participation: Have the viewpoints of both stakeholders and experts been taken into account in the development of the design?	Design approach and methodologies Lynch's approach to design polls and surveys Workshops, meetings and consultation
Economical	Efficiency and economic appraisal	Futurity: Has a long-term financial appraisal been undertaken?	Life-cycle costing of buildings

	It is not concerned so much with finance, but rather with wise use of limited resources	Equity: What is the financial distribution for the stakeholders? Has employment of the local labour force in construction activities been considered?	Cost–benefit analysis
	Efficiency is defined as the ability to achieve desirable goals by managing limited resources. It asks developers and designers to consider how to make best use of all the available resources	Environment: Is there an efficient environmental management system? Is there an exhaustive city-wide recycling programme from which the development could benefit? Participation: How many of the stakeholders have committed themselves to the financial appraisal?	Community Impact Evaluation Multicriteria analysis
Social	Social climate, social relationship, social cohesion It refers to a relationship which links people together, developing cooperation and association. Key concepts related to it are 'Sociophilia', cohesion, synergy and plurality	Futurity: Does the plan enhance and sustain social interaction in the long term? Does it consider the impact of the development on the social climate in the long term? Equity: Does the plan favour cooperation and association between individuals and institutions? Does it improve the accessibility to social utilities for all the members of the community? Environment: Does the plan consider the impacts of tourism on the cultural and natural settings? Participation: Have social clubs, voluntary groups and cultural associations been involved in the development of the scheme?	Polls and surveys Questionnaire techniques Audit and monitoring
Communicative	Communication and the Media Advertising and urban signs, information facilities, media and networking are common means for transferring information in a built and urban environment. It may also refer to the communicative role of a planning activity with the meaning to inform	Futurity: Is a monitoring system for the area available? Will the communicative infrastructures be improved in the present and the future? Is a long-term programme for urban signs available? Equity: Does the plan improve the accessibility to communication facilities for all citizens, including poor and disadvantaged?	Monitoring and audit Argumentative approaches in planning evaluation

Table 3.3 (Continued)

Modal aspects	Sustainability aspects	Key questions	Evaluation tools
	and in turn to get information from stakeholders, developers and community in general	Environment: Does the plan include environmental audits? Is an environmentally oriented advertising available for the area? Participation: Is information on the development scheme available to all stakeholders? Are all relevant citizen groups able to take part in the discussion, argument and evaluation in planning? Does everyone understand the language used?	Technical and non-technical languages IT tools Virtual reality
Historical	Creativity and cultural development It means 'formative power' for a human community, change and creativity in planning and design. It deals with all those active, creative and designing activities within a community, such as conservation strategies for the built heritage, effective technologies employed in construction	Futurity: Does the urban plan include a restoration programme for cultural heritage? Is the innovation based on local practice? Equity: Does the plan improve the living standards of the poor and disadvantaged and their cultural aspirations? Environment: Are the technologies employed environmentally friendly? Participation: Does the city have a well-established consultation process? Has consultation successfully been undertaken in relation to the proposal?	Design approaches Technological analyses Goals achievement matrix
Analytical	Analysis, formal knowledge It governs the process of understanding, reasoning and deductive thinking. It refers to the activity of scientists, researchers and all those people who use scientific tools in their professional work It is related to quality of analysis for planning, research, education and teaching	Futurity: Has scientific analysis been applied to the problem, including consideration of the long-term perspective? Does the funding to support the solution in the long term?	Analytical hierarchy process Analytical approaches in planning evaluation

		Environment: Is there an educational programme relating to the environment available for the community? Participation: Has the developed analysis been accessed and agreed on by most of the stakeholders?	Logic, scientific reasoning and deductive thinking
Sensitive	Perceptions of people towards the environment It deals with senses, feelings and emotions, such as the feeling of well-being, the feelings engendered by living there, security, privacy, noise, comfort, etc.	Futurity: Is a long-term security scheme available for the area? Equity: Does the plan address the issues of crime and vandalism in the area and surroundings? Will every stakeholder feel comfort and confidence in the design for safety within the surroundings? Is the children's viewpoint taken into consideration? Environment: Does the plan solve the problems of noise in the area? Does it take into account the visual impact? Participation: Are the viewpoints of all stakeholders, including those who have no voice, taken into consideration? Have the groups for the rights of children been active in decision-making?	Lynch's theoretical outlook approaches IT tools Virtual reality Surveys and polls Questionnaire techniques
Biological	Health, bio-diversity and ecological protection It defines the 'vitality' of a system and its ability to survive, or to live, grow and develop. It refers to the carrying capacity of an urban environment. In terms of system ecology, it refers to the concept of 'autopoiesis' and of metabolism of a urban system	Futurity: What is the carrying capacity of the area? Does the development scheme for the area take into account the maintenance of available capital of non-renewable resources in the long term? Equity: Is every stakeholder able to enjoy an appropriate level of quality of air, water and soil in the developing area? Do they feel happy with the presence of green areas, hygiene, health and health services, hospitals, gyms, etc.? Environment: Is there an environmental planning scheme available for the area? Does the plan improve air, water and soil quality in the area? Does it increase or improve health services?	Ecological footprint approach Carrying capacity Environmental impact analysis

Table 3.3 (Continued)

Modal aspects	Sustainability aspects	Key questions	Evaluation tools
		Participation: Are the community groups active on environmental issues? Have all the stakeholders taken part in the development of the environmental planning scheme?	
Physical	Physical environment, mass and energy It is characterised by energy and mass which often represents the minimum level of functioning for a living entity. In planning, it refers to the physical environment, energy, water, air, soil, natural materials, resources and land on which to build. Within a quantitative meaning, it refers to the prosperity of the built environment, i.e. the amount of available capital of natural non-renewal resources	Futurity: Is an energy scheme available which takes into account a long-term perspective? Is a maintenance scheme for the buildings available? Equity: Does every stakeholder feel happy with the level of quality of housing and physical facilities? Environment: Has the development been based on an energy saving scheme? Participation: Have Local Environmental Action Groups such as Friends of the Earth, Greenpeace, Civic Trust association, WWFN, Ambiente Italia, etc. been involved in the development of the scheme?	Strategic environmental analysis Environmental impact analysis Multicriteria methods Energy planning schemes Physical indicators
Kinematics	Transport and mobility It deals with 'movement' (a concept derived from science and mechanics). It is related to: transportation, wildlife movement, accessibility to services and parking, drainage systems	Futurity: Does the development scheme for the area improve the mobility in and out of the area in the long term? Equity: Is every stakeholder able to move using public transport? Are transport facilities available to all stakeholders? Environment: Is the transport planning scheme environmentally friendly? Will it improve the air quality? Participation: Have all the stakeholders taken part in the development of the transport planning scheme?	Transport and traffic planning scheme Transport evaluation tools Infrastructure capacity

Spatial	Space, shape and extension It means 'continuous extension'. It deals with: shape and layout of buildings, terrain shape, density, location, geographical position, proximity, spatial differentiation, areas and form	Futurity: Is the development sufficiently flexible to take into account future development schemes for the area? Will the urban form be stable in time? Equity: Is the urban density appropriate for every stakeholder? Environment: Is the new urban density and form environmentally friendly? Participation: Have all the stakeholders taken part in the development of the shape and layout of the buildings and settings?	Design approaches Planning approaches GIS CAD
Quantitative	Numerical accounting It means 'awareness of how much of things'. It refers to the number of people, inhabitants, metre squares, hectares of ground on which to build, etc. It deals with numerical data, statistics and mathematics	Futurity: How long is the development process? Equity: How much redistribution of wealth is contained within the scheme? Environment: How much is the development in terms of natural and non-renewal resources? Participation: How many stakeholders have taken part in the decision-making?	Numerical indicators Mathematics and algebra Quantitative index

Source: Lombardi (2000)

of this development within the existing context; an assessment of the historical and cultural significance of the planning asset and of its social desirability; an analysis of the economic and juridical feasibility; a check of the visual appeal of this new (re)development and of its flexibility or adaptability which may allow the meeting of some future user's needs and an understanding of what interest or concern there is in the Local Agenda of the city.

OVERVIEW OF CASE STUDIES

The MS structure underlying this framework has been applied to three case studies related to different planning situations in order to show the flexibility of the proposed structure to different contexts and its potential generalisation (i.e. its replicability). As known, planning is a multi-aspect activity and generally proposes a continuous variety of different problems that challenge designers. These case studies cover some major current planning/management problems for sustainability (UNCHS, 1996) and are as follows: the management of technological systems at infrastructure level, the urban regeneration at district level and the strategic planning at city level.

The first example provides evidence for the comprehensiveness of the aspects included in the MS structure for the long-term planning of a situation by suggesting a decision-making problem which has been tackled previously by a traditional provisional evaluation method (i.e. multicriteria analysis). Thus, it is possible to compare the new approach with that one undertaken previously in order to see whether there is an improvement. In this example, it is shown that the multi-modal structure is able to render all the factors underlying the decision-making explicit, pinpointing the limitations of the method which was used in the case study. In turn, this helps to illustrate that the structure is comprehensive and able to sufficiently address the identified problems.

The second case study proposes a stakeholder's analysis of a decision-making process, adopting the modal aspects as a tool for detecting the stakeholders' views of the problem. The MS structure is used as a retrospective evaluation tool for understanding and learning about sustainability. A multi-stakeholder's decision-making problem is illustrated, which deals with the crucial sustainability problem of regenerating an ex-industrial area (Curwell and Lombardi, 1999).

Finally, the third example deals with sustainability indicators, structuring the 'social reporting' (or stakeholders' reporting) of the City of Modena (Italy) by means of the suggested multi-modal structure. It illustrates the relevance of the 15 structure components.

All three case studies are illustrated in Brandon and Lombardi (2005) and are based on previous applications of some traditional methodologies, respectively, 'multicriteria analysis', 'stakeholders analysis' and 'triple bottom–up approach' as documented, respectively, in: Lombardi and Zorzi (1993), Lombardi and Marella (1997) and Stanghellini and Lombardi (2002).

LIMITATIONS AND FUTURE DIRECTIONS OF RESEARCH

This chapter has presented a conceptual framework for understanding sustainability in urban planning and design for the built environment and the underlying theory. The framework is useful, not only because it recognises different levels of information (the so-called 'modalities') but also because it is able to make the relevant issues of a decision-making process explicit and transparent in the context of sustainability, identifying problems and providing a full check list of questions and assessment tools. This feature of the framework is particularly relevant in multicriteria evaluation for structuring decision-making problem (Nijkamp, 2003; Munda, 2004) and some experimental applications in this direction has been recently developed (Lombardi, 2005; Lombardi et al., 2006).

Although the framework is flexible and usable in different evaluation contexts, monitoring and ex-post planning situations, it is specifically developed for ex-ante evaluation. This is reflected in the selection of the assessment methods and procedures that are included in it.

However, it is worth remarking that technical information and scientific knowledge related to sustainability in the built environment is, at present, very limited. Moreover, experience in the field of sustainability in planning and the built environment is restricted to some good 'local' examples or case studies, whose applicability cannot always be generalised (Selman, 1996; Cooper and Palmer, 1999).

Research on sustainability is still experimental and still very fragmented since it requires joint effort, collaboration and continuous implementation; it requires multidisciplinary and multi-people working contexts over a long time period (Bentivegna *et al.*, 2002; Curwell *et al.*, 2005). A further major constrain is the lack of an existing database on sustainability so that application becomes extremely difficult. Current debates on sustainability tend to focus on statistical indicators and classification systems, but the information required for decision-making is not yet available (Mitchell, 1996; Deakin *et al.*, 2001, 2002).

The developed framework enables the linking of aspects for evaluation with questions for examining sustainability and, finally, with a number of problem-solving assessment methods. However, in order to operationalise the framework it needs further work and possibly the support of an IT tool, such as a knowledge-based system which can evolve and cope with incomplete and uncertain information. It requires pragmatic testing, revision, implementation and a convenient user-friendly interface.

Some major problems faced in decision-making for sustainability include the amount of information required for an evaluation of this type which is time-consuming and certainly costly; the variety of vocabulary employed and required by each assessment method; the elements of uncertainty included in the available data; and the difficult access to different databases; etc.

The framework, as it has been developed and illustrated in this chapter, does not overcome all of these problems directly but it shows how it is possible to use current assessment methods within the framework. However, it does provide new opportunities for collaboration between disciplines, experts and people; it adds new dimensions that were traditionally uncovered in the evaluation (e.g. aesthetics) and it links all the knowledge and the special contributions of science within the same structure, providing order, continuity and integration without falling into reductionism or lack of transparency. Thus, it can also act as a learning tool, answering current demands for higher education in the field of planning.

Future knowledge on sustainability, further implementation of the information on which the framework relies and pragmatic-testing in real worldwide contexts will certainly be required. Practical applications could also be improved if the model is linked to expert systems or GIS. (Geographical Information System). At present, research findings show that the framework is reliable as a model to be used for challenging planning towards greater sustainability in the built environment.

REFERENCES

Ashby, W.R. (1976), *An Introduction to Cybernetics*, Methuen, London.

Basden, A. (1994), *A Multi-modal Approach to Knowledge Based System*, Information Technology Institute, University of Salford, UK (unpublished).

Basden, A. (1996), 'Towards an understanding of contextualized technology', Proceedings of the International Conference of the Swedish Operations Research Society on Managing the Technological Society: The Next Century's Challenge to O.R., University of Lulea, Sweden, 1–3 October, pp. 17–32.

Basden, A. (2001), Cosmonomic Philosophy (with special relevance to Information Technology) (http://www.basden.demon.co.uk/Dooy/summary.html), October.

Beer, S. (1967), *Decision and Control*, John Wiley & Sons, Chichester.

Beer, S. (1981), *Brain of the Firm*, John Wiley & Sons, Chichester.

Bentivegna, V., Curwell, S., Deakin, M., Lombardi, P. and Nijkamp, P. (2002), 'A vision and methodology for integrated sustainable urban development: BEQUEST', *Building Research International, BRI*, 30(2): 83–94.

Bertalanffy, L. von (1968), *General Systems Theory*, Braziller, New York.

Brandon, P.S. and Lombardi, P. (2005), *Evaluating the Built Environment*, Blackwell Publishing, Oxford.

Clouser, R. (1991), *The Myth of Religions Neutrality*, University of Notre Dame, London.

Cooper, I. and Curwell, S. (1998), 'The implications of urban sustainability', *Building Research and Information*, 26(1): 17–28.

Cooper, I. and Palmer, J. (1999), 'Il programma di ricerca sulle città sostenibili', *Urbanistica*, 112: 83–86.

Curwell, S., Hamilton, A. and Cooper, I. (1998), 'The BEQUEST Network: towards sustainable urban development', *Building Research and Information*, 26(1): 56–65.

Curwell, S. and Lombardi, P. (1999), 'Riqualificazione urbana sostenibile', *Urbanistica*, n. 112, giugno 1999, pp. 96–103 (English version, pp. 114–115).

Curwell, S., Deakin, M. and Symes, M. (eds) (2005), Sustainable Urban Development: The Framework, Protocols and Environmental Assessment Methods, Vol. 1, E&FN SPON, London.

Deakin, M., Curwell, S. and Lombardi, P. (2001), 'BEQUEST: sustainability assessment, the framework and directory of methods', *International Journal of Life Cycle Assessment*, 6(6): 373–390.

Deakin, M., Curwell, S. and Lombardi, P. (2002), 'Sustainable urban development: the framework and directory of assessment methods', *Journal of Environmental Assessment Policy and Management*, 4(2): 171–197.

de Raadt, J.D.R. (1991), 'Cybernetic approach to information systems and organization learning', *Kybernetes*, 20: 29–48.

de Raadt, J.D.R. (1994), 'Expanding the horizon of information systems design', *System Research*, n. 3, 2: 185–199.

de Raadt, J.D.R. (1997), 'A sketch for human operational research in a technological society', *System Practice*, 10(4): 421–442.

Dooyeweerd, H. (1958), *A New Critique of Theoretical Thought*, 4 vols, Presbyterian and Reformed Publisher Company, Philadelphia, Pennsylvania.

Eriksson, D. (1996), 'System science: a guide for postmodernity? A proposition', *Proceedings of the International Conference of the Swedish Operations Research Society, Managing the Technological Society: The Next Century's Challenge to O.R.*, University of Lulea, Sweden, 1–3 October, pp. 57–71.

Hart, H. (1984), *Understanding our World*, University Press of America, USA.

Kalsbeek, L. (1975), *Contours of a Christian Philosophy*, Wedge Publishing Company, Toronto.

Le Moigne, J.L. (1994), *La théorie du systeme général*, PUF, Paris.

Lombardi, P. (2000), 'A framework for understanding sustainability in the cultural built environment', in P.S. Brandon, P. Lombardi and P. Srinath (eds), *Cities & Sustainability. Sustaining our Cultural Heritage*, Conference Proceedings, Vishva Lekha Sarvodaya, Sri Lanka, cap. IV, pp. 1–25.

Lombardi, P. (2005), 'How to identify the criteria for evaluating sustainable urban regeneration & design', Paper presented at the EUROXXI 2006, International Conference *OR for Better Management of Sustainable Development*, Reykjavik, 2–5 July (see: www.euro2006.org) and currently in press in: Stellin G. and Curto R. (eds), *La Ricerca Scientifica nel Campo dell'Estimo e della Valutazione*, Angeli, Milano.

Lombardi, P. and Marella, G. (1997), 'A multi-modal evaluation of sustainable urban regeneration'. A Case-Study Related to Ex-Industrial Areas in the Second International Conference on Buildings and the Environment, CIB-CSTB, Vol. 2, Paris, 9–12 June, pp. 271–279.

Lombardi, P. and Zorzi, F. (1993), 'Comparison between aggregated techniques for assessing the effects of decision-making processes in the environmental field', in A. Manso, A. Bezega and D. Picken (eds), *Economic Evaluation and the Built Environment*, Vol. 4, Laboratorio Nacional de Engenheria Civil, Lisbon, pp. 126–137.

Lombardi, P., Lami, I.M. and Bottero, M. (2006), 'Sustainable urban (re)development problem structuring at local planning level'. An application of the Analytic Network Process and the Multi-modal approach, Paper in preparation for the International Conference on *Whole Life Urban Sustainability and its Assessment*, 27–29 June 2007, Glasgow, UK.

May, A.D., Mitchell, G. and Kupiszewska, D. (1997), 'The development of the Leeds quantifiable city model', in Brandon *et al.* (eds), *Evaluation of Sustainability in the Built Environment*, E&FN SPON, Chapman & Hall, London, pp. 39–52.

Mitchell, G. (1996), 'Problems and fundamentals of sustainable development indicators', *Sustainable Development*, 4(1): 1–11.

Mitchell, G., May, A. and McDonald, A. (1995), 'PICABUE: A methodological framework for the development of indicators of sustainable development'. *International Journal of Sustainable Development and World Ecology*, 2: 104–123.

Munda, G. (2004), 'Social multi-criteria evaluation: Methodological foundations and operational consequences', *European Journal of Operational Research*, 158: 662–677.

Nijkamp, P. (2003), 'Il ruolo della valutazione a supporto di una sviluppo umano sostenibile: una prospettiva cosmonomica', in L. Fusco Girard, B. Forte, M. Cerreta, P. De Toro and F. Forte (eds), *L'uomo e la città*, Milano, Angeli, pp. 466–468.

Nijkamp, P. and Pepping, G. (1998), 'A meta-analytic evaluation of sustainable city initiatives', *Urban Studies*, 35.

Palmer, J., Cooper, I. and van der Vost, R. (1997), 'Mapping out fuzzy buzzwords – who sits where on sustainability and sustainable development', *Sustainable Development*, 5(2): 87–93.

Piaget, J. (1968), *Le Structuralism*, PUF, Paris.

Selman, P. (1996), *Local Sustainability*, Paul Chapman, London.

Stanghellini, S. and Lombardi, P. (2002), 'Il contributo dell'analisi SWOT e del Bilancio sociale alla pianificazione strategica: i casi di Trieste e Modena', in Archibugi F., Pianificazione strategica e Governance ambientale, Proceedings of the International Conference, Ministry of the Environment – Formez, 29–30 November, Rome.

United Nations Conference on Human Settlement (UNCHS) (1996), The indicators programme: monitoring human settlements for the global plan of action, paper – United Nations Conference on Human Settlement (Habitat II), Istanbul, June.

4

The Human Sustainable City: Values, Approaches and Evaluative Tools

Luigi Fusco Girard, Maria Cerreta, Pasquale De Toro and Fabiana Forte

INTRODUCTION

From sustainable development to human sustainable development

The rapid and increasing process of urbanization is leading to recognition of the increasingly vital role of the city. One half of the world's population lives in cities, while the other half depends on cities for its survival. Population growth, globalization and democratization are the three factors which have contributed to strengthen the role of the cities as centres of production, consumption and change, whether it be political or social (Hall, 2003), thus helping to modify our vision of sustainable development.

On the other hand, economic development, urbanization and democratization are linked by relationships which are certainly not simple, and demand that the new players and new tools be able to keep pace with the rapid changes generated by technological innovation (Gilbert, 2003).

The cities of the twenty-first century are spreading their tentacles, sucking food, energy, water and resources from the natural environment, without taking into due account the social, economic and environmental consequences generated at global level. Indeed, the city appears as a place of strong contrasts, promoting as it does consolidation of the wealth of the favoured few but the spread of poverty for others. Steady growth in the process of urbanization has led to the phenomenon of the urbanization of poverty and hence the spread of social exclusion, recognized as the main cause of social dysfunction and urban degradation, of crime and violence, above all in developing countries. We can state that the cities are the breeding grounds of the greatest social, ethnic and cultural changes consequent on significant movement of persons and the blending of social and cultural behaviour models.

The cities are becoming new frontier zones, where players with completely different interests meet and confront each other, where lacerating conflicts and social tensions may be born, where the contradictions of globalization concentrate.

But cities can also be seen as places where these conflicts can be resolved, where new development and 'human ecology' strategies can be born, new coalitions between civil society, public institutions and economic subjects can come to the fore: hence, the starting point for a new policy and a more vital democracy.

Redistributive strategies for innovative development, based on the promotion of equal opportunities for development and the redistribution of benefits, can transform the city from an *engine of economic growth* into an *engine of social change* (Hall and Pfeiffer, 2000).

Thus, in spite of difficulties due to globalization and urbanization, we believe that the city has a leading role to play, in both promoting and countering to the goals of 'human sustainable development'.

The demand for 'human sustainability' is a particular way of interpreting the task of 'human development' in a world marked by enormous inequalities in contemporary living conditions and by real threats to the prospects of human life in the future. It requires that in our anxiety to protect future generations, we do not overlook the pressing claims of the less privileged today. Human sustainable development is based on an elementary demand for impartiality, according to which human beings must be considered as persons with equal rights. It is therefore a synonym of 'distributional equity', able to distribute the conditions of well being among present and future generations, according to a vision of inter-generational and intra-generational solidarity (Anand and Sen, 2000). Having adopted this interpretation, it becomes important to articulate the concept of duty and responsibility towards present and future generations, but we also need to understand just how we must organize the way of life and relationships of our society, as well as identifying its reference values.

The paradigm of human sustainable development leads to a demand for a new type of city, that is one seen as a 'common good'. In this sense, the call for 'a new urban ethic' is linked to the theme of responsibility towards others, towards future generations, towards cultural and environmental resources, of solidarity with the weak and marginalized (whether human beings, communities or countries) and the recovery of a spiritual dimension. Indeed, sustainability as inspiration for the future suggests positive perspectives of commitment in transformation and highlights the requirement for a form of ethics able to make its mark in political, cultural and decision-making processes. On the other hand, we must recognize the fact that today the primary sources of urban change are to be identified in civil society and its organized forms of expression. Local actions, implemented in cooperation with the communities, individuals and groups on the basis of shared interests and values would appear to be the main means of humanizing, improving and transforming the quality of urban life.

As Zamagni (1999) observes, in our society there is a wall separating two spheres drastically and its polarization is one of the most serious dangers: State and the market; social justice and economic efficiency; assistance and production; etc. Thus what we need to do is replace an architecture based on 'walls' by an architecture based on 'bridges', which will allow the two spheres of State and market to interact and influence each other, generating mutually enriching synergies.

Thus, understanding the meaning and implications of human sustainable development means succeeding in identifying and interpreting which values, today, may be considered fundamental for the construction of the city of tomorrow.

Promoting humanization means rejecting the image of the one-dimensional human being in the name of the idea of 'integral and plural' individuals linked to other human beings and to the Earth, free in their ability for self-determination, in their uniqueness and irreproducibility, and marked by an 'intrinsic value' which makes them inviolable and never instrumental: human beings seen as *person*.

The dimensions of human sustainable development

Human sustainable development implies attention to certain value categories reflected in a multi-dimensional and integrated vision, grouped into six main dimensions (Nijkamp *et al.*, 1993; Fusco Girard *et al.*, 2003): *ecoware, hardware, finware, orgware, software* and *civicware*.

The improvement of *ecoware* means preserving the quality of the natural/built environment by urban ecological management. In the same way that the twentieth century was marked by an increase in productivity from work, the twenty-first century will be marked by ecological modernization and eco-efficient innovation (von Weizsäcker *et al.*, 1998). Considering the dimension of *ecoware* means, above all, attempting to safeguard a territory providing ecological support to the city, extensive enough to sustain the functioning of its economic system. It also means identifying the most sustainable form of use of a very scarce resource, such as natural capital.

The dimension of *hardware* includes the system of communications, transport, man-made capital and built stock. In order to make the city more eco-efficient and more equitable, an attempt has been made to improve: (1) efficiency in land use; (2) the efficiency of public transport; (3) availability of alternative modes of transport, through organizational or technological alternatives to the private car; (4) the network of pedestrian walkways and car parks; (5) equitable access. *Hardware* is the physical infrastructure of city.

Finware means the organization of financial support systems (loans and capital) integrating those already existing to combine economies of scale with purpose-oriented economies (productivity, quality, diversity). Cities need new resources to implement any sustainable development strategy. Naturally, development is first and foremost dependent on the upgrading of the urban economy, which in turn requires scientific and technological innovation centres, development incubators, etc., as well as local tax reforms for greater effectiveness. New financing mechanisms are also needed.

The *orgware* dimension implies shifting from production to promotion strategies. It is not so much a problem of controlling processes, but of turning them in a direction that overall is more desirable. This means not only imposing constraints, but rather providing incentives, stimulating, promoting, activating, convincing, communicating, acting jointly. Successful cities are those which have adopted institutional arrangements targeting several fronts in an integrated manner, according to a systemic approach, which recognizes the importance of governance and in particular of 'human urban governance'.

With the aim of promoting human sustainable development within the framework of this six-dimensional model, we must stress the priority role of *software* and *civicware* (Figure 4.1).

Indeed, the dimension of *software* means, above all, the improvement of human capital, including business skills, professional know-how and innovation, but also a cultural mindset. The challenge of improving urban *software* means first and foremost improving entrepreneurship and professional skills: there is a need for excellence in know-how to sustain continuous innovation. But scientific and professional competencies must be coupled with a capacity for critical analysis, i.e. identifying priorities, distinguishing what is important from what is only apparently so. In many cases, an overwhelming amount of information and knowledge is available, but what

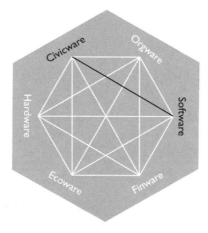

Figure 4.1 The dimensions of human sustainable development

is lacking is the ability to sort it and arrange it critically. Lack of critical knowledge is perhaps the most insidious form of poverty.

Urban *software* aims at providing the cultural basis for sustainability, that attempts to strike a balance between instrumental and intrinsic values, between present and future generations, between private interests and the general interest. It also recognizes the importance of gratuity and the gift. As such it is the exact antithesis of the culture of economic and financial globalization, founded on exchange between monetary equivalents.

The dimension of *civicware* expresses the attention to civil/social infrastructure. In the era of globalization, cities are experiencing progressive social fragmentation and a loss of collective consciousness, that is of social capital. At the same time, as the city consumes social capital, it has a growing need for it as a strategic element in its development. Today, the challenge facing the community may be summed up as the challenge to reproduce social capital at a rate at least equal to its rate of consumption. Social capital expresses the 'relational environment', that is the rules governing general interest and the common good which orient people in the direction of responsible choice, public spirit and legality. Social capital is the basic ingredient of civil society. *Civicware* and *software* are characterized by priority because they are the 'energy' for the change.

In order to design a human sustainable development project for the city, it is therefore necessary to act simultaneously on all these different levels, with opportune combinations. This implies succeeding in structuring a virtuous process of interdependence making it possible to achieve a balance between the six dimensions, explicating a multi-dimensional vision of value according to which the intangible components take on a determining role. Combining the various dimensions of value implies the need to consider as an essential condition for human sustainable development ethical and relational values, *intrinsic values*.

Widening the space of values

Which values can we assign to the natural environment and which to the built environment? What assumptions and theoretical constructs are able to guide us in the direction of the recognition of values? What are the key values facilitating human sustainable development?

By taking ethical values as theoretical bearings to help us confront the world, we can map the boundaries of our viewpoint, influencing research and the evaluation practice. Ethics has the potential as a 'meta-theory' to move us beyond its normative value as a scientific task or method and consider evaluation as a 'practical, moral undertaking' (Schwandt, 2002).

Recognizing the role of ethical values means admitting a need to move beyond the instrumental aspects of practice, proposing an 'equal foundation' for evaluation, starting from questions such as 'whose values?', 'values for whom?', 'values based on which point of view?'. Thus ethics seen as a basis for evaluation can provide a common language through which we can render values, creeds and dilemmas visible and communicable. But it also implies a move away from an anthropocentric vision, enriching evaluation by means of several types of approach such as: *systems thinking* (Capra, 1996); *learning organizations* (Senge, 1990); *self-organizing systems and complexity theory* (Kaufman, 1995; Wilber, 2000); and *eco-centric management* (Stead and Stead, 1996). Each of these approaches is coherent with the assumptions proper to environmental ethics which, in turn, may be considered a potential theoretical foundation to ensure the viability of multi-dimensional evaluation.

Indeed, it may be stated that 'environmental ethics presents and defends a systematic and comprehensive account of the moral relations between human beings and their natural environment' (Des Jardins, 2001, p. 13). According to environmental ethics, value theory distinguishes between *instrumental* and *intrinsic* values for single organisms and populations, for species, biomes, ecosystems, etc. Indeed, if evaluation is about making value statements, determining value and worth, and deciding which values are preferred, then addressing first utilitarian tradition we further define value as either *instrumental* or *intrinsic* (Scriven, 1983, 1986). The former term implies a means to further some ends, 'useful for Man' to obtain something else which has a value; and the latter means valuing things as ends in themselves.

In some countries such as New Zealand and Australia the importance of intrinsic value is recognized by legislation,[1] according to which only environmental capital that can be intrinsically evaluated can be monitored and included in the environmental decision-making process.[2]

These various statutory acts reflect as their assumption contemporary ethical thought on the environment which only in recent years has led us to assign Nature an intrinsic value, that is a value which goes well beyond the dimension of its usefulness for human beings and is thus in radical contradiction with Western philosophical tradition.

At the same time, environmental ethics recognizes different positions as to value type (instrumental or intrinsic) attributed to the natural environment and as to which entities (living beings, inanimate objects, ecosystems, natural processes, etc.) possess intrinsic value. Traditionally, a distinction is made between 'man-centred' and 'non-man-centred'.

In synthesis, the man-centred approach maintains that there is a separation between Man and Nature, that the latter exists for the well-being of Man, that Nature possesses instrumental value only and that it is permissible to apply differentiated treatment to human beings and non-human entities.

On the other hand, the non-man-centred approach maintains that there is no sharp distinction between Man and Nature and that Man is a part of Nature; Nature has intrinsic value and there is no justification for differentiated treatment between human beings and non-human entities (Bartolomei, 1995). According to Callicott (1984), all values are created by Man and may be defined as 'anthropogenic', but they do not necessarily centre on Man, thus they may well not be 'anthropocentric'.

Rolston (2003) maintains that environmental values are objective, pre-exist human beings and mark all species and ecosystems, and they continue to exist even without Man: Man discovers value in Nature, but he does not create it.

To be frank, the standpoints of environmental philosophers are not always so clear cut, so much so that we can also speak of anthropocentric and non-anthropocentric intrinsic value and anthropocentric and non-anthropocentric instrumental value (Hargrove, 1989, 1992; Turner et al., 2003).

On the basis of ethical reflection on the environment viewed in the framework of ecological economy, it has been pointed out that the value of any given resource cannot be limited to its Total Economic Value (TEV), since it is possible to evaluate only some ecosystem functions in economic terms, whereas for others this is not possible: the contribution of the species belonging to an ecosystem and its internal processes tending to make it into a life-support system cannot be defined in economic terms.

So what we need to do is adopt a new approach, founded on the recognition of use value (anthropocentric and non-anthropocentric) of natural resources. In point of fact, hitherto research on this question has not proven fully satisfactory, indeed we have not as yet identified a common reference value to replace the notion of TEV, nor methodologies universally accepted for its evaluation.

Following this possible line of research we may state that the total *output* of any given ecosystem addresses three different forms of utilization: development and maintenance over time of the ecosystem itself, *export* towards other ecosystems and/or *export* towards the human community. The first type of *output* refers to the self-organizing capacity of the system itself, whereas the other two express the capacity of acting as a life-support system for other systems (Gren et al., 1994).

In the first case we are looking at the Primary Value (PV) of the ecosystem and in the second Total Secondary Value (TSV): the complex of primary and secondary value constitutes the Total Value (TV) of an ecosystem (Turner, 1992; Turner *et al.*, 1993). It should be noted that TSV exists only as a function of PV, that is only insofar as the ecosystem continues to maintain the complex multi-functional structure which marks it out as a life-support system, able to provide a flow of functions from which a certain value accrues to society. Moreover, TEV is not always capable of incorporating TSV, since many ecosystem functions and processes cannot be evaluated in monetary terms, and it never incorporates PV. So TV is identified as a combination of bio-physical and economic evaluations where only part of the secondary value may be expressed in monetary terms.

Explicit recognition of the existence of multiple interdependent values establishes the foundations – both conceptual and empirical – for understanding just how these value categories may be applied to the urban ecosystem context. Turner *et al.* (2003) highlight the fact that TEV is not capable of including historical and cultural values, nor symbols, etc., and cannot express primary value. Thus, the notion of Total Value is extended to include the concept of Total Systems Value. This approach takes into account the constraints proposed by economic analysis for consideration of a multi-dimensional context. Indeed, Total Systems Value is an expression also of the complex system of relationships marking the urban ecosystem as closely linked to the social ecosystem, seen as a life relation support system, able to generate flows of immaterial functions of accepted intrinsic value for society.

In this view, we need to spread a new urban culture of sustainability, which must be promoted by making all the stakeholders aware of the intrinsic value of the ecosystems (natural and urban), which, with their autopoietic activity, sustain human life, as well as of the profound links between human beings and Nature, overcoming the culture of 'separation': between human beings and the environment; between human beings and the community. A new culture of sustainability means becoming aware of the 'complex social value' of resources (Fusco Girard, 1987). It also entails awareness of the fact that there is a common heritage of resources (natural, cultural, societal, etc.) available to all, which cannot be appropriated for individual purposes without damaging the rights of other human beings.

But how can we reconcile the intrinsic value of Nature with the intrinsic value of the city?

Environmental philosophy provides a foundation for a theory of ethics enabling us to face up to reality moving beyond an anthropocentric vision. It also suggests useful considerations for applying the intrinsic value model to the urban environment, starting from an eco-centric vision (Kortenkamp and Moore, 2001).

The city, indeed, may be seen as part of the wider biotic community (Callicott, 2003) and it is possible to establish an analogy between city life, seen as a complex, collective organism, and the life of an individual or a species. The city is *for living* – different, multiple, stratified – and is rooted deep in the subsoil, in the quality of the environment, in historical memory and cultural identity, able to generate lasting new balances, both environmental and social (Choay, 1992; Magnaghi, 1995). The city, from a systemic point of view, is the expression of the relationship of reciprocal interaction between 'content' (*social armature*) and the 'container' (*urban armature*) where the urban armature reflects organizational structure and represents the basis, material and immaterial, making it possible to reproduce the models proper to the natural environment; social armature, on the other hand, identifies the network of relationships which preserves the sense of identity and belonging, stimulates vitality and autopoietic capacity, promotes recognition of values and meanings.

The theory of autopoietic systems (Maturana and Varela, 1980), and in particular reference to the process of co-determination and co-evolution between environment and organism, highlights the way in which a system can subordinate its own changes to the conservation of the invariability of structural organization, drawing a sense of identity from the difference between itself and its context. Identity and difference, in turn, make it possible to recognize individuals in the complexity of the social system and keep to the fore the different combination of fundamental values proper to human sustainable development and their declination in space. Assigning priority to certain values allows us to distinguish between intrinsic values, seen as primary, and instrumental values, seen as secondary. Intrinsic values allow us to progress beyond the private sphere and reflect on benefits for the community, explicating a clear ethical dimension. Intrinsic value expresses the spirit of any given place, its specific character, unique, unrepeatable and its particular identity, the emotional link existing between social capital and built capital (Fusco Girard and Nijkamp, 1997, 2004).

The intrinsic value of a city is capable of constructing integration, reducing marginalization, overcoming fragmentation, stimulating vitality: it sustains life, promoting and regenerating it. It is a 'catalyst' of material and immaterial energies, able to blend various value dimensions, helping us to capture its deep unity.

The tension caused on the one hand by the wish to safeguard intrinsic values and on the other to maximize instrumental values complicates the management of human and social relationships and poses the need to explicate a moral judgement reflecting the more ample category of 'normative values' (Etzioni, 1988; Taylor, 1996; Tacconi, 2000). Recognizing a system with shared meanings, interpretations and social rules which the built environment incorporates and refers to through signals, universally understood and accepted over time, implies the need to interpret the organizational configuration of an urban ecosystem, on which adaptability to change and its autopoietic capacity depend, identifying 'the soul of the city' and its 'invariant structures'. Any estimation of the intrinsic value of an urban ecosystem must perforce include concrete definition of the integrity of the social ecosystem and should combine the possibility of evaluating organization types and differences, the level of stability and resilience, capacity for growth, renewal and development over time, tracing an all-inclusive 'assessment', both multi-dimensional and dynamic. In this sense the dimensions of integrity could be defined as *cultural/symbolic, social/relational, urban/architectural*. In turn, the three dimensions identified could be explicated through 'identity' recognition, in particular *cultural identity, social identity* and *urban identity*, which taken together with the 'differences' can help in understanding the terms of integrity. At the same time they contribute to the construction of a complex evaluation model able to express the meaning and role of the relationships between the various forms of built capital – natural, social and economic – which in differing degree contribute to the formation of a social ecosystem.

On the other hand, evaluating urban complexity means giving priority to the production of elements for re-founding the city and its relationship with the territory, highlighting the fact that it is a place equipped with temporal depth, scenic identity, aesthetic quality, social, economic and cultural stratification, capacity for self-presentation and self-reproduction. One essential assumption is a multi-dimensional vision of value, according to which it is possible to 'integrate' values belonging to different, multiple dimensions.

What type of answer can we formulate? How can we elaborate an integrated vision of development which pays due attention to human being and is capable of reconciling the different value dimensions? How can we establish adequate criteria to aid us in pinpointing priorities to face up to the crisis of values in concrete terms?

The city may be considered as a 'laboratory' in which ethical values and human resources constitute the elements of a process of ongoing transformation, in which physical, economical, social and cultural space takes shape, contributing to the identification of guidelines for possible change.

The 'human' city champions the rights of all, including disadvantaged groups, and curbs the growing inequalities, promoting integration. Similarly to individual human beings, the 'people-friendly city' (Lazzati, 1984) builds integration, combining material and non-material needs, utility, desires and hopes. The city where human beings are connected by a dense communicational/relational fabric behaves as a single body. And like every human body, it has a centre that unifies multiple activities and functions. Thus the 'human sustainable city' is the city which manages to integrate production, residence, consumption, mobility and leisure time in a single vital pulsing unit (Fusco Girard *et al.*, 2003).

TOWARDS HUMAN SUSTAINABLE PLANNING

Urban planning: Environmental and social issues

How can we construct a people-friendly city?

Bearing well in mind the different dimensions of sustainability and a multi-dimensional vision of value, with the aim of achieving rapid economic growth and activating the redistribution of wealth, the promotion of political and social integration and the protection of the environment are of course an indispensable premise for combating and reducing inequalities.

These objectives require identification of the relationships between different possible strategies, integrating environmental and social issues in the framework of the decision-making process.

The drawing up of suitable planning strategies should pursue the objective of making the cities of the world 'livable'. As the history of planning teaches us, 'good planning' may be defined above all as a 'question of balance' (Hall, 2003), and it becomes increasingly effective when it attempts to shape and modify economic and social trends, as well as operating in an efficient, convenient and sustainable manner. 'Good planning' must also be able to face up to the problems of the mega-cities, that is cities physically divided but arranged in a network from a functional point of view, dependent on a central nucleus which in turn determines the division of roles. We see the emergence of the need for adequate planning strategies to face urban growth and combat urban poverty, our aim must be to respond to elementary needs and affirm the principle of equity.

The critical role of the environmental and social dimensions forces us to take into account not only the city's 'ecological footprint', but also its 'social footprint', and this helps us reflect on the capacity of the city to support its social and ecological load, the aim being to combine strategies of the 'green agenda' with those of the 'brown agenda'. This implies promoting inclusive strategies, based on the recognition of ethical values, which consider individuals and society in relation to the environment, allowing the former to access the labour market and services, enjoy a quality existence, reduce their vulnerability, obtain respect of human rights without discrimination, live in harmony within and with communities in conditions of enabling and well being. For society it implies respecting human rights and the fundamental liberties, cultural and religious diversity, and social justice, providing for the needs of the vulnerable, allowing democratic participation and observance of regulations and laws.

Constructing an inclusive city means *re-constructing* its social capital which together with 'civil involvement' and 'governance' is one of the principles set out in the Habitat Agenda. Inclusion at social and urban level implies consideration of a new approach, defined as 'participatory urban governance' (UNCHS, 2001). This refers to a form of participatory planning and decision-making able to coordinate the efforts of local government, civil society organizations and the private sector. In this way it is possible to ensure sustainable urban and human development based on the active role of the community, on partnership, cooperation, and solidarity. Indeed, the structuring of a participatory approach for the drawing up of planning and programming strategies can assist us to face up to social and environmental issues, basing our actions on an integrated vision, starting from recognized shared values.

Harvey (2003) highlights the fact that the history of cities and the theories developed over time on the theme of the city have been marked by the attention shown to the capacity for transformation generated by the action of the community, and he stresses the fact that very often the true sources of urban change are rooted in civil society itself. The crumbling of institutional and ideological references determines a change in perspective, the new focal point is the individual, recognized as the 'main' tool for 'humanizing' the quality of life in the cities. The gap existing between actual transformations and planning theory is very often striking, and this highlights the need for a common language allowing us to overcome fragmented heterogeneity, but also implying respect for others, for differences, for culture in all its many facets.

The 'human' city: Ethics and planning

According to the traditional approach, 'land use planning' recognizes the requirement to satisfy multiple demands for resources and at the same time draw up a rational plan for their utilization making it possible to respond to different needs. In economic terms, this implies adopting an approach of the cost-effective type able to reduce externalities and achieve objectives which go well beyond mere efficiency.

In reality, for the construction of a people-friendly city, that is of a human sustainable city, the fundamental objectives of planning activity must be that of guaranteeing the 'common good' (Daly and Cobb, 1989). In this sense, it becomes essential that 'land use planning' goes beyond the traditional approach and be guided by considerations of an ethical nature and by participatory decision-making processes (Tacconi, 1997), combining intrinsic and instrumental values.

Indeed, we need to stress a new ethical dimension of the plan: its capacity to guarantee equal opportunities, permit socialization of land use, resolve the issue of the privatization of benefits and the publicizing of costs, identify the true needs/values of people (in terms of equipment, services, accessibility, etc.), stimulate awareness of the scarcity of resources and promote a sense of responsibility.

The plan's capacity should target the creation of common good, identifiable in physical terms as those spaces and collective equipment accessible to all, in which to construct a sense of community, of togetherness, interacting and relating, recovering the sensation of feeling part of a place, a city, a community.

If we analyse the cities of the industrialized countries and in particular European cities, it becomes evident that urban planning has addressed all too much the physical city and all too little the world of relationships. Today however with the accentuation of the problems of the physical city, an attempt is being made to find a balance between these two dimensions. The relevance of urban planning hinges mainly on recovery, re-qualification, enhancement of existing stock rather than on 'ex novo' production, as well as on the creation of material and immaterial relationships of varying kinds.

In urban planning, the importance of public spaces is generally accepted: urban parks, public gardens, squares, open spaces, all play a strategic role on the quality of our – increasingly urbanized – society. Different experiences show that the presence of natural resources (e.g. urban parks, gardens, green belts) in urban contexts contribute to the quality of life from many aspects (environmental, economic, social, psychological, etc.) (Nijkamp and Baycan-Levent, 2005). In the same way, public spaces such as squares and equipment of collective interest have in the past played the role of 'arenas' for social interaction, just as parks, schools, libraries, public buildings, etc., represent civic elements which determine the quality of the community's world, contributing to the construction of cohesion and relational interchange (Rogers, 2003). In projecting the future of the people-friendly city, a vital role is also played by its historical and cultural heritage, that is the collective memory of the city, its specific nature and identity. This is something that must be preserved and enhanced since it offers an essential contribution to the humanization of the cities (Choay, 1992).

So we can maintain that the people-friendly city plan must increasingly incorporate a 'relational' dimension to guarantee the production of common good, that is assets produced by individuals but which no one person can produce alone and which at a certain level of social differentiation may be classified more specifically as 'relational'.

An asset is 'relational' when it can be produced only by *a set of individuals or groups*, that is when it depends on the relationships generated by individuals amongst themselves and may be enjoyed only if they behave in an appropriate manner (Bruni and Zamagni, 2003). A relational asset is an asset produced together, excluding no-one, through a synergic function of the subjects and their overall relationships, both internal and external, which develop between day-to-day worlds and social institutions.

On the other hand, one particular category of 'social' effects, determined by the demand for urban sustainability, involves the 'relational' dimension itself. Over the past few years we have seen vis-à-vis this theme encouraging signals of interest on the part of economists who are starting to use expressions such as 'relational assets', thus indicating that in the sphere of interpersonal relationships, true 'assets' can indeed be created.

In this respect, we need to clarify two points: first, since we are not dealing with private assets (that is enjoyable in an exclusive sense), for their creation we cannot rely on the usual market incentives, but must rather focus on the voluntary contribution of resources (time, attention, money, etc.) by at least some of the subjects involved. Secondly, as regards interpersonal relationships, what count are not only objective aspects and actions but also the motivation which each person sees in the actions of his/her counterparts (Gui, 2001).

By including common and relational assets in the plan we acknowledge the relevance of some essential critical components, such as: a strong interest in strategic/collaborative planning; involvement of other players directly interested in the various phases of planning, decision-making and implementation; cooperation and partnership between public and private bodies; and the development of integrated approaches based on dialogue and participation.

Planning a human sustainable city

Planning may be interpreted as a process aimed at reducing inequalities and overcoming marginality, based on an ethical vision which recognizes the vital role of human rights, shared values, social responsibility and justice.

Diversity, community and sustainability are three themes which mark out the contemporary city and which form our starting point for the construction of the sustainable city of the twenty-first century. The promotion of diversity, community and sustainability are three objectives which explicate a common paradigm and, at the same time, challenge us to construct 'vital space'. The community and the vital space of the community are two essential aspects of physical and social development alike. The community is a place where people can feel sustained, involved and stimulated. The search for human sustainability also means activating processes of regeneration able to ensure that 'expert knowledge' can interact with 'common knowledge'.

Improvement in the conditions of the urban environment may represent a catalyzing element for activating a broader regeneration process. Indeed, renovation of the physical environment, the social context and economic mechanisms together with mobilization of the community may all assist in redefining a new vision of the 'good city'. Thus, working towards the creation of human sustainable cities means utilizing a 'therapeutic planning model' (Sandercock, 2003, 2004), and this implies *organizing hope, negotiating fear, mediating memory* and facilitating the search for and transformation of the community's soul. In this sense, planning is conceived as a process of 'social learning', of mutual learning, in which *dialogue* plays a key role as preferred means of communication facilitating interpersonal relations and creating thrust for overcoming conflicts and for the formation of coalitions (Friedmann, 1987).

Dialogue makes it possible to make *communicative action* explicit (Habermas, 1981), to construct awareness, recognize shared values and promote a sense of responsibility.

On the other hand, attention to the social micro-dimension and the role of individual players is an essential assumption for the inclusion of ethical and relational values in the planning process: taking them as our starting point, we can view 'listening procedures' as an integral part of the cognitive and operative scenario of planning (Fisher and Forester, 1993).

Communication, dialogue and listening, indeed, constitute the components of a pathway of knowledge and growth, of understanding of diversity and the conquest of new relationships, as well as the learning of values. In this perspective, the link between plan and action is oriented towards forms of interactive communication, argumentative and discursive alike, in which participation represents the means to activate 'communicative planning' processes (Innes, 1995).

Planning processes conceived in this manner are based on approaches proper to *collaborative planning* (Healey, 1997), which go beyond practices of regulative land use planning and focus on methods of promoting collaborative practices and the construction of consensus. Indeed, we see the structuring of strategic approaches linked to 'place governance', based on the importance of the quality of the 'process' rooted in a specific context and the need to strengthen the value of social and environmental justice.

Spatial planning, local environmental planning and practices of co-existence management in shared spaces become the ideal arena for experimenting and translating into reality this type of approach. A key role is played by the process of integration of competencies and knowledge, including the principles and models of interdependence between human being and Nature. At the same time, we must recognize the importance of stimulating the capacity of people to identify solutions rooted in their own culture, in social rules, in the system of values and the wisdom of traditions (Shah, 2003).

Indeed, it is commonly accepted that participation of citizens must form an integral part of the decision-making process, of planning and management of the city in a 'humanistic' approach which pursues objectives of sustainable development, highlighting the need to adopt a programmatic line to the process of city development.

Achieving the target of more human and sustainable cities requires new planning models that recognize the key role of the community, but also the need for special communicative skills able to transform the language of planning, recognizing the role of the deep emotions and experiences lived. The planning process must be able to introduce variety and diversity into a system of meanings, providing concrete answers to the needs of daily life and promoting rationally a way of 'living with dignity in harmony with Nature' (Laul, 2003).

Seen in this perspective, planning must utilize critical/evaluative and narrative/receptive models which assist in the creation of 'proactive' processes, the catalysts of wider transformations.

EVALUATIVE APPROACHES: METHODS AND TOOLS

From values integration to integrated evaluations

Recognition of values and evaluation methodologies are closely linked to planning activity since intended land use, the creation of infrastructure or the protection of Nature require suitable tools for the identification of priorities, especially in the light of the enormous conflicts which might well arise between the pursuit of economic and environmental objectives.

These conflicts emerge in a significant manner when, as in the case of 'strategic planning', there is a lack of sufficiently detailed information and it may well come about that: (1) alternatives are often too broad and abstract; (2) there is insufficient information about the affects of alternatives; (3) there is insufficient information about the possibilities and effects and 'flanking' policies; and (4) it is difficult to generate direct feedback from public and politics (Niekerk and Voogd, 1999).

In order to overcome the partial visions of sectoral studies, it is necessary to produce an 'integral impact assessment', targeting the creation of consensus taking into account the level of definition of alternatives, the possible degree of transparency of the decision-making process, the requirement to interest and involve the community in the discussion and formulation of possible solutions.

At the same time, we must have clear in our mind the fact that in a perspective of strategic planning and hence of 'strategic evaluation' very often we are not able to ensure appropriate recognition and consequent integration of environmental values, not forgetting that at this scale it is difficult to identify precisely and in quantitative terms all the effects of proposed options.

So what we need are new approaches able to provide an analytical and evaluative planning structure which will allow us to integrate objectives and environmental values in the decision-making process.

We must remember that any assessment of environmental impact does not, of itself, imply the integration of environmental values in the decision-making process, above all when there is a high degree of uncertainty as to the exact quantification of those impacts and a strong probability that unforeseen and/or unforeseeable impacts may take place (Dalkmann et al., 2004).

So it is necessary to develop an evaluation strategy not focused exclusively on the analysis of the environmental and/or economic and social consequences of the different options, but which weighs the nature of the questions in play, identifying priorities and values which influence the decision-making process. The interdependence between values, levels, roles and methods may be considered a means of interpretation, both interpretative and evaluative, able to express a reflexive cognitive approach. So there is a need to utilize regulatory and instrumental – but also explorative – approaches open to plurality.

Evaluation may be seen as the capacity to identify adequate responses, but also to explore wider systems and domains, capable of taking into account the profound differences, polarizations, contrasts and disparities which mark spatial, economic, social and human networks.

Evaluation based on an integrated approach implies weighing the interdependencies which may exist between economy, ecology and justice, in a construction of the future which implies attention to complexity and uncertainty. What does integration mean in operational terms? How can we integrate economic, non-economic and intrinsic values? How can we evaluate the common good? How can we best bear in mind the principles of ethics and justice in our evaluation?

Evaluation for planning, as an exercise in reason and democracy, addresses the facts and values definable in specific descriptive domains. Including in this evaluation ethical principles and moral reasoning implies the need to utilize interpretative and experiential domains, in which the objective and subjective are closely correlated.

The sphere of evaluation becomes more extensive, takes into account domain 'fluidity' and embraces the principles of 'good environmental governance' and 'good human governance', which cannot ignore the ethical role of the values in play.

In a perspective of social and environmental ethics, the link between ethics and economy is not limited to recognition of reference values but becomes an integral part of the decision-making process (Zamagni, 2003). In this sense it is essential to redefine the 'game rules' which guide collective choices, taking note of the limits of traditional economic analysis (such as cost–benefit analysis) and developing new approaches of the holistic type, based on the centrality of the role of values and which follow a pathway targeting the idea of 'strong sustainability'.

Attention to conservation of the values of natural capital and cultural built capital, as well as to the well being of present and future generations are the key issues in which we can identify values, explicate objectives and pinpoint any existing conflicts.

Values, integration and tools

Planning and strategic evaluation imply the need to operate in the framework of 'integrated environmental evaluation' defined as 'procedures to arrive at an informed judgment to different courses of action with regard to environmental problems; the information required refers to physical, chemical, biological, psychological, socio-economic and institutional phenomena, including the relevant decision-making process' (Munda, 1996, p. 157).

Constructing a balanced vision between conservation and progress requires integrated evaluative and complementary approaches which can utilize *combinatorial assessment methodologies* (Nijkamp and Medda, 2003), seen as flexible tools able to overcome the limits of each single method and strengthen the validity of the evaluation process to improve the coherence and internal consistency of the evaluation itself.

Working within integrated evaluative approaches, it is vital to establish an initial evaluation framework where initial integration is required between the diverse evaluation tools, such as the environmental, social and ethical balance sheets, but also Economic Valuation, Input–Output Analysis, Life Cycle Assessment, Risk Assessment, Ecological Impacts, Ecological Footprint, Mass/Energy Valuation, Multi-criteria Decision-Aid Methods, Future Studies (Finnveden *et al.*, 2003).

Other innovative tools which it could be of use to incorporate are those covering the possibility of combining multi-criteria analysis with Geographical Information Systems, Internet Technology, Spatial Decision Support Systems, Cellular Automata Models (Rotmans, 2000). Moreover, integration of differing evaluation models with GIS (Malczewski, 1999) becomes decidedly important in the construction of a Spatial Decision Support System (Geneletti, 2004). A variety of territorial information (social, economic and environmental) may be easily combined and correlated to the characteristics of the different options of territorial use, facilitating the construction of appropriate indicators and favouring impact forecasting, leading up to the preparation of a preference priority list of the various options.

But integration between multi-criteria analysis and GIS may prove exceptionally fruitful in land management where very often we find strong conflicts in which the role of local players, their relations and objectives may be considered a structuring element in the process of information construction in a spatial and dynamic evaluative model (Joerin and Musy, 2000).

In this way, as compared to traditional forms of utilization of GIS it should also be possible to evaluate data covering not only the current situation but also: (1) the spatial characteristics of options proposed; (2) temporal modification of data following implementation of the options; (3) the expressed preferences of local players; (4) analysis of the conflicts between the various stakeholders; and (5) evaluation of various options for the preparation of a preference priority list.

Moreover, the notion of 'integrated evaluation' assumes particular importance when we pass from the territorial to the urban scale, in which sustainability objectives are more difficult to pursue, in view of the complexity and nature of urban ecosystems, for which planning and evaluation of actions thus becomes particularly significant and urgent.

With reference to urban ecosystems, Ost (2003) proposes an innovative approach, starting from economic analysis, for the conservation of the architectural and cultural heritage, structuring a model for analyzing the attractiveness of an historic area and the way in which any given type of intervention can act as a magnet through possible spin-off activities. The perfecting of specific spatial indicators may assist in visualizing the impact of the decisions and in 'mapping' different area typologies based on several project variables connected to the potential attractiveness of the built heritage in accordance with an integrated evaluative approach.

It is indeed felt that Integrated Assessment may be defined as an 'interdisciplinary process of combining, interpreting and communicating knowledge pieces from diverse scientific disciplines in such a way that insights are made available to decision makers' (Rotmans, 1998, p. 155) or even as an 'interdisciplinary process of combining, interpreting and communicating knowledge from diverse discipline in such a way that the entire cause–effect chain of a problem can be evaluated from a synoptic perspective with two characteristics: (1) it should have added value compared to assessment based on a single disciplinary; and (2) it should provide useful information to decision makers' (van Asselt and Rotmans, 1996). This approach was applied initially to problems of the environmental type but subsequently was considered viable for addressing complex issues of urban planning in which economic, social and environmental questions are closely interrelated.

Indeed, integrated evaluations constitute an ongoing process, both iterative and interactive, able to stimulate dialogue between expert and common knowledge, starting from recognition of the relevance of two fundamental questions: 'technical indeterminacy' and 'value multiplicity' (Ravetz, 2000).

Indeterminacy represents one of the key elements of modern science; on the one hand it regards technical uncertainty and on the other refers to structural uncertainty, that is the impossibility of forecasting impacts (above all those of a cumulative nature) on the environment or the exact behaviour of natural and social ecosystems when exposed to certain stimuli.

Multiplicity, on the other hand, takes account of the fact that in evaluating the effect of possible actions on the environment there exist different perceptions and value systems which condition the choice of objectives and reference criteria, so that the decision-making process is influenced and, in its turn, influences definition of the problem and its solution.

Once again it emerges clearly that recognition of the values in play (economic, non-economic, intrinsic) is at the base of the identification, integration and/or ideation of methods and tools for the evaluation of policies, plans and projects.

In this perspective a possible approach pathway for making the notion of 'integrated evaluation' operational is offered by the Integrated Sustainable Cities Assessment Method which provides a 'scenario accounting system for the total metabolism of a city or region' (Ravetz, 2000, p. 31). According to this approach it is possible to construct a framework within which to identify the relations existing between human being and the environment (i.e. between what we need and what we get), taking into account criteria which do not refer only to 'efficacy', 'efficiency' and 'effectiveness', but also to 'ethicality' (*Four Es*), that is to the ethical values which constitute the assumption for any proposal, evaluation or choice.

The Integrated Sustainable Cities Assessment Method consists of three key stages:

1   *Vision*: exploration of values, goals, priorities, problem definition and system boundaries;
2   *Scenarios*: systems analysis and accounting, both for present conditions and for future possibilities;
3   *Action*: implications for policy, strategy, programmes and projects within practical constraints.

In this method, value recognition (economic, non-economic and intrinsic) assumes a fundamental role within which objectives and evaluation criteria themselves are identified, scenarios constructed, decisional rules deduced and sectoral evaluations are implemented to prioritize alternative options.

When examining the level of sustainability/non-sustainability of a city very often we are asked to analyse its ecological footprint, but today other tools are emerging. They make reference to the analysis of material and energy flows which enter/exit the city, i.e. what a city requires for its existence and what subsequently it returns to the environment in the form of waste product.

Rijkens-Klomp *et al.* (2003) propose the SCENE-Model (Social-Cultural, Environmental, Economic Model) which interprets the city as a dynamic system of *stocks* and *flows*, whose sustainability is described in terms of the interaction between economic, ecological and social capital, based on the concept of flows and the relations and interrelations which take place between the various capital stocks. This interpretive model of the city includes both temporal development dimensions: the long term covering various forms of capital (economic stocks, socio-cultural stocks, environmental stocks) and the short term covering flows, i.e. interaction between the various forms of capital. The integrated evaluation proposed is not a technique but rather an interdisciplinary and participatory process of combination, interpretation and communication of knowledge among the various scientific disciplines to promote the understanding and management of complex problems. The SCENE Model stresses the importance of integrated evaluations as a trans-disciplinary process, able to combine scientific, contextual and experiential knowledge, thus promoting understanding of how to orient shared sustainability strategies. Furthermore, particular importance is attached to the interaction–integration relationship between physical, socio-cultural and economic infrastructure and the labour market, in an attempt to identify appropriate indicators.

Among these new indicators we can certainly list the following: (1) intensity of resource consumption; (2) inflow/outflow ratio; (3) urban livability; (4) efficiency of urban metabolism; and (5) energy evaluation of urban metabolism (Huang and Hsu, 2003). This leads us to view the city as a complex, dynamic system, whose components are economic, social and cultural subsystems in reciprocal relation, enabling us to evaluate its degree of sustainability/non-sustainability (Newman, 1999). But in this case too evaluation cannot be limited to a neutral form of bookkeeping of material and energy flows; it must be accompanied by explanations as to the needs of its inhabitants and the values underlying those needs.

The evaluation of intangible assets takes on a key role and makes it possible to analyse the social concept of value in a multi-dimensional scenario. In this regard, Roca Cladera *et al.* (2003), starting from recognition of the limits of the evaluation techniques created for the determination of the economic value of public assets and of the unavoidability of the social dimension, show how it is possible to assess the social use value of urban public spaces through identification of different degrees of attractiveness (residential, commercial, cultural, etc.) perceived by users on the basis of subjective evaluation criteria independent of market forces. On the other hand, when examining the values which any given society attributes to the natural or built environment we must take into account three different meanings: (1) a set of philosophical, ethical, moral and emotional principles that order a society, as 'traditional values' and 'family values'; (2) intrinsic proprieties associated with particular environments, as 'wetlands values'; and (3) economic significance (often measured in monetary terms) of a given environment (Rapport *et al.*, 1998).

But we need to bear in mind that ecosystems are complex structures which it is not easy to interpret and model since they are 'conceived as conceptually open, self-modifying systems, which constantly ("on-line") produce novelty and new parameters and which cannot be severed from their environment' (Haag and Kaupen-johann, 2001), so much so that forecasting of the consequences of intervention on ecosystems (natural and cultural alike) is marked by several forms of uncertainty – technical, methodological and epistemological (Funtowicz and Ravetz, 1993) – which indeed constitute the principal characteristic of the decision-making process.

So we can say that the collective choices of our time are marked by facts uncertain, values in dispute, stakes high and decisions urgent (Funtowicz and Ravetz, 1991), which require the adoption of evaluation tools which are both rigorous from the scientific point of view, transparent in reference to the decision-making process but also of the participatory type: in this prospective 'social multi-criteria evaluations' (SMCE) have been proposed (Munda, 2004). These evaluation methodologies extend the field of social cost–benefit analysis to incorporate different aspects referring both to impact evaluation and to the participation of local communities in the decision-making process (Figure 4.2).

Faced with difficult choices whose outcome it is impossible to foresee, and because it is necessary and urgent to act (including in cases in which issues are marked by a high degree of uncertainty), it is important to widen the decision-making

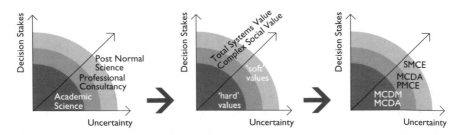

Figure 4.2 From the theoretical approach to the operative tools

field to involve new social players who, together with the experts, form a new 'extended community', within which we may achieve elaboration of new solutions through 'debate and dialogue' (Funtowicz and Ravetz, 1997). In this perspective, integrated evaluations, intrinsically 'participatory', constitute an essential tool for the support of the decision-making process in those cases in which uncertainty, complexity and the values in play, sponsored by the various social groups, are multiple, different and conflicting.

Social multi-criteria evaluations constitute inter/multi-disciplinary approaches insofar as they require differing technical competencies and public participation in collective choices from the start of the decision-making process but, above all, they must provide judgements of an ethical nature representing the inevitable and fundamental components of the process itself, thus influencing evaluation results. Once again we see that evaluation processes rest on values underlying evaluation objectives and criteria which need to be appropriately recognized and spelled out.

FINAL REFLECTIONS

Human sustainable development may be truly achieved only if we place the human being in pole position, at the centre of concern and priority interests, evolving a new paradigm founded on ethical values, coherent with the principles of 'good human governance' and 'good environmental governance'. This implies a need to change our way of thinking, overcoming the pragmatic logic of the market, productivity and profit and adopting a polycentric development model (Hall, 2003), marked by integrated solutions able to blend policies of sustainability and public acceptance focusing on the role of 'local preferences' in the implementation of concrete sustainability strategies.

Promoting human sustainable development also imposes the imperative of adopting appropriate approaches and tools enabling us to structure and elaborate suitable intervention choices, linked to the context and able to take account of differing levels of complexity and uncertainty.

Integration and interdependence between values, approaches and tools may be recognized as key concepts making it possible to embrace a pluralistic approach based on a multi-dimensional interpretation of value. At the same time, however, we must identify a common language to facilitate dialogue between knowledge and differing viewpoints. In this sense, shared values, and in particular ethical, relational and intrinsic values constitute the assumption for activating communication and structuring appropriate strategies of change. 'Value-focused thinking' (Keeney, 1992) implies reflecting on human being and his/her milieu, but also on his/her relationship with others and with Nature. It implies overcoming radical individualism and viewing the human being as a 'person-in-community'.

So the challenge becomes just how to transform global threats into new opportunities for the cities which must be safer, healthier, more sustainable and more human. The stakes are the construction of a people-friendly city in which the individualistic and utilitarian moral targeting exclusively the interests of the individual and the few can be opposed by an ethic of truth (Forte, 2003), open to values founded on common humanity and the transcendent dignity of the human being.

NOTES

1   For New Zealand reference may be made to the Environmental Act of 1987 and the Resource Management Act of 1991.

2   In Italy too, Law 394/1991 introduces a concept of the preservation/conservation of Nature, no longer seen solely as the protection of natural beauty and the landscape, but also as protection of naturalistic/ecological values. In particular, this law makes reference to the 'naturalistic and environmental values' (article 1) of the protected areas, where the former see Nature as an asset in itself (intrinsic value) and the latter address the relationship between Man and Nature (relational value).

REFERENCES

Anand, S. and Sen, A. (2000), 'Human Development and Economic Sustainability', *World Development*, 28(12): 2029–2049.

Bartolomei, S. (1995), *Etica e natura. Una rivoluzione copernicana in etica?*, Laterza, Roma-Bari.

Bruni, L. and Zamagni, S. (2003), 'Un'economia civile per città felici', in L. Fusco Girard, B. Forte, M. Cerreta, P. De Toro and F. Forte (eds), *L'uomo e la città. Verso uno sviluppo umano e sostenibile*, Angeli, Milan, pp. 595–609.

Callicott, J.B. (1984), 'Non-anthropocentric Value Theory and Environmental Ethics', *American Philosophical Quarterly*, 21: 299–309.

Callicott, J.B. (2003), 'The Role of Intrinsic Values for Naturalization of the City', in L. Fusco Girard, B. Forte, M. Cerreta, P. De Toro and F. Forte (eds), *The Human Sustainable City. Challenges and Perspectives from the Habitat Agenda*, Ashgate, Aldershot, pp. 107–120.

Capra, F. (1996), *The Web of Life: A New Scientific Understanding of Living Systems*, Anchor Books, New York.

Choay, F. (1992), *L'Allegorie du Patrimoine*, Editions du Seuil, Paris.

Dalkmann, H., Herrera, R.J. and Bongardt, D. (2004), 'Analytic Strategic Environmental Assessment (ANSEA). Developing a New Approach to SEA', *Environmental Impact Assessment Review*, 24: 385–402.

Daly, H. and Cobb, J. (1989), *For the Common Good*, Beacon Press, Boston.

Des Jardins, J.R. (2001), *Environmental Ethics: An Introduction to Environmental Philosophy*, 3rd edn, Wadsworth/Thomson, Belmont, CA.

Etzioni, A. (1988), *The Moral Dimension: Towards a New Economics*, The Free Press, New York.

Finnveden, G., Nilsonn, M., Johansonn, J., Personn, Å., Moberg, Å. and Carlsonn, T. (2003), 'Strategic Environmental Assessment Methodologies – Application within the Energy Sector', *Environmental Impact Assessment Review*, 23: 91–123.

Fisher, F. and Forester, J. (1993), *The Argumentative Turn*, Duke University Press, Durham and London.

Forte, B. (2003), 'An Open Conclusion', in L. Fusco Girard, B. Forte, M. Cerreta, P. De Toro and F. Forte (eds), *The Human Sustainable City. Challenges and Perspectives from the Habitat Agenda*, Ashgate, Aldershot, pp. 541–546.

Friedmann, J. (1987), *Planning in the Public Domain: From Knowledge to Action*, Princeton University Press, Princeton, NJ.

Funtowicz, S.O. and Ravetz, J.R. (1991), 'A New Scientific Methodology for Global Environmental Issues', in Costanza, R. (ed.), *Ecological Economics*, Columbia, New York, pp. 137–152.

Funtowicz, S.O. and Ravetz, J.R. (1993), 'The Emergence of Post-Normal Science', in R.V. Schomberg (ed.), *Science, Politics and Morality*, Kluwer, Dortrecht, pp. 85–126.

Funtowicz, S.O. and Ravetz, J.R. (1997), 'The Poetry of Thermodynamics: Energy, Entropy/Exergy and Quality', *Futures*, 29(9): 791–810.

Fusco Girard, L. (1987), *Risorse architettoniche e culturali: valutazioni e strategie di conservazione*, Angeli, Milan.

Fusco Girard, L. and Nijkamp, P. (1997), *Le valutazioni per lo sviluppo sostenibile della città e del territorio*, Angeli, Milan.

Fusco Girard, L. and Nijkamp, P. (2004), *Ecologia, economia, energia: valutazioni integrate*, Angeli, Milan.

Fusco Girard, L., Forte, B., Cerreta, M., De Toro, P. and Forte, F. (eds) (2003), *The Human Sustainable City. Challenges and Perspectives from the Habitat Agenda*, Ashgate, Aldershot.

Geneletti, D. (2004), 'A GIS-Based Decision Support System to Identify Nature Conservation Priorities in a Alpine Valley', *Land Use Policy*, 21: 149–160.

Gilbert, A. (2003), 'Is Urban Development in the Third World Sustainable?', in L. Fusco Girard, B. Forte, M. Cerreta, P. De Toro and F. Forte (eds), *The Human Sustainable City. Challenges and Perspectives from the Habitat Agenda*, Ashgate, Aldershot, pp. 71–88.

Gren, I.M., Folke, C., Turner, R.K. and Bateman, I. (1994), 'Primary and Secondary Values of Wetland Ecosystem', *Environmental and Resource Economics*, 4: 55–74.

Gui, B. (2001), *Economic Interactions as Encounters*, University of Padova, mimeo.

Haag, D. and Kaupenjohann, M. (2001), 'Parameters, Prediction, Post-Normal Science and the Precautionary Principle – A Roadmap for Modelling for Decision-Making', *Ecological Modelling*, 144: 45–60.

Habermas, J. (1981), *The Theory of Communicative Action*, Beacon Press, London.

Hall, P. (2003), 'The Sustainable City in a Age of Globalization', in L. Fusco Girard, B. Forte, M. Cerreta, P. De Toro and F. Forte (eds), *The Human Sustainable City. Challenges and Perspectives from the Habitat Agenda*, Ashgate, Aldershot, pp. 55–69.

Hall, P. and Pfeiffer, U. (2000), *Urban Future 21. A Global Agenda for Twenty-first Century Cities*, E&FN Spon, London.

Hargrove, E.C. (1989), *Foundations of Environmental Ethics*, Prentice Hall, Englewood Cliffs.

Hargrove, E.C. (1992), 'Weak Anthropocentric Intrinsic Value', *The Monist*, 75: 183–207.

Harvey, D. (2003), 'City and Justice: Social Movements in the City', in L. Fusco Girard, B. Forte, M. Cerreta, P. De Toro and F. Forte (eds), *The Human Sustainable City. Challenges and Perspectives from the Habitat Agenda*, Ashgate, Aldershot, pp. 235–254.

Healey, P. (1997), *Collaborative Planning: Shaping Places in Fragmented Societies*, Macmillan, Houndmills.

Huang, S. and Hsu, W. (2003), 'Material Flow Analysis and Energy Evaluation of Taipei's Urban Construction', *Landscape and Urban Planning*, 63: 61–74.

Innes, J. (1995), 'Planning Theory's Emerging Paradigm: Communicative Action and Interactive Practice', *Journal of Planning Education and Research*, 14(3): 183–190.

Joerin, F. and Musy, A. (2000), 'Land Management with GIS and Multicriteria Analysis', *International Transactions in Operational Research*, 7: 67–78.

Kaufman, S. (1995), *At Home in the Universe: The Search for the Laws of Self-organization and Complexity*, University Press, New York, Oxford.

Keeney, R.L. (1992), *Value-Focused Thinking. A Path to Creative Decision-making*, Harvard University Press, Cambridge, MA, USA.

Kortenkamp, K.V. and Moore, C.F. (2001), 'Ecocentrism and Anthropocentrism: Moral Reasoning about Ecological Commons Dilemmas', *Journal of Environmental Psychology*, 21: 261–272.

Laul, A. (2003), 'Sustainable Urban Strategies for Developing Countries', in L. Fusco Girard, B. Forte, M. Cerreta, P. De Toro and F. Forte (eds), *The Human Sustainable City. Challenges and Perspectives from the Habitat Agenda*, Ashgate, Aldershot, pp. 141–164.

Lazzati, G. (1984), *La città dell'uomo*, Ave, Rome.

Magnaghi, A. (1995), 'Ecologia e...urbanistica. Urbanistica e...ecologia', in E. Tiezzi (ed.), *Ecologia e...*, Laterza, Bari, pp. 43–60.

Malczewski, J. (1999), *GIS and Multicriteria Decision Analysis*, Wiley, New York.

Maturana, H.R. and Varela, F.J. (1980), *Autopoiesis and Cognition*, D. Reidel, Boston, MA.

Munda, G. (1996), 'Cost–Benefit Analysis in Integrated Environmental Assessment: Some Methodological Issues', *Ecological Economics*, 19: 157–168.

Munda, G. (2004), 'Social Multi-Criteria Evaluation: Methodological Foundations and Operational Consequences', *European Journal of Operational Research*, 158: 662–677.

Newman, P.W.G. (1999), 'Sustainability and Cities: Extending the Metabolism Model', *Landscape and Urban Planning*, 44: 219–226.

Niekerk, F. and Voogd, H. (1999), 'Impact Assessment for Infrastructure Planning: Some Dutch Dilemmas', *Environmental Impact Assessment Review*, 19: 21–36.

Nijkamp, P. and Baycan-Levent, T. (2005), 'Evaluation of Urban Green Spaces', in D.H. Miller and D. Patassini (eds), *Beyond Benefit Cost Analysis. Accounting for Non-market Values in Planning Evaluation*, Ashgate, Aldershot, pp. 63–88.

Nijkamp, P. and Medda, F. (2003), 'Integrated Assessment of Urban Revitalization Projects', in L. Fusco Girard, B. Forte, M. Cerreta, P. De Toro and F. Forte (eds), *The Human Sustainable City. Challenges and Perspectives from the Habitat Agenda*, Ashgate, Aldershot, pp. 417–428.

Nijkamp, P., Oirschot, G. and Oosterman, A. (1993), *Regional Development and Engineering Creativity: An Instrumental Comparison of Science Parks in a Knowledge Society*, Free University, Amsterdam.

Ost, C. (2003), 'Can Economic Help Preserve and Conserve Heritage? And if so, Can Economics Help to Improve Quality of Life and of the Environment?', in L. Fusco Girard, B. Forte, M. Cerreta, P. De Toro and F. Forte (eds), *The Human Sustainable City. Challenges and Perspectives from the Habitat Agenda*, Ashgate, Aldershot, 491–504.

Rapport., D.J., Gaudet, C., Karr, J.R., Baron, J.S., Bohlen, C., Jackson, W., Jones, B., Naiman, R.J., Norton, B. and Pollock, M.M. (1998), 'Evaluating Landscape Health: Integrating Societal Goals and Biophysical Process', *Journal of Environmental Management*, 53: 1–15.

Ravetz, J.R. (2000), 'Integrated Assessment for Sustainability Appraisal in Cities and Regions', *Environmental Impact Assessment Review*, 20: 31–64.

Rijkens-Klomp, N., van de Lindt, M., van Asselt, M.B.A. and Rotmans, J. (2003), 'Integrative Policymaking for the Improvement of the Quality of Urban Life', in L. Fusco Girard, B. Forte, M. Cerreta, P. De Toro and F. Forte (eds), *The Human Sustainable City. Challenges and Perspectives from the Habitat Agenda*, Ashgate, Aldershot, pp. 141–164.

Roca Cladera, J., Burns, M.C. and Almirall, P.G. (2003), 'The Social and Economic Attractiveness of the Urban Environment: An Exercise in the Valuation of Public Space in Barcelona', in L. Fusco Girard, B. Forte, M. Cerreta, P. De Toro and F. Forte (eds), *The Human Sustainable City. Challenges and Perspectives from the Habitat Agenda*, Ashgate, Aldershot, pp. 505–517.

Rogers, W. (2003), 'The Excellent City Park System', in P. Harnik (ed.), *What Makes it Great and How to Get There*, The Trust for Public Land Pub, Washington, DC.

Rolston, H. (2003), 'Value in Nature and the Nature of Value', in A. Light and H. Ralston (eds), *Environmental Ethics: An Anthology*, Blackwell Publishers, Oxford, pp. 143–154.

Rotmans, J. (1998), 'Methods for Integrated Assessment: The Challenges and Opportunities Ahead', *Environmental Model Assessment*, 3: 155–181.

Rotmans, J. (2000), 'An Integrated Planning Tool for Sustainable City', *Environmental Impact Assessment Review*, 20: 265–276.

Sandercock, L. (2003), 'The Sustainable City and the Role of the City-Building Professions', in L. Fusco Girard, B. Forte, M. Cerreta, P. De Toro and F. Forte (eds), *The Human Sustainable City. Challenges and Perspectives from the Habitat Agenda*, Ashgate, Aldershot, pp. 375–385.

Sandercock, L. (2004), *Cosmopolis II. Mongrel Cities of the 21ˢᵗ Century*, Continuum, London, New York.

Schwandt, T.A. (2002), *Evaluation Practice Reconsidered*, Peter Lang Publishing, New York.

Scriven, M.S. (1983), 'The Evaluation Taboo', in E.R. House (ed.), *Philosophy of Evaluation*, Jossey-Bass, San Francisco, pp. 75–82.

Scriven, M.S. (1986), 'New Frontiers of Evaluation', *Evaluation Practice*, 7: 7–44.

Senge, P. (1990), *The Fifth Discipline: The Art and Practice of the Learning Organization*, Doubleday, New York.

Shah, K. (2003), 'Agenda 21 for Sustainable Construction in Developing Countries: The Indian Case', in L. Fusco Girard, B. Forte, M. Cerreta, P. De Toro and F. Forte (eds), *The Human Sustainable City. Challenges and Perspectives from the Habitat Agenda*, Ashgate, Aldershot, pp. 263–295.

Stead, R. and Stead, J. G. (1996), *Management for a Small Planet*, 2nd edn, Sage, Thousand Oaks, CA.

Tacconi, L. (1997), 'An Ecological Economic Approach to Forest and Biodiversity Conservation: The Case of Vanuatu', *World Development*, 25(12): 1995–2008.

Tacconi, L. (2000), *Biodiversity and Ecological Economics*, Earthscan, London.

Taylor, R. (1996), 'Forms of Capital and Intrinsic Values', *Chemosphere*, 33(9): 1801–1811.

Turner, R.K. (1992), 'Speculations on Weak and Strong Sustainability', *CSERGE Working Paper GEC*, 92–26: 3–41.

Turner, R.K., Folke, C., Gren, I.-M. and Bateman, I.J. (1993), 'Wetland Valuation: Three Case Studies', *Joint CSERGE/Beijer Institute, Working Paper*, pp. 1–26.

Turner, R.K., Paavola, J., Cooper, P., Faber, S., Jessamy, V. and Georgiou, S. (2003), 'Valuing Nature: Lessons Learned and Future Research Directions', *Ecological Economics*, 46: 493–510.

UNCHS (United Nations Centre for Human Settlements) (2001), *The State of the World's Cities 2001*, UNCHS (Habitat), Nairobi.

van Asselt, M.B.A. and Rotmans, J. (1996), 'Uncertainty in Perspective', *Global Environmental Change*, 6(2): 121–157.

von Weizsäcker, E.U., Lovins, A.B. and Lovins, L.H. (1998), *Factor Four: Doubling Wealth, Halving Resource Use*, Earthscan, London.

Wilber, K. (2000), *A Theory of Everything: An Integral Vision for Business, Politics, Science, and Spirituality*, Shambahala, Boston.

Zamagni, S. (ed.) (1999), *No profit come economia civile*, Il Mulino, Bologna.

Zamagni, S. (2003), 'Suotainablo Dovolopmont, the Struggle against Poverty and New Structures of Governance in the Era of Globalization', in L. Fusco Girard, B. Forte, M. Cerreta, P. De Toro and F. Forte (eds), *The Human Sustainable City. Challenges and Perspectives from the Habitat Agenda*, Ashgate, Aldershot, pp. 121–139.

5

The Role of Evaluation in Supporting a Human Sustainable Development: A Cosmonomic Perspective
Peter Nijkamp

INTRODUCTION

This chapter offers a new perspective on the issue of urban sustainability. Starting from a positive perspective on city life, it makes a typology of critical roles of the city which are to be considered with a view to urban sustainability. Next, it is argued that a sine qua non for a structured view on sustainable cities is the use of a more integrated perspective, as offered inter alia by cosmonomic philosophy. Then the chapter argues that the use and choice of indicators in multicriteria analysis for urban sustainability may usefully be based on this integrative methodology.

THE CITY AS A HUMAN CONSTRUCT

The modern city is not a recent invention. It has a long history and it has manifested itself in a great variety of appearances. The city has meant the centre of open democracy, as witnessed by the Greek concept of polis. But it has also shown its military significance, as exemplified by fortifications and walls around the city. At present, the city mirrors part of a global network society by acting as a nodal point in an interlinked information and communication configuration (see Castells, 1996). But whatever appearance a city may have had in the history of mankind, it has always formed the cradle of civilization. The key role of the city in ancient times is eloquently presented in a fascinating study of Tulleken (1988), when he argues:

> Yet by 3000 BC, an astonishingly different panorama was unfolding. Along the length of the valley, magnificent cities sprawled on the riverbanks. Around them, fields of grain spread like a tide of fecundity across the once desolated flatlands. Groves of date palms swayed in the wind, offering fruit and shade. Within the massive walls that ringed the cities, temples towered over both streetscape and plain. There were brick places and mansions and street after street of comfortable houses. People thronged the avenues and; in hundreds of workshops artisans turned out all manner of goods, from pottery to sparkling jewelry. On holy days, processions of the worshipful wound through the streets

to the temples. What had happened in this land the Greeks later called Mesopotamia, 'between the rivers', was the most crucial event in human history: the birth of civilization.

(p. 1)

Clearly, the city has also played a critical role in the economic development of a country or region. The grandfather of economics, Adam Smith (1776), has already drawn attention to the strategic position of cities, as exemplified by the following quotation on Italian cities:

> The cities of Italy seem to have been the first in Europe which were raised by commerce to any considerable degree of opulence. Italy lay in the centre of what was at that time the improved and civilized part of the world. The crusades too, though by the great waste of stock and destruction of inhabitants which they occasioned, they must necessarily have retarded the process of the greater part of Europe, were extremely favourable to that of some Italian cities. The great armies which marched from all parts of the world to the conquest of the Holy Land, gave extraordinary encouragement to the shipping of Venice, Genoa, and Pisa, sometimes in transporting them thither, and always in supplying them with provisions. They were the commissaries, if one may say so, of those armies: and the most destructive frenzy that ever befell the European nations, was a source of opulence of those republics.

(p. 406)

Cities seem to be an open intrinsic part of society and hence they carry all the evils and all the merits of human society. They are a centre of socio-economic interplay, human confrontation, political dialectics, birthplaces of civilization, centers of science and art and a melting pot of cultures. According to Jane Jacobs (1969), cities generate economic growth inter alia from the disordered order of human interaction. In the urban economics literature, we find the concept of agglomeration advantages, which means that a spatial clustering of economic activities (industries, households, public services) leads to various types of economies of scale, which cannot be generated elsewhere. Sometimes a distinction is made into localization advantages, urbanization advantages, scale advantages, urban externalities and the like. They all point at the fact that a geographic juxtaposition may lead to win–win situations for all actors involved.

In this paper we start from a positive perspective on the city as an appropriate spatial organization of human activities. On the basis of a typology of different roles of the city, we will then question whether and how the concept of a sustainable city can be employed and operationalized. Next, on the basis of the principles of the cosmonomic philosophy of the Dutch philosopher Herman Dooyeweerd, we will try to create an analytical framework for judging urban sustainability. This result will then be used to test whether multicriteria methods are appropriate tools for urban sustainability planning. The chapter will be concluded with some retrospective remarks.

ROLES OF CITIES

Urbanization has become a common spatial organization of human activity world-wide, in both the developing and developed countries. A few hundred years back, only a small portion of a nation's population lived in the city, but at present we observe an average urbanization rate of about 70 per cent. The geography of our world has clearly exhibited a major transition towards urban forms of life. Clearly, some authors have questioned this ongoing historical trend by referring to the phenomenon of suburbanization or even de-urbanization. It is of course an undeniable fact that a process of urban sprawl has taken place, but this phenomenon did not destroy urban functions, but on the contrary reinforced urban functions. This spatial distribution only meant that the action radius of the city was increasing, but the people leaving the city centre were in their economic activity still largely – directly and indirectly – depending on central urban functions.

It has to be admitted that city life does not only have positive benefits, but also several disadvantages. A discussion on city life is often witnessing uneasy feelings. O'Sullivan (2000) quotes two authors who express contrasting views on the merits of the city: 'Cities have always been the fireplace of civilization, whence light and heat radiated out into the dark' (Theodore Parker) and 'I'd rather wake up in the middle of nowhere than in any city on earth' (Steve McQueen) (p. 1). Despite the existence of mixed feelings about the city, the idea that the city is a 'blessing in disguise' is still prevalent. This has also to do with the great variety of roles cities are able to play. We will mention here a few of such important roles of cities, without striving for an exhaustive list.

Shelter role

The city is offering settlement facilities for numerous people, based on its scale advantages in housing many citizens. Shelter has even become a human right, and cities are able to care for the housing needs of people. From this perspective, cities offer a significant contribution to a sustainable human habitat.

Religious role

In the early biblical history the city was often regarded as the source of evil (Babylon, Nineveh). But in the later history we observe a more positive appreciation of the city. Jerusalem was the seat of King David and the New Jerusalem became even a metaphor for a total re-birth of mankind.

Cultural role

Historically, the city was the place where arts and sciences were flourishing. Venice, Bologna, Padua, Paris, Augsburg, Amsterdam and many other places offer an over-whelming evidence of the favourable seedbed conditions of an urban way of life for the advancement of culture.

Political role

Democracy was a new type of governance which found its seedbed in the city. And still nowadays political power is largely concentrated in cities and governments have established their premises in cities. Deconcentration of physical government facilities (e.g., premises) has never become very successful. Administrative functions are usually executed in capital cities of countries, or at least in cities with a critical political mass.

Economic role

The city is the marketplace for economic activity. It is also the place where usually products are designed and often manufactured. Furthermore, it is a marketplace where capital is supplied and advisory services are offered. In addition, the city is – as a result of various types of agglomeration advantages – a very efficient way of organizing production and consumption.

Social role

Cities house thousands of people who are through the associative nature of city life able to communicate with a great number of others, intensively or less intensively. But they have a social contact and communication spectrum which far exceeds that of a random distribution of people.

Engineering role

The city is the cradle of technological inventions and innovations. It brings together craftsmanship, technical expertise, hardware, software and orgware. As a result, cities are still the breeding places for the genesis of new products and services.

Network role

In an emerging network society cities become more and more the virtual centres of global network forces. The city brings together a triple-C potential: communication, competence and creativeness. Despite doomsday scenarios on the 'death of distance' and on the threats to city life, it is more plausible that cities continue to reinforce their role in local, regional, national and international networks.

The manifold strategic functions of the city have also attracted many negative forces which might erode city life. Congestion, pollution, poor health conditions and criminality are examples of phenomena which exert a threat for survival of the modern city. The worldwide concern on cities has led to the popularity of the concept of urban sustainability. This will be further discussed in the next section.

THE SUSTAINABLE CITY

Sustainable development as a general concept has already a long history and dates back to 1987, when the World Commission on Environment and Development (WCED), headed by Gro Harlem Brundtland, published its report under the title 'Our Common Future'. Ever since, a worldwide debate is going on, addressing the concept of sustainable development. Despite political consensus on the importance of this notion, there was no scientific agreement on the definition of this concept. Gradually, however, it became clear that sustainability should incorporate at least economic, social and environmental dimensions. This has led to a distinction into economic sustainability (EcS), social sustainability (SS) and environmental sustainability (ES). The various characteristics and their linkages have been clearly outlined by Goodland (1994) and are represented in Figure 5.1.

Clearly, the distinction into three types of sustainability leads also to a distinction into three classes of objectives, namely economic objectives (e.g., growth, equity, efficiency), social objectives (e.g., social participation, cohesion, cultural identity) and environmental objectives (e.g., biodiversity, carrying capacity, resilience).

It was, in the past years, increasingly recognized that sustainable development was not only referring to global issues, but also to more manageable policy directions, such as sectors or regions. Hence, notions such as sustainable agriculture, sustainable tourism, sustainable transport, sustainable regions and sustainable cities came to the fore (see for a broader exposition also Giaoutzi and Nijkamp, 1995; Capello et al., 1998; Satterthwaite, 1999).

In this section we will address in particular the concept of a sustainable city. A sustainable city is more than an environmentally benign city; it should also fulfil

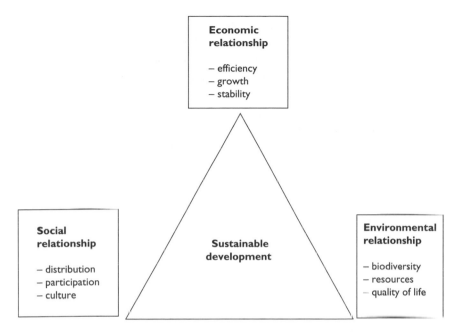

Figure 5.1 Description of social, economic and environmental sustainability
Source: Goodland, 1994, p. 277

economic goals and act as a home for man. Thus, a sustainable city is based on a symbiosis between various, sometimes conflicting objectives (see also Priemus, 1999). It has been extensively argued in Capello *et al.* (1998) that a city – through its potential for agglomeration advantages – has far more opportunities for sustainable development than dispersed ways of living and working. Examples are environmental benefits from public transport instead of private modes, or energy efficiency for concentration of households. Clearly, there are also bottlenecks as a result of massive densities of people or economic activities.

From an environmental perspective, urban sustainability has also played an important role in recent discussions on urban spatial configurations, such as 'the resourceful city', 'the green city', 'the garden city', 'the ecological city', 'the edge city' and 'the virtual city'. Thus far, no unambiguous concept has emerged and, in reality, we observe a parallel development of various contemporaneous urban policy concepts (Nijkamp and Perrels, 1994). Although it is likely that environmental quality problems may become more severe with urban size, there is no clear evidence that urban size as such causes environmental decay. This is also evident from new developments in smart growth and new urbanism.

Some authors have interpreted a sustainable city in a rather narrow sense by addressing predominantly urban form (for instance, in a compact city perspective, see Jenks *et al.*, 1996) or urban transport (in relation to energy consumption, see Newman and Kenworthy, 1989). It should be noted, however, that the urban environment is a multi-faceted phenomenon ranging from 'hard' pollution indicators to 'soft' quality-of-life indicators. The urban environment is, in addition, the playing ground of many conflicting interests, institutionally, sectorally and geographically, so that the concept of the sustainable city is an interesting test case for the notion of 'civitas' or civil society (Selman, 1996). This paper will, therefore, adopt a broad perspective on urban sustainability.

It also ought to be recognized that the efficiency of the city in achieving sustainability goals is partly due to the ecological footprint of the city: a significant share of the environmental burden caused by activities taking place in the urban territory is exported to other areas (see also Wackernagel and Rees, 1995).

An evident major problem in urban sustainability analysis is the definition and operationalization of proper indicators, e.g. on density, green areas, pollution emission, waste water, energy consumption, waste noise, etc. (see also Finco and Nijkamp, 2000). Many indicators are used and collected on an ad hoc basis and lack a clear policy and methodological foundation. In various planning evaluation studies, such indicators form the input for a multicriteria analysis. There may thus be a need for a more rigorous and thorough basis for sustainability indicators. In the next section, we will present some ideas based on the cosmonomic philosophical school.

TOWARDS A METHODOLOGICAL UNDERPINNING

The design of a typological framework for mapping out the manifold dimensions of modern city life – and of urban sustainability in particular – is not an easy matter. The development of a theoretical, ontological system as a basis for classifying urban sustainability indicators is fraught with many problems, because of the multiplicity of characteristic aspects involved and the varied nature of all relevant aspects in modern city life. Such a classification should provide a relevant differentiation of key factors and an operational framework for multidisciplinary work in urban planning. The cosmonomic philosophy of Dooyeweerd (1953–1955, 1968), though theoretical in nature, may provide a useful framework for tackling more properly these issues. It is explicitly transdisciplinary; yet it provides integration rather than fragmentation between disciplines. It may offer a very useful checklist to guide urban development planning, ensuring that not only one, but all aspects of the environmental system and human life, from the numerical to the credal, be present in urban planning research (Lombardi and Basden, 1997). It finally helps to understand the nature of a city in such a way that it not only presents a multi-faceted ideal, but also may be able to provide specific guidance in planning theory and practice (see also Lombardi and Nijkamp, 2000).

The theory of Dooyeweerd has been postulated in a number of recent studies related to cybernetics, information systems and organizational learning (see also Basden, 1990). It has been studied and developed by other contemporary authors, such as Clouser (1991) and Hart (1984), who illuminated some of its benefits in understanding and explaining how social systems and institutions work. Finally, it has been applied to urban planning and design for understanding urban sustainability in the built environment (Lombardi, 1995, 1999, 2001; Lombardi and Brandon, 1997; Lombardi and Basden, 1997).

This theory proposes a pluralist ontology, in which temporal reality has 15 aspects or dimensions (named 'modalities'), each of which has a kernel meaning (in brackets): Quantitative (amount), Spatial (continuous extension), Kinematic (movement), Physical (energy and mass), Biotic (life functions), Sensitive (sense, emotion), Analytical (distinction), Historical (including technological-cultural) (formative power), Communicative or Lingual (symbolic meaning), Social (social intercourse), Economic (frugality), Aesthetic (harmony, beauty), Juridical (rights, what is due), Ethical (self-giving love), Pistic-credal (faith, vision, commitment). Each modality in this sequence presupposes the existence of one or more previous modalities thus creating a hierarchical structure.

Each aspect provides a set of 'laws' (including norms and regularities) – e.g. laws of arithmetics, laws of physics, laws of aesthetics, laws of ethics, etc. – which not only guide but also enable entities or species (people, animals, etc.) to function in a variety of ways. The laws of the earlier aspects are more determinative, while those of subsequent aspects are more normative. Although each aspect is irreducible to each other, there are definite relationships between the modalities which define their position. For instance, the economic modality is dependent on the social, the social on the communicative, the communicative on the historical, and so on (Lombardi and Basden, 1997).

These relationships between modalities allow an entity (or a system) to function in a coherent rather than fragmented manner. In other words, there are two ways a 'thing' or object may possess properties of a modality: 'actively' and 'passively'. The two functions are not mutually exclusive. All 'things' function simultaneously passively in all the modalities, so that it is only the active functions of certain modalities that a 'thing' may lack and which exhibit the sequential order of appearance noticed above (Hart, 1984).

Though each system is subject to the specific law(s) of every modality (either as subject or object), there is one modality that qualifies the system, i.e. it endows the system with its ultimate mission character and uniqueness, distinguishing it from other types of system. The way 'things' of a particular type are 'qualified' by its associated modality and are governed by the laws of their qualifying modality is named their 'qualifying functions'. The qualifying aspect of a 'thing' is the modality whose laws guide and regulate the internal organization or development of the 'thing' considered as a whole and which is also the highest aspect in the above mentioned sequential order in which the 'thing' functions actively. For example, a rock is qualified by the physical modality, a tree by the biotic, a dog by the sensitive, while a man having all the 15 modalities active is qualified by the credal one (the highest in the list). It is noteworthy that there is no direct causal link between modalities, e.g. better lingual communication does not automatically bring better social relations (Lombardi and Basden, 1997).

Finally, the correspondence between the orders of different modalities allows one modality (named 'source') to be used as a metaphoric representation of another or several other modalities (named 'idiom'). For example, the quantitative modality is often used for explaining the functioning of other systems, such as the social system. Social scientists can then use the laws of mathematics to manipulate aspects related to the social modality or the economic modality and derive conclusions which have been difficult to arrive at without the aid of these laws. However, it is important to note that these conclusions rest upon the laws of the numeric modality and not on the basis of the spatial or social modality. Therefore, while they may be mathematically valid, they need not be necessarily valid in the other spheres. In particular, though every modality can be an 'idiom' for another, its effectiveness as an idiom varies and the degree of correspondence declines as the distance between one modality and another increases. Therefore, the numeric modality is not a very suitable idiom for the ethical modality and it would be better to use a closer modality such as the juridical modality.

In the context of spatial development, this ordered structure of aspects may offer a useful classification system for spatial development and a guide for the identification of potential barriers to interaction between regions. It may provide the theoretical underpinning of a new taxonomy of sustainable cities which is able to support decision-making processes and the mapping of qualitative factors in an urban sustainability context.

This classification is concisely summarized in Table 5.1. It provides a systematic and logic design, which is comprehensive, but avoids an overload of unprocessed information. The various items may also constitute the basis for urban sustainability planning.

Table 5.1 Classification of urban roles/functions by means of modality order

Modalities	Nucleus of meaning	Taxonomy of urban roles/barriers (examples)
Quantitative	Knowledge of 'how much' of 'things'	Low volume of resources Large population size
Spatial	Continuous extension/ expansion	Connectivity potential Spatial distance
Kinematic	Movement, flows	Missing links in traffic infrastructure Opportunities from telecommunication
Physical	Energy, mass	Natural obstacles Due access to energy sources
Biological	Life function	Overpopulation High environmental sustainability
Sensitive	Senses, feelings	Sense of safety Criminality
Analytical	Discerning of entities, logic	Educational and training backlog High skills of network actors
Historical	Formative power, technology and cultural development	Long-term isolated location Distinct evolution of human systems
Communicative	Informative, symbolic representation, linguistic	Language and vocabulary backlog Network externalities
Social	Social intercourse, social exchange	Ethnic segmentation Socio-economic harmony
Economic	Prudence in handling limited resources	Low entry cost to network participation Lack of monetary integration
Aesthetic	Harmony, beauty	Disparities in creative arts Abundance of cultural heritage
Juridical	Retribution, fairness, rights	Harmonization of legal system Administrative and bureaucratic rules
Ethical	Love, moral, code of conduct	Internal social group protection Political and ideological protection
Credal	Faith, commitment, trustworthiness	Cultural-religious segmentation Work ideology and trust

The various elements of Table 5.1 can be re-grouped for sustainability purposes into three major clusters:

A.   *Spatial-physical*

- quantitative
- spatial
- kinematic

- physical
- biological

B. *Socio-cultural*

- sensitive
- analytical
- historical
- communicative
- social

C. *Institutional-behavioural*

- economic
- aesthetic
- juridical
- ethical
- credal.

If one takes for granted that this cosmonomic approach offers a comprehensive framework for scientific research, then also our analytical apparatus should be tested on its ability to meet the above classification. This will be discussed in the next section with a particular view to multi-criteria analysis.

A MULTIPLE CRITERIA FRAMEWORK

Multicriteria analysis has become a useful tool in evaluation and planning studies, also in regard to urban sustainability analysis (see Finco and Nijkamp, 2000). In public decision-making, normally a wide range of decisions has to be made without a clear reliance on the market system. This is partly caused by the nature of choices in the public sector (with emphasis on multi-actor participatory democratic modes of decision-making) and partly by the complexity of government projects (with long-lasting and often uncertain implications) and it is indeed increasingly recognized that decisions based on market forces alone do not necessarily lead to optimal results. In the context of urban policy, structural market failures as well as unexpected external factors may need a policy system that ensures an improvement of socio-economic and environmental conditions.

In the past, several methods have been developed and applied in policy analysis, in which a market evaluation played a prominent role. The most well-known example of such a market evaluation method is based on cost–benefit analysis (as an operational application of welfare theory). This method forms the foundation for many policy assessment methods and has been successfully applied in many case studies in the public sector. Despite its great many merits, it is increasingly recognized in modern policy analysis that it also has severe limitations, because not all relevant welfare implications of public sector initiatives can be expressed using the 'measurement rod of money' (Nijkamp et al., 1991).

Cost–benefit studies seem to be most applicable and appropriate if the decision concerns a well-demarcated and a priori precisely defined project which does not generate many unpriced or qualitative externalities. If, however, the decision concerns a more general policy programme (of which the details and even sometimes the major features are unknown), then the translation of the impacts into precisely measurable and quantitative consequences and subsequently into monetary figures is often rather problematic. Similarly, if a public investment is likely to generate a wide diversity of social costs (e.g. landscape destruction, loss of safety, health effects, loss of biodiversity or rare species, destruction of archaeological sites), it is often a heroic research task to come up with reliable figures which are broadly accepted in the policy area. This does not mean that cost–benefit analysis would have to be discredited; but it would have to be complemented with more appropriate evaluation tools.

As a response to the shortcomings of conventional evaluation studies, a great diversity of modern assessment methods has been developed over the last 10 years in order to extend the range of and to provide a complement to conventional cost–benefit analysis and to offer a perspective for procedural types of decision-making in which various quality aspects are also incorporated. Many of these methods simultaneously investigate the impacts of policy strategies on a multitude of relevant criteria, partly monetary, partly non-monetary (including qualitative facets). They are often coined multicriteria methods and are also known as multi-assessment methods (Nijkamp et al., 1991).

It is noteworthy that, in the past few years, an avalanche of assessment and evaluation studies has been undertaken in the regional, transportation and environmental field, but unfortunately an integral study and a systematic comparison of findings of previously undertaken assessment studies have proven to be difficult due to different analytical approaches and differences in presentation. Several problems underlying a decision-making process in an urban sustainability context have to be coped with, such as:

- the relevant urban information or available data always contain a component of uncertainty;
- the data or information may be stored in different statistical databases that may be difficult to access, manipulate, compare and study;

- a large set of often conflicting urban objectives or targets has to be taken into account;
- the decision-making process itself might be influenced by power relations or selfish motivations of urban stakeholders; and
- a decision-making process has to take place within the shortest time possible to avoid countervailing effects from the side of various urban actors.

The above considerations highlight that the policy objective of urban sustainability is not unambiguous, but may lead to conflicting actions. Is it possible to devise a decision support system that is able to shed clear light on this difficult issue? The answer to this question may be given by referring to conflict management techniques development in the multi-assessment literature. The existence of multiple objectives means that, in a given societal setting, the best possible alternative or policy has to be determined that also creates sufficient public acceptability or at least social feasibility. In other words, the basic question is: how to determine the optimal policy?

It is generally accepted nowadays that most decisions – certainly in the public domain – can be typified as multiple objective or multicriteria problems (Janssen, 1991; Nijkamp *et al.*, 1991; Beinat and Nijkamp, 1998). This means that an optimal – or most acceptable – compromise alternative from a set of competing alternatives has to be identified which best satisfies a number of – often conflicting – objectives or decision criteria. Another complicating factor is that usually in the public policy domain, besides a set of quantitative criteria, qualitative criteria must also be taken into account in a multi-actor decision-making process. Examples are the interest of the biotic and abiotic environment, the protection of school children, accessibility conditions of the elderly generation, or the risk of criminality in public transport.

As mentioned above, cost–benefit analysis has severe shortcomings when it comes to an operationalization of intangible aspects, so that this theoretically elegant method has often limited applicability. In most public policy evaluation studies, especially the assessment of environmental impacts turns out to be troublesome, since all advantages and disadvantages of policy options would have to be translated into a common monetary unit. Hence, incommensurable criteria of an unpriced and intangible nature cannot be included in a decision-making procedure based on a standard cost–benefit analysis. Furthermore, in the current policy practice in many countries there is hardly any applicable and meaningful way of including distributional impacts on welfare (e.g., through a weighting system for different groups) into policy evaluation. Therefore, a proper decision-making tool is needed that is able to handle qualitative and intangible information in a proper way. Consequently, for our analysis of urban sustainability initiatives, it seems useful to resort to multi-criteria analysis (MCA) as a modern decision support method in the public sector and elsewhere.

It also seems plausible that the great many aspects of urban sustainability can meaningfully be checked on completeness, consistency, duplication and internal logic by deploying the classes A to C (and its 15 constituents) from Dooyeweerd's cosmonomic methodology. Clearly, a more rigorous empirical test framework would be needed to do this.

CONCLUDING REMARKS

Although the city forms the heartland in a modern network society, local or urban sustainability is seemingly a small-scale policy objective in a large world. But it ought to be recognized that it plays a crucial role in the wider context of international climate and environmental policy. Each city has a vast range of policy options ranging from the built environment to public transport, from waste management to energy policy, from information campaigns to efficient water use. The responsibility of local authorities far exceeds the boundaries of their city, as is witnessed by the urban ecological footprint indirectly. But the challenge is to bring the issue of the global environment close to the citizen, as they are the key actors in any sustainability policy. Local instruments should, therefore, appeal to the individual household and at the same time refer to a broader environment. This idea is also convincingly reflected in the Local Agenda 21 (see also Selman, 2000). Urban sustainability management is thus a complex undertaking, as it has to address a formidable number of aspects. In the paper we have tried to offer a novel approach to multicriteria analysis of sustainability initiatives by referring to cosmonomic philosophical thoughts offering a systematic typology for multidimensional urban planning issues. They offer at least a coherent and rather complete framework for judging and designing a multicriteria analysis by way of a meta-experiment.

ACKNOWLEDGEMENT

The author is indebted to Patrizia Lombardi who has provided the intellectual input for this chapter.

REFERENCES

Basden, A. (1996) 'Towards an Understanding of Contextualized Technology', *Managing the Technological Society: The Next Century's Challenge to O.R.*, International Conference of the Swedish Operations Research Society, 1–3 October 1996, University of Lule, Lule, Sweden.

Beinat, E. and Nijkamp, P. (eds) (1998) *Multicriteria Analysis for Land-Use Management*, Kluwer, Dordrecht.

Capello, R., Nijkamp, P. and Pepping G. (1998) *Sustainable Cities and Energy Policy*, Springer-Verlag, Berlin.

Castells, E. (1996) *The Rise of the Network Society*, Blackwell, Malden.

Clouser, R. (1991) *The Myth of Religions Neutrality*, University of Notre Dame, London.

Dooyeweerd, H. (1953–55) *A New Critique of Theoretical Thought*, vol. 1–4, Philadelphia, Presbyterian and Reformed Publisher Company, Pennsylvania.

Dooyeweerd, H. (1968) *In the Twilight of Western Thought*, Nutley, New Jersey, USA.

Finco, A. and Nijkamp, P. (2000) 'Towards a Sustainable Future of Cities in Europe', *Land Use Simulation in Europe* (J. Stillwell and H. Scholten, eds), Kluwer, Dordrecht, pp. 173–192.

Giaoutzi, M. and Nijkamp, P. (1995) *Decision Support Systems for Sustainable Regional Development*, Avebury, Aldershot, UK.

Goodland, R. (1994) 'Environmental Sustainability and the Power Sector', *Impact Assessment*, vol. 12, Fall, pp. 275–299.

Hart, H. (1984) *Understanding Our World*, University Press of America, USA.

Jacobs, J. (1969) *The Economy of Cities*, Penguin, London.

Janssen, R. (1991) *Multiple Decision Support for Environmental Problems*, Kluwer, Dordrecht.

Jenks, M., Burton, E. and Williams, K. (eds) (1996) *The Compact City: A Sustainable Urban Form*, FN Spon, London.

Lombardi, P. (1995) 'Evaluating Sustainability at a Local Planning Level', Proceedings of the International Workshop CIB TG-8, *Linking & Prioritising Environmental Criteria*, 15–16 November, Toronto, Canada, pp. 89–100.

Lombardi, P. (1999) *Understanding Sustainability in the Built Environment*, PhD Dissertation, University of Salford, Salford.

Lombardi, P. (2001) 'Responsibilities towards the Coming Generation: Forming a New Creed', *Urban Design Studies*, vol. 7, pp. 89–102.

Lombardi, P. and Basden, A. (1997) 'Environmental Sustainability and Information Systems', *Systems Practice*, vol. 10, no. 4, Hull, UK.

Lombardi, P. and Brandon, P. (1997) 'Toward a Multimodal Framework for Evaluating the Built Environment Quality in Sustainability Planning', *Evaluation in the Built Environment for Sustainability* (P. Brandon, V. Bentivegna and P. Lombardi, eds), Chapman & Hall, London.

Lombardi, P. and Nijkamp, P. (2000) 'A New Geography of Hope and Despair for the Periphery', *New Trends in Human Geography*, University of the Aegean, Lesvos, pp. 276–306.

Newman, P. and Kenworthy, J. (1989) *Cities and Automobile Dependence*, Gower, Aldershot.

Nijkamp, P. and Perrels, A. (1994) *Sustainable Cities in Europe*, Earthscan, London.

Nijkamp, P., Rietveld, P. and Voogd, H. (1991) *Multicriteria Analysis for Physical Planning*, Elsevier, Amsterdam.

O'Sullivan, A. (2000) *Urban Economics*, Irwin McGraw-Hill, Boston.

Priemus, H. (1999) 'Sustainable Cities: How to Realize an Ecological Breakthrough', *International Planning Studies*, vol. 4, no. 2, pp. 213–236.

Satterthwaite, D. (ed.) (1999) *Sustainable Cities*, Earthscan, London.

Selman, P. (1996) *Local Sustainability*, Paul Chapman, London.

Selman, P. (2000) 'A Sideways Look at Local Agenda 21', *Journal of Environmental Policy and Planning*, vol. 2, no. 1, pp. 39–53.

Smith, A. (1776) *An Inquiry into the Nature and Causes of the Wealth of Nations*, Liberty Classics, Indianapolis (English translation, 1981).

Tulleken, K. (1988) *The Age of God-Kings, 3000–1500 BC*, Time-Life Books, Amsterdam.

Wackernagel, M. and Rees, W.E. (1995) *Our Ecological Footprint*, New Society Publishers, Philadelphia.

WCED (1987) *Our Common Future*, Oxford University Press, Oxford/New York.

6

The Role of Modelling in Urban Sustainability Assessment
Gordon Mitchell

INTRODUCTION

Three hundred years ago, few people lived in a city. Globally, just five cities had a population over half a million people, and even by 1800, only 3 per cent of the world population lived in settlements of more than 25,000 people (Table 6.1). Cities were mostly small with a densely populated core with intense environmental impacts, surrounded by a mid zone acting as the main resource base, followed by a distant but largely untouched peripheral zone. Today, half the global population is urban, and collectively they exert an unprecedented impact upon the environment, from local to global levels (Table 6.2). Delivering urban sustainability is thus critical to improving the lives of urban people, and the rest of the planet, people and ecosystems, impacted upon by their activities.

In 'Southern' cities urbanisation occurs at 10 times the rate of the developed world (UN, 1995), and the overriding sustainability concerns are basic quality of life issues – livelihood and survival. Of the 1 billion people with no access to proper sanitation, 1.7 billion with no safe drinking water, and 700,000 annual deaths due to poor air quality, most occur in southern cities (Gladwin et al., 1995). One-third of the urban population here have no access to basic amenities, education or healthcare, and communicable and vector borne disease account for a high proportion of all deaths, particularly in the poor and the young. Residents of southern cities experience the worst economic and environmental impacts of urbanisation, hence steps to promote environmentally sustainable urban development here must address the pressing needs of the poor through provision of basic services.

In cities of the developed 'North', livelihood issues are less pressing, and more attention is given to limiting urban environmental impact. Such impacts are considerable. A European Environment Agency (EEA) assessment (Stanners and Bordeau, 1995; EEA, 1998) reveals that an EU city of 1 million people typically consumes, each day, 11,500t of fossil fuels, 320,000t of water and 2000t of food, whilst producing 25,000t of CO_2, 300,000t of wastewater and 1600t of solid waste. The consequences of such material flows are serious and well documented (see e.g. Douglas, 1983; Giradet, 1992; and Haughton and Hunter, 1994). For example, 70–80 per cent of large EU cities do not comply with health-based air quality standards due to growth in road traffic, which has proved difficult to constrain, and

Table 6.1 Changes in city size distribution, 1700–2000

Date	Number of cities exceeding specified sizes (population in thousands)					
	>100	>200	>500	>1000	>10,000	>20,000
1700	34	14	5	0	0	0
1800	50	17	6	1	0	0
1900	287	142	43	16	1	0
1950	950	NE	179	76	NE	0
1975	NE	NE	422	191	7	1
2000	1699	NE	859	440	20	NE

Note: NE – no estimate

Table 6.2 Environmental impacts and issues of urbanisation

Environmental impacts and issues of urbanisation	Local	Regional	Global
Climate			
Reduced solar radiation at ground surface due to airborne particulates	•		
Higher air temperature due to energy use, and heat storage in buildings	•		
Lower humidity as less transpiration and water retaining surface soil	•		
Cloud and fog is more frequent and intense, wind speeds are lower	•		
Precipitation higher with more extreme rainfall events	•		
Water			
Replacement of permeable with impermeable surfaces	•		
Reduced evapo-transpiration loss and higher water yield potential	•		
Faster runoff response with higher peak discharge and flood risk	•		
Reduced groundwater replenishment, subsidence and saline intrusion risk	•		
Reduced discharge at times of low flow	•		
Land inundation for water supply and hydro-power	•	•	
Land and resources			
Loss of productive agricultural land, Soil erosion	•	•	
Overbuilding of mineral reserves	•		
Deforestation	•	•	•
High dependence on non-renewable energy; depletion of fossil resources	•	•	•
Energy efficiency of distribution networks, buildings and production	•	•	
Risks from nuclear energy, waste disposal and facility decommissioning	•	•	

Table 6.2 (Continued)

Environmental impacts and issues of urbanisation	Local	Regional	Global
Conservation of built heritage	•		
Waste and Pollution			
Emission of ozone depleting gases (CFCs, HCFSs)			•
Emission of greenhouse gases (CO_2, NH_4, CFCs, NO)			•
Emission of acid gases (SO_X, NO_X)	•	•	
Emission of toxic gases (CO, VOCs, Ozone)	•	•	
Emission of toxic metals (Pb, Cd, Hg, Ar, Ni)	•	•	
Noise	•		
Pollution of water by sewage, industrial effluent and non-point sources	•	•	•
Contamination of land otherwise suitable for food production	•	•	
Solid waste production exceeds capacity of available disposal sites	•	•	
Hazards			
Road traffic accidents	•		
Elevated flood risk, coastal inundation, water supply failure	•		
Land instability: subsidence, land slip and earthquake	•	•	
Residential proximity to industrial processes	•		
Non-conformity of buildings to construction standards	•		
Crime and civil unrest			
Health and welfare issues			
Vector borne and communicable diseases	•	•	
Respiratory diseases	•		
Cancer, cardiovascular disease and long-term genetic effects of toxins	•		
Adequacy of basic services (water, sanitation, waste disposal)	•		
Accessibility to adequate shelter	•	•	
Accessibility to basic health, education and welfare services	•	•	
Accessibility to green areas and open spaces	•		
Employment and income opportunities	•	•	
Accessibility to work and service opportunities	•	•	
Ecological issues			
Reduction of habitat space	•	•	•
Toxicological effects on plants and animals	•	•	
Reduced species abundance and diversity (extinctions)	•	•	•
Biomass appropriation (reduced carbon fixation capacity)	•	•	

which creates further problems of CO_2 emission, noise (65% of the EU population are exposed to unacceptably high noise levels) and accidents (1.7 million injuries and 55,000 deaths each year). EU cities also face major challenges related to water, with demand rising in a time of climate change and a less reliable supply, flood frequency increasing, and surface waters degraded through persistent combined sewer overflows and diffuse discharges.

In northern cities, tackling these problems, and others such as rising waste production and declining green space and biodiversity, is part of the 'green agenda', whose goal is to ensure human activity is conducted within ecologically defined limits, but without an unacceptable decline in the socio-economic benefits those activities deliver (i.e. 'living within the carrying capacity of supporting ecosystems'). Environmental efficiency thus dominates the literature on northern sustainable cities, with works taking a variety of perspectives, including: holistic (e.g. Elkin et al., 1991; Tjallingi, 1995); sectoral (e.g. Nijkamp and Perrels (1994) on energy; Rees (1993) on water); and discipline-based (e.g. Blowers (1993) on land use planning; Barton et al. (1995) on architecture and urban design). This efficiency objective is encapsulated in the urban metabolism concept in which materials flow must be reoriented from their current linear flow (extract, use, dispose), to cyclical flows with lower resource demand, and waste used as a resource, thus reducing impact upon the environment (Wolman, 1965; Boyden et al., 1981; Di Castri et al., 1984; Giradet, 1992). The EEA assessment (op.cit.) found that the metabolic efficiency and environmental quality are not simply a function of city size, nor are they directly related to economic development, as both growth and decline cause environmental impact. Rather, they are products of complex patterns of urban activity related to form and function, mobility and lifestyle, themselves products of an elaborate mix of economic, geographical, social and political factors developed over the history of the city.

Assessing the sustainability of development processes and management interventions is thus clearly a challenging task. The complexity must be 'unpacked' and understood to such a degree that reasonable projections of city futures can be made, and appraised against sustainability objectives. Many factors contribute to this complexity. Some urban processes are well understood, but there is no definitive theory of the urban process to act as a reference framework for analysis. Rather, there are multiple theories from different disciplines (demography, economics, social science) which are in practice intimately linked, often in ways which are poorly described. The sustainability concept itself also adds to the complexity. Differing ethical perspectives on what constitutes sustainable development (Pearce et al., 1989) result in widely differing valuation of environmental capital, and hence agreed sustainability objectives. Urban sustainability assessment must also address more prosaic problems of spatial scale (what is a city, how are city activities related to impacts beyond their boundary?), lack of data describing basic processes, and inadequate knowledge of environmental thresholds, including carrying and assimilative capacities.

If urban regions are to develop sustainably, we do not have time to wait for a full understanding of urban processes. Rather, we must apply the available tools, and work towards their more effective application as our understanding of cities grows. The 'kit-bag' of policy tools is fortunately extensive, comprising numerous specific instruments in the broad areas of strategic planning, legislation, economic instruments, technology and education (see Table 6.3 for examples with reference to energy, and examples from other areas in CEC, 1990; Elkin et al., 1991; Giradet, 1992; Blowers, 1993; CEC, 1994; Barton et al., 1995; Stanners and Bordeau, 1995; Roseland, 1998). Assessing the effectiveness of these tools is, however, challenging due to the size and complexity of the urban system. Effects on the environment are also often indirect, and may not be realised for several years. Thus highly uncertain environmental assessments may result, and counterintuitive or unintended side effects may be missed altogether. These problems are exacerbated

Table 6.3 Instruments for sustainable development

Policy instrument	Example application in energy sector
Strategic planning is the co-ordination of key urban functions at local and regional level. It often addresses land-use planning to manage competing economic, social and environmental needs. It also seeks to provide the appropriate infrastructure required to address identified needs, and deliver key services. Infrastructure may include transport and utility networks, public buildings housing key services (schools, hospitals) and central functions such as waste disposal facilities.	• Land-use control to locate energy source near use point to reduce transmission loss (e.g. district heating schemes). • Land-use control to reduce travel demand. • Provision of facilities to recover energy from waste (digesters, landfill biogas collection, incinerators). • Development and exploitation of renewable energy sources. • Public transport infrastructure provision.
Technology Technological solutions to development problems have often merely created new problems or shifted the costs of development elsewhere, often impacting on the environment or populations that gain no direct benefit from the development. Nevertheless, there is a role for technology in promoting sustainable development, particularly through clean technologies and those that promote the efficient use of resources, and exploitation of renewable energy.	• Efficiency in production of energy. • Design and construction of energy-efficient buildings (insulation, passive energy use, heat exchangers). • Energy-efficient processes (e.g. reuse of breaking energy in vehicles, thermostatic controls). • Renewable energy sources; solar, bio-gas, wind and waves. • Telematics to reduce travel demand.

Economic instruments are increasingly been seen as powerful tools with which to promote sustainable development, and may take several forms, including direct manipulation of price (e.g. pollution charges, resource use taxes); indirect alteration of price or cost using subsidies; and market creation (e.g. tradable permits).

- Subsidies for energy conservation measures.
- Demand management through price control.
- Internalisation of environmental and social costs in charges.
- Public transport subsidy.
- Carbon taxes.

Legislative controls involve the establishment and policing of minimum standards. Often the prevailing social, economic or cultural circumstances mean that such standards are routinely ignored.

- Implement and police emission standards.
- Implement and police energy-efficiency standards.
- Mandatory purchase by power companies of energy supplied derived from non-fossil fuel sources.

Education and awareness-raising is required so that individuals and organisations are better able to make informed decisions about their activities which have sustainability implications.

- Energy efficiency advice.
- Driver advice for fuel economy.
- Encourage attitudinal change through education (e.g. feedback on costs/impacts of energy use).

---

when addressing combinations of tools, which may prove antagonistic, but which when applied in an appropriate mix have the potential to deliver far greater benefits than when applied individually. Assessing the long-term impact of policy instruments on city sustainability is thus a significant challenge, but one that is greatly assisted by a systematic approach in which modelling is employed as a key approach to handling system complexity.

THE FALL AND RISE OF URBAN MODELLING

Whilst modelling inevitably represents an abstraction of a system, so long as significant elements and the relationships between them are correctly identified, then this simplification can help assess how changes in one part of the system affect another. Models are very relevant to sustainable development, a concept which implies numerous interacting subsystems, and multiple, potentially conflicting, objectives. Thus modelling can help bring order to the 'messiness' of urban sustainability appraisal. There is, of course, a long history of urban modelling, typified by Lowry (1964), Harris (1968), Wilson (1974, 1984), Batty (1976), Echenique (1994) and Anas (1994). The models developed by this school focus on the city as a system in which interactions take place between people, land-use and services, and how and where in the city these interactions manifest themselves. The main elements addressed are population, employment and housing, residence and workplace location, and the provision and use of services and infrastructure.

These models were developed to advance understanding of urban form, internal structure and process, and so support urban planning. However, in *Requiem for Large-Scale Urban Models*, Lee (1973) criticised modellers for failing to meet these objectives, describing seven fundamental flaws he believed led to the collapse of the urban modelling effort. He believed models were too comprehensive, trying to replicate complex processes in a single step, particularly when there was a fundamental lack of understanding of urban structure and process. Conversely, the models were too gross, with spatial scale at a too aggregate level to represent processes of interest to policy makers. Models were also criticised on the grounds that they contained little theoretical structure, required huge amounts of unavailable data, were too complicated, error prone and expensive.

In light of these highly influential criticisms, and the perceived failure of the urban modelling efforts of the 1950s and 1960s, it might be assumed that there was no longer any interest in urban modelling. However, advances continued to be made, particularly in Europe, where a scientific approach that included computer modelling was being taken increasingly seriously by planners (Batty, 1994), possibly due to a more centralised planning system than the USA (Klosterman, 1994a). Theory developed in three areas (Batty, 1994). First, existing models, particularly of land use and transport, were refined through defining optimal zone sizes, disaggregating models to better reflect the available data, and in estimation and calibration of parameters. Secondly, mathematical developments, theories of catastrophe, chaos, complexity and non-linear dynamics meant that models were more dynamic, able to represent time-dependent processes more effectively. The city need no longer be viewed as a system in equilibrium, and urban processes thought to be in equilibrium were found to have previously unseen dynamism. Impacts of shock changes, such as a stock market crash, could also be explored. Thirdly, location optimisation theory advanced sufficiently, through economic theory, gravity and network equilibrium models, to define linkages between the disaggregate and aggregate, giving an improved representation of actual behaviour.

Technology also advanced: computers are many orders of magnitude faster, can handle very large databases, and are capable of presenting data in graphical formats from CAD to multi-media visualisation. Geographical information systems (GIS) have developed, allowing information to be manipulated through a combination of spatially referenced data and attributes characterising the data. Whilst developed separately from urban modelling, GIS are used widely in the field, although applications were initially largely limited to mapping, with few spatial decision support systems integrating GIS and model functionality. One early example includes Geertman and Ritsema van Ecks (1995) GIS-gravity model, used to investigate accessibility of jobs and services, and so inform land-use policy that sought to minimise travel demand. Such developments are increasingly supported by improvements in the availability of digital data.

These advances have done much to address the criticisms of urban modelling outlined in *Requiem*. However, Lee (1994) questions whether urban modelling has made real progress: few models have been formally validated and proven demonstrably useful, and most fail the tests of 'transparency and replicability'. Transparency is essential for understanding results and communicating them to other technical professionals and public decision-makers. Even good ideas, if represented by a black box, are insufficient grounds for making choices. Replicability is needed so that results can be duplicated by others, with or without the computer code, allowing analysts to change model assumptions and parameters, and see how results differ, clearly important if models are to be applied in different geographical or cultural settings. Lee believes that these standards can be met, but only through pragmatic testing that makes it possible to tell which models perform best, and if the models in general contribute more to urban theory and planning practice than their alternatives. Advocates of urban modelling should find little to dispute in these conclusions, thus Klosterman (1994b) concludes that, while progress has been made, the biggest difficulty remains the development of practical applications accessible to planners.

From this implementation perspective, Wegener (1994) identifies key opportunities for urban modelling. Increasingly powerful but inexpensive computers with user-friendly interfaces can be exploited to make models more accessible. Model performance can be improved through linkage to expert systems, whilst micro-simulation can be used to allow the functional potential of GIS to be realised. However, the greatest challenge is to open the field to new problems. Urban modellers have been concerned with a narrow set of planning problems, and while models do address aspects of urban development they feature few of the critical issues implied in the phrase *sustainable* urban development. There has been insufficient attention to resource use or pollution, quality of life issues are considered simply as issues of employment or income, and scant attention is given to the effects of urban activities on ecological systems. Thus Wegener (1994) states: 'in particular, models should be made more sensitive to issues of equity and environmental sustainability. Only if the models prove able to give meaningful answers to the urgent questions facing cities on these matters can they establish for themselves a firm position in the planning process of the future'.

OUTPUT VARIABLES FOR SUSTAINABLE DEVELOPMENT MODELS

If modelling is a valid sustainability appraisal tool, then sustainability measures are needed to act as model output variables. Given the comprehensive, ill-defined nature of sustainability, this is clearly a significant challenge in itself. Fortunately, following a call for sustainability measures (UNCED, 1992; CEC, 1993) many programmes have sought to devise sustainable development indicators (SDIs). Although none of these indicators were developed expressly for sustainability modelling, many have potential for use in such models. These SDIs come in two forms, either as an index (see Mitchell et al., 1995), or as a suite of indicators addressing specific issues (see Mitchell, 1996).

Sustainability indexes commonly address one of three theoretical perspectives. Ecological indexes quantify the appropriation by society of environmental carrying capacity. Measures include net primary production sequestration (Vitousek et al., 1986), the ecological footprint (Rees, 1992), which expresses resource consumption as land area required to support an activity or place, and Environmental Space (Spangenberg, 1994), a material's use intensity measure. These indices quantify the degree to which countries are not sustained by their own resource base, and the extent to which consumption must be reduced to deliver ecological sustainability (e.g. FoE (1995) find that Europe requires a 10-fold reduction in consumption by 2060). These measures remind us that our welfare is based on exploitation of the environment. However, they are crude measures due to our poor knowledge of environmental capacities (Holmberg et al., 1999). They are also subject to problems of averaging, treatment of spatial scale and unproven assertions relating to resource use targets (Moffat, 1996), and have a limited ability to address pollutant emissions and equity issues (but see McLaren, 2003).

Economic sustainability indexes address the problem where 'a country can exhaust its minerals and forests, erode its soil, pollute its water, and hunt its wildlife to extinction but the loss of these assets would not show up in current measures of income' (Repetto et al., 1989). Measures include Green GDP (Repetto et al., 1989; Young, 1990), the Z-value (Pearce and Warford, 1993) environmentally adjusted net national product (Hartwick, 1990) and the index of sustainable economic welfare (ISEW) (Daly and Cobb, 1989). These measures internalise the environmental and social costs of development within conventional economic accounts. Using the ISEW as a consistent departure from GDP in the 1970s is evident, illustrating declining sustainability at a time of economic growth, due to resource depletion and rising social and environmental costs (Daly and Cobb, 1989; Jackson and Marks, 1994; Moffat and Wilson, 1994). These measures are flawed as there are difficulties in valuing environmental capital, and because ecosystem function, critical thresholds and irreversible effects are not addressed (Constanza et al., 1997), hence taken to a logical conclusion, they suggest all environmental capital can be consumed so long as it is substituted with human capital (assets, knowledge) of equivalent value.

Socio-economic indexes are quality-of-life indexes constructed from multiple subjectively weighted factors addressing human needs (food, shelter, income, clean environment, social relations, etc.). Such indices like the Human Development index (UN, 1998) are used to predict social need and are explicit in their treatment of quality-of-life issues including less tangible psycho-social elements. They are also better at addressing social equity issues than the other indices, but there is no consensus on which variables to include, there are difficulties in quantifying intangible variables and weighting them, and little attention is given to ecological elements, particularly those without a direct resource value.

Although good at conveying the status of a whole system, indexes aggregate data which inevitably leads to loss of information about specific problems. In addition, application of several indices to the same place and period can yield different sustainability trajectories (Moffat et al., 1994), limiting the confidence in the information they convey. A well-constructed suite of issue-specific indicators can overcome these problems, being conceptually simple, closely reflecting the data and communicating well to end-users. Numerous suites of SDIs have been developed, many prompted by the Local Agenda 21 process. These suites often give an extensive coverage of issues, but it can be difficult to get a sense of overall progress towards sustainability. There is also a danger of ignoring ecological limits (carrying or assimilative capacities), although methodologies to counter this are available (Mitchell et al., 1995). Overall, both indexes and suites of SDIs offer improvements over conventional performance measures of societal development, and are powerful sustainable development tools, used in assessment at many levels. Whilst developed principally to assess and monitor sustainable development, they clearly have potential to strengthen decision-making through their application in predictive models.

SUSTAINABLE DEVELOPMENT MODELS

Because sustainability indices are a relatively recent innovation, none of those described above have yet been embedded within operational models. However, models in which a single measure is used to assess the sustainability of economic–ecologic systems have been developed, based on thermodynamic laws. Here, the law of energy conservation applied to balance material flows in an economy (energy flow implies resource depletion and pollution), and the most sustainable option is one in which the rate of entropy change is lowest. Applications use both input–output analysis and dynamic simulation. Input–output models attempt to account for all energy required in production, distribution and consumption of goods, often using national economic statistics (see the Polestar model of Raskin (1992), and Moffat (1997) for other examples). In dynamic simulation models, relationships within the system are described in more detail, most notably feedback mechanisms connecting major state variables. Models that address greenhouse gas emission are often of this type (e.g. Edmonds *et al.*, 1991). In some dynamic models, thermodynamic laws are explicitly addressed, and all processes are expressed in units of energy, as in ECCO – Enhancement of Carrying Capacity Options (Gilbert and Braat, 1991), a national scale model using 700 equations. In others, such as the World3 model of Meadows *et al.*, (1972, 1992), thermodynamic laws are obeyed, but stocks and flows are described using units appropriate to the resources and pollutants of interest.

From a review of such models, the International Institute for Applied Systems Analysis (IIASA) drew general conclusions about the desired structure of sustainability models (Sanderson, 1994). First, models needed to be better specified. The models they examined were poorly specified in terms of the conceptual structure and often vague in the way in which relationships between variables were expressed. For example, World3 was unreliable as it too readily flipped between growth and collapse because variables and their linkages were poorly specified and were too sensitive to parameter changes. Secondly, they concluded that such nebulous relationships occurred as models were not built for any specific place where states and relationships could be verified, hence place-specific models permitting verification were essential. SOCIOMAD (Picardi in Sanderson, 1994), a reliable model of population, grazing and livestock in the North African Sahel fulfilled these criteria, but represents a system with a simplicity not found in urban economies. Considering this complexity, they concluded that sustainability models should concentrate on common property resources (air, water, land), as problems here are difficult to manage, have complex causes and wide-ranging impacts. Finally, they concluded that sustainability models must permit a broad range of specific policy options to be tested. Some models, such as Poma (Aricia *et al.*, 1991), a USAID population–development model of Costa Rica, could test only the effect of population policies on development, and so ignores potential solutions from other policies or policy mixes.

The approach advocated by IIASA is found in the regional sustainable development model (RSD) of Giaoutzi and Nijkamp (1993), and the population–development–environment (PDE) model of Lutz (1994). RSD is a dynamic simulation of the Greek Sporades islands, addressing freshwater and coastal resources by linking an economic input–output model to a water resource model and a dynamic model of sustainable fish yield. PDE is based on a well-specified population model, linked to an input–output economic model, itself linked to modules describing impacts on land, energy, air quality, water and biodiversity. PDE allows feedback between modules where relationships are poorly defined (e.g. between human fertility and economic parameters), by enabling the user to define the relationship, within limits, thus giving the model greater relevance to local policy and cultural processes. PDE was applied to Mauritius, addressing key resources of fresh water and coral reefs (a driver of tourist revenue) and has proved demonstrably useful in setting local sustainability policies.

URBAN SUSTAINABILITY MODELLING

The examples above suggest that there is much interest in using models to support sustainable development. However, given how important it is for cities to achieve sustainability at all levels, it is surprising how few models of sustainable urban development there are. This may be attributed to the double challenge of addressing two difficult topics: urban modelling and sustainability assessment. For example, whilst sustainable development indexes can be readily evaluated at the national scale, their application in city models first has to deal with a lack of suitable data at the appropriate scale. Data issues may be less problematic when using SDI suites (where relevant data is often collected for other purposes), but modelling them implies that very many system elements must be addressed, increasing both model complexity and data demands.

A greater challenge to urban sustainability modelling is the implied need to build a comprehensive model that addresses social, economic and environmental concerns in sufficient depth to inform policy. Figure 6.1 illustrates a high-level conceptual model of this kind. Note that conventional urban modelling has to date largely been limited to the human economy subsystem, whilst sustainability models have largely addressed the metabolic system, but at the regional not urban scale. Marrying the economic and metabolic systems at the urban scale is an obvious goal, but note how other areas, including ecological integrity, ecological vitality (including biodiversity) and the more intangible quality-of-life issues are relevant and important, but increasingly difficult to model. As Lee (1973) points out, if done too crudely, urban models will not reflect reality and will have little chance of yielding defensible policy guidance. However, modelling urban sustainability implies greater complexity than conventional urban models, and even without data problems, our limited understanding of relationships within the urban system hampers development of a sound comprehensive model.

Such problems do not imply that urban sustainability modelling is fruitless. Rather, the criticisms of Lee must be addressed, and models developed which

systems) and pricing (e.g. subsidies/taxes on areas where development is to be promoted/restricted, road user charging). Combinations of levers were used to design seven development options for Cambridge: minimum growth; densification; satellite development; green swap; public transport links; virtual highway; and a new town (Cambridge Futures, 1999). The impact of the policy restrictions represented in these options were then assessed using a model of the Cambridge sub-region.

The Cambridge model recognises that whilst policy levers influence future development, it is the development market that determines actual outcomes, thus the model comprises interacting sub-models of land use and transport. The land use model represents the interaction between the demand for and supply of property, which determines property prices and hence the location of firms and households. This then determines transport flows (e.g. between home and work), which given the supply of transport infrastructure, determines the level of congestion, and in turn, the accessibility of locations, which determines their attractiveness of land for development. The system integrates MENTOR (based on MEPLAN – Echenique and Owers, 1994) which simulates the market for land and includes a multi-modal transport model able to address policies such as park and ride or light rail development, and SATURN (Van Vliet, 1982), a highway assignment model that simulates traffic flow on the road network.

The model was calibrated for a base year, then projections of land use (7 categories of firm, 30 categories of household) and traffic flows made for up to 50 years ahead, under each development option. Options were then evaluated against the criteria of economic efficiency, social equity and environmental quality: economic efficiency is the impact on living costs (housing, transport, goods and services) and costs to firms (labour, rent, transport); social equity is represented by change in costs to each socio-economic group, and the extent by which these groups become spatially segregated; and environmental quality is represented by the availability of open space, use of greenfield land, pollution (vehicle emissions) and road safety. For these three categories, a summary score was produced for each option (environmental components were aggregated using subjective weighting), but no attempt was made to integrate them. Rather, each option is described in terms of its performance against all the evaluation criteria, and a summary table of option performance against the economic, equity and environment criteria presented. It is suggested that any option which performs badly against any one of the three criteria is unsustainable.

The results indicate that the 'business as usual' minimum growth option is the least sustainable option overall, and that other options (particularly densification, public transport and virtual highway-oriented development) offer preferable development alternatives. The team recognises that the model has limitations. For example, implementation costs that may vary between options are ignored, as some factors are impossible to predict, such as future tax policy. However, the sophisticated modelling approach simultaneously accounts for a range of impacts, and allows them to be systematically compared across a series of options. The results of the modelling exercise were presented to the public in Cambridge as a detailed report, animated video and a series of local exhibitions. The public were then invited to comment on their preferred development option. This combination of detailed analytical work and extensive public consultation were instrumental in modifying the Cambridge structure plan. The 50-year-old planning constraint on the size of Cambridge has been removed, and development is now permitted in the green belt, but separated by a series of green wedges. Cambridge Futures is now using the model to investigate more detailed transport options associated with this development plan (Echenique and Hargreaves, 2003).

SPARTACUS, the System for Planning and Research in Towns and Cities for Urban Sustainability (Anon, 1999; Lautso, 2003), also uses a land-use transport model as the basis of an investigation of urban sustainability futures. SPARTACUS models indicators in three categories: environmental quality (gaseous emissions, consumption of fuel and construction materials, land coverage); social equity (exposure to emissions and noise, segregation, accessibility, travel cost); and economic efficiency (total net benefit per capita). Unlike Cambridge Futures, however, policy options are evaluated using a quantified index for the environment, equity and economy categories. Within the USE-IT evaluation module, indicator values are converted to a standardised scale (0–1) using a value function curve, and indicators are weighted, using either direct proportional weighting or analytic hierarchy pairwise comparison. Value function curves and weights are derived through a Delphi exercise involving professional stakeholders. This differs from Cambridge Futures, in that no explicit public consultation over results took place, although in principle any group could participate in evaluation via derivation of weights and by commenting on results. SPARTACUS also differs from Cambridge Futures in that it gives greater attention to distributive issues, including the social distribution of environmental externalities (see also Chapter 22), and their evaluation under different theories of social justice.

SPARTACUS was used to conduct policy tests addressing land use and transport levers (pricing, regulation and investment) as well as scenario tests in which the implications of changes in exogenous factors, such as population, were explored. Over 70 options, representing combinations of land use and transport policy levers were tested for Helsinki, Bilbao and Naples. The study showed that in all three cities, the pressure for urban sprawl is very strong, and that measures designed to reduce travel demand (e.g. teleworking, car pooling) act to increase private car use in the long term, as congestion was reduced allowing households to move to more peripheral urban areas. Pricing levers (e.g. increasing car operating costs) were found to be most effective, whilst regulation (e.g. reduced car speeds) can have significant positive effects. Investment was found to have a limited impact on social and environmental sustainability, whilst land-use policies designed to encourage more mixed-use development did not produce positive benefits, except where residential and workplace land use were addressed together.

Overall, the study demonstrated that unless mobility by private car could be reduced, existing levels of sustainability could not be maintained. The model suggested that a good urban policy was one in which private car use costs and public transport provision are significantly increased, road speeds lowered on some routes, and residential development only permitted where there is ready access to employment areas or public transport infrastructure. Measures to mitigate any negative side effects should also be identified. For example, pricing policies working alone tend to concentrate people and work opportunities in city centres, leaving the suburbs deficient in services, but this side effect can be avoided by also promoting teleworking.

SPARTACUS continues to be used by planners in the test cities. Where common results were found they have provided the basis for generic recommendations for European sustainable city development. Where results were inconsistent between cities, they have been used to make recommendations for cities of relevant types, and have provided the basis for testing of further policy combinations.

The Quantifiable City (QC) programme also uses models to investigate urban sustainability issues. However, whilst land use and transport policy are an important element of the programmes integrative framework (May *et al.*, 1996), the focus of the QC has been common property problems (see the IIASA study above), which are addressed in more detail than has been possible to date using the large-scale urban models typified by Cambridge Futures and SPARTACUS. Three difficult to manage problems with complex causes and wide-ranging impacts have been addressed to date: water resource sustainability; urban air quality (including greenhouse gas emission and health impact); and diffuse urban water pollution. Each of these areas has been investigated for West Yorkshire, UK, using multiple linked models of urban processes, developed and applied in conjunction with end-users.

Demand forecasting is at the centre of the water sustainability module. The UK is often perceived to be a water-rich country, but availability per capita is amongst the lowest in Europe, and due to the difficulty of developing new resources, demand management is now a widely favoured approach to water sustainability. However, there are uncertainties over the level of demand control that is required, and the possible impact that demand management strategies, such as universal household metering, may have on low-income households. These problems are discussed further by Mitchell (1999a), who describes the QC approach to water resource sustainability. First, water use indicators were identified to address the inter-generational equity, social-equity and environmental aspects of water resource use. The indicators were developed using PICABUE (Mitchell *et al.*, 1995), an objective methodology, applied with stakeholders, and include: total annual regional demand (from currently developed resources) as a percentage of the estimated resource stock in a drought year with a 50-year return period (*c.* two generations); the percentage of households spending above a set proportion of household income on water services; and the number of days each year that flow in abstraction rivers falls below the minimum recommended to maintain the aquatic ecosystem. These indicators address sustainability concerns more directly than other programmes (which often use water use per capita) and provide the focus for subsequent model application.

Models were then identified, developed where needed, and linked so as to address the indicators, whilst ensuring that sufficient scenarios and policy options could be investigated. First, household demand was forecast using microsimulation in which chain conditional probabilities are used to quantify household characteristics for small areas, typically 10–20 houses (Clarke *et al.*, 1996). Characteristics related to water use (household size, number of occupants, socio-economic group, presence of a dishwasher, etc.) were estimated for each area, and associated with relevant water-use coefficients derived from household surveys. This allows region-wide, small-area household demand forecasting. The simulation is constrained by a regional-scale demographic model thus allowing demand forecasts up to 2025 (Williamson *et al.*, 2002). All non-domestic water demand was forecast using a new econometric model (Mitchell *et al.*, 2000a), built from long-term time-series records, in which demand in nine standard industrial classification groups is responsive to macro-economic drivers, water pricing policy, waste minimisation practice and climate. Inputs to this model are derived from models of the regional economy (MDM9, Barker, 1996), and climate change (DoE, 1996), whilst an internal sub-model allows investigation of the possible impact of industrial waste minimisation practice on water use (Mitchell, 1999b). Network losses are represented by measured losses and leakage targets.

The demand forecasting models are operational within the UK water industry, where they are applied in business planning and the investigation of water sustainability. Application in Yorkshire shows that, under a business-as-usual scenario, water demand will rise by about 1 per cent per annum over the next 20–30 years, whilst supply becomes more unreliable due to climate change. The surplus of supply over demand is thus declining, placing inter-generational equity on an unsustainable trajectory. Modelling indicates that demand management can offset projected increases in non-household demand through pricing policy and waste minimisation practice, but that domestic demand must also be constrained. UK household demand management strategies are not dependent upon compulsory water metering (the current focus is on voluntary measures and efficient technology), and bills for vulnerable groups are now capped under provisions in the 1999 Water Industry Act, indicating that social equity in water services should be sustainable [note, however, that 4 million UK households are estimated to spend more than 3 per cent of their income on water services, the government definition of water poverty (Fitch and Price, 2002)]. In Yorkshire, the impact of water resource management policies on the environment indicator is assessed by entering the small-area demand and supply forecasts to WRAPSIM (Likeman et al., 1995), a regional water network model that identifies optimum abstraction strategies based on constraints of demand, supply, pumping costs, and the minimum acceptable level of water in rivers or reservoirs.

Within the QC air quality is addressed through integrated models of transport, pollutant emission, pollutant dispersion and health impact. The SATURN tactical transport model (Van Vliet, 1982) is used to model vehicle flows, speeds and delays at each of several thousand junctions and road links for the Leeds urban road network. A second model, ROADFAC (Namdeo and Colls, 1994), uses SATURN output variables, to estimate emission of toxic air pollutants and CO_2 using emission factors recommended by CORINAIR and MEET, EU expert groups on emission factors. Estimates of emissions from buildings are made using land-use and economic activity data, discharge consent applications, or, where available, observed data collected for consent compliance monitoring. These stationary and mobile emission estimates, produced for roads, buildings and areas are combined within a GIS, using grid cells as a common data format. These combined emission estimates are then fed to a pollutant dispersion model (AirViro or ADMS urban), which when initialised with appropriate topography data is used to calculate air quality in 3D, given specified or typical meteorological conditions. This integrated transport emission modelling and mapping suite (TEMMS) is described further in Namdeo et al. (2002). A health impact module has been added which provides estimates of respiratory illness and premature deaths attributed to exposure to nitrogen dioxide and fine particulates (Mitchell et al., 2000b).

This series of linked models has been used to assess the impact of transport policy on urban air quality, green house gas emission and respiratory health in Leeds, UK. Transport policies of particular concern to the local authority were investigated, including investment (road improvements and a new highway planned to serve an economic development zone; promotion of clean fuel vehicles), road pricing (varied charge type, level and charging zone), and regulation (emission control). The model shows that under a do-nothing scenario, air quality will improve with respect to some pollutants, but that exceedences of standards will become more frequent for others (especially particulates) as the benefits of current emission control regulation are offset by rising travel demand. Road building results in a net decline in air quality due to additional trip generation, whilst all road-user charge options suppress trips, improving air quality and reversing the rapid upward trend in CO_2 emission. The distributional impacts of road pricing options proved highly variable, with some districts experiencing a decline in air quality as vehicles re-routed to avoid the charge zone. A low distance charge proved most sustainable, with the fewest number of people (in total, and the socially deprived) experiencing a decline in residential air quality, whilst also delivering economic benefits (shorter, faster trips) and environmental benefits (air quality improvement, respiratory health impacts, reduced CO_2 emission) (Mitchell et al., 2003). The study suggests that social equity concerns related to pollution redistribution following road pricing may be less significant than commonly assumed, although this remains to be proven more generically.

A third component of the QC is an urban diffuse pollution model (Mitchell, 2001). Diffuse pollution derives not from point sources but from areas (roads, car parks, roofs, etc.), and is forecast to be the most common cause of water quality objective failures in urban rivers by 2010 (SEPA, 2003). Sustainable urban drainage systems (SUDS), such as filter drains, swales and constructed wetlands are demonstrably effective in remediating diffuse pollution, but knowledge is needed on where to install SUDS for maximum effect in existing built areas. The QC urban diffuse pollution model has been developed to meet this demand, and to address the requirements specified in the Water Framework Directive for estimating pollutant loads at a basin scale, supporting load reduction planning within a water quality framework directive. The model has been applied to the Aire basin, West Yorkshire, allowing the identification of diffuse pollution 'hotspots', and assessment of load response to changes in climate, land use and traffic density on the region's road network.

All of the urban sustainability models described above can be improved. Refinements are clearly possible in the description of basic processes (e.g. the influence of environmental quality on locational decisions is poorly represented in land use-transport models), but the greatest progress is likely to be derived from cross-fertilisation of the various model approaches. In particular, there is clearly scope for integration of the large-scale urban models of the type that underpin Cambridge Futures and SPARTACUS (where environmental systems are relatively crudely described), with the more detailed 'common property' models character-istic of the QC, but where land use is treated statically. Such increases in model functionality should, however, be tempered with appropriate attention to end-users. This includes particular attention to the type of information that end-users need (e.g. addressing a singular but complex problem vs. a more comprehensive assessment; addressing indicators vs. indexes), so that models are demonstrably useful. Effort must also be made to ensure that end-users find models sufficiently accessible, such that they better understand their abilities and limitations, and so are able to make more informed decisions.

The examples presented above demonstrate that modelling is a useful tool for coping with some of the inherent complexity of urban sustainability. In particular, modelling is well suited to identifying combinations of policies that cumulatively have a positive effect, and which may otherwise go unnoticed. Unforeseen effects can also be identified, which without modelling may not be intuitively recognised. Models present an opportunity to explore alternate development paths, identifying the most promising options without recourse to costly or mistaken trials, and providing advance warning of possible deleterious or irreversible effects. It also emphasises the importance of long-term strategic planning over short-term problem manage-ment, and can address multiple, simultaneous processes so that optimal solutions for potentially competing social, economic and environmental objectives can be iden-tified. The process of modelling also helps to operationalise the sustainable devel-opment concept, by encouraging creative thinking about societal goals, expressed as sustainability indicators, and how they might be related to the root causes of societal problems. Thus models have an important role to play in supporting urban sustainability planning.

PROBLEMS AND PROSPECTS FOR URBAN SUSTAINABILITY MODELLING

Inevitably, differences of 'place' mean that models developed in one context cannot automatically be applied to another. McGee (1994), for example, shows how some Asian cities (Singapore, Kuala Lumpur) have followed a Western development model where differentiation in economic activity, administrative responsibility and ideology has produced a spatially defined urban–rural divide, whereas others (Bangkok, Shanghai, Beijing-Tianjin) are developing with multiple urban cores linked by fast transport routes, from which extensive mixed rural–urban land-use zones develop. The varied land-use patterns that result have very different implications for sustain-ability concerns, such as the efficiency of material flows. Similarly southern city problems cannot be explained simply as a consequence of rapid population growth, as cities like Tokyo and Los Angeles have grown at comparable rates to southern cities without similar problems, which in practice tend to be linked to poor governance structures and municipal debt (Hardoy and Satterthwaite, 1995). Urban geographers have also concluded that because of their dominant role in national economies, mega-cities require solutions to sustainability problems which cannot be derived simply by scaling up from small cities (Fuchs, 1994).

Clearly, it cannot be assumed that a sustainability model that works in one city also works in another – the underlying theories must be locally applicable. Other problems include those of adequately representing processes without oversimplification, drawing boundaries without treating key processes as exogenous to the model, treating scale appropriately, and tackling uncertainty (e.g. over the nature of interactions, in model parameters, or the assessment of assimilative capacities). Other prosaic but important problems relate to the scale of the modelling effort required. Integrating extant validated models within a common framework provides a short cut to a more extensive model, but only if practical problems of different computer languages and platforms, varied ownership of constituent models, and working practices between different disciplines can be overcome, in addition to problems of validation and integration across different scales.

Of course modelling is just one of many tools for evaluating urban sustainability, and the purpose of projects such as BEQUEST (Curwell et al., 1998) is to provide guidance on selection of an appropriate method. Whilst models are more difficult to apply than other techniques, it should be remembered that they can provide very powerful insights into the interactions within urban systems, and have the potential to simultaneously address economic, social and environmental concerns, with explicit consideration of intra- and inter-generational equity issues. There is, then, no reason why useful models cannot be developed for cities if the lessons of earlier efforts are learnt, for they have much to offer in terms of understanding complex systems and supporting appropriate long-term strategic management.

Batty (1994) forecasts the future of urban modelling as renaissance rather than revolution, with models playing a more modest role in urban studies than in the past. In effect, modelling limitations have been recognised, and urban sustainability models are likely to develop gradually, via improved subsystem models (of common property problems, and perhaps the more intangible quality-of-life issues) that can be integrated into a wider modelling framework. Urban sustainability models seem most likely to progress through the refinement of dynamic city simulation models (e.g. micro-simulation of population, land-use and transport; application of neural networks and fuzzy logic to describe relationships that defied description in earlier models), and enhancement of their ability to address key environmental quality problems, preferably with explicit attention to environmental capacities. Improved models of the city metabolism, addressing the urban region, would complement such models, and could be linked to sustainability indexes to provide a sustainability overview, and applied in a 'backcasting' mode to identify policy mixes that could bring the urban region within ecologically defined limits. Models are also likely to act as part of more extensive and flexible decision-support systems, comprising a mix of models, GIS, visualisation tools and expert systems embedded with local knowledge (see Geertman and Stillwell (2003) for a review of planning support systems).

These potential advances offer the prospect of a more robust means of identifying sustainable urban policies. Thus there is a belief amongst modellers that past difficulties can be overcome: 'We could in principle, if we wished to do so, model entire populations at the people level as well as zonal levels of resolution. Indeed, let's be quite clear here, there is probably no longer any human system that could not be modelled in all its spatial and aspatial complexity if we had good reason to do so' (Openshaw, 1994). Of course, it will not be sufficient just to overcome the 'technical' problems – modellers will have to ensure that tools are useful, addressing the needs and capabilities of planners and end-user organisations.

CONCLUSION

Correcting urban 'sustainability failures' is difficult due to the complexity of the urban system and the major challenges posed by the sustainability paradigm itself. Modelling offers a powerful means of addressing these failures, through evaluation of urban sustainability trajectories and management intervention options. Thirty years after its initial decline, there is optimism that urban modelling can rectify past problems and prove useful in city management through a focus on sustainability concerns. Progress has been made here, but there is potential for much greater integration between the urban modelling and the sustainable development assessment communities. In particular, urban modelling needs to give greater attention to issues of sustainable resource use, environmental quality and social equity.

It is recognised that urban management in the past has been too rationalist and reductionist, with a poor ability to cope with uncertainty, insufficient attention given to cross-sectoral issues, and institutions established on narrow concerns that were too often preoccupied by technical solutions. More adaptive management is needed with a move away from functional experts working in 'silos' to institutional frameworks supportive of multi-function teams working in collaboration with stakeholders. However, decision-makers working within this adaptive strategy must be supported by sound assessments of policy options. Undoubtedly, perceptions on the role of modelling in shaping city futures will be coloured by attitudes towards past failures of rational comprehensive planning. However, rationality should be seen simply for what it is, the ability to distinguish between good and bad actions on the basis of logic, best available data and analysis. In this light, a rational systems approach and modelling, one expression of that approach, have much to offer via the appraisal of possible solutions to complex urban sustainability problems.

REFERENCES

Anas, A. (1994). *NYSIM (The New York Area Simulation Model): A Model for Cost–Benefit Analysis of Transportation Projects*. Regional Plan Association, New York.

Anon (1999). *SPARTACUS. System for Planning and Research in Towns and Cities for Urban Sustainability*. Summary of Final Report to CEC DGXII, LT Consultants, Helsinki, 21pp.

Aricia, G., Merino, L., Mata, A. and O'Hanlon, B. (1991). *Modelo Interactivo de Poblacion y Medio Ambiente en Costa Rica – Análisis y Proyecciones para el Valle Central*, Asociación Demográfica Costarricense, San José, Costa Rica.

Barker, A. (1996). 'Multi-sectoral Dynamic Model 9.0'. In: Anon, *Regional Economic Prospects*, Chapter 6, February, Cambridge Econometrics.

Barton, H., Davis, G. and Guise, R. (1995). *Sustainable Settlements: A Guide for Planners, Designers and Developers*. Local Government Management Board, 260pp.

Batty, M. (1976). *Urban Modelling*. Cambridge, UK: Cambridge University Press.

Batty, M. (1994). 'A Chronicle of Scientific Planning: The Anglo-American Experience'. *Journal of the American Planning Association*, 60(1): 7–16.

Blowers, A. (ed.) (1993). 'Planning for a Sustainable Environment. A Report by the Town and Country Planning Association'. London: Earthscan, 239pp.

Boyden, S., Millar, S., Newcombe, K. and O'Neil, B. (1981). *The Ecology of a City and its People: The Case of Hong Kong*. Canberra: Australian National University Press.

Cambridge Futures (1999). *Cambridge Futures*, Cambridge University Press, Cambridge, 48pp.

CEC (1990). *European Green paper on the Urban Environment*. Committee of the European Community. Office for official publications of the European Community, Luxembourg.

CEC (1993). *Towards Sustainability: A European Community Programme of Policy and Action in Relation to the Environment and Sustainable Development*. Commission of the European Communities. Directorate General for Environment, Nuclear Safety and Civil Protection, Luxembourg.

CEC (1994). *European Sustainable Cities*. Draft report of an EC expert group on the Urban Environment, Sustainable Cities Project, Commission of the European Community, Brussels.

Clarke, G.P., Kashti, A., McDonald, A. and Williamson, P. (1996). 'Estimating Small Area Demand for Water: A New Methodology'. *Journal of the Institute of Water and Environmental Management*, 11: 186–192.

Constanza, R., d'Arge, R., de Groot, R., Farber, S., Grasso, M., Hannon, B., Limburg, K., Naeem, S., O'Neill, R.V., Paruelo, J., Raskin, R.G., Sutton, P. and van den Belt, M. (1997). 'The Value of the World's Ecosystem Services and Natural Capital'. *Nature*, 387(15): 253–260.

Curwell, S., Hamilton, A. and Cooper, I. (1998). 'The BEQUEST Network: Towards Sustainable Urban Development'. *Building Research and Information Journal*, 26(1): 56–65.

Daly, H.E. and Cobb, J.B. (1989). *For the Common Good: Redirecting the Economy Towards the Community, the Environment and a Sustainable Future*. Boston: Beacon Press.

Di Castri, F., Baker, F.W.G. and Hadley, M. (eds) (1984). *Ecology in Practice: The Social Response*, Volume 2. International Conference on Ecology in Practice – Establishing a Scientific Basis for Land Management, September, 1981. Dublin: UNESCO/ICSU, Tycooly International publishing.

DoE (1996). *Review of the Potential Effects of Climate Change on the United Kingdom: Conclusions and Summary*. Department of the Environment, HMSO.

Douglas, I. (1983). *The Urban Environment*. London: Edward Arnold.

Echenique, M.H. (1994). 'Urban and Regional Studies at the Martin Centre: Its Origins, Its Present, Its Future', *Environment and Planning* B, 21: 517–533.

Echenique, M.H. and Hargreaves, T. (2003). 'What Transport for Cambridge?' *Cambridge Futures* 2. Cambridge University Press, Cambridge, 78pp.

Echenique, M.H. and Owers, J. (eds) (1994). 'Research into Practice: The Work of the Martin Centre in Urban and Regional Modelling', *Environment and Planning B: Planning and Design*, 21(5): 513–650.

Edmonds, J., Pitcher, H.M., Barnes, D., Baron, R. and Wise, M.A. (1991). *Modelling Future Greenhouse Gas Emissions: The Second Generation Model Description*, Paper Prepared for the United Nations University Conference on Global Changes and Modelling, Tokyo, October, Pacific Northwest Laboratory, Washington DC, USA. UN University Press.

EEA (1998). *Europe's Environment: The Second Assessment – An Overview*. European Environment Agency, Office for Official Publications of the European Union, Luxembourg, 43pp.

Elkin, T., McLaren, D. and Hillman, M. (1991). *Reviving the City: Towards Sustainable Urban Development*. London: Friends of the Earth/Policy Studies Institute, 278pp.

Fitch, M. and Price, H. (2002). *Water Poverty in England and Wales*. Centre for Utility Consumer Law, University of Leicester.

Friends of the Earth Europe (FoE) (1995). *Towards Sustainable Europe: The Study*. Brussels: FoE.

Fuchs, R.J. (1994). 'Introduction'. In: Fuchs, R.J., Brenbma, E., Chamie, J., Lo, F. and Uitto, J. (eds) *Mega-City Growth and the Future*. Tokyo: United Nations University Press.

Geertman, S.C.M. and Ritsema van Eck, J.R. (1995). 'GIS and Models of Accessibility Potential: An Application for Planning'. *International Journal of Geographical Information Systems*, 9(1): 67–80.

Geertman, S. and Stillwell, J. (eds) (2003). *Planning Support Systems in Practice*. Berlin: Springer-Verlag.

Giaoutzi, M. and Nijkamp, P. (1993). *Decision Support Model for Regional Sustainable Development*. Aldershot, England: Avebury.

Gilbert, A.J. and Braat, L.C. (eds) (1991). *Modelling for Population and Sustainable Development*, Routledge, London, UK.

Giradet, H. (1992). *The Gaia Atlas of Cities: New Directions for Sustainable Urban Living*. London: Gaia books Limited.

Gladwin, T.N., Krause, T.S. and Kennelly, J.J. (1995). 'Beyond Eco-efficiency: Towards Socially Sustainable Business'. *Sustainable Development*, 3: 35–43.

Hardoy, J. and Satterthwaite, D. (1995). 'Urban Growth as a Problem'. In: Kirkby, J., O'Keefe, P. and Timberlake, L. (eds) *The Earthscan Reader in Sustainable Development*. London: Earthscan, pp 197–199.

Harris, B. (1968). 'Quantitative Models of Urban Development: Their Role in Metropolitan Policy Making'. In: Perloff, H.S. and Wingo, L. (eds) *Issues in Urban Economics*. Blatimore: John Hopkins Press.

Hartwick, J.M. (1990). 'National Resources, National Accounting and Economic Depreciation'. *Journal of Public Economics*, 43: 291–304.

Haughton, G. and Hunter, C. (1994). *Sustainable Cities*. Regional Studies Association. London: Jessica Kingsley.

Holmberg, J., Lundqvist, U., Robert, K. and Wackernagel, M. (1999). 'The Ecological Footprint from a Systems Perspective of Sustainability'. *International Journal of Sustainable Development and World Ecology*, 6: 17–33.

Jackson, T. and Marks, N. (1994). *Measuring Sustainable Economic Welfare: A Pilot Index 1950–1990*. London: New Economics Foundation.

Klosterman, R.E. (1994a). 'Large-scale Urban Models: Retrospect and Prospect'. *Journal of the American Planning Association*, 60(1): 3–6.

Klosterman, R.E. (1994b). 'An Introduction to the Literature on Large-scale Urban Models'. *Journal of the American Planning Association*, 60(1): 17–29.

Lautso, K. (2003). 'SPARTACUS System for Defining and Analysing Sustainable Urban Land Use and Transport Policies'. In: Geertman, S. and Stillwell, J. (eds) *Planning Support Systems in Practice*. Berlin: Springer-Verlag, pp. 453–464.

Lee, D.B. (1973). 'Requiem for Large-scale Urban Models'. *Journal of the American Institute of Planners*, 39(3): 163–178.

Lee, D.B. (1994). 'Retrospective on Large-scale Urban Models'. *Journal of the American Planning Association*, 60(1): 35–40.

Likeman, M.J., Field, S.R., Stevens, I.M. and Fleming, S.E. (1995). *Applications of Resource Technology in Yorkshire*. Proceedings of the 5th National Hydrology Symposium, British Hydrological Society.

Lowry, I.S. (1964). *A Model of Metropolis*. Santa Monica: RM-4035-RC, Rand Corporation.

Lutz, W. (ed.) (1994). *Population, Development, Environment: Understanding Their Interactions in Mauritius*. Berlin: Springer-Verlag.

May, A.D., Mitchell, G. and Kupiszewska, D. (1996). *The Quantifiable City: The Development of a Modelling Framework for Urban Sustainability Research*. European Union Council on Science and Technology Urban Civil Engineering C4 Workshop. Information Systems and Processes for Civil Engineering Applications, Rome, November 1996.

McGee, T.G. (1994). 'Labour Force Change and Mobility in the Extended Metropolitan Regions of Asia'. In: Fuchs, R.J., Brenbma, E., Chamie, J., Lo, F. and Uitto, J. (eds) *Mega-City Growth and the Future*. Tokyo : United Nations University Press.

McLaren, D. (2003). 'Environmental Space, Equity and Ecological Debt'. In: Agyeman, J., Bullard, R.D. and Evans, B. (eds) *Just Sustainabilities: Development in an Unequal World*. London: Earthscan, pp. 19–37.

Meadows, D.H., Meadows, D.L., Randers, J. and Behrens III, W.W. (1972). *The Limits to Growth*. New York: Universe Books.

Meadows, D.H., Meadows, D.L. and Randers, J. (1992). *Beyond the limits*. London: Earthscan.

Mitchell, G. (1996). 'Problems and Fundamentals of Sustainable Development Indicators'. *Sustainable Development*, 4(1): 1–11.

Mitchell, G. (1999a). 'Demand Forecasting as a Tool for the Sustainable Development of Water Resources'. *International Journal of Sustainable Development and World Ecology*, 6: 231–241.

Mitchell, G. (1999b). 'The Long-term Impact of Waste Minimisation'. *The Demand Management Bulletin*, Environment Agency, 37, p. 5.

Mitchell, G. (2001). 'Assessing a Pointless Pollution Hazard'. *Geo:Connexion*, 1(1): 2–5.

Mitchell, G., May, A.D. and McDonald, A.T. (1995). 'PICABUE: A Methodological Framework for the Development of Indicators of Sustainable Development'. *International Journal of Sustainable Development and World Ecology*, 2: 104–123.

Mitchell, G., McDonald, A., Williamson, P. and Wattage, P. (2000a). 'A SIC Coded Strategic Planning Model of Non-household Water Demand for UK regions'. *Journal of the Chartered Institution of Water and Environmental Management*, 14(3): 226–232.

Mitchell, G., Namdeo, A. and Kay, D. (2000b). 'A New Disease-burden Method for Estimating the Impact of Outdoor Air Quality on Human Health'. *Science of the Total Environment*, 246(2–3): 153–163.

Mitchell, G., Namdeo, A., May, T. and Milne, D. (2003). 'The Air Quality Implications of Urban Road User Charging'. *Traffic Engineering and Control, The International Journal of Traffic Management and Transportation Planning*, 44(2): 57–62.

Moffat, I. (1996). 'An Evaluation of Environmental Space as the Basis for Sustainable Europe'. *International Journal of Sustainable Development and World Ecology*, 3(4): 49–69.

Moffat, I. (1997). *Sustainable Development: Principles, Analysis and Policies*. London: Parthenon, 200pp.

Moffat, I. and Wilson, M.D. (1994). 'An Index of Sustainable Economic Welfare for Scotland, 1980–1991'. *International Journal of Sustainable Development and World Ecology*, 1(4): 264–291.

Moffat, I., Hanley, N. and Gill, J.P.S. (1994). 'Measuring and Assessing Indicators of Sustainable Development for Scotland'. *International Journal of Sustainable Development and World Ecology*, 3: 170–177.

Namdeo, A. and Colls, J. (1994). 'ROADFAC: A Computer Program to Calculate Automobile Emission for UK Roads'. Paper to *The 3rd International Symposium on Transport and Air Pollution*, Arignon, France, 6–10 June.

Namdeo, A., Mitchell, G. and Dixon, R. (2002). 'TEMMS. An Integrated Package for Modelling and Mapping Urban Traffic Emissions, Air Quality and Respiratory Disease'. *Journal of Environmental Modelling and Software*, 17(2): 179–190.

Nijkamp, P. and Perrels, A. (1994). *Sustainable Cities in Europe: A Comparative Analysis of Urban-Energy Environmental Policies*. London: Earthscan, 141pp.

Openshaw, S. (1994). 'Computational Human Geography: Towards a Research Agenda'. *Environment and Planning* A, 26: 499–508.

Pearce, D.W. and Warford, J.J. (1993). 'World Without End: Economics, Environment and Sustainable Development'. New York: Published for the World Bank [by] Oxford University Press.

Pearce, D.W., Markandya, A. and Barbier, E.B. (1989). *Blueprint for a Green Economy*. London: Earthscan.

Raskin, P.D. (1992). *PoleStar. Introduction, Current Status, Future Directions*. Working Paper. Stockholm Environmental Institute, Stockholm.

Rees, W.E. (1992). 'Ecological Footprints and Appropriated Carrying Capacity: What Urban Economics Leaves Out'. *Environment and Urbanisation*, 4(2): 121–130.

Rees, J. (1993). *Water for Life: Strategies for Sustainable Water Resources Management*. Council for the Protection of Rural England, London.

Repetto, R., McGrath, W., Wells, M., Beer, C. and Rossini, F. (1989). *Wasting Assets: Natural Resources in the National Income Accounts*. Washington: World Resources Institute.

Roseland, M. (1998). *Towards Sustainable Communities: Resources for Citizens and their Governments*. New Society, Gabriola Island, Canada.

Sanderson, W.C. (1994). 'Simulation Models of Demographic, Economic and Environmental Interactions'. In: Lutz, W. (ed.) *Population, Development, Environment: Understanding their Interactions in Mauritius*. Berlin: Springer-Verlag.

SEPA (2003). Scottish Environmental Protection Agency Diffuse Pollution Initiative website (http://www.sepa.org.uk/dpi/), accessed December 2003.

Spangenberg, J.H. (1994). *Towards Sustainable Europe: The Study*. Europe: Wuppertal Institute for Climate, Environment and Energy; Friends of the Earth.

Stanners, D. and Bordeau, P. (eds) (1995). *Europe's Environment: The Dobrís Assessment*. Copenhagen: European Environment Agency.

Tjallingi, S.P. (1995). *Ecopolis: Strategies for Ecologically Sound Urban Development*. Leiden: Backhuys, 159pp.

UNCED (1992). *Agenda 21*. An action plan for the next century, endorsed by United Nations Committee on Environment and Development, Rio de Janeiro. United Nations Association.

United Nations (1995). *World Urbanisation Prospects: The 1994 Revision*. New York: UN.

United Nations (1998). *Human Development Report*. United National Development Programme.

Van Vliet, D. (1982). 'SATURN – A Modern Assignment Model'. *Traffic Engineering and Control*, 23(12): 578–581.

Vitousek, P.M., Ehrlich, P.R., Ehrlich, A.H. and Matson, P.A. (1986). 'Human Appropriation of the Products of Photosynthesis'. *Bioscience*, 36: 369–373.

Wegener, M. (1994). 'Operational Urban Models: State of the Art'. *Journal of the American Planning Association*, 60(1): 17–29.

Williamson, P., Mitchell, G. and McDonald, A.T. (2002). 'Domestic Water Demand Forecasting: A Static Microsimulation Approach'. *Journal of the Chartered Institution for Water and Environmental Management*, 16(4): 243–248.

Wilson, A.G. (1974). *Urban and Regional Models in Geography and Planning*. London: Wiley.

Wilson, A.G. (1984). 'Making Urban Models More Realistic: Some Strategies for Future Research'. *Environment and Planning* A, 16: 1419–1432.

Wolman, A. (1965). 'The Metabolism of Cities'. *Scientific American*, 213(Sept.): 179–188.

Young, M.D. (1990). 'Natural Resource Accounting'. In: Common, M. and Dovers, S. (eds) *Moving Towards Global Sustainability Policies and Implications for Australia*, Canberra: Australian National University, pp. 13–28.

Part 3

Methods for Environmental Valuations

7

Evaluation of Sustainable Urban Development: Cost–Benefit Analysis and Multicriteria Analysis
Ron Vreeker, Peter Nijkamp and Giuseppe Munda

INTRODUCTION

This chapter focuses on project evaluation, physical planning and the usefulness of various evaluation methods such as Cost–Benefit Analysis (CBA) and Multicriteria Analysis (MCA) in the light of Sustainable Urban Development (SUD). The main objective of this chapter is to provide a systematic overview of the characteristics of SUD and various evaluation methods. We first begin this chapter with a discussion of the concept of Sustainable Urban Development and evaluation processes in the next section. The third section of this chapter describes the economic evaluation method CBA as well as its roots in welfare economic theory. However, the application of CBA in an SUD context is not without complications. This has led to the development of alternative methods to overcome the limitations of CBA. The fourth section is dedicated to these alternative evaluation methods often referred to as MCA. Finally, the examination concludes with a comparison of CBA with MCA methods.

SUSTAINABLE URBAN DEVELOPMENT

Since the publication of the Brundtland Report in 1987, the concept of sustainable development has become central in research and policy. With regard to sustainable development, it became increasingly apparent that it should be addressed in close co-operation with local stakeholders. Furthermore, the awareness has grown that many environmental problems have a local origin, while also global environmental decay often manifests itself at a local level. This awareness has led to the formulation of Local Agenda 21, in which a plea is made for the need for dedicated local actions which combine the reduction of environmental decay with an improvement of local socio-economic conditions. Local Agenda 21 placed cities at the centre of research and policies concerning sustainable development.

It has been argued by various authors that urban sustainable development is more than environmental protection, and the city is seen by them as the result of three intersecting forces, namely the social, the environmental and the economic (Camagni *et al.*, 1998). Sustainable cities are therefore cities where socio-economic interests are brought together in harmony with environmental concerns in order to ensure continuity in change (Capello and Nijkamp, 2002).

According to Capello and Nijkamp (2002), various other reasons exist for why the urban level is the most suitable level for policy-makers to target in order to strive for global sustainable development. Since most production and consumption takes place in urban areas, a clear focus on sustainable development at the urban level may enhance the effectiveness of resource and environmental policies. Cities are also able, as a result of scale advantages, to create conditions for the efficient provision of public services or the implementation of measures to achieve the objectives of sustainable development. This urban focus is furthermore supported by the decentralisation of environmental and resource policy-making (Capello and Nijkamp, 2002). Other advantages are the increased possibilities for direct local involvement in policy-making, thus creating support from the general public for changes in resource use and lifestyles. The urban level also provides advantages in terms of efficiency in data gathering and availability. The increasing role of local authorities in environmental policies is stressed by various policy initiatives related, for example, to Local Agenda 21.

Finco and Nijkamp (2001) note that urban sustainability policies are often developed at the edge of various – sometimes conflicting – objectives, and cover multiple fields like urban rehabilitation, urban land use, urban transport systems, urban energy management, urban architecture and urban cultural policy. An illustration of the multidimensional character of such policies is depicted in Figure 7.1.

The multidimensional nature of SUD makes clear that conflicts will be present in the design of policies aiming at an ecologically sustainable economic development of urban areas. This multidimensional character of SUD might result in *inter-actor* conflicts (e.g. industrialist versus environmentalists), *inter-regional* conflicts (e.g. the geographical transfer of pollution) and *inter-temporal* conflicts (e.g. present resource use may be detrimental to the interest of future generations). This intertwined nature of urban sustainability calls for an adequate evaluation methodology that is able to reconcile – to some extent and in principle – economic and ecological paradigms from a steady state and a long-term perspective. In the remainder of this chapter we take a close look at various instruments planners have at hand to evaluate the consequences of urban sustainability policies.

Evaluation is defined as the systematic analysis of the extent to which a project or policy measure contributes to a set of objectives (e.g. social welfare). Evaluation processes therefore aim at rationalising decision problems by systematically structuring the relevant aspects of choices. Nijkamp et al. (1990) refer to the notion of 'evaluation process' as a set of coherent activities which involve the simultaneous evaluation of a set of alternatives.

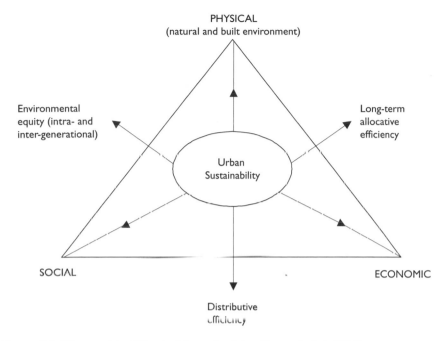

Figure 7.1 Urban sustainability principles and policies (Camagni *et al.*, 1998)

Evaluation processes have a cyclic nature, which entails possible adaptations of elements of the evaluation process due to continuous consultations between the different actors involved. Moreover, the degree of complexity of an evaluation process depends *inter alia* on the evaluation problem at hand, the resources available and the organisational context (Nijkamp *et al.*, 1990).

In the literature on evaluation, various types of evaluation are distinguished. A major distinction is often made between *ex post* and *ex ante* evaluation. *Ex post* evaluation is focused on the analysis of the effects of projects or policies which have already been implemented. An *ex ante* evaluation deals with expected and foreseeable effects of projects that are not yet implemented. Both types of evaluation can be subdivided into a monetary and a non-monetary evaluation. A monetary evaluation is characterised by an attempt to measure all effects in monetary units, whereas non-monetary evaluation utilises a wide variety of measurement units to assess the effects.

Finally, a distinction can be made between implicit and explicit evaluation. In the case of explicit evaluation, a distinct systematic analysis is pursued, whereby the activities are focused on the transparency and accountability of the final results. An implicit evaluation focuses on reaching consensus among stakeholders, whereby attention is directed towards the participation of all parties concerned (Nijkamp *et al.*, 1990).

Before the Second World War, evaluation showed a strong tendency towards financial trade-off analysis. After the Second World War, CBA gained increasing popularity in public policy evaluation. Especially in countries with a market or mixed economy, CBA became the leading evaluation instrument.

In the 1970s, due to an increased awareness of the negative external effects of economic growth and the emergence of distributional questions regarding welfare, there arose the need to cope in a systematic manner with multiple goals and multiple actors in decision problems. These trends led to the development of multicriteria evaluation methods. In this chapter, we will discuss both stances in evaluation. We start, however, with a discussion about welfare economics and CBA in the next section.

COST–BENEFIT ANALYSIS AND WELFARE ECONOMICS

The standard framework for evaluating policies and investments from an economic perspective is CBA.

The French engineer Dupuit laid the theoretical foundations for CBA in 1844 (Dupuit, 1844). In his article, Dupuit introduced the concept of consumer's surplus, which has since played a crucial role in welfare economic theory (see, among others, Marshall, Pigou, Keynes, Kaldor, Hicks, Wicksell and Samuelson).

The basic concept in welfare economics is known as the Pareto principle. According to this principle, a policy measure is socially desirable if every member in society is made better off (the weak Pareto criterion), or at least some members are made better off while no member is made worse off (the strong Pareto criterion). When the opportunities to make such changes are exhausted, we are left with a *Pareto-optimal* allocation (Johansson, 1991).

However, the Pareto criterion is useless in a situation where there are both gainers and losers. The reason is that valuing such a change would require an interpersonal utility comparison. To overcome this problem, the compensation principle was introduced. Hicks (Hicks, 1939) and Kaldor (Kaldor, 1939) separately introduced the compensation principle. According to the compensation principle, a project or policy measure is desirable if, with the project, it is hypothetically possible to redistribute welfare so that everyone becomes better off. In other words, gainers should be able to compensate losers.

The aim of CBA as an evaluation instrument is to locate and include all the costs and benefits of a project and to express the unobservable change in social welfare in observable monetary units (Varian, 1992). In conducting a CBA, various steps need to be taken.

In the first step, the project is defined, along with the relevant population (those individuals whose welfare is considered relevant and affected).

In the second step, the relevant impacts of the project are identified, using the criterion of whether they constitute a cost, benefit or a redistribution of welfare. In the third step, relevant costs and benefits are valued in monetary units. Where price changes are involved, this necessitates the calculation of changes in consumers' and producers' surpluses. For changes in the supply of public goods, estimates of compensating or equivalent variations are necessary. When no market prices exist to value costs and benefits, non-market valuation techniques can be used. Costs are measured as social opportunity costs. Where market imperfections or government interventions create differences between market prices and marginal social costs or benefits, shadow prices are calculated to reflect costs and benefits in an accurate way.

In the fourth step of a CBA, benefits and costs are aggregated over time by means of discounting. However, establishing the correct discount rate is still a matter of great dispute.

The fifth step involves the comparison of total discounted benefits with total discounted costs in order to produce a Net Present Value (NPV). If the NPV is positive, then the project has passed the CBA test. Alternatively, information may be presented in terms of Benefit–Cost ratios, or as an Internal Rate of Return (IRR), which is the discount rate that yields a Net Present Benefit of zero.

The final step in a CBA consists of conducting a sensitivity analysis of important parameters such as the discount rate, project life span and costs and benefits estimates.

The application of CBA has several problems which can be summarised as: (1) distorted markets or 'second best' conditions'; (2) the valuation of unpriced effects; (3) the determination of the discount rate; (4) the spatial scope of CBA; (5) risk and uncertainty; and (6) equity concerns. In the remainder of this section, we will discuss the topics of unpriced effects, the spatial scope of CBA and equity concerns.

Valuation of unpriced effects

The inclusion of unpriced effects, such as environmental effects, in a CBA requires the monetary valuation of these effects. Since no markets exist for these goods, it is difficult to observe market prices that reflect marginal costs or benefits related to these effects. In order to overcome this problem, various valuation methods have

Table 7.1 A classification of environmental values

	Use value *(related to the 'use' of the good as a consumption good or production factor)**			Non-use value *(not related to the 'use' of the good as a consumption good or production factor)*		
	Direct use value (the use of the good itself)	*Indirect use value* (the existence of the good improves the quantity or quality of other consumption goods or production factors)		*Option value* (related to possible future use of the good)	*Quasi-option value* (related to possible future information on the importance of the good)	*Existence value*
As a consumption good		Affecting consumption goods	Affecting production factors			Philan-thropic value (for contemporaries)
As a production factor						Bequest value (for future genera-tions)

* Note that 'consumption' need not always deplete the good: enjoying a scenic view is also a form of consumption.

been developed that aim to identify shadow prices for these effects. Various types of values can be distinguished. Nijkamp *et al.* (2002) provide us with an overview (Table 7.1).

Valuation methods aim to estimate the individuals' marginal 'willingness-to-pay' (WTP) (or 'willingness-to-accept' (WTA) a decrease) in monetary terms for an improvement in the quantity or quality of the good concerned. A brief outline of possibilities to derive estimates of the value of effects is set out here. Table 7.2 gives a concise overview of the valuation methods (Munasinghe, 1992; Verhoef, 1996).

In this table, market or behavioural-based valuation methods are depicted on the left-hand side. Two main categories of behavioural techniques can be distin guished. Revealed preference techniques can be applied when surrogate markets for the good to be valued exist; that is, when consumers' marginal WTP for changes in the effect can be measured by looking at their behaviour on other, related, markets by means of hedonic techniques, travel cost approaches or household production functions.

When the aim is to obtain non-use values, or when surrogate markets are non-existent, stated preference techniques could be used to infer consumers' WTP or WTA by confronting them with hypothetical markets. Contingent valuation studies try to ask for a WTP or WTA directly.

This overview shows that, in the absence of markets for certain goods and services, tools exist to value these goods and services. However, these tools have some limitations. A first limitation concerns *absolute imperfect information* (Van Pelt, 1993). In order to apply a valuation method, environmental effects need to be assessed in physical terms. Due, for example, to the complexity of environmental

Table 7.2 An overview of valuation methods

Valuation approaches		Short-cut approaches		
Behavioural		*Non-behavioural*		
Surrogate markets (revealed preference)	*Hypothetical markets (stated preference)*			
• Hedonic techniques • Travel cost methods • Household production functions	• Contingent valuation • Conjoint analysis	• Damage costs • Costs of illness	• Prevention costs: hypothetical defensive, abatement or repair programmes	• Actual defensive abatement or repair programmes

Source: Verhoef, 1996

problems, a significant degree of uncertainty is likely to exist in the determination of these physical effects.

The WTP principle underlying all valuation techniques constitutes a second limitation. *Relative imperfect information* hampers comprehensive valuation by individuals. For example, due to a lack of awareness, people may appear to be willing to pay relatively little for a certain good (Hueting, 1980). Furthermore, no valuation method exists to account for the interests of future generations that may be affected by a project or policy. This problem particularly refers to the estimation of option, bequest and existence values and, to a lesser extent, to direct and indirect use values.

A third limitation is that most valuation techniques are *partial approaches*, focusing on a single aspect. For example, whereas the travel cost method is especially useful to value recreation areas or urban green spaces, the cost of earnings technique is only applicable if human health is affected. Because most techniques focus on (environmental) effects that can be linked to existing markets, they may fail to incorporate other values resulting in an inadequate valuation of these effects.

A fourth limitation is *method uncertainty*. Apart from method-specific shortcomings, several studies have shown that, if a number of valuation techniques are applied in a certain case, (significantly) different results are obtained. A related problem in the case of Contingent Valuation Methods is the divergence between WTP and WTA measures.

Finally, the application of these methods can be criticised from an *equity* point of view (Van Pelt, 1993). As CBA is indifferent with regard to existing income distributions, so too are WTP and WTA indicators. These indicators may also be inappropriate in the light of inter-temporal equity.

When resources are lacking to conduct market-based valuation studies, short-cut approaches are sometimes used. These techniques are often criticised on many grounds. Important considerations are that circularity may plague the estimated values (e.g. if an externality is considered unimportant by an authority, this would induce small public defensive outlays, which would subsequently produce a low estimate of the value of the externality); that defensive outlays may not always be possible; that defensive outlays by private parties are typically carried out up to the point where marginal benefits equal marginal costs, so that external costs remain in existence which are not measured using the method; and that hypothetical 'full defence' programmes may, on the one hand, consider too large a reduction of the externality, but, on the other, bear no relation to the true external costs if they are not actually carried out.

Spatial scope of CBA

Projects or policies may affect the welfare of people living nearby, but also of people further away. From the welfare economic literature it is well known that the impacts on economic welfare may include substantial *distributive* effects, in addition to the *generative* effects. As a result, a project's desirability, as well as the ranking of alternatives, may depend on the definition of the 'planning area' and, with that, of the (spatial) set of individuals whose welfare is assumed to matter in the CBA.

The geographical boundaries for a CBA may in some instances be defined by the jurisdiction that commissions the appraisal and that finances the prospective project. In other cases, official guidelines may exist which stipulate that the national level is the appropriate level of spatial aggregation. This is often motivated by the desire to avoid wasteful investments by lower-level authorities that would merely redistribute – rather than generate – national welfare. From an overall efficiency viewpoint, it is obvious that one would eventually benefit if all CBAs took a global perspective, and hence considered welfare impacts 'world wide', and if lump-sum redistributions between and inside jurisdictions were possible (Nijkamp *et al.*, 2002). But it is probably a rather theoretical consideration that may not be viable in the practice of decision-making. In any case, the spatial demarcation is an important aspect for the design and interpretation of CBAs.

Equity concerns

In the previous section, attention was devoted to the inclusion of environmental and unpriced effects in CBA. However, the distribution of impacts should also be accounted for in the analysis.

In principle, there are two ways to account for equity objectives in CBA. The first is social CBA, whereby the outcomes of economic CBA are adjusted for income distribution objectives by means of quantitative weights.

The second possibility is to score project alternatives on a separate equity criterion. Sometimes it may be possible to develop *quantitative* indicators, which are usually based on the same philosophy underlying (in)equality measures for countries, such as the Lorenz curve and the Gini-concentration ratio.

At the project level, less data-demanding indicators are needed. Focusing on relative income, one possible indicator is the ratio between that of net efficiency benefits that accrues to target groups and the total net efficiency benefits. Alternatively, changes in absolute poverty measures may be used as scores on the equity criterion. This requires the definition of a poverty line, representing minimal acceptance levels of income or basic needs. To overcome the data requirements of the above-mentioned indicator, some alternative tools for equity analysis have been developed. Lichfield, for example, has developed the *Planning Balance Sheet Method* (Lichfield, 1964) to integrate distributive impacts in assessments.

From the discussion above it becomes clear that various limitations do exist in applying CBA in evaluating SUD-policies. Although some of these limitations were relaxed by the introduction of amendments to the method such as the planning–balance sheet method, goals-achievement method or shadow-project methods, alternative evaluation methods were developed during the 1970s and 1980s. This new class of evaluation methods is often referred to as MCA. Various reasons can be mentioned for the increasing influence of multicriteria evaluation techniques vis-à-vis conventional evaluation tools (Nijkamp *et al.*, 1990):

- The impossibility to include intangible and incommensurable effects in conventional evaluation methods, such as CBA.
- The conflicting nature of modern planning problems, so that – instead of a single decision-maker – various formal and informal decision-makers determine the final choice.
- The shift from conventional 'one-shot' decision-taking to institutional and procedural decision-making where many political aspects play a major role
- The desire in modern public decision analysis not to be confronted with a single and 'forced' solution but with a spectrum of feasible solutions.

The above-stated reasons have led to the popularity of MCA in public planning. In the 1970s and 1980s a vast number of methods were developed. We will discuss the main types of classes in the Section 'Multicriteria evaluation'.

MULTICRITERIA EVALUATION

It has already been discussed in the preceding sections that the presence of externalities, risks, long-term effects, spatial spillovers, irreconcilable interests and qualitative information generally preclude a meaningful application of one-dimensional evaluation methods, such as CBA. Consequently, in the recent decades, attention has been devoted to the development of alternative evaluation methods such as multicriteria evaluation methods. These methods aim to take into account the heterogeneous and conflicting dimensions of decision problems. An essential difference between MCA and CBA is that CBA takes consumer preferences as the starting point and tries to achieve market conformity. In MCA, the preferences of the main actor (often the government) are not modelled as the sum of individual preferences. Instead, the government is assumed to have its own preferences and responsibilities.

Rather than a specific appraisal method, MCA is a family of methods. This family comprises a collection of around 100 techniques that share some basic principles, but differ in other, mainly technical, aspects.

Janssen and Munda (1999) offer a typology of evaluation methods which helps us to classify methods according to various characteristics (see Figure 7.2). They based their typology on the following four distinctions (Janssen and Munda, 1999):

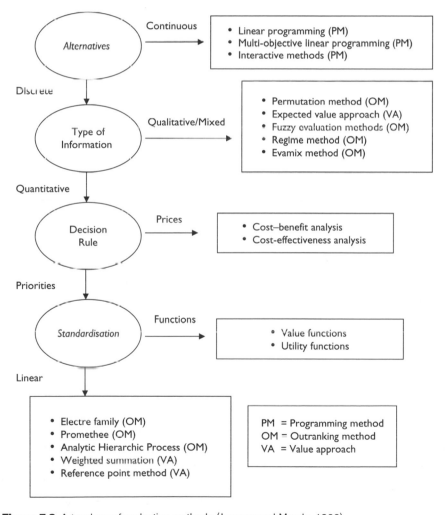

Figure 7.2 A typology of evaluation methods (Janssen and Munda, 1999)

1   *The set of alternatives: discrete versus continuous problems.* In evaluation practices, a distinction is often made between discrete and continuous problems. Discrete decision problems involve a finite set of alternatives. Continuous problems are characterised by an infinite number of feasible alternatives.

2   *The measurement scale: quantitative versus qualitative attribute scale.* Some problems include a mixture of qualitative and quantitative information. Qualitative and mixed evaluation methods can handle this type of information to analyse the alternatives. If the information concerned is not exact, fuzzy evaluation methods can be applied.

3   *The decision rule: prices or priorities.* The decision rule is unique for each method. Priorities used in MCA reflect the relative importance of the criteria considered in the analysis. In CBA, prices are used to calculate Benefit–Cost ratios. These prices are derived directly or indirectly from market prices or are assessed by means of valuation methods, as was described above.

4   *The valuation functions: standardisation versus valuation.* In order to make quantitative scores comparable, they must be transformed into a common dimension or into a common dimensionless unit. This can be done by transforming the scores into standardised scores by means of a linear standardisation function, or by using value or utility functions. Utility and value functions transform information measured on physical measurement scales into a utility or value index.

In the last 25 years developments in multicriteria techniques are reflected in the progress of the three main theoretical schools: (1) Utility or value system approach, MAUT and MAVT; (2) Programming methods; and (3) Outranking techniques. In this chapter, we will describe the main characteristics of the above-mentioned groups of MCA methods.

Utility and value system approaches

The first school of thought regarding MCA is the American School or Value System Approach. This approach contains Multiattribute Utility Theory (MAUT) and Multiattribute Value Theory (MAVT).

These approaches are based on the hypothesis that for any decision problem, a value or utility function can be defined for the considered alternatives which the decision-maker wishes to maximise (Vincke, 1992). The role of the researcher is to determine this function.

The MAUT and MAVT differ in the sense that MAVT uses a value function to represent the outcomes for the alternatives considered, while MAUT relies upon the definition of utility functions, which allows the computation of an expected utility derived from each alternative. Although a utility function is also a value function, a value function is not necessarily a utility function. By constructing a value or utility function a multicriteria problem is reduced to a unicriterion optimisation problem.

In MAUT and MAVT, decision-makers are twice involved in the decision-making process. The first involvement concerns the development of the utility function for each criterion. The second involvement is related to the calculation of the expected utility by means of an aggregated utility function. In this phase of the decision-making process, decision-makers are asked to assign probabilities to certain outcomes. Preferences are assigned directly, aggregated and used to develop the utility function.

Programming methods

Multiobjective programming (MOP) is an MCA method which simultaneously maximises or minimises several objectives subject to a set of constraints. In contrast to the value system approach, the value or utility function is unknown. Although it is assumed that a value function exists, it is regarded as unknown and no assumptions are made about this value function.

However, due to conflicts between the various objectives included in the analysis, a simultaneous optimisation of these objectives is impossible. Therefore, instead of optimisation the aim of the decision-maker is to achieve a set of predefined goals as closely as possible (satisfying behaviour). Multiobjective programming is aimed to find the set of efficient solutions and divides the feasible set of solutions in a set of efficient solutions and a subset of inefficient solutions (Ballestero and Romero, 1998).

> A set of solutions in a MOP problem is efficient or non-dominated, if their elements are feasible solutions such that no other feasible solution can achieve the same or better performance for all the criteria being strictly better for at least one criterion. This is a necessary condition to guarantee the rationality of any solution to a MOP problem.
>
> (Ballestero and Romero, 1998)

As long as we do not have additional information regarding the preference structure of the decision-maker, any choice from the set of efficient solutions is acceptable and reasonable. The final or best solution is the solution preferred by the decision-maker above all other efficient solutions.

Outranking methods

The third school of thought in MCA is the French school (see, for example, Roy, 1968, 1972). The French school in MCA is based on pair wise comparisons between alternatives, and tries to build an outranking relationship between them. The associated techniques are not based on utility theory and do not try to construct a mathematical model in order to represent the decision-maker's preference structure.

The foundation of the French school is that it is better to accept a result less strong than one yielded by MAUT or MAVT, by avoiding introducing mathematical hypotheses, which are too strong, and asking the decision-maker questions which are too complicated.

Outranking allows for the performances of the alternatives according to each criterion to be compared with respect to a margin of error or indecision. It is obvious that some differences in the scores of the alternatives are irrelevant and that any difference needs to be of a certain magnitude before it has some meaning in the comparison of alternatives. Therefore, outranking methods often make use of thresholds. Well-known outranking methods are ELECTRE, PROMETHEE, NAIADE and REGIME.

CONCLUSIONS

Whereas CBA is linked to the principles of welfare economics, this is not the case with MCA. Although the basic principles of welfare economics and CBA are straightforward, several difficulties play an important role in the application of CBA. These include second-best conditions, difficulties related to the discounting principle, equity concerns and non-priced effects. This has led to the development of alternative evaluation techniques such as MCAs (Table 7.3).

The first difference between the two approaches is the decision rule used in the evaluation process. CBA uses prices to make efficiency attributes compatible, whereas MCA is characterised by a weighting system implicitly or explicitly involving relative priorities of decision-makers.

The second difference concerns the type of criteria used in the evaluation. In contrast to CBA, which is focused on efficiency and therefore an IRR, Benefit–Cost ratios or NPV, MCA does not impose any limits on the number and nature of criteria. This poses, however, a serious risk for 'double counting' of effects.

Furthermore, to apply CBA, prices need to be known. CBA, therefore, requires that effects on efficiency attributes are measured in quantitative terms. MCA does

Table 7.3 Differences between CBA and MCA

Criteria	CBA	MCA
Systematic comparison of alternatives	Yes	Yes
Explicit use of weights in the analysis	Yes	Yes
Evaluation of effects	Market-based	Political
Possibility for political abuse of technique	By means of manipulating inputs	By means of manipulating inputs and weights
Degree of compensation of effects	Every negative effect can be compensated by means of a bigger positive effect	Depends on chosen multicriteria method
Risk of 'double counting'	Limited, applies to indirect effects	Yes
Inclusion of weights to reflect stakeholder preferences	Not in the basic form of CBA	Yes

not impose such strict requirements regarding the measurement of effects. There are three groups of MCA techniques with respect to effects: one that requires quantitative data, a second that processes only qualitative data, whereas a third type of method can deal with both types of effects simultaneously.

The SUD policies are multidimensional in nature and the design of such policies is essentially conflict analysis characterised by technical, socio-economic, environmental and political value judgements. Therefore, in the process of designing SUD policies it is difficult to arrive at straightforward and unambiguous solutions. This implies that such a multidimensional planning process is characterised by the search for acceptable compromise solutions. MCA provides a framework to obtain such acceptable compromise solutions. However, MCA is not a panacea, it has its own limitations and problems.

Although both CBA and MCA differ in many aspects and most debate has been on which method is most suitable in project evaluation, the debate nowadays regards these two approaches as complementary analytical tools rather than competitive methods. Seen from this perspective, a mixture of monetary and non-monetary methods may be a fruitful way to proceed in evaluation research and processes.

It should be stressed that both types of methods are useful as tools in decision-making processes, as long as policy-makers and evaluators are aware of the limitations of the methods.

The role of experts in evaluation processes is therefore of paramount importance. Rather than employing evaluation methods in a technocratic manner, the expert's responsibility is to confront decision-makers with the consequences of their priorities and choices, so that such methods serve as an aid to improve the quality of decisions. Decision-support techniques should therefore have a learning character, based on interplay between suppliers and users of information regarding a broad spectrum of consequences and scarce resources used.

REFERENCES

Ballestero, E. and Romero, C. (1998), 'Uncertainty and the Evaluation of Public Investment Decisions'. *American Economic Review*, 60: 364–378.

Camagni, R., Capello, R. and Nijkamp, P. (1998), 'Towards Sustainable City Policy an Economy, Environmental, Technology Nexus'. *Ecological Economics*, 24(1): 103–118.

Capello, R. and Nijkamp, P. (2002), 'In Search of Sustainable Human Settlements; Prefatory Remarks'. *Ecological Economics*, 40(2): 151–155.

Dupuit, J. (1844), 'On the Measurement of Utility of Public Works', in D. Murphy (ed.) *Transport*. London: Penguin.

Finco, A. and Nijkamp, P. (2001), 'Pathways to Urban Sustainability'. *Journal of Environmental Policy & Planning*, 3: 289–302.

Hicks, J.R. (1939), 'The Foundation of Welfare Economics'. *Economic Journal*, 49: 259–279.

Hueting, R. (1980), *New Scarcity and Economic Growth*. Amsterdam: North-Holland.

Janssen, R. and Munda, G. (1999), 'Multi-Criteria Methods for Quantitative, Qualitative and Fuzzy Evaluation Problems', in J.C.J.M. Van den Bergh (ed.) *Handbook of Environmental and Resource Economics*. Aldershot: Edgar Elgar.

Johansson, P.-O. (1991), *An Introduction to Modern Welfare Economics*. Cambridge: Cambridge University Press.

Kaldor, N. (1939), 'Welfare Propositions and Interpersonal Comparisons of Utility'. *Economic Journal*, 49: 549–552.

Lichfield, N. (1964), 'Cost–Benefit in Plan Evaluation'. *The Town Planning Review*, 35: 160–269.

Munasinghe, M. (1992), *Environmental Economics and Valuation in Development Decision-Making*. Environment working paper, 51. Washington, DC: Environment Department, World Bank.

Nijkamp, P., Rietveld, P. and Voogd, H. (1990), *Multicriteria Analysis for Physical Planning*. Amsterdam: Elsevier.

Nijkamp, P., Ubbels, B.J. and Verhoef, E.T. (2002), 'Transport Appraisal and the Environment', in D.A. Hensher and K.J. Button (eds) *Handbook of Transport Strategies, Policies and Institutions, Handbooks in Transport 4*. Amsterdam: Elsevier/Pergamon.

Roy, B. (1968), 'Classement Et Choix En Presence De Points De Vue Multiple (La Methode Electre)'. *R.I.R.O.*, 2: 57–75.

Roy, B. (1972), 'Decision Avec Criteres Multiple'. *Metra*, 11: 121–151.

Van Pelt, M.J.F. (1993), *Ecological Sustainability and Project Appraisal*. Aldershot: Averbury.

Varian, H. (1992), *Microeconomic Analysis*. New York, NY: Norton.

Verhoef, E.T. (1996), *The Economics of Regulating Road Transport*. Cheltenham: Edward Elgar.

Vincke, P. (1992), *Multicriteria Decision-Aid*. New York, NY: John Wiley & Sons.

8

Economic Valuation, Values and Contingent Method: An Overview
Paulo A.L.D. Nunes and Peter Nijkamp

INTRODUCTION

Urban planning is a complex force field with a multiplicity of actors, a variety of – often conflicting – interests, and a great deal of site-specific circumstances or features. In the history of urban planning, various methodological strands have emerged, such as purely economic perspectives (reflected inter alia in urban land rent theories or social cost–benefit analyses), ecological perspectives (dealing with historical driving forces of the city), evolutionary perspectives (considering the city as a dynamic and self-organising entity), or interactive-democratic perspectives (emphasising the city as a joint workshop with distinct responsibilities of urban agents). In recent years we have witnessed the emergence of a new paradigm for urban planning, such as the microcosmic perspective, in which individual actors represent part of the urban interest and shape together the urban future. The methodological challenge is then to design a toolbox through which mutually complementary and mutually contrasting interests can be integrated in a decision support method that helps to identify a common pathway for the urban future.

From an economic perspective, one might argue that the city makes up a local market which is able to shape its own pathway as the result of 'invisible hand' forces. This would certainly justify a case for a non-interventionist policy, provided all conditions for a market equilibrium in the city would be fulfilled. However, the city is a complex spatial entity characterised by a great deal of positive and negative externalities. The positive externalities emerge from the economies of spatial density such as scale and agglomeration advantages. The negative externalities are related to the decay in urban quality of life (e.g. congestion, criminality, socio-economic equality). Such externalities can be analyzed at the meso-level of urban or local economies, but are essentiality related to micro-decisions of individual actors. How do urban citizens value their environment? Which information is needed by urban planners to design a pleasant quality of life? A micro-cosmic approach may be helpful in mapping out the environmental wishes and the willingness-to-pay (WTP) of urban actors. Seen from the perspective or urban quality of life, the present chapter resorts to lessons from environmental economics, in particular modern evaluation techniques which have proven to offer a new analytical angle for studying the complex relationship between urban actors and their environment, not only the social costs but also the benefits of an urban mode of living.

Conceptually, the total economic value of benefits of an urban mode of living consists of use and non-use values. The monetary value assessment of the total economic value of an urban mode of living requires the use of special valuation tools. We pay special attention to non-market valuation, i.e. on how to place a monetary value on benefits, such as urban environmental quality, that are not routinely traded in regular marketplaces. Contingent valuation method (CVM) is one of the valuation tools suggested in the literature and this method will be the focus of our analysis.

This chapter is organised as follows. The Section 'Economic Values and Valuation methods' presents the concept of total economic value of an environmental asset, such as the protection of a green urban area, reviewing the different valuation methods available to put a monetary value on environmental resources as a non-market good. The Section 'A Brief History on Contingent Valuation' focuses on the contingent valuation method and its significant importance to policy makers since it is the only valuation method that is able to assess the non-use value component of environmental resources. The Section 'Theoretical Underpinning on the Use of Contingent Valuation' presents the link of contingent valuation method to standard economic theory. The Section 'Contingent Valuation in Practice' discusses the application of the contingent valuation and respective state-of-art research work guidelines. The Section 'Respondent's Strategic Behaviour and Value Measurement Bias' reviews potential measurement bias that the contingent valuation estimates are likely to embed and how these can be addressed in terms an efficient survey design and alternative micro-economic formulations that underpin consumer behaviour. The Section 'Conclusions' concludes with some retrospective remarks.

ECONOMIC VALUES AND VALUATION METHODS

The concept of total economic value of an environmental benefit has its foundations in welfare economics: the basic premise of economic valuation is its effect on the well-being of the individuals who make up society. Therefore, if society wishes to make the most in terms of individuals' well-being maximisation, the issue of the monetary assessment of the total economic value of an environmental benefit is a key issue in terms of policy decisions. Conceptually, the total economic value of an environmental benefit, such as the protection of an urban green area, consists of its use value and non-use value (Table 8.1).

Use values are what they seem to be: values arising from the actual use/consumption made of the urban green area. Use values are further divided into direct use values, indirect use values and option values. Since we focus on the

Table 8.1 Classification of benefits derived from the protection of an urban green area

Total economic value	Use	direct use value	Recreation benefits e.g. jogging, bird watching, walking (with the dog)
		indirect use value	ecosystem functional benefits e.g. carbon sequestration, timber production
		option value	safeguard of use benefits e.g. future visits
	Non-use	bequest value	legacy benefits e.g. conservation for the use of the future generations
		existence value	existence benefits e.g. knowledge of protection of urban green area

value assessment of the benefits derived from the protection of a green park in a urban context (the emblematic case is the Central Park in New York), the direct use value refers to the various forms of recreation possibilities available to the park's visitors; the indirect use value refers to benefits deriving from ecosystem functions such as the park's role in terms of carbon sequestration; the option value refers essentially to the individual's WTP for the preservation of the park against some (subjective) probability that the individual will make use of it at a future date. In addition, the conservation of an urban park has impacts on the well-being of the individuals that are not directly associated with recreational consumption. These are referred to in the literature as the non-use values, i.e. anthropocentric values which are not associated with current or expected use. The non-use values are usually divided between the bequest value and the existence value.

The bequest value refers to the benefit accruing to any individual from the knowledge that others might benefit from the park in the future; the existence value refers to the benefit derived simply from the knowledge of continued protection of the urban green area. The non-use values have typically a public good character for which no market price is available to disclose accurate monetary valuation. The lack of such market price information may convey the impression that benefits of conservation policies are unimportant, when compared to the market priced allocation alternatives (e.g. urbanisation and commercial development of the area). As a consequence, most of the time, policy makers have based their decisions on an undervaluation of the environmental resources which has thus resulted in a misallocation of scarce environmental resources.

The monetary assessment of the use and non-use benefits involved with the conservation policy is, therefore, an important step in policy decisions about environmental resources use. The money value assessment of such environmental assets requires special tools. These are discussed in the following section.

Monetary valuation methods

Various valuation methods are available to put an economic value on environmental benefits. We can distinguish two groups of valuation methods: the direct and indirect or dose response valuation methods (Table 8.2). The dose response methods have in common that they put a price on environmental commodities without retrieving people's preferences for these commodities. The production cost techniques such as the dose response methods rely on the presence of physical input–output relationships. For example, if one is willing to estimate the monetary value of the benefits of clean air on human health, one can take into account the relationship of air pollution on the number of visits to physicians and purchase of drugs. Conversely, the direct methods rely on individual preferences. On the basis of the process by which these methods retrieve individuals' preferences, these methods are further divided into revealed preference methods and stated preference methods. The group of revealed preference valuation methods consists of three methods: travel cost, hedonic pricing and averting behaviour (see Braden and Kolstad, 1991). The common underlying feature is a dependency on a relationship between a market good and the environmental benefit. For example, when using the travel cost method, researchers estimate the economic value of recreational sites by looking at the costs of the trips made by the visitors to these sites. When using the hedonic price method to estimate the economic value of clean air, the researchers explore the analysis of house market prices and surrounding air characteristics. Researchers who use the averting behaviour method try to estimate the economic value of clean air on the basis of expenditures on technological equipments made to avert or mitigate the adverse effects of air pollution.

Whereas economists who use revealed preference valuation methods have to carry out estimation exercises bearing in mind the existent market price data, economists who use stated preference valuation methods have to collect their own

Table 8.2 A classification of economic valuation methods

Revealed preference	Stated preference	Dose response
Travel cost	Contingent valuation	Production cost
Hedonic pricing	Contingent ranking	Production factor
Averting behaviour	Pairwise allocation games	

data by means of questionnaires. The underlying feature is the use of the questionnaire to ask directly the individuals to state their economic values for environmental commodities (Mitchell and Carson, 1989). The use of questionnaires require economists to work closely with experts from market and survey research, sociology and psychology in order to guarantee the authority of the stated choice methods as a valid instrument to assess economic value of an environmental benefit (Carson *et al.*, 1992; NOAA, 1993). In contrast, revealed preference methods have remained an exclusive valuation tool for economists. Stated preference valuation methods are the contingent valuation, contingent ranking, pair-wise comparison and allocation games. The respective differences relate to the way in which the economic values are elicited. For example, whereas the contingent valuation method asks respondents to express directly their preferences in monetary terms for some defined environmental benefit, the contingent ranking method asks the respondent to rank a number of described environmental quality alternatives. The pair-wise comparison is closely related to the contingent ranking method, yet respondents are asked to compare a series of pairs of alternatives. Finally, in an allocation game, respondents are asked to allocate a fixed budget among a set of environmental benefits. This method is frequently used in experimental economics.

The contingent valuation methodology

The CVM is a stated preference valuation method that uses questionnaires to ask directly the individuals to state their preferences for environmental commodities. Mitchell and Carson defined the method as follows:

> The CVM method uses survey questions to elicit people's preferences for public goods by finding out what they are willing to pay (WTP) for specified improvements in them. The method thus aims at eliciting their WTP in dollar amounts. It circumvents the absence of markets for public goods by presenting consumers with hypothetical markets in which they have the opportunity to buy the good in question. The hypothetical market may be modelled after either a private goods' market or a political market. Because the elicited WTP values are contingent upon the hypothetical market described to the respondents, this approach came to be called the contingent valuation method.
>
> (Mitchell and Carson, 1989, pp. 2–3)

The typical CVM survey consists of three sections. The first section is characterised by the description of the environmental change as conveyed by the policy formulation and the description of the contingent market. The policy formulation involves describing the availability (or quality) of the environmental commodity in both the 'reference state' (usually the status quo) and the 'target state' (usually depicting the policy action). Since all monetary transactions occur in a social context, it is also crucial to define the contingent market – most of the time rather unfamiliar to the respondents – by stating to the respondent both the rules specifying the conditions that would lead to policy implementation and the payment to be exacted from the respondent's household in the event of policy implementation. The second section is where the respondent is asked to state their monetary valuation for the described policy formulation. This part is the core of the questionnaire. The major objective of this section is to obtain a monetary measure of the maximum WTP that the individual consumers are willing to pay for the described environmental policy action. The third section of the CVM instrument is a set of questions that collect socio-demographic information about the respondents. The answers to these questions help to better characterise the respondent's profile and are used to understand the respondent's stated WTP responses. The third section finishes with follow-up questions. The follow-up questions are answered by the interviewers. The goal is to assess whether the respondents have (well) understood the CVM survey in general, and the valuation question in particular.

Today, the CVM is one of the most used techniques for valuation of environmental benefits. This is partly due to the advantages of CVM compared to other valuation methods. First, the CVM method gives immediately a monetary assessment of respondents' preferences. Secondly, the CVM method is the only valuation technique that is capable of shedding light on the monetary valuation of the non-use values, i.e. the benefit value component of the environmental commodity that is not directly associated with its direct use or consumption. These values are characterised by having no behavioural market trace. Therefore, economists cannot glean information about these values relying on market-based valuation approaches. For environmental resources such as the protection of natural parks or biodiversity sensitive areas, which play an important role in guaranteeing the protection of local wildlife diversity, the non-use value component may account for the major part of the conservation benefits. Ignoring such values will be responsible for a systematic bias in the estimation (an underestimation) of the total economic value of the related environment resource. Thirdly, CVM brings with it the advantage that environmental quality changes may be valued even if they have not yet occurred (*ex ante* valuation). This implies that the CVM can be a useful advisory tool for policy decision-making. Fourthly, and as result that environmental changes may be valued even if they have not yet occurred, CVM offers a greater potential scope and flexibility than the revealed preference methods since it is possible to specify different states of nature (policy scenarios) that may even lie outside the current institutional arrangements or levels of provision. Furthermore, the constructed nature of the CVM method permits to test various methodological issues concerning the measurement validity of the individual's stated valuation responses. Indeed, a great deal of today's research efforts is concerned with the validity of CVM responses. We start, however, with a brief history of CV, exploring the link of survey valuation answers to standard economic theory.

A BRIEF HISTORY ON CONTINGENT VALUATION

The first CVM published reference dates from 1947 (Ciriacy-Wantrup, 1947). We refer to the Ciriacy-Wantrup article published in the *Journal of Farms Economics*. The study focuses on the valuation of the economic effects of preventing soil erosion. The author suggested that one way to obtain information on the demand for these favourable effects would be to ask directly the individuals how much they would be willing to pay for successive soil conservation increments. However, no empirical valuation was attempted. However, the first CVM design and implementation only occurs two decades later when Robert Davis assessed the economic value of the recreational possibilities of the Maine Woods by exploring the survey technique (Davis, 1963). Davis simulated a market behaviour situation by putting the interviewer in the 'position of a seller who elicits the highest possible bid from the users of the services being offered'.

Since these early beginnings, the CVM has been used to measure benefits of a wide range of environmental goods including recreation, amenity value, scenery, forests, wetlands, wildlife, air and water quality. More recently, there has been a trend to conduct CVM studies not only to value environmental goods, but also to investigate the various methodological issues involved in the valuation exercise, including the study of the impact of consumer's attitudes and motivations on CVM estimates – see section on the purchase of warm glow. Furthermore, throughout these decades, the CVM has gone through several phases, emerging from the academy into the rough and tumble of the outside world. Strong development stimulus was given by the Reagan Executive Order 12291, introduced in 1981; the re-interpretation of CERCLA in 1989; the Exxon Valdez damage assessment in 1992, and, more recently, the National Oceanic and Atmospheric Administration (NOAA) panel.

Reagan Executive Order and the re-interpretation of CERCLA

The Reagan Executive Order 12291, introduced in 1981, constitutes a strong stimulus for the development of the monetary valuation methods of environmental commodities. In concrete terms, the Executive Order stipulated that all federal regulations on environmental policy should be submitted to a cost–benefit analysis. All regulations, including both the promulgation of new regulations and the review of the existing ones, would only be carried out if a positive present value for the society could be achieved. Therefore, the social benefits had to be monetised. The flexibility and generality of CVM's application was the main reason why this valuation method received most of the EPA's 'demands' in the monetary assessment of the social costs and benefits associated with the new regulations on environmental policy. Thus, the appearance of Executive Order 12291 had a major impact in the development of the CVM.

Another important benchmark in the CVM is the District of Columbia Court of Appeals re-interpretation in 1989 of the US Comprehensive Environmental Response, Compensation and Liability Act of 1980 (USDI, 1989). This governmental decision not only expressed the legitimacy of non-use values as a component of the total resource value, but also granted equal standing to stated and revealed preferences evaluation techniques. Since then, the CVM is being widely used by academic institutions as well as by governmental agencies as a crucial tool in cost–benefit analysis and damage cost assessment.

The Exxon Valdez valuation report

Another important benchmark in the history of the CVM is the massive oil spill due to the grounding of the oil tanker Exxon Valdez in the Prince William Sound in the Northern part of the Gulf of Alaska on 24 March 1989. This oil spill was the largest oil spill from a tanker in US history: more than 1300 km of coastline were affected and almost 23,000 birds were killed (Carson et al., 1992). After the oil spill, the State of Alaska commissioned various studies to identify the physical damage to the natural resources. The follow-up economic damage assessment studies also take into account, in addition to water purification costs, economic losses such as the decrease in revenue from recreation and fisheries. Moreover, the State of Alaska appointed an interdisciplinary group of researchers to design and implement a national CVM study to measure the loss of non-use values to US citizens as a result of the oil spill. This study constitutes one of the major contingent valuation applications and represents an important methodological reference for all contingent valuation researchers' work. The loss of non-use values resulting from the Exxon Valdez oil spill is estimated at 2.8 billion dollars. However, anticipating these high financial consequences, Exxon commissioned a group of researchers to verify whether non-use values could be accurately measured by means of CVM. The main argument of critics of CVM is that this method is not capable of resulting in valid and reliable monetary measures of non-use values. Hausman's well-known argument 'is some number better than no number' fully expresses the scepticism towards the CVM method. Therefore, according to Hausman, assessments of lost non-use values by means of the CVM method should not be used in court. In order to address Hausman's critique, NOAA set a group of experts in order to evaluate the reliability of the use of CVM in the natural resource damage assessments.

The NOAA panel

A panel of experts, with the Nobel Laureates Kenneth Arrow and Robert Solow as chairmen, provided advice to the NOAA on the following question: 'Is the contingent valuation method capable of providing estimates of lost non-use or existence values that are reliable enough to be used in the natural resource damage assessments?' The final advice of the NOAA panel may be summarised by the following sentence:

> The Panel concludes that well conducted CVM studies can produce estimates reliable enough to be the starting point of a judicial process of damage assessment, including lost passive values.
>
> (NOAA, Federal Register, Vol. 58, No. 10, p. 4610)

This conclusion cheered all researchers who wish to use the contingent valuation method. However, the Panel was rather prudent with its conclusion and qualified such a statement by establishing a set of guidelines, recommended to all future CVM applications, concerning the design and execution of the survey instrument. The six most important guidelines, also well known as the six pillars of the NOAA, are summarised as follows:

1   CVM should rely on face-to-face interviews rather than telephone interviews, and whenever this is not possible (especially because of the high costs associated with the personal interviews) telephone interviews are preferable to mail surveys.
2   CVM should elicit the respondent's WTP to prevent a future incident rather than WTA for an incident already occurred.
3   CVM should use a dichotomous choice referendum elicitation format, i.e. the respondents should be asked how they would vote (favour or against) upon a described environmental quality change. The main reason for the dichotomous choice is that such a take-it-or-leave-it survey valuation question is more likely to reflect real daily world market decisions which individuals are confronted with. Moreover, the dichotomous choice referendum reveals itself to be less vulnerable to strategic bidding behaviour than, for example, the open-ended elicitation format.

4   CVM should contain an accurate and understandable description of the programme or policy under consideration and the associated environmental benefits in each of the two scenarios, i.e. with and without the policy. Inter-disciplinary work with other research areas, namely the biological sciences, is recommended here.

5   CVM should include reminders of the substitutes for the commodity in question as well as its budget. In a context where the respondents are being asked how they would vote on a financial contribution to protect a natural area, the respondents should be reminded of the existence of the other areas that exist. Moreover the respondent should be reminded that such contribution would reduce the amount of money that he or she has available to spend on other things. The major idea here is to make such a (hypothetical) valuation exercise resemble as closely as possible an actual market transaction.

6   CVM experiments should include a follow-up section at the end of the ques-tionnaire to be sure if the respondents understood (or not) the choice that they were asked to make.

According to the Panel, this set of guidelines contributes to guaranteeing the quality of the CVM survey as a measurement instrument and the validity of the respective monetary measures for cost–benefit analysis and damage cost assessments. In the following section, we show how the behaviour of CVM respondents can be analysed with standard micro-economic models of choice and explore the demand for environmental quality with respect to alternative measures for assessing welfare changes.

THEORETICAL UNDERPINNING ON THE USE OF CONTINGENT VALUATION

Neo-classical theory attempts to model the demand for goods given, certain assumptions. The central assumption pertains to the behavioural characteristics of the individual, i.e. the consumer. The theory assumes that consumers act ratio-nally. This behavioural premise implies two things. First, individual consumers have coherent preferences over the different states of the world. These states can be defined so broadly that they can encompass the distribution of private goods and services or the provision of public goods like environmental quality. Secondly, when making choices among alternative states of the world, the individual does this on the basis of her preferences, choosing the state that is most preferred. The underlying intuition that one can draw from the rationality premise is that if an outside observer knew the preferences of any given individual as the individual knows them, that knowledge could be used to explain the human behaviour as it relates to choices. It is important, however, to see that the prior 'rationality' does not mean 'unbounded rationality': surely there are cognitive constraints to any respondent's ability to make complex choices such as the economic valuation of environmental changes (seldom thought in monetary terms). The important thing is that respondent answers to the CVM questionnaire in general, and to elicitation questions in particular, in a manner consistent with the respondent's preferences.

The basic model

The present section draws on the theoretical perspective that individuals make welfare-optimising consumption decisions. These decisions are captured in the consumer-demand functions with respect to available goods and services. Environmental attributes enter those demands. For some environmental benefits, such as the recreational visits to an urban green park, the consumer exercises direct choice over the amount consumed, assuming that the park is open to all residents. To illustrate this setting, we consider an individual whose utility function has the following form:

$$V = V(x, q, z) \qquad (1)$$

where x is the consumption of the private good, q is the quantity of the environmental attribute and z is the quality of that attribute. For example, q could represent the number of visits and z the level of protection of the urban green area. We assume that all commodities, including the number of visits, have prices. Moreover, we assume that x is a composite private good whose price is normalised to one, and p is the price associated with q, and that p is fixed. We also assume that the consumer exercises direct choice over q but not over z. The consumer maximises utility subject to a budget constraint:

$$p.q + x \leq M \qquad (2)$$

where M is money income. Assume non-satiation, i.e. assume that the consumer uses the available budget fully. For a particular level of M and z, the consumer solves:

$$\underset{\{x,q\}}{\text{Max }} V(x, q, z)$$
$$s.t.$$
$$p.q + x = M \qquad (3)$$
$$q, x \geq 0$$

yielding some level of utility, V^*, and an optimal consumption bundle, (q^*, x^*), both of which are functions of p, M and z. To investigate a change in z, holding utility constant, we proceed to the total differentiation of $V(x^*, q^*, z)$ and $p.q^* + x^* = M$. Formally, we have:

$$dV = \frac{V}{q}dq + \frac{V}{z}dz + \frac{V}{x}dx \qquad (4)$$

and

$$dM - qdp + pdq + dx \qquad (5)$$

We focus how changes in q and z can be compensated by changes in M. Thus, we let $dV = 0$. The assumption of fixed prices means that $dp = 0$, so the first term in Equation (5) drops out. Rearranging Equations (4) and (5), we get:

$$-dx = \frac{V/q}{V/x}dq + \frac{V/z}{V/x}dz \qquad (6)$$

and

$$-dx = pdq - dM \qquad (7)$$

Now let z be the attribute for which a change is contemplated. Setting equal the right-hand sides of the Equations (6) and (7) gives:

$$\frac{\partial V/\partial q}{\partial V/\partial x}dq + \frac{\partial V/\partial z}{\partial V/\partial x}dz - pdq - -dM \qquad (8)$$

Equation (8) establishes that the monetary payment must equal the difference between the personal worth of the change in quantity and quality, the first two terms on the left-hand side, and the change in the expenditure on q, the last term on the left-hand side. A fundamental condition in consumer theory is that the consumers that make welfare-optimising consumption decisions equate the marginal rate of substitution to the ratio of product prices. In the present case, p is normalised with respect to the price of composite commodity x:

$$\frac{V/q}{V/x} = p \qquad (9)$$

Substituting Equation (9) into Equation (8) and cancelling the terms results in:

$$\frac{\partial V/\partial z}{\partial V/\partial x} = -\frac{dM}{dz} \qquad (10)$$

i.e. the marginal rate of substitution between z and x must equal the change in income that will keep utility constant as z changes, which can be interpreted as the introduction of a set of new regulations on the protection of the green natural park (e.g. stricter regulations on the use of the park and banning the use of scooters inside the park). That income change is the 'price' that reflects the consumer's maximum WTP to avoid an undesirable change in z. In other words, the theoretical economic measure of welfare change, as described by Equation (10), is the payment that will make a consumer indifferent between having and not having a particular change in the quality or quantity of the environmental attribute. This is the measure of welfare change that CVM researchers look for through the use of direct questioning.

Alternative measures of welfare change

The literature suggests two alternative measures that can be used to assess the magnitude of the welfare change as described by Equation (10), respectively the Hicksian compensating measure and the Hicksian equivalent measure are theoretical refinements of the ordinary consumer's surplus (Hicks, 1943). Before introducing the Hicksian compensating and the Hicksian equivalent as alternative welfare measures of welfare change, we return to the model as presented in the last section and investigate the welfare change associated with a non-marginal decrease in the quality level of the environmental attribute, z. This environmental change may be interpreted as the introduction of a set of new regulations designed to allow partial commercial development of the urban green area, zoning areas for bars and restaurants that did not exist before. In the original situation, i.e. before the setting of the new regulations policy, the individual consumer faces a particular quality level of the environmental attribute. Let us denote such a level by z^0. For an environmental quality level z^0, and given an amount M of monetary income, the consumer solves (3) yielding an optimal consumption bundle (q^0, x^0) and the utility level $V^0 = V(q^0, x^0, z^0)$. Inserting the demand functions into the utility function gives the indirect utility function $V(q^0(p, M, z^0), x^0(p, M, z^0), z^0) = v(p, M, z^0)$. Inverting the indirect utility function for the term M yields the expenditure function on market goods required to produce utility level V, given p and z^0. This is $e(p, z^0, V^0)$. Table 8.3 summarises the notation.

This welfare measure equals the compensating payment, i.e. an offsetting change in income, necessary to make the individual indifferent between the original situation (status quo) and the new environmental regulation policy (after the environmental quality change). In terms of the indirect utility function, the Hicksian compensating variation (HC) is the solution to:

$$v(p, M, z^0) = v(p, M + \text{HC}, z^1) = V^0 \qquad (11)$$

Table 8.3 Summary of results

Variables	Original situation	New regulation (introduction of bars and restaurants)
Environmental attribute quality	z^0	z^1
Utility level	V^0	V^1 with $V^0 > V^1$
Indirect utility function	$v(p, M, z^0)$	$v(p, M, z^1)$
Expenditure function	$e(p, z^0, V^0)$	$e(p, z^1, V^1)$

i.e. the HC measures what must be paid to the individual to make that person indifferent to the new environmental quality level. In other words, if the new regulation is adopted, the individual's income could be increased by the amount of HC and that person would still be as well off as in the original situation. Alternatively, HC can also be defined in terms of the expenditure function. In terms of the expenditure function, HC is the difference between the expenditures required to sustain utility level V^0 at the new environmental quality level, i.e.

$$HC = e(p, z^1, V^0) - e(p, z^0, V^0)$$
$$= e(p, z^1, V^0) - M \tag{12}$$

Since spending M at the new environmental attribute quality level yields a lower level of utility, V^1, we can also write

$$M = e(p, z^1, V^1) \tag{13}$$

and by substitution

$$HC = e(p, z^1, V^0) - e(p, z^1, V^1) \tag{14}$$

i.e. although the HC is defined in terms of V^0, it also measures the amount of money required to raise the utility from V^1 to V^0 at the new quality level of the environmental attribute.

The Hicksian equivalent measures the change in income (given the original quality level) that would lead to the same utility change as the change in the quality of the environmental attribute. In terms of the indirect utility function, the Hicksian equivalent (HE) is the solution to

$$v(p, M, z^1) = v(p, M - HE, z^0) = V^1 \tag{15}$$

i.e. the HE measures the income change equivalent to the welfare lost due to the decrease in the quality of the environmental attribute. In other words, and if we admit that the implied property rights are assigned to the change and not to the status quo, the HE translates the maximum amount that the individual would be willing to pay to avoid the changes in the quality level of the environmental attribute. The HE can also be defined in terms of the expenditure function. It is the difference between the expenditures required to sustain utility level V^1, at the original environmental quality level:

$$HE = e(p, z^0, V^0) - e(p, z^0, V^1)$$
$$= M - e(p, z^0, V^1) \tag{16}$$

Substituting Equation (13) into (16), we get:

$$HE = e(p, z^1, V^1) - e(p, z^0, V^1) \tag{17}$$

i.e. although the HE is defined in terms of the monetary equivalent of a change from V^1 to V^0, it can also be measured by the change in the expenditure function associated with the environmental quality changes (given the utility level V^1).

These two Hicksian welfare measures can also be interpreted in terms of the implicit rights and obligations associated with alternative environmental quality levels. The HC carries with it implicitly the assumption that the individual has the right to the original environmental quality level in case of environmental quality deterioration. In contrast, the HE contains the assumption that the individual has an obligation to accept the decrease in the quality in the environmental attribute and thus will have to make a payment if the new quality level is not to be attained. Based on the interpretation of the two measures, we are able to argue that the choice between them is, basically, an ethical one, i.e. one that depends on the value judgement as to which underlying distribution of property rights is more equitable (Krutilla, 1967). The results can be summarised as shown in Table 8.4.

Table 8.4 Welfare measures and the property rights distribution

Attribute quality	Hicksian Equivalent measure: Implied property rights in the change	Hicksian Compensating measure: Implied property rights in the status quo
Increase	WAC to forgo	WTP to obtain
Decrease	WTP to avoid*	WAC to accept

* The preferred welfare measure according to the suggestions of the NOAA panel (1993).

CONTINGENT VALUATION IN PRACTICE

In 'standard' private market exchanges, an individual evaluates the alternative market prospects given their previous experience and market information. The nature of the CVM application, in terms of policy choice appraisal, makes the value formulation problem more difficult relative to ordinary market decisions (Mitchell and Carson, 1993). First, in CVM, an individual formulates a valuation given the experience and the information provided by the contingent market, i.e. as described in the survey instrument. Secondly, CVM is usually applied to assess the monetary valuation of alternative protection choices that, most of the times, are unfamiliar to the citizens. However, these are precisely the cases where the lack of public information for policy choice is the greatest. Thirdly, the time devoted to contingent choices may be more limited than in market situations. This time constraint occurs for two reasons: (1) the research strategy may seek to reduce data collection costs by limiting the time devoted to gathering each set of observations; (2) the respondent may choose to limit their time resources devoted to value formulation. Therefore, the value formulation process in the contingent market is submitted to sources of error. Information errors may arise as complex information is communicated to the respondents. Information errors may be left uncorrected due to time constraints on review or repetition. Thus the time-constrained process of communicating complex information is an important source of error in the value-formulation process.

The question is then: what is the level of information necessary to be provided in the survey instrument? How much information should be provided in a CVM questionnaire so that the respondents are able to make a valid value formulation? These questions are addressed in the following sections.

Definition of the survey contingent market

The description of the contingent market is very important in guaranteeing a successful valuation exercise and, this way, can produce estimation results that can be interpreted in economic terms (Carson *et al.*, 1999; Nunes, 2002). The description of the contingent market involves three major design tasks. The CVM researcher has in one first stage to: (1) identify the set of environmental attributes to which the policy formulation is addressed and measure the respective levels in each of the 'reference' and 'target' states; then (2) describe the social context that involves the hypothetical transaction; and finally (3) recognise the circumstances under which the environmental change is made available to the respondents.

In the first stage, which concerns the identification and measurement of the set of environmental attributes, it is crucial to work together in a multi-disciplinary team, making the best use of the scientific information available. This work goes usually hand-in-hand with the use of focus groups, i.e. small groups of citizens, from all educational levels and varied life experiences, who are invited to discuss the degree of understanding of the material proposed to be used in the description of the public policy. Their comprehension feedback is crucial since it is very important that all the individuals potentially affected by the change in public policy are able to understand the described contingent market. Therefore, careful wording has to be provided without making the questionnaire so complex that its understanding would be beyond the ability, or interest, of many respondents. Finally, the CVM survey communicates the policy formulation as much as possible in visual form, making use of photos, images and computer-manipulated images: this makes it possible to the respondent to better 'visualise' the range of changes involved.

In a second stage, the CVM researcher has to choose the payment mechanism and the number of the years involved in the transaction. This means that the respondent has to be informed both about the way in which the described environmental changes are financed and about the number of years over which payments are collected. The best recommendation is to choose a plausible payment vehicle, i.e. one that is perceived as a likely way to pay the environmental change. This improves the credibility of the contingent market: if the respondent finds the payment vehicle believable, ceteris paribus, then they will take the choice situation more seriously.

Finally, the respondent has to be informed how the survey results are likely to be used. This involves describing to the respondent the capacity of the government in providing the described environmental service(s) as well as the ability of the government to (coercively) collect the payment for the described environmental service(s). The underlying idea is to make the respondents care about the policy outcomes described in the survey instrument as well as to make the respondents perceive that their responses to the survey will potentially influence the final outcome(s).

The level of survey information

On one hand, enough information must be provided to enable the respondents to make sound choices (Fischhoff and Furby, 1988). Naturally, it is easier to make a valuation of a 'red car' if information is also available about the brand, its age, mileage, etc., than to make a valuation of a 'red car' without such additional information. Most probably, one could expect that such 'variations' in the information set are associated with different value estimates. Empirical evidence from CVM studies supports this assertion. Samples *et al.* (1986) tested the proposition that an individual's reported WTP to preserve a particular species would be significantly influenced by information about the species and its endangered status. The test results confirmed that the estimated values of wildlife conservation were indeed dependent on the level of information conveyed. Hanley (1988) found that the WTP to preserve biodiversity increases significantly as the level of information provision increases, but at a decreasing rate – 'what is out of sight, is out of mind' (Tversky and Kahneman, 1973; Woo, 1996). But, on the other hand, the need for information must be balanced with the need to keep surveys to a reasonable length and easily comprehensible. If enough information is required to communicate alternative policy formulations that, most of the time are unfamiliar to the citizens, too much information will drive the respondent's attention away. The challenge is, therefore, to reach an appropriate level of information. This involves two tasks: an accurate description of the environmental changes associated with the proposed policy formulation as well as an accurate description of the contingent market.

Survey elicitation question

Once the respondent is given the description of the environmental change(s) and the contingent market involving such a provision, the respondent is asked to report their monetary valuation. This involves the choice of information support in which the respondent is able to report their valuation responses, i.e. the choice of the elicitation question format. We review five elicitation formats, respecting more or less a chronological order, and discuss the various pros and cons associated with each of these methods – see Table 8.5.

One the earliest elicitation formats was developed by Davis (1963) and is called the 'bidding game'. The bidding game format was also applied by CVM studies in the 1970s (for example, Randall et al., 1974; Brookshire et al., 1976). The assumption is that the individual's WTP will be obtained after a series of questions has been asked, i.e. letting the interviewer iteratively raise, or lower, the proposed bid until the respondent alters her 'yes' or 'no' answer. A fine-tuning of the bidding game format may be achieved by rising, or lowering the bids in the reverse direction after a change in the 'yes/no' answers. An advantage of the bidding game is that respondents get some assistance to arrive at a WTP value; moreover, the choice process of the respondent is simplified, so that the number of non-responses may be reduced. These desirable features are, however, obtained at high costs. The principal disadvantage is the phenomenon of 'anchoring' or 'starting-point-bias' (Mitchell and Carson, 1989). This occurs when the respondent sees the initial bid as a clue, or reference point, for her final valuation. Thus the respondents who start with a lower initial bid will end up, ceteris paribus, with a lower WTP than the ones who start with a higher bid. To make matters worse, the bidding game format is highly vulnerable to a 'yea-saying', i.e. the fact that respondents tend to agree with increasing bids

Table 8.5 Comparative analysis of alternative elicitation formats

	Advantages	Disadvantages
Bidding game	Simple and assisted iterative process High participation rate	Anchoring Yea-saying Boring
Open ended	Displays the WTP in the format that the research is looking for Higher accuracy of the relevant statistics	Low participation rates Vulnerable to strategic behaviour No valuation 'assistance' Procedure not familiar to consumers
Payment card	No anchoring Displays the WTP in the format that the research is looking for	Limited range of the cards Vulnerable to strategic behaviour
Dichotomous choice	Simple and assisted iterative process High participation rate No anchoring Incentive compatible Procedure familiar to consumers	Yea-saying Too expensive Low accuracy of the relevant statistics
Dichotomous choice with follow-up	Simple and assisted iterative process High participation rate No anchoring Incentive compatible Procedure familiar to consumers Higher accuracy of the relevant statistics	Yea-saying Too expensive Complexity of the involved estimation procedures

regardless of their true valuations (Kanninen, 1995). Consequently, the bidding game may be expected to result in an overestimation of the environmental change. Finally, the respondents become bored during the bidding game, especially if the iterative process is particularly long, meaning that their motivation will decline, so that the respective answers will be less accurate.

The open-ended, or direct questioning, format consists of one single question that straightforwardly asks for the maximum amount that the respondent is willing to pay for the described environmental change: 'What is the maximum amount of money that you are willing to pay for (. . .)'. The main advantage of this format is that it immediately gives the information that the researcher is looking for. However, this method opens up the possibility of some form of strategic behaviour: many respondents may immediately state zero WTP although the amenity has value for them, simply because the respondent may attempt to misreport their preferences by bidding untruthfully and thus affecting the outcome (Hoehn and Randall, 1989). That is to say, there is a possibility that the respondents will reveal a WTP that is biased downward in the hope of getting 'something for nothing'. The reluctance of individuals to contribute to the support of public goods is a well-known phenomenon in the literature and referred to as the free rider problem. Furthermore, the open-ended question may be very difficult to answer for the individual because most of the time the described environmental change is not particularly familiar to them (Hoevenagel, 1992). In this context, Mitchell and Carson argue that 'respondents often find it difficult to pick up a value out of the air, as it were, without some form of assistance' (Mitchell and Carson, 1989, p. 97). Finally, individual consumers are not used to this procedure in normal market behaviour; generally speaking, consumers make choices about buying (or not) a given good at fixed market prices.

The payment card was developed as a response to the large proportions of non-responses and protest 'zeros' which were obtained in the CVM applications with open-ended formats (Mitchell and Carson, 1989). The payment card format means that the respondents are offered a card that contains a list of bid amounts. Then the respondents are asked to indicate which amount of money on the card they are willing to pay for the described environmental change. According to Mitchell and Carson the payment card would give the respondents some assistance in searching for their valuation. Furthermore, it would avoid the phenomenon of start bid 'anchoring', as described in the bidding game, and still maintain the positive feature of the open-ended format, i.e. measure the respondent's WTP by means of a single question. However, the validity of the stated WTP amounts may be questioned because the range of the payment card, specially the maximum bid amount, may influence the final WTP answers of the respondents (Hoevenagel, 1992). From an economic point of view, the range of the payment card should be irrelevant: the different maximum amounts on the payment card do not reduce the set of choices of the respondents because each card contains the category 'other, namely: (...)'.

The dichotomous choice referendum format, also known as the take-it-or-leave-it (TIOLI) approach, asks the respondents how would they vote (in favour or against) upon a described programme (and associate environmental benefits) upon the payment of an individual cost which is specified in the question format (e.g. 'Is your household willing to pay $xx for...'). The main reason for the dichotomous choice is that such TIOLI valuation question is more likely to reflect real daily world market decisions which individuals are confronted with, rather than, for example, when respondents are facing an open-ended question. Technically speaking, the dichotomous choice elicitation format is simply the first round of the bidding game: the respondents are asked to accept or reject a specific bid amount in return for an environmental change. Therefore, one of the properties of the bidding game is kept: it burdens the respondent less than the open-ended question formats. This elicitation format also avoids most of the disadvantages of the bidding game.

First, the dichotomous choice elicitation uses various bid amounts and randomly assigns them to the respondents thus minimising the 'starting-point' phenomenon. Secondly, this elicitation format has the characteristic of being incentive compatible, i.e. truth telling is the individually optimal strategy (Hoehn and Randall, 1989). Nevertheless, when compared to the elicitation question formats mentioned above, the dichotomous choice format involves a stronger financial effort in interviewing since it requires substantially larger samples to obtain the same degree of accuracy of the relevant statistics and thus the same level of value estimation precision. The dichotomous choice format may also encourage the 'yea saying' phenomenon where the posted bid is accepted as a hint of what is a reasonable payment (Kanninen, 1995).

The dichotomous choice with one follow-up elicitation format, also called the double-bounded dichotomous choice, was first proposed in 1986 (Carson *et al.*, 1986) and is an extension of the (single-bounded) dichotomous choice format. This elicitation format involves the simple addition of one extra dichotomous choice question, containing a proposal for a bid that is dependent on the first bid. So, if the respondent answers 'yes' ('no') to the initial bid, then the bid amount proposed in the second question is increased (decreased). As in the single-bounded dichotomous choice, a nice property of this elicitation format is that the empirical survival function can be estimated from which the mean and median can be assessed (Kriström, 1990; Cameron, 1991; Cameron and Quiggin, 1994). It has also been proved that the follow-up greatly improves the statistical efficiency of the dichotomous choice format (Hanemann *et al.*, 1991). This means that for each observation, i.e. for each respondent, the CVM researcher has more information about the 'location' of the respondent's WTP. In econometric terms, this additional information is reflected (1) in a higher precision in the estimation of the truncated intervals of the cdf and (2) more robust valuation estimates. In other words, this means that it is possible to get more precise WTP value estimates with the same sample dimension and thus, without incurring additional interviewing costs.

RESPONDENT'S STRATEGIC BEHAVIOUR AND VALUE MEASUREMENT BIAS

The CVM researchers, borrowing from Samuelson's notion of 'false signals', maintain a priori that different payment scheme provides different incentives for engaging in strategic behaviour and thus influencing the expected valuation results. As Samuelson argued 'It is in the selfish interest of each person to give false signals to pretend to have less interest in a given collective activity than she really has'

(Samuelson, 1954, p. 388). He made specific reference to the possibility of strategic behaviour with respect to the use of surveys. Samuelson's point, repeated in many textbook discussions of public goods, had a strong effect on how economists view the survey questions. The wrong inference made by many CVM critics is to equate strategic behaviour with lying. As the term is used in the modern mechanism design literature in economics, 'strategic behaviour is merely synonymous with a rational agent maximising (broadly defined) self-interest' (Carson et al., 1999, p. 3). Mechanism design theory has shown that the optimal strategic behaviour for the individual consumers in many instances is to truthfully reveal their preferences. Whether this is the case or not depends upon the particular format of the survey elicitation question and other aspects of the scenario, including the payment vehicle and the level of information. These issues are discussed in the following sub-sections.

The choice of the elicitation question

Much of the attention focused on the binary choice question elicitation format in recent years is due to the NOAA Panel on Contingent Valuation's recommendation for its use. One of the reasons underlying the Panel's recommendation is related with the fact that the dichotomous (binary) choice format is an 'appropriate elicitation mechanism for estimating the demand for public goods' because of its (defensive) properties with respect to strategic bidding behaviour. Indeed, one of the core results in mechanism design theory as derived by Gibbard and Satterthwaite (Gibbard, 1973; Satterthwaite, 1975) is that the binary choice question is the only response format that is potentially incentive compatible in the sense that truthful preference revelation represents an optimal (and the dominant) strategy for the respondent. It has been long known that in some settings the binary choice question format is incentive compatible (Farquaharson, 1969). The best-known examples are political races with only two candidates and binding (approve/disapprove) referendums with plurality (usually majority approval) vote requirement. The discussion of whether the binary choice question meets the incentive compatible property raises two questions.

The first question is whether it is the binding nature of the referendum that makes it incentive compatible. Carson et al. (1999) considered 'an advisory referendum vote', i.e. the government is more likely to undertake an action the larger the percentage in favour, and showed that such vote rule is incentive compatible. The second question is whether substituting an 'advisory survey' for an 'an advisory referendum' alters the incentive properties of the mechanism. Green and Laffont (1978) have shown that the economic mechanism geared by the binary choice question can be implemented using a sampling approach rather than complete information.

These two arguments were reiterated in a recent paper by Carson, Groves and Machina:

> It is possible to replace the binding nature of an incentive compatible referendum with the more general assumption that the government is more likely to undertake the action the higher the percentage in favour. It is also possible to substitute a survey of the public good for a vote of the public on the issue. Neither of these changes, alone or together alter the original incentive structure of the binding referendum.
>
> (Carson *et al.*, 1999, p. 11)

In a paper Hoehn and Randall (1989) illustrated the case for truth telling as the individually optimal strategy in a policy referendum model. The authors conclude that the 'values elicited with parametric cost referendum format weakly dominate the valuations obtained with a [open ended] willingness to pay format' (pp. 237, 239). The authors consider that when choosing within the dichotomous choice referendum, the respondent is informed that: (a) the proposed policy is implemented if the majority of the respondents approves it, and that (b) for each respondent, approval is conditional on an individual cost as stated in the survey instrument. Since the respondent is uncertain about how others will vote, and (a) holds, then they face an incentive for participation. Therefore, the respondent considers their vote as decisive to approve (or reject) the environmental improvement. If the survey stated cost is lower than the individual's subjective WTP, then the respondent attains a welfare gain if the project is approved, and thus it is optimal to report approval. Conversely, the survey stated cost is higher than the individual's subjective WTP, the respondent suffers a welfare loss if the project is approved and it is optimal to report disapproval. It is important to remark, however, that it is not casting the preference question as a referendum that provides its desirable incentive properties. It is the cast of the preference question in terms of being able to influence a government decision with a binary agree/not agree format.

On the contrary, when choosing for open-ended elicitation question format, the respondent is informed that: (a) the proposed policy is implemented if the sum of the reported aggregated benefits exceed the costs; and that (b) each respondent pays in proportion to the sample mean bid. This setting may lead respondents to misrepresent preferences and stating a bid that is not their true bid but a bid sufficiently small enough to manipulate the sample mean bid in the hope of getting 'something for nothing' (Bohm, 1972, p. 113). In other words, the respondent may attempt to give 'false signals' and wait to see if the good is provided without their contribution. The empirical evidence shows that, on average, the open-ended estimation results are, on average, lower when compared to the dichotomous choice referendum estimates. This empirical finding suggests that understating may be the overwhelming bidding force in the open-ended elicitation question format and this is interpreted as free-riding to the supposed lower overall mean.

The choice of the payment vehicle

A key assumption is being made in the preceding discussion of the binary choice question as an incentive compatible mechanism. The assumption is that the government can compel payment for a good if provided. The ability to coercively collect payment for the provision of the public good is the property that causes the agent to try to influence the government's decision in the desired direction taking into account both the costs and the benefits of the action to the respondent. Relaxing such an assumption will destroy the incentive properties of the referendum advisory survey – see Table 8.6.

To illustrate Table 8.6, let us consider the case where an (charitable) organisation wants to provide an increase in the environmental quality of a natural park (e.g. creation of a habitat reserve) via voluntary contributions. A 'yes' to the question of the form 'Is your household willing to pay $xx to purchase the habitat reserve if we started the fund' will encourage the charitable organisation to undertake the fund-raising effort. Given the public nature of the environmental quality – once the habitat reserve is created there is no way that any individual could be excluded from its benefits – the optimal strategy of an agent who wants to visit the forest is to contribute less than her maximum WTP for the good and, in many instances, sit back and wait to see if the good is provided without her contribution. The reluctance of individuals to contribute to the support of public goods, the free rider problem, is a well-known phenomenon in the literature.

One of the first CVM studies focused on the study of strategic bidding behaviour was presented by Swedish economist Peter Bohm. Bohm conducted a CVM experiment with the objective of testing whether value estimates are sensitive to the alternative configurations of the payment rules. Bohm's results do not rule out the hypothesis that different payment decision rules engage different strategic

Table 8.6 Incentive properties of binary discrete choice questions

Type of good and nature of the payment obligation	Incentive property
New public good with coercive payment	Incentive compatible
New public good with voluntary payment	Not incentive compatible

Source: Adapted from Carson et al. (1999, p. 17)

behaviour incentives, but the empirical evidence makes it unlikely that these differences are 'very large' – and this result is of considerable practical importance (see Bohm, 1972). More recently, Champ et al. (1997) set up an experiment involving contingent donations and actual donations for an environmental project along the North Rim of the Grand Canyon. The project involved old, unpaved roads that must be removed before it can be officially designated as a Wilderness Area. The experiment was characterised by the use of two survey versions: one posed a dichotomous choice question which gave the opportunity to actually donate a specific amount for road removal, whereas the second asked a parallel contingent donation question. The estimation results showed that '23 per cent of the contingent donation respondents were inconsistent in the sense that they said yes to the dichotomous choice contingent donation question but our model predicts that they not actually donate if they had been in the dichotomous choice actual donation treatment'.

The hypothetical nature of the survey payment

Hypothetical bias is defined as the systematic difference between the stated payments response in a hypothetical market and the actual payments when individuals are presented with the opportunity in reality. Hypothetical bias may occur in the CVM responses because respondents may not be able to visualise the described scenario situation, or it may not seem realistic enough to spend time thinking it through. Respondents may also not believe that their answers will have any effect on the policy. More recently, the divergence between actual and survey behaviour may also be interpreted (and expected) as additional empirical evidence of strategic behaviour in CVM surveys.

To see this, let us return to the case where the government wants to provide a forest recreation area. The incentive structure is illustrated in Table 8.7. If one takes a compulsory tax as the payment vehicle, the government can compel payment for the public good if the majority of the electors vote for the provision of the forest recreation area. Therefore, the agent perceives that they are able to influence a government decision and their optimal strategy is to state their true valuation of the public good. On the contrary, if we consider that an (charitable) organisation wants to provide the forest recreation area via voluntary contributions, the optimal strategy of an agent who wants to visit the forest is to contribute less than their maximum WTP for the good and, in many instances to contribute nothing. This is the classic free-riding incentive behaviour – see arrow (a) in Table 8.7. However, Carson et al. (1999, p. 12) argue that 'the same incentive structure which should cause free-riding with respect to the actual contributions should induce respondents in a survey to over pledge because doing so helps to obtain the latter opportunity

Table 8.7 Strategic behaviour, payment vehicles and payment settings

	Actual payment setting (with cash transaction)	Hypothetical payment setting (no cash transaction)
Compulsory tax	Voluntary contributions	Survey-based contributions
Ability to coercively collect payment for the provision of the public good	Agent sits back and waits to see if the good is provided without her contribution	Agent over pledges (Carson et al., 1999)
Agent is able to influence a government decision	Agent contributes less than her own WTP	Agent contributes more than her own WTP
	⟶ (a)	⟶ (b)
⟹ Incentive compatible	⟹ Not incentive compatible	⟹ Not incentive compatible

Source: Nunes (2002)

to free ride'. Therefore, according to these authors the survey based predictions of contributions, when compared to the actual contributions, are influenced by an over pledge incentive – see arrow (b) in Table 8.7. The hypothetical bias is difficult to test, except by comparison with real-payments. But clearly, if it was possible to obtain real-cash-payments for the good in question, the CVM method would not be necessary. However, there are some CVM experiments that combine the use of the hypothetical market value elicitation with actual payments. The empirical evidence has not always supported Carson et al.'s 'over pledge' argument.

One of the possible reasons for the discrepancy between the intended and the actual behaviour is that an individual may judge their consumption from a public good (e.g. preserve a habitat reserve) as something quite different from consuming the same good as a private one (e.g. WWFN membership fee). Hence, 'the transformation of a public good into a private good may be considered highly inefficient'. Another possible reason explaining the difference between hypothetical and actual behaviour is the respondent's lack of foreknowledge of an obligation to pay in accordance with one's verbal statements. According to Navrud, 'a carefully constructed CVM survey should contain an explicit payment obligation' (Navrud, 1992, p. 245).

In contrast, other studies provide considerable evidence that hypothetical bias may not be a problem. Sinden (1988) conducted 17 experiments comparing the hypothetical and actual money donations to a fund for soil conservation and an eucalyptus planting programme. He found that there was no statistical difference between the two markets in any of the experiments. Finally, some studies found that hypothetical estimates may even be slightly smaller than actual payments. Bateman et al. (1993) cite experiments that 'clearly show that stated willingness to pay in a hypothetical market may be below the willingness to pay in a real market' (p. 39). Furthermore, Majid *et al.* (1983) obtained lower WTP responses from hypothetical markets. A possible reason for this situation is that in the 'real market', the version of the good as a 'private' (excludable and rival) good introduces elements of competition, exclusivity and 'auction fever' completely absent from the good conceived as a 'public good'. More recently, Nunes (2002, 2005) puts forward the idea that two valuation mechanisms, of opposite sign, emerge simultaneously when answering survey-based contributions. The first refers to free-riding, and thus reflecting in an incentive to lower WTP responses from the survey. The second refers to the purchase of warm glow, i.e. an expression embedded in the WTP so as to acquire a sense of moral satisfaction. The latter is reflecting in an incentive to increase WTP responses from the survey. Nonetheless, the only problem with such cases, from the perspective of economic theory, is not whether there should be a divergence between the actual behaviour and the survey estimate, but rather whether the magnitude of the divergence empirically observed should be even larger, i.e. to assess whether 'the incentive in a survey to over pledge' is indeed a statistically significant driving force of the stated WTP responses. Arrow *et al.* (NOAA, 1993) suggest that the response to the issue of the hypothetical nature of the CVM method is to make both the hypothetical market and the payment vehicle as credible and realistic as possible. Moreover, the members of the NOAA Panel also recommend that CVM survey should contain, together with the explicit payment obligation, the use of budget constraint reminders and substitute reminders before eliciting the WTP question.

The purchase of warm glow

Despite the fact that CVM survey design has been a target of extensive methodological research and quality improvements, this valuation method is an object of diverse critiques. The embedding effect is a major critique of the CVM method. Embedding is attributed to the possibility that CVM is insensitive to the scope of the public policy formulated in the instrument survey. Consider the question of the preservation of two natural areas: area 1 and area 2. Suppose that the WTP for the two areas jointly is $(X + C)$, where X is the economic value of preserving the areas and C is the value attached to the warm glow of giving. Now suppose the answer to the question for area 1 individually is $(Y + C)$ and the answer to the question for area 2 individually is $(Z + C)$, where $X = Y + Z$. Then, the sum of the answers for the areas individually will be $(X + 2C)$, which is greater by the amount C than the answer for the two areas jointly. The argument for criticising the CVM method goes as follows: how can cost–benefit analysis and damage cost assessment rely on a valuation tool that discloses, for the same public good, different value estimates, whether the public good is valued alone or included in a wider policy programme? Kahneman and Knetsch (1992) offered an explanation for embedding that has its roots in the individual consumer behaviour. According to these authors, embedding is not in conflict with the standard value theory; according to Kahneman and Knetsch, embedding can be explained in terms of an impure altruistic motivation of the individual consumer, and that aspect of consumer behaviour was not considered in the standard valuation framework. In other words, Kahneman and Knetsch proposed an explanation that maintains that the WTP for public goods is also an expression of WTP to acquire moral satisfaction: 'respondents express a willingness to contribute for the acquisition of many public goods, and there is no reason to doubt their sincerity or seriousness (. . .) What is the good that respondents are willing to acquire in CVM surveys? We offer the general hypothesis that responses to CVM questions express a willingness to acquire a sense of moral satisfaction, also known as warmglow of giving'.

Moreover, the moral satisfaction valuation transmission can be interpreted in the light of the general model formulation for private donations as initially developed by Andreoni (1989, 1990). According to Andreoni, the individual consumer contributes to the provision of a particular public good for two reasons. First, because the individual consumer simply wants more of it – no satiety axiom. Second, because the individual consumer derives some private benefit from giving to the good. Therefore, the individual consumer contribution to the public good enters into her utility function twice: once as a private good and once as a contribution to a public good. By inference, it seems plausible that the act of participating in a CVM market so as to assist in the supply of an environmental good could provide a mixture of private, warm-glow benefits and public services from the increased supply of the good. More recently, Nunes and Schokkaert (2003) explore the use of factor analytic information so as to characterise respondent's motivational profile, showing that the embedding problem in CV applications is linked to the warm-glow effect. Moreover, the use of direct attitudinal information played a crucial role to get a better understanding of the real content of CV answers. In fact, it allowed for operationalising and estimating that a 'cold' WTP, i.e. a WTP measure for the case in which all respondents would be free from a general feeling of well-being or satisfaction generated by the act of giving, has worked reasonably well. The 'cold' WTP estimates are lower than the original estimates and formal testing has shown that they do not violate the adding-up property. Therefore, if one takes the view that the original WTP estimates do not reflect 'economic preferences' because they contain an altruistic motive and should therefore not be used for cost–benefit exercises (Milgrom, 1993), this procedure of 'cooling down' the altruistic motive might offer a way out. Further refinement of our method could even lead to a better distinction between the different components of 'altruism'. One could as well argue, however, that 'warm glow' is a legitimate component of WTP and should therefore not be disregarded. Since our results suggest that the problems with the embedding effect do not necessarily point to inconsistent response behaviour but can be explained by the existence of a stable and measurable warm-glow component in individual preferences, they also give support to the direct use of the uncorrected original WTP measures.

CONCLUSIONS

An environmental resource asset, such as the conservation of a natural area, provides a wide range of benefits. Generally speaking, the conservation benefits are classified in terms of the natural area's provision of use and non-use service flows. The use benefits, like the name suggests, refer to a set of recreational possibilities that the individuals are able to experience when visiting the natural area, e.g. hiking or simply enjoying the aesthetic satisfaction of being in such natural environment. The non-use benefits refer to the set of activities – not necessarily associated with any human use – that the natural area is also able to provide, e.g. areas closed to the general public and created to guarantee the protection of the local biodiversity in their natural habitat. Different valuation instruments are available to the researcher as to assess such conservation benefits. CVM is an important valuation technique and since it is the only one capable of assessing the value of the non-use benefits – which are characterised by having no behavioural market trace – therefore, economists cannot glean information regarding these values by merely relying on market-based valuation approaches. Today the CVM method is a well-known benefit valuation technique of non-market goods and services and is widely used within the framework of cost–benefit analysis and natural damage assessment. The CVM method consists of implementing a market with the help of a survey directed to the individual consumer. The principal idea underlying this method is that individuals not only have preferences defined over the described environmental good, but also are capable of transforming these preferences into monetary units. In the present work, we present the link of contingent valuation method to standard economic theory as well as carry out a survey on CVM, discussing the state-of-art survey design guidelines. The overall goal is to ensure the validity of the proposed survey as a measurement instrument. In the valuation exercise, we are particularly interested in the study of possible behavioural incentives underlying respondent's behaviour, paying particular attention to strategic behavioural issues, such as free-riding, and the purchase of warm glow. Free-riding and the purchase of warm-glow display opposite effects on individual respondent's bidding. Whereas free-riding is characterised by an incentive to understate individual willlingness to pay, the presence of warm-glow signals the occurrence of a potential overpledging. Recent attempts to introduce attitudinal information into the analysis of CV answers reveal the warm-glow effect has an important influence on the WTP answers seems to be rather robust. The use of direct attitudinal information may play a crucial role to get a better understanding of the real content of CV answers.

All in all, these developments have led to an increase in popularity of CV methods in recent years. CVM has proven empirically valid in a wide variety of environmental economic problems. It is noteworthy that the city – the place par excellence for both positive and negative externalities – has received far less attention in the great many efforts to introduce CV methods as a powerful analytical tool. This offers a great challenge for research, as almost all issues studied in modern CV analysis are present in urban quality of life, such as conservation issues, ecological diversity, etc. More research would be needed to make CV a well-accepted analytical tool for studying urban quality of life. The prospects are favourable as CV methods incorporate a wealth of solid economic perspectives apparent in urban life.

REFERENCES

Andreoni, J. (1989) 'Giving with Impure Altruism: Applications to Charity and Ricardian Equivalence', *Journal of Political Economy*, 97: 1447–1458.

Andreoni, J. (1990) 'Impure Altruism and Donations to Public Goods', *The Economical Journal*, 100: 464–477.

Bateman, I.J., Langford, I.H., Willis, K.G., Kerry, R. and Garrod, G.G. (1993) 'The Impacts of Changing Willingness to Pay Question Format in Contingent Valuation Studies', *CSERGE Working Paper*, University of East Anglia and University College London, UK.

Bohm, P. (1972) 'Estimating the Demand for Public Goods: An Experiment', *European Economic Review*, 3: 111–130.

Braden, J.B. and Koldstad, C.D. (eds) (1991) *Measuring the Demand for Environment Quality*, Elsevier Science Publishers, North-Holland.

Brookshire, D.S., Ives, B.C. and Schulze, W.D. (1976) 'The Valuation of Aesthetic Preferences', *Journal of Environmental Economics and Management*, 3: 325–346.

Cameron, T. A. (1991) 'Interval Estimates of Non-Market Resource Values from Referendum Contingent Valuation Surveys', *Land Economics*, 67(4): 413–421.

Cameron, T. A. and Quiggin, J. (1994) 'Estimation Using Contingent Valuation Data from a Dichotomous Choice with Follow-up Questionnaire', *Journal of Environmental Economics and Management*, 27: 218–234.

Carson, R.T., Hanemann, W.M. and Mitchell, R.C. (1986) 'Determining the Demand for Public Goods by Simulating Referendums at Different Tax Prices', *San Diego Department of Economics Working Paper*, University of California.

Carson, R.T., Mitchell. R.C., Hanemann, W.M., Kopp, R.J., Presser, S. and Ruud, P.A. (1992) 'A Contingent Valuation Study of Lost Passive Use Values Resulting from the Exxon Valdez Oil Spill', *Report Prepared for the Attorney General of the State of Alaska*, Washington.

Carson, R.T., Groves, T. and Machina, M.J. (1999) 'Economic Response to Survey Questions', mimeo, Department of Economics, University of California San Diego, La Jolla, US.

Champ, P.A., Bishop, R.C., Brown, T.C. and McCollum, D.W. (1997) 'Using Donation Mechanism To Value Nonuse Benefits From Public Goods', *Journal of Environmental Economics and Management*, 33: 151–162.

Ciriacy-Wantrup, S.V. (1947) 'Capital Returns from Soil Conservation Practices', *Journal of Farms Economics*, 29: 1180–1190.

Davis, R.K. (1963) 'The Value of Outdoor Recreation: An Economic Study of the Maine Woods', *PhD Dissertation*, Department of Economics, Harvard University.

Farquaharson, R. (1969) *Theory of Voting*, Yale University Press, Yale, US.

Fischhoff, B. and Furby, L. (1988) 'Measuring Values: A Conceptual Framework for Interpreting Transactions with Special Reference to Contingent Valuation of Visibility', *Journal of Risk and Uncertainty*, 1: 147–184.

Gibbard, A. (1973) 'Manipulation of Voting Schemes: A General Approach', *Econometrica*, 41: 587–601.

Green, J.R. and Laffont, J.J. (1978) 'A Sampling Approach to Free Riding Problem', in Agnar Sandmo (ed.), *Essays in Public Economics*, Lexington Books.

Hanemann, M.W., Loomis, J. and Kanninen, B. (1991) 'Statistical Efficiency of Double-bounded Dichotomous Choice Contingent Valuation', *American Journal of Agricultural Economics*, 73(4): 1255–1263.

Hanley, N.D. (1988) 'Using Contingent Valuation to Value Environmental Improvements', *Applied Economics*, 40: 541–549.

Hicks, J.R. (1943) 'The Four Consumer Surpluses', *Review of Economic Studies*, 11(1): 31–41.

Hoehn, J.P. and Randall, A. (1989) 'Too Many Proposals Pass the Benefit Cost Test', *American Economic Review*, 79: 544–551.

Hoevenagel, R. (1992) 'An Assessment of Contingent Valuation Surveys', in S. Navrud (ed.), *Pricing the European Environment*, Oslo, Scandinavian University Press, pp. 177–194.

Kahneman, D. and Knetsch, J.L. (1992) 'Valuing Public Goods: The Purchase of Moral Satisfaction', *Journal of Environmental Economics and Management*, 22(1): 57–70.

Kanninen, B.J. (1995) 'Design of Sequential Experiments for Contingent Valuation Studies', *Journal of Environmental Economics and Management*, 25(1), Part 2, S1–S11.

Kriström, B. (1990) 'A Non-Parametric Approach to the Estimation of Welfare Measures in Discrete Response Valuation Questions', *Land Economics*, 66: 135–139.

Krutilla, J.V. (1967) 'Conservation Reconsidered', *American Economic Review*, 57: 777–786.

Majid, I., Sinden, J.A. and Randall, A. (1983) 'Benefit Evaluation of Increments to Existing Systems of Public Facilities', *Land Economics*, 59(4): 377–392.

Milgrom, P. (1993) 'Is Sympathy an Economic Value? Philosophy, Economics, and the Contingent Valuation Method', in J.A. Hausman (ed.) *Contingent Valuation: A Critical Assessment*, Contributions to Economic Analysis, Chapter XI, North-Holland, New York, US.

Mitchell, R.C. and Carson, R.T. (1989) 'Using Surveys to Value Public Goods. The Contingent Valuation Method', Washington DC, Resources for the Future, p. 97.

Mitchell, R.C. and Carson, R.T. (1993) 'Current Issues in the Design, Administration, and Analysis of Contingent Valuation Surveys', *San Diego Department of Economics Working Paper*, University of California.

National Oceanic and Atmospheric Administration (NOAA) (1993) 'Report of the NOAA Panel on Contingent Valuation', *Federal Register*, 58(10): 4601–4614.

Navrud, S. (1992) *Pricing the European Environment*. Oslo, Scandinavian University Press/Oxford University Press.

Nunes, P.A.L.D. (2002) 'The Contingent Valuation of Natural Parks: Assessing the Warmglow Propensity Factor', *New Horizons in Environmental Economics Series*, Edward Elgar Publishing, UK.

Nunes, P.A.L.D. (2005) 'Payment Schemes, Signalling and Warm Glow: An illustration of the Joint Characteristic Model to a CV Exercise', in C.S. Russell and S. Krarup (eds) *Environment, Information and Consumer Behaviour, New Horizons in Environmental Economics Series*, Edward Elgar Publishing, UK.

Nunes, P.A.L.D. and Schokkaert, E. (2003) 'Identifying the Warm Glow Effect in Contingent Valuation', *Journal of Environmental Economics and Management*, 45: 231–245.

Randall, A., Ives, B. and Eastman, C. (1974), 'Bidding Games for Valuation of Aesthetic Environmental Improvements', *Journal of Environmental Economics and Management*, 1: 132–149.

Samples, K.C., Dixon, J.A. and Gowen, M.M. (1986) 'Information Disclosure and Endangered Species Valuation', *Land Economics*, 62(3): 306–312.

Samuelson, P. (1954) 'The Pure Theory of Public Expenditure', *Review of Economics and Statistics*, 36(4): 387–389.

Satterthwaite, M. (1975) 'Strategic-Proofness and Arrow Conditions: Existence and Correspondence Theorems for Voting Procedures and Welfare Functions', *Journal of Economic Theory*, 10: 187–217.

Sinden, J.A. (1988) 'Empirical Tests of Hypothetical Bias in Consumers' Surplus Surveys', *Australian Journal of Agricultural Economics*, 32: 98–112.

Tversky, A. and Kahneman, D. (1973) 'Availability: A Heuristic for Judging Frequency and Probability', *Cognitive Psychology*, 5: 207–232.

United States Department of Interior (USDI) (1989) District of Columbia Circuit Court of Appeals, Re-interpretation of the Comprehensive Environmental Response, Compensation and Liability Act of 1986.

Woo, L.G. (1996) *Out of Site, Out of Mind: A Contingent Valuation Analysis of the Siting of a Sanitary Landfill*, University of North Carolina, Raleigh.

9

The Hedonic Price Method
René van der Kruk

INTRODUCTION

The hedonic price method is commonly applied in real estate economics in order to determine the added value of housing characteristics on parcel and housing sales prices. In environmental economics, the hedonic price model is used as a revealed preference economic valuation method. Application of the hedonic price method yields estimates of the implicit prices of the quality of environmental functions. For example, Harrison and Rubinfeld (1978) analyse the relation between housing prices and air quality, while Leggett and Bockstael (2000) consider the impact of water quality on residential land prices.

In this chapter the most fundamental features of environmental valuation using the hedonic price method are discussed. This chapter is structured as follows. In the Section 'The Hedonic Price Method', the hedonic price theory is discussed and a three-stage approach is introduced that can be followed in the application of the hedonic price method. In the Section 'Valuing Land Use Patterns Using the Hedonic Price Method' the focus is on important issues that arise if the hedonic price method is used in order to determine the impact of land-use patterns on parcel and housing transaction prices: spatial-temporal heterogeneity; multicollinearity; and spatial autocorrelation. In the Section 'Application: Economic Valuation of Dutch Wetlands' the hedonic price method is applied to determine the impact of the presence of Dutch wetlands on the transaction prices of neighboring houses. This chapter ends with the main conclusions in the Section 'Conclusions'.

THE HEDONIC PRICE METHOD

A price index of 'usefulness and desirability'
Consider two products that are exactly identical in all respects with the exception of a single characteristic. The difference between the selling prices of these two commodities is assumed to reflect the revealed willingness to pay for this distinctive feature. For example, consider a passenger car that is for sale on the market with and without a voice navigation system. In this case the difference between the sales price of a car with the voice navigation system and the market price of an identical

car without this attribute reflects the willingness of customers to spend extra money for this distinguishing feature.

In the general case, in which goods or services differ along several dimensions, one may seek to identify the monetary effect of each and every attribute. The pioneering analysis of this problem dates back to Court (1939). Inspired by utilitarianism, Court sought to determine the potential contribution of a commodity to the welfare and happiness of its purchasers and the community (see Goodman, 1998). Court introduced the term 'hedonic' to describe the weighting of the relative importance of various automobile components, such as horsepower, braking capacity, and window area, in constructing a price index of 'usefulness and desirability'.

Most of the recent work in environmental valuation literature using hedonic price models is based on an article by Rosen (1974), who provides a theoretical model to analyse hedonic markets in a perfectly competitive setting. Consider a housing market setting. Buyers and builders of houses are assumed to have heterogeneous preferences and productivities. Let z be an attribute vector characterizing dwellings. $p(z)$ is the market price of a property with characteristics z. Equilibrium in the hedonic market requires that housing supply and demand are equal at each vector z. For each value of z, the equilibrium price of the corresponding property depends on the distribution of the preferences of the consumers and the technologies of the builders. See Rosen (1974) for a formal theoretical hedonic price model.

The next section gives a description of the three stages that are part of an empirical application of the hedonic price method.

Applying the hedonic price method

A typical application of the hedonic price approach consists of three consecutive stages. The first stage of a hedonic price analysis is the identification and delineation of a class of homogeneous products. At the same time, these products should be sufficiently heterogeneous, i.e. to such an extent that there is a sufficient number of degrees of freedom in order to be able to analyse the price effect of distinctive features. If the goods or services are not distinctive with respect to certain features, the identification of implicit prices of these particular attributes is not possible. From an economic perspective, a straightforward approach is to select products that serve a single 'generic need', a term which is used often in the marketing literature. If this class covers a range of products which is too broad, one could decide to narrow down the range of products by focusing on a subclass or even a set of brands or types of products within a subclass. For example, a voice navigation system adds value to a passenger car. However, the same attribute will not serve any need if it is built into a formula one racing car.

In the second stage of the hedonic price method, all attributes of the chosen class of homogeneous products should be identified and quantified in physical terms. Moreover, even in this early stage of the hedonic analysis, it is often useful to construct summary statistics of the characteristics, including a table with sample correlation coefficients.

In the third stage of the hedonic price method, one tries to isolate the impact of each product characteristic on the price of a single unit of this product class from the influence of all other features of the same commodity. Such a decomposition of a transaction price can be particularly problematic if several product features are closely related to each other. For example, the maximum speed limit of a sports car is strongly linked to its design and engineering. This means that it is extremely difficult to determine the pure or supplementary value of the maximum speed limit by splitting the price effect of this feature from both design and engineering of the car. The values of the correlation coefficients mentioned above should give an indication of the difficulties one can expect to encounter in a multiple regression analysis.

VALUING LAND-USE PATTERNS USING THE HEDONIC PRICE METHOD

Introduction

If the hedonic price method is applied to urban planning, one often encounters theoretical and empirical problems that are related to the spatial context of the economic valuation problem. Several of the issues discussed above will be illustrated here in a spatial framework of land-use patterns.

There are three econometric issues that are particularly important in connection with the economic valuation of land-use patterns by means of hedonic models: spatial-temporal heterogeneity, multicollinearity, and spatial autocorrelation. These concepts are discussed below.

Spatial-temporal heterogeneity

The identification and delineation of a set of dwellings is not straightforward in a housing market context. Estimation results of hedonic price models are usually dependent on the choice of the type of house (e.g. single-family home, apartment), the type of area (e.g. urban, sub-urban, greenbelt, or agricultural area), the time period, and the spatial scale of the study. Therefore, it is important to take account of the possible presence of spatial-temporal heterogeneity or variation of model parameters. This heterogeneity is caused by factors which have an effect on supply and demand. Examples of these causes are volatility over time of mortgage interest rates and local excess housing demand due to spill-over effects from land-use zoning regulations in nearby districts. Housing market prices may, however, also be different because of heterogeneous housing preferences of residents.

Each house can be described by two categories of features: physical attributes and neighborhood characteristics. Physical attributes concern the internal features of a property, e.g. lot size, number of rooms, length of the garden, and type of garage. Neighborhood characteristics comprise the social, cultural, economic, and environmental background of the surrounding area of the house. This area can be the housing block, street, district, or city in which the house is located, depending on the scale of the spatial impact of the feature. For example, the presence of both urban green and air quality levels might be local factors of great importance for the value of a house, while the accessibility of natural areas, business parks, and airports are more likely to have an effect within a region. In summary, housing prices are a reflection of the preferences of potential buyers with respect to physical and neighborhood features of properties.

As a consequence of the latter observation, if neighborhood properties of houses vary over space, people will seek to move to those areas that best match their wishes. Whether or not an individual housing consumer will succeed in buying a house within this region will depend on his or her purchasing power. Thus, preferences of consumers over housing attributes will be reflected in a spatial pattern of housing prices.

Multicollinearity

The danger of multicollinearity is acknowledged by Belsey (1976), Maddala (1979), and Stewart (1984). Fickel (2000, 2001) reasons that if the degree of multicollinearity is high, partial coefficients are not only very bad measures of influence but even useless.

In the third stage of the hedonic price method, the individual impact of each attribute on the housing price has to be estimated. It was argued above that such a decomposition of the transaction price is challenging if a number of features are closely related to one another. By definition, the fundamental feature of the sale of a property with multiple attributes is that a combination of housing attributes is provided simultaneously in a package deal. In hedonic price analysis, this issue is particularly relevant for the incorporation of amenity effects of neighborhood variables, since these effects are often spatially interconnected.

For example, there is a positive relation between the presence of natural areas and good air and water quality levels in close proximity of these regions. Moreover, if a wetland or forest is characterized by a beautiful landscape as well as by a diverse animal and plant life, it makes the area an ideal location for recreation and tourism. As another example, consider people living in the city center of Amsterdam. They are surrounded by several positive externalities such as scenic views of canals and the proximity of shopping areas, theatres, and the city concert hall. One can also think of negative externalities that are associated. Hanley and Spash (1993) note that if a house is sited near a quarry both dust and noise levels are closely correlated with each other. Correlations in housing characteristics obscure a clear analysis of the influence of a single explanatory variable on property prices. The additional influence of housing variables can be determined only by taking account of this correlation.

Leaving characteristics out of the set of correlated neighborhood variables will often generate spatial autocorrelation in the disturbance terms of the regression model. This issue will be discussed in the next section. Moreover, it will lead to omitted variable bias of implicit price estimates of the remaining regressors. For example, if one would like to determine the added value of accessibility of the main railway station in the central business district of a major city, one should bear in mind that this accessibility index will probably be correlated with a host of other (positive externality) neighborhood variables. Even if the pure or supplementary price effect of the railway station would be negative, for example due to high noise levels, the partial effect of the accessibility index could be found to be positive.

Spatial autocorrelation

Another important issue in the hedonic price analysis of land and housing markets is related to the influence of unobserved spatial variables on property prices. 'Spatial autocorrelation' is the term that is used in spatial econometrics (see, for example, Cliff and Ord, 1981; Anselin, 1988; and Cressie, 1993) to describe the case in which the covariance between spatial variables is not equal to zero for different spatial units. In the spatial economic context of the hedonic price method these spatial units are parcels or dwellings. If the spatial arrangement of the values of unobserved variables is not random, the disturbance terms of the hedonic price model are correlated. If spatial autocorrelation is present in the disturbance terms, one of the Gauss-Markov assumptions of the classical linear regression model is violated. As a result, ordinary least squares estimates of the classical linear regression model are inefficient. Moran's I, Lagrange Multiplier, Wald, and Likelihood Ratio tests can be applied to detect the presence of spatial autocorrelation (see Anselin, 1988).

If spatial autocorrelation is confirmed by the test results, spatial models can be used to improve estimation of the hedonic price analysis. Spatial models include terms that account for the presence of spatial autocorrelation between disturbance terms. The identification problem of such a spatial model is very similar to the one frequently encountered in the estimation of simultaneous equations models. Spatial weight or link matrices are used to structure relations between spatial units.

In hedonic price analysis, the elements of these matrices are often based on the distance between spatial units. See Hordijk (1974), Cliff and Ord (1981), and Stetzer (1982) for more information on spatial weight matrices.

APPLICATION: ECONOMIC VALUATION OF DUTCH WETLANDS

In the next paragraph the results will be discussed of an application of the hedonic price method with the aim of determining the housing price effect of Dutch wetlands. In the Section 'A Literature review', a review of the impact of wetlands on property prices is presented. In the Section 'Data', the data are described. In the Section 'Ordinary least squares estimation results', multiple regression model results are presented. The issues of multicollinearity and spatial autocorrelation are addressed in the Sections 'Multicollinearity' and 'Spatial autocorrelation' respectively.

A literature review

The hedonic pricing technique has been applied only a few times to value wetland functions, i.e. amenity values for local residents. Thibodeau and Ostro (1981) use this method to value wetlands in Massachusetts's Charles River Basin. They find that these wetlands add value to adjacent properties. Batie and Mabbs-Zeno (1985) estimate the opportunity cost of prohibiting the development of recreational housing lots in order to preserve the wetlands at Captain's Cove, Virginia. Lupi et al. (1991) value wetlands in Ramsey County, Minnesota. They apply the hedonic price method by including a variable that expresses the total wetland acreage in a property's section. Doss and Taff (1996) argue that since the data used by Lupi et al. do not include point location data a relationship between the distance to a wetland and the value of a property can not be estimated. Because Doss and Taff do have such data they are able to value the proximity to several types of wetlands in Ramsey County, Minnesota, as expressed by housing prices. These authors estimate distance parameters to express the marginal value of houses, which are located 10 and 200 meters closer to a wetland. Leggett and Bockstael (2000) consider waterfront property sales in Anne Arundel County, Chesapeake Bay, Maryland. They estimate both non-spatial and spatial models that include, among other land use categories, a variable corresponding to the percentage of wetland within 3/4 mile of a house. Mahan et al. (2000) estimate the relationship between property prices and wetlands in the Portland metropolitan area, Oregon. Bin and Polasky (2002) analyse the effect of coastal and inland wetlands in Carteret County, North Carolina on nearby residential property values. They find a positive (negative) relationship between proximity to coastal (inland) wetlands and nearby property prices. However, the authors admit that the total amount of wetland near the property would probably be more relevant than the distance to the nearest wetland and its size.

Data

The data that are used for the hedonic pricing analysis in this chapter cover large and distinctive parts of the Netherlands. The study area, which is shown in Figure 9.1, is about 170 × 225 km. It includes both highly populated areas such as the *Randstad* (metropolitan area that includes the cities of Amsterdam, The Hague, Rotterdam, and Utrecht) and regions with relatively low population densities in the north of the country. The following data from the year 1996 are used:

- housing transaction data from NVM (Dutch Association of Real Estate Agents);
- land-use data from CBS (Statistics Netherlands);
- land-use data from Alterra (a research institute in Wageningen, the Netherlands);
- a zip code map from Geodan (a firm using GIS techniques);

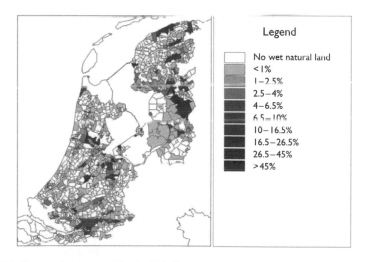

Figure 9.1 Shares of wet natural land within Dutch zip code areas

- cadastral data from Kadaster (Dutch land registry office); and
- employment figures on a district level from LISA (a Dutch foundation that supplies these data primarily for research and policy issues).

Address information of individual property transactions are linked to spatial point (x, y) coordinates using cadastral data. Sequentially, these coordinates can be used to calculate percentages of land-use classes within certain distance ranges of the house. Alternatively, a zip code map can be used to construct shares of land-use categories within zip code areas. In this case, each dwelling within the same zip code area is assigned similar neighborhood characteristics. Note that this method is less accurate that the one mentioned above as it does not use exact point coordinates of properties. However, most zip code areas in the study area are relatively small and homogeneous with respect to land-use classes. Figure 9.1 depicts the shares of wet natural land within a zip code area of the study area. The Statistics Netherlands definition of wet natural land includes nature reserves and other natural areas such as wet heathlands, peat bogs, salt marshes, and surrounding waters that are narrower than 20 m or smaller than 2 ha. Note the spatial distribution of wet natural land over the country. Most of the wetlands in the western part of the country have disappeared over time because of human (peat) exploitation. The *Naardermeer* (lake near the city of Naarden) is one of the few remaining wetlands in the *Randstad* metropolitan area.

The big wetland in the south (*De Biesbosch*) was created in 1421 during a heavy storm with spring tide. Other wetlands including *De Weerribben* and *Bargerveen* can be found in the northern parts of the Netherlands.

Apart from the land-use data from Statistics Netherlands, geographical land-use data from Alterra are used in this chapter. Currently, Alterra is the owner of four land-use databases which span a time period from 1986 to the year 2000, which are called LGN 1 through LGN 4, where LGN (Landelijk Grondgebruiksbestand Nederland) stands for national land-use database for the Netherlands. Data from the third version of LGN are used in this chapter. LGN 3 is based on observations from the years 1995 and 1997. The LGN data have a category 'natural areas', which includes wetlands such as salt marshes in coastal areas, raised bogs, swamps, and peat meadow areas.

Ordinary least squares estimation results

In this section the ordinary least squares estimation results of a multiple regression model of Dutch property values is presented. Within the hedonic price framework, the property transaction price (in thousands of euros) is regressed on housing characteristics. The average value of transaction prices of all other houses within the same zip code area as the house under consideration is also included as an explanatory variable. It represents the overall housing price level within a clearly defined spatial submarket that is characterized by specific supply and demand conditions. In addition, there are no less than 28 independent variables that provide shares of land-use categories in the zip code area. Moreover, there is a variable that contains information regarding employment on a district level.

Table 9.1 shows the ordinary least squares estimates. The average price level within a district is a key explanatory variable. The monthly dummy parameters pick up the gradual upward trend in housing prices in 1996. The construction quality of Dutch houses differed quite a lot over the 20th century. In the period between the First and the Second World War (1918 until 1940) the quality of new houses was relatively good. After the Second World War the issue of quality was of secondary importance because of large-scale housing shortages. The model parameters confirm these observations. All garage type dummy parameters are positive. The built-in garage is clearly preferred. Insufficient or even bad (outside) maintenance reduces the value of a house. The presence of a (maintained) garden is also contributing to the housing price, especially if its length is over 15 m. The sales condition dummy parameter is positive and the variable lease dummy parameter is negative as expected. Both capacity and parcel size do not add much value to the price. However, the number of rooms seems to be an important price determinant. The through room dummy parameter does not have the expected (positive) sign. However, the room and suite combination is indeed valued positively. The fact that a house is a monument increases the transaction price by about 40,000 euros. A small proportion of houses have more than one bathroom. The fact that a house has a gas fire, i.e. no central heating, has a negative impact on the price. A fireplace has a positive added value.

Employment is an important explanatory variable of the housing price. For an additional number of 1000 jobs in a district the average price of a house goes up with approximately 40 euros. The parameters that correspond to the presence of wet natural land are insignificant. However, the parameter of the land-use category 'other waters broader than six meters' is positive. While water reservoirs seem to have a positive impact on housing prices, waters with a recreational function do not. Other land-use variables such as car-wreckage lands and, remarkably, parks and public gardens have a negative impact on the price. Positive externalities correspond to the presence of long-stay recreation sites, dry natural land, and even dumping sites.

Table 9.2 contains the model statistics. The addition of 28 land-use variables by definition improves the fit of the hedonic price model to 0.71. F-tests reject the joint hypothesis that the parameters of the land-use variables are equal to zero.

Table 9.1 OLS regression results of the hedonic housing price model

Variable	Parameter	t-value	Variable	Parameter	t-value
Constant	−12.18	−54.19	*Other variables (continued)*		
Average price level in district[1]	0.47	74.78	Capacity (cubic meters)	0.12	83.34
Month dummy[2]			Parcel size (square meters / 10^3)	6.07	36.53
January	−11.93	−11.08	Number of rooms	7.83	37.04
February	−11.40	−10.61	Through room dummy[3]	−4.82	−9.47
March	−9.02	−8.43	Room and suite dummy[4]	7.41	7.08
April	−6.72	−6.21	Monument dummy[5]	37.09	15.02
May	−5.76	−5.41	Number of bathrooms	14.26	28.96
June	−3.83	−3.62	Gas fire dummy	−7.08	−9.33
July	−4.64	−4.33	Fireplace dummy	15.41	26.66
August	−3.33	−3.05	*Employment*		
September	−2.53	−2.34	Employment (thousands of jobs)	0.04	39.28
October	−1.16	−1.11	*Wetland variables*		
November	0.16	0.15	Wet natural land	2.02	0.30
Construction year dummy[6]			Other waters broader than 6 m	26.89	6.97
Constructed in the 1910s	−0.27	−0.20	*Water-related variables*		
Constructed in the 1920s	0.39	0.35	Water reservoir	203.10	2.44
Constructed in the 1930s	4.33	4.11	Water with recreational function	−13.10	−0.83
Constructed in the 1940s	−0.23	−0.09	*Other land use variables*		
Constructed in the 1950s	−2.64	−2.09	Cultivation under glass	21.29	6.63
Constructed in the 1960s	−6.45	−5.87	Forest	20.64	8.20
Constructed in the 1970s	−5.56	−5.39	Residential area	18.49	17.71
Constructed after 1979	5.32	5.29	Extraction of minerals	116.81	2.94
Type of garage dummy			Industrial area	6.31	1.80
Undetached stone garage	29.36	41.24	Service facilities	16.22	2.67
Detached stone garage	21.94	30.34	Other public facilities	15.68	1.28

Wooden garage	12.20	8.26	Socio-cultural facilities	45.06	7.21
Built-in garage[7]	33.54	34.72	Railway	39.53	4.34
Maintenance dummy			Asphalted road	−8.08	−1.16
Insufficient maintenance inside	−6.54	−3.41	Unpaved road	−284.50	−1.73
Bad maintenance inside	−9.94	−2.06	Airport	−27.17	−0.42
Insufficient maintenance outside	−12.17	−5.67	Park or public garden	−16.58	−3.68
Bad maintenance outside	−20.76	−3.95	Sports park	13.47	2.57
Garden length dummy			Day trip location	39.75	3.81
5–10 m garden	1.20	1.40	Allotment gardens	36.71	1.92
10–15 m garden	3.99	4.57	Long-stay recreation site	158.52	5.09
15–20 m garden	20.20	19.19	Dry natural land	32.12	9.31
20–50 m garden	37.25	30.68	Dumping land	293.99	4.54
> 50 m garden	64.12	34.49	Car wreckage land	−590.62	−3.73
Other variables			Cemetery	18.31	0.95
Sales condition dummy[8]	14.38	5.09	Construction site (firms)	5.63	0.38
Fixed lease dummy[9]	0.57	0.55	Construction site (other)	−8.21	−1.21

[1] The average price level within a district allows for specific local housing market conditions such as scarcity and unobserved neighborhood characteristics (e.g. crime).
[2] The monthly dummy variables are included in order to correct for structural price changes over time. December 1996 is the default month.
[3] 26 percent of houses in the Netherlands have a through room so that inhabitants can enjoy the presence of the sun for a long time during the day.
[4] Approximately 6 percent of Dutch houses have a room and suite.
[5] Only about 1 percent of all houses are on the list of monuments.
[6] The construction year dummies allow for heterogeneity in prices of houses built in different time periods due to distinctive quality levels, materials used, designs, etc.
[7] About 6 percent of the houses have a garage that is part of the house.
[8] The dummy sales condition refers to the buy and sales conditions where the seller of the house pays the conveyance tax and notarial and land register costs. These costs are about 8 percent of the price (10,650 euros in case of an average transaction price). The dummy variable equals one in the rare case when the costs are not paid by the buyer.
[9] The dummies fixed and variable lease refer to the long-term lease costs if the land is leased from the local government. Approximately 7 percent (1%) of the Dutch transactions have a fixed (variable) lease contract.

Multicollinearity

Although the inclusion of land-use variables improves the fit of the model, it is more likely to suffer from the presence of multicollinearity. The sample correlation coefficients of wetland variables and other explanatory variables reveal that the share of wet natural land within an area is positively related to the presence of other waters broader than

Table 9.2 OLS regression model statistics

Model statistics	
Number of observations	36,491
Number of regressors	75
Standard error of the regression	39,869
R^2	0.71
Adjusted R^2	0.71
Sum of squared residuals	5.79E+13
Log likelihood	-438,303
Mean-dependent variable	133,190
Standard deviation–dependent variable	74,232
Akaike criterion	24.03
Schwarz criterion	24.04
F	1217.34
p-value corresponding to F	0.0000

6 m and unpaved roads. Moreover, it is negatively related to residential dwellings, parks and public gardens, socio-cultural facilities, asphalted roads, and employment within the same area.

The presence of multicollinearity is analysed using an approach suggested by Fickel (2000). The total price effect, i.e. the parameter of a linear regression of a single variable on housing prices, of the share of 'wet natural land' within a zip code area is negative. By definition, the total price effect of the wetland variable is the sum of its pure or supplementary effect and a number of other effects which are present due to the multicollinearity between the wetland variable and other regressors. The supplementary effect of 'wet natural land' is found to be, only slightly, positive. The fact that the relationship between housing prices and wet natural lands in the Netherlands, as expressed by the total effect, is negative is caused by the lack of the presence of positive amenity effects of dry natural land, forests, and employment possibilities in wet natural areas. In other words, even though the pure amenity effect of wetland functions is positive, the absence of other positive neighborhood features within the same areas dominates the price effect. Thus, shares of wetlands are found to be negatively correlated with housing prices in a simple linear regression model. In summary, by isolating the pure effect of wetland variables it can be shown that the average transaction price levels of dwellings in Dutch wetland areas are positively influenced by wetland amenities.

Spatial autocorrelation

The estimated error terms of the ordinary least squares hedonic price model can be used to test for spatial autocorrelation. Using different model specifications, the null hypothesis of no spatial autocorrelation is rejected by a Lagrange Multiplier test.

Therefore, a spatial hedonic price model with an autoregressive error structure is estimated using maximum likelihood estimation.

Using either CBS or Alterra land-use data, the share of 'wet natural land' or 'natural areas' is added as an independent variable to the physical attributes of the house, while all other land-use variables are left out of the model. Using spatial coordinates, wetland shares are calculated for circular areas within a distance of 50, 125, 250, or 500 m from a dwelling. The first (last) two numbers out of this set of four roughly correspond to viewing (walking) distances. The housing price impact of wet natural areas as defined by Statistics Netherlands is slightly positive and statistically different from zero for the 125- and 250-m distance parameters of the spatial model. If the natural areas variable as defined by Alterra is used the transaction price effect is found to be positive and statistically significant for all distance parameters.

CONCLUSIONS

The hedonic price method is a useful tool in assessing the usefulness and desirability of certain land-use patterns. In particular, it is possible to determine the revealed willingness to pay for neighborhood characteristics. Sustainable urban development can be achieved only if residential preferences for environmental, natural, and ecological quality are taken into account.

In this chapter, the hedonic price method is discussed and applied to determine the impact of Dutch wetlands on the housing price of surrounding properties. It is argued that the amenity effect of wetlands can only be determined within a general land-use framework, as certain land-use combinations often rule out other patterns. Evidence is presented that both multicollinearity and spatial autocorrelation are important econometric problems in hedonic models. The economic importance and value of neighborhood characteristics of residential areas can only be determined if these issues are dealt with adequately. It is found that the share of wetlands within an area is 10 percent, and that their functions add approximately 2–7 percent to the value of nearby houses, depending on the distance range and the wetland definition used.

REFERENCES

Anselin, L. (1988). *Spatial Econometrics: Methods and Models*. Kluwer Academic Publishers, Dordrecht.

Batie, S.S. and Mabbs-Zeno, C. C. (1985). 'Opportunity costs of preserving coastal wetlands: A case study of a recreational housing development'. *Land Economics* 61(1): 1–9.

Belsey, D.A. (1976). 'Multicollinearity: Diagnosing the presence and assessing the potential damage it causes least-squares estimation'. *NBER Working Paper Series No. 154*.

Bin, O. and Polasky, S. (2002). *Valuing Coastal Wetlands: A Hedonic Property Price Approach*. Department of Economics, East Carolina University, Greenville, NC.

Cliff, A.D. and Ord, J.K. (1981). *Spatial Processes: Models and Applications*. Pion Limited, London.

Court, A.T. (1939). 'Hedonic price indexes with automotive examples'. *The Dynamics of Automobile Demand*. General Motors Corp., New York.

Cressie, N. (1993). *Statistics for Spatial Data*. Wiley, NY.

Doss, C.R. and Taff, S.J. (1996). 'The influence of wetland type and wetland proximity on residential property values'. *Journal of Agricultural and Resource Economics* 21(1): 120–129.

Fickel, N. (2000). 'Sequential regression: A neodescriptive approach to multicollinearity'. The paper is downloadable from http://www.lsw.wiso.uni-erlangen.de/frames/forschung/D0033.pdf

Fickel, N. (2001). *Sequenzialregression: Eine neodeskriptive Lösung des Multikollinearitätsproblems mittels stufenweise bereinigter und synchronisierter Variablen*. University of Erlangen-Nürnberg, Berlin: Verlag für Wissenschaft und Forschung.

Goodman, A.C. (1998). 'Andrew Court and the invention of hedonic price analysis'. *Journal of Urban Economics* 44: 291–298.

Hanley, N. and Spash, C. (1993). *Cost Benefit Analysis and the Environment*. Edward Elgar Publishing, England.

Harrison, D. and Rubinfeld, D.L. (1978). 'Hedonic housing prices and the demand for clean air'. *Journal of Environmental Economics and Management* 5: 81–102.

Hordijk, L. (1974). 'Spatial correlation in the disturbances of a linear interregional model'. *Regional and Urban Economics* 4: 117–140.

Leggett, C.G. and Bockstael, N.E. (2000). 'Evidence of the effects of water quality on residential land prices'. *Journal of Environmental Economics and Management* 39(2): 121–144.

Lupi, F., Graham-Tomasi, T. and Taff, S.J. (1991). 'A hedonic approach to urban wetland valuation'. *Staff Paper* P91–98. Department of Agricultural and Applied Economics, University of Minnesota, St. Paul, Minnesota.

Maddala, G.S. (1979). *Econometrics*. McGraw Hill, Tokyo.

Mahan, B.L., Polasky, S. and Adams, R.M. (2000). 'Valuing urban wetlands: A property price approach'. *Land Economics* 76(1): 100–113.

Rosen, S. (1974). 'Hedonic prices and implicit markets: Product differentiation in pure competition'. *Journal of Political Economy* 82: 34–55.

Stetzer, F. (1982). 'Specifying weights in spatial forecasting models: The results of some experiments'. *Environment and Planning A* 14(5): 571–584.

Stewart, J. (1984). *Understanding Econometrics*. Hutchison, London.

Thibodeau, F.R. and Ostro, B.D. (1981). 'An economic analysis of wetland protection'. *Journal of Environmental Management* 12: 19–30.

Part 4

Methods for Environmental, Economic and Social Assessments

Part 4.1

Simple, Complex and Advanced Evaluations

10

The Analytic Hierarchy Process

Patrizia Lombardi

INTRODUCTION

Decision-making at different planning (both regional and local) levels is usually concerned with evaluation of alternatives and selection of a preferred action. The alternatives can also vary in their type of effects and in the intensity of them.

This process can be improved via the use of Multicriteria analysis (MCA) which provides a systematic process for trading off effects of various alternatives, taking into account all the aspects and values involved in the decision and synthesising individual contributions. Originally developed in the field of Operations Research, discrete MCA is able to determine lists of priorities from a finite series of choice options (alternatives) which are assessed and compared in relation to identified characteristics of the problem (criteria) when it is appropriately broken down into its fundamental elements (Voogd, 1983).

Compared with cost–benefit analysis, MCA does not require a quantification of the services rendered by the resources in monetary terms but only cardinal and/or ordinal score indices to be assigned when comparing the alternatives with the criteria and when weighting the criteria considered in the assessment (Arrow and Raynard, 1986). In MCA the measure of benefits are not related to the concept of 'willingness to pay' but to the 'goal achievement level', which involves the evaluation of performance against a number of criteria. Both performance and criteria can only be defined by a value-based judgement; they are not empirically verifiable. Indeed, the term performance must be a goal-oriented behaviour, i.e. a behaviour rendered meaningful by the existence of a criterion that specifies when a goal has been attained (Francescato, 1991).

In particular, MCA provides the following benefits: a clear definition of the criteria used in the selection of an option between alternative solutions; a weighting of the criteria to be used in the evaluation, in accordance with different point of views; a combination of multiple aspects which have a different nature; a comparison between objectives, strategies of the various subjects involved, and available resources; a transparent and explicit evaluation approach (Roy and Bouyssou, 1993).

By taking into account different point of views and a weighting of the criteria to be used in the evaluation of alternative options, MCA provides the possibility to realise a meaningful and pluralistic evaluation of planning proposals, synthesising all the contributions of the different experts and the point of views of the actors involved (stakeholders and decision-makers).

In the field of planning evaluation, the most applied MCA methods are of a 'discrete' type since they are able to manage a limited number of alternatives, corresponding to few projects, and multiple indicators, quantitative and qualitative in nature. Decision-makers can express their views, assigning individual preferences to the various criteria of evaluation. Therefore, discussion and negotiations should be encouraged where exponents of different groups of opinion, political currents and lobbies, as well as the promoters and executors of the proposed actions, may be represented.

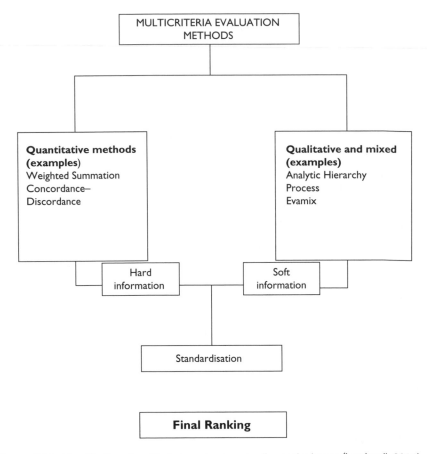

Figure 10.1 Classification of multicriteria methods according to the inputs (Lombardi, 2001)

Literature presents a wide range of MCA methods which can be grouped in families, as quantitative, qualitative and mixed (Hinloopen *et al.*, 1983; Voogd, 1983; Nijkamp *et al.*, 1990; Bazzani *et al.*, 1993; Bentivegna *et al.*, 1994; Bravi and Lombardi, 1994; Lombardi, 1995; Fusco Girard and Nijkamp, 1997; Lombardi, 2001; Roscelli, 2005). These differ from each other in the nature of information they are able to manage, i.e. cardinal (hard), ordinal (soft) or mixed data (see Figure 10.1).

Following this typology, a well-known example of a mixed-data method is the *Analytic Hierarchy Process* (AHP model), developed by Saaty (1980, 1992, 1993, 1994, 1995, 1996a, 2001) which translates expert judgements in a 9 points-scale, providing cardinal indices for operationalizing.

This chapter specifically focuses on this method. It illustrates the methodological approach (Section 'The methodological approach'), the main examples and fields of application (Section 'Case studies and examples of application') and the recent development of the approach, named 'Analytic Network Process' (Section 'Recent developments').

THE METHODOLOGICAL APPROACH

The mathematician Thomas L. Saaty developed the AHP as an aid to managers in making decisions. Subjective assessments and objective facts are incorporated into a logical hierarchical AHP framework to provide decision-makers with an intuitive and common-sense approach in quantifying the importance of each decision element through a comparison process. This process enables decision-makers to reduce a complex problem to a hierarchical form with several levels (Saaty and Forman, 1993).

The AHP allows the investigation to reach a set of ratings for the decision alternatives by aggregating the relative weights of decision elements. The procedure starts by breaking down the decision problem into a hierarchy of interrelated decision elements. At the top of the hierarchy lies the most macro-decision objective, such as that of selecting the best alternative. The lower levels of the hierarchy contain attributes which contribute to the quality of the decision. Details of these attributes increase at the lower levels of the hierarchy. The last levels of the hierarchy contain decision alternatives.

In setting up the decision hierarchy, the number of levels depends on the complexity of the problem and on the degree of detail the analyst requires to solve the problem. Generally, the hierarchy has at least three levels: goal, criteria and alternatives (Saaty, 1995). Criteria may have sub-criteria (Figure 10.2). Since each level entails pairwise comparison of its elements, Saaty suggests the number of

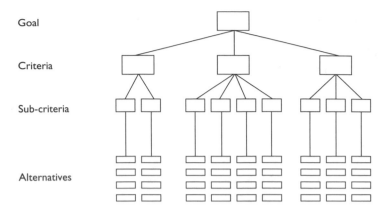

Goal

Criteria

Sub-criteria

Alternatives

Figure 10.2 A hierarchical model structure

elements at each level to be limited at a maximum of nine (Saaty and Vargas, 1987, 1991).

The process starts by determining the relative importance of particular alternatives with respect to the criteria and the sub-criteria (Saaty and Kearns, 1991). Then the criteria are compared with respect to the goal. Finally the results of these two analyses are synthesized by calculating the relative importance of the alternatives with respect to achieving the goal.

The process of comparison is represented by forming a comparative matrix (see Figure 10.3). If the analyst has at his disposal n alternatives, or criteria that form the comparative matrix, then he must make $n(n-1)/2$ evaluations. Pairwise comparison data are collected for only half of the matrix elements: diagonal elements always equal one, and the lower triangle elements of the matrix are the reciprocal of the upper ones.

Pairwise comparisons give to the user a basis to reveal his/her preference by comparing two elements. Furthermore, the user has the option of expressing preferences between the two as equally preferred, weakly preferred, strongly preferred, or absolutely preferred, which would be translated into pairwise weights of 1, 3, 5, 7 and 9, respectively. The numbers 2, 4, 6 and 8 are used as intermediate values when there is not agreement between preferences. The reciprocal numbers $1/2, 1/3, \ldots, 1/8, 1/9$ complete the matrices (see Table 10.1).

The technique of the AHP takes as input the above comparisons and produces the relative weights of elements at each level as output using the 'eigenvalue'

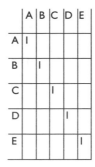

Figure 10.3 Comparative matrix

Table 10.1 The fundamental scale

Intensity of importance	Definition	Explanation
1	Equal importance	Two activities contribute equally to the objective
3	Moderate importance	Experience and judgment slightly favour one activity over another
5	Strong importance	Experience and judgement strongly favour one activity over another
7	Very strong or demostrated importance	An activity is favoured very strongly over another; its dominance is demonstrated in practice
9	Extreme importance	The evidence favouring one activity over another is of the highest possible order of affirmation
2,4,6,8	Intermediate judgments	
Reciprocals of above	If activity i has one of the above non-zero numbers assigned to it when compared with activity j, then j has the reciprocal value when compared with i	
Rationals	Rations arising from the scale	If consistency were to be forced by obtaining n numerical values to span the matrix

method. The eigenvector of each comparative matrix is the priority list, while the eigenvalue gives the measure of consistency in making the assessment or comparison. The synthesized eigenvector is the global sequence of the alternatives with respect to achieving the goal.

The eigenvector and the maximum eigenvalue of the comparative matrix are determined by solving the general problem of eigenvalues:

$$AW = \lambda_{max}W$$

Table 10.2 The Random Inconsistency for different size matrix – IR

Size matrix – n	1	2	3	4	5	6	7	8	9
Random Consistency Index – IR	0	0.52	0.89	1.11	1.25	1.35	1.40	1.45	1.49

where

A = comparative matrix,

$W = (W_1, W_2, W_3, W_4, W_5)^T$ = eigenvector, and

λ_{max} = maximum eigenvalue.

The consistency index (CI) of a matrix of comparisons is given by

$$CI = (\lambda_{max} - n)/n - 1$$

The consistency ratio (CR) is obtained by comparing the CI with the appropriate one of the set of numbers shown in Table 10.2, each of which is an average random consistency index derived from a large sample of randomly generated reciprocal matrices using the scale $1/9, 1/8, \ldots, 1, \ldots, 8, 9$. The resulting vector is accepted if CR is about 0.10 or less. For $n = 3$, it is 0.05 and for $n = 4$, it is 0.08. If it not less that 0.10, study the problem and revise the judgements. The AHP has a systematic procedure for better judgements (Saaty, 1996a).

The last step of the procedure aggregates relative weights of various levels obtained from the previous step in order to produce a vector of composite weights which serves as ratings of decision alternatives in achieving the most general objective of the problem.

The use of AHP is facilitated by the availability of an user-friendly supporting software *Expert Choice* (2000).

CASE STUDIES AND EXAMPLES OF APPLICATION

Because of its flexibility, this approach has been successfully applied in different areas. In the words of Saaty (1996b, p.70), 'It has been used extensively in the economics/management area for auditing, data-base selection, design, architecture, finance, macro-economic forecasting, marketing (consumer choice, product design and development, strategy), planning, portfolio selection, facility location, forecasting, resource allocation (budget, energy, health, project), sequential decisions, policy/strategy, transportation, water research, and performance analysis. In political problems, the AHP has been used in such areas as arms control, conflicts and negotiation, political candidacy, security assessments, war games, and world influence. For social concerns, it is applied in education, behaviour in competition, environmental issues, health, law, medicine (drug effectiveness, therapy selection), population dynamics (interregional migration patterns, population size), and public sector. Some technological applications include market selection, portfolio selection, and technology transfer. Additional applications are discussed in Golden *et al.* (1989), Saaty and Vargas (1994) and Saaty (1990).

In the field of regional and urban planning, including urban regeneration and sustainable development, AHP has been often used for evaluating alternative courses of action and/or design solutions, assessing their impacts on the built and natural environment. A number of Italian contributions can be mentioned, such as Roscelli (1990, 2005), Realfonzo and Barbanente (1992), Fusco Girard and Nijkamp (1997), Lombardi (1997), etc.

In the Italian context, this method has been also suggested in the recent Law for 'Public Work', named 'Merloni' (L.109/1994 and subsequent versions, and the executive document DPR 554/1999), during the bidding stage of the urban development process, as a transparent procedure to be adopted by the public authority for selecting the most appropriate designer (Lombardi, 2001).

A more recent field of application of AHP is risk analysis. This is an evolving activity area which has an evident impact on sustainable development. It is a multicriteria problem in which it is not possible to precisely quantify how alternatives impact decision-making. Mustafa and Al-Bahar (1991), Dey *et al.* (1994), Dey (1999), Dey (2001) and more recently Brandon and Ceric (2005) used the AHP in qualitative risk analysis. A synthetic illustration of the application developed by Brandon and Ceric (2005) is provided as follows.

The risk priority list is calculated in five steps. The first step in applying this model is dividing the problem into one or more criteria which will be used to weight the alternatives offered. This means that it is necessary to define the hierarchical levels: goal, criteria, sub criteria and alternatives (see Figure 10.4).

The second step is forming comparative matrices for all hierarchical levels.

The third step is calculating regional eigenvectors and eigenvalues for the comparative matrices for all hierarchical levels. On the level of criteria the regional eigenvector defines the priority, with respect to weight, of the individual criteria for achieving the goal, while on the level of alternatives the regional eigenvector defines the priority of the alternatives with respect to the given criterion.

The fourth step is calculating the consistency coefficient for each comparative matrix on all levels, and this is determined from the eigenvalue of the comparative matrix. If the consistency coefficient exceeds 0.10, then inconsistent assessments were made in forming the comparative matrices on particular hierarchical levels and

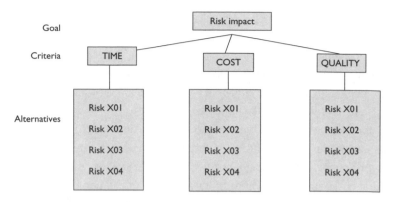

Figure 10.4 Hierarchical structure for risk impact (Brandon and Ceric, 2005)

such matrices must be formed anew. If the consistency coefficient is smaller than 0.10, then it is possible to move on to the next step.

The fifth step is synthesising the calculation results from all levels and weighting each alternative in relation to achieving the goal. The global eigenvector and the global consistency index are calculated. If the global consistency index exceeds 0.10, then inconsistent judgments still exist and the comparative matrices must be redefined. If the consistency index is smaller than 0.10, then the process of defining the weight and interdependency of the alternatives with respect to the given goal has been concluded.

In AHP the risk priority list, that is risk impact on time, cost and quality, is calculated through their comparison. When there is not enough data to quantify particular values a qualitative approach is used. It is therefore more natural and intuitive for the decision-maker to compare those values with one another than to try to determining their edge values, or at least their minimum, most likely, and maximum values. For example, available information and experience often make it easier to assess that an event will do twice more damage than another event, than to try to quantify the extent of the actual damage caused by either or both of them.

The risk exposure of one risk is of no usable value and gains significance only when compared with the risk exposure of one or several other risks. Since the goal parameter in the proposed framework is risk exposure, used to determine risk acceptability and risk response, comparing the elements that make up the risk exposure of all the identified risks in a phase imposes itself as the most natural technique. In AHP no knowledge is necessary of statistics, probability distribution functions or fuzzy numbers and their meaning. It is only necessary to consistently compare alternatives with respect to criteria and criteria with respect to the goal.

RECENT DEVELOPMENTS

The AHP has been generalized into the Analytical Network Process (ANP) (Saaty, 1996b, 2005). This is based on the observation that many decision problems cannot be structured hierarchically because they involve the interaction and dependence of higher-level elements on lower-level elements. In other words, the feedback structure does not have the linear top-to-bottom form of the hierarchy but looks like a network, with cycles connecting its clusters of elements and with loops that connect a cluster to itself.

In a network model, usually not only the importance of the criteria determine the importance of the alternatives but also the importance of the alternatives themselves determines the importance of the criteria. However, in general, if there is no feedback, and to diminish complexity, the alternatives can be excluded and the influence among the remaining clusters may be examined.

The ANP makes use of supermatrices of components with their elements displayed vertically on the left side and horizontally at the top. A supermatrix represents interactions of the elements in different components within themselves and with elements in other components. A component consists of elements specialized in a certain type of activity. The matrix must be column staochastic to yield meaningful results.

Assume we have a system of N clusters $(C_1, C_2, \ldots, C_n)$ or components whereby the elements in each component interact or have an impact on or are influenced by some or all of the elements of another component with respect to a property governing the interactions of the entire system (see Figure 10.5).

Assume that component h, denoted by Ch, $h = 1, \ldots, N$, has n_h elements, which we denote by $e_{h1}, e_{h2}, \ldots, e_{hn_h}$. The impacts of a given set of elements in

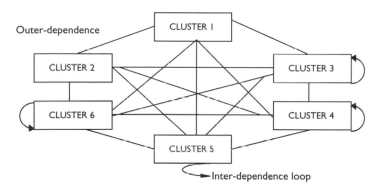

Figure 10.5 A network diagram

a component on another element in the system is one represented by a ratio scale priority vector derived from paired comparison in the usual way.

Each such priority vector is introduced in the appropriate position as a column vector in a supermatrix of impacts displayed as in Figure 10.6a, where the ij block of this matrix is given by the matrix represented in Figure 10.6b, each of whose columns is a principal eigenvector that represents the impact of all elements in the ith component on each of the elements in the jth component.

In the ANP procedure for structuring the decision problem (with or without dependence and feedback), users can rely on available information and understanding to develop control hierarchy: benefits, opportunities, costs and risks and then combine their results for the alternatives in the usual way. In each control hierarchy under each criterion or sub-criterion, a hierarchy or a network is developed that is appropriate for that criterion. The same set of alternatives must be included in all these structures.

The following steps are suggested (Saaty, 1996b):

1   perform four types analyses: one for benefits, one for opportunities, one for costs and one for risks;
2   in each, use a control hierarchy of criteria and sub-criteria to separate the kinds of interactions;
3   for each of the criteria or sub-criteria, create a hierarchy or network of the different clusters. Identify the elements in each cluster and draw arrow connecting clusters, indicating which cluster affects which other cluster. If there is inner dependence, draw a loop for that cluster.

The ANP has been applied to a variety of decision problems in different field, including prediction of business and sports competition outcomes. Brief summaries of the studies made with ANP in the period 1990–95 are illustrated in Saaty (1996b) (Chapter 5).

Recent developments of the AHP/ANP are applied to four fundamental areas of knowledge, as follows: neurology, genetics, physics–chemistry and cosmology. A specialized approach has been established, named Neural Network Process (NNP), based on the same ratio measurement scale of AHP/ANP, which is specifically directed to the study of the brain functionality.

The NNP makes use of superkernels, which are a generalization of the supermatrices and it allows to determine the form of neural firings and to deduct some of their critical properties. However, having determined all this, the question which arise is the following: 'How do we go from neural firing to describing the world

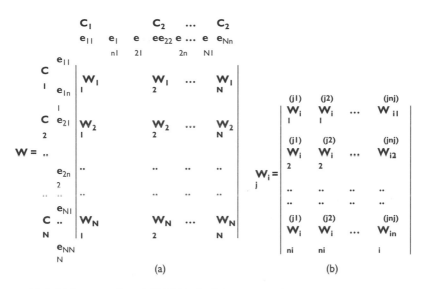

Figure 10.6 (a) Supermatrix and (b) i, j block of the supermatrix

of experience, feelings, emotions, abstract thought, and science' (Saaty, 1996b, p. 336).

As explained by Saaty (1996b), 'Time is the basic magnitude related to which the existence of all things is defined' (p. 337). The firing of neurons is essential for recognising the things which can exist in the mind only by stimulating feelings of a certain duration; otherwise they are nothing. Therefore, time and neural firing are two sides of the same concern with respect to cognition. 'But even as we analyse the firing of some neurons over time, time is also needed to sort the firings of other neurons that do the analysis.'

Time is a key concept not only in decision-making but also in the history of science and human thoughts and many philosophers and experts have managed to define it. In Kant's view, for example, neither time nor space exists outside the boundaries of the sensory perception (Kant, 1988). The reality we think and we see around us does exist only in our consciousness; the structural formation of the whole is derived from human knowing itself. In contrast with this conception, Dooyeweerd (1958) places time in isolation with respect to space and to all the other aspects of reality, or modalities, linking it with progress and sustainability.

Time, to Dooyeweerd, is like a 'prism' that separates out the aspects. There is a direction to the history of the cosmos, not just a set of random or contingent events, and that direction is towards the 'opening up' of the aspects so that the potential of all is fulfilled. What this means is that if an (urban) environment or a community is to be sustainable (i.e. 'healthy'), then it must be so over as long a term as is necessary for all the effects of functioning in all the aspects to be manifest – for good or ill (Lombardi and Basden, 1997; Brandon and Lombardi, 2005).

Our final unsolved question is, knowing that, 'how does this lead us to create mathematics?'

REFERENCES

Arrow, K. and Raynard, H. (1986), *Social Choice and Multicriterion Decision Making*, MIT, Boston.

Bazzani, G., Grillenzoni, M., Malagoli, C., and Ragazzoni, A. (1993), Valutazione delle risorse ambientali. Edagricole, Bologna.

Bentivegna, V., Mondini, G., Nati Poltri, F., and Pii, R., (1994), 'Complex Evaluation Methods. An Operative Synthesis on Multicriteria Techniques', Proceedings of the IV International conference on Engineering Management, Melbourne, Australia, April 1994.

Brandon, P. and Ceric, A. (2005), 'La gestione del rischio nel processo di costruzione', in Roscelli, R. (ed.), *Misurare nell'incertezza. Valutazioni e Trasformazioni Territoriali*, II edition, CELID, Torino, pp. 109–122.

Brandon, P. and Lombardi, P. (2005), *Evaluating Sustainable Development in the Built Environment*, Blackwell, Oxford.

Bravi, M. and Lombardi, P. (1994), *Tecniche di valutazione. Linguaggi e organizzazione di database*, CELID, Torino.

Clough, D.J. (1984), *Decisions in Public and Private Sectors: Theories, Practices and Processes*, Prentice-Hall Inc., New Jersey.

Dey, P.K. (1999), 'Process re-engineering for effective implementation of projects', *International Journal of Project Management*, 17(3): 147–159.

Dey, P.K. (2001), 'Decision support system for risk management: a case study', *Management Decision*, 39(8): 634–649.

Dey, P.K., Tabucanon, M.T. and Ogunlana, S.O. (1994), 'Planning for project control through risk analysis: a petroleum pipeline-laying project', *International Journal of Project Management*, 12: 23–33.

Dooyeweerd, H. (1958), *A New Critique of Theoretical Thought*, 4 vols, Presbyterian and Reformed Publisher Company, Philadelphia, Pennsylvania.

Expert Choice Software (2000), Expert Choice Inc., 4922 Ellsworth Ave., Pittsburgh, PA 15213.

Francescato, G. (1991), 'Housing quality: technical and non-technical aspects', in Bezelga, A. and Brandon, P. (eds), *Management, Quality and Economics in Buildings*, CIB Proceedings of European Symposium held in Lisbon, E&FN Spon, London, Part 2, pp. 602–609.

Fusco Girard, L. and Nijkamp, P. (1997) *Le Valutazioni per lo Sviluppo Sostenibile della Città e del Territorio*, Franco Angeli, Milano.

Golden, B.L., Harker, P.T. and Wasil, E.A. (1989), *Applications of the Analytic Hierarchy Process*, Springer-Verlag, Berlin.

Hinloopen, E., Nijkamp, P. and Rietveld, R. (1983), 'Quantitative discrete multiple criteria choice models in regional planning', *Regional Science and Urban Economics*, 13: 77–102.

Kant, I. (1988), *Critique of Pure Reason*, J.M. Dent & Sons Ltd, London.

Lombardi, P. (1995), 'Non-market and multicriteria evaluation methods for public goods and urban plans', Proceedings of the International Conference on 'Financial management of property and construction' held in Newcastle, Northern Ireland, May 1995.

Lombardi, P. (1997), 'Decision making problems concerning urban regeneration plans', *Engineering Construction and Architectural Management*, 4(2): 127–142.

Lombardi, P. (2001), La valutazione delle prestazioni professionali nella legge Merloni. Problematiche applicative, Consulente Immobiliare, no. 654 (maggio), pp. 1159–1180.

Lombardi, P.L. and Basden, A. (1997), 'Environmental sustainability and information systems', *Systems Practice*, 10(4): 473–489.

Mustafa, M.A. and Al-Bahar, J.F. (1991), 'Project risk assessment using the Analytic Hierarchy Process', *IEEE Transportatin Engineering Management*, 38(1): 46–52.

Nijkamp, P., Rietveld, P. and Voogd, H. (1990), *Multicriteria Evaluation in Physical Planning*, North Holland Publ., Elsevier, Amsterdam.

Realfonzo, A. and Barbanente, A. (eds) (1992), *The Evaluation in Urban and Regional Planning*, IRIS-CNR, n. 8, v. 2, Bari.

Roscelli, R. (ed.) (1990), *Misurare nell'incertezza*, CELID, Torino.

Roscelli, R. (ed.) (2005), *Misurare nell'incertezza. Valutazioni e Trasformazioni Territoriali*, II edition, Celid, Torino.

Roy, B. and Bouyssou, D. (1993), *Aide Multicritére à la Décision: Méthodes et Cas*, Economica, Paris.

Saaty, T.L. (1980), *The Analytic Hierarchy Process*, McGraw Hill, New York.

Saaty, T.A. (1990), *Decision-Making for Leaders*, RWS Publications, 4922 Ellsworth Ave., Pittsburgh, PA.

Saaty, T.L. (1992), *Multicriteria Decision Making – The Analytic Hierarchy Process*, RWS Publications, 4922 Ellsworth Ave., Pittsburgh, PA 15213, Vol. I, AHP Series.

Saaty, T.L. (1993), What is a relative measurement? The Ratio scale phantom, Mathematical and Computer Modelling, 17/4–5, 1–12.

Saaty, T.L. (1994), *Fundamentals of Decision Making and Priority Theory with the Analytic Hierarchy Process*, RWS Publications, 4922 Ellsworth Ave., Pittsburgh, PA 15213. Vol. VI, AHP Series.

Saaty, T.L. (1995), *Decision Making for Leaders*, RWS Publications, 4922 Ellsworth Ave., Pittsburgh, PA 15213. Vol. II, AHP Series.

Saaty, T.L. (1996a), *Decision-making with Dependence and Feed-back – The Analytic Hierarchy Process*, RWS Publications, Pittsburg.

Saaty, T.L. (1996b), *The Analytic Network Process*, RWS Publications, Pittsburgh, USA (completed revision 2001).

Saaty, T.L. (2005), *Theory and Applications of the Analytic Network Process: Decision Making with Benefits, Opportunities, Costs, and Risks*, RWS Publications, Pittsburgh.

Saaty, T.L. and Forman, E. (1993), *The Hierarchon*, RWS Publications, 4922 Ellsworth Ave., Pittsburgh, PA, 15213. Vol. V, AHP Series.

Saaty, T.L. and Kearns, K. (1991), *Analytical Planning*, RWS Publications, 4922 Ellsworth Ave., Pittsburgh, PA 15213. Vol. IV, AHP Series.

Saaty, T.L. and Vargas, L.G. (eds) (1987), The Analytic Hierarchy Process. Theoretical developments and some applications, Mathematical Modelling, Vol. 9, n. 3–5, pp.161–395.

Saaty, T.L. and Vargas, L.G. (1991), *Prediction, Projection and Forecasting*, Kluwer Accademic, Boston.

Saaty, T.L. and Vargas, L.G. (1994), *Decision Making in Economic, Political, Social and Technological Environments*, RWS Publications, 4922 Ellsworth Ave., Pittsburgh, P.

Voogd, H. (1983), *Multicriteria Evaluation for Urban and Regional Planning*, Pion, London.

11

Ecological Footprint Analysis: A Useful Method for Exploring the Interaction Between Lifestyles and the Built Environment
Craig Simmons

INTRODUCTION

More than 200 years ago, US Founding Father Benjamin Franklin wrote that 'There seems to be but three ways for a nation to acquire wealth: (1) by war – which permits taking by force the wealth of other nations; (2) by trade – which to be profitable requires cheating; and (3) by agriculture – through which we plant the seeds and create new wealth as if by miracle.' Franklin's wry observations are as true today as they were then. Just and sustainable wealth arises only from nature – a point fundamental to an understanding of ecological economics and the resource flows that underpin modern economies.

Our global store of resources is often likened to a bank account. This capital account cannot be depleted without consequences for future generations. If we are to live sustainably we must aspire to a quality of life which is within the means of nature. To put it another way, we must learn to live – along with other peoples and species – within the interest on nature's global capital account.

The case of fossil fuel-derived energy is perhaps the clearest example of where our demands are being met from unsustainable capital rather than renewable revenue. Pre-nineteenth-century man lived by harvesting sunlight stored by plants. In the last century we have increasingly consumed energy capital – fossil fuels, ancient 'stored sunlight'.

Many notable environmentalists and ecological economists, including Lovins, Hawken, Capra, Henderson, and Korten (see, for example, Capra, 1988; Weizsacker et al., 1997; Henderson, 1999; Korten, 1999; Hawken et al., 2000) have highlighted the need to create an economy based on natural limits which acknowledges the basic laws of thermodynamics.

MEASURING ENVIRONMENTAL SUSTAINABILITY

There have been few attempts to operationalise the measurement of 'nature's interest' to provide an indicator suitable for widespread use. Energy flow analysis is complex, hard to communicate, and difficult to relate to natural limits. Perhaps because of this, the literature on carrying capacity has proven, quite literally, a more fertile ground for research into a unified indicator of environmental sustainability.

Measuring the availability and bio-productivity of land, and therefore the capacity to sustainably support life, is one way to express captured sunlight and therefore nature's available 'interest'.

One such area-based indicator is the 'ecological footprint' (EF), a term first coined in the early 1990s by Mathis Wackernagel and Bill Rees while working at the University of British Columbia. It is defined as the area (usually expressed in global average productive hectares) required to sustainably provide the required resources and absorb any wastes (Wackernagel and Rees, 1996).

The theoretical foundations of footprinting date back at least 200 years to Malthus' *Essay on the Principle of Population* and beyond (see Malthus and Gilbert, 1999). Historian Fernand Braudel has pointed out that, in the 16th century, the hectare was preferred as a more reliable measure of economic activity across the diverse Mediterranean basin than the ducat, whose exchange rate and net worth varied wildly (Braudel, 1996).

Though pre-industrial writers were solely interested in the agricultural uses of land, Wackernagel and Rees had the insight to incorporate other area-based uses – including the accounting of fossil fuel energy through carbon sequestration by forested land. In doing so they created a powerful methodology able to aggregate a range of environmental impacts into a single indicator of sustainability.

The work of Wackernagel and Rees, directed mainly at calculating national and global impacts, has since been refined and extended to enable the use of footprinting in a wide variety of applications (Chambers et al., 2000). For example, substantial projects have been completed which calculate the footprints of regions, lifestyles and organisations (BFF, 2005c).

LIVING ON ONE WORLD – A LOW FOOTPRINT

The surface of the global is approximately 51 billion hectares. Only about 15 billion hectares of this is dry land. Of this, just over 5 billion hectares is unproductive desert, ice or mountain leaving close to 10 billion hectares which can reasonably expected to yield useful materials; food, timber, grazing and so on. About 3 billion hectares can be considered as productive sea (Chambers et al., 2000).

Assuming a population of 6 billion, then the area available for each person on the planet is little more than 2 hectares – without including any allowance for other plant or animal life.[1] This area, just $200 \times 100\,\text{m}$, is often referred to as the average 'earthshare' – the productive area each person would get if the planet were divided up equally.

If the global average footprint was less than, or equal to, this earthshare then humanity could live sustainably within the earth's carrying capacity. Latest calculations show that consumption is exceeding this sustainable level by about 20 per cent (WWF, 2004).

Footprints vary between nations – with consumption in high-income countries four times that of middle and low-income nations. The typical European lifestyle is neither the most wasteful nor extravagant. Yet, if everyone on the planet consumed as much as the Europeans, then we would need between two and three planets to support global consumption.

Living on One World, which Best Foot Forward have termed a LOW footprint lifestyle, has become a sustainability imperative. A LOW footprint is a benchmark against which individuals, organisations and communities can be judged (ref. South West report).

CALCULATING ECOLOGICAL FOOTPRINTS

In essence, the footprint is a simple accounting tool which estimates the area (land and sea) that would be required to sustainably support a particular community, lifestyle, activity, product or service. Area types included in the calculation are pasture, arable, sea, forest and energy land (areas of forest dedicated to carbon sequestration). As previously mentioned, land is also 'set aside' for biodiversity (see Figure 11.1). For example, how much land is required to grow all the bananas consumed by the average UK resident?

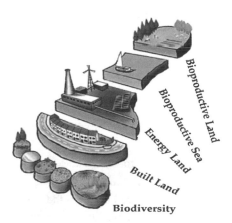

Figure 11.1 Ecological footprints

Assuming a consumption of 12 kg of bananas per person per year, and a world average annual yield of 12,000 kg (12 t) per hectare, the land area required can be simply derived by dividing 12 by 12,000 which equals 10 m² or 0.001 a per year.

This figure then needs to be converted to world average productive hectares (global hectares or gha) by adjusting for the higher productivity of arable land. Since arable land is 2.19 times more productive than world average productive land (GFN, 2004), the final footprint is 0.00219 gha/capita.

The same basic approach can be taken to calculate the footprints of a whole range of 'services'; the provision of mobility (travel), nourishment (food and drink), shelter (buildings), goods (materials) and direct services (e.g., health care, education, leisure, etc.).

INFLUENCE OF POPULATION, AFFLUENCE AND TECHNOLOGY

The ecological footprint of any population is a product of population, affluence and technology.

The IPAT model proposed by Ehrlich and Holdren (1972) neatly expresses this relationship,

$$\text{Impact} = \text{Population} \times \text{Affluence} \times \text{Technology}$$

The impact, or footprint, is affected by the number of consumers, the throughput of energy and materials and the efficiency of the technologies involved. This can be applied just as easily to providing mobility as it can to providing nourishment.

Returning to the earlier example, the footprint of the UK's banana 'habit' can be expressed in an IPAT format thus

$$\text{Footprint (I)} = \text{UK population (P)} \times 12\,\text{kg (A)} \times \frac{1}{12,000}\,\text{kg/ha (T)}$$

(*Note*: Here the footprint is calculated in hectares. The formula excludes the normalisation required to convert from arable hectares to global average productive hectares.)

It can be seen how increasing either population, the weight of fruit consumed or the efficiency factor (equivalent to reducing yield) will increase the total footprint.

Meadows *et al.* (2005) have pointed out how the Southern hemisphere would seem to have the most room for improvement in P, the West the potential for reducing A and the East the opportunity to reduce T.

A somewhat extended example follows which puts the points about consumption and technology in more of a lifestyle context.

Imagine two households. The Smiths are a family of four (two adults, two children) and the Jones' a young couple without children. The Smith household owns two very efficient petrol cars with *each* clocking up 40,000 km per year. Each car uses just 0.03 l of petrol per kilometre. The Jones' household owns one gas-guzzling sports utility vehicle (SUV) but they do not travel as much as the Smiths. In one year they drive about 20,000 km. However, their less efficient vehicle uses 0.16 l of petrol for each kilometre.

Measuring their footprint, it is easy to see how the trade-off between number of cars, distance travelled and vehicle efficiency translates into impact on the environment. For simplicity in this example, only direct fuel use is considered using a footprint figure per litre of petrol obtained from Best Foot Forward (BFF, 2005a). The impacts relating to vehicle manufacture, maintenance and disposal are ignored, as is the footprint of the built infrastructure (roads, garages, factories) that car use requires.

GENERIC FORMULA

Footprint (I) = number of car owners (P) × distance travelled each car (A)

× fuel efficiency (T) × gha per litre fuel

Smith Household: I = 2 × 40,000 km × 0.03 l/km × 0.00063 = 1.69 gha

Jones Household: I = 1 × 17,000 km × 0.16 l/km × 0.00063 = 1.75 gha

Note that the travel footprint of the two-car Smith family is less than the one-car Jones household. This is despite having two cars which each travel further than the SUV. Although their Affluence (the distance travelled) and the Population (the number of car owners) is greater, the Technological efficiency of their chosen mode of travel more than makes up for this. Overall their Footprint (I) is lower and can therefore be considered more environmentally sustainable.

The per capita footprint is also worth calculating for comparison with the average earthshare. The average travel footprint for the four-person Smith household is 1.69/4 = 0.42 gha/capita. The equivalent footprint for the two-person Jones household is 1.75/2 = 0.87 gha/capita. This is equivalent to 23 and 47 per cent respectively of each household member's earthshare – not taking into account, of course, all their other impacts. If the households wish to adopt a LOW footprint lifestyle then, clearly, travelling these sorts of distances by car would use a significant portion of the available resources. This is especially the case for the Jones' with close to half their footprint used up.

In the Smith and Jones example the consumption of only one resource, petrol, is considered. The benefits of footprinting become more apparent when a range of resources are included in the calculation.

LANDRAKE CASE STUDY

This footprint analysis is more sophisticated again than the previous examples. It includes modelling of three complete lifestyles and was undertaken to determine whether the small eco-housing development proposed would deliver a LOW footprint. The software used for these calculations was Personal Stepwise version 1.5 (BFF, 2005b).

Wishing to stimulate 'novel and sustainable solutions' to the shortage of affordable homes, the Cornwall Sustainable Building Trust ran a competition to design a development for a small site provided by Caradon District Council in Landrake near Plymouth in England.

The competition winner, architect Bill Dunster, proposed a 'carbon neutral construction strategy' producing a development with zero fossil fuel energy demand and built to the emerging Zero Energy Development (ZED) standards (BDA, 2005), which aim to reduce a broader range of environmental impacts relating to water use, transport, waste, food supply and material consumption.

Designed to be both affordable and environmentally benign, whilst providing a high quality of life for residents, the Landrake development is ideal to illustrate the potential for sustainable new build. The site comprises two blocks of high density, low rise housing (containing five homes), which surrounds a communal green space and allotments. The site is surrounded on two sides by wildlife planting, and on another by existing housing. An access road runs along the remaining boundary.

DESIGN FEATURES

The design reduces energy demand to 16,800 kWh/year (2,800 kWh per home) through super insulation and massive construction,[2] maximising solar gain, and the incorporation of passive cooling.

The residual energy demand is met by a mix of on-site renewable energy sources; a communal woodchip boiler, two wind turbines, solar water heating panels, and photovoltaics. Surplus electrical energy (estimated at 9200 kWh/yr) is used to charge electric pool cars, and will provide an estimated 31,000 miles of fossil fuel-free motoring.

Other features of the site include rainwater collection, storage and recycling. This is combined with water-efficient fittings to reduce water consumption. The retention of perimeter hedgerow, the inclusion of space for wildlife on the site and the use of sedum as a 'living' roofing material combine to maximise biodiversity. Private gardens and communal space, unusual on a high-density site, good interior daylighting and high levels of soundproofing all contribute to a high quality of life for residents.

RESIDENTIAL CONSUMPTION

Monitoring data from the Dunster-designed BedZED development, the prototype for the ZED Standards, provides a sound basis on which to estimate the consumption of the Landrake homes. Using this data we can explore the ecological footprints for future Landrake residents with reference to the South West regional average for residents moving into new build. To illustrate the range of lifestyles possible at Landrake, three character profiles are introduced here. They are referred to as Eco-zero, Eco-hero and Eco-willing. Their basic characteristics are described below.

Eco-zero is resistant to change or subject to heavy constraints on their time, which results in them taking the path of least resistance (real or perceived) when it comes to lifestyle choices. For example, Eco-zero will typically use a car – rather than public transport – but *would* probably use an electric vehicle if it was at least as accessible as a conventional alternative.

Eco-hero is at the opposite end of the spectrum. Eco-hero will always make an effort to take the most sustainable course of action and environmental criteria feature when making lifestyle choices. Eco-hero would, for example, seek to reduce the need to travel when seeking a new job and aim to use public transport even if it meant a slightly longer journey time. Eco-hero sees benefit in not owning a car and is likely to belong to a car club – where these exist – so that when needed, they can hire one.

Eco-willing lifestyle fits somewhere between that of zero and hero. Eco-willing is responsible, but not well informed about sustainability issues and these do not therefore feature when making major lifestyle decisions. However, when put in a particular situation, and informed as to the most environmentally friendly option, Eco-willing will generally comply even if this means some additional effort. For example, Eco-willing would not consider access by public transport when seeking a new job but, once the job were secured, they may well use public transport if it were available. However, Eco-willing is more likely than Eco-zero to be drawn to the idea of car-sharing or a car club, although they would most likely retain their own car for occasional use.

The consumption data for these three profiles is given – along with the carbon dioxide and footprint results – in Table 11.1.

As can be seen, the Eco-hero profile produces a footprint close to the Living on One World (LOW) benchmark. Together, the profiles demonstrate the range of lifestyles possible within a single eco-house design situated within a small zero carbon development.

Table 11.1 Landrake case study summary lifestyles

	Eco-Zero	Eco-Hero	Eco-Willing
Diet	Average UK diet	Vegetarian	Low meat
% local/ unprocessed/ fresh food	25%	50% – takes advantage of on-site allotments and box scheme	25%
Commuting	125 vehicle-km per week commuting to Plymouth/Liskeard by car	Works from home or lives within commuting distance by bike or electric pool car (powered by renewable energy)	125 passenger-km by bus each week commuting to Plymouth/Liskeard
Holiday	1 long haul air flight per year (10,000 km)	European holiday by train (1500 km)	1 short haul air flight per year (2000 km)
Other travel	50 additional car-km per week	25 additional bus and 25 additional train passenger-km per week	25 car-km per week using electric pool car/25 car-km using own car
Domestic energy use	856 kWh (from wind energy) based on 2800 kWh per dwelling at average occupancy of 3.4 people/house. Hot water – 356 kWh (50% provided by solar water heating, 50% by wood fuel)	As per Eco-zero	As per Eco-zero
Domestic waste	8 kg/wk (c. UK average) no recycling	4 kg/wk – 63% recycling/composting	8 kg/wk (c. UK average) – 31% recycling/composting
Spending on services	£219/month	£175/month	£219/month
Carbon Dioxide emissions (tonnes)	12.1	3.2	7.5
Annual ecological footprint (gha)	6.44	2.11	3.97

The Eco-hero profile requires the adoption of certain lifestyle changes; waste minimisation and high levels of recycling, reduced spending, a vegetarian diet, 50 per cent local, fresh food, limited car use and vacation by train. Whereas it is perfectly possible to enjoy a high quality of life at these reduced levels of consumption, it is acknowledged that such living might not appeal to everyone. Certainly, living within a conventionally designed house in a typical urban environment such a lifestyle would be inconvenient.

A more acceptable Landrake lifestyle is that of Eco-willing. This less 'extreme' lifestyle has a footprint which exceeds that of the Eco-hero but is still well below the UK average footprint of 5.35 ha/capita.

Reductions from the UK average footprint as due to higher levels of recycling (encouraged by the integrated recycling facilities at the development), reduced use of a petrol-fuelled car (assisted by the convenient location of the development on a main bus route and the provided solar-charged car), a diet consisting of more plant-based foods (as a result of the local food availability) and last, but not least, the zero carbon house.

ENVIRONMENTAL ECONOMIES OF SCALE

It became apparent to the author when modelling the interactions between lifestyles in the built environment that large developments offer the opportunity to more easily deliver LOW footprint communities.

This is because many factors which are outside of the control of designers considering small developments can be integrated into larger schemes. For example, average commuting distances can be reduced by providing workplaces near to housing. Similarly, the provision of education, health and other services can be brought into the zero emission fabric (see Figure 11.2).

With the assistance of architect Bill Dunster, one of his 500-unit ZED Standards-compliant 'urban block' designs (referred to as LandZED) was evaluated. One aim of this design was to make the most environmentally friendly lifestyle

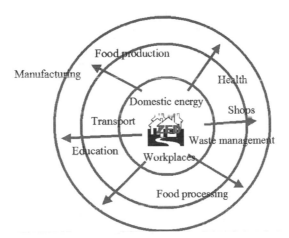

Figure 11.2 Scales of development (*Note*: As the scale of development expands more and more functions can be included within the ZED fabric)

The 21 Steps Chart 2004

Step	Description	Saving (ha)	Total Eco Footprint (ha)	Carbon Saving (t/yr)	Total Carbon Emission (t/yr)
Start	Start with UK typical housing built to 2000 BRegs, built at average density. Average ecofootprint of residents is 5.45ha. (UK typical would be 5.62ha)		5.45		11.9
1	Location	If the site can be located within 10 minutes walk of good public transport links, this will allow savings from reduced car dependence	0.05	5.40	0.10	11.8
2	Density	Increase housing density by 30%, reduce road, paving and lawn areas from 80m² to 15m²/person. Introduce sky gardens and sedum roofs to maintain amenity.	0.09	5.31	0.10	11.7
3	Domestic Electrical	Introduce electrical energy efficiency measures (A-rated white goods, low energy lighting) that reduce consumption to 3kWh/person/day.	0.09	5.22	0.30	11.4
4	Building Fabric	Introduce ZED specification building fabric that reduces space heating to 16.2kWh/m²/year (12% UK typical or 27% BRegs 2000) and hot water consumption to 6kWh/household/day (43% UK typical or 56% BRegs 2000)	0.12	5.10	0.50	10.9
5	Provide workspace opportunities on-site	Introduce offices, home working IT infrastructure and other non-residential uses. A proportion of residents will be able to work on site and avoid the need to commute. The larger the development, the more scope for people both living and working on site: 100 Homes (BedZED size), say 10% of workers - save 0.02ha; 400 Homes (ZED quarter), say 25% of workers - 0.04ha	0.04	5.06	0.10	10.8
6	Energy efficient workspace	Build workspace in the shade zone of the south facing homes, built to ZED specification. Energy use is 40% less than comparable conventional offices. Provide enough workspace for all the working population of the development. Even though many residents will work off site and other workers will commute in to their jobs, the energy efficiency savings in the buildings are the same per occupant.	0.22	4.84	0.40	10.4
7	Primary school	On 400 home developments upwards, include a primary school, built to ZED energy efficiency specification and allowing residents to avoid using the car for school run.	0.04	4.80	0.15	10.25
8	Mixed use facilities	A good mix of community, sports, childcare, retail and health facilities appropriate to the site will help to further reduce the residents' need to travel. Assume that an equivalent of 50% of services needed to support the population of the development are brought within the boundaries of the site and built to ZED specification.	0.06	4.74	0.15	10.10
9	Car club	Introduce car club service, allowing members to give up their private vehicles without sacrificing mobility. Assume 25% of car owners give up their car and so reduce their annual mileage to one fifth.	0.10	4.64	0.20	9.9
10	Green travel plan	In addition to mixed use facilities and a car club, introduce bicycle storage facilities and a programme of cycle promotion. Promote public transport and home delivery services.	0.05	4.59	0.10	9.8

#					
11	Alternative vehicles	Introduce alternative fuel vehicles and ultra efficient vehicles for further reductions.	0.08	4.51	9.6
12	Eco-travel agent	Introduce green travel agent on site, promoting eco-tourism, with special deals for UK and European destinations, Eurostar deals, links with WWOOFers (willing workers on organic farms) and networks of European farm accommodation. Reduce average air miles from UK average of 14km/wk to 10km/wk.	0.07	4.44	9.45
		On overall transport impact, BedZED has achieved monitored savings of 0.38ha. A larger ZEDQuarter (a community of around 400 homes that could be mixed use regeneration of an existing urban quarter, a new build development, or both) offers greater potential for a wide range of services and facilities and so greater potential for reducing the need to travel. Overall savings on transport could be 0.43ha (1.0 t CO_2/year)			
13	Renewable heat	Generate all domestic heat demands from renewables – either wood or solar thermal.	0.09	4.35	9.15
14	Renewable electricity	Generate all domestic electricity demands from renewables – mixture of wind and PV or from wood-fired CHP.	0.12	4.23	8.65
15	Non-residential renewables	Generate all energy for workspace and non-residential facilities from renewables.	0.14	4.09	8.35
16	Construction materials	Introduce a policy of low impact, local, low embodied energy construction materials (that perform to the ZED spec), sourced from reclaimed and recycled sources where possible.	0.10	3.99	8.07
17	Low impact food programme	Introduce farmers markets, space for growing food on site, links with local farms and local organic box schemes. Promote vegetarian and ever vegan diets. Eco-saint vegans who buy 70% fresh local produce and waste 40% less than average can save 1.25ha; Moderate eco-samaritans who are vegetarian and get 50% of their food locally and fresh and waste 2% less than average can save 0.82ha; Carnivorous eco-angels who eat a low meat diet, buy 70% fresh local produce and waste 40% less than average save 0.88ha; Eco-part-timers who eat a low meat diet, take part in the weekly box scheme and reduce food waste by 20% can save 0.6ha.	0.82	3.17	7.74
18	Bakery	On site bakery where waste heat is tapped and used for heating.	0.01	3.16	7.74
19	Waste reduction programme	Campaign and advice on reducing the amount of packaging, introduction of community composting scheme with compost used on site for gardens and food growing displacing manufactured fertilizers.	0.74	2.42	7.40
20	Recycling facility	Introduce easy, convenient recycling facilities and information on what to recycle where.	0.51	1.91	6.95
21	Reduce impact of remaining goods and facilities	Encourage residents to purchase fewer goods & services and/or to buy them from low impact sources. 10% reduction - 0.05 ha (0.2t CO_2); 30% reduction - 0.15ha (0.4t CO_2); 50% reduction - 0.24ha (0.7t CO_2)	0.15	1.76	6.50
Total Savings			3.69		5.40

Figure 11.3 The 21 Steps Chart 2004

choices the behavioural path of least resistance thus maximising the potential for voluntary behaviour change. Although design choices clearly interact, a useful set of guidelines was developed which became known as the 21 Steps (see Figure 11.3).

Although a range of lifestyle choices are available to those inhabiting such as development, one LOW footprint lifestyle profile was developed (see Table 11.2)

Table 11.2 LOW footprint communities

	UK Typical	LandZED
Nourishment		
• Diet	38% animal-based	15% animal-based
• Local/unprocessed/fresh food	25%	70%
• Reductions in food waste	0%	5%
Mobility		
• average UK petrol car (vkm/wk)	122	0
• ultra-efficient petrol car (vkm/wk)	0	7
• solar-powered car (pass. km/wk)	0	25
• bus and coach (pass. km/wk)	15	25
• rail, metro etc. (pass. km/wk)	15	40
• ship, ferry etc. (pass. km/wk)	1	1
• air (pass. km/wk)	14	10
Shelter		
• electricity consumption kWh/yr	1756	0
• gas/LPG consumption kWh/yr	5808	0
• oil consumption litres/capita/yr	664	0
• coal consumption kg/capita/yr	528	0
• consumption of renewables (excl. wood) kg/capita/yr	2	554
• wood fuel consumption kg/capita/yr	0	0
• CHP (water heating & electricity) kWh/yr	0	386
• How much space does your home - occupy? m^2/capita	100	35
• How large are the paved/lawn/gravel areas? m^2/capita	100	15
• Area left managed for wildlife/food production m^2/capita	0	5
Domestic waste (kg)		
• . . . to landfill	6.75	1.00
• . . . to recycling	0.9	1.25
• . . . to composting	0.7	1.25
• . . . to incineration	0	0.00
• . . . to chp	0	1.00
Services		
• Spending (£/month)	219.36	197.00
• % goods procured from ZED sources	0	10
• % services procured from ZED sources	0	30
• Footprint gha/capita/yr	5.29	1.96
• CO$_2$ t/capita/yr	11.20	3.00

to illustrate one possibility for sustainable living. The LandZED profile is shown alongside UK Typical data for comparative purposes.

The use of ecological footprint analysis in the case studies provided demonstrates the potential for achieving LOW footprint communities and provides pointers to those seeking to make developments more sustainable.

NOTES

1   The exact 'earthshare' for a global population of 6 billion (the figure for year 2000) is 2.13 ha/capita. This reduces to 1.87 ha with a biodiversity allowance of 12 per cent. Of course, as population increases the earthshare reduces. A population of 9.5 billion would decrease the earthshare to 1.35 ha or 1.19 ha with 12 per cent reduction for biodiversity.

2   Massively constructed buildings store heat during the day for slow release at night (or over even longer periods) to minimise the need for supplementary heating. Absorbing heat in this way can also reduce overheating on hot days.

REFERENCES

BDA (2005) www.zedstandards.com

BFF (2005a) Corporate Stepwise version 1.3. Best Foot Forward, www.bestfootforward.com.

BFF (2005b) Personal Stepwise version 1.5. Best Foot Forward, www.bestfootforward.com.

BFF (2005c) Various examples of the application of ecological footprints can be found on the Best Foot Forward website www.bestfootforward.com.

Braudel, F. (1996) *The Mediterranean and the Mediterranean World in the Age of Philip II: Vol I.* University of California Press, Berkeley and Los Angeles, California.

Capra, F. (1988) *The Turning Point: Science, Society, and the Rising Culture*. Simon & Schuster, New York.

Chambers, N., Simmons, C. and Wackernagel, M. (2000) *Sharing Nature's Interest: Using Ecological Footprints as an Indicator of Sustainability*. Earthscan, London.

Ehrlich, P. and Holdren, J. (1972) Review of the closing circle, *Environment*, 14: 24–39.

GFN (2004) National Footprint and Biocapacity Account – United Kingdom 2001. Global Footprint Network, www.footprintnetwork.org.

Hawken, P., Lovins, A.B. and Lovins, L.H. (2000) *Natural Capitalism: The Next Industrial Revolution.* Earthscan, London.

Henderson, H. (1999) *Beyond Globalization: Shaping a Sustainable Global Economy.* Kumarian Press, Bloomfield, CT, USA.

Korten, D.C. (2000) *The Post-corporate World: Life After Capitalism.* Berrett-koehler Publishers, San Francisco.

Malthus, T.R. and Gilbert, G. (eds) (1999) *An Essay on the Principle of Population* (*Oxford World's Classics*). Oxford University Press, Oxford. [*Note*: Original essay published in 1798.]

Meadows, D., Randers, J. and Meadows, D. (2005) *Limits to Growth – The 30 Year* Update. Earthscan, London.

Wackernagel, M. and Rees, W. (1996) *Our Ecological Footprint: Reducing Human Impact on the Earth.* New Society, Philadelphia, PA.

Weizsacker, E. von, Lovins, A.B. and Lovins, L.H. (1997) *Factor Four: Doubling Wealth – Halving Resource Use: A Report to the Club of Rome*. Earthscan, London.

WWF (2004) *Living Planet Report 2004.* WWF, Switzerland.

12

Urban Spiders: A Comparative Framework for Evaluation and Scenario Analysis

Tüzin Baycan-Levent, Frank Bruinsma and Peter Nijkamp

INTRODUCTION

This chapter reviews the 'spider analysis' and its applications in comparative and scenario studies. The experiences of several comparative case studies, stemming from the applications of spider analysis, show the effectiveness of the model as a visualization tool in the decision-making process, in particular for complex issues.

Evaluation is a scientific approach that is based on several methodologies used in social science research on complex decision-making. The concept of 'evaluation' is frequently accompanied by the concept of 'valuation' and the related concept of 'value', which is concerned with an object of the valuation. A single unifying definition of value does not exist and more precise definitions have evolved in different disciplines to meet different needs. However, at a generic level, valuation methods can be defined as methods that define and measure the importance or desirability of the object of valuation and the results of the interaction between it and humans.

The literature on evaluation has drawn attention to the combination of methods, tools and data and the integration of results from evaluations that use different strategies, carried out from different perspectives, and using different methods (Nijkamp et al., 1990; Bingham et al., 1999; Turner et al., 1999; Trochim, 2003; Baycan-Levent and Nijkamp, 2004). It is emphasized in many studies that valuation requires other – and in particular additional – methods such as scenario studies, which may contribute to a better understanding of the interactions, for example between the development process and the environment. Applying different techniques may provide insight into the robustness of the results.

The complex and multidimensional structure of many problems and development processes makes necessary an informative database and an integrated approach that require comparative analyses and scenario approaches in order to better understand the similarities and differences among factors and potential consequences of the general policy or exogenous change. Illustration and visualization of the potential alternatives, scenarios or comparisons are of importance in the decision-making process. Figures, maps, charts and diagrams can be used to illustrate the consequences of the analyses in a clearer way. In terms of illustration, the so-called 'spider model' can be a relevant method for a better understanding of the relationships among the factors and also for developing and evaluating 'hypo-thetical scenarios' for planning and management. Recent experiences have shown that the spider model can be used as an effective instrument in comparing different scenarios.

This chapter reviews the 'spider analysis' and its applications in comparative and scenario studies. The Section 'Spider Analysis' introduces spider analysis and explains the steps of the model on the basis of a hypothetical example. The Section 'Applications of Spider Analysis in Comparative Studies' gives examples from the applications of spider analysis in comparative studies whereas the Section 'Applications of Spider Analysis in Scenario Studies' addresses applications of spider analysis in scenario studies. The Section 'Concluding Remarks' concludes with an evaluation about strengths and weaknesses of spider analysis.

SPIDER ANALYSIS

The Spider model is an analytical tool, which can be used to visualize the relative strengths and weaknesses of the selected case studies or different scenarios for various chosen factors (see Rienstra, 1998). The advantage of this visualization is that it is easy to show the relative score of the various factors and thereby makes it possible to compare different case studies or scenarios. However, the most important thing to keep in mind is that the spider model is not a real model in the sense that there are no real mathematics or econometrics behind it; it is just a helpful tool for visualizing the results of analysis.

In a spider model, scores on each factor are mapped out on an axis starting from the interior towards the outer boundary of the spider, in which the lowest scores are to be found in the centre of the spider. The scores may be qualitative (i.e. ordinal rankings) or quantitative (e.g. standardized on a 10-point scale), in which the centre of the web represents a score of zero, whereas the outer edges represent the highest score (e.g. 10). All factors are scored on this range under the assumption that a higher score represents a better performance. Nevertheless, there is no mutual weighing between the factors. A score of 7 on one factor does not necessarily mean that it is a better score than a score of 6 on another factor.

The extreme points on each axis usually have a qualitative meaning; they often do not present numerical information, but rather a rank order (in terms of 'more' or 'less'). This is important for scenario design or comparative analysis since experts are more concerned with statements that make system options and underlying forces viable, than with precise assessments of all consequences of such options.

The envelope composed of all scores per factor forms a connecting line resulting in a surface representing the integral representation of these factors per option type (case study or scenario). In general, one might state that the larger the surface, the better the option type in question scores. However, it should be recognized that the size of the area formed by linking the points on all axes has no statistic significant meaning, because (i) the information on the axes has only a qualitative (and not a cardinal data) meaning and (ii) the size of the resulting area is also dependent on the order in which the axes are positioned in the spider.

We will explain the steps of the spider model for a hypothetical example to make things more clear. In our hypothetical model we will compare the availability of urban green spaces in different cities. The spider model will enable us to visualize the relative scores of different cities in terms of availability of urban green spaces. We will use three kinds of data: (1) general data, which contains socio-economic data such as population, population density, unemployment, etc., (2) general land use, which contains land-use data such as built-up area, residential area, water surfaces, etc., and (3) green land use, which contains data such as parks, recreation areas and sport fields, etc. We will assume that there are four cities called A, B, C and D (see Table 12.1).

The first step of the spider model is to standardize the quantitative data as explained previously. For standardization of quantitative data, we use total surface and population. We use population as a standardization tool for the general data, whereas we use total surface to standardize general land use. For green land use we also use population as a standardization tool – because of the importance and availability of urban green space per inhabitant. First, we calculate the share of each factor. For example, for general land use, we calculate the share of the total surface of city A in the total surface of the four cities (A, B, C and D). For the other land-use factors such as built-up area, we calculate the built-up area as a percentage of the total surface of the city (equal to 36%), which we correct for the share of the surface of city A in the total surface of the four cities (equal to 0.11). Then we standardize the scores for A (0.11), B (0.15), C (0.06), and D (0.04) on a 10-point scale. In our example, city B has the highest score (0.15) so we give a score of 10 to city B and we calculate the relative scores for the other cities. According to this calculation, the scores are 7.3 for city A, 3.8 for city C and 2.8 for city D. For the general data and green land-use data we follow the same method, but this time we use population as a standardization tool instead of total surface area (see Table 12.1).

After this first step that is based on the standardization of primary data, we use the standard values (10-point scores) of each factor for visualization by means of the spider model. This visualization module of the spider model can be found in Excel among the alternatives of chart (choose type 'Radar', and then the left sub-type).

Table 12.1 Spider explanation data

GENERAL LAND USE

CITIES	Total surface	Share	Spider value	Total built-up area	Total built-up area/total surface	Share	Spider value	Total area for housing	Total area for housing/total surface	Share	Spider value	Total agri.	Total agri./total surface	Share	Spider value
A	200000	0.31	**6.7**	72000	0.36	0.11	**7.3**	45000	0.23	0.07	**10.0**	27500	0.14	0.04	**9.2**
B	300000	0.47	**10.0**	99000	0.33	0.15	**10.0**	45000	0.15	0.07	**10.0**	30000	0.10	0.05	**10.0**
C	80000	0.13	**2.7**	38000	0.48	0.06	**3.8**	29000	0.36	0.05	**6.4**	4700	0.06	0.01	**1.6**
D	60000	0.09	**2.0**	28000	0.47	0.04	**2.8**	17000	0.28	0.03	**3.8**	14000	0.23	0.02	**4.7**
	640000	1.00													

GENERAL LAND USE

CITIES	Total forest	Total forest/total surface	Share	Spider value	Total recr.	Total recr./total surface	Share	Spider value	Total water	Total water/total surface	Share	Spider value
A	1100	0.01	0.00	**2.8**	21000	0.11	0.03	**10.0**	50000	0.25	0.03	**5.7**
B	3500	0.01	0.01	**9.0**	20000	0.07	0.03	**9.5**	95000	0.32	0.05	**10.0**
C	3900	0.05	0.01	**10.0**	9000	0.11	0.01	**4.3**	14000	0.18	0.01	**2.1**
D	1100	0.02	0.00	**2.8**	6000	0.10	0.01	**2.9**	2500	0.04	0.00	**0.4**

Table 12.1 (Continued)

GENERAL DATA

CITIES	Population	Share	Number of inhabitants 60+	Number of inhabitants 15-	%60+	Share	Spider value	%15-	Share	Spider value	Average disposable income per inhabitant	Share	Spider value
A	500000	0.37	75000	80000	15.0	5.6	**9.4**	16.0	5.9	**10.0**	6750	2500	**10.0**
B	400000	0.30	80000	68000	20.0	5.9	**10.0**	17.0	5.0	**8.5**	6200	1837	**7.3**
C	300000	0.22	60000	51000	20.0	4.4	**7.5**	17.0	3.8	**6.4**	6600	1467	**5.9**
D	150000	0.11	24000	22500	16.0	1.8	**3.0**	15.0	1.7	**2.8**	6300	700	**2.8**
	1350000	1.00											

GENERAL DATA

CITIES	Registered unemployment	Share	Spider value	Population density/km²	Share	Spider value	Housing density/km²	Share	Spider value
A	39	14.44	**10.0**	4000	1481	**10.0**	2000	741	**10.0**
B	33	9.78	**6.8**	2500	741	**5.0**	1000	296	**4.0**
C	21	4.67	**3.2**	6000	1333	**9.0**	3000	667	**9.0**
D	9	1.00	**0.7**	3500	389	**2.6**	1500	167	**2.3**

GREEN LAND USE

CITIES	Population	Share	Total recreation	#hectares recreation/inhabitant	Share	Spider value	Parks	Parks/inhabitant	Share	Spider value	Sport fields	Sport fields/inhabitant	Share	Spider value
A	500000	0.37	15000	0.03	0.011	**10.0**	7000	0.01	0.005	**10.0**	5000	0.01	0.004	**10.0**
B	400000	0.30	14000	0.04	0.010	**9.3**	7300	0.02	0.005	**10.0**	4000	0.01	0.003	**8.0**
C	300000	0.22	6000	0.02	0.004	**4.0**	2300	0.01	0.002	**3.3**	2200	0.01	0.002	**4.4**
D	150000	0.11	4000	0.03	0.003	**2.7**	1700	0.01	0.001	**2.4**	1800	0.01	0.001	**3.6**
	1350000	1.00												

GREEN LAND USE

CITIES	Total nature fields	Total nature fields/inhabitant	Share	Spider value	Forest	Forest/inhabitant	Share	Spider value
A	350	0.00	0.000	**0.9**	800	0.00	0.001	**3.0**
B	1000	0.00	0.001	**2.5**	2500	0.01	0.002	**9.3**
C	4000	0.01	0.003	**10.0**	2700	0.01	0.002	**10.0**
D	0	0.00	0.000	**0.0**	800	0.01	0.001	**3.0**

The application of the second step of the spider model for our hypothetical example, drawing the spiders, can be seen in Table 12.2 and Figure 12.1 for available urban green spaces. In our example, City B has the highest score for almost every factor, except for forest and recreation. On the other hand, city C, for example, has the highest score on forests. Table 12.3 and Figure 12.2 show the same step of drawing the spiders for available urban green spaces per inhabitant. In this example, City A has the highest scores for recreation, parks and sport fields whereas City C has the highest scores for nature fields and forest per inhabitant. On the other hand, City D, for example, shows the worst performance in all factors. Similar comparisons between the factors and also cities can be made in this way.

The spider model can be used for visualization of hypothetical scenarios as well. For example, if we increase the share of urban green spaces and/or if we increase also the budget for maintaining urban green spaces, then we might observe

Table 12.2 Standardized scores for general land use (spider values)

CITIES	GENERAL LAND USE						
	Surface	Built-up area	Residential area	Agriculture	Forest	Recreation	Water
A	6.7	7.3	10.0	9.2	2.8	10.0	5.7
B	10.0	10.0	10.0	10.0	9.0	9.5	10.0
C	2.7	3.8	6.4	1.6	10.0	4.3	2.1
D	2.0	2.8	3.8	4.7	2.8	2.9	0.4

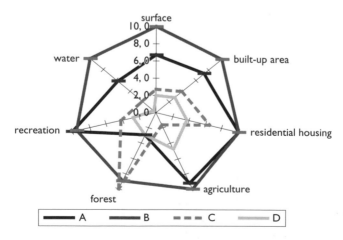

Figure 12.1 The hypothetical spider model for available urban green spaces

Table 12.3 Standardized scores for green land use (spider values)

CITIES	GREEN LAND USE				
	Recreation/ inhabitant	Parks/ inhabitant	Sport fields/ inhabitant	Nature fields/ inhabitant	Forest/ inhabitant
A	10	10	10	0.9	3
B	9.3	10	8	2.5	9.3
C	4	3.3	4.4	10	10
D	2.7	2.4	3.6	0	3

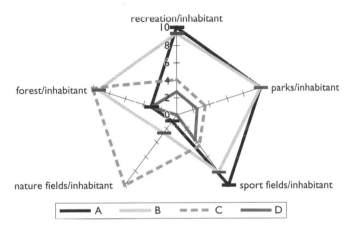

Figure 12.2 The hypothetical spider model for available urban green spaces per inhabitant

a decrease in air pollution, or some changes in other land use. But, keep in mind, these changes are based on calculations; the spider model is only a means for visualizing the calculated changes. It does not calculate changes itself. Therefore, with the help of the spider model we can evaluate the effectiveness of the suggested policies.

APPLICATIONS OF SPIDER ANALYSIS IN COMPARATIVE STUDIES

After an explanation on a hypothetical example, in this section we will give the empirical results of several case studies stemming from the applications of spider analysis. These case study researches are additional studies that we have conducted in parallel to the EU project on 'Development of Urban Green Spaces to Improve the Quality of Life in Cities and Urban Regions' (URGE).[1] With the applications of spider analysis we aimed to compare the similarities and differences in and between European and Dutch cities especially to point out the availability of green spaces per inhabitant in cities. For these comparative case study researches we used factor analysis and the spider model as methodologies. Factor analysis enabled us to understand the relationship that exists between urban green areas and the other types of land use. The spider model, on the other hand, enabled us to visualize the relative scores of different cities and city groups in terms of availability of urban green spaces. Therefore, our previous comparative case study researches brought to light important characteristics of urban green spaces in different size classes of cities.

Comparative case study I: Availability of natural and urban green in European cities

A comparative factor-analytic approach to European cities in terms of urban green spaces has shown that a strong relationship exists between urban green areas – built-up areas and urban green areas – and water (Baycan-Levent *et al.*, 2002). The results of this study indicated that the availability of 'urban green' is relatively high in metropolises and big cities, whereas the availability of 'natural green' such as forest and agricultural area is relatively high in medium-sized and small cities (see Table 12.4).

Another comparison on European cities by means of a so-called 'spider model' concluded that parallel structures in terms of built-up area and urban green spaces can be observed in big and medium-sized cities (Baycan-Levent *et al.*, 2002). Cities having higher scores on built-up areas have also higher scores on urban green spaces. Similarly, higher scores on urban green spaces imply also having higher scores on water in the same city groups (see Figure 12.3). The results of this study demonstrate that there is an order from a small city to a metropolis in

Table 12.4 Availability of natural and urban green in European cities

Metropolises population >1,000,000		Big cities population 500,000–1,000,000		Medium-sized cities population 100,000–500,000				Small cities population <100,000	
Berlin	U	Birmingham	U	Antwerp	–	Leipzig	N	Alphen aan de Rijn	–
Budapest	U	Cracovia	N	Bern	–	Montpellier	–	Freiberg	–
Istanbul	N	Genoa	–	Chemnitz	N	Salzburg	–	Gorlitz	–
Vienna	U	Helsinki	U	Dresden	N	Sarajevo	–		
Warsaw	U	Lodz	N	Edinburgh	U	Tallinn	–		
		Turin	–	Espoo	U	Zurich	–		

U – **U**rban Green, **N** – **N**atural Green
Source: Baycan-Levent *et al.*, 2002

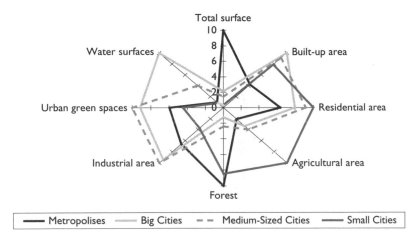

Figure 12.3 General land use within the four European city groups (Baycan-Levent *et al.*, 2002)

terms of available green per inhabitant, where a metropolis constitutes the most disadvantaged city group.

Comparative case study II: Availability of natural and urban green in Dutch cities

Recent comparative case studies on Dutch cities show also interesting links and patterns for different city groups such as Big cities, New cities, Intermediate cities and Peripheral cities in the Netherlands (see van Leeuwen *et al.*, 2006). A comparative factor-analytic approach (see Table 12.5) shows that Big Dutch cities have a

Table 12.5 Availability of urban green in Dutch cities

Big cities		New cities		Intermediate cities		Peripheral cities	
Amsterdam	U	Almere	L	Breda	–	Deventer	–
Rotterdam	U	Alphen aan de Rijn	L	Ede	S	Den Helder	S
The Hague	U	Zaanstad	L	Eindhoven	U	Emmen	S
Utrecht	U	Zoetermeer	U	's-Hertogenbosch	L	Middelburg	–
				Leiden	–	Roermond	L
				Nijmegen	L	Enschede	S
				Tilburg	–	Groningen	–
				Zwolle	–	Maastricht	–

U: **U**rban Recreation Areas, **S**: **S**tructural, Long-term Recreation Areas, **L**: Daily **L**eisure Areas
Source: van Leeuwen *et al.* (2006)

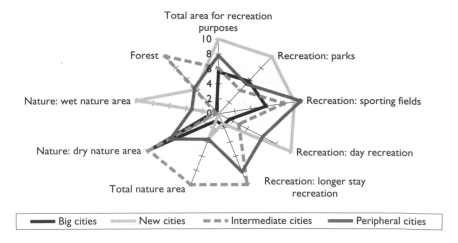

Figure 12.4 Green land use within the four Dutch city groups (van Leeuwen *et al.*, 2006)

high score in terms of urban recreational factors, whereas New cities have higher scores on the daily leisure factor, and Peripheral cities tend to have high scores on the structural, longer-stay recreational areas (van Leeuwen *et al.*, 2003).

Another comparison by means of spider models shows that Dutch Big cities have the lowest scores on the availability of different types of urban green (Leeuwen *et al.*, 2006). They accommodate less green space, especially less natural green space, not only as a percentage of the total land use, but also in terms of availability per inhabitant (see Figure 12.4).

Comparative case study III: Availability of natural and urban green in Dutch and European cities

A final comparison by means of spider model was applied to European and Dutch cities (Baycan-Levent *et al.*, 2002). The results of this comparison show that small cities in both Europe and the Netherlands have better conditions in terms of urban green and non-built-up area. A high population density goes together with a low availability of total recreational and urban green areas. While Big-European and Big-Dutch cities have a relatively higher population density and lower total recreational and urban green areas, Small-European and Small-Dutch cities have higher total recreational and urban green areas and a lower population density (see Figure 12.5). This comparative framework shows once more that a sufficient availability of urban green spaces is more problematic for big cities.

These experiences from several case studies have enabled us to understand the different relationships that exist between urban green spaces and other factors.

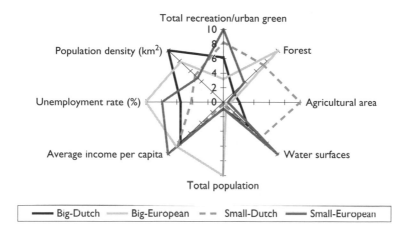

Figure 12.5 Availability of urban green spaces in European and Dutch cities (Baycan-Levent and Nijkamp, 2002)

They have also shown us the effectiveness of the methods applied to define relevant methodologies and techniques for future studies to evaluate urban green spaces. As a result of our experiences we can recommend these methods in order to understand that different relationships exist between urban green spaces and other factors, and also to understand the relative strengths and weaknesses of the possible different scenarios and policies.

APPLICATIONS OF SPIDER ANALYSIS IN SCENARIO STUDIES

Another widespread application of spider models is in scenario analysis on transport and regional development issues (see, for instance, Rienstra, 1998; Nijkamp *et al.*, 2000; and Bruinsma *et al.*, 2001). In this section we will concentrate on a case study experiment with spider models applied for the design of a regional development plan for the province of Utrecht, located in the centre of the Netherlands (see Bruinsma *et al.*, 1998). In this experiment spider models were used as a visualization of four extreme development paths. By showing these development paths in a visual way, the doorway was opened that led to the development of an expected and desired development path. Policy measures had to close the bridge between the expected and the desired development.

The future regional development is surrounded by uncertainties, because the development of the region is influenced by many factors, which can progress in various ways. We only mention the uncertainty about the general economic development, demography and environmental quality. The scenario approach is a decision support tool to reduce uncertainty regarding the likelihood of decision-makers' future developments in the region. Scenarios reduce complexity and facilitate discussion about future events by arranging and classifying information and preventing information overload (Rienstra, 1998). A scenario can be defined as 'a tool that describes pictures of the future world within a specified framework and under specified assumptions. The scenario approach includes the description of at least two or more scenarios, designed to compare and examine alternative futures' (EU, 1994).

In our application, four contrasting qualitative scenarios representing extreme development directions are constructed to draw the edges of the planning field in which regional economic development will take place for the Dutch region of Utrecht (see Bruinsma *et al.*, 1998). In this way the scenarios provide a reference framework for less extreme scenarios, and may also clarify policy choices and their impacts (Rienstra, 1998). Based on regional interviews and Delphi-sessions, a final scenario is constructed in which the expected and desired future developments and policy measures (and their impacts) are presented.

Spider models are used to visualize the different scenarios. In the context of our experiment two axes are drawn, dividing the spider field into four quadrants: one for each main spatial economic issue: firms, labour market, infrastructure and spatial economic quality. Each quadrant covers four key factors (see Table 12.6).

As discussed in the Section 'Spider Analysis', each factor in each quadrant is represented by an axis starting from the interior towards the outer boundary of the spider. For the present situation the score of each factor is often based on statistical information or other quantitative information. The direction and the size of the changes in the scores of the factors are mutually consistent for the constructed future scenarios. So, the direction and the relative size of the impacts of each future scenario is comparable to the direction and size of the impact of all other scenarios. Nevertheless, the absolute size of each impact remains qualitative and by that it is disputable. In this respect the independent position of the scientist proposing the scenarios – and its effects – should be indisputably accepted by all parties involved in the planning process.

Table 12.6 Key factors of the main spatial economic issues

Firms	Labour market	Infrastructure	Spatial economic quality
Quality (sectoral structure)	Quality (education)	Quality	Economic growth
Quantity	Quantity	Quantity	Living environment
Location (dispersion)	Location households	Mobility	Natural environment
Land-use	Land-use dwellings	Net external effect	Multiple land use

We have constructed four reference scenarios describing the boundaries of the playing field. In order to construct those reference scenarios one needs insight in the strengths, weaknesses, opportunities and threats of the region. Such a SWOT-analysis took place by desk-research and a first round of interviews with stakeholders in the region. This SWOT-analysis resulted in two contrasting paths – critical success and failure factors – for the spatial economic development of the region

The following four contrasting scenarios are constructed:

Scenario 1: welfare and conventional transport infrastructure;
Scenario 2: welfare and knowledge infrastructure;
Scenario 3: well-being and conventional transport infrastructure;
Scenario 4: well-being and knowledge infrastructure.

Each scenario is visualized by means of a spider model in which the present situation is represented by a grey field, and the scenario situation by a black line. In this way the positive and negative developments compared to the present situation can be seen immediately (see Figure 12.6 for the present situation and scenario 1: welfare and conventional transport infrastructure).

Not only the present situation is of importance for the future scenarios but also the autonomous developments – both mega-trends and regional-specific trends – as far as their implications can be overseen.

Some developments in the spatial organization are already given by existing spatial plans, in which the expansion of residential and industrial areas are indicated. In the light of these developments an increasing economic expansion and an increasing use of the road (highway) and rail network might be expected.

The four extreme scenarios were the input for a discussion session with stakeholders, politicians and policy makers. In a plenary session the pros and cons of each scenario were given. The pros and cons represented indirectly the strong and the weak spots of the interests of most stakeholders, so everyone was aware of the interests of each of the participants, and each stakeholder was aware of the weak spots linked to his own interests. In this way, an atmosphere was created, where there was mutual understanding of each other's interests, as well as a willingness to discuss the relative importance of their own interests in relation to other – contrasting – interests. The doorway to achieve consensus was opened. After the plenary session a discussion in three groups took place and each group had to present its expected and desired regional development path in a final plenary session. The outcome of this session led to the construction of an expected and desired development scenario for the Utrecht region, which may boost a reasonable degree of consensus by the stakeholders (see Figure 12.7).

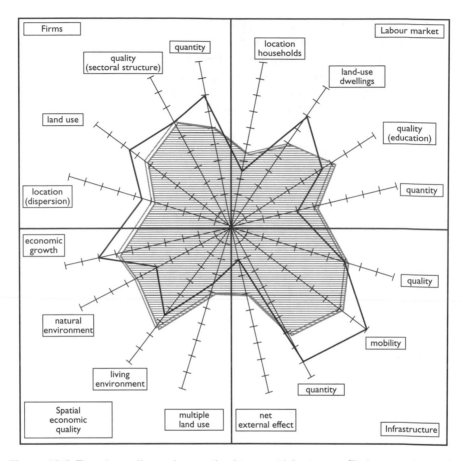

Figure 12.6 The edge welfare and conventional transport infrastructure (Bruinsma *et al.*, 2001)

The last stage of research concerns the construction of the expected and desired spatial economic development paths for the Utrecht region and the formulation of a set of policies on how to achieve the desired development by additional measures, given the present performance and the expected development path of the region.

With this experiment we made clear that spider models are useful tools in scenario analysis. The visualization of the complex scenarios by spider models led to an open discussion between stakeholders in the region. Furthermore, it stimulated the discussion on how to move from the expected to the desired development path by the design of additional policy measures.

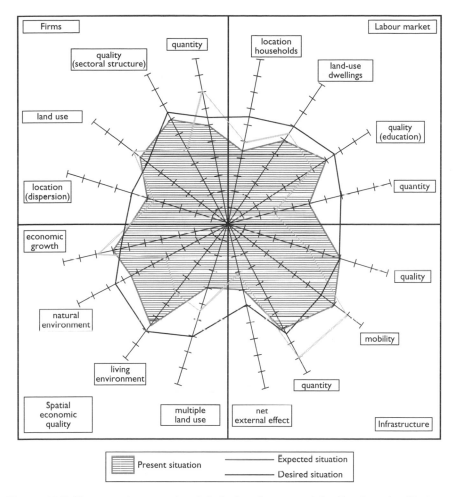

Figure 12.7 The present, expected and desired performance of the Utrecht region (Bruinsma *et al.*, 2001)

CONCLUDING REMARKS

The spider model is a very helpful tool for visualizing the results of analysis. This visualization enables us to compare different case studies or scenarios by means of their relative strengths and weaknesses. The comparative framework of the spider model is important since experts are more concerned with statements that make system options and underlying forces viable, than with precise assessments of all consequences of such options. Therefore, the model makes the decision-making process easier, in particular for complex issues.

However, the spider model is not a real model. There are no real mathematics or econometrics behind it. The model has a qualitative meaning only; it does not present numerical information and it has no significant statistic meaning. On the other hand, the spider model is only a means of visualizing the calculated changes. It does not calculate changes itself. These weaknesses reduce and limit the use of the model.

NOTE

1   This project is funded under Key-Action 4 'The City of Tomorrow and Cultural Heritage' of the Program 'Energy, Environment and Sustainable Development' of the 5th Framework Program of the European Union.

REFERENCES

Baycan-Levent, T. and Nijkamp, P. (2002) 'Planning Urban Green Space: European and Dutch Cities', *Australasian Journal of Regional Studies*, 8(2): 129–142.

Baycan-Levent, T. and Nijkamp, P. (2004) 'Evaluation of Urban Green Spaces', in *Accounting for Non-Market Values in Planning Evaluation: Alternative Methodologies and International Practices*, D. Miller and D. Patassini (eds), Ashgate Publishing Limited, Aldershot.

Baycan-Levent, T., van Leeuwen, E.S., Rodenburg, C. and Nijkamp, P. (2002) 'Development and Management of Urban Green Spaces in European Cities: A Comparative Analysis', in *The Pulsar Effect in Urban Planning*, E. Beriatos and J. Colman (eds), ISoCaRP, Athens, pp. 237–247.

Bingham, G., Bishop, R., Brody, M., Bromley, D., Clark, E.T., Cooper, W., Costanza, R., Hale, T., Hayden, G., Kellert, S., Norgaard, R., Norton, B., Payne, J., Russell, C. and Suter, G. (1999) 'Issues in Ecosystem Valuation: Improving Information for Decision Making', in *Ecosystems and Nature: Economics, Science and Policy*, R.K. Turner, K. Button and P. Nijkamp (eds), Environmental Analysis and Economic Policy: 7, An Elgar Reference Collection.

Bruinsma, F.R., Nijkamp, P., Ubbels, B., Smit, S. and Vreeker, R. (1998) *Strategie-Nota REOS Utrecht*, Vrije Universiteit, Amsterdam.

Bruinsma, F.R., Nijkamp, P. and Vreeker, R. (2001) 'Experts at Arm's Length of Public Policy Makers: A Case Study on Utrecht', in *Recent developments in evaluation*, H. Voogd (ed.), Geo Press, Groningen, pp. 123–152.

EU (European Union) (1994) *Strategic Transport Glossary*, Brussels.

Leeuwen, E.S. van, Rodenburg, C. and Nijkamp, P. (2003) 'Urban Green and Integrative Urban Sustainability: Concepts and Their Relevance in Dutch Cities', *European Spatial Research and Policy*, 10(1): 5–26.

Leeuwen, E.S. van, Rodenburg, C.A. and Vreeker, R. (2006) 'A Framework for Quality of Life Assesment of Urban Green Areas in Europe: An Application to District Park Reudnitz Leipzig', *International Journal of Environmental Technology And Management*, 6(1–2).

Nijkamp, P., Rietveld, P. and Voogd, H. (1990) *Multicriteria Evaluation in Physical Planning*, North Holland, Amsterdam.

Nijkamp, P., van Delft, H., Geerlings, H. and Van Veen-Groot, D. (2000) 'Transportation Between Globalization and Localization', *Innovation*, 13(1): 11–25.

Rienstra, S.A. (1998) *Options and Barriers for Sustainable Transport Policies*, PhD Thesis, Vrije Universiteit, Amsterdam.

Rodenburg, C.A., van Leeuwen, E.S. and Nijkamp, P. (2004) 'Environmental Assessment Indicators for Urban Green Spaces: A Comparative Study on Dutch cities', in *Marktdynamik und Innovation – Beiträge im Gedenken an Hans-Juergen Ewers*, M. Fritsch (ed.), Duncker & Humblot (Volkswirtschaftliche Schriften), Berlin, pp. 365–382.

Trochim, W.M.K. (2003) *The Research Methods Knowledge Base*, The Research Methods Knowledge Base website www.trochim.human.cornell.edu/kb/

Turner, R.K., Button, K. and Nijkamp, P. (eds) (1999) *Ecosystems and Nature: Economics, Science and Policy*, Environmental Analysis and Economic Policy: 7, An Elgar Reference Collection.

13

A Sustainable Test Method for Urban Green Areas Using the Flag Method: A Comparative Study of Leipzig

Eveline van Leeuwen and Peter Nijkamp

INTRODUCTION

Urban sustainability is an important but also a complex issue. Sustainability cannot be identified by a single criterion, but requires multiple criteria, often subdivided into a biophysical, an economic and a social dimension. Sustainability and quality of life are closely related phenomena and are both critical topics to policy-makers in urbanised areas. In order to improve urban sustainability and quality of life by a better provision with 'green' facilities, public and private decision-makers need better information regarding the quantity and quality of urban green available in their city.

The aim of this chapter is to develop an operational framework that can be used for the practical evaluation of sustainable urban green spaces by means of relevant criteria linked to urban quality of life. The evaluation framework in this paper is built upon a particular multicriteria analysis method called the Flag Model and will be demonstrated by means of a comparison of green areas in Leipzig. In our case study, the Leipzig 'District Park Reudnitz' and 'Green Belt Grünau' will be evaluated and compared against a set of benchmark values related to policy objectives.

SUSTAINABLE DEVELOPMENT

Sustainable development has in recent years become an important anchor point for policy-makers worldwide. A major issue in sustainability policy is the question of how sustainability can be identified as a normative orientation for policy. Sustainability became a fashionable topic after the publication of the report of the World Commission on Environment and Development (WCED), titled 'Our Common Future' (1987). The publication calls for a view of the earth as an integrated social, economic, ecological and political system, which needs joint initiatives and actions in order to ensure continuity under changing conditions (Finco and Nijkamp, 2001).

Sustainability can usually not be specified via one single indicator, but it requires multiple judgement criteria. Because of the normative nature of sustainability, it requires, in general, a framework of analysis and expert judgement which should be able to test actual and future states (or developments) of the economy and the ecology against a set of reference values (Nijkamp and Ouwersloot, 1998).

According to the WCED's 1987 definition, 'sustainable development' means meeting the needs of the present without compromising the ability of future generations to meet their own needs. It involves the interrelationship between poverty, economic development and the state of the natural environment (Perman *et al.*, 1999). This means that an analytical framework aiming at evaluating sustainability in every kind of situation or context should distinguish these three dimensions: ecological, social and economic.

The first dimension incorporates such aspects as biodiversity, pollution or scarcity of resources. The second dimension is more related to aspects like the distribution of income and public health. The final dimension related to the economic world focuses on e.g. investments or market developments. To be able to evaluate these dimensions in a general way, it is necessary that meaningful and measurable sustainability indicators be identified and specified. However, the difficulty with sustainability indicators is that they are always context-specific and site-specific and never unambiguous. This holds for economic–social–ecological analysis in general, but also for specific urban planning issues.

THE URGE PROJECT

This chapter is based on the results of the European Union research project 'Development of Urban Green Spaces to Improve the Quality of Life in Cities and Urban Regions' (URGE[1]). An important goal of this project is to analyse to what extent urban green areas are able to contribute to urban sustainability and to an improvement of quality of life. To be able to do so, a set of indicators as well as an evaluation framework is required. Clearly there is a variety of evaluation methods available, but in our specific case we needed to have a simple, unambiguous and appealing approach that could readily be applied in an empirical urban planning context.

The following will describe the evaluation tool used to assess the effects of urban green spaces on spatial sustainability and quality of life. This evaluation shall involve a comparison of two urban green spaces situated in the city of Leipzig. In the next section the Flag Model will be described.[2]

THE FLAG MODEL

The Flag Model is a multicriteria decision method, which aims to evaluate one or more alternatives, while using an a priori set of constraints formulated as sustainability evaluation classes for the empirical outcomes of the choice possibilities (see Figure 13.1). It assigns different coloured flags (e.g., green, red) to relevant indicators according to their compliance to, for example, policy objectives. The model requires measurable indicators as well as a corresponding set of reference values, the so-called

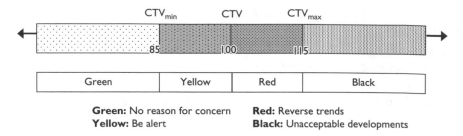

Green: No reason for concern | Red: Reverse trends
Yellow: Be alert | Black: Unacceptable developments

Figure 13.1 The relation between Critical Threshold Values and the colour of the flags

'critical threshold values' (CTV). These CTVs ensure compliance with certain objectives; exceeding such a value means no-compliance and results in unacceptably high social costs (Nijkamp and Vreeker, 2000).

A distinction can be made between two types of indicators, namely cost and benefit indicators. If, for example, an indicator is characterised as a cost condition (i.e., 'a lower value is better'), a score above the benchmark signals a dangerous or threatening development with regard to sustainability. This type of indicator is labelled as a *cost indicator*. The reverse reasoning applies to *benefit indicators* (Leeuwen *et al.*, 2006).

As sustainability indicators are usually not unambiguous, it is at the same time very difficult to generate unambiguous CTVs. In certain areas and under certain circumstances different experts and decision-makers may have different views on the precise level of an acceptable CTV.

This uncertainty problem can be handled by introducing a bandwidth for the corresponding value of the CTV, defined as CTV_{max} and CTV_{min}, respectively. CTV_{max} refers to the maximum, in case of a cost indicator, allowable value of the sustainability indicator beyond which an alarming development will certainly start (Nijkamp and Ouwersloot, 1998). On the other hand, the CTV_{min} indicates there is no reason for concern (see Figure 13.1[3]).

The Flag Model provides instruments to analyse alternatives in two complementary ways. First, it can be used to focus on a single alternative in order to find out whether an alternative is acceptable or not. Secondly, the model can compare several choice options and classify which alternative scores best. The standard model consists of four steps:

1	Identifying a set of measurable indicators.
2	Assessing the impact of the alternatives on these indicators.
3	Establishing a set of normative reference values (CTVs).
4	Evaluating the relevant alternatives.

In Step 1 of the Flag procedure, the set of measurable indicators has to be identified. Criteria can be measured with the help of indicators. Indicators are pieces of information designed to communicate complex messages in a simplified, (quasi-) quantitative manner, so that empirical progress in achievements of policy goals can be measured (Rotmans, 1997). The number of relevant indicators is not restricted a priori; the Flag Model can include any number. Of course, the choice of the indicators is subordinate to the relevant choice problem at hand. In the second step, the impact matrix has to be filled with empirical information. This structured information table contains the values that the indicators assume for each alternative considered. The Flag Model contains various classes of policy-relevant indicators, which correspond in our urban green study to three dimensions: Environmental, Social and Economic. Furthermore, the attribute 'type' (benefit or cost) has to be distinguished for each indicator. In Step 3 of the procedure a CTV has to be defined for each indicator in the Flag Model. As mentioned before, these values represent the reference system for judging the alternatives. These values can consist of goals or critical standards set by the government, but they can also consist of values agreed upon by the stakeholders or by scientific experts. After the establishment of the indicators and the threshold values, the Flag model software[4] is used in Step 4 to evaluate the alternatives. There are essentially three approaches to this evaluation: a qualitative, a quantitative and a hybrid approach, which complement each other, rather than being a substitute (Vreeker et al., 2002).

The qualitative approach focuses on the colours of the flags. It counts the frequencies of outcomes in a certain class and it may make use of cross tabulation (when two alternatives are compared), pie charts and stack bars to visualise the number of different coloured flags. The various qualitative methods do not give different outcomes, but represent other ways to display the same information. It shows information such as the mean values per indicator group or the standard deviation. The hybrid form takes into account both qualitative and quantitative aspects.

DESCRIPTION OF THE URGE PROJECT AND ITS CRITERIA

The URGE project is a European Union (EU) research project, which aims to improve the provision of green spaces in cities, both qualitatively and quantitatively. In order to achieve this goal, the project focuses on the complex interactions between nature, economy and social systems in urban environments. New and integrated knowledge of these complex interactions should be considered as a premise to the development of modern strategies for the design and management of urban landscapes (URGE, 2001). The URGE project also elaborates and tests an interdisciplinary catalogue of criteria and indicators, based on experiences from various European cities. This catalogue comprises criteria to evaluate ecological, economic, social and planning issues regarding urban green spaces and quality of life. The knowledge gained will be used to improve existing green spaces and to optimise urban green policies in Europe.

In this examination of the URGE project, the evaluation framework presented will be applied to two urban green spaces in the German city of Leipzig. The first area considered is the district park Reudnitz, which is part of the former railway station 'Eilenburger Bahnhof'. The area was established as a terminal in 1874 for rail connections to the south. The area of the current district park itself was used for technical functions for the railways; for example, as an engine garage. The re-developed park was opened to the public in June 2001 and it provided new opportunities for daily recreation and north–south as well as east–west path connections. The second urban green area considered here is Green Belt Grünau. The district of Grünau is situated in the west of Leipzig and it was the third largest modern estate within the former DDR. The case study site is located in an area, which was relatively recently finished. It is bordered on the west by a densely built residential area, on the south by agricultural land, on the east by detached housing and on the north by another residential complex, divided by a main street (URGE, 2001).

For these two green spaces a set of indicators were chosen for which both data on the actual situation and relevant benchmark values are available (see Table 13.1). Some benchmarks are national values; some are values set by the municipality of Leipzig and some benchmarks are developed within the URGE project.

First, the ecological indicators have been selected. Examples of ecological indicators used are: isolatedness expressed by the distance to the next green space; soil quality measured by the possibility of contamination on the site; and edge effects, which take into account the ratio between the edge (the outline) and the surface.

The second group of indicators consists of economic indicators, for example, number of square meters green space per resident living within 500 m of the green space; the yearly actual expenditures per square meter; or the question whether an entrance fee has to be paid or not. The third subset of indicators, that is the social and planning indicators, is represented by, among others, the presence of sports facilities; the question of whether the urban green is used as a teaching aid or not; and safety indicating whether people feel safe during day and night while using the green space.

Table 13.1 The criteria, indicators and indicator values for Green Belt Grünau and District Park Reudnitz

Criteria	Indicators	Data	Value Grünau	Value Reudnitz
Ecological				
• Fragmentedness	• Isolatedness of the area	Quantitative	75 m	120 m
	• Connectivity to next green area	Qualitative	1	1
	• Edge effects (shape index)	Quantitative	3	6
• Soil quality	• Quality of the soil	Qualitative	3	1
	• Soil sealing	Quantitative	17%	24%
• Barrier	• Noise reduction from surroundings	Quantitative	40 dB	40 dB
• Naturalness	• Proportion of the surface which is heavily worn	Quantitative	2%	1%
Economic				
• Availability	• Number of m² green space per resident within a 500 m radius	Quantitative	5 4 m²	4.4 m²
• Accessibility	• Average distance between entrances	Quantitative	133	85 m
• Production	• Exploitation of natural resources	Qualitative	1	1
• Finance	• Do visitors have to pay an entrance fee?	Qualitative	No	No
	• Yearly actual expenditures	Quantitative	1.48 E/m²	4.45 E/m²
	• Activities to generate income	Quantitative	0	1
Social and Planning				
• Educational resource	• Is the area used as a teaching aid?	Qualitative	Yes	No
• Recreational facilities	• Presence of sports facilities	Qualitative	3	4
	• Presence of additional recreational facilities	Qualitative	3	3
	• Presence of facilities for children	Qualitative	3	3
• Safety	• Do people feel safe in the area?	Quantitative	56%	51%
• Citizens involvement	• Information available	Qualitative	2	2
	• Instruments to involve citizens	Qualitative	4	3
	• Co-operation between authorities and education and recreation providers	Qualitative	Yes	No
	• Thematic trails	Qualitative	No	No

RESULTS OF THE EVALUATION

As stated before, we will compare two urban green areas to illustrate the use of the Flag model and its ability to evaluate sustainability issues using the three dimensions. The two areas, District Park Reudnitz and Green Belt Grünau, are both situated in the city of Leipzig. Therefore, the policy objectives of the municipality are

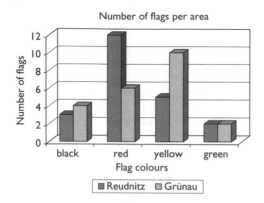

Figure 13.2 Number of flags per area

relevant to both areas. But since the needs of the surrounding residents differ as the social characteristics of the population differ, the design and the facilities of the two areas are likely to be dissimilar. This will, of course, affect the outcomes of the evaluation.

If we start looking at the number of flags per area (Figure 13.2), we see that from the total of 22 flags, Reudnitz scores 3 black flags and Grünau 4, i.e., one more. But at the same time, Reudnitz has 12 red flags and Grünau only 6. Concerning the yellow flags, 5 of them are assigned to Reudnitz and 10 to Grünau. Overall, from the first impression, it seems that the outcomes for Green Belt Grünau perform slightly better regarding the larger number of yellow flags, a smaller number of red flags and only one more black flag than the District Park Reudnitz scores.

To better understand the differences between the two areas, a cross-tabulation table can be helpful. Table 13.2 shows the number of different coloured flags for Grünau and Reudnitz. It shows, for example, that Reudnitz scores in total three black flags; for two indicators, Grünau also scores a black flag, while for one indicator a red flag is assigned to Grünau. On the other hand, four black flags are assigned to Grünau in total, while only two of these are red in the Reudnitz case. The green flags are all assigned to the same two indicators in both areas.

A next interesting step is to examine the dimensions of the coloured flags, in other words: are the flags of one colour all assigned to one dimension or are they spread over the three dimensions?

Figures 13.3 and 13.4 show the number and proportion of flags per dimension for Green belt Grünau and District Park Reudnitz respectively.

First of all, it appears that the two green flags are assigned to the biophysical dimension. This dimension also scores four yellow flags, no red flags and one black flag. The social dimension also scores one black flag, but no green flag, three red flags and five yellow flags. Finally, the economic dimension appears to score no green flags, two black flags, three red flags and only one yellow flag.

Because the three dimensions are not all represented by means of the same number of indicators per dimension, we also have to take into account the proportion of the different coloured flags. Again the proportion of green and yellow flags appears to be the highest for the biophysical dimension and the lowest for the economic dimension.

District Park Reudnitz shows a slightly different picture. The flags of the biophysical dimension are quite equally spread among the four colours. The social and economic dimensions received no green flags, only one black one and almost the same proportion of red and yellow flags.

Looking at both urban green areas we see that the biophysical dimension shows the best results and that hence there is a reason to argue that improvements may be made on the economic characteristics of the areas. But we do not yet know precisely which characteristics should be improved (black and red flags) and which of them (partly) applies to the needs of the users (yellow and green flags).

Table 13.3 shows the colour of the flag per indicator for the two areas (both for the evaluation and for the sensitivity analysis[5]). Concerning the biophysical indicators we find that only largeness, the ratio between the outline and the surface, causes problems. It would be better for ecological values, if the edge effects could be reduced, but of course this indicator cannot easily be adapted. Fortunately, on average, the noise from the surrounding area does not reach unfavourable levels and the naturalness (proportion of the surface which is heavily worn) is fine.

Looking at the economic dimension we see that for Grünau the indicator 'average distance between entrances' may have to be improved. This is a better performable task, although we should note that the counted entrances are only the official ones and that, as there are no fences, a lot of unofficial entrances exist, which improves accessibility. Concerning Reudnitz, the actual annual costs are too high.

Table 13.2 Cross tabulation table

1		Grünau				
		Black	Red	Yellow	Green	Total
Reudnitz	Black	2	1	0	0	3
	Red	2	4	6	0	12
	Yellow	0	1	4	0	5
	Green	0	0	0	2	2
	Total	4	6	10	2	22

But because the area is a rather recently established area, the costs will decrease in future. Also the safety, from the social dimension perspective, may have to be improved. Both areas score a black flag for this indicator.

CONCLUSIONS

As stated before, sustainability can usually not be specified via one single indicator, but requires multiple judgement criteria. Therefore it also needs an evaluation framework, which should be able to test actual and future states of, for example, urban green areas against a set of reference values. In our opinion the three dimensions

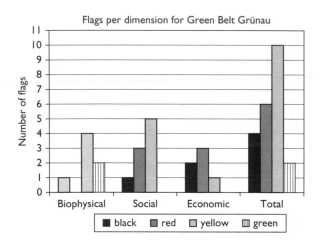

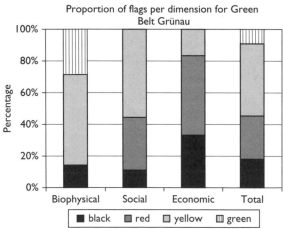

Figure 13.3 The number and the proportion of flags per dimension for Green Belt Grünau

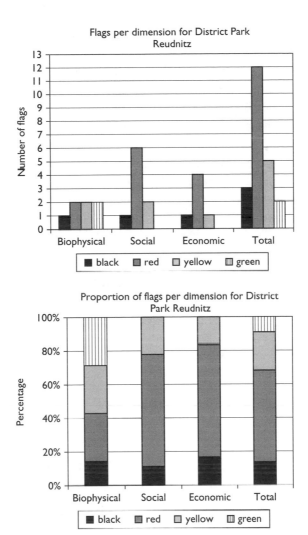

Figure 13.4 The number and the proportion of flags per dimension for District Park Reudnitz

extracted from the WCED's 1987 definition on sustainability is a very useful tool to classify the multiple criteria.

The Flag Model also adopted these three dimensions: the biophysical, the economic and the social dimension. The Flag Model is a multicriteria decision method, which aims to evaluate one or more alternatives while using an a priori set of constraints or evaluation classes. Furthermore, it is capable of evaluating both quantitative and qualitative indicators. The alternatives, which are evaluated in this chapter, form part of the EU research project 'Development of Urban Green Spaces to Improve the Quality of Life in Cities and Urban Regions' (URGE). The first area is district park Reudnitz, which is part of the former railway station 'Eilenburger Bahnhof'. The second urban green area is Green Belt Grünau. From these two green spaces a set of indicators and reference values or benchmarks are chosen. Some benchmarks are national values; some are values set by the municipality of Leipzig and some benchmarks are developed within the URGE project. The indicators are all generated within the project.

First of all it can be concluded that the Flag Model is a useful tool to evaluate a complex issue such as the sustainability of urban green areas. The indicators easily fit the three dimensions, while both the quantitative and the qualitative indicators can also be evaluated.

Table 13.3 Colour of the flags for District Park Reudnitz (S.1) and Green Belt Grünau (S.2), for the evaluation and the sensitivity analysis (G = Green, Y = Yellow, R = Red and B = Black)

		Evaluation		Sensitivity	
	Indicator	*S.1*	*S.2*	*S.1*	*S.2*
B	Isolatedness	R	Y	R	G
B	Connectivity	Y	Y	Y	Y
B	Soil sealing	Y	Y	G	G
B	Naturalness	*G*	*G*	G	G
B	Noise from surroundings	**G**	**G**	**G**	**G**
B	Soil quality	R	Y	R	Y
B	Largeness	**B**	**B**	**B**	**B**
E	Exploitation of national resources	Y	Y	Y	Y
E	Green space per resident within 500 m	R	R	R	R
E	Average distance between entrances	R	*B*	R	**B**
E	Entrance fee	R	R	R	R
E	Actual yearly costs	**B**	R	**B**	R
E	Activities to create income	R	**B**	R	**B**
S	Sports facilities	Y	R	Y	R
S	Additional recreation facilities	R	Y	R	Y
S	Facilities for children	Y	Y	Y	Y
S	Instruments to involve citizens	R	Y	R	Y
S	Green as a teaching aid	R	Y	R	Y
S	Information available	R	R	R	R
S	Co-operation	R	Y	R	Y
S	Thematic trails	R	R	R	R
S	Safety both day and night	**B**	**B**	**B**	**B**

Concerning the evaluation of the two urban green areas, it appears that Green Belt Grünau is the best performing or most sustainable green area in terms of the benchmarks used. Green Belt Grünau scores the same number of green flags, a larger number of yellow flags, a smaller number of red flags and only one more black flag than those assigned to District Park Reudnitz.

Looking at both urban green areas in the case study, we see that the biophysical dimension shows the best results, although some improvements may be made on the economic characteristics of the areas. Looking at the economic dimension it appears that for Green Belt Grünau the indicator 'average distance between entrances' may have to be improved, although we should note that the counted entrances are only the official ones and that, as there are no fences, a lot of unofficial entrances exist, which improves, of course, accessibility. Concerning District Park Reudnitz, the actual yearly costs are rather high. But because the area is a recently established area, the costs may decrease in the future. Also the safety, from the social dimension, should be improved. Both areas score a black flag for this indicator.

These empirical results show the practicability of the Flag Model for decision-makers. First of all it becomes clear which dimensions, the ecological, the economic or the social, comply with the benchmarks. If necessary, a certain dimension can be further examined and the indicators can be taken into account. This means that the decision-maker obtains a clear view of the current situation of an urban green area related to their own policy (benchmarks) and that, with the help of the different coloured flags, practical information is offered about which aspects of the area need to be improved.

NOTES

1   This project is funded under Key-Action 4 'The City of Tomorrow and Cultural Heritage' of the Programme 'Energy, Environment and Sustainable Development' of the 5th Framework Programme of the European Union.

2   The comparison of the two areas is used to illustrate the Flag model; the values of the indicators are provisional figures obtained in the URGE project.

3   In this figure the relationships between CTVs, flags and indicator values are illustrated. If the outcome value of this cost-indicator is lower than 85 units, e.g. 70 units, it receives a green flag, which means that there is no reason for concern. If the indicator has an outcome value of 110 units, it receives a red flag, which means that the trend should be reversed.

4   The Flag Model software has been developed as a deliverable of the European Union research project SAMI. SAMI, *Strategic Assessment Methodology for the Interaction*

of CTP-Instruments, Deliverable 5: SAMISoft, DG7 Transport Research (Strategic), European Union, 4th Framework Programme, 2000.

5   In order to obtain robust results, we evaluated the urban green area in two different ways. For the first analysis (evaluation) we used the planning targets provided by the city of Leipzig as benchmark values (CTV). The second analysis (sensitivity) can be seen as a sensitivity analysis or a robustness test, for which we used the various planning targets as CTV_{min} or CTV_{max} and imposed the next less strict threshold values on the indicators. As can be seen in Table 13.2, the evaluation offers quite robust results: only three yellow flags from the biophysical dimension turned into green flags, while the rest remained constant.

REFERENCES

Finco, A. and Nijkamp, P. (2001). 'Pathways to Urban Sustainability', *Journal of Environmental Policy and Planning*, 3: 289–302.

Leeuwen, E.S. van, Rodenburg, C.A. and Vreeker, R. (2006). 'A Framework for Quality of Life Assessment of Urban Green Areas in Europe: An Application to District Park Reudnitz Leipzig', *International Journal of Environmental Technology and Management*, 6(1–2).

Nijkamp, P. and Ouwersloot, H. (1998). 'The Flag Model, Theory and Implementation of Sustainable Development Modeling'. In: van den Bergh, J.C.J.M. and Hofkes, M.W. (eds), *A Decision Support System for Regional Sustainable Development*. Kluwer, Dordrecht.

Nijkamp, P. and Vreeker, R. (2000). 'Sustainability Assessment of Development Scenarios: Methodology and Application to Thailand', *Ecological Economics*, 33: 7–27.

Perman, R., Ma, Y., McGilvray, J. and Common, M. (1999). *Natural Resource and Environmental Economics*. Longman, Dorchester.

Rotmans, J. (1997). 'Indicators for Sustainable Development'. In: Rotmans, J. and de Vries, B. (eds), *Perspectives on Global Change – The TARGETS Approach*. University Press, Cambridge.

URGE (2001). www.urge-project.org.

Vreeker, R., Nijkamp, P. and Ter Welle, C. (2002). 'A Multicriteria Decision Support Methodology for Evaluating Airport Expansion Plans', *Transportation Research Part D*, Elsevier, 7: 27–47.

WCED (1987). *Our Common Future*, Oxford University Press, New York.

14

Evaluation of Mixed Land Use Using Regime Analysis
Ron Vreeker

INTRODUCTION

Planners envisage various effects resulting from mixed land use; for example, reduced transport and energy consumption, increased safety, and increased productivity of economic activities. In most cases it is difficult to express these effects in quantitative or monetary units and therefore the inclusion of these effects in Cost–Benefit Analysis (CBA) is limited or sometimes even impossible. Multi-criteria evaluation methods, however, offer opportunities to deal with this problem. In this chapter we compare Cost–Benefit Analysis and two multi-criteria evaluation methods on the South-Axis urban development plan in The Netherlands.

WEIGHTED SUMMATION AND REGIME ANALYSIS

The multi-criteria evaluation (MCA) methods discussed here are non-monetary evaluation methods as they can cope with a variety of measurement scales to assess effects of projects or policies. To assess the performance of alternatives, MCA techniques often combine a set of criteria with a set of weights reflecting the preferences of the decision-maker.

Rather than a specific appraisal method, MCA is a family of methods. The various methods are mostly classified according to their underlying aggregation procedure (Nijkamp et al., 1990; Vincke, 1992). This is the mathematical specification of how information is translated into overall performance scores. Three aggregation procedures are distinguished, namely *iterative, complete* and *partial aggregation*.

In this chapter we show the functioning of two multi-criteria evaluation methods by applying them to a case study. The first method concerns Weighted Summation which is based upon a complete aggregation method. The second method Regime Analysis is a so-called outranking method.

Weighted summation

Just as other complete aggregation methods, Weighted Summation has its roots in Multi-attribute Utility Theory (MAUT). MAUT assumes that for any decision problem, a utility function can be defined which a decision-maker wants to maximise (Keeney and Raiffa, 1976). MAUT also assumes that all impacts are comparable and weights are used to synthesise them into one utility measure. This means that a sufficiently high score on a criterion can compensate a poor performance on another. The weights used by these methods can therefore be interpreted as trade-offs.

Weighted Summation is the least complicated method based on MAUT; it is essentially the optimisation of the following linear utility function:

$$U_i = \sum_j^J \tilde{a}_j P_{ji} \quad (i = 1, \dots \dots \dots J)$$

where P_{ji} denotes the score of alternative i on criterion j, and $\tilde{a}_j$ the weight attached to this criterion by the decision-maker. Utility U_i is the summation of the weighted criterion scores of an alternative. A utility-maximising decision-maker will ultimately select the alternative that provides the highest utility. Weighted Summation allows full compensation between scores.

Regime analysis

Criticism to MAUT led to the development of methods based on partial aggregation. These methods do not aim to optimise a mathematical model but to find a compromise solution and allow alternatives to be incomparable.

Regime Analysis uses pair-wise comparisons to assess the performance of alternatives. Based on these pair-wise comparisons outranking relationships are built between the alternatives. An outranking relation exists when the performance of alternative a is better on one criterion and at least as good as b on all other criteria considered.

Regime Analysis calculates two indices to rank alternatives (Nijkamp et al., 1990). We describe here a choice problem with a set of alternatives k and a set of criteria l. After comparing alternative i with alternative j in relation to all criteria, we select all criteria for which the former performs better than, or is equal to, the latter. We call this set of criteria the 'concordance set'. Similarly, we define the class of criteria for which alternative i performs worse than, or is equal to, alternative j. This set of criteria is called a 'discordance set'.

To rank the alternatives, a concordance index is used. This is the sum of the weights that are related to the criteria for which i performs better than j (C_{ij}). One can see that the higher the value of C_{ij} the greater is the dominance of alternative i over j. We also calculate the concordance index for the same alternatives, but by considering the criteria for which j is better than i, i.e., C_{ji}. After having calculated these two sums, we subtract these two values in order to obtain the net concordance index $\mu_{ij} = C_{ij} - C_{ji}$.

An impact matrix consisting of ordinal and cardinal data is treated in Regime Analysis as ordinal data. As a consequence only the sign of the net concordance index μ_{ij} is of our interest. If the sign is positive, this indicates that an alternative outranks another. A complex situation arises when ambiguity exists in the sign of the index. As a consequence a complete ranking of alternatives cannot be determined. This problem is solved in Regime Analysis by introducing a performance indicator which indicates the probability that an alternative dominates another. This indicator is calculated for each alternative. By means of a linear combination of the calculated probabilities, an aggregate performance score for each alternative is determined and a ranking established (Hinloopen et al., 1982).

Pros and cons of both methods

Methods based on complete aggregation require intensive interaction with the decision-maker. This concerns the elicitation of weights and the estimation of utility and value functions. One important advantage of MAUT methods is the aggregation which is fairly transparent. In this case study we applied Weighted Summation as an exponent of MAUT methods. We in particular choose this method since its aggregation procedure is transparent and interaction with the decision-maker is less intensive than with other MAUT methods. Although Weighted Summation is an elementary MCA method, it exhibits the main characteristics of MAUT.

Most methods based on partial aggregation lack transparency and are difficult to understand for a non-expert. This drawback also applies to Regime Analysis. The fact that Regime Analysis can handle mixed data sets is an advantage. To apply Weighted Summation, the effect scores need to be transformed onto a cardinal measurement scale.

THE AMSTERDAM SOUTH-AXIS

The South-Axis is located in the southern part of Amsterdam. The southern districts of Amsterdam developed in two periods. The northern part of this area, consisting of the neighbourhoods Oud-Zuid and Rivierenbuurt, was built in the 1910s and 1930s and formed an integral part of the third city expansion designed by Berlage. The southern part, consisting of the neighbourhood Buitenveldert, was built in the 1950s and 1960s. This area formed a part of the General Expansion Plan for Amsterdam.

The South-Axis is the area between these two neighbourhoods and was initially kept as a green belt area. Nowadays, the South-Axis is crossed by massive road and rail infrastructure and has railway South/World Trade Centre as its focal point.

However, the infrastructure bundle forms a major barrier and divides the southern district in two parts (Projectbureau Zuidas, 2001b).

The South-Axis houses important economic activities, such as the World Trade Centre (WTC), The Free University and Hospital, The Court of Justice, the insurance market and the headquarters of ABN-AMRO bank and the ING-group. The area also contains many green spaces: a few sport clubs, a cemetery and a park. The adjacent areas are dominated by residential functions. At least 24,000 jobs are associated with these activities (Projectbureau Zuidas, 2001b). The area is dominated by offices (450,000 m^2) and housing does not have a prominent position (37,000 m^2).

PROBLEM DESCRIPTION AND SOUTH-AXIS DEVELOPMENT PLANS

Initially the municipality of Amsterdam aimed to develop the Southern IJ-banks as the major office location. However, this policy was not supported by trends in the market for office space. Real estate companies showed particular interest in the South-Axis area.

The growing demand for space in the South-Axis area did not remain unnoticed by the municipality of Amsterdam. In 1994 the municipality stated that an integral development plan for the South-Axis should be designed to prevent further uncoordinated and undesired developments in the area. It was aimed to develop the South-Axis as a top location for business activities that can compete with other office locations in Europe.

In the *Masterplan South-Axis* it is emphasised that the construction of the so-called 'dock-model' is a prerequisite for achieving the various objectives. The dock-model consists of the subterranean placement of all infrastructure present in the South-Axis area (dRo, 1998).

Another objective of the South-Axis project is to limit the barrier effect of the infrastructure and to increase the physical connection between the residential areas of Oud-Zuid and Buitenveldert. Furthermore, by placing the infrastructure subterranean, it is expected that the noise nuisance will be reduced and spatial quality raised.

In 1997 the South-Axis project was indicated as a Key Site Project by the Ministry of Spatial Planning and the Environment. Key Site Projects are linked to the introduction of high-speed trains in the Netherlands. In those projects emphasis is placed on the integral development of locations around those railway stations. The main aim is to revitalise the existing urban centres or to create new ones here.

The Key Site Project Amsterdam South-Axis includes the construction of a new urban centre, the renovation of the railway station and the expansion of rail and road capacities. The objectives stated in the *Masterplan* are summarised in Table 14.1. It is foreseen that the construction of buildings, roads and tunnels will take a period of around 20 years. It is expected that it will take 30 to 40 years until the project objectives are fulfilled and the South-Axis reaches its full potential as a new urban centre.

Updates of the *Masterplan* are frequently given by means of the so-called 'South-Axis Vision reports' (Zuidas Visie). The First Vision report (dRo, 1999) describes the development opportunities resulting from the subterranean placement of all infrastructure components over a length of 1.2 kilometres. Due to the construction of the Dock, space for the development of offices and houses will become available. The report also states that the development of the South-Axis should be based on the mixing of functions and high density. The building density in the central area, close to the public transport terminal, will be the highest in the plan (fsi of 5.5 to 6.5).[1] The height of buildings will vary between 30 and 100m. The development of the Eastern and Western edges will be based on lower densities (fsi of 3 to 4.5). It is foreseen that high-density development will create sufficient

Table 14.1 South-Axis development objectives

Aims	Masterplan (2000–2020)
Economy	• International top office location (650,000 m²) • Creation of 90,000 m² for non-office related activities • New regional economic impulse with a specific attention for office-related industries • Creation of additional regional employment • Establishing linkages with local knowledge centres • Financing subterranean infrastructure by means of area development revenues
Living	• Development of a high-quality living area • Significant reduction of annoyance caused by transport • Development of residential areas (215,000 m²) • Provision of amenities (141,800 m²)* • Development of high-quality public spaces • Expanding the existing green areas
Use of space	• Compact and high-density land use • Infrastructure will be placed on a subterranean level • Creating a mix of various land-use functions
Transport	• Current railway station becomes major public transport node and will accommodate high-speed trains • Expansion of A10 to deal with higher traffic intensities • Creating a critical mass for the usage of public transport • Expansion of capacity for trains and light-rail systems

*In the first step of the project approximately 6500 m² of amenities is developed. This is based on the subterranean placement of the southern part of A10 orbital motorway. The subterranean placement of other infrastructure components will offer additional space for development.
Source: dRo (1998)

Table 14.2 The urban development programme of the South-Axis

	Office (in m^2)	Housing (in m^2)	Amenities (in m^2)	Total (in m^2)
Masterplan	650,975	215,880	141,575	1,008,430
Vision Report 1999	1,241,000	548,000	167,000	1,956,000
Vision Report 2001	1,007,000	982,000	263,000	2,252,000
Vision Report 2004	1,091,700	1,171,700	485,020	2,748,420

Source: dRo (2001)

support for the various facilities in the South-Axis area and enhance social cohesion. In order to create an attractive urban area, a wide variety of high-quality amenities will be developed. The public space in the South-Axis should also be of a high quality. The Vision Reports of 2001 and 2004 (dRo, 2001, 2004) reflects the municipality's preference for an even presence of housing and office in the South-Axis.

To summarise, the aim gradually changed from the development of an office location to the development of a complete urban centre (Table 14.2). Furthermore, the project includes a major expansion of the infrastructure located in the area.

ALTERNATIVES CONSIDERED IN THE SOUTH-AXIS DEVELOPMENT PROJECT

In the planning phase of the South-Axis, three alternatives were investigated. The main differences between these alternatives are related to the location of the infrastructure components and not to the composition of the infrastructure bundle. However, the urban investment programme varies per alternative, since each type of infrastructure placement offers different building opportunities.

The *Dike* alternative is characterised by an infrastructure dike of 170-m width; this dike will accommodate the lanes of the orbital motorway A10 and the tracks of subway and trains. The motorway lanes will be placed on the outer part of the dike, while the railtracks will be placed in the middle of it. Extensive development of buildings will take place on both sides of the dike. Railway station South/WTC forms the main connection between both sides of the city. Within the Dike + alternatives, the terminal will be more compact and transfer distances will be shorter. Furthermore, the urban development programme is larger in the Dike + alternative than in the Dike alternative.

In the *Dock alternative* the infrastructure will be placed subterranean over a stretch of 1.2 kilometres and space is created for the urban development programme. The public transport terminal will form an integral part of the building area for facilities and commercial activities at surface level. Emphasis will be placed on the development of a new urban centre on top of the infrastructure.

In the *Combination*, alternative parts of the infrastructure will be placed at the surface level (railroad) with parts remaining subterranean (A10 and subway). This will result in an infrastructure dike that is less wide than the one in the Dike alternative. On both sides of the dike, space is used for offices and housing. Due to high disturbance and nuisance levels it is not feasible to place residential areas along the railroad corridor. We have summarised the alternatives considered in Table 14.3.

The planning phase has been concluded with a preliminary analysis of the effects of the three alternatives (Projectbureau Zuidas, 2001a). It was concluded that the combination alternative is not viable. As a consequence, this alternative was not included in the Cost–Benefit Analysis, conducted by the Central Netherlands Bureau for Economic Policy Analysis (CPB, 2003). However, in our Multi-criteria evaluation, we will analyse the effects of the combination alternative.

The scenario for autonomous developments in Table 14.3 reflects what will happen in the project area in case none of the alternatives will be implemented. This is not simply a 'policy-off' scenario but a continuation of already agreed policy-plans. When in the impact assessment phase, the alternatives are compared with this scenario to assess the various effects. The autonomous developments scenario is thus used as a so-called 'reference alternative'.

The project consists of the expansion of infrastructure and the construction of more than 4000 houses and 200,000 m² office space. As a consequence the

Table 14.3 Characteristics of the alternatives

	Autonomous developments	Dike	Dike+*	Dock	Combination
Railroad	Surface	Surface	Surface	Sub	Surface
Subway	Surface	Surface	Surface	Sub	Sub
A10	Surface	Surface	Surface	Sub	Sub
Terminal	Per public transport system	All modalities integrated in one terminal			
Offices	461,700 m²	461,700 m²	790,200 m²	984,600 m²	1,063,900 m²
Housing	334,900 m²	334,900 m²	466,900 m²	1,056,000 m²	717,200 m²
Facilities	165,700 m²	165,700 m²	209,900 m²	321,700 m²	223,700 m²
Total	961,300 m²	961,300 m²	1,467,000 m²	2,362,300 m²	2,004,800 m²

*The constructed square meters in the Dike+, Dock and Combination alternatives include the autonomous development.
Source: Projectbureau Zuidas (2001a,b)

project initiators are obliged to conduct an Environmental Impact Assessment (EIA). This study has been divided into two stages. During the stages, the various effects of the alternatives are assessed in scenario terms. The first stage was concluded with the selection of alternatives for which in the second stage a more detailed assessment will be made (Projectbureau Zuidas, 2001b). It was concluded that the combination alternative is not politically viable. As a consequence, this alternative was not included in the CBA, conducted by the Central Netherlands Bureau for Economic Policy Analysis in 2003 (CPB, 2003).

The CPB estimated how the project would affect the real-estate markets and the market for transportation services. The results of this study indicate that the Dike and Dock alternatives do not contribute to the augmentation of the Dutch welfare. Both alternatives show a negative Net Present Value[2] (NPV) of respectively 550 million and 1050 million Euro. This is mainly caused by the small transport benefits resulting from the project.

Although various remarks can be made regarding the CPB analysis, we will not discuss them here in detail. Instead we focus on effects which cannot easily be valued in monetary terms. Noise nuisance and traffic congestion during the construction phase are, for example, not expressed in monetary terms by the CPB. As a result they do not influence the NPV of the alternatives.

By placing the infrastructure subterranean, an uninterrupted urban area will emerge, resulting in a possible improvement of the urban quality. Such an improvement will lead to increased values of land, houses and offices. Although the CPB argues that this effect is fully reflected in prices prevailing on the associated markets, the researchers had difficulties in estimating effects of increased urban quality (CPB, 2003).

Although the formal EIA is not yet completed, various environmental (external) effects were considered by the CPB, such as noise and emissions resulting from traffic and safety issues. The CPB does not foresee any increase in these parameters and the monetary values of these effects were not estimated. The first stage of the EIA, however, indicated that the alternatives differ with regard to safety, noise and environmental impacts (Table 14.4).

From the above it becomes clear that various effects are not included in the presented CBA. Furthermore, the translation of certain effects in monetary terms is sometimes cumbersome and may lead to the exclusion of these effects in a CBA. In the remainder of this chapter we will address these issues by applying MCA techniques to qualitative measurements of those effects. Furthermore, we will link the evaluation closer to the project objectives and formulate indicators which reflect those objectives.

Table 14.4 CBA South-Axis project

	Dike	Dock
Costs		
Infrastructure	550	1800
Preparation of land	450	750
Nuisance during construction phase	PM	PM
Total costs	1000	2550
Benefits		
Land revenues–offices	150	350
Land revenues–housing	150	350
Land revenues–others	100	250
Urban quality	0	450
Transport benefits	100	100
Total benefits	500	1450
NPV	−550	−1050

Source: CPB (2003)

MULTI-CRITERIA EVALUATION OF SOUTH-AXIS ALTERNATIVES

In this section we evaluate the alternatives by means of Regime Analysis and Weighted Summation. The criteria, indicators and effects used in this analysis are based on the results of the first EIA-stage described previously. This study is conducted by the Project Office Amsterdam South-Axis and Ministry of Transport Public Works and Water Management (Projectbureau Zuidas, 2001a).

In this study the effects of the alternatives on seven indicator themes were assessed. These themes included traffic, urban quality, safety, project management, effects during the construction period, environment and economy. The impacts of the alternatives on these themes are measured by means of various indicators.

The indicators selected in the first stage of the EIA reflect the various objectives associated to the South-Axis development project. An important objective of the project is the facilitation of growth in passengers using the various forms of (public) transport that come together at or crosses the South-Axis area. This includes the construction of a new public transport terminal which will enable the transfer of passengers between various modalities. Furthermore, it is foreseen that the rail and road infrastructure will be expanded by means of additional tracks and lanes. These objectives are reflected in the evaluation by the indicator themes Rail, Terminal and Road.

It is also aimed to develop the South-Axis as a location which can compete with other top-office location in Europe. Furthermore, the project should result in an enhancement of the economic structure and should provide additional employment opportunities in the Amsterdam region. To achieve this goal the area will be developed by means of mixed land use at a high density. This objective is reflected by the indicator themes Urban Quality and Economy.

Indicator themes such as safety and milieu are related to various legal requirements stemming from the spatial planning act.

Most of the effects in the first stage of the EIA are assessed on a qualitative scale ranging from $---$ to $+++$. This especially applies to the themes Rail, Terminal, Safety and Construction. Others were assessed on a quantitative scale using measurement vehicles like average speed, number of m^2. We haven chosen to transform these effects on the proposed qualitative scale. The use of the qualitative scale will still enable us to show the functioning of two MCA methods.

In this evaluation we transformed the cost indicators into benefit indicators so that they fit on the proposed qualitative measurement scale. The assessed effects are depicted in Table 14.5 and, for every indicator in these tables holds the higher the score the better. Both tables form the basis for our evaluation with Regime Analysis and Weighted Summation.

We conducted two separate multi-criteria analyses. In the first one we evaluated the performance of each alternative on the distinctive themes. In the second one all criteria were taken into consideration to evaluate the overall performance of the alternatives. In both analyses we used the effect scores depicted in Tables 14.5 and 14.6 and a weight vector in which equal weight is given to each criterion. The results of the analyses are depicted in Tables 14.7 and 14.8. The overall performance of the alternatives is highlighted in the tables. The first row indicates the position each alternative takes in the final rankings. The second row gives the overall performance scores of the alternatives. While in Regime Analysis this score reflects the probability that a specific alternative will dominate the others, in Weighted Summation it is the utility of each alternative. The results of the analysis per theme are given by means of the performance score of Regime and the calculated utility by Weighted Summation.

From the tables it can be seen that both methods place the Dike+ on the first position in their rankings. The combination alternative appears in both rankings on the lowest position.

While Regime Analysis places the Dike above the Dock alternative, this is not the case with Weighted Summation. We will clarify this difference by means of the result of the evaluation per theme. Both methods indicate that the Dike alternative dominates the Dock alternatives on the themes *Rail, Safety, Milieu, Project Management* and *Construction Phase*. The Dock alternative performs better on the themes *Terminal, Urban Quality* and *Economy*. Due to the domination of the Dike alternative on the mentioned themes, Regime Analysis places it above the Dock in the overall ranking. Weighted Summation takes the (standardised) effect sizes into

Table 14.5 Evaluation criteria and scores

Theme	Indicator	Dike	Dike+	Dock	Combination
Rail*	Excess capacity	0	0	−	− −
	Flexibility	0	0	0	0
	Turn-track functionality	0	0	−	− −
	Maintenance	+	+	0	+
	Intervention	0	0	0	0
	Expandability	0	0	− −	−
Terminal[†]	Platform functionality	0	0	−	0
	Accessibility platforms	0	+	+	+
	Transfers	0	+ +	+ +	+
	Integration of modalities	0	+ +	+ +	+
	Social safety busstation	0	0	+ +	+
	Social safety platforms	0	0	− −	−
	Social safety transfer hall	0	0	+ +	+
	Quality layout surroundings	0	0	+ +	+
	Quality layout terminal	0	+ +	+ +	+
	Phasing and exploitation	+	+	− −	−
Road	Traffic flows	0	0	0	0
	Average speed rush hour	0	0	0	0
Urban quality[§]	Land use	0	+	+ + +	+ +
	Recreation	0	0	+ +	+
	Safety	0	+	+ +	+
	Physical barrier	−	0	+ + +	+ +
Safety	Internal risk	0	0	−	−
	Individual risk	−	−	0	0
	Group risk	0	0	−	−

* Effects assessed by comparing the outcomes with the autonomous developments.
[†] The Dike alternative is used here as the reference scenario.
[§] Effects assessed by comparing the outcomes with the autonomous developments
Source: Projectbureau Zuidas (2001a)

account and the high scores on the themes *Terminal, Urban Quality* and *Economy* compensate the other scores. As a result the overall utility calculated by Weighted Summation is slightly higher than for the Dike alternative.

One should be aware that we have given here the same weight to each indicator. In reality some effects/indicators are deemed more important than others. This is especially the case for indicators related to *Urban Quality* and *Economy* since they reflect the main project objectives. It is therefore reasonable to assign higher weight values to these themes. In such a situation the Regime Analysis places the Dock alternative above the Dike. The same result is produced by Weighted Summation as the difference in utility produced between both alternatives grows in favour of the Dock.

The results of Weighted Summation indicate that the difference between the Dike+ and the Dock model is small. When we take a close look at the main categories of criteria, we see that the Dock alternative performs better than the other alternatives

Table 14.6 Evaluation criteria and scores

Theme	Indicator	Dike	Dike+	Dock	Combination
Milieu	Noise (inhabitants affected)*	0	0	0	0
	Noise (severely affected)	0	0	0	0
	Resonance	0	0	−	−
	Area $NO_2 > EU$ threshold	0	0	+	+
	Water quality	−	−	++	+
	Surface water[t]	0	0	−	−
	Resource usage	−	−	−−	−−
	Sand extracted	0	0	−−	−
	Sand needed	−	−	−	−
	Disturbance of flora/fauna	−	−	−−	−−
Project management	Phasing of activities	0	0	−−	−
Construction phase	Accessibility of area	−	−	−−	−−
	Noise	−	−	−−	−−
	Resonance	−	−	−−	−−
Economy	Investment costs	−	−	−−	−−
	Temporary employment[§]	+	++	+++	+++
	Structural employment	+	++	+++	+++

* Prognoses are based on the noise produced by traffic on motorway A10. Effects are compared with legally binding threshold values.
[t] It is assumed that larger water-areas will facilitate the drainage of surface better.
[§] Temporary employment effects resulting from the construction of real estate. Effects of infrastructure construction are excluded.
Source: Projectbureau Zuidas (2001a)

Table 14.7 Results of Regime Analysis per overall and per theme

	Dike	Dike+	Dock	Combination
Position in overall ranking	2	1	3	4
Overall performance score	0.67	1	0.33	0
Rail	0.83	0.83	0.00	0.33
Terminal	0.00	0.83	0.83	0.33
Road	Alternatives perform equally well			
Urban quality	0.00	0.33	1.00	0.63
Safety	0.67	0.67	0.33	0.33
Milieu	0.83	0.83	0.33	0.00
Project management	0.83	0.83	0.00	0.33
Construction phase	0.83	0.83	0.17	0.17
Economic effects	0.00	0.33	0.83	0.83

on the themes *Terminal*, *Urban Quality* and *Economy*. This is also emphasised by the sensitivity analysis. If more emphasis is placed on indicators belonging to these themes and less on the other indicators, the Dock alternative will attain the first

Table 14.8 Results of Weighted Summation overall and per theme

	Dike	Dike+	Dock	Combination
Position in overall ranking	3	1	2	3
Overall performance score	0.48	0.52	0.50	0.48
Rail	0.53	0.53	0.39	0.42
Terminal	0.52	0.63	0.63	0.58
Road	0.67	0.67	0.67	0.67
Urban quality	0.46	0.58	0.92	0.75
Safety	0.44	0.44	0.39	0.39
Milieu	0.43	0.43	0.38	0.37
Project management	0.50	0.50	0.17	0.33
Construction phase	0.33	0.33	0.17	0.17
Economic effects	0.56	0.67	0.72	0.72

position in the overall ranking. This is due to the compensation mechanism present in the method. This is however not the case with Regime Analysis. No matter what weights applied, the Dike+ alternative will always take the first position in the final ranking.

To conclude, the multi-criteria analysis shows that the Dike+ and Dock alternatives are preferred above the combination alternative. Although the results of Regime Analysis indicate that the Dike alternative outranks the Dock alternative, the difference between both alternatives is smaller when the Weighted Summation is applied. This highlights that the robustness of the outcomes should always be checked for their dependence on the applied method (e.g. method uncertainty).

The results of our multi-criteria evaluation indicate that the decision to drop the Combination alternative is correct. In future stages of the South-Axis development, only the suitability of the Dike+ and Dock alternatives will be investigated and the effects will be assessed in more detail.

CONCLUSIONS

Planners envisage various effects resulting from MLU. The effects are sometimes expressed in quantitative or qualitative indicator scores. In cases where assigning monetary values to the effects is difficult, the application of CBA becomes cumbersome.

From the case study it can be concluded that the absence of quantitative effect estimations can be overcome by applying MCA methods. The evaluation conducted here showed the differences between methods based on different aggregation procedures. Especially the compensation feature of the complete aggregation methods was highlighted by the results.

Whether compensation between scores is allowed depends on the decision-problem at hand. One can imagine that decision-makers will not allow the compensation of severe environmental impacts by, for example, economic indicators. In such a situation it is reasonable to apply a non-compensatory outranking method. This does, however, not apply to the Amsterdam South-Axis case study, as the environmental effects are limited. Furthermore, MLU projects are surrounded by multiple actors with multiple, often conflicting, objectives. MCA methods allow decision-makers to take this particular feature into consideration.

The MCA approach is able to cope with the multiple goals of various stakeholders in the decision-making process. The approach makes it possible for the decision-making process to be interactive and carried out in close consultation with the decision-maker and other relevant stakeholders. This might result in the selection of compromise solution, which is supported by the relevant stakeholders, instead of an optimal solution that favours only one stakeholder.

Although CBA and MCA differ in many respects, nowadays these two approaches are regarded as complementary analytical tools rather than competitive methods. A combined application might, for example, include a CBA to calculate the efficiency effects of alternatives. The results of this exercise (e.g. Benefit–Cost Ratios, NPVs) can form an input in an MCA, in which, besides the efficiency effects, both the equity consequences and the un-priced effects also are taken into account. One should be aware that 'double-counting' of effects might be a serious threat to conduct a sound evaluation of projects and policies.

With regard to the Amsterdam South-Axis case study, a combined CBA–MCA approach might be conducted in two steps. In the first step, CBA can be applied to rank and select alternatives on the basis of their economic efficiency. In the second step, MCA might be applied. Based on the selected efficient alternatives, one can reach towards a compromise solution that is supported by all stakeholders. Furthermore, the application of MCA allows for the explicit treatment of distributional and un-priced effects in the decision-making process.

To conclude, there is no single evaluation method that can satisfactorily and unequivocally evaluate all complex aspects of choice possibilities. The choice of assessment methods in any given choice context therefore depends on the features of the problem at hand, on the aims of the analysis, and on the underlying information base.

NOTES

1   Floor Space Index is Gross Floor Area divided by the Lot Area.
2   The net present value of a project is the sum of the present values of the costs and benefits of that project. Each future cost and benefit is discounted, meaning that it is divided by a number representing the opportunity cost of holding capital from now (year 0) until the year in which the benefit or cost occurs.

REFERENCES

CPB (2003), *Kengetallen Kosten-Baten Analyse Project Zuidas Amsterdam*. Den Haag: Centraal Planbureau.

dRo (1998), *Masterplan Amsterdam Zuidas*. Amsterdam: Projectbureau Zuidas.

dRo (1999), *Concept Visie Amsterdam Zuidas*. Amsterdam: Projectbureau Zuidas.

dRo (2001), *Visie Zuidas Stand Van Zaken Maart 2001*. Amsterdam: Projectbureau Zuidas.

dRo (2004), *Visie Zuidas Stand van Zaken 2004*. Amsterdam: Projectbureau Zuidas.

Hinloopen, E., Nijkamp, P. and Rietveld, P. (1982), 'The Regime Method: A New Multicriteria Method', in: P. Hansen (ed.), *Essays and Surveys on Multiple Criteria Decision Making*. Berlin: Springer.

Keeney, R. and Raiffa, H. (1976), *Decision with Multiple Objectives: Preferences and Value Trade-Offs*. New York, NY: John Wiley & Sons.

Nijkamp, P., Rietveld, P. and Voogd, H. (1990), *Multicriteria Analysis for Physical Planning*. Amsterdam: Elsevier.

Projectbureau Zuidas (2001a), *Alternatievennota Zuidas; Basis Voor Trajectnota/Mer*. Amsterdam: Projectbureau Zuidas.

Projectbureau Zuidas (2001b), *Startnotitie Integrale Trace/Mer Studie Zuidas*. Amsterdam: Projectbureau Zuidas.

Vincke, P. (1992), *Multicriteria Decision-Aid*. New York, NY: John Wiley & Sons.

Part 4.2

Advanced Evaluations of Urban Land Use

15

The Assessment of Multi-Functional Land Use
Caroline Rodenburg and Peter Nijkamp

INTRODUCTION

Economic science has traditionally shown a great interest in land use. This interest stems from three economic characteristics of land: (i) land is scarce, (ii) land has alternative use options, and (iii) land has a social value in the economy. The scarcity of goods is important from an economic point of view, as scarce resources may be depleted or even subjected to irreversible destructive processes. This poses the question of how these resources can be dealt with in a sustainable way, in order to make sure that future generations can still use them. Scarcity of land also raises policy questions concerning its efficient usage, since land can be produced only to a limited extent. At the same time, spatial claims are often conflicting, resulting in a need for conflict management. Such conflicting spatial claims stem from physical scarcity, since the choice of a certain form of land use implies the sacrifice of production factors that could be used in an alternative way. This feature is related to the second characteristic of land, namely it has alternative use options, which means that land (and other production factors) can be deployed for different – sometimes complementary, sometimes conflicting – purposes. As this chapter will show, in practice, a multiplicity of different land use functions can be distinguished. As soon as a particular function is no longer practised at a given site, the location can be used for other purposes. However, if land use is exclusively oriented towards a single function, the land often can no longer be used for other purposes, except when different functions can be combined or merged, like in multi-functional land use. The third characteristic of land, its social value, is determined by the interaction of supply and demand in the market. If the population density is increasing, the price of using scarce space will, in accordance with economic theory, increase. Since the total supply of land can in the short to medium term be regarded as fixed, the value of land may be seen as determined by demand (apart from institutional and policy interventions). However, if particular locations are considered for specific uses (e.g., the city centre), the supply of land cannot be regarded as completely inelastic, since alternative – though less preferable – locations do exist, especially when individuals accept to be located outside the city centre. One could say that the pattern of land use reflects competition in the market between alternative uses for sites. Land values and land use are therefore determined simultaneously (Harvey, 2000).

Economists have typically focussed on questions of efficiency and (more recently) sustainability of land use. These studies are generally concerned with 'mono-functional' land use patterns. In recent years, however, also the concept of multi-functional land use has gained the interest of economists. This and similar concepts have been mentioned already in earlier literature (see, e.g., Jane Jacobs (1961), Coupland (1997) and Hoover (1948)), but the economic attention for multi-functional land use arose more recently, at least in The Netherlands. Multi-functional land use attempts to combine several socio-economic functions in the same area, so as to conserve scarce space and to exploit economies of synergy. The aforementioned characteristics of land use can also be used to study the concept of multi-functional land use from a socio-economic perspective. The present chapter aims to analyse the concept of multi-functional land use in greater detail by focussing on specific land use functions and by analysing the opportunities for benefiting from multi-functionality in designated land use projects. Therefore, in the Section 'Identification of land use functions' a set of different land use functions is defined, along with the relationships between them. Since this chapter focuses mainly on urban areas, not all land use functions will be taken into account. To offer more focus, this chapter concentrates mainly on multi-functional land use projects that include, at least, an infrastructure function. Definitions of the most important concepts dealt with in this chapter (land use and multi-functionality) are presented in the Section 'Definition of land use concepts'. Before the relationship between these concepts is analysed, the factors that determine urban land use are examined in the Section 'Factors determining land use decisions'. These are investigated from a multi-functional point of view as well. The Section 'Actors in multi-functional land use' then provides an overview of the main actors in the planning and management process of multi-functional land use projects. These analytical contributions form the basis for the indicators framework presented in the Section 'Framework for analysis', through which multi-functional land use projects may be quantitatively analysed in terms of the degree of multi-functionality. The Section 'Amsterdam South-axis' is a provisional attempt to explore a multi-functional land use project (the so-called South-Axis ('Zuidas') in Amsterdam). The Section 'Concluding remarks' offers some conclusions.

IDENTIFICATION OF LAND USE FUNCTIONS

An empirical analysis of multi-functional land use, of course, requires unambiguous definitions of its elements, i.e. of the different land use functions to be distinguished. Our study will distinguish nine such (rather aggregate) typical functions (Rodenburg, 2001), namely:

1   *Residential housing* is defined as the space that is used for (permanent) living.
2   *Work and business* refers to the space that is used for commerce and industry. This includes, e.g. office locations and industry locations.
3   *Amenities* include non-profit organisations (hospitals, schools, museums, churches, etc.) as well as shopping facilities.
4   *Infrastructure* refers to the space (including safety buffers) that is used to facilitate movement of goods and persons. This includes the transport infrastructure (roads, railways, waterways, terminals, ports and airports), the communication infrastructure (data-communication networks), energy facilities (electricity network) and the water infrastructure (dikes, bridges, locks, sea walls, etc.).
5   *Recreation and culture* has a broad definition. However, specific small-scale amenities such as benches along public roads are not included. Relevant areas included are day trip destinations, campgrounds and amusement parks. Space consumed by cultural functions is also included.
6   *Water* refers to the space taken up by rivers, watercourses, lakes and territorial waters that have a 'water management' function. This also includes areas that have a drinking water function, e.g. storage of drinking water and filtration areas.
7   *Agriculture* refers to the space that is used for cropland, pasture, orchards, vineyards or horticulture, but also to the space needed for intensive, non land-constricted cattle breeding.
8   *Nature and landscape* means, in its broad definition, the space needed to maintain or guarantee the current quality of nature (biodiversity). In a more specific setting, it may refer to the Main Ecological Structure: a policy concept used in the Netherlands to indicate a spatially connected network of larger units of nature (including water). The broad definition will be used here.
9   *Remaining* includes the use of the land area that cannot be classified under one of the land use functions described above.

These individual spatial functions are meant to be mutually exclusive. This means that the sum of the total land area cannot be exceeded by the sum of the land area consumed by the different functions. The initial starting point is therefore a mono-functional land use situation in which each type of land use has its own characteristics of demand and supply.

Figure 15.1 shows the relations between the various functions (except for the function 'remaining land') and the external forces that affect the system of land use and vice versa. Examples of external forces are the actual spatial organisation,

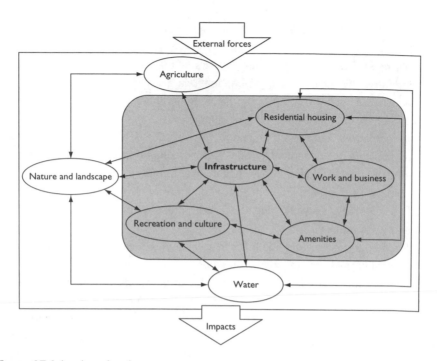

Figure 15.1 Land use functions

as well as demographic and geographic influences. The highlighted part shows the focus of this chapter: those land use functions that are most common in a multi-functional metropolitan context. Remaining land is not included in this figure, since there are no direct relations to be indicated between remaining land and other functions. This will be dependent on the activities exercised on the remaining land.

A few remarks are in order here. First, time is an important aspect of this figure for two reasons: (i) The arrows all point in two directions, but this does not necessarily mean that both influences take place at the same time. For example, the influence of residential housing on amenities is direct, since people want shops, schools, etc. close to their homes, but the development of a big shopping centre does not necessarily mean that houses will soon be established near it; (ii) Also, more generally, different arrows may refer to different time spans. For example, infrastructure has an influence on all other functions, but not necessarily at the same moment. Secondly, it is very well possible that certain relationships are more likely to occur than others.

Urban spatial structure consists of the layout of the physical components of an urban area and their interrelationships. These are continually evolving, so that spatial structure is a dynamic phenomenon, changing over time and in space

(Dowall, 1978). In determining urban structures and location behaviour, the land use system and the transportation system (regarded here as the system of transport infrastructure) are highly interdependent. Briefly stated, location decisions made as a result of land use activities are, to a large extent, the result of the relative cost of travel to various opportunities. Given the structure (layout, capacity, geographical position, etc.) of the transportation system, the pattern of trips generated by these activities affects the costs of travel in the region. It can be said, therefore, that the spatial organisation of land use determines and, at the same time, is determined by the design and characteristics of the transportation system. It is interesting to analyse this dual relation in greater detail, especially in light of multi-functional land use.

DEFINITION OF LAND USE CONCEPTS

Before discussing the dual relation between land use and transport infrastructure, it is important to determine the main concepts that will be dealt with in this chapter: land use, multi-functional land use, and factors determining land use decisions. The latter category will be discussed in the Section 'Factors determining land use decisions'.

Land use generally refers to 'how land is put to use' (Chapin and Kaiser, 1979). As has been explained in the Section 'Identification of land use functions', nine different land use functions are distinguished here, one of which is infrastructure.

When multiple functions emerge at the same location, there is a shift from mono-functional land use to *multi-functional land use*. To define multi-functional land use adequately, it is important to identify its time dimensions and its geographical scale levels. The longer the time span, the greater the extent of multi-functional land use. The larger the scope of the geographical scale, the greater the extent of multi-functional land use.

There are several current definitions of multi-functional land use. That of Lagendijk and Wisserhof (1999) is the most commonly used. It states that one can speak of multi-functional land use if at least one of the following four conditions are satisfied: (1) intensification of land use (an increase in the efficiency of the land use for a function); (2) interweaving of land use (use of the same area for several functions); (3) using the third dimension of the land (e.g. the underground along with the surface area); and (4) using the fourth dimension of the land (use of the same area for several functions within a certain time frame).

However, there are some remarks to be made that mainly concern the first element of the definition. In comparison with the other elements, intensification is a process, whereas the other three elements represent a state. This means that intensification itself cannot be observed in a static sense, but only in relation to developments over time or between different land use alternatives. Interweaving as well as the use of the third and fourth dimension can be observed as being present or not, at a certain moment. Furthermore, intensification may strictly spoken be also a matter of mono-functional land use. Only above a certain scale level intensification can lead to multi-functional land use, since more land becomes available for other functions. The interweaving of land use is defined by 'use of the same area for several functions', but it is preferable to call this 'diversity'. Interweaving, then, can be seen as the degree in which different functions touch upon other functions. For example, within a project area of 400 m², four different functions of 100 m² each may be less interwoven than the same number of functions having in total 100 m² per function as well, but scattered over the project area.

The combination of different land use functions at one location means that the land use intensity increases. Since in many countries the intensity of land use has increased in the last decades and will probably increase further, it is difficult to develop a clear definition of multi-functional land use. The concept of multi-functional land use is very broad. It can range from a combination of two economic functions to the combination of all nine economic functions shown in Figure 15.1, depending on the chosen scale level. In this chapter, for practical reasons, the project level has been chosen as the scale level. The boundaries of the project define the area that will be analysed. When seen from a project perspective, it is very hard to indicate whether projects are multi-functional or not. A practical definition of multi-functional land use should therefore reflect that the concept is best understood as a relative, non-binary one: it is better to define a degree of multi-functionality than to make a strict demarcation between mono- and multi-functional land use patterns. A more suitable definition of multi-functional land use from a developmental perspective would be: A land use pattern is said to become more multi-functional when the average number of functions and/or units of land increases in the area considered. An increased degree of multi-functionality may therefore result from the addition of functions to the area (multi-functionality by diversity) or from a decrease in the average size of mono-functional areas (multi-functionality by interweaving).

Clearly, increased multi-functionality may be the result of market forces, government policies or both. From an economic perspective, market forces can be subdivided into demand factors (such as an increased preference for diversity of products and services and marketing externalities) and supply factors (such as agglomeration externalities).

It is important to identify specific focal points in order to design an operational definition of multi-functional land use in actual situations (case studies). Nijkamp et al. (2000) have carried out an electronic interactive consultation about the definition of multi-functional land use. The consultation made clear that when applying the definition of multi-functional land use to actual situations, the time dimension and geographical scale level must be specified, but also the following aspects need explicit consideration:

- The *efficiency* of the multi-functional land use project, compared to the current use of the land, not only as far as the costs of space and space-saving are concerned, but, especially, as far as quality of space and sustainability are concerned.
- The *diversity* of the project's appearance: this can be an extension, such as a new development or an intensification, which means a change in the organisation of space.
- The *synergy* of the economic and spatial functions that are brought together, leading to increasing returns to scale.

FACTORS DETERMINING LAND USE DECISIONS

The most important concepts in this chapter were defined in the previous section; now it is important to analyse why and how the concept of multi-functional land use originated. Theories on urban land use address the factors that determine urban growth and spatial structure, and analyse their interactions with respect to their impact on spatial configurations. Urban growth and spatial structure are closely related phenomena, since changes in spatial structure are heavily influenced by the observed or expected growth rate. Urban spatial structure consists of the layout of the physical components of an urban area and their inter-relationships. These are continually evolving, so that spatial structure is a dynamic phenomenon, changing over time and in space (Dowall, 1978). Urban land use is determined by the various decisions made by firms, households and the government (Fujita *et al.*, 1999; Harvey, 2000). Firms occupy land with offices and factories. They must continually decide whether or not to expand, and, if so, whether to move to a new site or redevelop the existing one. When new firms come into being they have to choose where to locate themselves. The main element influencing this decision is profit maximisation. More or less the same thing holds true for households. They have to decide where to live, and usually make this decision in order to maximise utility. The government influences land use by controlling development, overall transport policy and the location of roads. The government also makes decisions about housing construction and redevelopment. Government does not strive towards profit or utility maximisation, but tries to find the most optimal way of determining land use for society.

When undesirable consequences arise from land use choices thought to be economically desirable, the decision about whether or not to implement the choices must be based on a policy value judgement (Lean, 1969). On the basis of this value judgement, it has to be decided whether the economic gain from the land use decision outweighs the social, political or other undesirable consequences. Outlining the economic costs and benefits of alternative land use decisions can support this process of decision-making.

To understand land use decisions, we must consider the factors determining profitability and utility. Five main factors can be identified (based on Harvey, 2000): *accessibility, agglomeration economies, historical development, topographical features* and *technological development.*

1   *Accessibility* can be defined as 'the money, time and trouble costs of getting anywhere' (Harvey, 2000), where accessibility increases if these costs decrease. Firms require accessibility to factors of production (especially labour) and to markets. Households, on the other hand, require accessibility to work opportunities, shops, schools and recreational facilities. Accessibility is largely dependent upon transport facilities; transport costs are therefore an important determinant of the location of firms and households. Other determinants are the money, time and trouble costs of travel as well as communication costs. These costs result from the fact that spatial interaction – in a general sense – involves the movement of people, goods, production factors or services, or the transfer of ideas and information.

2   *Agglomeration economies*, in the broadest sense, may also influence location decisions. This means, e.g., that by locating closer together, firms can produce at lower cost. In agglomeration economies, activities compete for scarce space. There are various types of agglomeration economies, such as localisation economies, urbanisation economies and shopping externalities (e.g. O'Sullivan, 2000). To create localisation economies, firms locate themselves close to other firms in the industry, clustering in order to decrease their production costs. Urbanisation economies occur if the production cost of an individual firm decreases as the total output of the urban area increases. Shopping externalities arise if shops selling comparable goods profit from their mutual proximity by offering consumers greater choice and improving the location's reputation as a source for a particular good.

3   *Historical development*: Current and future development is often dependent on past development and on the current function of an area. At some geographical locations, land use patterns may be heavily influenced by location decisions

made by the Romans or by nineteenth-century industrialists; other land use patterns are clearly the product of twentieth-century planning. This path dependency means that present spatial organisation is a logical starting point for an analysis of the future land use of certain areas.

4   *Topographical features*: Geographical heterogeneity is an important factor in the location decisions for certain activities. An activity's ultimate location is often dependent on physical features such as rivers, mountains, plains, slopes, wind, climate and geology.

5   *Technological developments*, together with increases in real income, are important factors that determine land use decisions. The widespread ownership of cars and freezers, together with new retailing techniques, largely accounts for the setting up of out-of-town hypermarkets, retail warehouses and shopping centres. The development of road transport has also resulted in the construction of residences on the land between the major transport routes of urban areas and in the movement of households towards the peripheries. For offices, the effects of technological development are mixed. New building techniques have reduced the cost of upward building, leading to more intensive development of the CBD. Improved information technology, in contrast, enables the majority of office procedures to be carried out at sub-centres.

The aforementioned factors influencing ultimate land use decisions can also be used to explain the increasing attention now being paid to multi-functional land use. If different land use functions are combined, *accessibility* becomes even more important. In every urban area there are locations where the transport routes and systems converge. These locations are the positions with the greatest accessibility for the population of the urban area (Lean, 1969) and are therefore very suitable for multi-functional land use. At these locations, transport costs are lower (shorter distances, but also multipurpose trips), enabling firms and households to save time and money on transport. Concerning the *agglomeration economies*, their size could increase with an increase in multi-functional land use. Urbanisation economies and shopping externalities are particularly likely to result from multi-functional land use. Obviously, *historical development* and *topographical features* do not change as a result of the combination of functions in space. The final factor *technological development* is an important reason for the development of the concept of multi-functional land use. Not only improvements in construction techniques, but also developments in ICT possibilities have created new insights into opportunities for combining economic activities.

Another important element must be taken into account concerning location decisions and multi-functional land use: *scarcity of land*. The scarcity of land is an important reason for the development of multi-functional land use. People do not want only to live in densely populated areas, but also want to be able to work, shop, move around, etc. in order to maximise their utility. If all these different activities have to be carried out in a limited space, land use functions will have to be combined (e.g., by using the third and/or fourth dimension). This type of development corresponds with one of the main characteristics of the urban economy – the interdependence of land uses, which is largely created by external economies and diseconomies of production and consumption. These interdependencies bring about entirely different uses and values in areas with the same level of general accessibility. The theories on the concentric ring pattern of the spatial distribution of land use and the smooth pattern of the rent gradient may, therefore, have to be modified. The spatial distribution of land use patterns can be expected to become far more patchy as complementary land use patterns are gathered together in specific parts of the city where they can more easily enjoy the benefits of their proximity. The rent gradient will consequently show 'bumps' – temporary rises in land values reflecting areas of land use where neighbourhood economies are very favourable (Newell, 1977).

ACTORS IN MULTI-FUNCTIONAL LAND USE

Next to the aforementioned factors influencing land use decisions of firms and households, there are also general economic market factors that influence both ultimate land use decisions and possible opportunities for multi-functional land use. Examples are demand and supply factors, costs involved with spatial interaction, existence of negative spatial external effects as well as policies influencing land use. This broad spectrum of factors underlying land use decisions indicates that there are many different parties involved, especially in multi-functional land use where different land use functions are combined. To be able to understand the success and failure factors as well as the complexities that might arise in a multi-functional urban setting it is important to know who is involved as share- or stakeholder in the process of realisation and exploitation of multi-functional land use projects.

There are four main parties to be distinguished: investors, corporate organisations, individuals and government. *Investors* are parties investing in infrastructure and real estate. Examples of investors are the public sector, municipalities, landowners, speculators, real estate developers, banks, brokers and real estate agents. *Organisations* are parties that operate infrastructure, but also parties that rent office/retail space, or institutions that manage the operationalisation of public and private facilities or amenities. Examples of operators are railway and bus companies, housing associations, retailers and tenants of office space. *Individuals* are the people who make use of the different land use functions and the related activities offered after realisation of the multi-functional project. Examples of users are dwellers, employees, travellers and shoppers. The final stakeholder is the *government*, whose main aim is to take care of the social interest. Besides, government can play a role as investor, organisation and individual as well. Examples are national, regional and local governments.

The presence of different stakeholders leads to organisational complexities. Not only because each stakeholder has its own interest, but also because there is a dependency of governments with regard to certain land use elements of the location. Since there is often publicly owned infrastructure involved in multi-functional land use projects (which often contain a majority of privately owned land use functions), in many cases there is a certain form of public–private partnership necessary in order to develop the site. In a perfect situation, such a partnership should lead to the realisation of value added and efficiency gains. This could be realised by a more proportional distribution of means between public and private parties, the use of market knowledge in the early stages of the process and by carrying out the project more efficiently. However, in practice, the uncertainty about the character of the co-operation, the juridical and financial consequences for both public and private parties and the participation of governments often lead to more complexity without evidence of the value added and the efficiency gains. The degree of multi-functionality of projects may also influence the complexity of development of and co-operation within projects.

Redevelopment of Dutch railway station sites (often having a high degree of multi-functionality when an additional floor level is built on top of the rail infrastructure) shows erratic results due to the former mentioned complexity. To realise a program that meets the needs of every party involved is difficult. The emphasis on financial feasibility of the projects on the level of co-operation between municipalities and real estate developers often leads to a homogeneous programme with emphasis on office development. Aims such as improving the social safety and contributing to the stimulation of the use of public transport are often not explicitly addressed.

FRAMEWORK FOR ANALYSIS

The observations so far form the basis of a framework for the analysis of multi-functional land use projects. The analysis attempts to identify criteria that measure the degree of multi-functionality of a certain land use project. There are various publications about relevant kinds of criteria and indicators to measure, for example specialisation, diversity and intensification (see, e.g., Fouchier, 1996; Harts *et al.*, 1999; McCann, 2001; and Piepers, 2001). However, the criteria used in this chapter do not have to be assigned only to the different land use functions, but have to be also adjusted for the scope of a specific multi-functional project. The adjustment of criteria will mainly be dependent on the specific land use functions involved in the multi-functional project concerned.

Operational indicators to measure the degree of multi-functionality of a certain land use project have to be related to the elements of the definition of multi-functional land use as presented in the Section 'Definition of land use concepts'. As a starting point, it is important to define what we want to measure, or, in other words, from which viewpoint we want to reason. A logical starting point is the creation of a distinction between input and output (performance) of land use. Since this chapter deals mainly with the supply side of land use, our starting point will be the input side.

A first multi-functionality indicator that complies with the definition of multi-functional land use is *diversity*, representing 'the different land use functions that can simultaneously be found in the project area at hand'. These can simply be counted as frequencies according to the definitions of land use functions as presented in the Section 'Identification of land use functions':

$$\text{Diversity} = \frac{\text{Actual number of functions}}{\text{Maximum number of feasible functions}}$$

The actual number of functions in our case cannot exceed 9; the maximum number in our classification. Clearly, the maximum value of diversity is always 1. This indicator is a tentative one, but could be made more precise by identifying and assessing sub-functions.

An indicator that is closely related to diversity is *dispersion*. This indicator is based on the Herfindahl-Hirschman index (HHI) (see Hannan, 1997; and Lijesen *et al.*, 2002) and dependent on the actual number of functions as used for the diversity indicator. Dispersion measures 'the degree to which each function is present in equal proportions within the project area (in m^2 land use)', as represented by the following formula:

$$\text{Dispersion} = \frac{1}{I * \sum_{i=1}^{I} (M_i/S)^2}$$

where
M_i = the amount of m² land used by a single function i (input)
S = the total amount of m² land use of the project area
I = the actual number of functions (where I has a maximum of 9 (according to the definition of land use functions in the Section 'Identification of land use functions')).

This indicator has a maximum value of 1, indicating that there is maximum dispersion within the project area, or, in other words, the proportion of each individual function is equal to that of the other functions. The minimum value of this indicator varies with the number of functions that are present within the project area. According to our maximum of nine land use functions as defined is this chapter, the minimum dispersion value will be 1/9. This indicator will, ideally, be measured in m² land use, since this shows the proportion of territories of land used within the project area by the different functions, and with that the spatial dispersion of the functions in a flat surface.

The second element in the definition of multi-functional land use is *interweaving*, which is defined as 'the degree to which different functions touch upon other functions'. This case of interrelatedness can be represented by the following formula:

$$\text{Interweaving} = \sum_{i=1}^{I} \frac{B_i}{S}$$

where
B_i = the length of physical boundaries with other functions within the project area
S = the total amount of m² land use of the project area
I = the actual number of functions (where I has a maximum of 9 (according to the definition of land use functions in the Section 'Identification of land use functions')).

This indicator does not reckon with the third (vertical) dimension yet and is therefore only measured in a flat surface. To solve this shortcoming, the surface of boundaries between land use functions could be measured for B_i, and S could then be expressed in m³. However, these are just tentative ideas that have not been crystallised yet in empirical work.

Another relevant feature is concerned with intensity of functions. Although *intensification* – as a process – in itself is difficult to observe in a static sense, it is useful and illustrative to show the land use intensity for different land use alternatives. Therefore, it will be used here as one of the indicators representing the degree of multi-functionality of a specific land use project. Only in the case of a comparison between different alternatives we may draw conclusions about the degree of multi-functional land use (possibly related to the third dimension). Intensification should, in the first instance, be measured for each single land use function ($i = 1, \ldots, I$), which can be represented by the following formula:

$$\text{Intensification} = \frac{Q_i}{M_i}$$

where
Q_i = the amount of non-land input of a certain land use function (houses, employment, etc.)
M_i = the amount of m² land used by a single function i (input)
I = the actual number of functions (where I has a maximum of 9 (according to the definition of land use functions in the Section 'Identification of land use functions')).
 Intensification may also be measured for the project area as a whole:

$$\text{Intensification} = \sum_{i=1}^{I} \frac{Q_i}{S}$$

where
Q_i = the amount of non-land input of the project area
S = the total amount of m² land use of the project area
I = the actual number of functions (where I has a maximum of 9 (according to the definition of land use functions in the Section 'Identification of land use functions')).
 In this case, in measuring the intensification for the project area as a whole we need to have a common unit of measurement to express the non-land inputs of the different land use functions. For example, in the first indicator for intensification, the input for working and business and amenities is measured via the number of jobs created, and the input for residential housing is measured via the number of houses to be realised. These units cannot be summed up and should therefore be expressed in a common unit of measurement. An example of such a unit is to express all non-land inputs in Euro (€).
 For future studies, it will be interesting and necessary to analyse the ceteris paribus influence of the aggregation level of the land use functions on the indicators.
 In the next section, an example of a multi-functional land use project will be analysed in terms of 'degree of multi-functionality'. The aforementioned criteria will be applied to the different alternatives for developing the so-called South-Axis ('Zuidas') in Amsterdam, which will be presented in the next section.

THE AMSTERDAM SOUTH-AXIS

The Amsterdam South-Axis ('Zuidas') is in general regarded as a location with a high development potential for offices, houses and amenities. It is intended to become a location with an adequate mix of functions, which should not have a negative effect on the functioning of the city centre of Amsterdam. The development of the South-axis is intended to create a new urban environment with its own identity. There are a number of goals for the development of the South-axis, in particular to eliminate the barrier effect of the ring road around Amsterdam, to prevent mono-functionality, and to create a solid and consistent public space. With the South-axis project, this part of the city is intended to undergo enormous improvements in quality. Currently, there is already a certain mix of functions available at the South-axis. There are housing areas of high quality on both sides of the ring road, as well as an international exhibition centre and conference facilities (RAI), the World Trade Centre, a university (Free University) and an academic hospital, the Court of Justice and various office buildings. The Masterplan South-axis (DRO, 1998) aims at strengthening this mix of functions in order to increase the status of the location.

In the planning process thus far three alternatives for the development of the South-axis are distinguished: the Dock alternative, the Dike alternative and the Combination alternative. These alternatives will be compared here with a reference situation, assuming an autonomous development of the area (DRO, 1998).

The *Dock alternative* puts all infrastructure underground over a length of 1.2 km, providing a huge extra amount of available building space.

In the *Dike alternative*, all through traffic will be guided on an elevated dike infrastructure. The latter will be situated at the current level on a broadened dike body of width 170 m. This alternative has a compact terminal for public transport with short transfer distances; the external architecture of the dike is on a qualitatively sophisticated level, and there is an extra underpass for slow traffic.

The *Combination alternative* combines different aspects of the Dock and the Dike alternative. The essence of this alternative is that only parts of the infrastructure will be brought underground: road traffic will be positioned underground, whereas the rail infrastructure will stay at its current level. In this alternative, the dike will become narrower, allowing for construction of offices and houses on both sides of the dike on top of the road infrastructure (that has been constructed underground).

Table 15.1 shows the number of m² floor space occupied by certain functions as well as the number of planned jobs and houses within the project area.

With the data in this table we can try to calculate the indicators as developed in the Section 'Framework for analysis' (see Table 15.2). The first indicator is diversity. The value of this indicator is for all four alternatives the same, namely 1; there are seven land use functions (offices, residential housing, amenities, infrastructure,

Table 15.1 The three alternatives for the Amsterdam South-Axis ('Zuidas') and autonomous development in m^2

	Autonomous	Dock	Dike	Combination
Total built-up area	962,300	2,362,300	1,467,000	2,004,800
Offices	461,700 (48%)	984,600 (42%)	790,200 (54%)	1,063,900 (53%)
Residential housing	334,700 (35%)	1,056,00 (45%)	466,900 (33%)	717,200 (36%)
Amenities	165,700 (17%)	321,700 (13%)	209,900 (14%)	223,700 (11%)
Infrastructure	1,374,091	1,423,031	1,374,091	1,397,454
Green	309,153	370,328	309,153	335,190
Water	80,000	100,000	120,000	90,000
Remaining	827,626	562,926	787,626	723,921
Planned jobs	24,600	35,000	40,500	53,100
Planned houses	2680	8450	3730	5730

Table 15.2 Indicator values for the four alternatives for the Amsterdam South-Axis ('Zuidas')

	Autonomous	Dock	Dike	Combination
Diversity	1	1	1	1
Dispersion	0.60	0.71	0.67	0.69
Interweaving	NA	NA	NA	NA
Intensification:				
(1) Q_i/S Offices	0.009	0.013	0.015	0.019
Residential housing	0.001	0.003	0.001	0.002
Amenities	0.001	0.001	0.001	0.001
(2) Floor space created/total project area	0.35	0.85	0.53	0.72
(3) Floor space created/total 'commercial' land use	4.97	7.20	7.57	8.42

water, nature and landscape, and remaining) out of seven possible, feasible functions (according to the definitions used in the Section 'Identification of land use functions'). Agriculture is not a feasible land use function at the Amsterdam South-axis and recreation and culture will in this case be assigned to 'remaining' since there is no detailed information available.

The second indicator, dispersion, is more difficult to calculate. The only alternative for which all necessary data are readily available is the Dock alternative. For the other alternatives, the data for the Dock alternative have been adapted to the characteristics of the alternative concerned. This means that with the help of a land use map for the Dock alternative, the proportions of land that will be lost by applying the Combi alternative, Dike alternative or Autonomous development (in which only a part of the layer on top of the infrastructure will be realised (Combi alternative) or no extra layer at all (Dike alternative and Autonomous development)) are attributed to the respective land use functions. Furthermore, as a result of a lack of data, the dispersion has been calculated by means of the amount of m^2 floor space instead of land use, for the individual land use functions as well as the total project area. The result shows that the Dock alternative has the highest value for dispersion. A value of one would mean that all functions occupy the same share of the project area. Therefore, its value of 0.71 means that, of all alternatives, the total land use by the different land use functions in the Dock alternative is most evenly spread over the different functions.

Also, the calculation of interweaving creates some difficulties. There are no data available on the length of physical boundaries with other functions within the project area for any of the four alternatives. This means that this indicator can only be judged qualitatively. However, since there is as yet no information on the distribution of the functions over the project area (to which extent will the functions be realised in a flat surface or will the third dimension be used), nothing can be said about the qualitative value of this indicator either.

The final indicator of intensification cannot be calculated for each single land use function, since there are no detailed data on land use per function. However, the second indicator for intensification as presented in the Section 'Framework for analysis' can be calculated, but only for work and business, residential housing and amenities. It shows some differences between the alternatives as a result of differences in the number of planned jobs and houses in the project area. Since the distribution of m^2 floor space for houses, offices and amenities differs per alternative as well, the values for intensification for offices, houses and amenities can best be considered in combination.

Another calculation that could be made with the available data and that is illustrative for intensification is the amount of m^2 floor space created for work and business, residential housing, and amenities divided by the amount of m^2 floor space of the total project area, and by the land used for these functions (variants on floor space index (FSI)). These values show which alternative creates the biggest amount of m^2 floor space within the project area, and which alternative uses the area for offices, housing and amenities most intensively. It is not surprising that the Dock alternative has the highest value on the first indicator (0.85), since it has more space available to built offices, houses and amenities, due to bringing the infrastructure underground. However, for the second indicator, the highest value can be found in the Combi alternative (8.42). This shows that in this alternative, the buildings will have to be higher in order to create the planned floor space within the planned area. This alternative uses the land for offices, houses and amenities most intensively, which is also reflected in the value for intensification on offices (Q_i/S).

Table 15.3 Performance scores of
alternatives based on Regime analysis

Alternative	Score
Autonomous	0.00
Dock	0.82
Dike	0.35
Combination	0.83

We have distinguished in an illustrative case study four development alternatives, each characterised by distinct numerical indicators which may be seen as
quantitative approximations of attributes of these plan alternatives. This is a clear
case of a multi-criteria evaluation problem, which aims to identify the most promising
choice possibilities. The four alternatives have been evaluated by means of the
so-called 'Regime analysis', which is a discrete multi-criteria method (Hinloopen
et al., 1983; Nijkamp *et al.*, 1990). This method is based upon two kinds of input
data: an impact matrix and a set of political weights. The impact matrix shows the
effect of each alternative on the indicators considered. The set of weights provides
information about the relative importance of the indicators considered. In this analysis no policy weights have been given to the indicators, so we used a uniform
weight factor. On the basis of these inputs, the Regime method provides us with a
ranking of the alternatives in terms of degree of multi-functionality (see Table 15.3).

This table shows that the Combi alternative has the highest score on multi-
functionality, although the difference with the Dock alternative is negligibly low. The
Dike alternative has a much lower score, whereas the Autonomous development
shows the lowest score. A sensitivity analysis attributing different weights to different
indicators does not give really different results. Depending on the indicator that will
be attributed the highest score, the Combi alternative or the Dock alternative has
the highest score. The Autonomous development always has a score of 0, whereas
the Dike alternative always has an intermediate score.

Table 15.3 shows furthermore that – given the current available database –
the Combi and the Dock alternatives are obvious examples of alternatives with a
high multi-functionality value. The two others are inferior and do not offer a clear
contribution to multi-functionality. It should be added that multi-functionality in itself
is not a policy goal. It serves merely to realise other objectives, such as a keen
management of scarce space. In our particular case, both the Dock and the Combi
options reduce the barrier function of the infrastructure and may therefore be attractive policy options, while the multi-functionality is just the instrument through which
this objective is met.

These results show that a subterranean infrastructure option creates favourable opportunities for multi-functional land use. The choice for the Dock alternative as the most optimal filling in of the project area, however, is mainly based on the increase in connectivity between the different areas of Amsterdam, which, in this alternative, will no longer be separated by the infrastructure. The importance of infrastructure for the Amsterdam South-Axis is recognised and travellers are best facilitated in the Combi and Dock alternatives.

CONCLUDING REMARKS

The concept of multi-functional land use has turned out to be a very interesting one in urban and infrastructure planning. Economic research has traditionally put great interest in mainly mono-functional land use based on issues of efficiency and (more recently) sustainability. Multi-functional land use, however, attempts to combine several socio-economic functions in the same area, so as to conserve scarce space and to exploit economies of synergy. A practical definition of multi-functional land use should reflect that the concept is best understood as a relative, non-binary one: it is better to define a degree of multi-functionality than to make a strict demarcation between mono- and multi-functional land use patterns. In order to operationalise the concept of multi-functional land use, a functional typology of specific land use functions is needed, along with the development of criteria and indicators to measure the degree of multi-functionality of specific land use projects. From a critical analysis of common definitions of multi-functional land use, the most important elements for measuring the degree of multi functionality became clear in the present study. Applying these indicators to a case study (the Amsterdam South-Axis) showed that different project alternatives might have different degrees of multi-functionality. It is interesting to analyse this in further detail in the light of underlying assumptions regarding the ultimate choice for one of the alternatives. This is also dependent upon the preferences of the actors in multi-functional land use projects. The degree of multi-functionality will have consequences for investment costs (investors), for the number of functions that can be exercised at the location (organisations), and on how people experience and value the site (individuals). Another future research challenge is to adjust the current indicators for a comparison between different projects, instead of an analysis of different alternatives for one project as presented in this chapter. Therefore, a reflection on the nature of indicators concerning factors such as aggregation level of land use functions, dispersion, concentration, diversity, interweaving and intensity, taking into account the state of affairs in other disciplines, is likely to be a very interesting exercise.

ACKNOWLEDGEMENT

This research was sponsored by HABIFORUM, the Dutch expertise network on multi-functional land use.

REFERENCES

Chapin, F.S. and Kaiser, E.J. (1979), *Urban Land Use Planning*. University of Illinois Press, Urbana.

Coupland, A. (1997), 'An introduction to mixed use development', in: Coupland, A. (ed.), *Reclaiming the City; Mixed use Development*. Spon, London.

Dowall, D.E. (1978), *Theories of Urban Form and Land Use: A Review*. Working Paper 295. Institute of Urban & Regional Development. University of California, Berkeley.

DRO (Dienst Ruimtelijk Ordening) (1998), *Masterplan Zuidas*. Gemeente, Amsterdam.

Fouchier, P. (1996), *Measuring the Density: But Which Density?* Evry New Town Corporation. French Institute of Town Planning. Paper presented at the Norwegian Ministry of Environment Workshop on 'Density and Green Structure' in Oslo, 25–27 January.

Fujita, M., Krugman, P. and Venables, A.J. (1999), *The Spatial Economy, Cities, Regions and International Trade*, MIT Press Mass., Cambridge.

Hannan, T.H. (1997), 'Market share inequality, the number of competitors and the HHI: an examination of bank pricing'. *Review of Industrial Organisation*, Vol. 12, pp. 23–35.

Harts, J.J., Maat, C. and Zeijlmans van Emmichoven, D. (1999), *Meervoudig Stedelijk Ruimtegebruik; methode en analyse*. Stedelijke en Regionale Verkenningen 20. Delft University Press, Delft.

Harvey, J. (2000), *Urban Land Economics*. MacMillan Press Ltd., London.

Hinloopen, E., Nijkamp, P. and Rietveld, P. (1983), 'Qualitative discrete multiple criteria choice models'. *Regional Planning, Regional Science and Urban Economics*, Vol. 13, no. 1, pp. 77–102.

Hoover, E.M. (1948), *The Location Theory of Economic Activity*, McGraw-Hill, New York.

Jacobs, J. (1961), *The Death and Life of Great American Cities*, Penguin, Harmondsworth.

Lagendijk, A. and Wisserhof, J. (1999), Geef Ruimte de Kennis, Geef Kennis de Ruimte, deel 1: Verkenning van de kennisinfrastrcutuur voor meervoudig ruimtegebruik. Rapport aan de Raad. RMNO-nummer 136.

Lean, W. (1969), *Economics of Land Use Planning; Urban and Regional*. The Estates Gazette Limited, London.

Lijesen, M.G., Nijkamp, P. and Rietveld, P. (2002), 'Measuring competition in civil aviation'. *Journal of Air Transport Management*, Vol. 8, pp. 189–197.

McCann, P. (2001), *Urban and Regional Economics*. Oxford University Press, Oxford.

Newell, M. (1977), *An Introduction to the Economics of Urban Land Use*. The Estates Gazette Limited, London.

Nijkamp, P., Rietveld, P. and Voogd, H. (1990), *Multi-criteria Analysis for Physical Planning*. Elsevier, Amsterdam.

Nijkamp, P., Vreeker, R. and van Delft, H. (2000), Electronische Interactieve Consultatie EMR: Een gezelschapsdiscussie over het begrip Meervoudig Ruimtegebruik. Vrije Universiteit, Amsterdam.

O'Sullivan, A. (2000), *Urban Economics*. Irwin McGraw-Hill, Boston.

Piepers, P. (2001), Financiële Haalbaarheid van Meervoudig Ruimtegebruik bij Infrastructurele Knooppunten. Afstudeeronderzoek Technische Universiteit Delft, Delft.

Rodenburg, C.A. (2001), *Multi-functional Land Use in The Netherlands*. Paper presented at the ERSA Conference of the European Regional Science Association, August 29–September 1, Zagreb.

16

The PROPOLIS Model for Assessing Urban Sustainability
Klaus Spiekermann and Michael Wegener

INTRODUCTION

The notion of each generation's duty to its successors is at the heart of the concept of sustainable development and was captured by the Brundtland Commission (WCED, 1987) in its report 'Our Common Future', which defined sustainable development as 'development that meets the needs of the present generation without compromising the ability of future generations to meet their own needs'. Many definitions have followed that of the Brundtland Commission. For example, Daly (1991) defines sustainable development as one that satisfies three basic conditions: (1) its rates of use of renewable resource do not exceed their rates of regeneration; (2) its rates of use of non-renewable resources do not exceed the rate at which sustainable renewable substitutes are developed; and (3) its rates of pollution do not exceed the assimilative capacity of the environment.

However, many definitions of sustainability are broader in concept and seek to extend the definition beyond environmental considerations and include issues of social equity and justice. Different weight is often also given to the importance of economic growth. For instance, the 'Charter of European Cities and Towns Towards Sustainability' states that the main basis for sustainable development is 'to achieve social justice, sustainable economies, and environmental sustainability. Social justice will necessarily have to be based on economic sustainability and equity, which require environmental sustainability' (ICLEI, 1994).

In the sustainability discussion, often a distinction is drawn between major environmental threats to human life on the planet earth on the one hand and local concerns which are more amenable to trade-offs on the other. In this discussion, cities and urban regions play an important role. Cities contribute to a large extent to global environmental problems, but at the same time people living in cities are confronted with environmental damage, pollution, health and social and economic problems.

Consequently, goals to make cities more sustainable have been formulated (e.g. European Environment Agency, 1995):

- minimising the consumption of space and natural resources;
- rationalising and efficiently managing urban flows;

- protecting the health of the urban population;
- ensuring equal access to resources and services;
- maintaining cultural and social diversity.

Also, different policies including transport, land use, regulatory, investment, fiscal and pricing policies to improve the urban situation have been designed and partly implemented. However, actual urban developments show that these policies have not been able to stop the decrease of sustainability of our cities. Even to maintain the existing level of sustainability will probably require the introduction of more radical policy measures. But such policies will not be implemented if their effects cannot be clearly demonstrated. Policies might have very different effects. Besides direct environmental, social or economic impacts many policy options may have negative side effects. Some policy options may work against each other, whereas some may reinforce each other. Some policy options may improve the situation in part of the region, whereas in other parts the situation may get worse. Hence, the design of policies to improve urban sustainability is anything else than a straightforward task. Because the direct and indirect, the short-term and long-term effects have to be identified and measured in a transparent way, this calls for advanced methods of policy impact assessment and policy evaluation.

To develop and implement such a system is the objective of the EU research project PROPOLIS. The goal is to assess urban strategies and to demonstrate their long-term effect in European cities with respect to sustainability. To reach this goal, a comprehensive framework of methodologies including integrated land use, transport and environmental modelling as well as indicator, evaluation and presentation systems have been developed.

PROPOLIS is part of the Key Action 'City of Tomorrow and Cultural Heritage' of the 5th Framework Programme for Research and Technology Development of the European Union. Project partners are IRPUD and S&W (Dortmund), LT (Helsinki), ME&P (Cambridge), MECSA (Bilbao), STRATEC (Brussels), TRT (Milan) and UCL (London).

The objective of the EU research project PROPOLIS (Planning and Research of Policies for Land Use and Transport for Increasing Urban Sustainability) is to assess urban strategies and to demonstrate their long-term effect in European cities. To reach this goal, a comprehensive framework of methodologies including integrated land use, transport and environmental models as well as indicators, evaluation and presentation systems has been developed.

Sustainable development is viewed as comprising the environmental, socio-cultural and economic dimension. To measure the three dimensions of sustainability, 35 key indicators were defined – such as air pollution, consumption of natural resources, quality of open space, population exposure to air pollution and noise, equity and opportunities and economic benefits from transport and land use.

Indicator values are derived from state-of-the-art urban land-use and transport models. A number of additional modules, including a justice evaluation module, an economic evaluation module and a GIS-based raster module, were developed and integrated to provide further indicator values. Both multicriteria and cost–benefit analysis methods are used to consistently evaluate the impacts of the policies. The environmental and social dimensions of sustainability are measured using multicriteria analysis for the evaluation of the indicators, whereas cost–benefit analysis is used for the economic dimension. The modelling and evaluation system is currently being implemented in seven European urban regions: Bilbao (Spain), Brussels (Belgium), Dortmund (Germany), Helsinki (Finland), Inverness (Scotland), Naples (Italy) and Vicenza (Italy).

A large number of policies are being tested with the modelling and evaluation system in the seven urban regions. Policies investigated are land-use policies, transport infrastructure policies, transport regulation and pricing policies and combinations of these. Besides a common set of policies examined in all seven urban regions, also city-specific local policies are being assessed in each urban region.

The first part of the chapter introduces the methodology and the model system developed. The second part presents the first results of the policy-testing and evaluation. The chapter concludes with reflections on how successful strategies to enhance the long-term sustainability of urban regions can be developed.

INDICATORS OF URBAN SUSTAINABILITY

As definitions of sustainability have broadened in scope over time, the number of possible indicators has grown to an extent where virtually all aspects of life are covered. Consequently, a vast number of sustainability indicator systems are in use today.

In PROPOLIS, sustainable development is viewed as comprising the environmental, socio-cultural and economic dimension. For the three components, key indicators have been identified by using a set of criteria:

- *Relevance*. The indicator should be relevant for describing important aspects of sustainability.
- *Representativeness*. In order to keep the indicator system manageable, not every suitable indicator can be included – the focus is on key indicators representing different domains of sustainability.
- *Policy sensitiveness*. Only indicators that are sensitive to the policies investigated are of interest.

- *Predictability.* There exist a large number of indicators suitable for monitoring but, as the objective is to model future policy impacts, it is essential that the indicator values can be forecast into the future by the model system.

The resulting PROPOLIS indicator system is presented in Table 16.1. To allow a structured evaluation, the three sustainability components are subdivided into themes. Then appropriate indicators are related to these themes.

Table 16.1 PROPOLIS indicator system

	Theme	*Indicator*
Environmental indicators	Global climate change	Greenhouse gases from transport
	Air pollution	Acidifying gases from transport
		Volatile organic compounds from transport
	Consumption of natural resources	Consumption of mineral oil products, transport
		Land coverage
		Need for additional new construction
	Environmental quality	Fragmentation of open space
		Quality of open space
Social indicators	Health	Exposure to PM from transport in the living environment
		Exposure to NO$_2$ from transport in the living environment
		Exposure to traffic noise
		Traffic deaths
		Traffic injuries
	Equity	Justice of distribution of economic benefits
		Justice of exposure to PM
		Justice of exposure to NO$_2$
		Justice of exposure to noise
		Segregation
	Opportunities	Housing standard
		Vitality of city centre
		Vitality of surrounding region
		Productivity gain from land use
	Accessibility and traffic	Total time spent in traffic
		Level of service of public transport and slow modes
		Accessibility to city centre
		Accessibility to services
		Accessibility to open space
Economic indicators	Total net benefit from transport	Transport investment costs
		Transport user benefits
		Transport operator benefits
		Government benefits from transport
		Transport external accident costs
		Transport external emissions costs
		Transport external greenhouse gases costs
		Transport external noise costs

To measure the three dimensions of sustainability, 9 themes and 35 key indicators have been defined – such as greenhouse gas emissions, air pollution, consumption of natural resources, quality of open space, population exposure to air pollution and noise, equity and opportunities and economic benefits from transport. The present indicator list lacks indicators related to land use, such as greenhouse gas emissions, air pollution, noise, energy use or economic benefits. Some of these indicators are tested in individual case-study cities, but it was outside the scope of PROPOLIS to implement these indicators in all case-study cities.

PROPOLIS METHODOLOGY

This chapter presents the main components of the PROPOLIS model system and shows how the policy-testing and evaluation process is organised.

The PROPOLIS model system

For a systematic evaluation of policies with respect to their long-term impacts on urban sustainability, a model system was designed in which different models and tools are integrated. Figure 16.1 illustrates the main components and data flows of the model system from input through behaviour and impact modelling to output in the form of indicators and their evaluation and presentation.

The *input data* include policy packages, GIS databases and model databases. Policy packages to be tested are transformed to 'model language' by changing some of the model parameters or model data. GIS databases contain georeferenced data of zone boundaries, transport networks, land-use categories, etc. in a geographic information system (GIS). All land-use transport models used are fully GIS-integrated, i.e. each model zone or model network link is represented in the GIS database.

In the *modelling part* the land-use transport models are the driving engines of the system. They have been previously calibrated to correspond to the observed behaviour in the test cities. The land-use transport models simulate the effects of policies on zonal activities, such as population or employment, and on mobility patterns, such as modal shares and link flows. The indicator modules receive the outputs of the land-use transport models and calculate the sustainability indicators.

The *output part* consists of sustainability indicator values which are further processed in the sustainability evaluation module. Other important information that helps to understand the behaviour of the system but is not used in the evaluation is stored as background variables. Examples for background variables are zonal population and employment, modal shares, car-km travelled, etc. A Web-based

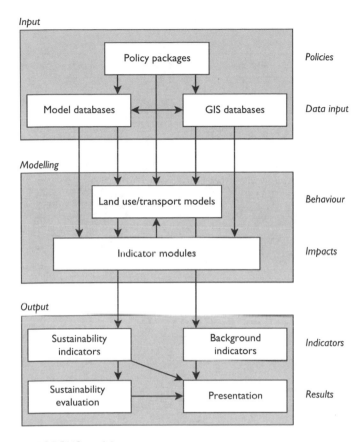

Figure 16.1 PROPOLIS model system

presentation tool shows the results of each policy in a standard form for comparisons between policies and between cities.

The land-use transport models

The PROPOLIS model system is implemented in seven European urban regions: Bilbao (Spain), Brussels (Belgium), Dortmund (Germany), Helsinki (Finland), Inverness (United Kingdom), Naples (Italy) and Vicenza (Italy). For each region an operational land-use transport model existed before the project. Table 16.2 presents the seven urban regions, their land-use transport models and their zoning systems. Figure 16.2 shows their location.

The seven case study regions differ in many respects. Their sizes range from 130,000 to over 3 million inhabitants. Some have experienced strong growth while others are old declining cities, sometimes in the process of restructuring. Some have

Table 16.2 Case city regions and land-use transport models

Case city	Bilbao	Brussels	Dortmund	Helsinki	Inverness	Naples	Vicenza
Area (km²)	2217	4332	2014	764	4152	1171	2722
Population (1000)	1140	2841	2516	946	132	3099	787
Density (inh/km²)	514	656	1249	1238	32	2647	289
Average household size	3.2	2.7	2.1	2.1	2.8	3.1	2.7
Unemployment rate	25.0%	11.0%	12.6%	6.0%	8.1%	27.8%	2.8%
Income/inh/month (Euro)	750	713	1570	1100	NA	695	1079
Cars/1000 inh	418	461	492	345	332	526	591
Land-use transport model	MEPLAN	TRANUS	IRPUD	MEPLAN	TRANUS	MEPLAN	MEPLAN
Land-use zones	111	139	246	173	153	179	102
Transport zones	111	139	246	173	153	39	27

Figure 16.2 PROPOLIS case-study regions

high and some very low unemployment rates. Income per person and car ownership differ considerably. The spatial structures range from highly compact and centralised to dispersed or polycentric patterns. With different conditions of transport supply, the modal shares vary significantly; however, car travel is always dominant.

The models applied belong to three different types of urban land use transport model: the MEPLAN model (Hunt, 1994; Williams, 1994; Martino and Maffii, 1999) is implemented in four urban regions, the TRANUS model (de la Barra, 1989) in two and the IRPUD model (Wegener, 1996, 1998, 1999) in one. The models simulate the effects of policies on the location behaviour of households and firms and on the resulting mobility patterns in the case study regions. Common base year of the models is 1996, the final forecast year is 2021.

Output of the land-use transport models is provided in a common data format for a predefined set of variables. Because the models are implemented in very different ways, harmonisation of the model outputs is necessary. The harmonisation is performed by aggregation to the 'lowest common denominator'. This means that the land-use transport models work with as much detail as they were implemented and that subsequent stages of the model system work with less detail but with a common set of variables in order to allow comparisons between cities. Socio-economic groups are aggregated to three types, employment sectors to four types, land and floorspace to three types, trips to five types, transport modes to five types and transport links to ten types.

The indicator modules

The indicator modules calculate the sustainability indicators. They post-process the output of the land-use transport models. Four indicator modules are implemented in the system: the *Raster Module*, the *Economic Indicator Module*, the *Justice Indicator Module* and the *Other Sustainability Indicator Module*. The output of the indicator modules are values of the sustainability indicators listed in Table 16.1.

The *Raster Module* calculates indicators for which a disaggregate treat-ment of space is required. The land-use transport models are not directly capable of capturing important aspects of urban sustainability because their zone-based spatial resolution is too coarse to represent other environmental phenomena than total resource use, total energy consumption or total CO_2 emissions. In particular emission-concentration algorithms such as air dispersion and noise propagation, but also land coverage, landscape fragmentation or the exposure of population to pollutants and noise, require a much higher spatial resolution than large zones. In all cases, the information needed is configurational. This implies that not only the attributes of the components of the modelled system such as quantity or cost are of interest but also their physical *micro locations*. This is where the Raster

Module comes into play. It maintains the zonal organisation of the aggregate land-use transport model but complements it by a disaggregate representation of space in 100 × 100 m raster cells for the calculation of local environmental and social impacts of policies (Spiekermann and Wegener, 1999, 2000; Spiekermann, 1999, 2003). The Raster Module calculates most environmental indicators, the exposure indicators and an indicator of accessibility to open space. In addition the Raster Module feeds the Economic Indicator Module with information on emission and noise exposure and the Justice Indicator Module with information on exposure of different socio-economic groups to air pollution and noise.

The *Economic Indicator Module* performs a cost–benefit analysis of the transport sector. Single indicators address transport investment costs, user, operator and governmental benefits as well as external costs of transport. In addition the module provides an indicator describing the efficiency of the urban system measured on the basis of variables, such as the size of the city, the speed at which people and goods are moved in the city and the sprawl of jobs and home following Prud'homme and Chang-Woon (1999).

The *Justice Indicator Module* addresses equity implications of the investigated policies. It translates the per cent of people of different socio-economic groups who are exposed to air pollution and traffic noise into equity indicators. Four different theories of justice are incorporated in the module: the equal-shares principle, the utilitarian principle, the egalitarian principle and the Rawlsian difference principle.

The *Other Sustainability Indicator Module* calculates a small set of indicators which is not covered by the previous modules but may be of general interest for understanding the behaviour of the urban system, such as zonal population and employment, modal shares and car-km travelled.

The evaluation and presentation modules

Finally, the indicators are evaluated by a multicriteria evaluation tool and are analysed and presented in a harmonised way for comparisons between policies and between cities.

The multicriteria evaluation tool *USE-IT* determines the sustainability of policies with respect to environmental, social and economic sustainability. It calculates the contribution of each indicator to sustainability and aggregates them to the sustainability themes and components defined in Table 16.1.

Value functions are used to transform the indicator values to a scale from zero to one by taking existing target values into account. Indicators are given weights for aggregation to indices. The weights are the outcome of an internal expert survey performed to determine a common set of weights for all case-study cities. In addition, local value systems are explored to determine weights in the local contexts. Indices are formed as weighted averages of the evaluated indicators. Aggregation is performed separately for the environmental, social and economic components of sustainability. A single index aggregating the three components is not calculated to avoid double-counting, because some aspects are considered in more than one component, i.e. are treated from different viewpoints.

An Internet-based *Analysis and Presentation Tool* presents the results of the policy-testing for all cities in a standardised format. The tool analyses and displays sustainability indicators and background variables for comparison between policies and between cities. The Internet tool is designed to be used by planners and policy-makers in the case-study regions to make it easier for them to understand the impacts of policy decisions and so aid them in the process of selecting the most appropriate policy measures.

Implementation and policy-testing

The PROPOLIS model system is currently being implemented in the seven European urban regions. Figure 16.3 shows how the system is used to define strategies

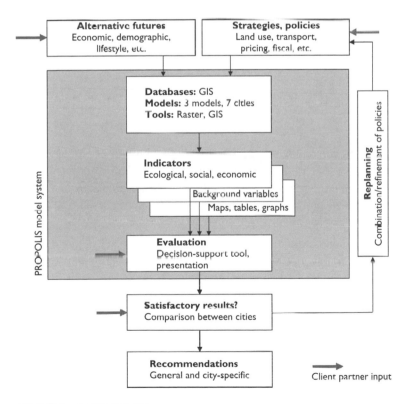

Figure 16.3 Policy-testing process

that increase urban sustainability. The model system is the core of the policy analysis. First single policies are defined and introduced into the system. Policies include land use, transport, pricing and regulatory and investment policies. The evaluation of policies and the comparison between policies and between cities may lead to a reformulation of policies ('Replanning'). Replanning includes the refinement of policies, e.g. finding an optimal level of a pricing policy, but also experimenting with policy combinations to improve the results. The final output of the systematic policy tests are general and city-specific recommendations of which policies or combinations of policies are likely to contribute most to sustainable development.

There are various points in the system at which planners and policy-makers in the case-study regions may intervene and introduce their ideas and values into the modelling and evaluation process. They may contribute to the formulation of the assumptions about external developments for the models, such as assumptions about the likely overall economic development of the region or about migration flows across the regions' borders. Or they may want to test the impacts of alternative assumptions about external developments. An important task of the local partners is to contribute to the formulation of strategies and policies common for all case-study cities or specific to their regions. Finally, the local experts are asked to indicate their values, i.e. enter their own weights into the evaluation system.

TYPICAL RESULTS

In this section typical preliminary results of the modelling work for the Dortmund case-study region are presented. The first part will discuss typical output indicators of the land-use transport model, the second will focus on some key sustainability indicators calculated with the tools introduced in the previous section.

The Dortmund case-study region is the urban region of Dortmund consisting of the city of Dortmund and its 25 surrounding municipalities. The region is subdivided into 246 statistical areas or zones. However, as it was explained in the previous section, the spatial resolution of 246 zones is not sufficient for the simulation of environmental impacts, such as air quality and traffic noise. Therefore the zone-based and link-based results of the land-use transport model are disaggregated to raster cells by the *Raster Module* (see the Section 'PROPOLIS Model System'). Raster cells of 100×100 m size are used to model environmental impacts. In total, about 207,000 raster cells cover the study area. The same spatial reference system will be used in a microsimulation model currently developed for the Dortmund region.

Land-use transport model indicators

Figures 16.4–16.6 show selected results of altogether 22 policy scenarios modelled in PROPOLIS. The policy scenarios included, besides local infrastructure improvement policies specific for each case-study city, policies for car pricing, speed limits, public transport and land use as well as policy packages consisting of several land use and transport policies combined. All policy scenarios are compared with a reference or base scenario, in which no policy changes are assumed after the year 2001. All policies in the policy scenarios start after 2001, i.e. all policy scenarios are identical with the reference scenario until that year.

Each of the three diagrams shows trajectories for one system variable between the base year 1970 and the target year 2030. Each line in the diagrams corresponds to one policy scenario. The heavy line represents the development of the variable in the reference or base scenario 000. After the year 2000, the lines representing the policy scenarios diverge from the line of the reference scenario; the numbers attached to each line is the scenario number. The policies modelled in each policy scenario are listed in short form on the diagram.

Figure 16.4 shows the development of mean travel cost per trip in the scenarios. The increase in mean travel cost in the reference scenario is the combined effect of inflation, increasing fuel costs and public transport fares, longer distances travelled and growing fuel efficiency of cars (see Figure 16.4).

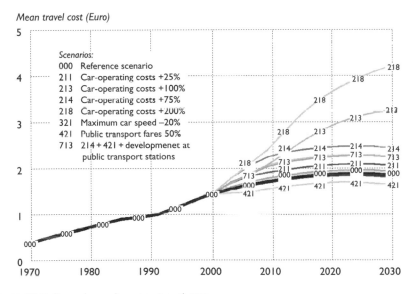

Figure 16.4 Scenario results: mean travel cost

The differences in mean travel cost between the policy scenarios and the reference scenario indicate the effect of the pricing policies. There is only one scenario, scenario 421, in which mean travel costs are lower than in the reference scenario, whereas in all other scenarios they are higher. The highest increases are shown in scenarios 213 and 218, in which significant increases of fuel taxes are assumed.

Figure 16.5 shows the development of mean trip lengths. In the reference scenario mean trip lengths increase from under 10 to about 15 km between 1970 and 2030. This is the combined result of growing affluence, decentralisation of population through suburbanisation and only moderate increases of fuel prices, which have in effect made fuel less expensive in real terms during the forecasting period. The differences between the policy scenarios and the reference scenario are as expected. Scenario 421, in which travel by public transport is made less expensive, longer trips are made – something not always expected by proponents of subsidisation of public transport. All other scenarios result in shorter average trip lengths, which is in line with economic theory.

A similar picture emerges if only car-km travelled is considered. Figure 16.6 shows that only car pricing policies have a significant effect on car distances travelled. All other policy types, including the land-use policies, have only insignificant effects.

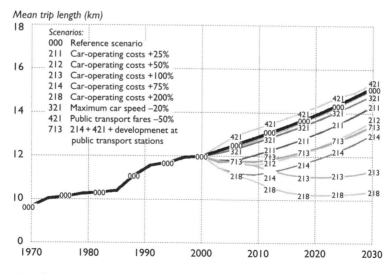

Figure 16.5 Scenario results: mean trip length

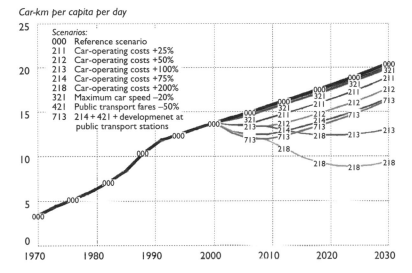

Figure 16.6 Scenario results: car-km

Sustainability indicators

The land-use transport models predict long-term changes in the urban land use and transport system. The indicator modules (see Figure 16.1) use the output of the land-use transport models (zone data and link flows), disaggregate it to raster cells using GIS information and produce the sustainability indicators. If the land-use transport model results are translated into sustainability effects the same overall picture with respect to the policy impacts holds true.

Only by making car travel more expensive, significant reductions in greenhouse gas emissions can be expected (Figure 16.7). However, the diagram also shows that equally important are efforts to make cars more energy efficient: the decline in CO_2 emissions after 2000 in the reference scenario is due to the assumptions about growing energy-efficient car technology built into all of the scenarios.

Figures 16.8–16.11 show examples of raster-based output of environmental and social indicators in the Dortmund urban region for the year 2021 for the base scenario 000.

Figure 16.8 shows a forecast of air quality in the Dortmund urban region as it would result in the reference scenario. Based on a forecast of number and type of vehicles on the links of the road network, emission functions are used to determine the volume of pollutants, in this case of NO_2, emitted along the links. An air distribution model is used to forecast the dispersion of the pollutant on adjacent areas – the predominant south-west wind direction in the Dortmund area is clearly visible. As also population by socio-economic group is disaggregated to

CO_2 emissions transport per capita per day (g)

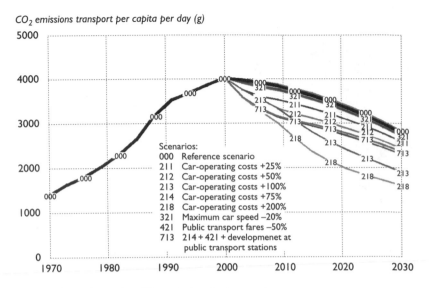

Scenarios:
000 Reference scenario
211 Car-operating costs +25%
212 Car-operating costs +50%
213 Car-operating costs +100%
214 Car-operating costs +75%
218 Car-operating costs +200%
321 Maximum car speed −20%
421 Public transport fares −50%
713 214 + 421 + developmenet at
     public transport stations

Figure 16.7 Scenario results: CO_2 emissions by transport

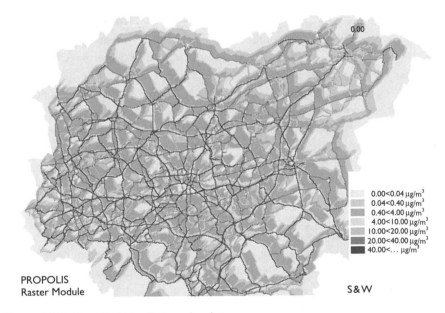

0.00

0.00<0.04 μg/m³
0.04<0.40 μg/m³
0.40<4.00 μg/m³
4.00<10.00 μg/m³
10.00<20.00 μg/m³
20.00<40.00 μg/m³
40.00<... μg/m³

PROPOLIS
Raster Module

S&W

Figure 16.8 Air quality in the Dortmund region

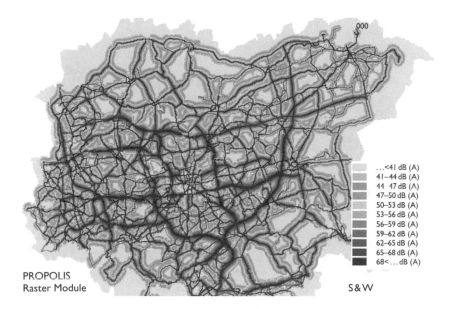

Figure 16.9 Traffic noise in the Dortmund region

raster cells, it is possible to calculate how many people in each neighbourhood and in each socio-economic group are exposed to this type of air pollution. This information is used for the health and equity indicators in the system of indicators (see Table 16.1).

Figure 16.9 shows exposure to traffic noise. Again link loads by vehicle type are used to calculate traffic noise emissions along links. A noise propagation model is used to calculate the dispersion of noise on both sides of the links. To take into account that buildings along the roadways act as noise barriers, assumptions about the reduction of noise propagation in areas of higher density are made. As with air quality, exposure to noise can be related to residences of population by socio-economic group and used in the health and equity evaluations.

Figure 16.10 is a raster-based representation of open space, i.e. all land that is neither a built-up area nor a transport link. In the map the traffic noise corridors of Figure 16.7 are overlaid with the open space. Red raster cells are disturbed by traffic noise, green areas are not. It is assumed that only the remaining open space, which is not disturbed by traffic noise, is of value for recreation and can therefore serve as an indicator of the quality of open space in a zone.

Figure 16.11 shows accessibility to open space. The indicator is calculated by a potential accessibility model using open space as mass term and walking distance as impedance. The average accessibility to open space is influenced

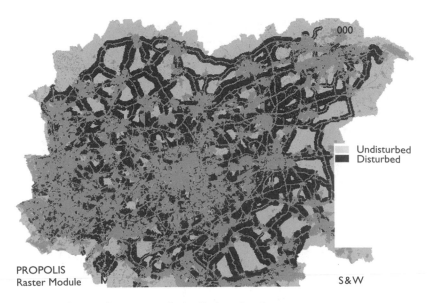

PROPOLIS
Raster Module

Undisturbed
Disturbed

S&W

Figure 16.10 Quality of open space in the Dortmund region

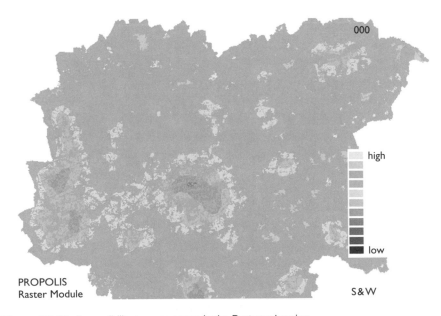

PROPOLIS
Raster Module

high

low

S&W

Figure 16.11 Accessibility to open space in the Dortmund region

Table 16.3 Scenario results: selected sustainability indicators

Scenario		Year	Quality of open space	Exposure to NO_2	Exposure to noise	Accessibility to open space
Number	Policy		Index 2001 = 100	Percent of population above EU guidelines	Percent of population disturbed	Index 2001 = 100
000	Base scenario	2001	100.0	20.5	39.5	100.0
000	Base scenario	2021	89.4	12.3	37.6	88.7
211	Car-operating costs +25%	2021	90.1	12.0	37.4	88.7
212	Car-operating costs +50%	2021	91.3	11.7	37.1	88.6
213	Car-operating costs +100%	2021	92.9	10.8	36.5	88.5
214	Car-operating costs +75%	2021	92.1	11.4	37.0	88.7
218	Car-operating costs +200%	2021	91.3	8.9	34.4	88.6
321	Maximum car speec −20%	2021	95.1	13.0	35.6	88.5
421	Public transport fares −50%	2021	89.8	12.0	37.5	88.8
713	214+421+development at public transport stations	2021	95.0	11.0	36.7	88.1

in the different scenarios by settlement activities, infrastructure development and movement of households.

The maps presented are used as a means to understand the spatial distribution of effects of a certain policy. For the policy evaluation, the indicator numbers are used. Table 16.3 presents for selected sustainability indicators the outcome of the selected policies presented in the previous sections. Emission of air pollutants will clearly go down in all scenarios because of new emission standards for new vehicles replacing old ones assumed already in the base scenario. The increase in car-operating costs will result in even lower numbers of population exposed to air pollution and traffic noise. However, most significant effects can only be achieved by a clear increase in costs as in Scenario 218. Quality of open space and also the accessibility to open space are becoming worse in the future, mainly because of the fact that the ongoing trend of land consumption will continue in all scenarios. However, quality of open space might be improved compared to the base scenario by appropriate policies such as increase of car-operating costs, reduction of speeds or combinations of policies.

CONCLUSIONS

This chapter presented a model system developed to simulate and evaluate the impacts of land use and transport policies on sustainability in seven European urban regions.

The PROPOLIS system of sustainability indicators differs from other sustainability indicator systems. Other systems are based on monitoring approaches in which the quantities in question are directly observed or measured, whereas in PROPOLIS the indicators are modelled, i.e. can be forecast. Another distinction is that the PROPOLIS indicators were chosen as near as possible at the tail-ends of causal chains. For example, vehicle kilometres or average travel times are not presented as indicators for sustainability but emissions or numbers of residents in the most polluted areas.

The land-use transport models implemented in PROPOLIS are integrated with geographic information systems. All model zones and network links have their direct correspondence in a GIS. Tools were developed to exchange information back and forth between the models and the GIS, such as tools for editing links and link attributes in the GIS and to load them into the models. In this way the land-use transport models follow the trend to link spatial models to georeferenced data (Fotheringham and Wegener, 2000). GIS integration is a precondition for linking land-use transport models with environmental impact modules.

The PROPOLIS model system is one of the first attempts to address the issue of urban sustainability in a comprehensive long-term forecasting framework. The model system moves from two-way land-use transport modelling towards three-way land-use transport environment modelling (LTE), even though the feedback from environment to land use and transport, i.e. the way by which changes in environmental quality affect location decisions of investors, firms and households and so indirectly also influence activity and mobility patterns, has so far been only poorly developed (Spiekermann and Wegener, 2003).

The few results presented suggest that a clear increase in car-operating costs might be the single best policy to support sustainability and might also suggest that other policies such as regulatory policies or land-use policies are not important. However, the latter would be a misleading conclusions. High-density, mixed-used settlement patterns are an essential precondition for less car-dependent cities. Therefore land-use policies supporting high densities and smaller distances between residences and workplaces are a necessary ingredient of sustainability-oriented urban planning.

The PROPOLIS system is currently being implemented in seven European urban regions. Therefore, only typical preliminary results could be presented in this chapter. All case city model systems are expected to calculate all PROPOLIS sustainability indicators and test the same set of policies. This will allow the systematic comparison of policy scenarios and individual policies with respect to their impact on urban sustainability. This comparison will lead to recommendations as to which policies should be adopted to improve urban sustainability in the long term.

ACKNOWLEDGEMENTS

The authors are grateful to their colleagues of the PROPOLIS project at IRPUD (Dortmund), LT (Helsinki), ME&P (Cambridge), MECSA (Bilbao), STRATEC (Brussels), TRT (Milan) and UCL (London) for the permission to use material they have contributed to the project.

REFERENCES

Daly, H.E. (1991), *Steady State Economics*. Island Press, Washington.
de la Barra, T. (1989), *Integrated Land-Use and Transport Modelling. Decision Chains and Hierarchies*. Cambridge University Press, Cambridge.
European Environment Agency (1995), *Europe's Environment: The Dobris Assessment*. European Environment Agency, Copenhagen.
Fotheringham, A.S. and Wegener, M. (eds) (2000), *Spatial Models and GIS: New Potential and New Models*. GISDATA 7. Taylor & Francis, London.

Hunt, D. (1994), 'Calibrating the Naples land use and transport model', *Environment and Planning B: Planning and Design*, 21: 569–590.

International Council for Local Environmental Initiatives (ICLEI) (1994), *Charter of European Cities and Towns Towards Sustainability* (Aalborg Charter). http://www.iclei.org/europe/echarter.htm.

Martino, A. and Maffii, S. (1999), 'The integrated land-use and transport model of Naples: from the master transport plan to the EU policy tests' in Rizzi, P. (ed.) *Computers in Urban Planning and Urban Management on the Edge of the Millennium*. F. Angeli, Milan.

Prud'homme, R. and Chang-Woon, L. (1999), 'Size, sprawl speed and the efficiency of cities', *Urban Studies*, 36(11): 1849–1858.

Spiekermann, K. (1999), *Sustainable Transport, Air Quality and Noise Intrusion – An Urban Modelling Exercise*. Paper presented at the ESF/NSF Transatlantic Research Conference on Social Change and Sustainable Transport, University of California, Berkeley.

Spiekermann, K. (2003), *The PROPOLIS Raster Module*. Deliverable D4 of PROPOLIS. Spiekermann & Wegener Urban and Regional Research (S&W), Dortmund.

Spiekermann, K. and Wegener, M. (1999), 'Disaggregate environmental modules for modelling sustainable urban development' in Rizzi, P. (ed.) *Computers in Urban Planning and Urban Management on the Edge of the Millennium*. F. Angeli, Milan.

Spiekermann, K. and Wegener, M. (2000), 'Freedom from the tyranny of zones: towards new GIS-based models' in Fotheringham, A.S. and Wegener, M. (eds) *Spatial Models and GIS: New Potential and New Models*. GISDATA 7. Taylor & Francis, London, pp. 45–61.

Spiekermann, K. and Wegener, M. (2003), *Environmental Feedback*. Deliverable D2 of PROPOLIS. Institute of Spatial Planning, University of Dortmund and Spiekermann & Wegener Urban and Regional Research (S&W), Dortmund.

Wegener, M. (1996), 'Reduction of CO_2 emissions of transport by reorganisation of urban activities' in Hayashi, Y. and Roy, J. (eds), *Land Use, Transport and the Environment*. Kluwer Academic Publishers, Dordrecht, pp. 103–124.

Wegener, M. (1998), *The IRPUD Model: Overview*. http://irpud.raumplanung.uni-dortmund.de/irpud/pro/mod/mod_e.htm.

Wegener, M. (1999), *Die Stadt der kurzen Wege – müssen wir unsere Städte umbauen?* Berichte aus dem Institut für Raumplanung 43. Dortmund: Institute of Spatial Planning, University of Dortmund.

Williams, I.N. (1994), 'A model of London and the South East', *Environment and Planning B: Planning and Design*, 21: 517–533.

World Commission on Environment and Development (WCED) (1987), *Our Common Future*. Oxford University Press, Oxford.

Part 4.3

Advanced Evaluations of Urban Land Use, Buildings and Estates

17

Sustainability Assessment of Building Design, Construction and Use

Pekka Huovila and Steven Curwell

INTRODUCTION

The operation of buildings within the built environment has a major impact on environment. Important decisions, that have consequences over a long life span, are made already in the design phase. Changes to design in construction are restricted due to their capital cost effects. On the other hand, optimization due to construction often has important implications to the life cycle performance and sustainability of constructed assets.

Cole (1998) states that we are clearly still very much in our infancy of understanding and practising environmental responsibility and, more significantly, are far from developing the means to affect significant positive change. He defines environmental assessment as those techniques developed to specifically evaluate the performance of a building design or completed building across a broad range of environmental considerations. Cole (2000) has studied the assessment of construction impacts from building design, management and process issues. He concludes that there is little formally structured information about procedures associated with the inclusion of environmental issues in the construction procurement process. Today's design, construction and operation practice is still, therefore, very much handicapped by the poor assessment of building design, insufficient use of appropriate assessment methods, problems with access to relevant data and lack of competence in making sustainable decisions.

Responding to this challenge, BEQUEST (Sunikka et al., 2000) delivers a tool (Bequest Toolkit, 2001) consisting of

- a framework to map the sustainability assessment (see Figure 17.1);
- a protocol for sustainable procurement;
- a list of sustainability assessment methods.

This chapter discusses the classification of assessment methods and presents some of them that are already in use. The applicability of these methods in different process phases and their suitability to cover various sustainability dimensions are

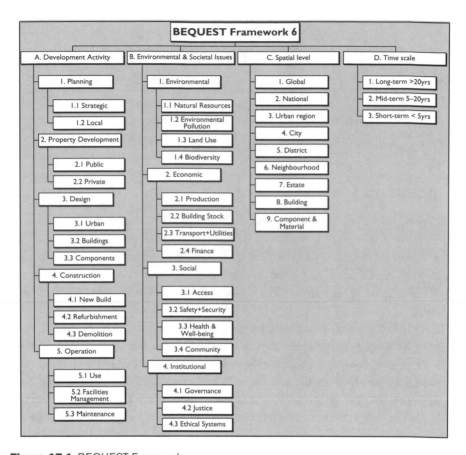

Figure 17.1 BEQUEST Framework

then presented. The BEQUEST contribution and remaining future challenges are finally concluded.

CLASSIFICATION OF THE ASSESSMENT METHODS

To understand better how assessment methods work they should be structured in a comprehensive way. Trusty (2001) divides assessment systems and tools into three levels as follows:

- Level 1 – Product comparison tools and info sources (e.g. BEES).
- Level 2 – Whole building design or decision-support tools (e.g. Eco-Quantum, Envest).

- Level 3 – Whole building assessment frameworks or systems (e.g. BREEAM, GBC).

Level 1 – Product comparison tools are used at the procurement stage. They may include economic as well as environmental data. They may have a life cycle analysis in the background or they can be used to construct LCA.

Level 2 – Decision-support tools have a narrow focus, like environment, cost or operating energy. They are objective, used by design team members and may involve weighting or scoring. They provide input to Level 3 tools.

Level 3 – Whole building systems tools have a broad coverage: environment, economic or social. They mix objective and subjective data and use scoring or weighting systems. These tools may apply to new design or existing buildings. They may require external auditors and may yield certificate or label.

Deakin et al. (2001) divides assessment methods into two classes: environmental in general and those augmenting into particular forms of life cycle assessments. The environment in general tends to focus on assessments of eco-system integrity. Those augmenting into particular forms of life cycle assessment in turn tend to focus on assessing how to build the environmental capacity needed to not only qualify the integrity of eco-systems, but evaluate the equity, participation and futurity of the economic, social and institutional structures underlying the city of tomorrow and its cultural heritage. That is, qualify and evaluate if forms of human settlements which develop from the design and construction of buildings are sustainable.

The REQUEST Framework set out in Figure 17.1 covers different development activities at different spatial levels in different time scales. The classification of environmental and societal issues (in environmental, economic, social and institutional categories) is based on the UN Working list of Indicators of Sustainable Development (1996) that follows the chapters of Agenda 21.

The Level-classification provided by Trusty (2001) provides a rough picture where different assessment methods are applicable (product comparison, building design evaluation, systems analysis). The PICABUE definition of sustainable development that is offered by Deakin et al. (2001) can be used to differentiate assessment methods relative to the ecological integrity (environment), and the broader sustainability content (environment + equity, participation and futurity) of the systems which they evaluate.

The definition of sustainability used by Deakin et al. (2001) is set out in Figure 17.2.

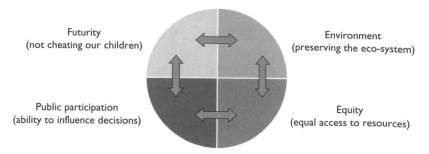

Figure 17.2 PICABUE definition of sustainable development

SUSTAINABILITY ASSESSMENT METHODS IN THE BEQUEST TOOL

Some building level assessment tools that are used in daily practice are briefly presented in the following as examples of current sustainability assessment practice for building design, construction and use. A full list of sustainability assessment methods included in the BEQUEST tool is shown in the Appendix.

BREEAM is taken as an example of a method for assessing existing buildings. Since its development in the United Kingdom, it has been exported also to other countries. Green Building Challenge (GBC) is an international, ongoing project resulting in new tool versions every two years that are in the meanwhile tested by participating national design teams. Eco-Quantum is the Dutch system for design evaluation with a detailed version for researchers. Two methods are selected from Finland: PIMWAG, which the City of Helsinki has used to award building permits for sustainable housing; and EcoProP, a software tool to produce design briefs with sustainability requirements incorporated. The UK Ecopoints, and the Green Guide and Envest, that are based on Ecopoints, are then given as supplementary examples of assessment tools that can be of a different nature.

BREEAM – THE BRE'S ENVIRONMENTAL ASSESSMENT METHOD

BREEAM (Baldwin *et al.*, 1998; Dickie and Howard, 2000) was first launched in 1990 as an independent methodology for assessing the environmental quality of buildings. There are currently four versions covering different building types: offices, homes, industrial units and supermarkets/superstores. BREEAM is a design stage assessment; however, clients can request a post-construction audit to verify that the design requirements have been implemented in the construction.

For the Offices version, the management and operation of the building can also be assessed. In this case, a set of core issues are assessed, along with those specific to either the design stage or the management and operation. This allows the performance of the building to be compared throughout its life.

Assessments are carried out by licensed assessors, who are trained by BRE. The assessor reviews the building against a broad range of environmental issues to give an overall score, which is then translated into a BREEAM rating of Pass, Good, Very Good or Excellent.

Clients, design teams and building managers can use BREEAM in a number of different ways. Clients can use BREEAM to specify the environmental sustainability performance of their buildings in a way that is quick, comprehensive and visible in the marketplace. Letting Agents can use BREEAM to promote the environmental credentials and benefits of a building to potential clients. Building managers can benchmark their performance against others, both generally and within their own company. Design teams can use BREEAM as a tool to improve the performance of their buildings and their own experience and knowledge of environmental aspects of sustainability.

The framework of BREEAM can be used internationally – indeed versions of BREEAM have been developed in Canada, Hong Kong and New Zealand, as well

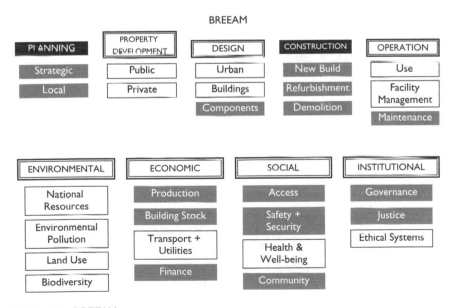

Figure 17.3 BREEAM

as it is being used as a starting point for many other schemes. However the details need to be tailored for specific application.

GBC – GREEN BUILDING CHALLENGE

GBC is a hierarchical system of environmental assessment criteria for buildings developed for international comparative purposes in order to select and analyse the environmental performance and impact of buildings, initially for Green Building Challenge '98 (GBC'98, 1998) and subsequently for the Sustainable Building 2000 (SB2000, 2000) conference. Three versions exist: multiunit residential buildings, office buildings and schools. In each version a very comprehensive list of environmental criteria in 19 categories is addressed and scored using a weighting system. The output can be presented in a concise graphical format, which can be seen as an Environmental Label.

Quantitative data include detailed statistics on the predicted consumption of energy, water, land use, materials, as well as emissions, waste and sewage, the measurable aspects of indoor environmental conditions. Some contextual factors are environmental loading on immediate surroundings, mainly in terms of the effects on neighbouring or adjacent properties.

Qualitative data include most aspects of indoor environment, health issues, design issues related to longevity, design and construction process, building operations planning and management provisions.

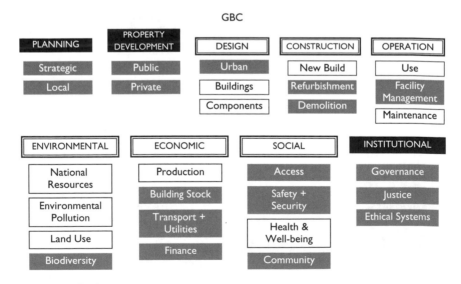

Figure 17.4 GBC

The system provides some flexibility to adjust the assessment criteria and thus the data requirements, as well as the scoring/weighting to respond to differing regional and national climatic and cultural conditions.

The method has been tested on a total of 34 buildings in 14 different countries by the 1998 Conference. A further tranche of results of the same order was presented in the 2000 Conference.

ECO-QUANTUM

The history of environmental assessment has to a large extent evolved in line with the developments in sustainable building. The type of environmental assessment originally promoted by the government under the Dutch environmental policy was strongly product-oriented. Therefore, it is not surprising that environmental assessment started focusing on building materials. For this environmental checklists were developed.

Nowadays, more comprehensive and quantitative methods are used. In addition to materials, also construction elements, buildings and urban plans can be evaluated with them. The building level can be assessed with Eco-Quantum, which was developed to measure the environmental performance of building on a basis of a life cycle assessment. It is a computer-aided tool, which calculates environmental effects during the whole life cycle of a building. Eco-Quantum takes into account extraction of raw materials, production, construction, operation and demolition or reuse

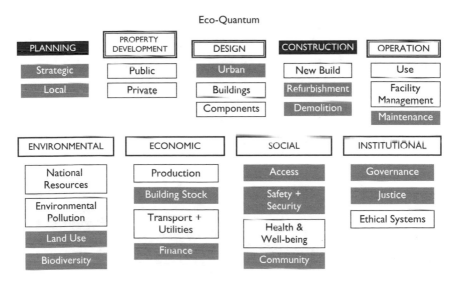

Figure 17.5 Eco-Quantum

phases. It expresses the evaluation results through 13 environmental effects: depletion of raw materials, fuels and the ozone layer, greenhouse effect, depletion, acidity, nutrification, human toxicity, ecotoxicity, photochemical oxidant formation, energy, harmless, harmful and radioactive waste. The flows of energy, materials and water are accounted. The objective is to determine, to analyse and to improve the environmental performance of a building (Mak *et al.*, 1997; Sunikka and Klunder, 2001).

Eco-Quantum is targeted for the design phase, and architects form the main target group. In the near future it may be adapted also for renovations.

PIMWAG

In Finland the experimental ecological areas that are currently under construction have gained a lot of attention and great expectations. Advancement in construction ecology is very much depending on the success of these areas. The most important project at the moment is Viikki, one of four new Nordic eco-cities, in Helsinki, where construction began in 2000.

In PIMWAG (Aaltonen *et al.*, 1998) ecological criteria have been developed to evaluate housing projects in the experimental housing area Viikki, where every project must reach a basic threshold level in order to get building permission. PIMWAG assesses environmental performance of a housing project from five aspects: pollution, natural resources, healthiness, bio-diversity of nature and nutrition. The data

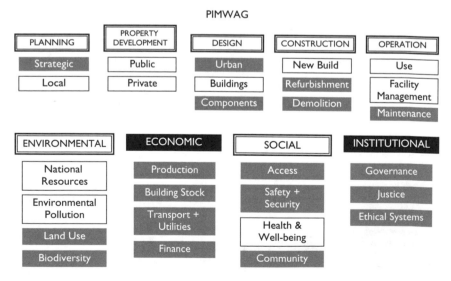

Figure 17.6 PIMWAG

output is a table, which presents the points that a project may achieve on a sliding scale 1–3 per criteria. The weakness of this method is that it is not a computer-aided tool, and the calculations have to be made with separate programs. The scope of the method is also quite limited in order to make it work as a practical tool. What makes PIMWAG interesting is that the measures which it introduces have the potential to become standard evaluations.

A surveillance group is currently collecting feedback from the users of the method, and if it is positive, in the future PIMWAG may be applicable to the governmental building projects more widely. Energy efficiency and life cycle issues will have more value in the next version.

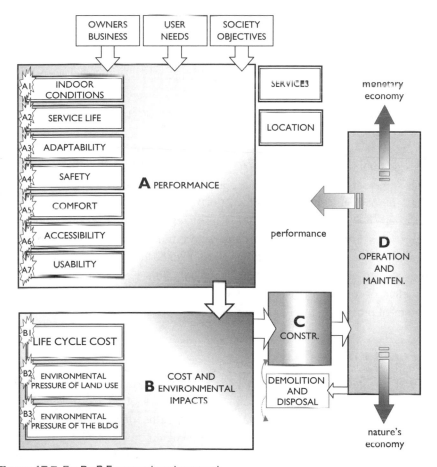

Figure 17.7 EcoProP Framework and approach

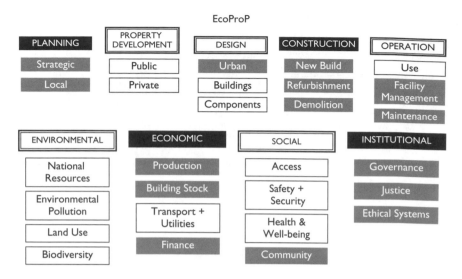

Figure 17.8 EcoProp

ECOPROP

EcoProP has been used in Finland in construction projects of different building types: housing, offices, nurseries, etc. Its main users have been building owners who, often together with the already selected design team, document the performance objectives for the building. The framework is universal, but the reference data is adopted to meet the Finnish building regulation and practice.

EcoProP (Huovila and Leinonen, 2001; Leinonen and Huovila, 2001) is a requirement management software tool used for setting performance objectives for a building to be designed and constructed, thus supporting and forming the design brief. It consists of a generic classification of building properties (VTT ProP®), reference data about environmental requirements (in a form of values or classes), information on relevant verification methods and automated procedures to scan requirement profiles and to form a design brief.

UK ECOPOINTS

The BRE initiated research to identify the relative importance of different sustainability issues with construction, from the perspective of all the industry's main stakeholders. Initially, the research was planned to further develop the environmental and ecological ratings used in BRE's environmental management and analysis tools. However, it was decided to broaden the scope of the project to address the emerging agenda of sustainable construction. Ecopoints are generally used

UK Ecopoints

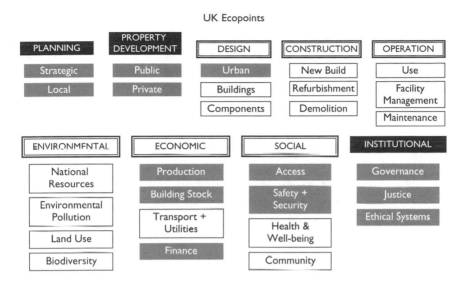

Figure 17.9 UK Ecopoints

as part of other tools, such as Envest, to allow different environmental issues to be compared. They can also be used by material producers or other parties to communicate the environmental performance of a product or service.

A UK Ecopoint (Dickie and Howard, 2000) is a single unit measurement of environmental impact. A UK Ecopoint score is a measure of the total environmental impact of a particular product or process expressed in units (ecopoints). It is calculated in relation to impacts on the environment in the UK and therefore applies to UK activities only. UK Ecopoints are calculated from a defined range of Life Cycle Analysis data. UK Ecopoints are derived by adding together the points calculated for each environmental impact, using weightings derived from a consultation exercise with UK construction industry representatives. A process of normalization is used so that the total number of Ecopoints for all the impacts that arise per UK citizen in one year amounts to 100. While Ecopoints are derived specifically for the UK, the methodology used can be applied in other European countries.

The Green Guide to Specification

The Green Guide to Specification (Howard et al., 1998; Anderson and Howard, 2000) is a simple guide to allow designers to consider the environmental implications of the material design choices made. There are two versions of the Green Guide, one for offices and one for housing.

Materials and components are arranged in product groups: External Wall Construction, Partitioning, Floor Finishes, etc., so that designers and specifiers can compare and select from comparable systems or materials as they compile their specification. As it is meaningless to compare the environmental profiles of, say, concrete floors and a particular type of paint, ratings are therefore based on product information from within each respective product group. The specifications are based on commonly found components, assemblies and materials selected to reflect the best available data and provide a representative range. For each specification, information has been gathered on the constituent materials, for the relative quantities per m². Using Life Cycle Analysis it is possible to calculate the environmental impact per ton of material and assess this over a 60-year life span.

The Green Guides cover issues primarily relating to environmental sustainability; however, information on indicative cost is also provided to give the designer or specifier an indication of the cost implications of any decisions at the earliest opportunity. The Green Guide will generally be used by designers who wish to have a simple way to use the most environmentally sound materials for the building design they are considering. Designers may just use the summary rating, which takes the performance of the element for each of the different environmental categories and weights them according to their relative importance. Alternatively they may wish to use those materials which perform best in specific areas of environmental performance.

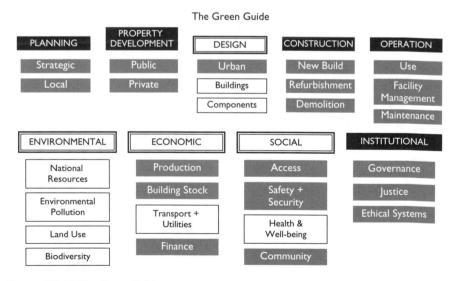

Figure 17.10 The Green Guide

The methodology used to derive the environmental impacts of the materials is applicable internationally; however the weightings used to produce the summary rating are specific to the UK. As too are the specifications, method of manufacture and resource usage are specific to the UK, although some may also be applicable in Europe.

ENVEST – ENVIRONMENTAL IMPACT ESTIMATING SOFTWARE

Envest is the first UK software for estimating the life-cycle environmental impacts of a building from the early design stage. Currently, Envest is designed for offices and commercial buildings and enables architects and designers to evaluate the environmental impacts of different design options for a chosen building. It considers the environmental impacts of materials used during construction and maintenance, and energy and resources consumed over the building's life.

Using minimal data entered through simple input screens, Envest allows designers to quickly identify those aspects of the building which have the greatest influence on the overall impact. All impacts are assessed using Ecopoints, a measure of total environmental performance, which allow the designer to compare different designs and specifications directly. Using Ecopoints to calculate the environmental impacts of the design, Envest considers the same environmental

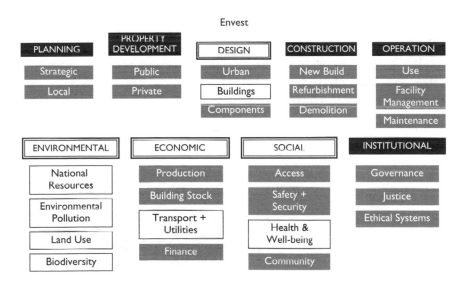

Figure 17.11 Envest

issues as the Environmental Profiles, with the exception of transport pollution and congestion.

Envest has been created principally for designers, to help them compare different options in terms of environmental performance. It is intended for use from the early design stages. Clients may also use Envest to establish an environmental performance requirement for their design team. The concept behind Envest, and the method of calculating the design parameters, is appropriate across Europe, where they use similar building design and construction. The environmental impacts derived are specific to the UK and the operational performance is based on benchmarks in UK buildings.

CONCLUSIONS

The given examples show that various sustainability assessment methods for building design, construction and operation are already in use. What is more the examination shows those methods already in existence mainly focus on assessment of building design and have some operational coverage. Construction, maintenance, local planning and property development issues are less included and strategic planning not at all.

The environmental issues are covered together with transport and health, which are classified as part of economic and social categories in the BEQUEST framework. Some methods relate with other social issues, such as access, safety and community, or ethical systems. Most of the economic (production, building stock, finance) and institutional (governance and justice) issues seem to be out of scope of these methods.

The focus is clearly on buildings, but with component and estate, even neighbourhood and global dimensions being partly encompassed. National, urban, regional or city level issues cannot be assessed by the same methods because the

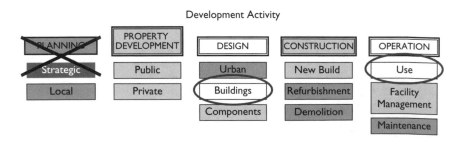

Figure 17.12 Development activity

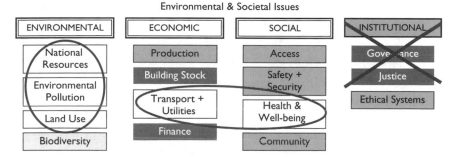

Figure 17.13 Environmental and societal issues

time scale does not seem to have a meaning in these sustainability assessment methods.

The challenge is to establish how all the sustainable development issues can be assessed.

REFERENCES

Aaltonen, T., Gabrielsson, J., Inkinen, R., Majurinen, J., Pennanen, A. and Wartiainen, K. (1998), *Ecological Building Criteria for Viikki*. City of Helsinki, Helsinki.

Anderson, J. and Howard, N. (2000), *The Green Guide to Housing Specification*. London: CRC.

Baldwin, R., Yates, A., Howard, N. and Rao, S. (1998), *BREEAM 98 for Offices: An Environmental Assessment Method for Office Buildings*. Construction Research Communications, Watford.

Bequest Toolkit (2001), http://www.surveying.salford.ac.uk/bqtoolkit/.

Cole, R. (1998), 'Emerging Trends in Building Environmental Assessment Methods', *Building Research and Information*, 26(1): 3–16.

Cole, R. (2000), 'Building Environmental Assessment Methods: Assessing Construction Practices', *Construction Management and Economics*, 18: 949–957.

Deakin, M., Curwell, S. and Lombardi, P. (2001), 'BEQUEST: The Framework and Directory of Assessment Methods', *International Journal of Life Cycle Assessment*, 6(6): 373–383.

Dickie, I. and Howard, N. (2000), Assessing Environmental Impacts of Construction; Industry Consensus, BREEAM and UK Ecopoints. CRC.

GBC'98 (1998), *Green Building Challenge'98 Conference Proceedings*. October 26–28, Vancouver, Canada. Natural Resources Canada, Ottawa, Canada.

Howard, N., Shiers, D. and Sinclair, M. (1998), *The Green Guide to Specification*. BRE.

Huovila, P. and Leinonen, J. (2001), *Managing Performance in the Built Environment*. CIB World Congress Proceedings, April. Wellington, New Zealand.

Leinonen, J. and Huovila, P. (2001), *Requirements Management Tool as a Catalyst for Communication*, Accepted Paper to be Presented in ECCE Conference, June, Espoo.

Mak, J., Anink, D. and Knapen, M. (1997), *Eco-Quantum, Development of LCA Based Tools for Buildings*, Proceedings of CIB Conference Buildings and the Environment, June 9–12, Paris.

SB2000 (2000), *Sustainable Building 2000*, Conference Proceedings. Maastricht, The Netherlands.

Sunikka, M. and Klunder, G. (2001), *Environmental Assessment in the Built Environment: The Dutch and the Finnish Approach*. Proceedings of the HAS Conference, April 18–19, York.

Sunikka, M., Huovila, P., Curwell, S. and Bentivegna, V. (2000), *Procurement Protocols for Sustainable Urban Development*. ILCDES 2000 Conference Proceedings, Helsinki.

Trusty, W. (2001), *Life Cycle Assessment (Athena Institute)*. An oral presentation at NRC – VTT seminar, 16 January, Ottawa.

UN (1996), The United Nations Working List of Indicators of Sustainable Development. http://www.un.org/esa/sustdev/worklist.htm.

APPENDIX

List of assessment methods

1   Analytic Hierarchy Process (AHP)

   The method allows users to reach a set of ratings for the decision alternatives by aggregating the relative weights of decision elements.

2   Building for Environmental and Economic Sustainability (version 2.0) (BEES 2.0)

   Building for Environmental and Economic Sustainability (version 2.0) (BEES) is an interactive computer design aid that helps users select building products for use in commercial office and housing projects in a way that balances environmental and economic criteria.

3   Building Research Establishment Environmental Assessment Method (BREEAM)

   The Building Research Establishment Environmental Assessment Method provides authoritative guidance on ways of minimising the adverse effects of buildings on the local and global environments. The assessment is based on 'credits' awarded for a set of performance criteria. The outcome of the assessment is a certificate or label that enables owners or occupants to gain recognition for their building's environmental performance.

4   BRE Environmental Profiles

Environmental Profiles are a method of gathering and presenting environmental data to compare the environmental performance of building materials. They enable architects, specifiers and clients to make informed decisions about construction materials and components, by providing a method for independent, 'level playing field' information about the relative environmental impacts of different design options.

5   Community Impact Evaluation (CIE)

CIE takes account of the total costs and benefits on a community and brings out the incidence of such costs and benefits on the various community sectors.

6   Contingent Valuation Method (CVM)

Contingent valuation deduces the value of a product not on the basis of the effective observed behaviour of subjects on the market, but with reference to an artificially structured market (hypothetical market).

7   Ecopoint

A UK Ecopoint is a single unit measurement of environmental impact. A UK Ecopoint score is a measure of the total environmental impact of a particular product or process expressed in units (ecopoints). It is calculated in relation to impacts on the environment in the UK and therefore applies to UK activities only.

8   Ecoprofile

Ecoprofile is a top–down method for environmental assessment of existing office buildings. It consists of three main areas: Outdoor environment, Use of resources and Indoor environment, focussing on energy flexibility and efficiency, use of hazardous materials (PCB, asbestos, etc.).

9   EcoProP

EcoProP is a requirements management tool, consisting of a generic classification of building properties, reference data about environmental requirements, information on relevant verification methods and automated procedures to scan requirements profiles and to form a design brief.

10   Eco-Quantum

Two versions of Eco-Quantum are available. Eco-Quantum Research is a tool for analysing and developing innovative and complex designs for sustainable buildings and offices. Eco-Quantum Domestic is a tool which architects can apply to quickly reveal environmental consequences of material and energy use of their designs of domestic buildings.

11   ENVEST

ENVEST is the first UK software tool for estimating the life cycle environmental impacts of a building from the early design stage. The first version is for office buildings.

12   Environmental Appraisal of Development Plans

This is an explicit, systematic and iterative review of development plan policies and proposals to evaluate their individual and combined impacts on the environment.

13   Environmental Impact Assessment (EIA)

Initiatives for large-scale facilities and structures likely to cause significant environmental impacts are subject to the Environmental Impact Assessment Procedure in EU (and quite widely worldwide).

14   Financial Evaluation of Sustainable Communities

The purpose of this assessment is to evaluate the financial viability of sustainable communities as a development option.

15   Green Building Challenge (GBC)

GBC is a hierarchical system of environmental assessment criteria for buildings developed for international comparative purposes in order to select and analyse the environmental performance and impact of buildings, initially for Green Building Challenge '98 and subsequently for the Sustainable Building 2000 conference.

16   The Green Guide

The Green Guide to Specification is an Environmental Profiling System for Building Materials and Components. The Green Guide provides a pointer to specification, which is both easy to use and soundly based on numerical data. These measure the environmental impacts of building materials in terms of 13 key parameters based around embodied energy, emissions, toxicity, wastes and use of resources.

17   Impact matrix techniques

Impact matrices are used to summarize the impacts of development activities in a tabular form.

18   MASTER (Managing Speeds of Traffic on European Roads)

The MASTER Framework is a set of guiding rules and principles for evaluating the impacts of a speed management policy so that the socioeconomic feasibility of the policy can be established.

19   Net Annual Return Model

As a form of income, net annual return (NAR) is defined as the difference between gross annual returns (such as rent received) and operating costs (including repairs, maintenance and other such outgoing payments). The annual returns and operating costs include those resulting from the introduction of experimental designs aimed at the construction of environmentally friendly, green land uses and building programmes.

20 Office, Schools and Local Authority Toolkits

These toolkits are designed to help facilities, building or office managers to improve the environmental performance of their buildings, and indicate where these activities will help them save money. It is possible to use the toolkits in their own right or as a stepping stone towards a formal accreditation system, such as EMAS or ISO 14001.

21 PIMWAQ

PIMWAQ is a method which defines minimum ecological levels for a residential building and assesses the eco-efficiency degree of various development projects.

22 Social Cost–benefit Analysis (SCBA)

SCBA aims at (1) identifying the actions that either minimise the social costs when outputs (objectives) are given or maximise the output (achievement of objectives) within a given budget; and (2) establishing the social distribution of the impacts.

23 Social impact assessment (SIA)

SIA is a method for assessing the impacts of policies, plan or projects on people. Its aim is to predict and evaluate those impacts before they happen.

24 SPARTACUS (System for Planning and Research in Towns and Cities for Urban Sustainability)

SPARTACUS is an indicator system and a decision-support tool for assessing sustainability implications of urban land use and transport policies. It is based on the results of a transport land-use interaction model.

25 System Dynamic Approach

A city can be viewed as a system whose purpose is to provide employment, housing and other social benefits for its inhabitants. The system's approach to studying systems such as these emphasizes the connections among the various parts that constitute a whole. System thinking is concerned with connectedness and wholeness.

Source: www.surveying.salford.ac.uk/bqtoolkit/ (22 April 2001).

18

Life Cycle Analysis of Buildings, Groups of Buildings and Urban Fragments

Niklaus Kohler

INTRODUCTION

In sustainability, assessment of different levels of the built environment – a specific family of methods – can be considered as life cycle-oriented. It encompasses Life Cycle Analysis (LCA), Life Cycle Costing (LCC) and to a lesser degree Mass Flow Accounting (MFA) and Risk Analysis (RA). These methods have their roots in system ecology (Odum, 1971) and its applications in urban and industrial metabolism, in thermodynamics, in process engineering, in energy calculations and finally in economy in the form of environmental accounting. They all share an explicit physical framework, extended system limits in space (interface to nature) and in time (past and future). Their stronghold in sustainability assessment is their capability to explicitly relate the different dimensions of SUD, to take long time frames both in the past and in the future into account and to be applicable at different levels from individual buildings to urban systems. They all use a large amount of input data (upstream and downstream flows, historical data, etc.) and they still have large domains of missing, uncertain or vague information. The communication of their complex results to concerned users needs new methods of multi-dimensional visualisation that do not yet exist in practice. Even if some of the methods are international standards, there is still a lot of ongoing transdisciplinary research.

LIFE CYCLE ANALYSIS (LCA)

Life Cycle Analysis is an evaluation method for the consumption of resources and of the impacts on the environment of a product, a system or a service during its life cycle, i.e. from the extraction of the raw materials to the elimination of waste. It is basically an accounting method of mass and energy flows using system ecological methods. The interest in Life Cycle Analysis has appeared over the last 20 years. The Society of Environmental Toxicity and Chemistry (SETAC, 1996) has produced methodological guides. ISO has developed and adopted a series of standards (ISO, 2000) dedicated to life cycle assessment. A new standard under development is the ISO 14048, providing a standardised format for LCA data, in paper-based or electronic media.

Step	Definition	Content
Goal definition and scoping	Objectives and framework of the LCA	Goal of the study, Content of the study Functional unit. Need of a peer review Form of communication
Inventory	Mass and energy balances	System definition (limits) Collection of data
Impact assessment	Study of the impacts on the environment, human health and depletion of resources	Classification Characterisation Evaluation (Valuation)
Improvement assessment	Proposition to reduce the system impact on the environment	Identification of options Evaluation of options Selection of options

Figure 18.1 The four steps of a Life Cycle Analysis (SETAC, 1996; ISO, 2000)

LIFE CYCLE COSTING (LCC)

The basic definitions can be derived from ISO 15686 (ISO, 2001) where Life Cycle Costs are defined as the total cost of a building or its parts throughout its life, including the cost of planning, design, acquisition, operations, maintenance and disposal, less any residual value.

> Life cycle costing (LCC) is a technique which enables comparative cost assessments to be made over a specified period of time, taking into account all relevant economic factors both in terms of initial capital costs and future operational costs. In particular, it is an economic assessment considering all projected relevant cost flows over a period of analysis expressed in monetary value.

Life Cycle Analysis and Life Cycle Cost (in the UK, the term 'Whole Life Costs' has also been used) share common basic data and partially common aims. They seek to assess impacts on the whole life of a building or an infrastructure and present the information in a manner which supports decision-making processes (SETAC, 2002; Task Group 4, 2003).

The key similarities between LCC and LCA are that both utilise data on the

- quantities of materials used;
- service life the materials could or will be used for;
- maintenance and operational impacts of using the products; and
- end-of-life proportions to recycling (and sale value) and disposal.

The key differences are that, first, conventional LCC methods do not consider the process of making a product; they are concerned with market costs whereas LCA considers production and disposal (from 'cradle to grave'). Since asset component costs for differing options occur at varying times throughout the asset's life cycle, expressing them as costs at a common base rate can only compare them. This can be achieved through the process of discounting. Because of difficulties of predicting inflation in the long term, it is recommended to use real costs (without inflation) and a realistic discount rate. Selecting a discount rate is one of the most contested areas of LCC study, from an environmental perspective, because it can be considered to be devaluing future resource consumption, which is in contradiction to intergenerational equity objectives. Over a long period of time, the real discount rate is usually assumed to be 0–2 per cent only. At low discount rates, long-term future costs and savings are immediately meaningful. Even in the current economic climate, the economic performance of environmentally sound building systems is usually superior to those of more traditional systems (with lower investment costs), compared over the life cycle of a building. As we can expect the cost of consuming resources to reflect, in the future, more accurately the true environmental and social costs, these arguments look set to become more convincing. When considering the scale of impact the built environment has on national and global scales, LCA and LCC should be seen as two common tools, which enable building designers and developers to recognise and demonstrate the benefits of environmentally sensitive construction.

MASS FLOW ACCOUNTING (MFA)

Mass flow accounting is applied in many domains like agriculture, private household consumption, regional planning, etc. In a very general way, it monitors processes in the anthroposphere. Mass flow accounting records, describes and interprets the process of metabolism in a defined geographic space during a certain period of time (Baccini and Brunner, 1991; Adriaanse et al., 1997). This type of model is sometimes also referred to as urban metabolism (Wolman, 1965). The Quantifiable City Project (May et al., 1997) follows the same direction, even if it is arguable whether a transport model should be the basis of a long-term urban development. There are interesting transdisciplinary approaches to the study of town development, in particular urban sprawl, regional development, urban and rural mass flow (Baccini and Oswald, 1998). Furthermore analogies between urban development and wild ecosystems have become a promising object of research recently: 'Energy and material flows through human settlements are conceived as urban metabolism, in which material inputs are transformed into useful energy, physical structure, and waste. Principles of ecosystem succession are used to explore ways in which city development differs from that of wild ecosystems' (Decker, 2000).

The process of mass flow accounting follows four main steps:

1   definition of the system (products, process, materials);
2   data capture of flows and concentrations;
3   calculation of the flows (by data processing);
4   schematic representation and interpretation of results.

As it is a practical approach, it has to react to actual constraints and results. This means that the analysis may have to go back to an earlier step before advancing to the next step. It might be necessary to repeat this process several times to achieve a well-evolved and stable result.

In the METAPOLIS model (Baccini and Oswald, 1998), the input and output data concerning private households in an urban system have been analysed. The data are divided into four main groups corresponding to the main activities of urban life: 'nourishing', 'cleaning', 'living' and 'transportation'. The flows of eight materials

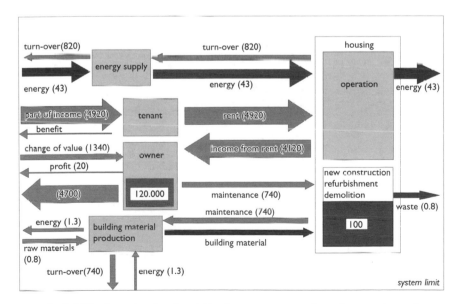

Figure 18.2 MFA of a regional system taking into account mass flows (input and waste), energy (use and embodied), costs and benefits (Brunner *et al.*, 1994)

(sulphur, carbon, phosphorus, chlorine, aluminium, iron, copper and zinc) are used as indicators. The assessment of the four activities gives a general overview of the characteristics of private households' consumption behaviour. The analysis of the eight substances shows where the materials enter the system, where they remain, and where they leave the system (Baccini and Brunner, 1991).

The main differences between LCA and MFA reside in different system limits. In life cycle analysis, the system limits are not determined geographically (in space) but by the interfaces to nature ('cradle and grave'). The time system limit in LCA is the life-time of a product (SETAC, 1996). LCA uses process and hybrid analysis whereas mass flow accounting uses generally statistical or macroeconomic data. The basic material data are identical for LCA and MFA but the functional unit and the system limits differ. MFA is generally used as part of an EIA procedure for towns and regions. The objectives are to identify limits or thresholds of critical flows and critical loads. LCA is more concerned with products and, in the case of buildings and infrastructure, with long living products. But building-LCA can also be linked with more detailed models of the environment at least on the emission level. Matsumoto (1999) has established a dynamic CO_2 flow model to simulate the carbon dioxide flow of wooden materials from production to disposal in Japanese houses; 7 stocks, 14 flows and 38 converters are identified. The model provides a complete simulation of the reuse of wood.

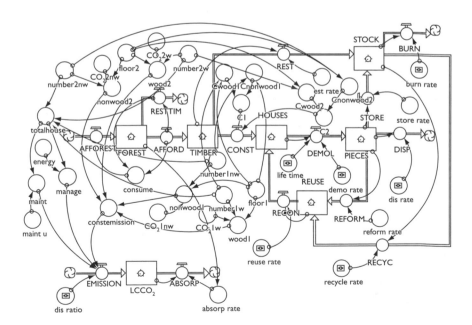

Figure 18.3 Carbon flow system dynamic model for wooden houses (Matsumota, 1999)

In urban life cycle assessment both methods are used and the results can be compared. LCA sets generally the inferior limit but allows attributing the causes whereas MFA gives the upper limits and allows judging effects in terms of concentrations and critical loads. Both LCA and MFA can be combined with economic data.

EXTENSION OF LCA TOOLS IN THE ASSESSMENT OF SUD

Most of the existing LCA tools are based on the standardised LCA framework (Moffatt, 2000; BEQUEST, 2001). The enlargement of the scope from the analysis of the life cycle to the assessment of sustainable development raises the question of how to relate physical results from LCA to general economic, social and cultural protection goals and their assessment. Taking these goals into consideration requires a considerable conceptual enlargement that cannot be met by a single tool. The protection goals of sustainable development can be formalised for buildings and urban fragments through a simple hierarchical structure of protection, environmental and operational objectives. Taking into account the different dimensions of sustainability in the assessment will only be possible through a whole set of methods. LCA, MFA and LCC tools are necessarily part of this set, above all, when they are combined in Integrated LCA (Kohler and Lützkerndorf, 2002). The direct

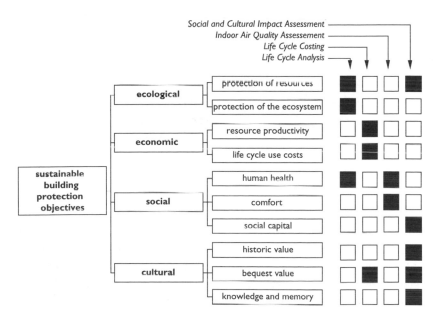

Figure 18.4 Sustainable objectives for buildings and urban fragments and the necessary assessment methods (Kohler and Moffatt, 2002)

consequences for human health (indoor air quality) and the local impacts on the ecosystem can be assessed through indoor air quality appreciations and local environmental impact assessment. Social and cultural impacts can be assessed through social and cultural impact assessment. Once again the system limits have to be adjusted and there must be a distinction between global impacts (LCA) and local impacts (Indoor Air Quality Assessment).

The crucial issue is to include several tools in the same performance assessment and to integrate them into the professional design and management environments (i.e. through sharing data with other design tools). Tools resulting from the combination of LCA and LCC are referred to as Integrated Building Life Cycle Analysis (Kohler and Lützkerndorf, 2002). The assessment can be applied in the case of individual buildings, both for new construction and for refurbishment. General sustainability studies have also drawn the attention to the importance of taking into account existing buildings and the building stock. The long-term maintenance and management of the building stock is certainly a societal issue with increasing importance (Hassler and Kohler, 2002). LCA has been applied in research projects (SUIT, 2001; IFIB, 2003) to groups of existing buildings forming urban fragments. Prototypical research tools at this level are by now on the way of becoming professional tools. All these applications are based on common assumptions, they use the same basic building representation (at different granularities), they share data in building inventories, they use the same modular data sets for LCA inventories (both upstream and downstream) and they use the same sets of evaluation criteria.

Common building representation

The extensive application of LCA, and to a certain degree LCC, has been retarded by the lack of an appropriate (and common) building representation. The usual geometrical representation of buildings through plans, sections, elevations and details is in this case of limited interest. It is more convenient to base an LCA on the textual process-oriented building description for cost calculation and for tender, i.e. to describe buildings as they are built. The building is decomposed into functional units (or cost elements like $1m^2$ of exterior wall), which are the result of all building processes proportionally necessary. This process-oriented specification contains the necessary quantities of materials (including all auxiliary materials and waste) as well as the type and working time of machines used (including their energy and material consumption as well as their capital and maintenance costs). Material and building process quantities can be linked to the basic inventory data and evaluation sets (mass flow, primary energy consumption, effect-oriented impact categories, aggregate indicators, etc.). In order to reflect the life cycle of a building element, additional information is needed on the life expectancy, maintenance and cleaning cycles, energy consumption during use, recycling behaviour and possible downstream paths. Element data contain also information on the succession and fixation of the different layers (and materials), which allows the calculation of heat flow, vapour diffusion, off gassing, toxicity, acoustic protection, fire resistance, construction time, deconstruction possibility, etc. When using such elements in a scaleable way, a complete list of elements and specifications exists at the end of the design process. These specifications can be grouped by traders or contractors as a basis for tender without the loss of the initial information.

For applications including groups of buildings the complete (element-) information of a building can be referred to as a new functional unit like 1m² of use surface (of a certain type, e.g. 1 m² of elementary school). Through these new functional units (1 m² of a typical elementary school-building of the period 1950 to 1975) it is possible to describe building stocks and urban fragments and to apply life cycle simulations and scenarios.

Common data sets

In LCA it is necessary to define system limits in a very explicit way, so that modular data sets from upstream and downstream processes can be used for the analysis

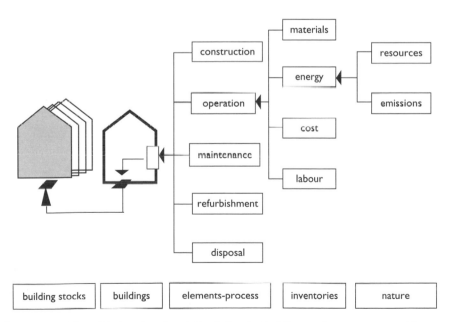

Figure 18.5 Hierarchical system description linking the building stock to resources and impacts through elements and specifications (IFIB, 2003)

of different energy carriers, materials, products and services. In the inventory, mass inputs (resources) and mass outputs (emissions) are identified. Mass flows are vectors to which effects are associated; they are not evaluation factors in themselves. They have to be referred to as a functional unit, which is the building (or part of it) during its life cycle. There are spatial, time and functional system limits inside this functional unit. The proposed reference frame for the functional unit allows allocating the different flows (and later effects and evaluations) to life cycle phases and responsibilities (for design, ownership, management, disposal, etc.). The same method can be used at any moment of a building's life cycle, alone or in combination with scenarios. The mass flows determined at the building site are only part of the mass flows which the building causes during its lifetime. Before the building process starts, there are upstream processes like resource extraction, energy preparation, transport, infrastructure, etc. Once the building has been demolished, there are downstream processes (deposit, combustion, reuse, etc.). It is not possible to establish all these flows every time a building LCA is realised. Only a modular approach, with general upstream, transformation, transport and downstream data sets, can meet the following guidelines:

- Use consistent upstream and downstream system limits and allocation proce-dures.
- Profit from consistent general process analysis data (if possible in a common format) for a multitude of domains.
- Avoid the extensive data collection and concentrate on the interpretation of LCA results.

Basic data sets like Ecoinvent (2000) refer to:

- Energy process analysis;
- Transport process analysis;
- Building material and building process analysis (LEGOE, 2002);
- Downstream process analysis.

In addition, auxiliary materials can be considered. They constitute approximately 5 per cent of the mass flow and are often not indicated in the inventories because these materials are added later in order to give specific properties to building products (e.g. plasticizer, concrete additives, etc.). It is however possible through general formulations (which exist in the professional literature) to estimate which and how much auxiliary materials are probably included in a building product (Kohler and Lützkendorf, 2002).

Evaluation methods

The LCA methodology distinguishes very clearly between the classification phase when certain effects are associated with causes and the aggregation of different impacts or effects (Hofstetter, 1998). On the level of effects there is a difference between unknown, potential and real effects. Unknown effects, above all combined effects, are by definition impossible to describe. One approach to handle this problem is to determine the overall mass burdens for every type of activity without any type of weighting and to use them as an indicator (proxy) for (yet) unknown impacts. Potential effects are considered as area-independent and media-independent. The inventory parameters (mass and energy balances) are not expressed under concentration type data. Moreover they are summed over the various phases of the life cycle without any consideration of location and calendar time. Potential effects do not assess any consequences or damage (mortality for example) but give only an indication of a hazard. The aggregation of several effect-oriented indicators needs a supplementary weighting with regard to more general categories (like effects on the ecosystem, human beings, etc.) This type of weighting can only result from expert or societal judgements.

Finally, real effects are quantified impacts which constitute risks for human beings or ecosystems. The distinction between potential and real impacts is of the same order as between the notions of 'hazard' and 'risk'. The term 'hazard' typically refers to the source of a risk. A hazard assessment is area-independent, as it will only give information on potential effect. To be able to perform a risk assessment, it is necessary to estimate the fate of the emitted substance, which means that site-specific data, both on the location of the emissions and on the location of the exposure, is needed. This means that all results are only valuable for certain locations and calendar time. It is no more possible to compare results from different locations and realisation time, which explains why this type of more detailed assessment is relatively rare.

The basic evaluation categories are:

- the use of resources (materials, energy, abiotic resources, land, water);
- the potential impacts on the ecosystem (global warming, acidification, ozone depletion, etc.);
- the combined effects on human health.

For the resource consumption, a certain number of approaches based mainly on the scarcity of raw materials exist (Hofstetter, 1998; Goedkoop and Spriensma, 1999). In the case of buildings, there is often an alternative to the consumption of raw materials taken from nature in the form of the continued use of existing buildings. The main problem is therefore the appreciation of existing buildings as resources. LCA tools should be able to handle the comparison of new construction versus continued use of existing buildings. Economically this can be expressed in the simple example of recycling steel when demolishing a building. The benefit from recycling is approximately €45/t versus the cost of new steel which is approximately €450/t and the cost of completed steel structure which is approximately €1500/t. The effect-oriented evaluation is the best-known evaluation domain through the quasi-standardised effect categories of CML (Guinée et al., 2001). For the last category, the burden of death, disease and disability can be used as an aggregation relevant for the effects on human health. It evaluates the number of 'years of life lost' (YLL) caused by an environmental effect or by accident, hunger, wars, etc. The more differentiated concept of 'disability-adjusted life years' (DALYs) has generated a comprehensive picture of the 'burden of disease', covering all major disease and injury categories (Murray and Lopez, 1996).

It is not possible to find scientific criteria for a weighted aggregation between resource conservation, impact on human health and impact on ecosystem health. The weighting is left to the end-user of LCA methods (Goedkoop and Spriensma, 1999).

Optimisation

Classical optimisation procedures tend to reduce the complexity by aggregating several evaluation criteria by simple weighting or other multi-criteria preference procedures. As cost parameters can be reduced by discounting methods to one single value, the resulting optimisation problem is of a simple cost–benefit type. The application of these methods in LCA has several drawbacks: through aggregation a large part of the initial information is lost; weighting procedures are by definition view- (and person-) dependent; and multi-criteria procedures suggest replacing fundamental societal choices with a impressive number of crunching procedures. Research in design and decision theory has shown that in complex situations constraint satisfying and other 'frugal' heuristics are preferable. The problem is considered as n-dimensional dimensions for which it is possible to define target and limit values constituting a solution space. Assisting design and decision tools allow situating a specific solution inside (or outside) the solution. It can then be decided if the solution or the solution space (the level of performance) has to be revised (Papamichael and Protzen, 1993). This approach has found a well-known visualisation method (Spider – see Baycan-Levent et al. in this volume).

In the spider, three design solutions are compared along ecological, energetic and economical criteria. The values take into account operation and embodied energy

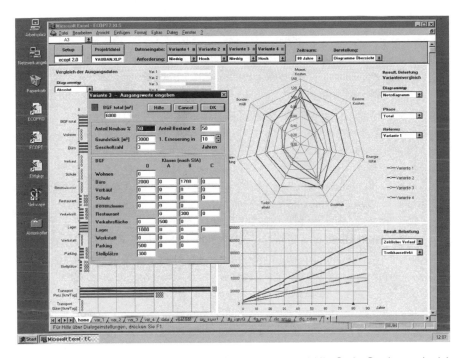

Figure 18.6 Example of an integrated Life Cycle Analysis and Life Cycle Costing method for design brief stage

as well as transport. The three central solutions of the spider represent buildings with different construction and performance alternatives in the city centre with a large part of public transport. The exterior solution corresponds to the best alternative but is situated outside town with users taking personal cars (ECOPT, IFIB).

INTEGRATED LCA OF INDIVIDUAL BUILDINGS

Integrated LCA methods can be used from the design brief stage on to the facility management and deconstruction of buildings. The impacts of the building during the life cycle phases can be estimated using the same basic upstream and down stream processes data. The simulation of large amounts of buildings shows that buildings of a certain function (housing, offices, hospitals, factory, etc.) are much more similar than generally thought to be. This opens a large field of using default values in early design stages when complete information is not available. The cost and environmental impacts during the lifetime of a building can already be determined during the design brief and through performance specification by associating average performance and functional units. The same simulation techniques can be used with more detailed data to verify if the initial performance targets are reached.

The lifetime of buildings is predicted by using scenarios of the aging and replacement process. Two models are possible. In general, a simple replacement model is used, where all elements are automatically replaced at the end of their assumed lifetime. This is problematic because the empirical knowledge about real replacement and refurbishment is low and the replacement and refurbishment depends on many technological, economical, legal, political and fashion (obsolescence) assumptions. A periodic refurbishment model is therefore closer to the real world. Three periods are distinguished:

1   Current maintenance (elements with a lifetime less than 12 years). The replacement of coatings, gaskets, paint, window glass, etc. is continuous and can be taken into account on an average yearly basis.

2   Partial refurbishment (elements with a life between 15 and 30 years). The partial refurbishment takes place in general between 20 and 25 years and concerns parts of the heating, sanitary and electrical system. Coatings and windows can be part of it.

3   General refurbishment (elements with lifetime between 35 and 60 years). The general refurbishment takes place between 40 and 60 years and concerns the heating, sanitary and electric system, windows and roof as well as coatings. A general raise of standard and transformation of the building often accompany it.

The total lifetime of an individual building is a purely conventional value. After 60 years it has no particular signification because the replacement flow becomes constant and the annual material 'pay back' of the basic structure (which can last a very long time) diminishes rapidly. From a resource conservation point of view, it is important that buildings last as long as possible, that they have small replacement flows (throughput), that they are easy to repair and that they can easily be adapted to other uses. In the central European climate, the impacts due to the operation of average existing buildings are by factors higher than the impacts due to construction and maintenance. For low energy buildings or passive buildings, the relation between operation and construction related impacts tends towards 1; in experimental low emission buildings or passive buildings a factor less than one is possible.

The objectives of the LCA and LCC tools are to assist the design or management teams in setting complex targets (energy, costs, impacts), in verifying at different levels of advancement if these targets are reached and, if they are not reached, to identify which building element or parameter has to be changed in order to make the building lie within the target or solution space again. Even if there is a growing number of internationally available LCA and LCC tools, a certain number

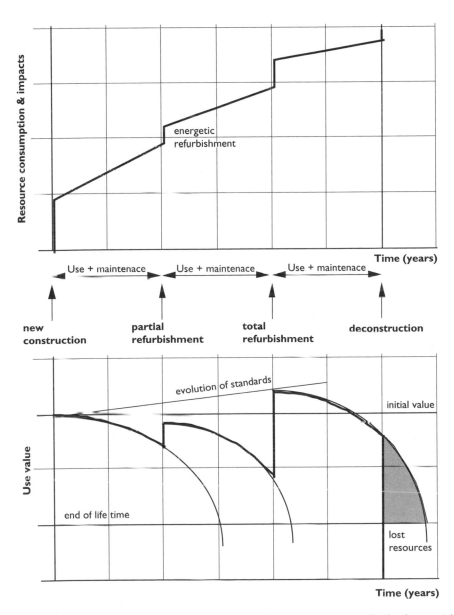

Figure 18.7 Periodic replacement model and cumulative resource consumption/environmental impacts over the lifetime [IFIB]

of problems are not yet solved. They include uncertainty and sensitivity analysis (Chouquet et al., 2003), difficulties to appreciate resource consumption, links to real impacts (indoor and local environment), missing reference data on different types of buildings and operational reliable interfaces to CAAD software.

INTEGRATED LCA OF GROUPS OF BUILDINGS (BUILDINGS STOCKS)

Groups of buildings (buildings stocks) can be defined by common ownership, common (facility) management or a common geographical (spatial) limit. They are composed of individual buildings with their own age and use-related behaviour. If the objective is to obtain general information on how a group of buildings will behave (e.g. how the refurbishment costs will evolve without intervention or with particular exterior intervention), the stock has to be modelled (described) in an appropriate way depending in particular on how much information is available on individual buildings and in which form it is. In practice, all cases from almost total lack of information to very complete information, which may however not be accessible because in paper form, exist. The crucial question is which objectives the group of buildings should match over time (functional, financial, energetic, human-toxic, etc. performance). Depending on the number of buildings, the type and granularity of the available information, a stock can be modelled by individual buildings (known or virtual). In general subgroups of buildings (which have the same function and have been built during the same period) with similar construction properties (types) are defined and the stock is simulated as resulting from the behaviour of the subgroups. Using different statistical and stochastical methods like survival analysis, population dynamics, cohort models, Markov chains, cluster analysis, etc. can simulate the evolution of buildings stocks. These methods can be used on different levels from the simulation of national buildings stocks with the objective to reduce the energy consumption, over to the management of social housing stocks with the objective to maintain the resource value, to the management of public communal stocks with the objective to predict the overall costs over the next decade. Tools based on such methods should allow defining targets for the sustainable management of buildings stocks, to assess if the objectives are achieved and to suggest what has to be done to realise the objectives over a longer period. The combination of LCA, LCC and social impact analysis allows evaluating the risks of negative feedbacks between building degradation and increasing social problems (Madanpour et al., 1997). Sustainable development strategies of social housing stocks are probably the only long-term strategy, which allows maintaining physical, social and economical capital.

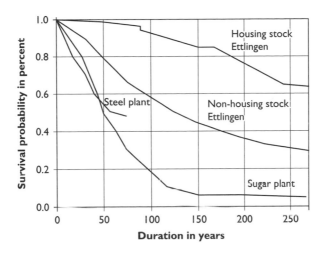

Figure 18.8 Survival functions of different building stocks

Figure 18.8 shows the housing stock and the non-housing stock of the small German town of Ettlingen with 7000 buildings – an industrial (steel plant) stock with 100 buildings and another industrial plant (sugar factory) with 500 buildings. The detailed historical analyses of buildings, refurbishment and demolition activities show that the survival curves of housing stocks are very different from those of industrial stocks (IFIB, 2003).

This type of application to integrated LCA is only at the beginning. The most efficient way to introduce these methods rapidly is to link LCA and LCC with the existing financial management tools of housing societies and facility management tools for non-housing applications. Sharing of design, quantity surveying and real estate management data, as a basis for integrated LCA, will considerably improve the possibility of implementing sustainability strategies in the building sector.

INTEGRATED LCA OF URBAN FRAGMENTS

Urban fragments and neighbourhoods are parts of towns, which are defined by limits resulting from property or a specific intention. This can occur on the level of real estate management, urban planning or project development. When decisions concerning a local project have larger impacts both in space (spillover) and in time (long-term development), new assessment questions appear (Lichfield, 1996). This is the case when new projects or plans are situated in existing urban contexts,

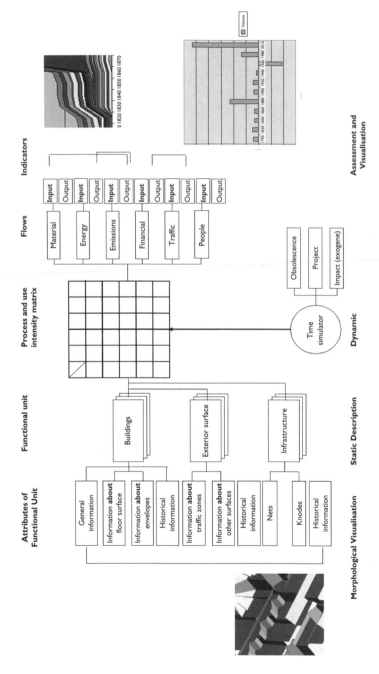

Figure 18.9 The structure of a simulation model for the development of urban fragments (IFIB, 2003)

which are often strongly characterised by their historical development. The term 'urban fabric' stands both for the physical and the non-material urban qualities. The multitude of cultural and social qualities related to the urban fabric, in particular in the case of the European historic towns, has to be considered as an almost non-renewable resource. The traditional instruments of EIA cannot handle complex long-term phenomena of urban development, in particular in the perspective of a sustainable development. The future application of Strategic Environmental Assessment (SEA) could certainly take into consideration time-dependant aspects. It will however also rely on basic assessment methods like integrated LCA and LCC applied to groups of buildings and urban fragments. These methods can use data from Life Cycle Analysis and Costing by aggregating it to the granularity of the urban fabric. At the urban level infrastructure, exterior surfaces and urban furniture must be taken into account.

A comprehensive assessment model on an urban fragment scale must allow the simulation of historical, present and future developments within the same conceptual framework and using the same basic data (IFIB, 2003). The historical information is necessary to understand the long-term dynamics (the historic time constants) and possible future options (solution corridor). The necessary comprehensive information on the buildings is referred to the use-floor surface (per building level) and all flow calculations are generated from this functional unit. The complexity of urban life produces a system of flows, which can be referred to several urban functions (e.g. traffic). For LCA applications it seems that the choice of the building floor surface reflects best the complex functions and becomes the 'origin' of a multitude of flows. The historical part of the analysis causes peculiar difficulties, as knowledge of historical functions and flows is often very limited. The only reliable information describes the built structure, which defines material inputs and outputs at a certain moment. There is little information about historic energy use or water supply.

All exterior surfaces, which are not occupied by buildings, have positive and negative effects on the urban ecological and social system. They also induce considerable life cycle costs. The using intensity of these surfaces has an influence on the noise level, microclimate or soil-use density. The urban furniture includes objects such as bus stops, benches, street lighting and power lines and trees and bushes. Apart from their function, they often have a strong social significance.

Infrastructure systems include waste water, storm water and fresh water, electricity, gas, district heating and communication systems. They have considerable impacts both through their construction-maintenance and through the material, energy and information flows, which they transport. Most systems in use today have a long history and sometimes high time constants. Their life cycle costs are considerable and due to administrative limits, it is often difficult to have a complete and up-to-date view of their state. Although hidden and often forgotten, they are part of the urban fabric and of the cultural heritage, as well.

The evolution of both past and future (scenarios) can be modelled through the extended life cycle of buildings and infrastructures. Basically, the functional units are use surfaces of buildings and exterior surfaces and the segments or nodes of infrastructure. They have states of use and transitions between states. At each moment flows are generated (materials, energy, transport, information, financial, etc.) and effects can be associated with them. The evaluation procedure is similar to individual buildings: the different performances or targets define an n-dimensional solution space, which becomes a solution corridor through the introduction of a time axis.

The speed of transformation is certainly one of the key parameters of a sustainable urban development. Towns, cities and urban contexts have historically evolved with a certain speed. There have been faster and slower developments, but the overall relatively low speed allowed at the same time a conservation of resources and a cultural continuity, which could be understood by the inhabitants and allowed social identification. There has always been a difference between the time constants of basic infrastructures (decades and centuries) and of their use (decades). The underlying physical transformation of the built environment (as expressed by different energy and mass-flow levels as well as by the overall appearance) stays within limits even if these limits evolve slowly over time. Recent developments show that when those limits are passed, urban (historical) areas either become unstable and enigmatic when the speed of transformation is too high – or they perish by dereliction when the speed of transformation is too low.

Assessment and indicators

The assessment leads to a large number of flows, effects and indications concerning the different parameters. These values have to be conserved as such; they are the basic un-aggregated data serving to constitute indicators. On the other hand, the determination of sustainability (protection) objectives leads to operational objectives. Indicators result from the detailed assessment, which they sum up. In an evaluation, several indicators are in general confronted with several operational objectives. Instead of an aggregation of all parameters into one single indicator it is more transparent for the decision process to choose specific indicators as proxy for a group of effects and to confront them with an operational objective. The information is not lost; it is always possible to go back to the complete list of indicators and objectives and to select other combinations. This process of choice has to be open and transparent for the concerned users.

Limits

The generic difficulty, to take into consideration cultural and social dimensions within economic and ecological evaluation frameworks, resides in the difficulty that only some cultural and social aspects can be characterised through material parameters. The objective cannot be to 'integrate' cultural values inside the frameworks, but to enlarge the scope of the evaluation in such a way that cultural, social and historic dimensions can be recognised. This can be achieved through the recognition of additional properties:

- time (age, history, historical dynamic);
- complexity (complexity of different historical dimensions);
- quality (of the parts, materials, architecture and construction);
- signification (including immaterial dimensions);
- resource value (material, use value, bequest value);
- collective memory (associated to material objects).

The large mass inputs illustrated in Figure 18.10 are from the period of construction at the end of the nineteenth century and the construction of shopping centre in 2003. The outputs were the subject of destruction during World War II and of the demolition to build the shopping centre. Whereas the buildings at the end of the nineteenth century densified and structured the urban fabric, the shopping centre destroyed the urban fabric – a classical case of overshoot (IFIB, 2003).

All information on these buildings is contained in a database. Different attributes (energy, costs, etc.) can be visualised in different time slots (calendar time and duration). The tool integrates CAD, GIS, LCA and LCC simulation (IFIB, 2003).

Existing tools

LCA of urban fragments and neighbourhoods is only at its beginning. The idea of sharing data with other professional applications and above all the link to data storage, communication and visualisation tools will allow a rapid development and implementation. This means also that as much data as possible will be stored in GIS as a basis for all time-space related simulations. The capacity of GIS to handle temporal information is improving due to intensive research in this field

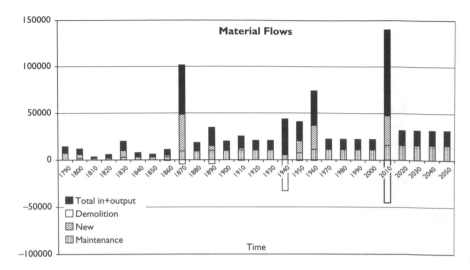

Figure 18.10 Historic evolution of mass flows in this example of an urban fragment in the historical centre of Karlsruhe

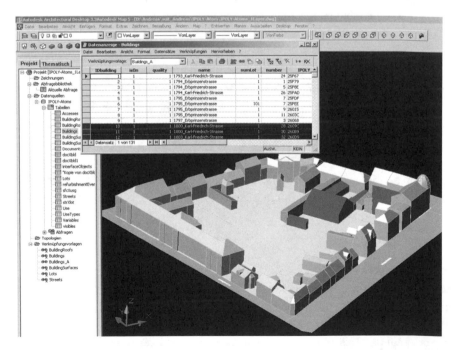

Figure 18.11 Representation of an urban fragment in a life cycle assessment

(Ott and Swiaczny, 2001). New forms of distributed data storage in geo portals and groupware applications are developed at present. Another crucial problem is the necessity for nD – visualisations in order to interpret and communicate a large amount of complex space-time related information.

CONCLUSIONS

LCA, LCC and MFA are comprehensive assessment methods based on physical models of buildings and the urban fabric. They can take into account directly or indirectly a multitude of different aspects and can encompass new system limits in time both going back in history and modelling possible futures through scenarios. As the methods need considerable data on both upstream and downstream processes as well as on the object (building or urban fabric), they should be combined with other planning tools (quantity surveying, CAAD, GIS) and exterior databases. This will allow to concentrate on the interpretation of complex results and on the discussion about the multiple hypotheses and assumptions in the methods. Classical optimisation and weighting techniques do not seem appropriate to cope with the complexity of the results. Constraint satisfaction techniques combined with new visualisation tools could assist both specialists and concerned users in taking decisions in democratic participation processes.

Even if these methods are not yet fully operational on the level of building stocks and urban fragments, they show a new dimension of understanding in sustainable urban development processes by integrating the past, the long-term dynamic and the issues of complex resource conservation in the public discussion.

REFERENCES

Adriaanse, A., Bringezu, S., Hammond, A., Moriguchi, Y., Rodenburg, E., Rogich, D. and Schütz, H. (1997) *Resource Flows – The Material Basis of Industrial Economies*, World Resources Institute, New York.

Baccini, P. and Brunner P.H. (1991) *Metabolism of the Anthroposphere*. Springer-Verlag, Berlin.

Baccini, P. and Oswald, F. (1998) *Netzstadt, Transdisziplinäre Methoden zum Umbau urbaner Systeme*. VdF-ETH, Zürich.

BEQUEST (2001) Building Environmental Quality Evaluation for Sustainability through Time. A concerted action. http://www.surveying.salford.ac.uk/bqpart/.

Brunner, Ph., Daxbeck, H. and Baccini, P. (1994) 'Industrial metabolism at the regional and local level: a case study on a Swiss region' in Ayres, R.U. and Simonis, U.E. (eds) *Industrial Metabolism: Restructuring for Sustainable Development*, pp. 163–193. United Nations University Press, Tokyo.

Chouquet, J., Kohler, N. and Bodin, O. (2003) *Dealing with Uncertainty in Life Cycle Analysis of Building Model by Using Experiment Design Methods.* IKM, Bauhausuniversität Weimar.

Decker, E.H. (2000) 'Energy and material flow through the urban ecosystem', *Annu. Rev. Energy Environ.* 25: 685–740.

Ecoinvent (2000) *The Swiss Centre for Life Cycle Inventories.* http://www.ecoinvent.ch.

Goedkoop, M. and Spriensma, R. (1999) *The Eco-indicator99 – A Damage Oriented Method for Life Cycle Impact Assessment. Methodology Report. Second edition.* http://www.pre.nl.

Guinée, J., de Bruijn, H., van Duin, M. and Huijbregts, M. (2001) *LCA – An Operational Guide to the ISO-standards*, Final report, May 2001. CML – University of Leiden. http://www.leidenuniv.nl/interfac/cml/ssp/.

Hassler, U. and Kohler, N. (2002) 'The building stock as a research object', *Building Research and Information* 30(4): 226–236.

Hofstetter, P. (1998) *Perspectives in Life Cycle Impact Assessment. A Structured Approach to Combine Models of Technosphere, Ecosphere and Valuesphere.* Kluwer, Boston.

Institut Für Industrielle Bauproduktion (IFIB) (2003) *Life Cycle Analysis of Urban Fragments.* Internal report for EifER – European Institute of Energy Research. University of Karlsruhe.

ISO 14040–14043 (2000) *Environmental Management – Life Cycle Assessment – Principles and Framework. ISO/FDIS/TC207SC514040/1997(E).*

ISO 15686 (2001) *Buildings and Constructed Assets – Service Life Planning.* ISO.

Kohler, N. and Lützkendorf, Th. (2002) 'Integrated Life Cycle Analysis', *Building Research & Information*, 30(5): 338–348.

LEGOE (2002) *Umweltorientierte Planungsinstrumente für den Lebenszyklus von Gebäuden.* Schlussbericht. DBU – Deutsche Bundesstiftung Umwelt. http://www.legoe.de.

Lichfield, N. (1996) *Community Impact Evaluation*, UCL Press, London.

Madanpour, A., Cars, C. and Allen, J. (1997) *Social Exclusion in European Cities, Regional Policy and Development.* Kingsley Publishers, London.

Matsumoto, H. (1999) *System Dynamics Model For Life Cycle Assessment (LCA) Of Residential Buildings.* Proceedings of Sixth International IBPSA Conference (Building Simulation '99), pp. 1013–1018.

May, A.D., Mitchell, G. and Kupiszewska, D. (1997) 'The Leeds Quantifiable City Model' in Brandon, P., Lombardi, P.L. and Bentivegna, V. (eds) *Evaluation of the Built Environment for Sustainability.* Spon, London, pp. 39–52.

Moffatt, S (ed.) (2000) *IEA Annex 31: The Environmental Effects of Buildings.* http://annex31.wiwi.uni-karlsruhe.de/

Murray, C.L.J. and Lopez, A.D. (1996) *The Global Burden of Disease: A Comprehensive Assessment of Mortality and Disability from Diseases, Injuries and Risk Factors in 1990 and Projected to 2020.* Harvard School of Public Health. Cambridge Mass.

Odum E.P. (1971) *Fundamentals of Ecology*, Saunders, Philadelphia.

OTT, Th. and Swiaczny, F. (2001) *Time-integrative Geographic Information Systems – Management and Analysis of Spatio-Temporal Data*, Springer, Berlin.

Papamichael, K. and Protzen, J.-P. (1993) 'The limits of intelligence in design', *Computer Assisted Building Design Systems*, 4th. Int. Symp. on System Research, Baden-Baden.

SETAC (1996) Society of Environmental Toxicology and Chemistry. *Towards a Methodology for Life-Cycle Impact Assessment*, Bruxelles.

SETAC (2002) *LCA in Building and Construction*. A State-of-the-art Report of SETAC-Europe.

SUIT (2001) *Sustainable Development of Urban Historical Areas Through an Active Integration Within Town*, 5th Framework key action 'The City of Tomorrow and Cultural Heritage'. http://www.suit.lema.be.

Task Group 4 (2003) EC – Working Group Sustainable Construction. *LCC in Construction*, Final Report. August. http://europa.eu.int/comm/enterprise/construction/index.htm

Wolman, A. (1965) 'The metabolism of cities', *The Scientific American* 213: 179–190.

Part 4.4

Very Advanced Evaluations of Neighbourhoods,
Districts and Cities

19

The AUSTIME Methodology: Quantifiable Sustainability Assessment Coupled with Multi-agent Simulation

Katherine A. Daniell, Bernadette A. Foley, Ashley B. Kingsborough,
Holger R. Maier, David J. Malovka and Heath C. Sommerville

INTRODUCTION

The inherent complexity of socio-ecological systems presents many challenges and opportunities for governments, policy-makers, businesses and researchers the world over. Due particularly to increasing environmental degradation, depletion of natural resources and rapid increases in population and urbanisation, a large focus has been placed on working towards 'sustainable development' as outlined in documents such as Agenda 21. Although these documents provide good guidelines and objectives for sustainable development, set methods for adhering to those principles are rather more elusive. In light of this problem, this chapter will outline a framework known as the AUSTIME methodology: 'Assessment of Urban Sustainability Through Integrated Modelling and Exploration', for analysing, assessing and consequently forming policy and management strategies to improve the sustainability of urban systems. The methodology uses a 'Sustainability Scale' for indicators that are derived from percentiles of a population with resource use above a predetermined sustainable level or threshold. It has been coupled with a technique for modelling complex housing development systems using multi-agent-based simulation, which also allows for exploration of possible system futures through scenario analyses. The holistic framework can be used as a multi-criteria decision-making tool by policy-makers, governments and planning authorities, as well as to discover potential risks and opportunities relating to achievement of sustainable urban development (SUD). The AUSTIME methodology is applied in the Christie Walk housing development of inner-city Adelaide, Australia. The results of this assessment demonstrate that the development compares favourably to the rest of the Adelaide metropolitan area. The case study also highlights, through behavioural scenario analyses, the importance of good infrastructure and design in reducing the impacts of human behaviour on housing development sustainability. It is envisaged that this new methodology for combining sustainability assessment with an integrated modelling technique will provide the basis for a solution to many of the challenges currently facing sustainability researchers, policy-makers and planning authorities of urban environments.

THE SEARCH FOR MORE SUSTAINABLE FORMS OF URBAN DEVELOPMENT

In order to combat the rapid degradation of the world's ecosystems and depletion of natural resources that follow larger world populations and increased urbanisation, governments and planning authorities are searching for more sustainable forms of urban development. The need to assess the 'sustainability' of development proposals and current urban areas is thus of great importance to policy and decision-makers worldwide. However, effective methods of assessing the overall sustainability of estates or 'housing developments' (proposed or existing) remain elusive. It is considered that the complexity of nature–society systems such as those of urban housing developments makes the understanding and consequent sustainability assessment of these systems difficult.

A large proportion of research into sustainable development over the past 15 years has attempted to assess various components of system sustainability without due respect for the complex interrelations between the components, which can have a significant effect on overall system behaviour (Clark and Dickson, 2003). This has led to an incomplete understanding at government and policy-making levels of what is required to achieve sustainable development for all communities. A consistent framework for sustainability assessment is therefore required for such decision-making purposes (Nishijima *et al.*, 2004).

A review of current literature into the assessment of the sustainability of housing developments (Daniell *et al.*, 2004a) found that:

- Governments and planning authorities worldwide require more holistic methods for sustainability assessment in order to develop future planning strategies (Tweed and Jones, 2000).
- Due to the narrow focus of current assessment tools, decision-makers find it difficult to make judgements which are consistent with sustainability goals for development (Macoun *et al.*, 2001).
- Current sustainability assessment tools do not adequately represent the temporal, spatial and behavioural aspects of sustainability.
- There is no common methodology which relates measures of resource use and other variables (referred to as indicators) to a measure of sustainability.
- There is a specific need for a methodology that can be used to assess the sustainability of complex housing development systems to be able to achieve sustainable urban development (Deakin *et al.*, 2002).

In order to address the shortcomings outlined above, a new methodology, AUSTIME: 'Assessment of Urban Sustainability Through Integrated Modelling and Exploration', is proposed. AUSTIME has currently been developed for the sustainability assessment of urban systems at the housing development or estate scale. The methodology uses a 'Sustainability Scale' for indicators that are derived from percentiles of a population with resource use above a predetermined sustainable level or threshold. It has been coupled with a technique for modelling complex housing development systems using multi-agent based simulation. The holistic framework can be used as a multi-criteria decision-making tool by policy-makers, governments and planning authorities, as well as to discover potential risks and opportunities relating to achievement of sustainable urban development (SUD). The AUSTIME methodology, although not specifically developed with Cooper's (1997) representation of sustainable development in mind, also allows for the inclusion of its four main axes: the environmental; equity; participation; and futurity aspects of sustainable housing developments. The application of the methodology to a case-study example, Christie Walk, an Australian eco-development, is presented in this chapter, with a special focus on determining the impacts of human behaviour on the housing development's sustainability.

AUSTIME METHODOLOGY

The proposed AUSTIME methodological framework for the sustainability assessment of housing developments is presented in Figure 19.1. The methodology can be used to foster the progression of sustainability of housing developments over time. It should be viewed as a dynamic process that needs to be integrated into a larger adaptive management and learning cycle or continuous improvement cycle. These cycles are similar to those promoted by Holling (1978) for adaptive environmental management and Deming (1986) for Total Quality Management. Stakeholder participation should be explicitly included in these cycles (Walker et al., 2002) and ongoing evaluation is required if real progress towards sustainable development is to be achieved (Bellamy et al., 2001). The AUSTIME methodological framework has been developed for use during several phases of the housing development cycle, depicted in Figure 19.2.

In the early planning stages of the development cycle, the AUSTIME methodology can be used to assess the effect of various policy alternatives on proposed urban housing developments, to inform and to set requirements and regulations in relation to available or appropriate resource use for these new developments. At these early planning stages, the methodology can also be used to assess the adequacy of proposed development plans in terms of their expected sustainability,

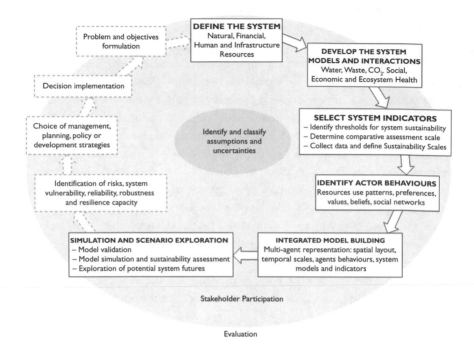

Figure 19.1 The AUSTIME methodology for housing developments

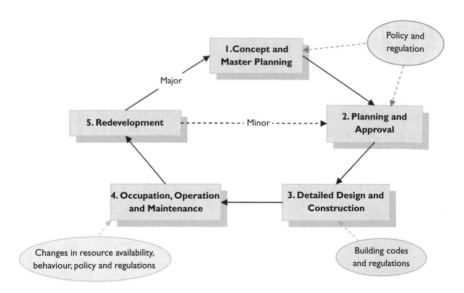

Figure 19.2 The urban development cycle

which, if found to be inadequate, can be improved before the detailed design and construction phases. In the later stages of the development cycle, the AUSTIME methodology, and associated integrated models, can either be refined through the collection of data or used during the occupation phase to assess how the occupants of existing developments are affecting the housing developments' sustainability. Based on the observations of these results, further action may be taken to encourage the improvement of sustainability in these developments through such measures as upgrading infrastructure, improving services, implementing education programmes, changing policy and regulations, or by administering subsidies and incentives for certain practices.

The AUSTIME methodology, like the urban development cycle, is a dynamic process that needs to be reviewed and refined over time as knowledge relating to the systems under consideration is explored and expanded. The principal stages of this methodology, highlighted in bold in Figure 19.1, are presented in more detail in the following sections of this chapter. The dashed stages of the methodology in Figure 19.1 have been included to illustrate the full cyclic nature of the AUSTIME methodology, and how it fits into the general problem formulation, problem-solving and decision-making context. These stages will only be implicitly treated and explained throughout this chapter.

Definition of housing development systems

A housing development is a system that can be defined, and its sustainability assessed, if the definition of sustainability presented by Gilman (1992) is adopted. Gilman stated that sustainability is:

> The ability of a society, ecosystem, or any such on-going system to continue func-
> tioning into the indefinite future without being forced into decline through exhaustion or
> overloading of key resources on which the system depends.

Using this Gilman definition, Foley et al. (2003) outlined that for a system to be sustainable, all of the resources upon which the system relies must be managed appropriately, including: natural; financial; social; and man-made (infrastructure) resources. Appropriate management requires knowledge relating to the system boundary, system resources, interactions between adjacent systems and allowable limits, or thresholds, for each resource, as well as the participation of the system's stakeholders. Each of these elements will be unique to the particular system under consideration, and each system must be assessed on its own merits. However, the process of assessment should be consistent for every system.

This general systems approach to sustainability can be applied more specifically to an urban development by viewing each urban housing development as a unique system. An example of such a system with its resources and interactions is shown in Figure 19.3.

To assess the sustainability of a housing development, all of the resources and their interactions represented in Figure 19.3 (both within and external to the system) need to be determined as specified in the methodology presented in Figure 19.1. As outlined by Foley *et al.* (2003), if each resource in the housing development is considered as a state variable x_i, at any time t_j, the state of the system can be expressed for *n* state variables in vector form as:

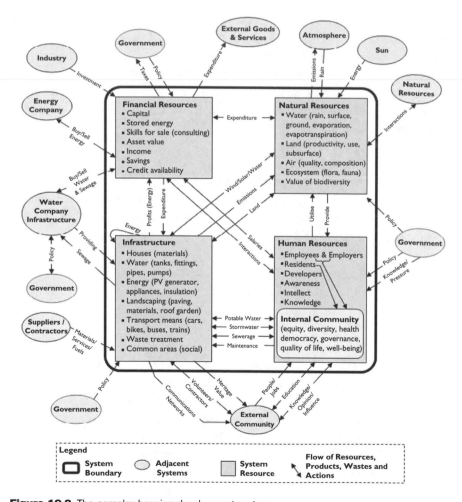

Figure 19.3 The complex housing development system

$$x(t_j) = \{x_1(t_j), x_2(t_j), \ldots, x_{i-1}(t_j), x_i(t_j), \ldots, x_n(t_j)\} \tag{1}$$

The changes to each state variable or resource can then be modelled over each specified time interval where $t_{j+1} = t_j + \Delta t_j$.

Housing development system models

Considering a complex urban housing development system as outlined in Figure 19.3, the key resources, processes and interrelations of a housing development can be defined in terms of six interrelated models, namely: water; carbon dioxide (CO_2); waste; ecosystem health; economic; and social. All of these models are affected by human behaviour and are represented in Figure 19.4. The role of human behaviour is discussed further in the Section 'Effect of human behaviour'.

In Figure 19.4:

- The water model incorporates all the water-related processes of the development, including rainfall-runoff, infiltration and potable and non-potable water use.
- The CO_2 model accounts for both embodied and operational energy use, calculated as an equivalent mass of CO_2, which incorporates the effects of

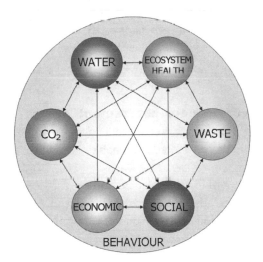

Figure 19.4 Framework of interrelated models for housing development sustainability assessment

building materials, infrastructure, electricity and gas use, as well as occupant transport use.

- The waste model accounts for all solid and liquid waste, both produced on site, and leaving the site, including: sewage; compost; waste to be recycled; and waste to be definitively disposed of (i.e. to landfill or incineration).

- The ecosystem health model encompasses environmental aspects of the development such as biodiversity and land-use changes, as well as pollution levels, air and water quality.

- The economic model accounts for both the microeconomic processes of each household based on income, expenditure and corresponding levels of debt, as well as the macroeconomic processes which affect the housing development, such as inflation, taxes, charges and interest rates.

- The social model incorporates levels of occupant satisfaction relating to comfort, living conditions, access to services (transport, health, education, shopping), social networks, environmental quality, employment and governance structures, as well as equity amongst occupants.

The state and adequacy of the infrastructural resources relating to each of these subsystem models is also intrinsically included in each of the models.

Through these interrelated models, all the key resources on which the system depends can be represented, allowing the sustainability of the whole housing development system to be analysed. Following the methodology presented in Figure 19.1, for each of these models an indicator representative of the model processes and consequent sustainability must be chosen for assessment purposes.[1]

Sustainability indicators and assessment

Once indicators are selected, it is important to determine the conditions under which an indicator is to be considered sustainable. Available assessment techniques for housing developments reviewed by Daniell *et al.* (2004a) use indicators that predominately present and collate resource use or resource quality data. There is little attempt to assess the adequacy of the data with respect to the level or condition of the resources available to the system under consideration (Fleming, 2005). Foley and Daniell (2002) recognised that the use of a sustainability satisfaction scale for indicators could allow the comparison of indicators not only against each other but also against sustainability criteria. This approach, together with the System Sustainability Conditions outlined in Foley *et al.* (2003), was further developed by Daniell *et al.* (2004b) to create the 'Sustainability Scale' for indicators, which is presented in this section.

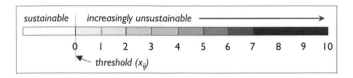

Figure 19.5 The sustainability scale

The Sustainability Scale is based upon a probability of exceedance of the ultimate sustainability threshold level, $threshold(x_{ij})$, for each resource, $x_i(t_j)$, as shown in Figure 19.5.

The sustainability threshold level is the resource level at which the system is deemed to be able to satisfy the following System Sustainability Conditions on an ongoing basis:

- Resource levels available to the system are sufficient to meet the requirements of the system.
- Resource levels within the system are maintained at levels that do not exhaust or overload the resources.
- Resources that are imported to, or exported from, the system do not compromise the ability of adjacent systems to be sustainable.

The Sustainability Scale ranges from 0 to 10, where 0 is considered as sustainable resource use, and the values between 0 and 10 represent increasingly unsustainable resource use. In other words, for a housing development system's resource use to be considered sustainable, Equation (2) must be satisfied:[2]

$$x_i(t_j) \leq threshold(x_{ij}) \tag{2}$$

Individual Sustainability Scale Ratings (SSRs) for indicators are based on the cumulative probability distribution of current resource use at a larger system scale exceeding the sustainable threshold level (i.e. a probability of threshold exceedance between 0 and 1).

The larger system chosen will depend on the purpose of the sustainability assessment. For example, a housing development might need to be compared to other developments within a local council area or to other housing developments in a larger metropolitan area.

Once this larger system scale has been chosen, a distribution of the resource use of the indicator to be assessed must be developed. An example of a cumulative distribution function (in this case where the indicator is mains water use in the

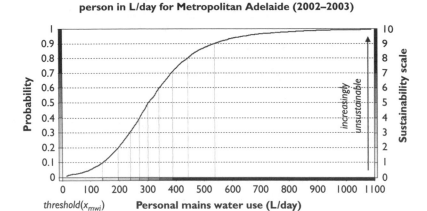

Figure 19.6 Cumulative distribution of mains water use exceeding the sustainability threshold level

metropolitan Adelaide area), from which the Sustainability Scale can be derived, is represented in Figure 19.6.

In order to create the cumulative distribution used to derive the Sustainability Scale, a number of steps need to be undertaken, depending on the form of data available. The example of mains water use in the Adelaide metropolitan area shown in Figure 19.6 will be expanded upon here to demonstrate the process.

Step 1: The frequency of people corresponding to each level of estimated mains water use in the Adelaide metropolitan area needs to be plotted, as shown in Figure 19.7.

Step 2: The sustainability threshold level for the resource, in this case mains water use, needs to be defined. For a housing development scale of sustainability assessment, the threshold for mains water use is defined as 0 L/person/day,[3] i.e. $threshold(x_{mwj}) = 0$ as denoted in Figure 19.7.

Step 3: Now consider all people with resource usage below the threshold to be sustainable and eliminate them from the distribution, in this case all people who do not use the mains water supply. This is equivalent to removing sustainability as an outcome from the original sample space.

Step 4: The probability density function (pdf) of the new sample space can be calculated (corresponding to the pdf of mains water use of only people exceeding the sustainability threshold in the example). Since being in the sustainable state has been removed as an outcome and the distribution has then been normalised on the remaining outcomes (i.e. being in an unsustainable state), a conditional probability

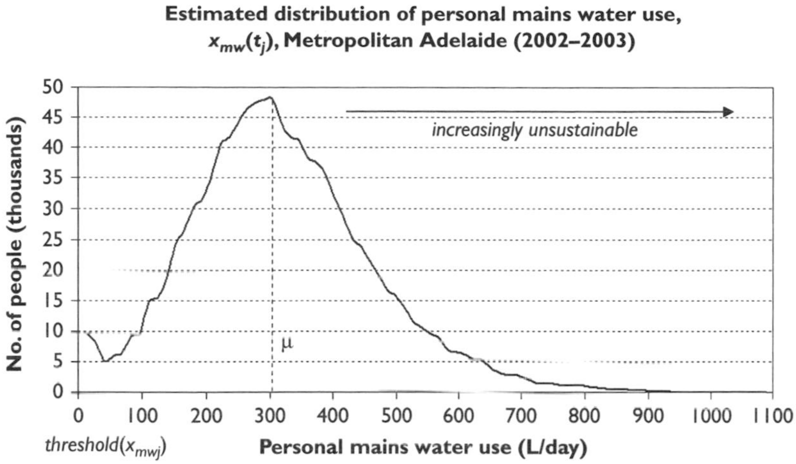

**Estimated distribution of personal mains water use,
$x_{mw}(t_j)$, Metropolitan Adelaide (2002–2003)**

Figure 19.7 Mains water use frequency distribution and the sustainability threshold level

density function has been calculated. If this pdf is defined as $f(x_{ij} \mid x_{ij} > threshold(x_{ij}))$ (for any resource), then:

$$P(a < X \leq b \mid X > threshold(x_{ij})) = \int_a^b f(x_{ij} \mid x_{ij} > threshold(x_{ij}))dx_{ij} \quad (3)$$

where X is a random variable within the sample space $[threshold(x_{ij}), \infty]$; and x_{ij} is the estimated value of resource usage of an unsustainable individual.[4]

Note: The order of steps 3 and 4 is very important in order to maintain the first Axiom of Probability, i.e. $\int_{-\infty}^{\infty} pdf = 1$. The relative frequencies (number of people/total population) must be calculated using only the portion of the population exceeding the threshold required for sustainability.

Step 5: Calculate the cumulative distribution function, $F(x_{ij} \mid x_{ij} > threshold(x_{ij}))$, corresponding to the pdf calculated in Step 4, namely the probability density given that resource use is in an unsustainable state:

$$F(x_{ij}) = P(X \leq x_{ij} \mid X > threshold(x_{ij})) = \int_{-\infty}^{x_{ij}} f(x_{ij} \mid x_{ij} > threshold(x_{ij}))dx_{ij} \quad (4)$$

where $x_{ij} \in [threshold(x_{ij}), \infty]$.

For the mains water example, the resulting cumulative distribution function is shown in Figure 19.6.

Step 6: The corresponding Sustainability Scale Ratings, SSRs, for a particular resource usage can now be directly calculated from the cumulative distribution function:

$$SSR = 10 \times F(x_{ij}) = 10 \times P(X \leq x_{ij} \mid X > threshold(x_{ij}))$$

$$= 10 \times \int_{-\infty}^{x_{ij}} f(x_{ij} \mid x_{ij} > threshold(x_{ij})) dx_{ij} \tag{5}$$

This can be performed without any loss of generality since a sustainable development has $SSR = 0$ (as in a sustainable state $x_{ij} \leq threshold(x_{ij})$ which leads to $P(X \leq x_{ij} \mid X > threshold(x_{ij})) = 0$).

This Sustainability Scale can be used to measure any indicator (provided that sufficient and equivalent data are available at both spatial scales) and thus produces a uniform method of sustainability indicator assessment. For example, waste production can be measured against water use for equivalent levels of sustainability (or, more correctly, unsustainability) or the same indicators can be compared between developments in the same larger system.

The indicator assessment concept can also be viewed in terms of system vulnerability (Hashimoto *et al.*, 1982). If the resource or indicator level fails to be sustainable, i.e. for the mains water example, if $x_{mw}(t_j) > threshold(x_{mwj})$, then the magnitude of failure or *vulnerability* of the system is quantified on the Sustainability Scale.

The proposed methodology also allows for the continuous assessment of system sustainability through time. For example, if a sustainability assessment is to be carried out on a housing development every year for a number of years, and data are available to create the resource distributions required for the larger system used for comparative assessment for each of these years, then the Sustainability Scale of resource use will change through time. The corresponding yearly resource use for the housing development being assessed can then be compared, based on the equivalent yearly Sustainability Scale. The threshold level of sustainability for a resource, $threshold(x_{ij})$, may also vary over time, depending on new scientific research or technological advances.

At the initialisation point, a sustainability assessment of the collection of six indicators for the interrelated models (water, CO_2, waste, economic, social and ecosystem health) may be performed to assess the current sustainability of the housing development system. Further modelling may then be performed to assess the potential sustainability of the housing development through time. As the sustainability analysis is based on a collection of indicators, it can be considered that the AUSTIME methodology belongs to the general class of multi-criteria assessment methods.

The development of the 'Sustainability Scale' for indicators is an advancement on existing assessment techniques as the indicators provide a measure of the proximity of the indicator to the sustainable or threshold level.

Continuous improvement or assessment of the adequacy and applicability of the threshold levels and resulting sustainability scales is essential to maintain the integrity of the AUSTIME methodology. Each of the threshold levels for sustainability is linked to the potential resilience of the system and its ability to respond to and absorb stress and shocks. The threshold levels are also dependent on current knowledge relating to what levels of resource use are possible to ensure the conservation or health of these resources for future generations (inter-generational equity). Knowledge relating to these elements of the process is only in its infancy and is specific to each system. As knowledge relating to these elements increases, the confidence in the outcomes of the process can also increase. The timeframe for review of these parameters will be dependent upon the individual system, the selected indicators and the length of response time for each of the system's variables. This concept is well illustrated in Holling's 'panarchy' process where an adaptive system is composed of various process scales: interacting small or fast cycles (or system variables) and larger and slower cycles that all have corresponding feedback loops that can affect each other (Holling, 2004).

The methodology to this point allows the assessment of sustainability at a given point in time but does not address other deficiencies in existing assessment techniques, such as the effect of human behaviour or changes in the system over time (the concept of futurity). The following highlighted steps of the methodology in Figure 19.1 address these aspects.

Effect of human behaviour

One of the criticisms of current urban simulation techniques is the lack of sufficient behavioural theory used in the modelling processes (Waddell and Ulfarsson, 2004). This view is confirmed by the findings from the review of current sustainability assessment tools presented by Daniell et al. (2004a), which showed that the effect of human behaviour in relation to resource use and sustainability was not adequately included. It has commonly been reported that human behaviour has a significant impact on resource use (Georg, 1999), although there has been very little research to date to quantify these effects (Jalas et al., 2001). To overcome the behavioural deficiencies of previous sustainability assessment methods, human behaviour, particularly related to resource use, has been included in the sustainability assessment framework developed as part of this research.

Behaviour relating to resource use can be analysed in many ways by studying both the causes and effects of human practices and actions. Study of behavioural patterns can be related back to sociological theory, where the normative (values and preferences), cognitive (representations and beliefs), operational (practices and actions) and relational (social interaction and relationship) aspects of individuals should be analysed.

Depending on the housing development to be assessed, several methods of defining behaviour relating to resource use may be applicable. If the housing development and occupants already exist, analysis of individual occupants can be performed. In such cases, questionnaires (or other forms of information-gathering such as interviews) can be used to determine occupants' preferences and practices relating to their resource usage, their beliefs and goals, as well as their social practices and networks. This information can then form the basis for a behavioural typology, and social structure of the housing development's occupants can be quantified as a series of rules for modelling based on sociological or psychological decision theory (Amblard *et al.*, 2001).

Another option for quantifying behavioural effects on resource usage is to use currently available sociological and resource use data from census collector districts or other area-specific surveys (Melhuish *et al.*, 2002). These data sets can be used to create synthetic distributions of resource use typical of the area's population. Further analysing these general resource use distributions with respect to socio-economic data can provide a good sample of what resource use relating to behavioural differences can be expected in the housing development.

The information obtained from these behavioural analyses can be integrated into the six interrelated models (water, CO_2, waste, ecosystem health, economic and social) as an initialisation point and driving mechanism to induce resource use changes for each model over time.

Multi-agent system modelling

In order to represent the six interrelated models in Figure 19.4, a suitable modelling platform is required. Multi-agent systems (MAS), an object-oriented programming method, traditionally used for artificial intelligence applications, can be used to combine the water, CO_2, waste, ecosystem health, economic and social models, and their relationships to human behaviour, for temporal sustainability assessment.

It has been recognised by many authors that multi-agent based simulation has many advantages over techniques currently used to model complex systems (Huigen, 2003). Multi-agent systems have the capability to explicitly incorporate human behavioural, spatial and temporal aspects into a more holistic model (Waddell and Ulfarsson, 2004). They can also incorporate both qualitative and quantitative data in the same model (Taylor, 2003), unlike many other modelling tools. This is of particular use in the field of sustainability assessment. The sustainability goals, or long-term objectives for resource use in housing developments, can be included in the framework of the multi-agent system as 'goals' or 'beliefs' of the agents (Krywkow *et al.*, 2002). The representation of human interaction processes, such as decision-making and learning based on changes witnessed in the surrounding environment, can be programmed into the individual agents in order to allow policy-makers to examine the total resulting system behaviour and evolution (Moss *et al.*, 2000). If required, multi-agent systems can also be coupled with Graphical Information Systems (GIS) for spatial data input (Batty and Jiang, 1999).

Housing development multi-agent representation

In the complex housing development systems to be assessed, each occupant or household can be modelled as an 'agent' that uses resources in the development 'environment' and can communicate with other occupant 'agents', as portrayed in Figure 19.8.

In the multi-agent representation of the housing development system shown in Figure 19.8, housing occupants can occupy the environment 'cells' (a cell being one unit of the multi-agent model's spatial environment), interacting with the environment through resource use. The information for each home relating to its infrastructure, location and occupants can all be included in the cells' information. Using a multi-agent systems approach, occupants can communicate with each other, exchange information and learn via community participation and interaction with other occupants. The households or 'occupant' agents will also be able to store specific

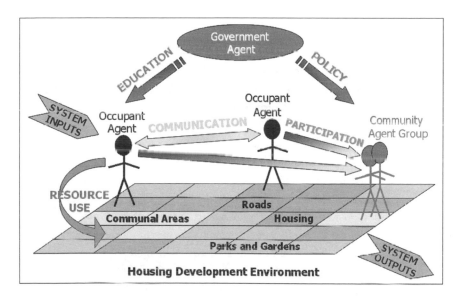

Figure 19.8 Multi-agent representation of a housing development

personal information on each of the agents, such as their beliefs, needs and decision processes. The government can also be created as an agent who can exert an influence on the housing development's occupants and environment through policy change and education programmes. The five resource-use models linked to the occupant behaviours can be incorporated directly into the multi-agent model using any number of readily available multi-agent modelling platforms, including: CORMAS (Common-pool Resources and Multi-Agents Systems); REPAST (REcursive Porous Agent Simulation Toolkit); and the DIAS/FACET (The Dynamic Information Architecture System/Framework for Addressing Cooperative Extended Transactions) platforms (ECAABC, 2004).

MAS for sustainability assessment and scenario analyses

After developing a multi-agent based model of the housing development that incorporates all of the resource models and the behavioural typology and interactions of the agents, the model can be run over a desired number of time-steps (potentially weekly, monthly or seasonally following the discussion in Daniell *et al.* (2004b)) to examine the emergent behaviour of the housing development system. Simulations of the multi-agent model can also be run to assess the impacts of various changes to the system, scenarios or policy 'options', and their impacts on the emergent behaviour of the housing development system and relative sustainability.

Model validation

Multi-agent models can be validated, at least in the preliminary time-steps of simulation, using a variety of methods, including the use of role-playing exercises, questionnaires and forums (El-Fallah *et al.*, 2004). Such methods can be used when the occupants of the housing development are willing to participate in the modelling process by either re-enacting the processes that take place in developments through games designed by the modeller or by answering questions to match the processes and attributes required by the multi-agent model. Other forms of validation of multi-agent models can include more qualitative methods of assessment, such as determining whether each output relates to what is seen in reality in similar housing developments, and by comparing relationships and trends obtained to trends found in the literature. Considering the complex nature of the systems being examined, it is highly advantageous to validate each relationship used in the modelling process before all the relationships are combined, a process which has been termed 'internal verification' (Vanbergue, 2003). As the use of multi-agent modelling for analysis of human ecosystems and natural resources management is still in its infancy, strict protocols for their validation are yet to be established. It is suggested that until such validation protocols are determined, modellers should use common sense in determining the accuracy of their results, even after preliminary validation exercises have occurred (Bousquet *et al.*, 1999).

MAS for scenario exploration

Once validation of the multi-agent model has taken place, further simulations of the model may be performed to assess the sustainability of, and explore the effects on, the housing development in its current state and for a range of other scenarios. For each simulation, the sustainability indicators chosen for each of the inner models of the multi-agent model can be shown on a common Sustainability Scale. At this point, a total assessment of the housing development's sustainability can be determined by an analysis of the collection of indicators. It is this step of the AUSTIME methodology that focuses on the futurity aspect of sustainable development. By analysing the long-term effects of certain policies or behavioural patterns on the housing development's sustainability relative to the larger region of comparison, decisions for policy, planning and maintenance or rehabilitation of the housing development can be made that aid in improving the intra-generational equity for all current and future inhabitants of the development area.

CASE STUDY APPLICATION

Introduction

To demonstrate how the methodology proposed in this chapter can be applied in practice to assess the sustainability of housing developments, the Christie Walk housing development was used as a case study.

The Christie Walk housing development, located in the Central Business District of Adelaide in South Australia, is a medium density urban housing develop-ment made up of 14 varied dwelling types (straw-bale cottages, aerated concrete and rammed earth construction) with other aspects of 'resource sensitive urban design' (Daniell *et al.*, 2004c). These aspects include: water-sensitive urban design; passive design of buildings to maximise energy savings; an inner-city location in close proximity to services; and designated community spaces (Downton, 2002).

Christie Walk is considered as a leading example of sustainable development due to the innovative nature of its design. However, until now, verification of this claim has been difficult. The nature of its design, combined with the accessibility of data, made Christie Walk an appropriate case study with which to test the methodology presented in the Section 'AUSTIME Methodology' of this chapter.

Christie Walk system and multi-agent representation

The first step of the assessment requires the system and system boundaries to be carefully defined, as outlined in Figure 19.1. As with any complex system, this is not necessarily a straightforward task. For example, Christie Walk currently relies upon numerous systems outside its spatial boundaries. For the development to be sustainable, it must be able to meet its requirements without compromising the ability of adjacent (or external) systems to be sustainable. The system boundary for the assessment of Christie Walk was considered to be its spatial boundaries (fence line). Any resource use sourced exterior to the system was considered to be unsustainable, as this allows the development to manage its own resources and minimises any impact on adjacent systems' ability to be sustainable.[5] The Adelaide metropolitan area was chosen as the larger system providing the resource-use comparisons against the resource use of Christie Walk for the construction of the Sustainability Scale as outlined in the Section 'Sustainability indicators and assessment'.

An analysis of the system, its resources and their interactions enabled detailed models representing the processes within the system to be developed as the second step of the assessment process. Models were developed for water, CO_2, waste, economic and social processes following the descriptions of Figure 19.4. An ecosystem health model was not created due to a lack of pollution, air and water quality and biodiversity data. However, the overall omission of this model is not considered to have a significant impact on the overall development's sustainability assessment. This is principally due to the fact that Christie Walk is located in the central business district of Adelaide and the site was previously used for commercial purposes with little to no biodiversity on the site. Any positive impact of improving the biodiversity on the site is considered as sustainable (and thus not quantified on the Sustainability Scale). Improvements in biodiversity may be shown through increased quality of life, which is processed through the social model. Similarly, other pollution and air quality and water quality factors not included in the ecosystem health model could be partially taken into consideration in the social model. A brief outline of each of the Christie Walk models and interactions, as well as graphical interpretations, is presented in following section.

Christie Walk conceptual models

The water model for Christie Walk was developed based on the current infrastructure, rainfall–runoff qualities, occupant behaviour and garden crop production of the site. Three sources of water are available to residents: the Adelaide mains water supply for potable uses and topping up of on-site non-potable water storage tanks; stormwater captured and stored on site for non-potable uses such

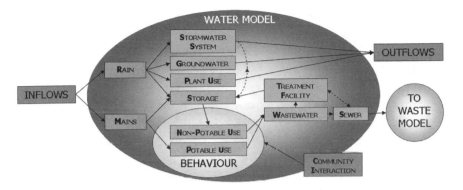

Figure 19.9 Christie Walk water model conceptualisation

as toilet flushing and garden watering; and treated wastewater for non-potable uses (although currently not used due to price of testing for water quality regulations compliance). The use of this water is dependent on occupant behaviour, which can also be potentially influenced by community interaction, as represented in Figure 19.9.

The two main inputs of CO_2 to the Christie Walk system model were embodied energy and operational energy, as shown in Figure 19.10. The only sink of CO_2 in the model is the on-site biomass. The embodied energy of the dwellings, the water, sewerage, pavement infrastructure and personal vehicles were included in the model as represented by the various categories of 'infrastructure' in Figure 19.10. Operational energy requirements and equivalent mass of CO_2 for each household

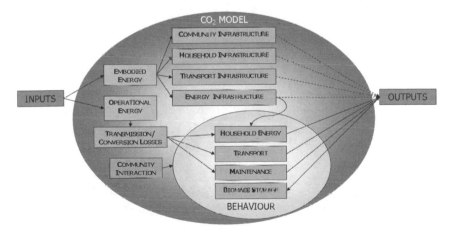

Figure 19.10 Christie Walk CO_2 model conceptualisation

were calculated to include the delivered electricity and gas, fuel for transportation, an allowance for ongoing infrastructure maintenance and also conversion and transmission losses. These energy uses are affected by behaviour and subsequent community interaction, as shown in Figure 19.10.

The waste model for Christie Walk was developed based on the current waste practices and facilities of the housing development. The site incorporates a community garden, which has the capability to compost all biodegradable waste, a community recycling initiative, which increases access to recycling facilities for a broad range of materials, as well as sewer mining and water recycling for liquid wastes. The waste model was divided into two main sections, as shown in Figure 19.11, including solid waste which is primarily created from general household consumption and garden production, and liquid waste, which is fed into the waste model directly from the water model. Materials use and subsequent household waste was divided into percentages of food which is composted, materials that can be recycled, and non-recyclable material, or garbage, that is sent to landfill. Each household's behavioural recycling and composting practices, as well as the effect of community interaction on these practices was determined based on survey responses of the residents relating to these issues.

The economic model for Christie Walk was based on cash flows for each household, all of which are influenced by the overriding macroeconomic environment, as shown in Figure 19.11. The micro-economy of each household within Christie Walk was based on effective household income which occupants distribute amongst a range of mandatory expenditures such as rates (based on resource usage from the water, waste and CO_2 models and current South Australian pricing structures), rent or mortgage payments, development strata fees and essential goods and services. Remaining disposable income use is then dependent on occupant behaviour, with

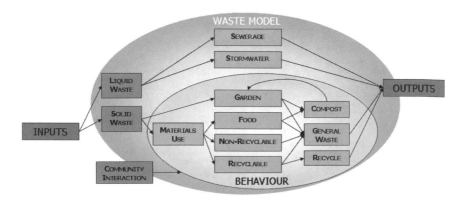

Figure 19.11 Christie Walk waste model conceptualisation

money being able to be borrowed or saved at interest rates affected by inflation and government policy in the macro-economy.

The social model for Christie Walk was devised based on five components of social sustainability: equity; diversity; quality of life; interconnectedness; and democracy and governance (McKenzie, 2004). The model allows for the assessment of individuals' 'social sustainability' through the seven key areas of the European Sustainable Cities programme 'citizen satisfaction' indicator. These seven areas of satisfaction – general comfort of living environment, social network, diversity of opportunities, city services, quality of environment, employment and community governance – were measured for each of the Christie Walk occupants as the difference between the current and desired state of each attribute, as shown in Figure 19.12. These satisfaction levels, as well as their relative importance, were obtained from occupant survey results. The range of individual occupants' satisfaction levels was then used to quantify the state of equity in the development, as represented in Figure 19.12.

A sustainability indicator for each of the water, CO_2, waste, economic and social models created for the Christie Walk housing development was then chosen as the next step in the methodology, as shown in Figure 19.1. These indicators and

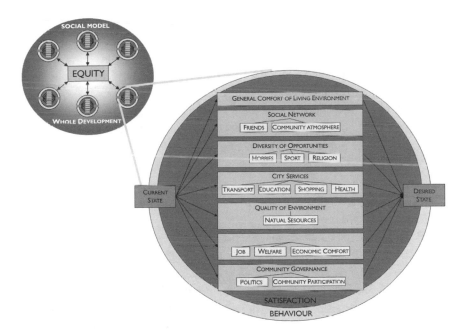

Figure 19.12 Christie Walk social model conceptualisation

Table 19.1 Model sustainability indicators

Model	Sustainability indicator	Equivalent measure
Water	Mains water use, $x_w(t_j)$	Litres/person/day
CO_2	Mass of equivalent CO_2, $x_c(t_j)$	Tonnes/person/year
Waste	Waste sent to landfill, $x_l(t_j)$	Kg/person/week
	Average per cent usage of available	
Economic	Household debt, $x_d(t_j)$	Percent usage of available debt
Social	Equitable satisfaction level, $x_s(t_j)$	Equitable satisfaction level

the equivalent measures used in the construction of the Sustainability Scales are presented in Table 19.1.

Defining behaviour

Behaviour for the Christie Walk occupants was defined using two methods based on those described in the section titled 'Sustainability indicators and assessment'. The first method was to examine the occupants' preferences and practices relating to resource usage, their beliefs and goals, and their social practices and networks through the use of a survey which was distributed to all Christie Walk residents. The second method was based on examining currently available sociological and resource-use data in order to quantify the behavioural aspects of the Christie Walk occupants with respect to their resource-use patterns, in comparison with the resource use of residents in the larger metropolitan Adelaide area.

The surveys distributed to the Christie Walk residents were used to obtain behavioural data regarding the occupants' values, preferences, practices and social interactions in a range of domains relating to resource utilisation and other aspects of the five models described in the Section 'Christie Walk system and multi-agent representation'. For the water, CO_2 and waste models, the resource-use distributions created for the metropolitan Adelaide area were used in conjunction with the survey information to assign general behavioural classifications to each household. In order to demonstrate the procedure for behavioural classification of occupants, the example of waste production will be outlined.

From the responses to the waste-related questions in the survey, the behavioural profiles of the occupants, relating to both quantity of waste produced and the amount of this waste they are likely to recycle and compost, were assessed. From these profiles, each occupant was assigned a grouping from the cumulative distributions of waste production and percentage waste diversion in the metropolitan Adelaide area. To simplify the process used in this case study, each distribution was only broken down into three levels of behavioural classification of resource usage

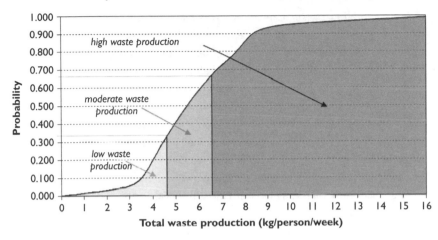

Figure 19.13 Occupant behaviour categories for total waste production

(33 percentile sections of the population). The cumulative distribution for total waste production in the Adelaide metropolitan area is shown with these waste production level groupings in Figure 19.13.

This division into behavioural categories enables the occupants' waste production to be assigned randomly in the multi-agent model from the appropriate category at each iteration. This allows the waste produced to fluctuate much like weekly household waste production in reality. Behavioural classifications for the other resource practices (for recycling, energy use, transport, water use and financial use) were formulated in the same way for the Christie Walk residents compared to the larger metropolitan Adelaide area.

Multi-agent model implementation

The multi-agent modelling platform, CORMAS (COmmon-pool Resources and Multi-Agent Systems), which uses the SmallTalk programming language, was used in order to combine all the required models and behavioural information for the sustainability assessment of Christie Walk. This modelling platform was developed by the French *Centre de Coopération Internationale en Recherche Agronomique pour le Développement* (CIRAD) in Montpellier, specifically for modelling the relationships between societies and their environments for natural resources management (Bousquet *et al.*, 1998). This particular platform was chosen as it is freely available and has a strong support network to help with any problems experienced with programming or the software.

Representation of the Christie Walk system in CORMAS was performed in several stages: representing the 'environment'; representing the 'agents'; and representing the models and interactions. After the model was created, it was calibrated, tested and validated before operational use.

The CORMAS platform allows for a spatial representation of a system as a grid of cells or 'spatial entities'. Each of these 'spatial entities' can have attributes such as area or land use, as well as processes such as rainfall or vegetation growth. For the purposes of the model, a grid was devised to mimic the land-use pattern of the Christie Walk development, including the land-use types of unit (home), garden, path/vegetation, car park, waste treatment plant and bike shelter. The conversion from the architectural plan drawings of Christie Walk, to the model environment is shown in Figure 19.14.

One agent was initialised per household with behavioural categories as outlined in the Section 'Defining behaviour', which could be graphically represented on the CORMAS model environment (in Figure 19.14 as pentagons in each home unit). Each agent was also pre-programmed with a specific behavioural category of community interaction, which was determined from the surveys and interviews with residents.

The five models previously defined in the Section 'Christie Walk system and multi-agent representation' (water, CO_2, waste, economic and social) and other processes for the Christie Walk model were written on several levels within the CORMAS platform. Methods relating to household resource use were written at the household level, for example in-house water use, energy use, transport

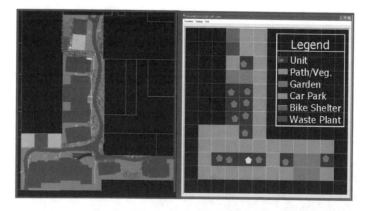

Figure 19.14 Architectural plan of the Christie Walk development and the CORMAS model environment representation

use, financial use and individual social sustainability. Other methods that related to the overall housing development situation were run at the main model level, for example the development's water use and the five sustainability indicators. At the government level, the methods for updating the interest rates and corresponding inflation rates, consumer price index (CPI), wages and tax brackets were performed.

A seasonal time-step (three months) was chosen for the model in order to ensure reasonable computational efficiency, as well as allowing seasonal variation to be gauged.

The model was validated to the greatest possible extent using several of the methods outlined in the Section 'Model validation', including internal verification (i.e. checking individual model outputs such as water and energy use against known meter readings), survey responses and general matching of the model outputs with observations of real-world housing developments.

Results of sustainability assessment simulations

Following the construction and validation of the CORMAS multi-agent Christie Walk model, simulations were run over a 30-year period with the sustainability indicators shown in Table 19.1 for the water, CO_2, waste, economic and social models being rated using the Sustainability Scale framework outlined in the Section 'Effect of human behaviour'.

A simulation of the Christie Walk multi-agent model over a 30-year simulation period assuming relatively stable economic, political and climatic conditions is illustrated in Figure 19.15, showing the five model indicators against the Sustainability Scale Ratings.

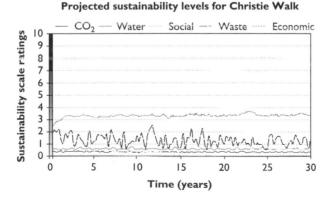

Figure 19.15 Sustainability scale ratings for Christie Walk for the five indicators

Sustainability indicators of mains water use, waste sent to landfill and CO_2 production are all based on distributions of the indicator variables within the metropolitan Adelaide area, according to the framework presented in the Section 'Effect of human behaviour'. It can be seen that for each of these indicators in Figure 19.15, Christie Walk is well within the lower 30th percentile of resource users in the Adelaide metropolitan area that exhibit unsustainable resource use. This demonstrates the effectiveness of some of the components integrated into the Christie Walk housing development design, when compared to other Adelaide residential developments.

As the modelling process adopted is stochastic (levels of uncertainty in many variables including resource-use behaviours, rainfall and levels of inflation are considered) every simulation performed will vary within reason. Outputs from each of the simulations give an overview of possible trends in the variation of the sustainability indicator ratings. These indicator ratings may be used to target specific areas for improvement and further analysis by government and planning authorities.

This simulation of the Christie Walk model through time reinforces the notion that the sustainability of a housing development will vary due to many parameters, including behavioural and climatic variation. For future government planning and assessment applications of this framework, both extreme and average Sustainability Scale values should be considered when such results are to be used for decision-making.

Scenario analyses

One of the greatest advantages of multi-agent modelling is the capability to perform 'what-if' scenario analyses. Using the Christie Walk model, a variety of scenario analyses were undertaken including assessment of the effects of droughts, changes to building materials, location, behaviour and community interaction on the sustainability of the Christie Walk development. Full details of these scenarios are given in Daniell *et al.* (2004b). In this chapter, the question of whether occupant behaviour is closely linked to the sustainability of housing developments is examined.

Behaviour scenarios

The effect of human behaviour on natural resources utilisation is often recognised, but rarely quantified (Curwell and Hamilton, 2003). Decision-makers such as governments and planning authorities have the ability to influence people's behaviour through legislation, education, increased awareness, information-sharing and price manipulation. However, the effectiveness of such campaigns has previously been difficult to analyse.

In order to analyse if occupant behaviour has a significant impact on the sustainability of Christie Walk, several scenarios were investigated, specifically focussing on waste production, recycling, water and energy use. In each case, high, moderate and low levels of each resource-use behaviour (see Figure 19.13) were initialised for all residents in the Christie Walk model and run for a 30-year simulation. These results were also compared to results for the current Christie Walk occupants (shown by 'CW' on the graphs). All other behavioural patterns were kept constant at the Christie Walk levels when an individual behavioural characteristic was analysed.

Figure 19.16 shows the effect of different behavioural levels of total waste production (total quantity of waste that needs to be reused, recycled, composted or disposed of to landfill) on the waste sustainability of a housing development (quantity of waste sent to landfill).

It can be seen from Figure 19.16 that the effect of total waste production behaviour on the waste sustainability of the housing development is substantial. Occupants with high waste production have Sustainability Scale Ratings as high as 7.3, while occupants with low waste production approach the threshold level for waste sustainability. A similar pattern, although with an improvement in ratings, is also observed for the behavioural effect of recycling on the amount of waste sent to landfill in Figure 19.17.

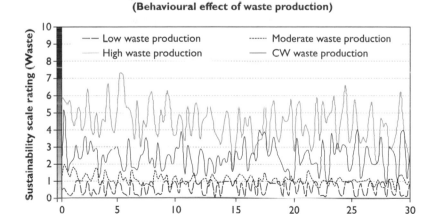

Figure 19.16 Effect of waste production behaviour on waste sustainability

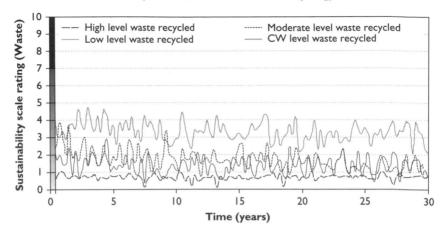

Figure 19.17 Effect of recycling behaviour on waste sustainability

These results show that both minimising waste at the source and recycling behaviour can have a significant effect on waste sustainability. It must also be noted that these results show that even with the worst recycling behaviour, the infrastructure at the Christie Walk development, including composting and recycling services, helps to reduce the effect of behaviour to below the 50th percentile of the greater Adelaide population.

A significantly different pattern is seen in Figure 19.18 for the effect of water use behaviour on water sustainability (based on mains water use) in Christie Walk. In this case, Sustainability Scale Ratings (SSRs) for water use show the effects of behaviour to be quite insignificant within the Christie Walk development. Figure 19.18 shows an average difference in water SSRs of less than 0.4 between low and high water use. This indicates that in the Christie Walk development, behaviour has very little effect on water sustainability compared to the rest of the metropolitan Adelaide water users. This is thought to be predominately due to the inclusion of water-saving devices and the use of stormwater for toilet flushing and garden watering, which reduces the overall mains water use in the housing development. Changes in behaviour therefore do not have the effect they might have in developments without water-saving infrastructure or small gardens.

The behavioural effects relating to in-house energy use on the CO_2 Sustainability Scale Ratings in Figure 19.19 show similar results to the water-use behaviour example. Once again, the small spread of SSRs indicates that in the Christie Walk environment, behavioural influence on energy use has very little effect on sustainability.

**Projected water sustainability rating time series
(Behavioural effect of water use)**

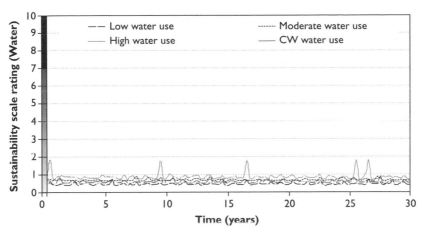

Figure 19.18 Effect of water use behaviour on water sustainability

**Projected CO₂ sustainability rating time series
(Behavioural effect of energy use)**

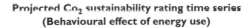
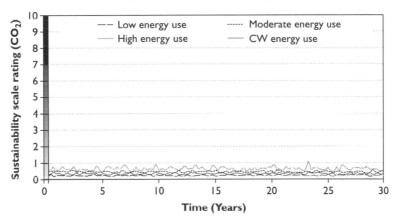

Figure 19.19 Effect of energy use behaviour on CO_2 sustainability

Due to the inclusion of energy-efficient appliances, solar hot water heaters, and building materials with high thermal efficiency, which lead to a lack of air conditioners, energy use in Christie Walk remains at very low levels for a range of behavioural types compared to metropolitan Adelaide users.

Discussion of behavioural results

The results of the behavioural analyses showed that for certain household factors, such as total waste production and waste recycling, changes in behaviour could significantly influence sustainability. Christie Walk includes basic infrastructure to encourage occupants to recycle and compost waste. However, because of their latent effectiveness, the infrastructure and design of other components of the development, such as water infrastructure and passive building design, are seen to drastically reduce the potential impacts of residents' behaviour on Christie Walk's sustainability.

These findings highlight the importance of good design and infrastructure in achieving sustainability in built environments. Although it is possible for governments and planners to potentially have an influence on occupant behaviour, it has been shown that attempts to change behaviour can be very difficult, time-consuming, and often met with extreme opposition. It could therefore be more effective for governments and planning authorities to concentrate on the improvement of infrastructure which will lead to a reduction in the effect of human behaviour on sustainability.

From the information obtained from the survey and the knowledge of the practices at Christie Walk, it was found that most residents had a high waste diversion to recycling (i.e. they recycled large percentages of the waste they produced, rather than disposing of it to landfill). Many residents had a low waste production, although it was interesting to note that quite a number of residents exhibited a moderate waste production, seeming to focus more on the reduction of their waste going to landfill through recycling, as opposed to the minimisation of waste generation (i.e. buying foods with less or no packaging, etc.). It could therefore be advantageous to focus any future education campaigns on buying produce with less packaging rather than focussing on the end solution of recycling.

From the results of the survey of Christie Walk residents, it was also found that community interaction can have a significant impact on improving resource-use behaviour (although not comparatively as large as the impacts of infrastructure and design), especially on recycling and energy use, and to a lesser extent on water use and waste minimisation. These findings highlighted that if it is not possible to improve infrastructure, then improvements to resource use through certain community programmes can be achieved. It has been stated by Marks *et al.* (2003) that the most effective way to introduce behavioural change is by including communities in the decision-making processes from the beginning of any plans for change. In this way, resistance can be reduced and the eventual uptake of practices and changes in behaviour can thus be made more quickly and smoothly. Increasing stakeholder participation in the sustainability assessment and consequent decision-making for policy, planning or redevelopment and mainte-nance of housing developments is thus of high importance for the achievement of sustainable urban development and forms an indispensable part of the AUSTIME methodology.

CONCLUSIONS AND FUTURE DIRECTIONS

The AUSTIME methodology presented in this chapter allows a housing develop-ment to be examined as a complex system rather than being broken down into components. It provides a method of assessing the sustainability of a housing devel-opment through time using multi-agent based simulation and incorporates the issues of environmental integrity, equity, participation and futurity in its framework. The multi-agent framework allows the integration of interrelated models including: water; CO_2; ecosystem health; waste; economic; and social; as well as their respective sustainability indicators. The methodology assists policy and decision-making within governments and planning authorities by examining and comparing the quantita-tive sustainability of housing developments using Sustainability Scale Ratings. The assessment process allows different indicators of sustainability to be compared on a common scale (i.e. water and waste can be directly analysed for their comparative sustainability) or indicators in different housing developments can be compared. Furthermore, simulations of the multi-agent based housing development model can be used to explore the emergent behaviour of the housing development system for various system changes and 'what-if' scenarios along with the corresponding sustainability assessment of the indicators on the Sustainability Scale. The AUSTIME methodology would provide an ideal decision-support system for stakeholders inter-ested in urban developments at all stages of the development cycle but particularly in policy and planning applications for the design, construction, operation and use of housing developments.

The methodology, shown to be operational in the case study application of the Christie Walk housing development, simultaneously overcomes identified deficiencies in existing assessment tools, specifically the inadequate inclusion of behavioural, spatial and temporal aspects within the sustainability assessment of complex housing development systems. Results from the Christie Walk case study with its many components of resource-sensitive urban design show that the devel-opment compares favourably with the rest of the Adelaide metropolitan area. The importance of good infrastructure and design in reducing the impacts of human behaviour on housing development sustainability is also highlighted through the behavioural scenario analyses. To maintain, improve and monitor the sustainability of Christie Walk, the parameters within AUSTIME can be refined and remodelled as knowledge relating to the systems, key resource limitations or variations and interactions, as well as behavioural patterns, increases. Such a continuation of the cyclic process will allow for increased stakeholder participation, evaluation and learning that is required to work towards the objectives of sustainable urban development.

From the success of this study, it is considered that the AUSTIME methodology outlined in this chapter could be applied to assess other developments throughout the world for comparative purposes or as part of planning and policy assessment. It is ideally to be used as part of a participatory framework for decision-making and to stimulate stakeholder discussions relating to sustainability agendas as represented in Figure 19.1.

Future directions for this research are numerous and could include the following:

- Further analysis of methods to model occupant behaviour based on more complex decision theory, game theory, role-playing games or other sociological and psychological theory.
- Further analysis of the impacts of resource pricing and markets on resource usage and behavioural changes.
- Studies of behaviour and the levels of occupant participation in community affairs and decision-making relating to the uptake of sustainable technologies and practices, as well as how policy-makers can better work with communities to ensure a successful uptake of such technologies and practices.
- Expansion of the methodology to assess the sustainability of larger urban areas, rural systems, companies or any other complex system, potentially with the integration of Graphical Information Systems (GIS).

ACKNOWLEDGEMENTS

Thank you to Paul Downton, the residents of Christie Walk, SA Water, Transport SA, Planning SA, the South Australian Office of Sustainability, Stephen Pullen, Monica Oliphant, Veronica Soebarto, Terry Williamson, Nils Ferrand, Pascal Perez, Anne Dray, Patrick Troy, Stewart Burn, Ian White, Ariella Helfgott, the School of Civil and Environmental Engineering at the University of Adelaide and everyone else who has helped and supported this work.

The fundamentals of this research were first presented at the CABM-HEMA-SMAGET Joint Conference on Multi-Agent Modelling for Environmental Management, 21–25 March 2005, in Bourg-St-Maurice, France.

NOTES

1   More than one indicator could be chosen for each model if desired, although various authors have outlined reasons for constraining the total number of indicators in an assessment, including Innes and Boother (2000) and Dodgson *et al.* (2000).

2   The reverse may be true when a system's resource level needs to be maximised (i.e. river flows for environmental requirements).

3   This considers that for a housing development to be sustainable, all water used must be collected on site if the site does not contribute to the mains water supply. Considering a different example, i.e. an urban development on an isolated island with no mains water, the threshold for water use could be set at a level that would not deplete the freshwater supplies or groundwater levels.

4   Here 'an individual' is an abstraction that can be interpreted as one individual person within a housing development or an 'equivalent average individual' of a development that can be compared to other developments within the larger community or system scale.

5   Although this assumption does not always hold true in reality, it is required to bound the assessment process for practicality of implementation.

REFERENCES

Amblard, F., Ferrand, N. and Hill, D. (2001), *How a Conceptual Framework can Help to Design Models Following Decreasing Abstraction*, Paper prepared for the 13th SCS-European Simulation Symposium, 18–20 October 2001, pp. 843–847, Marseille, France.

Batty, M. and Jiang, B. (1999), *Multi-Agent Simulations: New Approaches to Exploring Space–Time Dynamics within GIS*, Centre for Advanced Spatial Analysis – Working Paper Series, University College, London.

Bellamy, J.A., Walker, D.H., McDonald, G.T. and Syme, G.J. (2001), 'A systems approach to the evaluation of natural resource management initiatives', *Journal of Environmental Management*, 63: 407–423.

Bousquet, F., Bakam, I., Proton, H. and Le Page, C. (1998), *CORMAS: Common-pool Resources and Multi-Agent Systems*, Proceedings of the 11th International Conference on Industrial and Engineering Applications of Artificial Intelligence and Expert Systems, Springer-Verlag, Castellón, Spain, vol. 1416, pp. 826–838.

Bousquet, F., Barreteau, O., Le Page, C., Mullon, C. and Weber, J. (1999), 'An environmental modelling approach. The use of multi-agent simulations', *Advances in Environmental and Ecological Modelling*, Elsevier, Paris, pp. 113–122.

Clark, W.C. and Dickson, N.M. (2003), *Sustainability Science: The Emerging Research Program*, Proceedings from the National Academy of Sciences, Vol. 100, No. 14, July 8, pp. 8059–8061.

Cooper, I. (1997), 'Environmental assessment methods for use at the building and city scale: constructing bridges or identifying common ground', in P. Brandon, P. Lombardi and V. Bentivegna (eds), *Evaluation of the Built Environment for Sustainability*, E&FN Spon, London.

Curwell, S. and Hamilton, A. (2003), *Intelcity Roadmap – Version 4*, University of Salford, United Kingdom. Available at: www.scri.salford.ac.uk/icpart/documents/Docs/Roadmap/Roadmap%204.doc, 09/10/04.

Daniell, K.A., Kingsborough, A.B., Malovka, D.J., Sommerville, H.C., Foley, B.A. and Maier, H.R. (2004a), *A Review of Sustainability Assessment for Housing Developments*, Departmental Report R175, School of Civil and Environmental Engineering, The University of Adelaide, Australia. Available at: www.civeng.adelaide.edu.au/research/reports/R175.pdf, 03/02/05.

Daniell, K.A., Kingsborough, A.B., Malovka, D.J. and Sommerville, H.C. (2004b), *Assessment of the Sustainability of Housing Developments*, Honours Research Report, School of Civil and Environmental Engineering, The University of Adelaide, Australia.

Daniell, T.M., Foley, B.A. and Daniell, K.A. (2004c), *Sustainability in Water Resources Management – How Can it Help?* Proceedings of the 2004 International Symposium on Hydrological Environment, Daegu, Korea, International Hydrologic Society, 8–9 October 2004, pp. 7–26.

Deakin, M., Curwell, S. and Lombardi, P. (2002), 'Sustainable urban development: The framework and directory of assessment methods', *Journal of Environmental Assessment Policy and Management*, 4(2): 171–198.

Deming, W.E. (1986), *Out of the Crisis*. MIT Centre for Advanced Engineering Study, Cambridge, Massachusetts, USA.

Dodgson, J., Spackman, M., Pearman, A.D. and Phillips, L.D. (2000), *Multi-criteria Analysis Manual*, Office of the Deputy Prime Minister, London. Available at: www.odpm.gov.uk/stellent/groups/odpm_about/documents/pdf/odpm_about_pdf_608524.pdf, 31/07/05.

Downton, P.F. (2002), *Ecopolis: Towards an Integrated Theory for the Design, Development and Maintenance of Ecological Cities*, Thesis (PhD), Department of Geographical and Environmental Studies, University of Adelaide, Adelaide, Australia.

El-Fallah, A., Degirmenciyan, I. and Marc, F. (2004), *Modelling, Control and Validation of Multi-Agent Plans in Dynamic Context*, Paper prepared for the Third International Joint

Conference on Autonomous Agents and Multiagent Systems (AAMAS'04), 19–23 July, New York, USA.

European Co-ordination Action for Agent-Based Computing (ECAABC) (2004), *AgentLink – Agent Software* (website). Available at: www.agentlink.org/resources/agent-software. php, 09/07/04.

Fleming, N.S. (2005), *Systems Based Planning and Information Networks for Sustainability*, EIANZ Conference 'Working on the Frontier – Environmental Sustainability in Practice', 29 March–1 April, Christchurch, New Zealand.

Foley, B.A. and Daniell, T.M. (2002), *A Sustainability Tool for Intrasectoral and Intersectoral Water Resources Decision Making*, Paper prepared for the 27th Hydrology and Water Resources Symposium, 20–23 May, Melbourne, Australia.

Foley, B.A., Daniell, T.M. and Warner, R.F. (2003), 'What is sustainability and can it be measured?' *Australian Journal of Multidisciplinary Engineering*, 1(1): 1–8.

Georg, S. (1999), 'The social shaping of household consumption', *Ecological Economics*, 28: 455–466.

Gilman, R. (1992), *Sustainability*, from the 1992 UIA/AIA 'Call for Sustainable Community Solutions'. Available at: www.context.org/ICLIB/DEFS/AIADef.html, 04/02/03.

Hashimoto, T., Stedinger, J.R. and Loucks, D.P. (1982), 'Reliability, resiliency, and vulnerability criteria for water resource system performance evaluation', *Water Resources Research*, 18(1): 14–20.

Holling, C.S. (ed.) (1978), *Adaptive Environmental Assessment and Management*, John Wiley, New York, USA.

Holling, C.S. (2004), 'From complex regions to complex worlds', *Ecology and Society*, 9(1): Art. 11. Available at: www.ecologyandsociety.org/vol9/iss1/art11/print.pdf, 05/08/05.

Huigen, M.G.A. (2003), *Agent Based Modelling in Land Use and Land Cover Change Studies*, Interim Report IR-03-044. Available at: www.iiasa.ac.at/Publications/Documents/IR-03-044.pdf, 12/05/04.

Innes, J.E. and Boother, D.E. (2000), 'Indicators for sustainable communities: a strategy building on complexity theory and distributed intelligence', *Planning Theory & Practice*, 1(2): 173–186.

Jalas, M., Plepys, A. and Elander, M. (2001), *Workshop 10 – Sustainable Consumption and Rebound Effect*, Presented at the 7th European Roundtable for Cleaner Production, 2–4 May, Lund, Sweden.

Krywkow, J., Valkering, P., Rotmans, J. and van der Veen, A. (2002), *Agent-based and Integrated Assessment Modelling for Incorporating Social Dynamics in the Management of the Meuse in the Dutch Province of Limburg*, Published in: Integrated Assessment and Decision Support Proceedings of the First Biennial Meeting of the International Environmental Modelling and Software Society IEMSS, 24–27 June, University of Lugano, Switzerland, 2: 263–268.

Macoun, T., Mitchell, G. and Huovila, P. (2001), *Measuring Urban Sustainability: The Challenge of Integrating Assessment Methods and Indicators*, BEQUEST Lisbon Symposium, 26–27 April, Lisbon, Portugal.

Marks, J., Cromar, N., Fallowfield, H. and Oemcke, D. (2003), 'Community Experience and Perceptions of Water Reuse', *Water Science and Technology: Water Supply*, 3(3): 9–16.

McKenzie, S. (2004), *Social Sustainability: Some Definitions*, Hawke Research Institute Working Paper Series, No. 27. Available at: www.hawkecentre.unisa.edu.au/institute/resources/working%20paper%2027.pdf, 11/10/04.

Melhuish, T., Blake, M. and Day, S. (2002), *An Evaluation of Synthetic Household Populations for Census Collection Districts Created Using Spatial Microsimulation Techniques*, Paper prepared for the 26th Australia & New Zealand Regional Science Association International (ANZRSAI) Annual Conference, 29 September–2 October, Gold Coast, Queensland, Australia.

Moss, S., Downing, T.E. and Rouchier, J. (2000), *Demonstrating the Role of Stakeholder Participation: An Agent Based Social Simulation Model of Water Demand Policy and Response*, Centre for Policy Modelling Discussion Papers, Manchester. Available at: cfpm.org/~scott/water-demand/demand-pilot1.pdf, 12/05/04.

Nishijima, K., Straub, D. and Faber, M.H. (2004), *Sustainable Decisions for Life Cycle Costs Based Design and Maintenance*, Proceedings for the First Forum on Engineering Decision Making IFED, 5–9 December, Stoss, Switzerland.

Taylor, R. (2003), *Agent-Based Modelling Incorporating Qualitative and Quantitative Methods: A Case Study Investigating the Impact of E-commerce upon the Value Chain*, Prepared for the 1st International Conference of the European Social Simulation Association, Gronigen, The Netherlands, September. Available at: cfpm.org/papers/Taylor-abmiqaqm/Taylor-abmiqaqm.pdf, 12/05/04.

Tweed, T. and Jones, P. (2000), 'The Role of Models in Arguments about Urban Sustainability', *Environmental Impact Assessment Review*, 20: 277–287.

Vanbergue, D. (2003), *Conception de simulation multi-agents: application à la simulation des migrations intra-urbaines de la ville de Bogota*, Thèse de doctorat, Université Pierre et Marie Curie, Paris, France.

Waddell, P. and Ulfarsson, G.F. (2004), 'Introduction to Urban Simulation: Design and Development of Operational Models', forthcoming in Stopher P.R., Button K.J., Kingsley and Hensher D.A. (eds) *Handbook in Transport Geography and Spatial Systems*, Vol. 5. Pergamon Press, Oxford. Available at: www.urbansim.org/papers/waddell-ulfarsson-ht-IntroUrbanSimul.pdf, 12/05/04.

Walker, B., Carpenter, S., Anderies, J., Abel, N., Cumming, G., Janssen, M., Lebel, L., Norberg, J., Peterson, G.D. and Pritchard, R. (2002), 'Resilience Management in Socio-ecological Systems: A Working Hypothesis for a Participatory Approach', *Conservation Ecology*, 6(1): Art. 14. Available at: www.consecol.org/vol6/iss1/art14/print.pdf, 31/07/05.

20

HQE²R – Research and Demonstration for Assessing Sustainable Neighbourhood Development
Andreas Blum

INTRODUCTION

The acronym HQE²R (Haute Qualité Environnementale et Economique Réhabilitation/High Quality Environment and Economy in Regeneration) stands for a 30-month European research and development project on sustainable renovation of the built environment and the regeneration of urban neighbourhoods. HQE²R also stands for the decision-support toolkit for urban actors which was one of the major result of these works. The HQE²R approach (Figure 20.1) responds to the situation, that a large amount of sustainability research has been and is being done on the urban level as well as on the level of the single building while there is a lack of attention and experience on the intermediate level of urban neighbourhoods. This chapter reflects some of the related challenging questions and the experience and suggestions gained from this work.[1]

The following sections deal with six general issues of the project work: An explication of the core terms neighbourhood and sustainability, the question of 'how detailed is detailed enough?', the relation of quantitative measurements and qualitative talk, approaches to specific assessments, improvement of products and processes and finally the necessity for cross-border communication.

UNDERSTANDING NEIGHBOURHOOD SUSTAINABILITY

The neighbourhood is a real-life terrain – frequented daily, committed or not, but never neutral. As such it represents an effective scale of intervention for dealing with certain ecological or social problems and for implementing a participative approach. Nevertheless it is quite difficult to agree on a common definition of what is a neighbourhood – especially within an international project. So the first steps within the HQE²R project were concerned with clarifying the neighbourhood concept and the sustainability approach.

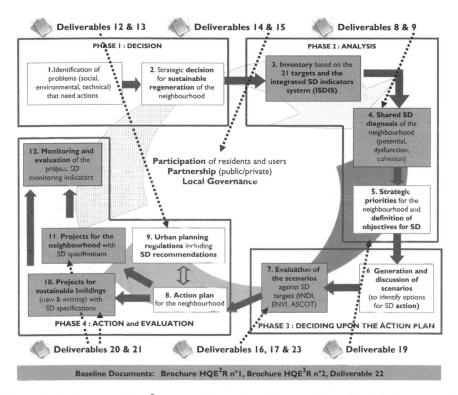

Figure 20.1 The general HQE²R approach towards sustainable neighbourhood development and the deliverables describing recommendations, tools, instruments and approaches for the different stages (www.hqe2r.cstb.fr; SD = sustainable development)

THE NEIGHBOURHOOD

The neighbourhood can be seen in as many ways as there are activity fields covering the subject, starting from sociology, via urban and regional planning and architecture to economy. To make it even more difficult, what is regarded as a neighbourhood may also differ with the different actors/users involved.

Therefore HQE²R started with the definition of a common subject of research. In the first instance this was defined as very formal and physical: The subject of HQE²R first of all is a cluster or ensemble of buildings/built urban environment with a need for renovation towards sustainability of the built environment. This may be an urban (residential) area framed by large roads or other (linear) structures or a more or less homogenous ensemble of similar types of buildings, etc. ('urban structural types', see below) and might be chosen quite liberally. Once having identified these clusters – roughly predefined by the case-study areas and structured along spatial elements (see below) – in the second step it is necessary to look a little closer at how far these 'micro-urban territories' are congruent with different possible notions of neighbourhood (social, economic, administrative, related to user groups, etc.). After that the scope of investigation can be widened or sharpened. Thereby especially the perception of 'neighbourhood' as represented by different user groups/stakeholders within these areas has to be taken in to account. This means the 'neighbourhood' may reach beyond the physical subject of investigation or the physical subject may encompass more than one neighbourhood.

Following this approach of explication rather than definition, HQE^{2}R identified the following issues as contributing to the identification, explanation and role of a neighbourhood within the urban context (Charlot-Valdieu and Outrequin, 2002).

- The inhabitants having a sense of community, or belonging to the community, derived from having local centres, services and a sense of place or specific symbolic elements, neighbourhood life, or the collective management of public property.
- Urban consciousness, social and political participation, founded on the history of the neighbourhood.
- Economic characteristics.
- The area functions and role of the area in the city.
- Physical cohesion created by the dominant architectural style and the arrangement of public space.
- Urban morphology as well as topography and natural aspects.

As already introduced above, these last two points describe the physically or rather spatially defined starting point when approaching a neighbourhood – at that time merely a 'micro-urban territory'. Since the HQE^{2}R-approach has 'renovation' in its core and 'renovation' in its core seemed to be directed towards the built environment, the elements for analysis of neighbourhood structures and uses were represented by different built and non-built structures:

- Residential space (the whole volume occupied by the residential uses including gardens and private spaces around housings).
- Non-Residential space (facilities and services other than housing including public, social, and cultural services including those directed towards a larger catchment area).

- Non-Built space (including all the parts of the neighbourhood which are not built even if they are not really natural).
- Infrastructure (including all the technical infrastructure present in the neighbourhood).

SUSTAINABLE DEVELOPMENT OBJECTIVES

To apply a procedure for sustainable neighbourhood development, it is necessary to define sustainable development objectives for the neighbourhood. These local objectives must finally be set by the local community, in accordance with joint consultation procedures that will have to be defined. As a starting point for this process within HQE²R a common set of sustainable development principles and objectives was defined on a general basis, and then had to be specifically adapted to the territorial scale of the neighbourhood.

Resting on a general concept of sustainable development with the idea of a triple dividend – economic efficiency, social solidarity and environmental caution – at its core, the following guiding principles of sustainable development were identified:

- Thinking global: Territorial approaches can only be sustainable when they are accompanied by an analysis of the territory in terms of its local (neighbourhood, city) and global (agglomeration, region, country, planet) environment.
- Taking long-term developments into consideration as well as relationships with the present (conceiving future changes and possible reversibility/adaptability.
- Principles of precaution and prevention, integration and solidarity.
- Participation of the population and co-operation in the decision-making process: Locally urgent problems have to be addressed first, before people are open for more general/global considerations.

With regard to these principles, five overall objectives are proposed for building and neighbourhood development towards sustainability: To preserve and valorise Heritage (natural and cultural), to improve the quality of the local environment, to improve diversity, to improve integration and to reinforce social life. Together with the general spatial elements of a neighbourhood these five overall objectives (and 21 more detailed general targets below them) define the basic framework of the HQE²R toolkit for analysis, diagnosis and action planning towards sustainability (Figure 20.2). This framework was at the same time the starting point and nucleus of the development work within the HQE²R-partner neighbourhoods.

Source: in progress table done by Foment of Ciutet Vella and CAATB (Spain) fot Raval neighbourhood case study from and original concept of the HQE²R Project (http://hqe2r.cstb.fr)

Figure 20.2 The HQE²R analysis grid for neighbourhoods in a visual adaptation by CAATB Barcelona: Sustainable development objectives by spatial neighbourhood-elements (Charlot-Valdieu *et al.*, 2004)

ASSESSING SUSTAINABILITY BETWEEN CITY LEVEL AND SINGLE BUILDING

At its core the HQE²R toolkit gathers recommendations, approaches and instruments to support the assessment of the situation and possible options of action for neighbourhood development against sustainability targets. Thereby the term assessment covers the three stages 'inventory', 'diagnosis' and 'evaluation'. General objectives of assessment are

- setting of a baseline/starting point;
- awareness-rising/awareness-giving ideas;
- identification of problems;
- suggestion of priorities for action;
- evaluation of the effects of action plans;
- identification of (monitoring-) indicators.

It was one of the first tasks within the HQE²R project to research and analyse existing assessment tools and approaches for the built environment which refer at least partially to the concept of sustainable development. As a general result it could be shown that none of the existing examples was designed specifically to operate on the neighbourhood scale. The methods were mostly optimised to work either on a larger scale – the city – or on a smaller scale – the single building. It therefore seemed reasonable to proceed to develop HQE²R as a toolkit conceived specifically for application on the neighbourhood scale.

So one of the major challenges for the HQE²R team was to find an answer to the question on 'how detailed is detailed enough?' On the one hand the level of the neighbourhood is too big for an assessment according to existing building-related approaches, on the other hand neighbourhood development and regeneration has to face very concrete issues that cannot be tackled by global approaches as used on an urban level. As a result of these considerations the HQE²R-approach generally suggests a two-level approach: fast screening and specific assessments.

Fast screening

To start with, a first package containing a limited set of indicators is to be used for cross-sectoral orientation with a minimum of direct field surveys and therefore with a limited use of resources. The aim of such 'fast screening' is to select the most critical issues and situations ('catch the big fish'), which can then be subjected to more thorough assessment. This entry-level package must, however, take account of social, economic and environmental issues, measuring at least some essential parameters for each. It also must be conceived for application at all phases of the HQE²R process: inventory, diagnosis and evaluation. A general framework is set up with the HQE²R analysis grid. The analysis grid is underpinned by the HQE²R 'Integrated Sustainable Development Indicators System' (ISDIS), which encompasses 51 key issues and 61 indicators for sustainable neighbourhood development. The respective assessment tool for measurement and comparison is HQE²R INDI ('Indicators Impact') which is introduced below.

Specific assessments

To support the selection of tools for deeper levels of investigation HQE²R provides a directory of tools for the assessment of the built environment suitable for specific tasks (e.g. the assessment of environmental impacts according to European Directive 2001/42/CE) or for details identified in the fast screening stage (as, for example, the energy efficiency of buildings, specific refurbishment needs, cost calculation of improved quality and so on). In the HQE^{2}R toolkit the ENVI (ENVironmental Impact) and ASCOT (ASsessment tool for additional construction COsT in sustainable building renovation) models are designed to support this second step of specific assessments at the neighbourhood level.

Besides concentrating specific assessments on thematic priority issues they may in addition and according to the local situation also be conducted for typical local situations (e.g. noisy main roads with residential vacancy) or relevant types of buildings/representatives of the building stock that can be considered as a sample in a wider field of interest. In this way it is possible to undertake well-targeted, detailed assessments with a lower input of resources than in a full survey of the entire neighbourhood. Based on experience from Germany the project team discussed for example possibilities of identifying 'Urban Structural Units' as representatives of the urban environment, for use in an assessment of land use, energy, and resource consumption issues (Schiller, 2003). This is certainly one of the fields that are worthwhile pursuing in future research activities.

QUANTITATIVE MEASUREMENTS AND QUALITATIVE TALK

The implementation of sustainable development policies at different territorial scales and in different structures is creating, from politicians and economic decision-makers, a persisting demand for indicators which will measure the state of the situation and its evolution. At the same time urban reality is subject to interpretation from very different viewpoints. Neighbourhood development in fact has to refer to and take account as widely as possible of all the different realities as they are perceived by different stakeholder groups. To this end, the discussion/negotiation of an appropriate system of indicators on the one hand and its implementation on the other are of equal importance for a robust process (Figure 20.3). The HQE^{2}R approach with its above-mentioned ISDIS system and INDI model has been proven to support both.

The ISDIS was developed as a set of core indicators based on an evaluation and synthesis of experience from the partner countries and beyond. In ISDIS, HQE^{2}R provides recommendations with reference to a baseline assessment on the neighbourhood level. Each indicator is described by a comprehensive data sheet, providing background information, suggested measurement methods and references. With the INDI model a calculable framework exists, which can help put ISDIS into operation.

Neighbourhood regeneration activities can build on the INDI model by directly using it for inventory, diagnostic and evaluation purposes. Each indicator is underpinned by a suggestion for measurement and a calculation algorithm leading to

General concept of sustainability

HQE²R INDI model of issues and indicators*

N°		Definition of indicator	Neighbour-hood value	INDI value [–3, +3]	
			0%	model	modified
				–3	
1A		% of buildings with a standard of heating/cooling or insulation above legal norms			
1B		Measures to save electricity consumption in the residential sector			
1C		% of housing units and public buildings using renewable energy in the neighbourhood.			
1D		Measures to reduce emissions of greenhouse effect gases from heating of housing unit.			
2Aa		Consumption of drinking water in the residential sector of the neighbourhood			
2Ab		% of public facilities saving water			
2B		% of buildings using rainwater			
2C		% of rainwater from the water-proofed areas which are locally managed			
2D		Sewerage network quality			
3Aa		Urban density			
3Ab		Useful surface area or open public spaces per resident			
3B		Surface of brown-fields or polluted sites in %			
3C		Number of targets attained in the urban planning instructions (on a total of the 21 HQE²R targets).			
4A		% of buildings built, renovated or demolished including an approach which takes into account recycle materials, environmental labels, certifications, or norms, as well as the lifetime of materials and equipments and the easiness of maintenance and operation			
4B		% of public infrastructures built, renovated or demolished including an environmental approach (idem 4A)			
5A		Measures to preserve and enhance the architectural patrimony			
5B		% of open spaces subject to measures to preserve and enhance the natural heritage and biodiversity			
6A					
6B	…				
7A	…				
7B	…				
7Ca	…				
7Cb	…				

To preserve and enhance heritage and conserve resources

…

Neighbourhood profiles*

Evolution du profil du quartier

1 – Energy
2 – Water
3 – Land
4 – Materials
5 – Patrimony
6 – Landscape
7 – Housing quality
8 – Hygiene & Health
9 – Safety & Risk
10 – Air quality
11 – Noise pollution
12 – Waste
13 – Diversity of population
14 – Diversity of functions
15 – Diversity of housing
16 – Education
17 – Accessibility to S&E
18 – Attractivity of neigh.
19 – Mobility
20 – Social Cohesion
21 – Solidarity Networks
Heritage
Environmental Quality
Diversity
Integration
Social Life

Identification and Communication of priority fields*

Environmental Quality
Diversity
Integration
Social Life
Heritage

■ Initial Value
□ Value (T)

* Images for illustration only

Figure 20.3 Levels of the HQE²R INDI model assessment (Blum and Morgenstern, 2004)

scores between -3 and $+3$ which are cumulated by objectives, targets and key issues. In practice, the INDI model was tested for the HQE²R demonstration neighbourhoods. Although for some of the HQE²R demonstration neighbourhoods – in particular the French neighbourhoods – the INDI model was fully applied and even used to compare development alternatives (Outrequin and Charlot-Valdieu, 2004), some other cases showed that certain problems occurred especially with data availability but also concerning the selection of indicators. In these cases the practical experience has also shown that – before quantitative assessments take place – valuable use of ISDIS and INDI can also be made by using them as 'tools to talk'. The different players concerned with or by neighbourhood development usually have very different if not conflicting positions, perspectives and priorities. In this situation ISDIS and INDI provide an impartial playground for the discussion of development scenarios in order to define, sharpen and harmonise the local perception and understanding. By using as well as contesting and adapting the suggested general set of indicators the local actors are encouraged to and supported in defining the most suitable and consensual sustainable development indicator framework for their specific context. In fact the quantitative INDI model also has the possibility of qualitative adjustment. When analysing the results calculated by the model, the tool offers an option to adapt the judgements according to the perception of local actors/stakeholder representatives and thus 'correct' the neighbourhood profile. As an example the waste target of the neighbourhood profile for the German HQE²R neighbourhood Dresden Loebtau scored 2.8, partly because waste separation facilities are a standard feature of urban infrastructure in Germany (CD-ROM with case-study results included in Charlot-Valdieu et al., 2004). At the same time there is an increasing general discussion of the sustainability of waste separation by households and separate collection services compared to new technological options of mechanical separation of unsorted household waste. As a result, differing from the optimistic suggestion of the INDI model, the waste issue for the Loebtau neighbourhood was interpreted as average. The involved actors thereby enter a discussion of different appreciations and weightings of seemingly 'objective' facts. In this way ISDIS and INDI help to open up the minds, create new ideas. Thus the ground is prepared to step back from routines, which is one of the preconditions for a change of action patterns.

SPECIFIC ASSESSMENTS: HQE²R ASCOT AND ENVI

Besides routine action often also the cost issue has to be tackled in every day work as a barrier to sustainable development options. HQE²R supports this with the ASCOT tool (Assessment of Sustainable COnstruction and Technologies cost).

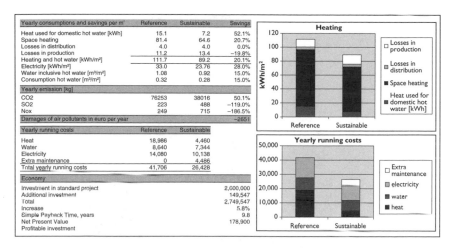

Figure 20.4 Example for an HQE²R ASCOT results page (Mørck, 2004)

The ASCOT model allows a comparison between traditional approaches (Mørck, 2004) to building renovation and different sustainable concepts for the renovation of the building (Figure 20.4).

This comparison takes into account savings in use during the total lifetime of the building and the frequency of future replacement of building components and systems. The tool is primarily intended for use in the early stage of the design process. It can be used both for new construction and for renovation projects. It was initially designed for use in single building renovation projects but can also be used for larger properties or ensembles of buildings. There are strong indications given that at least in the long term also the economic efficiency of sustainable refurbishment measures is much better than usually expected.

Concerning a more detailed analysis of environmental issues on the neighbourhood level, the HQE²R ENVI model (ENVironmental Impact) has been worked out.[2] The aim of the ENVI model is to provide local authorities with a tool for an ex-ante evaluation and support their choice of projects and scenarios.

The model supports the description of the neighbourhood and the assessment of impacts of potential actions according to six variables: Energy consumption, greenhouse gas emission, water consumption, space consumption, waste not recycled or reused and the use of renewable energy sources (Figure 20.5).

As with the INDI model, the ENVI model defines pre-existing neighbourhood profiles at the diagnosis phase to assess the neighbourhood's initial state. The description of the neighbourhood is undertaken for seven fields: Buildings,

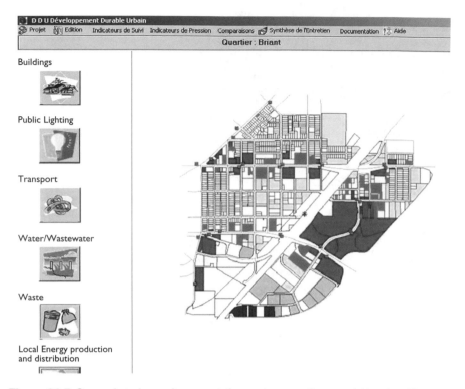

Figure 20.5 Screenshot of a results presentation waste generation on neighbourhood level from the French pilot-version of the HQE^{2}R ENVI model (Outrequin, 2004)

Transportation, Ground occupancy, Public lighting and Networks, Local energy production, Water and sewerage and Waste.

For each field, the required data can be either quantitative or qualitative. If the input is qualitative, the model proposes a default value. Once all inputs are entered, the ENVI model displays environmental profiles for the neighbourhood (Figure 20.6). Five output variables have been defined:

- Energy consumption, pollutants and greenhouse gas emission;
- Water consumption and rainwater re-use;
- CO_2 emissions;
- Waste quantities (not recycled or re-used);
- Land consumption.

For each of these variables, the model provides an absolute value and also provides the distribution of the loads according to the different actors or sectors in the neighbourhood. For example, related to energy consumption in the neighbourhood,

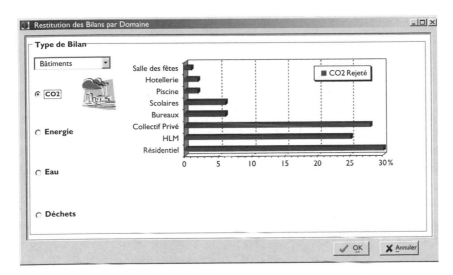

Figure 20.6 Example for an HQE^{2}R ENVI balance page: CO_2-emissions from buildings distinguished for event locations, hotels, swimming pools, offices, private multi-family homes, social housing and single family homes (Outrequin, 2004)

the model gives the distribution of this consumption for the different sectors like housing, tertiary uses and transport and where appropriate also for sub-sectors.

All in all the experience from the HQE^{2}R project, conferences and workshops show that the HQE^{2}R assessment models and tools provide a very helpful starting point for inventory and analysis as well as for monitoring approaches undortaken using the general concept of sustainable development. Even if comparable approaches are locally under development or already used, HQE^{2}R works as an overarching framework for review, positioning and improvement.

IMPROVEMENT OF PRODUCTS AND PROCESS

The HQE^{2}R toolkit provides also practical recommendations for the enhancement of the quality of the built environment. On the one hand these recommendations strive to encourage good practice solutions ('products') when specifying sustainable development projects. Structured along typical questions, the documents list relevant references and examples for each of the HQE^{2}R targets and key issues (Charlot-Valdieu and Outrequin, 2003a,b). On the other hand the complexity and diversity of sustainable development initiatives require also procedural improvements. The existence of routines (e.g. within the planning administration) was already mentioned as one of the barriers to practical changes. The HQE^{2}R 'Recommendations for specifying sustainable development in the building process' (Grossi and Mattarozzi, 2004) are designed to catalyse the reshaping of the framework of perceptions of building quality and to provide guidance on redirecting action towards sustainable development.

In traditional construction processes the key to achieving an excellent building is understanding the client's needs (which the Anglo-Saxon world refers to as the 'briefing process') and then controlling the results during the design and the construction phases. In a construction process aimed at sustainable development the client must or should take into consideration the (future) users' needs and thus the key to achieving a sustainable building is the process of understanding all the users' needs: To this end the briefing process becomes a cooperative process, involving all actors concerned and aimed at consensually defining sustainable development priorities and ensuring their achievement (Figure 20.7). The briefing participation process must continue beyond the initial phase of conceiving the building and permeate also the phases which follow: design, construction and use. There should be a well-defined series of participatory reviews.

This is the core of the recommendations which the HQE^{2}R team has produced for the briefing process. They also contain indications of the key activities which should be carried out if the client authority, that is the organisation or person in charge of the project, is to be assured of achieving a sustainable building. Specific datasheets give recommendations which guide actors on how to incorporate sustainable development issues in these key activities of the building process through its main phases:

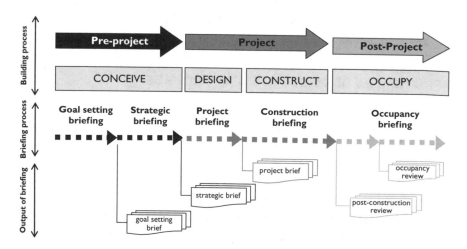

Figure 20.7 The briefing process following the stages of the building project (Grossi and Matarozzi, 2004)

- the pre-project phase (conception);
- the project phase (schematic design, detailed design, construction);
- the post-project phase (occupancy and use, maintenance).

For each of the key activities at all stages of the process a recommendatory datasheet describes the objectives and concerns (what?), the key actors (who?), how to proceed (how?) and the targeted output. The aim is to help client authorities (municipalities or the owners of social building, schools, offices, etc.) first to identify the relevant elements, secondly to carry out key activities related to sustainable development (SD) in the building process phases and thirdly to manage the entire process from the first fundamental decision ('to adopt a SD approach') up to periodic occupancy reviews without omitting any fundamental aspects.

CROSSING BORDERS

A consensus on quality moving towards sustainable development needs the involvement of the actors concerned. For this reason at the centre of the HQE^2R approach stands 'good governance': this is read as a cooperative approach to neighbourhood development. A crucial element of the HQE^2R approach to this end is the 'Shared Diagnosis'. The term stands for an intensive transversal communication process and consensus between involved actors, supported by the general HQE^2R-sustainable development framework and aiming to bring in line the three basic issues of sustainability: social, economic and environmental demands. 'Transversality' in this context means not only to involve concerned actors but also to aim for and facilitate communication between them. Thereby different settings of involved actors and levels of transversality were experienced and supported during the HQE^2R project work in the different case-study areas: transversal communication within the public administration as a first important step, transversal public–private communication with professional stakeholders (real estate owners, investors, etc.) and transversal communication integrating municipal officials, private professionals and the general public via either representatives of stakeholder-groups or even individuals. Similarly with discussions on participation processes ('ladder of participation') it is obvious that decisions aiming towards sustainable development should rest on the highest possible, but at the same time appropriate, level of transversality. To be confronted with other viewpoints, attitudes and interests – especially if arranged on the basis of an impartial framework – helps to 'de-centralise' individual concerns. The latter is a basic precondition to coming to a mutual understanding and opens the process up for consensual solutions. In this context and especially when discussing the roles and relationship of research and practice, an important experience of the HQE^2R

project is, that for an urban neighbourhood development aiming for sustainability it is essential, to dismiss the distinction between 'experts' and the 'public': All actors concerned are experts in their own case and are of equal importance for the definition of a sustainable consensus on neighbourhood development needs and options.

CONCLUSIONS

The HQE^{2}R case-study experience shows that in everyday practice of urban neighbourhood development the concept of sustainability still is somewhat unwieldy for the actors involved. The complexity of issues and their interrelation on the one hand and the usually limited resources (time, budget, manpower . . .) together with the urgency of problems on the other hand often take effect by favouring routine decisions and action: The 'Doeners' – term used in the Netherlands by and for 'People who are doing' implicitly distinguishing them(selves) from waverers – are suspicious, fearing a great deal of extra paper work. For that the co-operation of research, consultancy and practice has been proven fruitful. The HQE^{2}R approach follows the idea of 'constructive irritation': It is designed to contest the usual patterns of procedure and at the same time it provides a comprehensive, well-structured and impartial framework and toolbox for action, which complies with urgent contemporary demands. To follow the HQE^{2}R approach means to introduce the principle of sustainable development, to widen the scope of the involved actors and to raise awareness and thereby to support engaged and skilled participation by the public.

Although the HQE^{2}R experience also shows that in general local urgent problems have to be addressed before the actors involved are open to sustainable development considerations, the comprehensive HQE^{2}R framework is very useful as a 'foot in the door': Once on the table it helps to keep sustainable development – as well as issues of good governance – on the agenda. It is for certain that the HQE^{2}R toolkit could still use some improvements – e.g. the treatment of externalities within the cost calculation model or the sampling of urban structural units for assessment at the neighbourhood level. But where the HQE^{2}R approach does not provide the perfect answer it helps at least to ask the right questions. This is an important purpose especially if we realistically keep in mind that sustainable development – although scientifically discussed for some time – in practice is still a young concept and we are only at the beginning of a long process.

NOTES

1   The HQE^{2}R project with the full title 'Sustainable renovation of buildings for sustainable neighbourhoods' was co-ordinated by CSTB, France and gathered 10 research

partners and 14 neighbourhoods in Denmark, France, Germany, Great Britain, Italy, Spain and The Netherlands. For more detailed information and contact details of national partners, see the project website: http://hqe2r.cstb.fr/.

The findings presented in this paper are based on results of extensive teamwork within the HQE²R project. Some parts of the text are taken from HQE²R deliverables written by other partners. Nevertheless the author of this paper remains responsible for the correctness of the presentation.

2   The ENVI Model was designed in a partnership of the HQE²R Partners CSTB and LA CALADE with the EDF (Electricité de France) R&D department according to an additional contract reaching beyond the initial HQE²R consortium.

REFERENCES

Blum, A. and Morgenstern, D. (2004). HQE²R – Ansatz und Instrumentarium für nachhaltige Entwicklung von Stadtteilen; Zusammenfassung wesentlicher Projektergebnisse, HQE²R Deliverable 22 de, IOER, Dresden [*HQE²R – Approach and toolkit for sustainable development of urban neighbourhoods; Overview of major project results*].

Charlot-Valdieu, C. and Outrequin, P. (2002). Global HQE²R Methodology, HQE²R Deliverable 4, CSTB, Sophia Antipolis (internal report).

Charlot-Valdieu, C. and Outrequin, P. (2003a). HQE²R Recommendations for the integration of sustainable development in action plan specifications, HQE²R Deliverable 19, CSTB, La Calade, Sophia Antipolis.

Charlot-Valdieu, C. and Outrequin, P. (2003b). Sustainable development integration in specifications for non-built elements, HQE²R Deliverable 20, CSTB, La Calade, Sophia Antipolis.

Charlot-Valdieu, C., Outrequin, P. and Robbins, C. (eds) (2004). The HQE²R toolkit for sustainable neighbourhood regeneration and European application overview, Brochure HQE²R N°2 and interactive CD-ROM , QUASCO, Milan (available through the national HQE²R partners: www.hqe2r.cstb.fr).

Grossi, A. and Mattarozzi, S. (2004). 'Recommendations for specifying sustainable development in the building process', HQE²R Deliverable 21, ICIE, Bologna.

Mørck, O. (2004). The ASCOT model: Assessment of Sustainable COnstruction and Technologies cost, HQE²R Deliverable 17–3, CENERGIA, Ballerup.

Outrequin, P. (2004). The ENVI model: ENVironmental Impact assessment of neighbourhood regeneration scenarios from an environmental point of view, HQE²R Deliverable 17–2, La Calade, Valbonne.

Outrequin, P. and Charlot-Valdieu, C. (eds) (2004). ISDIS system and INDI model: Integrated Sustainable Development Indicators System (ISDIS) and INDicators Impact – Assessment of neighbourhood regeneration scenarios with a sustainable development indicators system – methodological presentation, HQE^{2}R Deliverable 17–1, CSTB, La Calade, Sophia Antipolis.

Schiller, G. (2003). The Urban Structure Unit Approach – A suitable frame for environmental and spatial urban investigations, Proceedings of the 8th International Conference on Environmental Science and Technology, Lemnos Island, Greece, Vol. A, pp. 775–781.

21

Assessing Sustainable Community Development Proposals
Mark Deakin

INTRODUCTION

Sustainable communities are seen as developments offering the opportunity to manage growth in plan-led and environmentally-friendly patterns of settlement. This chapter examines the settlement model put forward for the development of sustainable communities in the United Kingdom and shows that while in Scotland, the growth management strategy is clearly plan-led, the degree to which the design solution can be seen to be environmentally friendly is questionable. The chapter suggests this is because in its current form the model is not able to show whether the design solution advanced is ecologically sound; whether, in particular, the solution is ecologically sound and, because of this, efficient not only in greening economic development, but also in making it financially viable for plan-led experiments of this kind to produce environmentally-friendly patterns of settlement.

THE ON-GOING REVIEW

The on-going review of planning in the United Kingdom has highlighted the attractiveness of new settlements as an alternative to cramming, peripheral expansion and urban sprawl. What follows examines the argument for new settlements appearing in the United Kingdom. The examination goes on to establish how one of the experiments going on in Scotland is transforming the new settlement phenomenon into the search for a plan-led, environmentally friendly and sustainable pattern of settlement.

The examination draws attention to the Interim Development Framework put in place to support the plan-led, environmentally-friendly experiment in the South East Wedge of Edinburgh. After subjecting the settlement model and design solution to a critique, the chapter goes on to address the outstanding matter of assessment and how to evaluate the environmentally-friendly nature of the plan-led experiment in question. Here attention is drawn to the assessment methodology needed for the settlement model to show whether the plan-led experiment is ecologically sound and efficient in greening economic development. This in turn draws attention to the need for the methodology to clarify if the design solution advanced is financially viable. That is to say, produces an environmentally-friendly pattern of settlement which is sustainable because it has the ecological, economic and financial qualities needed to safeguard communities against the kinds of development traditionally seen as threatening their well-being.

Previous papers on the subject have looked at the settlement model and design solution put forward for the plan-led experiment in question (Deakin, 2000, 2002). This chapter examines the 'environmental-friendly' nature of the settlement pattern the plan puts forward for the development of sustainable communities. It draws attention to the strategic issues the plan has sought to address during the first 5 years of development (1995–2000) and highlights the questions this raises about the environmentally-friendly nature of the settlement pattern the model advances as a design solution. This is done in the interests of exposing the limitations of such 'state-of-the-art' models and drawing attention to the shortcomings of the design solutions they advance. The limitations and shortcomings that in turn raise particular questions about the manner in which such models and the design solutions they advance address the matter of environmental assessment.

THE NEW SETTLEMENT PHENOMENON IN THE UNITED KINGDOM

As Ward's (1992) review of new settlements in the United Kingdom establishes, with the privatisation of the New Towns Commission, private consortiums have sought to develop new settlements as an alternative to peripheral expansion and urban sprawl. It is a development Glasson et al. (1994) also examine. Their research shows that during the review of structure plans, carried out between 1988 and 1993, 46 new settlement proposals had been submitted to planning authorities throughout England and Wales and out of this only 2 developments were successful in receiving outline planning consent. As Ratcliffe and Stubbs (1996) also note, while the tight fiscal regime operating in local governments during this period made the development of new settlements by private consortiums attractive, they were too speculative, not supported by the planning system and unable to allay fears the public had about their impact on the environment.

THE POSITION IN SCOTLAND

In Scotland the new settlement phenomenon is a matter that has found its way into the statutory planning system and review of the structure plan for the City of Edinburgh. In respect of this review, the Lothian Regional Council (1995) *Structure Plan Review* document states, 'the development of Edinburgh can no longer be accommodated within the existing boundaries of the City'. The 'cramming of development in brown field sites is no longer an option for Edinburgh', neither is development by peripheral expansion around the edge of the City's greenbelt seen as a viable option. This is because there are 'simply not enough brown field sites to develop in Edinburgh and peripheral expansion around the edge of the City would put too much pressure on the greenbelt and result in urban sprawl' (p. 14). The solution, the statement suggests, rests with the development of new settlements and in particular with the 'development of new settlements on a 1600 hectare site at the periphery of Edinburgh and in an area of the City's greenbelt known as the South East Wedge' (p. 15).

As an exercise in the management of growth, the statement suggests that plan-led experiments of this kind can protect the environment and the proposal to 'develop new settlements in the South East Wedge of Edinburgh, provides the City with just such an opportunity' (p. 15). The reasons put forward to explain why the development provides such an opportunity are as follows:

- representing less than 10 per cent of the greenbelt, the site has the capacity to accommodate 35 per cent of Edinburgh's land use requirements, 60 per cent of the City's population growth, 15 per cent of additional households and 30 per cent of future employment opportunities;
- the site is able to carry such a level of growth due to spare capacity in both the utility and the transportation networks and because it is already well serviced with out-of-town shopping centres, retail and warehouse parks, leisure and entertainment facilities;
- in releasing pressure for speculative development around the edge of the City and protecting the greenbelt, the site provides the opportunity for Edinburgh to make sure the use of land, utilities, transportation networks and both retail and leisure services is environmentally friendly and fosters a more sustainable pattern of settlement.

It is noticeable that the proposal to develop new settlements in Edinburgh's South East Wedge goes a long way to avoid the difficulties experienced by many of its predecessors. In comparison with the experiences of new settlements in England and Wales, it is noticeable that the proposal to develop sustainable communities in the South East Wedge of Edinburgh is not only supported by a written statement, but is an experiment which also has the advantage of being plan-led and environmentally friendly. While going a long way to distinguish the development of new settlements in Edinburgh from previous experiments of this type, it is not these qualities that mark it out from its predecessors. As a more advanced experiment in the modelling of alternatives to peripheral expansion and urban sprawl, the qualities that distinguish this proposal from its predecessors lie elsewhere. They lie in the advantages it has of being not only plan-led and environmentally friendly, but able to produce a pattern of settlement which is also sustainable in terms of the communities it develops.

THE SETTLEMENT MODEL AND DESIGN SOLUTION

The search for a pattern of settlement that is sustainable in terms of the communities it develops is a matter the 1996 Interim Development Framework addresses (Chesterton, 1996). The settlement model the document puts forward as a design solution appears under the heading of 'sustainable communities'. Under this heading attention is drawn to the principles of sustainable development which the document argues such settlements should be based upon. Modelling the development of sustainable communities, the document proposes that Edinburgh's experiment in managing growth through plan-led, environmentally-friendly patterns of settlement in the South East Wedge should be based on the following:

- a distinctive urban culture;
- a spatially compact form;
- a strong landscape framework in a countryside setting;
- a set of neighbourhoods;
- a high density of population;
- a balance of land use, economic and social structures;
- an energy conscious public transportation network;
- high levels of infrastructure and shared service provision;
- a pattern of settlement that is able to integrate existing communities with those emerging from the development; and
- a financial structure that is viable in the short-, medium- and long-term horizons.

These design features reflect the findings of Breheny (1992a, 1992b), Breheny and Rookwood (1993) and Breheny et al.'s (1993) study of settlements models in the UK. The settlement model and design solution also draw attention to the experiences of sustainable developments from a number of UK cities. The experiences of Cambridge, Portsmouth and Swindon are reported on by Selman (1996) and Brown (1998). Hall and Ward's (1998) examination of such developments draw particular attention to the fiscal regimes regulating the infrastructures needed to service the settlement's high quality living and working environments. Similar examinations are also provided by Roberts et al. (1999) and the Urban Task Force (1999). What these examinations all have in common is their tendency to represent the settlement models and design solutions advanced as prototypes for the development of sustainable communities.

THE DEVELOPMENT OF SUSTAINABLE COMMUNITIES

In Edinburgh the plan-led experiment focuses on the development of sustainable communities in the City's South East Wedge and defines the qualities of the settlement model and design solution it advances, in terms of the following six key features.

Distinctive urban culture

Within the settlement model the proposal to design a distinctive urban culture is of general concern. This is defined as an alternative to the suburban lifestyle with its particular brand of resource-intensive consumerism, linked to demands for expansion into the periphery through the speculative development of green field sites; the speculative development of green field sites that results in the coalescence of settlements around the edge of the city and which leads to the break-up of communities.

Spatially compact form, strong landscape framework and countryside setting

The settlement model proposes that such an outcome can be avoided by restricting development around the edge of the city and concentrating it in a spatially compact form. The design solution allows for the development to build from existing peripheral housing estates and a former mining village. Set in a strong landscape framework, the model goes on to propose the countryside setting should make use of natural features, woodlands and country parks, to separate the existing and new settlements from one another. The model also proposes an urban regeneration programme and limited town centre expansion for the former mining village, so as to retain its identity and position in the settlement pattern.

Neighbourhoods, high population densities and balanced land uses

Elsewhere, it is proposed that up to 20,000 people should be accommodated within three new settlements. The model also proposes these should be designed as neighbourhoods of approximately 5000 residents. The model allows for the neighbourhoods to have a high population density (forecast to be between 50 and 200 persons per hectare) and a balanced set of land uses, comprising residential, commercial (light industrial, business, warehouse and distribution and retail) and community services (transportation, recreational, education and health). The design also allows for each neighbourhood to have a balanced (low, middle and upper income) economic and social structure in a diverse structure of tenure. That is to say, a mix of owner-occupied, private and social-rented accommodation at affordable rates of occupation.

Living and working environment

In the interests of providing a 'high quality working and living environment', the model allows for the development to have an energy-conscious transportation system. It suggests the transportation system should incorporate a number of measures: for example, a public transport corridor, bus priority proposal, park and ride system and traffic calming scheme. It also suggests that some of the neighbourhoods should be car-free and that residents should be within easy walking distance of public transport facilities.

Infrastructure requirements

The infrastructure requirements are considerable. They include land consolidation works, sites and service provision, transportation, recreation, education and health provision. In view of this, the model proposes the transportation, recreation, education and health services should be shared between the peripheral housing estate, former mining village and neighbourhoods forming the settlement pattern it puts forward for the development of sustainable communities. This is because the neighbourhoods emerging from the development will not be able to provide either the employment, recreational, education, health or retail services needed to support the high quality working and living environment the model suggests is required for the development of sustainable communities. It is this sharing of the infrastructure and service provision that is seen to represent the key factor integrating the peripheral housing estate, former mining village and neighbourhoods into a settlement pattern which is sustainable.

Financial viability

The financial viability issue tackles particular difficulties associated with the geology of the site and high level of both infrastructure and service provision needed for the settlement pattern to develop. Given the abnormal preparation costs, high infrastructure and service content, the framework sets out what the development will yield in the form of land receipts. The cash flows making up these land receipts are analysed over the short-, medium- and long-term horizons and discounted at the opportunity cost of capital. The income takes the form of receipts from the sale of sites making up the mixed set of land uses (residential, light industrial and retail). The income represents the development value of the sites with planning permission. The costs include the purchase of land at existing use value (i.e. without the development proposal) and capital expenditure on the infrastructures required to service the sites. The existing use value is taken to represent the sum of agricultural and 'hope value'. The capital expenditure represents the cost of site preparation and providing the recreation, education, health and public transportation networks. The discounted cash flow analysis supporting the appraisal illustrates the project should yield an 11 per cent internal rate of return (i.e. surplus of income over cost of development). The details of this discounted cash flow analysis are documented in the Interim Development Framework (see Chesterton, 1996).

As a development appraisal, the exercise follows the guidelines set out in the DoE's (1991) publication on *Policy Appraisal and the Environment*. It also makes use of DoE's (1993a) document on *Making Markets Work for the Environment* and publication from the Local Government Management Board (1994) on *Greening Economic Development*. Drawing upon these sources a number of economic instruments – for example, cash flow analysis, discounting procedures and cost benefit analysis techniques – are made use of to establish whether the quality of the working and living environments making up the development produce enough planning gain for the land market to fund the infrastructure services upon which the settlement pattern is based and the sustainable communities are seen to rest.

THE ENVIRONMENTALLY-FRIENDLY NATURE

The immediate difficulties faced in trying to establish the development's environmentally-friendly nature, rest with the effective absence of the data needed for such an assessment. This is because

- despite drawing upon the DoE's Planning Research Programme (DoE, 1993a,b, 1994) and using NPPG 1 (Scottish Office, 1994) to guide the on-going review of the structure plan, strategic environmental assessment and appraisal of how to manage growth, the IDF document provides very little evidence to support the claim that the plan-led development produces an environmentally-friendly settlement pattern;
- while placing a great deal of emphasis on the capacity the site has to carry a distinctive urban culture in spatially compact forms, set within strong landscape frameworks and countryside settings, the model and design solution it puts forward offers no formal assessment of its ecological footprint, biodiversity or natural capital.

In its current form the model and design solution it puts forward are vulnerable to many of the criticisms Glasson *et al.* (1994) and Ratcliff and Stubbs (1996) have previously made about the new settlement phenomena and the sometimes less than friendly way that plan-led developments of this kind treat the environment. These criticisms are also echoed by Lichfield (1996). The criticisms suggest that little has been learnt about the environmental values of the urban culture, spatially compact forms, strong landscape framework and countryside setting the model sets out, or how this in turn leads to a position where the population densities, socio-economic structures, energy-conscious public transport, high levels of both infrastructure and service provision advance a design solution which is efficient in greening economic development (also see Beatley, 1995; Campbell, 1996; Gibbs *et al.*, 1996; Cosgriff and Steinmann, 1998).

LITTLE MORE THAN AN AESTHETIC?

Set against the said criticism of such models and the design solutions they advance, the environmentally-friendly nature of the settlement pattern might be seen to add up to little more than an aesthetic; an aesthetic about the value of distinctive urban cultures, spatially compact forms and strong landscape frameworks in countryside settings – about, in this instance, the value of distinctive urban cultures, spatially compact forms and strong landscape frameworks, whose countryside settings have the population densities, land uses, socio-economic structures and public trans-portation systems forming the infrastructures needed to service high quality living and working environments.

THE VALUE OF THIS AESTHETIC

The value of this aesthetic may be seen to lie in the abilities it has to develop high quality living environments which are 'friendly'. If this is where the value of the aesthetic is seen to lie, then both its limitations and shortcomings need to be recognised. This is because in its current form it is not possible to say whether the high quality environments appearing in the model are friendly because they are ecologically sound, or because the design solution allows the land market to produce the level of planning gain needed to be efficient in greening economic development.

ITS LIMITATIONS AND SHORTCOMINGS

Asking whether the high quality living environments are friendly because they are ecologically sound, or efficient in greening economic development is instructive because it exposes the limitations of the model and shortcomings of the design solution the aesthetic rests upon. It reveals that the limitations of the model rest with the inability of the design solution to illustrate whether the high quality living environments are friendly because they are ecologically sound. It also goes a long way to contrast this shortcoming with the considerable lengths the model goes to in order for the design solution to show how the land market produces the level of planning gain needed to efficiently green the economic development in question.

ECOLOGICALLY SOUND AND EFFICIENT?

The question that remains unanswered is where the true value of the aesthetic lies. Whether it is with the value of models that are ecologically sound, or if it lies with the ability of design solutions to efficiently green economic development. Ultimately, the question that remains unanswered is whether it is the former or the latter that has the right to make claims about the environmentally-friendly nature of the settlement pattern and sustainability of the communities which the model and design solution propose to develop.

With the former – even though the model does not raise them – the questions are to do with the site's ecological footprint, bio-diversity and environmental loading (Barton *et al.*, 1995). They are to do with environmental values and matters concerning bio-mass, the levels of energy consumption, waste and emissions. They are questions about levels of energy consumption, waste and emissions, whether the high quality living and working environments are friendly and whether this is because they are ecologically sound (Barton, 1997; Breheny and Archer, 1998; Barton and Kleiner, 2000; Stead, 2000; Guy and Marvin, 2001). With the latter the questions are not to do with the aforesaid, but concern the land market and level of planning gain needed to be efficient in greening economic development. They are about the land market, the levels of planning gain needed to efficiently green the economic development and make it financially viable.

THE QUESTION OF INTEGRATION

If such concerns about energy consumption, waste and emissions are seen to be key, then it shows there is a pressing need for these matters to be integrated into such models. It also illustrates there is a critical requirement for the designs which follow to demonstrate whether they are ecologically sound; whether they are ecologically sound and because of this able to use land markets (and the levels of planning gain they in turn produce) in a manner that is not only efficient in greening economic development, but also has the effect of making it financially viable to produce an environmentally-friendly pattern of settlement. These needs and requirements are pressing, because as soon as a critical distinction is drawn between the environmental values of ecologically sound designs, land markets and the levels of planning gain needed to not only be efficient in greening economic development, but make it financially viable, questions arise about

- the science and technologies needed to make the energy consumption, waste and emissions of the high quality living and working environments friendly;
- how the said technologies provide the infrastructures required for the high quality living and working environments to be friendly because they are ecologically sound;
- the degree to which it is the science and technologies of the infrastructures and ecologically sound designs, rather than articulation of the said land markets and planning gain, that efficiently green economic development;
- how the science, technologies, infrastructures and ecologically sound designs in turn use the said market and levels of planning gain to efficiently green economic development and make it financially viable;
- how this particular, ecologically sound use of land markets and planning gain is efficient in greening economic development and making it financially viable for experiments of this type to produce environmentally-friendly patterns of settlement;
- how this environmentally-friendly pattern of settlement is sustainable in terms of the communities that develop from plan-led experiments of this type;
- how the said settlement pattern is sustainable in terms of the relationship the communities in turn have to the city and its surrounding region (Deakin, 2000, 2002).

Against the science and technology of ecologically-sound designs, it can be seen that matters concerning the articulation of land markets and planning gain reveal little about where the real issues associated with the transformation of the new settlement phenomenon currently lie. This is because by effectively reducing the environmental values of the settlement model to an aesthetic about the virtues of good design, it is simply not possible to say whether the solution advanced is friendly because of its ecological footprint, bio-diversity or natural capital. Nor is it possible to say so in terms of the environmental loading, levels of energy consumption, waste and emissions the settlement pattern produces.

As a result and as ridiculous as it may seem, it is currently not possible to say whether the plan-led experiment is an environmental good or not. This is because in line with the conventions and traditions built up since the 1980s (under the policy of privatisation, resulting 'boosterism' of civic privatism and drive towards the all pervasive marketisation of the public sector), the main point of concern lies else-where (Deakin, 1996, 1997, 1999a); not so much with plan-led experiments aimed at assessing the ecology, bio-diversity, natural capital and environmental loading of distinctive urban cultures, having spatially compact forms and strong landscaping frameworks in countryside settings, as with the need to provide accountability, value for money, economic, efficiency and effectiveness disclosures (Deakin, 1999b).

THE OUTSTANDING MATTER

The matter still outstanding is that of assessing whether plan-led experiments of this kind are environmentally-friendly and able to produce a pattern of settlement which is sustainable because the model and design solution are both ecologically sound and efficient in greening economic development. In meeting this challenge there are the following matters to consider:

- the terms of reference adopted as a framework to develop the settlement model and design solution it advances as sustainable communities (Deakin *et al.*, 2001);
- how this framework structures the relationship between the environmental values of the settlement model the design solution advanced to efficiently green economic development (Bentivegna *et al.*, 2002);
- the protocol(s) adopted to assess the sustainability of the communities under-going development and evaluate how ecologically sound the settlement model is (Deakin, 2002);
- the environmental assessments methods needed to evaluate the sustainability of the communities and to model whether the ecology of the design solution is not only sound, but efficient in greening economic development (Deakin, 2000, 2002);
- if this in turn makes it financially viable for plan-led experiments of this kind to produce environmentally-friendly patterns of settlement (Deakin *et al.*, 2002a,b);
- the question of what methods should be used in undertaking such an envi-ronmental assessment (Deakin *et al.*, 2002a,b).

These considerations are particularly challenging because they demand a shift of attention away from understanding the environment as an aesthetic and towards a knowledge of its status as a ecological system; as an ecological system that has a set of values which in turn make it possible to measure the environmental loading, levels of energy consumption, waste and emissions, as opposed to the land markets and levels of planning gain needed to be efficient in greening economic development.

THE MATTER OF ENVIRONMENTAL ASSESSMENT

In recognising this, the problem that surfaces is over the methods adopted to carry out such an environmental assessment. This task is particularly difficult because there are two classes of environmental assessment methods: those providing environmental valuations and those assessing the sustainability of development. With the former it is important to recognise this class of methods provide an index of the problems that have been experienced when the environment is reduced to little more than an aesthetic and not represented as an ecological system (Deakin *et al.*, 2002a,b). With the latter the emphasis is firmly upon assessing the environment as an ecosystem logically connected to the economy. This requires a systematic modelling of the relationship between the ecology of design solutions and their economic structures. This in turn requires that the models and design solutions which are advanced are themselves subjected to an environmental assessment and capable, in this instance, of evaluating whether the ecology of the model is sound and if the resulting design solution is efficient in greening economic development.

At present very few such models exist and their design solutions tend to be city-wide rather than district- or neighbourhood-based. However, those that can be made use of include the following:

- the NAR (Net Annual Return) model;
- the eco-neigbourhood model; and
- the transit-orientated settlement model.

These models illustrate a strong environmental inheritance and constitute serious attempts to assess the sustainability of communities in terms of their eco-systems and underlying economic structures.

The NAR model provides a critique of the discounting mechanism underlying the greening of economic development (Deakin, 1996, 1997, 1999a). It offers an environmental assessment of the impact this has upon the eco-system and provides a model of how the discounting mechanism can be rehabilitated to provide a design solution producing the levels of planning gain needed to make any greening of economic development financially viable (Deakin, 2000, 2002). The eco-neigbourhood model focuses on assessing the ecological footprint, biodiversity and natural capital of such proposals in terms of the environmental loading, levels of energy consumption, waste and emissions such a greening of economic development produces (Stead, 2000; Barton and Kleiner, 2000; Deakin *et al.*, 2002a,b). The transit-related settlement model provides a design solution which assesses whether eco-neighbourhoods have the environmental loading, levels of energy consumption, waste and emissions that are friendly because the infrastructures required to service such high quality living and working environments have the land markets and levels of planning gain needed to be efficient in greening economic development and make such a course of action financially viable.

The value of approaching the matter as an assessment rests with the potential such exercises have to evaluate the environmentally-friendly nature of settlement patterns in terms of whether their sustainability develops from the ecological, economic and financial qualities needed to guard communities against changes which are seen to threaten them; in particular, the coalescence of settlements, loss of identity and break-up of communities resulting from the type of infill development traditionally associated with peripheral expansion.

CONCLUSION

This chapter has reviewed a plan-led experiment aimed at developing sustainable communities and has found the 'state-of-the-art' settlement model put forward for such purposes wanting. The review has also found that in its current form the model is unable to tell us whether the high quality living and working environments which the design advances are ecologically sound.

The chapter has also suggested that asking whether the high quality living and working environments are friendly because they are ecologically sound, or due to the fact the land market produces enough planning gain to be efficient in greening economic development, exposes the limitations of the model and shortcomings of the design solution it puts forward. It has gone on to suggest that in its current form the model is limited because the design solution it advances is not able to say whether the high quality living and working environments in question are ecologically sound, only if the land market produces the level of planning gain needed to efficiently green economic development and make it financially viable to take such a course of action. As the discussions have gone someway to point out, the challenge which remains outstanding is that of establishing whether models of this kind and the type of design solution they advance are able to represent the environment as an eco-system and something more than an aesthetic for greening economic development.

To meet this challenge, the chapter has looked at the environmental assessments methods that can be made use of to overcome the problems which are associated with the existing models and design solutions currently put forward.

In meeting this challenge, the chapter has outlined the main elements of the assessment methodology it is possible to adopt for the purposes of evaluating whether such models are ecologically sound and if the design solutions they advance are efficient in greening economic development. Having outlined the assessments in question, the chapter has gone on to examine how it is possible to integrate both the ecological and the economic dimensions of the said methodology. Here attention has been focused on how to integrate such qualities into an assessment methodology that is able of evaluate whether the model adopted is ecologically sound, not only because the design solution advanced is efficient in greening economic development, but for the reason that this also makes it financially viable to produce patterns of settlement which are sustainable.

As the examination has also gone some way to demonstrate, the contribution integrated – ecologically sound, efficient and financially viable – assessments of this kind can make is noticeable, and this is because with such a methodology it becomes possible to evaluate not only whether the model is environmentally-friendly, but if the design solution advanced produces a pattern of settlement which is sustainable.

REFERENCES

Barton, H. (1997). 'Environmental capacity and sustainable urban form' in Farthing, S. (ed.), *Evaluating Local Environmental Policy*, Avebury, Andover.

Barton, H. and Kleiner, D. (2000). 'Innovative eco-neighbourhood projects' in Barton, H. (ed.), *Sustainable Communities*, Earthscan, London.

Barton, H., Davies, G. and Guise, R. (1995). *Sustainable Settlements – A Guide for Planners, Designers and Developers*, Local Government Management Board, Luton.

Beatley, T. (1995). 'Planning and sustainability: the elements of a new (improved?) paradigm', *Journal of Planning Literature*, 9 (4): 383–395.

Bentivegna, V., Curwell, S., Deakin, M., Lombardi, P., Mitchell, G. and Nijkamp, P. (2002). '"A vision and methodology for integrated sustainable urban development": BEQUEST', *Building Research and Information*, 30 (2): 83–94.

Breheny, M. (1992a). 'The Compact City', *Built Environment*, 18 (4): 241–246.

Breheny, M. (1992b). *Sustainable Development and Urban Forms*, Pion, London.

Breheny, M. and Archer, S. (1998). 'Urban densities, local policies and sustainable development', *International Journal of Environment and Pollution*, 10 (1): 126–150.

Breheny, M. and Rookwood, R. (1993). 'Planning the sustainable city-region' in Blowers, A. (ed.), *Planning for a Sustainable Environment*, Earthscan, London.

Breheny, M., Gent, T. and Lock, D. (1993). *Alternative Development Patterns: New Settlements*, HMSO, London.

Brown, F. (1998). 'Modelling urban growth', *Town and Country Planning*, pp. 334–337.

Campbell, S. (1996). 'Green cities, growing cities, just cities?', *Journal of the American Planning Association*, 62 (4): 296–312.

Chesterton (1996). *Edinburgh's South-East Wedge* in Final IDF Document, Chesterton Consulting, London.

Cosgriff, B. and Steinemann, A. (1998). 'Industrial ecology for sustainable communities', *Journal of Environmental Planning and Management*, 41 (6): 661–672.

Deakin, M. (1996). 'Discounting, obsolescence, depreciation and their effects on the environment of cities', *Journal of Financial Management of Property and Construction*, 1 (2): 39–57.

Deakin, M. (1997). 'An economic evaluation and appraisal of the effects land use, building obsolescence and depreciation have on the environment of cities' in Brandon, P., Lombardi, P. and Bentivegna, V. (eds), *Evaluation of the Built Environment for Sustainability*, Chapman and Hall, London.

Deakin, M. (1999a). 'Valuation, appraisal, discounting, obsolescence and depreciation: towards a life cycle analysis and impact assessment of their effects on the environment of cities', *International Journal of Life Cycle Assessment*, 4 (2): 87–94.

Deakin, M. (1999b). 'Financial instruments for capital accounting in local authorities', *Journal of Property Investment and Finance*, 17 (1): 89–107.

Deakin, M. (2000). 'Developing sustainable communities in Edinburgh's South-East Wedge', *Journal of Property Management*, 4 (2): 72–88.

Deakin, M. (2002). 'Modelling the development of sustainable communities in Edinburgh's South-East Wedge', *Planning Practice and Research*, 17 (3): 331–336.

Deakin, M., Curwell, S. and Lombardi, P. (2001). 'BEQUEST: sustainability assessment, the framework and directory of methods', *International Journal of Life Cycle Assessment*, 6 (6): 373–390.

Deakin, M., Huovila, P., Rao, S., Sunikka, M. and Vrekeer, R. (2002a). 'The assessment of sustainable urban development', *Building Research and Information*, 30 (2): 55–65.

Deakin, M., Curwell, S. and Lombardi, P. (2002b). 'Sustainable urban development: the framework and directory of assessment methods', *Journal of Environmental Assessment Policy and Management*, 4 (2): 171–197.

DoE (1991). *Policy Appraisal and the Environment*, HMSO, London.

DoE (1993a). *Making Markets Work for the Environment*, HMSO, London.

DoE (1993b). *Environmental Appraisal of Development Plans*, HMSO, London.

DoE (1994). *Guide on Preparing Environmental Statements for Planning Projects* [draft], HMSO, London.

Gibbs, D., Longhurst, J. and Braithwaite, C. (1996). 'Moving towards sustainable development: integrating economic development and the environment in local authorities', *Journal of Environmental Planning and Management*, 39 (3): 317–332.

Glasson, J., Therival, R. and Chadwick, A. (1994). *Environmental Impact Assessment*, University College, London.

Guy, S. and Marvin, S. (2001). 'Urban environmental flows: towards a new way of seeing' in Guy, S. and Marvin, S. (eds), *Infrastructure in Transition*, Earthscan, London.

Hall, P. and Ward, C. (1998). *Sociable Cities*, John Wiley, London.

Lichfield, N. (1996). *Community Impact Evaluation*, University College, London, London.

Local Government Management Board (1994). *Greening Economic Development*, LGMB, Luton.

Lothian Regional Council (1995). *Structure Plan Review*, LRC, Edinburgh.

Ratcliffe, J. and Stubbs, M. (1996). *Urban Planning and Real Estate Development*, University College, London, London.

Roberts, M., Lloyd-Jones, T., Erickson, B. and Nice, S. (1999). 'Place and space in the networked city: concepualising the networked metropolis', *Journal of Urban Design*, 4 (1): 51–65.

Scottish Office (1994). *National Planning Policy Guideline: The Planning System*, Scottish Office, Edinburgh.

Selman, P. (1996). *Local Sustainability*, St. Martin's Press, New York.

Stead, D. (2000). 'Unsustainable settlements' in Barton, H. (ed.), *Sustainable Communities*, Earthscan, London.

Urban Task Force (1999). *Towards an Urban Renaissance*, E&FN Spon, London.

Ward, S. (1992). *Garden Cities, Past, Present and Future*, Spon, London.

Part 5

Evaluating the Sustainability of Urban Development

22

Methodological Issues in the Assessment of Environmental Equity and Environmental Justice
Gordon Mitchell and Gordon Walker

ENVIRONMENTAL JUSTICE AND SUSTAINABLE DEVELOPMENT

The distribution of the costs and benefits of development is an issue central to sustainable development, with its objectives of inter- and intra-generational equity, and is also the core concern of growing calls for environmental equity and environmental justice (EJ). Cutter (1995) defined EJ as 'equal access to a clean environment and equal protection from possible environmental harm irrespective of race, income, class or any other differentiating feature of socio-economic status'. However, EJ advocates are increasingly concerned with a broader view of the environment, as issues such as access to environmental resources and participation in decisions affecting the environment are important quality-of-life determinants. Thus EJ is concerned not just with the distribution of environmental 'goods and bads' amongst minority populations, but also with how those distributions have come about, and how they can and should be addressed. Such 'procedural equity' issues make the distinction between environmental equity and environmental justice.

In *Just Sustainabilities* Agyeman *et al.* (2003) argue that environmental quality and human equality are inextricably linked in three ways. First, they note that, from global to local scales, higher environmental quality is associated with a more equitable income distribution, greater civil liberties, political rights and higher levels of literacy. Secondly, environmental problems impact disproportionately upon the poor, who often do not have the economic power to avoid environmental 'bads' (or access to environmental 'goods'), whilst at the same time, it is the affluent that make the greatest contribution to environmental degradation. Thirdly, they point to environmentally sustainable development, which, they argue, cannot be achieved unless society achieves greater social and economic equality within and between nations.

This last point is, however, contested territory. Dobson (2003) argues that social justice and environmental sustainability are not always compatible objectives, and hypothesises that the EJ movement does not necessarily share the same goals as the environmental movement. For example, the EJ movement might advocate a more even redistribution of waste by income or racial group, whereas the environmental movement would advocate a reduction in total waste arising. Agyeman *et al.* (2003) respond to this criticism by noting that the EJ movement adopted the term 'EJ' in the early 1990s, as environmental equity implies an equal sharing of burdens, whereas EJ is concerned with reducing the level of unacceptable environmental burden imposed on a minority group. Furthermore, the EJ movement is characterised as one that does not wish to alleviate environmental burdens by putting them in 'someone else's backyard', but rather seeks EJ through a reduction in the total burden to be distributed (Faber and McCarthy, 2003), achieved through such means as clean production, waste minimisation and phasing out of persistent toxic pollutants. Through application of the Environmental Space method (similar in concept to the ecological footprint discussed in Chapter 11), McLaren (2003) describes further how such tools, applied within an equity framework, contribute to environmentally sustainable development.

Environmental human rights are increasingly seen as a mechanism for achieving environmental sustainability. These rights include the right to a clean and safe environment, the right to act to protect the environment, and the right to environmental information and participation in decisions affecting the environment (Adebowale *et al.*, 2001). Such rights would likely benefit marginalised people most, and provide a platform for environmental improvement. Under principle 10 of the 1992 Rio declaration, environmental rights are now being established via the 1998 Human Rights Act, and particularly the 1998 UNECE convention on access to information, public participation and access to justice in environmental decision-making (the Aarhus convention), whose objective is to 'contribute to the protection of the right of every person of present and future generations to live in an environment adequate to his or her health and well-being' (UNECE, 1999). Whilst environmental human rights did not feature as strongly in the implementation plan of the World Summit on Sustainable Development as the EU had hoped, legislation being developed in response to the Aarhus convention will give EU citizens greater access to information and judicial procedures, allowing minority groups avenues to address procedures and breaches of environmental laws which contribute to environmental inequality and injustice.

Whilst EU legislation developed to address environmental rights does not mandate evaluation of the environmental equity implications of development programmes and plans (as is the case in the US – see below), environmental equity is likely to become an increasingly significant criteria upon which developments are assessed; hence assessment tools are required to allow stakeholders to consider the social distribution of environmental consequences, and participate in decisions over the most sustainable options. This chapter addresses the practice of environmental equity assessment as an essential input to assessment of EJ.

THE EMERGENCE OF ENVIRONMENTAL JUSTICE CONCERNS

The EJ approach has its roots in the work of Freeman (1972), who first proposed that environmental risk could be integrated within a theory of individual choice and welfare. Freeman found a relationship between pollution and income for US cities, and argued that, as the distribution of environmental quality was theoretically produced by its interaction with income and market forces, improving the distribution of wealth would lead to an improved distribution of environmental quality. Such research, however, did not gain significant momentum until the 1980s when US civil rights activists were concerned that landfills and hazardous industries were invariably sited within predominantly black communities or indigenous peoples' reservations. Dozens of studies, many conducted by the activists themselves, reported that minority populations were exposed to a disproportionate burden of environmental hazards and associated adverse health effects. Such exposure was considered unjust, as exposed minority populations gained a disproportionately small share of the benefits of the polluting industries (see reviews in Bullard, 1990; Lavelle and Coyle, 1992).

Despite the wealth of environmental equity research, class actions brought against US civil authorities on the grounds of unjust planning decisions were largely unsuccessful, due to poor empirical foundations (Bowen, 2002) or an inability to demonstrate intentional discrimination on the part of the developer or responsible authority where inequality was found (Taylor, 1999). Nevertheless, EJ is now an important part of environmental and public health policy assessment in the USA, mandated by a Presidential Executive order (President, 1994). The order requires Federal agencies 'to address EJ as part of their overall mission, and to identify and address disproportionately high adverse human health or environmental impacts of policies, programmes and activities on minority and low income populations'. The US Environmental Protection Agency, for example, now addresses EJ in planning and decision-making, defining 'fair treatment' as that where no group of people bears a disproportionate share of the environmental and adverse health impact of development (Wilkinson, 1998).

In neither the UK nor Europe more widely is there an EJ movement to compare with that of America. However, European Community legislation driven by the Aarhus convention will ensure that EJ issues are taken more seriously than ever before. Directives on public access to environmental information and public participation in environmental decision-making are well advanced in the EU legislative process. A third Aarhus goal, access to justice in environmental matters, aims to give the public access to judicial and independent procedures to challenge acts or omissions by public authorities and private persons which contravene environmental laws. This area is under formal discussion to clarify the legal standing of groups who might wish to bring a challenge (UNECE, 2002).

The UK is one country where an EJ discourse is emerging. Here, environmental issues once firmly allied to a 'green' agenda are increasingly addressed in the political process via concerns for equity and justice. Statements such as – 'Environmental problems are serious and impact most heavily on the most vulnerable members of society, the old, the very young and the poor' (introduction to Boardman *et al.*, 1999), made by the Environment Minister – are typical concerns expressed by senior politicians from most political parties (see quotes in Stephens *et al.*, 2001; McConnell, 2002) and addressed via national and devolved regional policy on environment and social justice (Cabinet Office, 2002; EA, 2002; SDC, 2002).

In addition to the timing of the developments, there are a number of clear differences between the EJ discourse in the UK and US. First, whilst EJ is a core concern of UK advocacy groups such as the Black Environment Network, the greatest equity concerns relate to poverty. There is little evidence of environmental inequality with respect to race (Walker *et al.*, 2000; Mitchell and Walker, 2003) and where ethnic communities do bear a greater environmental burden, this is probably a result of an association between poverty and ethnicity, rather than any racial bias in the planning system, although this remains to be proven. Thus the UK discourse has a less prominent civil rights element (Agyeman, 2003; Agyeman *et al.*, 2003). Secondly, UK EJ advocates seek to address a broader range of environmental issues than just hazardous facilities. These include physical needs (clean air and water, food, shelter, warmth); economic needs (transport infrastructure, access to work and services); and aesthetic, mental and spiritual needs (quiet, access to the countryside) (Stephens *et al.*, 2001). We note, however, that US EJ concerns are beginning to address EJ implications in other development areas, including transport systems and urban sprawl (FHA, 2000; Liu, 2001).

A further notable difference relates to public advocacy for EJ, which may lead to different institutional responses to environmental inequality. In the US the EJ issue grew out of the mutual interests of the civil rights and environmental movements. In contrast, environmental equity issues in the UK have emerged largely through critical analysis and integration of policy agendas and national-level NGO advocacy, rather than through grassroots campaigning (although initiatives such as Friends of the Earth's 'Pollution Injustice' campaign have been influential and there is a more substantial profile of local-level activism in Scotland). The US also has greater public access to environmental information, a more litigious culture, and a very much greater proportion of the population are non-white. Such differences indicate that countries may differ in their approach to EJ issues, dependent upon their national, environmental, cultural and institutional contexts. Nevertheless, the

US experience can usefully inform research and policy development elsewhere, including with respect to the methodological issues that are the focus of this chapter.

ENVIRONMENTAL JUSTICE ANALYSIS

The EJ movement in the US gained major impetus in the early 1980s following the now celebrated cases of Warren County, N. Carolina, and Love Canal, New York, where black and low-income residents fought against toxic waste disposal in their communities. Since then, a substantial body of research has emerged assessing the relationships between environmental hazard and socio-demographic characteristics (see reviews in Bowen, 2002; Agyeman *et al.*, 2003). Oft-cited studies include that of the US General Accounting Office (GAO, 1983) that found hazardous waste facilities in the EPA study region were disproportionately located in black communities; the United Church of Christ Commission for Racial Justice study (UCC, 1987), the first national study to correlate waste facility siting and race; and Anderton *et al.* (1994), a similar study to that of the UCC, but which used different methods and concluded that evidence for environmental inequity was weaker than previously suggested.

Environmental Justice concerns are more recent in the UK, hence the body of supporting empirical research is much smaller than that of the US. As part of the first major UK study of environmental equity conducted by the Environment Agency (EA), Mitchell and Walker (2003) reviewed this research, addressing a broad range of environmental issues. They found that, despite the broader expressions of concern, most explicit EJ research is pollution-oriented, addressing similar issues to those investigated in the USA: hazardous facilities and air pollution. Friends of the Earth's 'Pollution Injustice' campaign, for example, found that 662 of the UK's largest factories are located in areas with an annual average household income of less than £15,000, with only 6 factories in areas where average annual incomes were greater than £30,000, a very different distribution to that which would be expected if factories were randomly distributed (FoE, 2000). They also found that 82 per cent of carcinogen emissions from Part A processes (large facilities regulated by the EA) occurred in the most deprived 20 per cent of wards (FoE, 2001). Other studies investigating the social distribution of environmental risk from hazardous facilities and landfill sites include those of Walker *et al.* (2000, 2003), Elliott *et al.* (2001), EA (2002) and Cambridge Econometrics (2003).

Within the UK, air quality has been the subject of more environmental equity research than any other environmental issue, with at least a dozen studies conducted since 1998. These studies (see Mitchell and Dorling, 2003; Walker *et al.*, 2003) have addressed a range of pollutants, study area (country to city), spatial unit, social characteristics (deprivation, ethnicity, age) and analytical method. They therefore represent a small, heterogeneous body of research from which no consistent conclusion is drawn, although there is an indication that more minority communities, particularly the poor, are located in areas of worst air quality. The most recent studies have investigated the social distribution of air quality addressing the whole nation, but using a ward-level analysis (EA, 2002; Mitchell and Dorling, 2003; Mitchell and Walker, 2003). These studies reveal that air quality is worse than average in more deprived areas, but that there is no simple linear relationship between deprivation and air quality, with the affluent also bearing an above-average burden of poor air quality.

Mitchell and Dorling (2003) went on to include vehicle emission in their equity analysis. They found no relationship between emission and deprivation, as affluent wards have high rates of car ownership and use, but vehicles are newer and hence less polluting than those used by residents of more deprived wards. This is significant from a polluter-pays perspective, suggesting that statements like 'traffic pollution is mainly caused by the better off, but the poor feel its effects' (Higman, 1999) require careful scrutiny. They did, however, find evidence of environmental inequality when deprivation, air quality and emission were considered collectively. A series of wards were identified that were amongst the poorest in Britain, and where total vehicle NO_x emissions were very low, but where levels of NO_2 were amongst the highest observed. This is interpreted as unjust as the residents contribute little to the pollution problem, but can do little about it (i.e. move home).

National, small area analyses clearly overcome some of the problems experienced in US research, such as representative sampling and selection of comparison areas. This approach was adopted for the UK EA study (Mitchell and Walker, 2003), addressing IPC sites (large hazardous facilities regulated by the EA), air quality and flood hazard. Nevertheless, UK EJ research is still at an early stage, and so has not been subject to critical appraisal. In contrast, US EJ research has been more systematically reviewed (Liu, 2001; Bowen, 2002; Bowen and Wells, 2002) with reviewers concluding that the evidence for environmental injustice in the USA is less substantive than often thought, largely due to the limited quality of the empirical analyses. Bowen and Wells (2002) are particularly critical describing a 'rhetoric–reality gap' in which the many claims for environmental injustice, of which some have significantly influenced national policy, have not been adequately supported by evidence of inequality drawn from thorough, systematic research. Whilst others are less damning (e.g. Brown, 1995; Szasz and Meuser, 1997), it is clear that many of the US equity studies, particularly those early studies undertaken by policy advocates, are not sufficiently rigorous to support the conclusion drawn from them.

Therefore, in the rest of this chapter, we describe seven common methodological issues of environmental equity analysis as an aid to the more robust study of environmental justice.

SEVEN METHODOLOGICAL ISSUES IN ENVIRONMENTAL JUSTICE EVALUATION

Selection of study population

Environmental equity studies must identify a social or demographic group of concern, the people amongst who the distribution of environmental risk or benefit is measured. The selection of this group is largely a political one, based upon concerns expressed at national level, or by communities in the study area. In the USA, the 1994 Presidential Order required that state and federal agencies conducting environmental assessments address equity impacts with respect to 'minority and low income communities'. Minority and low income are not defined by the order, hence the US EPA interpret minority based on the Civil Rights Act. This prohibits discrimination against people on the grounds of race, colour, national origin, sex, age or disability. In practice most US equity studies address ethnicity and income, although it has been argued (Greenberg, 1993) that a wider range of socio-demographic variables should be addressed. Disability, for example, might be particularly relevant when considering access to green space, whilst age may be important when considering hazards whose effects are more pronounced in children (e.g. neurotoxic pollutants). Mitchell and Dorling (2003), for example, showed that very young children in Britain bear a disproportionately high burden of NO_2 pollution. This has implications for public health policy, as children are generally more susceptible to respiratory irritants than adults.

In the UK, there has been little debate over which demographic characteristic should be included in environmental equity assessment, and most studies have addressed the social distribution of environmental hazard with respect to deprivation. The focus on deprivation arises as interest in environmental equity assessment has developed in parallel with the government's social exclusion agenda, which focuses upon deprivation, and because there is relatively little grassroots pressure for assessments addressing other socio-demographic characteristics. This is in contrast to the USA where environmental equity analyses were first conducted at grassroots level by groups concerned about the disproportionate environmental burdens on predominantly coloured communities. UK studies addressing ethnicity have been made, but have not been motivated by grassroots concerns, or produced strong evidence for environmental inequality – partly as ethnic communities tend also to be more socially deprived and spatial segregation by ethnicity is less marked than in the US. Thus selection of the study population should reflect expressions of concern and the possibility of differential susceptibility to the environmental threat of under-study.

Impact assessment

Environmental equity studies assess a variety of impacts (on health, safety, amenity and economic welfare). With hazards, these are often addressed in an assessment chain comprising: location of hazard; emission; concentration of pollutant in environmental media; exposure; received dose; and effect on human or environmental systems. Ideally, equity studies address the later stages of the impact chain, with estimates of exposure or health impact used as the basis of assessment. However, most equity analyses address the start of the chain, implicitly assuming that greater proximity to a hazard is associated with higher exposure or health impact. Proximity studies are nevertheless valuable in their own right, particularly as a scoping tool followed by more detailed local analysis (e.g. Harner et al., 2002), or for identification of non-health equity impacts, such as the social distribution of compliance with environmental legislation, the resource investment of regulatory bodies or economic impact on property values. Their application is also simpler and more economical.

Where health is the principal equity concern, more sophisticated approaches addressing the later stages of the assessment chain are clearly desirable. Such equity studies (e.g. Bowen et al., 1995; Bolin et al., 2000; Baden and Coursey, 2002) apply simulation models of environmental and demographic processes, and do not make the implicit assumptions of proximity studies (facilities are equally noxious, emitting equal quantity of pollutants with equal toxicity, at a uniform rate over a uniform plane). Consequently, modelling provides an alternative to proximity analysis that gives increasingly better estimates of health risk and health impact. However, whilst models are used in developing public health standards (e.g. the total human exposure studies of Ott et al. (1988) and Lurmann et al. (1989)), the range of pollutants addressed is very limited, uncertainty in estimates increases along the assessment chain, and models tend to be applied to determine how large a risk is, with little or no attention given to its spatial or social distribution. In addition, models are also demanding in terms of data, time, knowledge and cost, to apply. Thus when designing environmental equity studies, it is necessary to match the adopted approach to the available resources and programme objectives. Table 22.1 details the strengths and weaknesses of different assessment techniques applicable to the environmental equity assessment chain.

Table 22.1 Features of equity assessment approaches

Approach	Strengths	Weaknesses
	Environmental risk	
Proximity analysis	• Easiest to apply • Economical • Able to capture non-health impacts	• Poorest approximation to actual health risk
Emission monitoring or modelling	• Easy to apply • Economical • Widely available data often supportive of longitudinal analysis	• Very poor approximation to health impact
Concentration monitoring or modelling	• Good spatial coverage • May have publicly agreed standards to address	• Poor substitute for human exposure and health impact • Lack of data
Concentration monitoring or modelling of micro-scale environments	• Good estimates of exposure and health risk	• Establishment of time-activity patterns of target populations difficult and costly
Internal dose assessment using personal monitors or biological markers	• Best estimate of health risk	• Difficult and costly • Problems of small samples
Epidemiological assessment of received dose	• Most accurate measure of health risk	• Difficult and costly • Limited knowledge of dose–response
	Economic impact	
Contingent valuation	• Simple to implement and interpret	• Biases and methodological problems
Hedonic pricing	• Summarises multiple using single value	• Some impacts neglected due to imperfect information

Source: Developed from Liu, 2001

Note that most environmental equity studies analyse the social distribution of individual environmental hazards. That is, no account is taken of possible cumulative impacts from multiple hazards in the same place. Those few studies that have attempted an analysis of multiple hazards (Mitchell and Walker, 2003) or cumulative burden of risk (Bolin *et al.*, 2002) have found that 'peaks' of accumulated inequity emerge. This suggests that multi-hazard analysis may be warranted if policy responses to environmental inequality have a spatially targeted component.

Data quality

Environmental equity studies are often constrained by the available data that are usually collected for purposes other than equity analysis (Krieg, 1998). For example, environmental equity assessments often use data on hazardous facilities recorded in national databases maintained for regulatory purposes (e.g. US waste transfer, storage and disposal facilities (TSDF) database) or spill and emergency response planning (e.g. US Toxic Release Inventory, UK Chemical Release Inventory). Such data presents difficulties to environmental equity analysis (Box 22.1) and indicate that environmental databases used in equity studies usually act only as a surrogate, and arguably a weak one, for risk or health impact. Clearly the best available data should be used (e.g. data on health impact would be preferred to hazard proximity) but the key objective is to be fully aware of the limitations and uncertainties of data that are used.

BOX 22.1

Data constraints in environmental equity analysis

Sampling. There is incomplete coverage of facilities handling a chemical (e.g. US TRI exempts SMEs such as dry cleaners, small waste handling or engineering firms) that cumulatively may emit more than a single large facility on a register.

Quantification of emissions. Emissions are not usually monitored, but are estimated using non-standardised assessment techniques.

Verification of emissions. No independent verification is made of self-reported emissions; reports may be partial (by site, type of chemical, etc.) or erroneous.

Exposure. Data usually addresses the quantity of emission, and is unable to indicate the degree of exposure for particular populations from the emission.

Temporal distribution. Emission estimates are usually annual aggregates, with no data on the temporal distribution of releases. 'Acute' releases could have much more significant health impact than the same amount released evenly over a year.

Health impact. Little is known about the health impacts of many chemicals addressed by release inventories, especially in specified minority populations that may be more or less susceptible than average.

Spatial analysis

Results of environmental equity analyses are sensitive to the spatial design of the study. Liu (2001), for example, describes three studies in which the social distribution of hazardous facilities in the US was found to vary with the spatial scale of analysis. This scale dependency, known as the modifiable area unit problem (Openshaw and Taylor, 1981), is well known to geographers, and is one of several spatial analysis issues that should be recognised by the environmental equity analyst. However, so long as these issues and the limitations they present are recognised, even the simplest proximity analysis can provide meaningful information for policy-makers (Maantay, 2002).

Amongst the most common spatial problems in equity analysis are the ecological and individual fallacies. The ecological fallacy occurs when results from analysis of large spatial units (counties, districts) are not true for smaller units (census wards, postcode units), but are assumed to be so. For example, the landmark United Church of Christ study (UCC, 1987) concluded from a zip code analysis that TSDF sites were disproportionately sited in minority and low-income communities, whilst Anderton et al. (1994), repeating the study for the smaller census tract, found no such association. The ecological fallacy likely explains why results of McLeod et al.'s (2000) UK local authority district air quality analysis conflict with similar national studies addressing the much smaller census ward.

The individual fallacy is the opposite of the ecological fallacy. Here, the error is 'inappropriate extrapolation', with results from one study used to infer patterns of inequity for other places, times or situations. The individual fallacy can occur when results from a case study are used to draw conclusions about inequalities for other areas or more aggregate scales. It conclusions do not hold true for these areas or scales (this is rarely tested), then measures to tackle inequality are not based on sound evidence, and may be seriously flawed. Thus in environmental equity studies the spatial unit of analysis should reflect the distribution of environmental risk as closely as possible. Failure to achieve this may lead to apparently statistically significant results that are meaningless as a basis for further decision-making.

A common spatial problem in proximity studies is the boundary problem. This occurs where the surrogate for exposure or health impact is the presence of a noxious facility or land use within a geographical unit such as a census ward. Clearly, households could be located very close to a noxious facility, say just across the street, but are located in a neighbouring geographical unit, and hence not linked to that facility in the equity analysis. One US study (GAO, 1995) identified the exact location of 295 major landfills, and found that 35 were within one mile of at least one other county, and 101 within 3 miles of at least one other county, illustrating a potential problem of a national analysis that address counties. Conversely, house-holds could be located in the same geographical unit as the noxious facility, but on the opposite side, perhaps many miles away, where they are unaffected, yet assumed to be exposed in the analysis. The boundary problem becomes less of an issue at finer geographical scales, and illustrates that proximity analysis is a poor surrogate for exposure.

Equity analyses uses social or demographic data that is routinely available for administrative or census units. The irregular shape and size of these units introduces a further source of error when proximity is used as a surrogate for exposure. This is illustrated in Figure 22.1, where noxious facilities have a buffer zone of uniform distance surrounding them, and affected zones are associated with the facility according to different rules. Ideally the buffer zone radius relates to the extent of the facility impact, but in practice this is rarely known, and buffer distance is set arbitrarily. It is also assumed that facilities are adequately represented by a point, whilst in reality some (e.g. a large landfill) are better represented as an area.

With polygon containment (Figure 22.1a) census units with all or part of their area within the buffer zone are associated with the facility. This can lead to an over-estimate of affected population, hence a preferred method is centroid containment (Figure 22.1b) where populations are only associated with the facility if the census unit centroids are 'captured' by the buffer zone. A further refinement is buffer containment (Figure 22.1c) where demographic data is only included for those parts of the census unit within the buffer zone. This gives a better approximation of exposure but relies on aggregation of within unit demographic data (not always available), or areal interpolation. The latter applies an area weight to the census units, and assumes a homogeneously distributed population within them (rarely the case). Maantay (2002) illustrates the effect of zone definition in an equity assessment of waste facility siting in the Bronx, New York (Figure 22.2). Polygon containment is considered least effective, as many facilities are on tract boundaries and not included in the analysis. Buffer containment is assumed to be more reliable, but note that distance remains a poor surrogate for exposure.

Understanding how inequalities arise (see the section on 'Understanding causality') is important in the assessment of environmental injustice, and is assisted by longitudinal studies that compare past and present social distributions of envi-ronmental hazard. A particular difficulty faced by longitudinal analysis is that of boundary stability, where the spatial units change over time, making comparison difficult. Many census units, for example, are designed to contain roughly equivalent numbers of people, and hence their boundaries are periodically revised to reflect changes in population density. A related problem is that of data stability, where variables used in longitudinal analysis are inconsistently described over the time

(a)

(b)

(c)

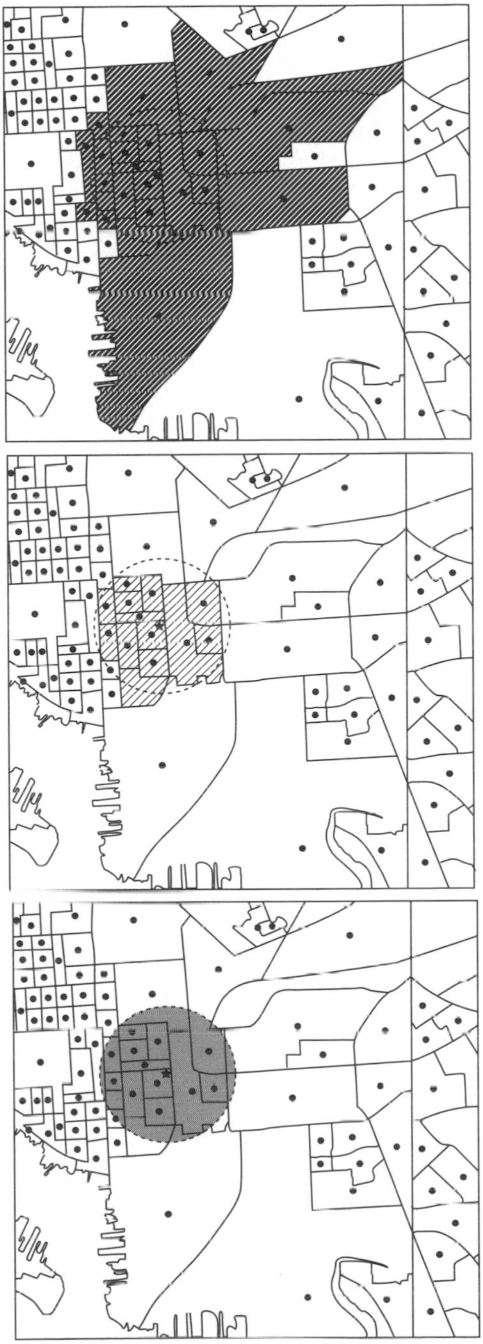

Figure 22.1 Defining units of analysis through buffering. (a) Polygon containment, (b) centroid containment and (c) buffer containment (Liu, 2001)

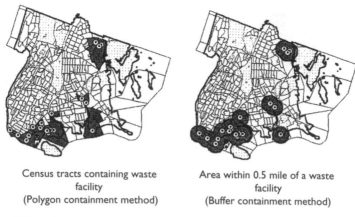

Census tracts containing waste
facility
(Polygon containment method)

Area within 0.5 mile of a waste
facility
(Buffer containment method)

Geographic method	Minority Population (%)	Mean Household Income ($/yr)
Polygon containment	71	35,400
Buffer containment	87	26,200
All county (reference)	76	29,200

Figure 22.2 Comparison of polygon containment and buffer containment (0.5 mile buffer) for hazard waste facilities in Bronx County, New York (Maantay, 2002)

series under investigation (e.g. UK government preferred measures of deprivation which have undergone several revisions).

A final spatial issue concerns the use of comparison areas. Environmental equity studies often assess the social distribution of a hazard for one area, say an urban district, and compare that distribution to a similar distribution for another area, say the city or city region. A high occurrence of hazard in the study area relative to the comparison area is then used to conclude that environmental inequity exists. However, if the study and comparison areas are not selected carefully, the conclusion may simply reflect differences in confounding factors between study and comparison areas. Significant differences in patterns of industrial location occur between rural and urban areas, for example, which are not a product of injustice perpetrated against a minority group, but the product of wider economic processes (see below). Thus poorly designed studies may conclude that environmental inequities occur, when in reality differences in the distribution of confounding factors between urban and rural areas have been highlighted (Bowen and Wells,

2002). National analyses using small spatial units (e.g. Mitchell and Dorling, 2003; Mitchell and Walker, 2003) are an effective means of eliminating the comparison area problem (and the individual fallacy), although these are naturally more resource-intensive.

There are then a series of spatial analysis issues that the environmental equity analyst must address. There is, for example, no ideal spatial unit, and impact zones vary according to the hazard source and characteristics of the receptor (contrast health, psychological and economic impact zones for example). There are no prescriptive solutions for addressing such problems (although GIS facilitates more sophisticated analysis than ever before), hence it is up to the analyst to ensure that spatial analysis issues are recognised in the study design.

Statistical methods

All environmental equity analyses must establish the degree of association between the environmental and social variables. This is sometimes done by visual comparison of mapped social and environmental distributions, but a confident assessment requires statistical analysis, for which a variety of procedures are applicable (Table 22.2). Appropriate use of these statistics is important as equity assessments are sensitive to the test applied (Greenberg, 1993).

A common first task is to characterise differences between populations. With categorical data, such as the presence or absence of a facility, population characteristics can be summarised using univariate statistics, and inferential statistics applied (if sample data is used) to assess the significance of any differences. With non-categorical data, differences can be assessed visually using histograms, and statistically using Pearson correlation (if underlying assumptions are met), or less powerful non-parametric tests. Note that because of possible confounding variables, association identified using bivariate statistics may be false. Studies often fail to account for the correlation between ethnicity and income for example, and wrongly conclude that environmental inequality occurs with respect to race, rather than poverty. Thus once there is evidence to indicate that environmental inequality occurs, multivariate analysis is desirable to control for the effects of other variables and to determine their relative importance in explaining the distribution of environmental risk.

Of the multivariate techniques used in environmental equity analysis (Table 22.2) linear regression is by far the most popular (and logit or probit models for discrete dependent data). In practice, however, few studies adequately report on diagnostic tests (non-linearity, multi-collinearity, heteroskedasticity, etc.), hence their usefulness in supporting development of appropriate policy is questionable (Bowen, 2002). Finally we find that the Gini Coefficient, routinely used

Table 22.2 Statistics used in environmental equity analysis

Statistic	Comments
Univariate statistics Central tendency measures (mean, median, mode)	• Used to provide description of distributions • The underlying probability distribution should be considered – the mean is very sensitive to extreme values, whilst there are dangers in using median values (e.g. when aggregating zones) • Data subject to sampling and non-sampling errors
Inferential statistics z-test, t-test, Rank tests	• Bivariate inferences to evaluate significance of relationships between two variables • Test must consider data distribution (e.g. t- and z-tests require normality, Wilcoxon does not, but is a less powerful test)
Correlation and regression Pearson, Spearman and Kendall correlation, linear regression, multiple regression	• Most popular tests in environmental equity literature • Stronger correlation tests have stricter underlying assumptions • Regression has five strong assumptions that are rarely tested for in equity studies rendering results unreliable (Bowen, 2002) • Regression used to infer causality in equity studies often suffers from model mispecification (e.g. relevant variables not included, linear regression used to address non-linear relationships (e.g. exposure and distance)
Probability and discrete choice Logit, Probit, Poisson	• Common to equity studies addressing facilities (e.g. where geographical units have discrete data, such as presence or absence of a hazardous facility) • Models determine probability of discrete event occurring based on random utility theory
Spatial statistics Spatial association, geostatistics, pattern analysis	• Based on theory that points are more alike when they are close together, thus it is possible to infer values for a point in space from its neighbours • Difficulties in deciding what constitutes a neighbour • Rarely used to date in environmental equity studies

Source: Developed from Liu, 2001

by economists to describe income distributions, proves to be a useful means of depicting and comparing the social distribution of different environmental variables (Mitchell and Walker, 2003). Note, however, that no level of statistical significance can be attached.

UNDERSTANDING CAUSALITY

When developing responses to environmental inequality, an understanding of how the inequality has arisen is helpful in judging how 'unfair' the inequality is and in ensuring that corrective measures are appropriate and efficient. The complexity of processes involved makes demonstration of cause and effect difficult, hence three criteria (Lazarsfeld, 1959) should be met: (i) demonstrate co-variation (variables are empirically correlated); (ii) demonstrate relationships are not spurious (correlation between variables cannot be explained away by a third variable); and (iii) establish time order of occurrences (cause precedes effect).

Most environmental equity studies are cross sectional, investigating associations at one point in time by addressing the first two criteria. Temporal changes in environmental equity are addressed in a few site-based longitudinal studies (e.g. Been and Gupta, 1996; Baden and Coursey, 2002), that seek to determine which came first, the environmental hazard or the minority community. If the minority community arrived after the siting of, say a noxious facility, then logically, malicious intent in siting decisions is not possible, and the observed inequality has arisen in another way. Some studies of this type have concluded that policy to reduce environmental inequality should focus not on siting decision but housing or employment policy (Been, 1994; Been and Gupta, 1996).

Baden and Coursey (2002) provide a simple list of scenarios (Table 22.3) that introduce a temporal dimension to the discovery of risk, and the relative timing of housing and risk at a site. Of the scenarios presented, it is argued that 4 and 6 suggest discriminatory intent, 5 is the least unjust and that for 1–3 any charge of discriminatory siting practice is tenuous. These are plausible (if sometimes controversial) alternatives to discrimination, for the development of environmental inequality, but have yet to be tested thoroughly. Table 22.4 describes the main theories for the evolution of site-based environmental inequalities, addressing how

Table 22.3 Scenarios for the creation of environmental inequity

Scenario	Event 1	Event 2	Event 3	Description
1	Siting	Danger	People	People move into an area known to be dangerous
2	Siting	People	Danger	People move into an area which is later determined to be dangerous
3	Danger	Siting	People	A dangerous facility is sited then people move into the area
4	Danger	People	Siting	People live in an area then a facility known to be dangerous is sited near them
5	People	Siting	Danger	A facility assumed safe is sited where people live and is later found to be dangerous
6	People	Danger	Siting	A dangerous facility is sited in a community

Source: Baden and Coursey, 2002

Table 22.4 Geographical and sociological theories for environmental inequality

Theory	Characteristics
'Economic' theory	• Owners of risky facilities site them where collective action against them, or compensation from damages, is likely to be minimised.
Location theory	• Households move to areas that meet a 'package of needs' (Tiebout model). The affluent place a higher value on environmental quality, hence the poor tend to occupy areas of lower environmental quality. When environmental decline occurs, the affluent move away and are replaced by the less affluent who find the area better meets their package of needs than their previous location • Industry locates where land, labour and transport costs are minimised. Low income areas tend to have cheaper land and provide the appropriate labour force, hence are more likely to house hazardous facilities
Risk theory	People perceive risk in different ways depending upon personal and social group characteristics: • Those that value the environment less than average perceive environmental risk as less than average, so will locate closer to the risk than average • Different cultural groups perceive risk in different ways • An individual's response to risk is mediated by other attributes which include their social group values
Neighbourhood change	Neighbourhoods change via processes which may put minority groups closer to hazards: • Invasion succession: Minorities arrive in a neighbourhood, survive, and make it more attractive for other minorities to move in. Social-spatial transition spills over into area with hazardous facilities • Neighbourhoods have a life cycle in which ageing and decline occurs naturally, presenting more housing opportunities for people of lower socio-economic status • Neighbourhood conditions act as a pull factor for some and a push factor for others. An industrial facility may push affluent people away, but attract others to the area for its better housing and employment • Large institutions (e.g. universities) influence the local economy (e.g. providing benefits that offset the risk due to local undesirable facilities).

Table 22.4 (Continued)

Theory	Characteristics
Planning and land use change	Land use planning protects high quality environments by directing threats to environmental quality towards areas that are already degraded. Risks and environmental 'bads' are agglomerated and via the housing market, people with resources to live in higher quality protected environments do so. Developers select within planning land parcel allocations which areas are to be developed for high quality housing and lower quality 'social' housing, directing lower quality developments into less attractive environments.

Source: Developed from Liu (2001)

industry and housing locate, how different people perceive risk, how planning shapes land use and how neighbourhoods evolve over time.

Bowen and Wells (2002) note that whilst the complexity of these processes makes causality difficult to demonstrate, understanding causality remains a valid goal, and that in the meantime studies should have an 'intellectual modesty and healthy scepticism' about causality. Some authors consider demonstration of discriminatory intent in siting processes to be less important, or that it should be examined not through inference from temporal statistical associations, but by the direct examination of processes of decision-making (Weinberg, 1998). Some authors (Hurley, 1995; Pulido *et al.*, 1996) adopt a strongly historical and contextual approach to understanding the development of patterns of inequity through the detailed description of patterns of community and industrial evolution.

Any judgement of inequity cannot just be concerned with proving or disproving discriminatory intent in siting (Williams, 1999). Maantay (2002), for example, argues that environmental inequity arising from land and housing market processes is equally unjust as minority communities are often restricted in where they can locate. Walker *et al.* (1998) also point out that those people reliant on council or social housing are often allocated accommodation rather than exercising the personal choices assumed in locational theory. Jerrett *et al.* (1997) argue that where there are lower levels of education, risks to health may be less well understood and so outwardly more 'tolerated', but that protecting people from making decisions that may harm themselves is an established rationale for public health interventions. This amply demonstrates that the assessment of environmental inequality includes ethical and political as well as technical considerations (see the next section).

WHAT IS 'FAIR'?

Having established that a significant environmental inequality exists, it is appropriate to ask to what extent this inequality is unfair, and what should be done about it? There are no technical answers to this question, rather it is a matter for debate between policy-makers, analysts and the affected community. We have seen, for example, that some believe it essential to understand how inequalities arise, whilst others are concerned with reducing inequality to a more acceptable level, regardless of how it has arisen. This is evidenced by practice in USA, where despite Federal legislation on environmental equity, guidance on valuing inequalities is limited: 'the analyst need(s) to exercise informed judgement as to what constitutes disproportionate as well as high and adverse (effects)' (EPA, 1998). The guidance suggests that this judgement be informed by quantitative comparative analysis, including that of alternative options to the development or policy under proposal.

Developing appropriate responses to environmental inequality should also consider justice theory, which provides guidance on how benefits can be distributed to make a more equitable society (e.g. benefits can be distributed according to merit or input, need, or entitlement). These ideas are formalised in theories of utilitarianism (maximise net benefit to society), egalitarianism (distribute benefits equally to all), contractarianism (improve conditions of least well off) and libertarianism (maximise freedom of choice and action). Thus depending upon the justice theory applied, a policy or development may be seen to be more or less just (Beatley, 1984; Been, 1993). If the goal is to improve the condition of the most disadvantaged, for example, then measures that deliver higher net benefit may be inappropriate. LT et al. (1998) show that, when assessing the environmental equity of land use and transport planning options, application of different justice theories leads to selection of different options. Note that allocating equal shares of a benefit to everyone may increase inequality if inequality already exists (e.g. a one per cent cut in income tax gives most money to the wealthy).

Clearly it is important to pursue sound science in evaluating the status of environmental inequality. However, the very best technical assessment only provides an input to subsequent evaluation in which wider philosophical issues are addressed. Bowen and Wells (2002) characterise this as a distinction between *means* (data gathering, modelling, etc.) and *ends*, the latter including some 'explicit and meaningful normative statements regarding fair treatment and meaningful involvement of all people... in the development, implementation and enforcement of environmental laws'.

CONCLUSION

This chapter began by noting that the distribution of the costs and benefits of development is a central concern of both the sustainable development and environmental justice movements. We have been careful, however, not to imply that social justice and sustainable development are mutually compatible for, as Dobson (2003) argues, this has yet to be firmly tested in the 'crucible of empirical practice'. By first deconstructing the concepts of sustainable development (e.g. what is to be sustained, for whom, for how long?) and social justice (e.g. what is a benefit or burden, what is a fair distribution, who/what belongs in the community of justice, is it the distribution process or its outcome that is important?), Dobson is able to construct a series of conceptions of environmental justice (e.g. what is a fair distribution of, say, critical natural capital) that unpacks the social justice – sustainable development nexus. In doing so, he provides a basis upon which the common assertion that environmental justice promotes sustainable development can be tested.

Dobson notes, however, that empirical analysis of these conceptions of environmental justice is lacking, and hence it is unknown to what extent objectives for social justice and sustainable development are compatible. Clearly we can identify examples where they are compatible (e.g. waste minimisation, phasing out of persistent toxic materials), and where they conflict (e.g. conserving water supplies through compulsory metering without recognising need of low-income households), but the evidence base for assessing the overall contribution of social justice measures to sustainable development is currently inadequate. The evidence that we do have mostly derives from studies that address a narrow range of Dobson's conceptions of EJ – the social distribution of risk from hazardous facilities, and as Bowen (2002) concludes, only tentative conclusions can be drawn from this research due to a lack of empirical rigour.

A clear lesson of the US experience is then the need for environmental assessment to include more robust empirical analysis of the social distribution of environmental costs and benefits. Studies must be precise about what is being analysed, match method to objectives, and express uncertainties. In doing so, sound evidence can be developed to guide policy-makers and communities faced with environmental justice concerns. This is a fundamental objective in itself, but, as we have seen, there is a larger goal to consider too – developing an understanding of how promoting social justice contributes to environmentally sustainable development. Ensuring that studies are conducted in an empirically robust manner is clearly critical for both the EJ and sustainable development movements, hence this chapter has described a number of key methodological issues that require consideration.

REFERENCES

Adebowale, M., Church, C., Kairie, B.N., Vasylkivsky, B. and Panina, Y. (2001), *Environment and Human Rights: A New Approach to Sustainable Development*. International Institute for Environment and Development, London, 7pp.

Agyeman, J. (2003), 'Constructing environmental injustice: transatlantic tales', *Environmental Politics*, 11(3): 31–53.

Agyeman, J., Bullard, R. and Evans, B. (2003), *Just Sustainabilities: Development in an Unequal World*, Earthscan, London.

Anderton, D.L., Anderson, A.B., Oakes, J.M. and Fraser, M.R. (1994), 'Environmental equity: the demographics of dumping', *Demography*, 31(2): 229–248.

Baden, B.M. and Coursey, L. (2002), 'The locality of waste sites within the city of Chicago: a demographic, social and economic analysis', *Resource and Energy Economics*, 24: 53–93.

Beatley, T. (1984), 'Applying moral principles to growth management', *Journal of the American Planning Association*, 504: 459–469.

Been, V. (1993), 'What's fairness got to do with it? Environmental justice and siting of locally undesirable land uses'. *Cornell Law Review*, 78 (September): 1001–1085.

Been, V. (1994), 'Locally undesirable land uses in minority neighbourhoods: disproportionate siting or market dynamics?' *Yale Law Review*, 103(6): 1383–1422.

Been, V. and Gupta, F. (1996), 'Coming to the nuisance or going to the barrios? A longitudinal analysis of environmental justice claims', *Ecology Law Quarterly*, 241: 1–35.

Boardman, B., Bullock, S. and McLaren, D. (1999), *Equity and the Environment,* Catalyst Trust, London.

Bolin, D., Nelson, A., Hackett, E.J., Pijwaka, K.D., Smith, S.C., Sicotte, D., Sadalla, E.K., Matranga, E. and O'Donell, M. (2000), 'Environmental equity in a sunbelt city: the spatial distribution of toxic hazards in Phoenix, Arizona', *Environmental Hazards*, 2: 11–24.

Bolin, D., Matranga, E., Hackett, E.J., Sadalla, E.K., Pijwaka, D., Brewer, D. and Sicotte, D. (2002), 'The ecology of technological risk in a Sunbelt city', *Environment and Planning A*, 24: 317–339.

Bowen, W. (2002), 'An analytical review of environmental justice research: what do we really know?' *Environmental Management*, 29(1): 3–15.

Bowen, W.M. and Wells, M.V. (2002), 'The politics and reality of environmental justice research: a history and considerations for public administrators and policy makers', *Public Administration Review*, 62(6): 688–698.

Bowen, W.M., Salling, M.J., Haynes, K.E. and Cyran, E. (1995), 'Towards Environmental Justice: Spatial Equity in Ohio and Cleveland', *Annals of the Association of American Geographers*, 85(4): 641–663.

Brown, P. (1995), 'Race, class and environmental health: a review and systemisation of the literature', *Environmental Research*, 69: 15–30.

Bullard, R. (1990), *Dumping on Dixie: race, class and environmental quality*, Westview Press, Boulder, Colorado.

Cabinet Office (2002), *Making the connections: Transport and social exclusion*. Interim findings from the Social Exclusion Unit, 68pp.

Cambridge Econometrics, EFTEC and WRc (2003), *The disamenity costs of landfill*, Department of the Environment and Rural Affairs, HMSO.

Cutter, S. (1995), 'Race, class and environmental justice', *Progress in Human Geography*, 19(1): 111–122.

Dobson, A. (2003), Social Justice and Environmental Sustainability: Ne'er the Twain Shall Meet?' in Agyeman, J., Bullard, R. and Evans, B. (eds) Just Sustainabilities: Development in an Unequal World, Earthscan, London, pp. 83–95.

EA (2002), The Urban and Environment in England and Wales: A Detailed Assessment, The Environment Agency.

Elliott, P., Morris, S., Briggs, D., de Hoogh, C., Hurt, C., Jensen, T.K., Maitland, I., Lewin, A., Richardson, S., Wakefield, J. and Järup, L. (2001), Birth Outcomes and Selected Cancers in Populations Living Near Landfill Sites, Report to the Department of Health, Imperial College, London.

EPA (1998), Final Guidance for Incorporating Environmental Justice Concerns in EPA's NEPA Compliance Analyses, Environmental Protection Agency, Washington DC.

Faber, D.R. and McCarthy, D. (2003), 'Neo-liberalism, globalisation and the struggle for ecological democracy: linking sustainability and environmental justice' in Agyeman, J., Bullard, R. and Evans, B. (eds) *Just Sustainabilities: Development in an Unequal World*, Earthscan, London.

FHA (2000), *Transportation and Environmental Justice Case Studies*. Federal Highway Administration, FHWA-EP-01-010.

Freeman, A.M. III (1972), 'Distribution of environmental quality' in Kneese, A.V. and Bower, B.T. (eds) Environmental Quality Analysis: Theory and Method in the Social Sciences, John Hopkins Press, Baltimore, pp. 243–278.

Friends of the Earth (2000), *Pollution Injustice*, www.foe.co.uk/pollution-injustice/Friends of the Earth.

Friends of the Earth (2001), *Pollution and Poverty – Breaking the Link*, Friends of the Earth, London.

General Accounting Office (1983), Siting of hazardous waste landfills and their correlation with racial and economic status of surrounding communities. US General Accounting Office, Washington DC.

General Accounting Office (1995), Hazardous and nonhazardous waste: demographics of people near waste facilities, GAO/RCED-95-84. Washington DC.

Greenberg, M.R. (1993), 'Proving environmental inequality in the siting of locally unwanted land uses', *Risk: Issues in Health and Safety*, 43: 235–252.

Harner, J., Warner, K., Pierce, J. and Huber, T. (2002), *Urban Environmental Justice Indices, Professional* Geographer, 543: 318–331.

Higman, R. (1999), *Poor hit hardest by transport pollution*, Press release from Friends of the Earth, 16th June 1999.

Hurley, A. (1995), 'The social biases of environmental change in Gary, Indiana 1945–1980', *Environmental Review*, 12(4): 1–19.

Jerrett, M., Eyles, J., Cole, D. and Reader, S. (1997), 'Environmental equity in Canada: an empirical investigation into the income distribution of pollution in Ontario', *Environment and Planning A*, 29: 1777–1800.

Kreig, E.J. (1998), 'Methodological considerations in the study of toxic waste hazards', *The Social Sciences Journal*, 35(2): 191–201.

Lavelle, M. and Coyle, M. (1992), (eds) 'The racial divide in environmental law: unequal protection', *National Law Journal, Supplement*, 21 September.

Lazarsfeld, P. (1959), 'Problems in methodolgy' in Merton, R.B. (ed.) *Sociology Today*, Basic Book, New York.

Liu, F. (2001), Environmental Justice Analysis: Theories, Methods and Practice, CRC Press, Boca Raton.

LT, ME and P, MECSA, IRPUD and TRT (1998), *SPARTACUS: System for Planning and Research in Towns and Cities for Urban Sustainability*, Final Report, CEC DG XII. Environment and Climate Research Programme – Human Dimensions of Environmental Change.

Lurmann, F.W., Winer, A.M. and Colome, S.D. (1989), Development and application of a new regional human exposure (REHEX) model. Proceedings from the US Environmental Protection Agency and Air & Waste Management Association Conference on Total Exposure Assessment Methodology: New Horizons, Las Vegas, NV, 27–30 November, Air & Waste Management Association, Pittsburgh, PA.

Maantay, J. (2002), 'Mapping environmental injustice: pitfalls and potential of geographic information systems in assessing environmental health and equity', *Environmental Health Perspectives*, 110(2): 161–171.

McConnell, J. (2002), 'Speech on the Scottish executive policy on environment and sustainable development'. Dynamic Earth Conference, Edinburgh, 18 February.

McLaren, D. (2003), 'Environmental space, equity and ecological debt' in: Agyeman, J., Bullard, R. and Evans, B. (eds) *Just Sustainabilities: Development in an Unequal World*, Earthscan, London, pp. 19–37.

McLeod, H., Langford, I.H., Jones, A.P., Stedman, J.R., Day, J.R., Lorenzoni, I. and Bateman, I.J. (2000), 'The relationship between socio-economic indicators and air pollution in England and Wales: implications for environmental justice', *Regional Environmental Change*, 12: 78–85.

Mitchell, G. and Dorling, D. (2003), 'An Environmental Justice Analysis of British Air Quality', *Environment and Planning A*, 35: 909–929.

Mitchell, G. and Walker, G. (2003), *Environmental Quality and Social Deprivation. Phase I: A Review of Research and Analytical Methods*. R&D Project Record 12615 XX, The Environment Agency, Bristol, 107pp.

Openshaw, S. and Taylor, P.J. (1981), 'The modifiable areal unit problem', in Wrigley, N. and Bennett, R.J. (eds) *Quantitative Geography: A British View*, Routledge and Kegan Paul, London, pp. 60–69.

Ott, W., Thomas, J., Mage, D. and Wallace, L. (1988), 'Validation of the simulation of human activity and pollutant exposure (SHAPE) model using paired days from the Denver, Colorado, carbon monoxide field study', *Atmospheric Environment*, 22: 2101–2113.

President (1994), Proclamation: *Federal actions to address environmental justice in minority populations and low income populations*, Executive order 12898/59 C F R 7629. 103rd Congress, Second Session. US Code Congressional and Administrative News, 6: B7–B12.

Pulido, L., Sidawi, S. and Vos, R.O. (1996) 'An archaeology of environmental racism in Los Angeles', *Urban Geography*, 17(5): 419–439.

Stephens, C., Bullock, S., and Scott, A. (2001), *Environmental justice: Rights and mean to a healthy environment for all*, Special Briefing Paper 7, ESRC Global Environmental Change Programme.

Sustainable Development Commission (2002), *Vision for sustainable regeneration. Environment and poverty – breaking the link?* The Sustainable Development Commission, London.

Szasz, A. and Meuser, M. (1997), 'Environmental inequalities: literature review and proposals for new directions in research and theory' *Current Sociology*, 453: 100–120.

Taylor, D. (1999), 'Mobilizing for environmental justice in communities of color: an emerging profile of people of color environmental groups' in Aley, J., Burch, W., Conover, B. and Field, D. (eds) *Ecosystem Management: Adaptive Strategies for Natural Resource Organisations in the 21st Century*, Taylor and Francis, Philadelphia.

UCC (1987), Toxic waste and race in the United States: A national report on the racial and socio-economic characteristics of communities with hazardous waste sites. United Church of Christ Commission for Racial Justice, New York.

United Nations Economic Commission for Europe (1999), Convention on Access to Information, Public Participation in Decision Making and Access to Justice in Environmental Matters UNECE, Geneva.

United Nations Economic Commission for Europe (2002), *Access Justice in Environmental Matters*, Working document UNECE, Geneva.

Walker, G.P., Simmons, P., Irwin, A. and Wynne, B. (1998), *Public perception of risks associated with major accident hazards*, Research Report 194/1998, HSE Books, Sudbury.

Walker, G., Fairburn, J., and Bickerstaff, K. (2000), Ethnicity and risk: the characteristics of populations in census wards containing major accident hazard sites in England and Wales, Occasional Paper 15 (Department of Geography, University of Staffordshire).

Walker, G., Mitchell, G., Fairburn, J. and Smith, G. (2003), *Environmental Quality and Social Deprivation. Phase II: National Analysis of Flood Hazard, IPC Industries and Air Quality.* R&D Project Record 12615 XX, The Environment Agency, Bristol, 133pp, ISBN to be allocated.

Weinberg, A.S. (1998), 'The environmental justice debate: a commentary on methodological issues and practical concerns', *Sociological Forum*, 13(1): 25–32.

Wilkinson, C.H. (1998), 'Environmental justice impact assessment: key components and emerging issues' in Porter, A.L. and Fittipaldi, J.J. (eds) Environmental Methods Review: Retooling Impact Assessment for the New Century, AEPI/IAIA, The Press Club, Fargo, North Dakota, pp. 273–282.

Williams, R.W. (1999), 'Environmental justice in America and its politics of scale', *Political Geography*, 18: 49–73.

23

Participative and Interactive Evaluation: A Review of the Methodologies
Andrea De Montis

INTRODUCTION

According to many research studies on the relationships between impact evaluation and planning, the reaction to so-called 'rationalism' has led professionals and scholars to search for alternative assessment methods. One of the main lessons drawn from the criticism of rationalism is that assessment should not become a process mastered by an independent actor, such as a planner, a professional, or a technician. Instead it is generally agreed evaluation should be more participative and based on the capacity for social interaction, mutual learning, and communication.

This examination of more participative and inter-active evaluation is organized as follows: first of all, the shift towards interactive methodologies is introduced. Secondly, the concepts of mutual learning, social interaction and communication are set out. Following this, a number of case studies of interactive planning support systems are described. Finally, conclusions are drawn about the interactivity of decision-support systems.

A RADICAL SHIFT TO INTERACTIVITY

Evaluation and planning are intertwined activities. Many scholars (Khakee, 1998; Lawrence, 2000; Secchi, 2000) would agree, even from their different points of view, to the statement that evaluation and planning, like two sides of the same coin, have evolved over time in a similar pattern. Thus the reflections on evaluation in this chapter shall mainly be linked to the associated planning process.

Both Khakee (1998) and Lawrence (2000) depict an historical evolution of planning and evaluation as a reaction to the so-called 'rational-comprehensive' approach. According to Lawrence (2000), this reaction has been concentrated so far on the following negative tendencies:

- autocracy (where 'experts' dominate the process, with only a peripheral role for the public);
- failure to consider resource and cognitive limits;

- overestimation of the ability to predict and control the environment (weakness in implementation);
- insufficient consideration of non-rational aspects (creativity), of synthesis (compared to analysis) and of non-technical and non-scientific knowledge, experience, and wisdom (scientific, technical, and quantitative bias);
- failure to consider the collective nature of planning and the central role of dialogue adequately.

Despite these pointed criticisms, rationalism has persisted until now for many reasons, but mainly due to the 'psychological reassurances it provides practitioners' (Lawrence, 2000: 610).

The shift from rationalism in planning and evaluation has resulted in a range of practices, concepts, and behaviour, which can be grouped under different 'styles' or philosophies. Khakee identifies seven variations on the theme: incremental planning, implementation-oriented planning, strategic planning, advocacy planning, transactive planning, negotiative planning, and communicative planning. Lawrence, on the other hand, provides the readers with a different aggregation of the same concepts in four approaches: pragmatism, socio-ecological idealism, political economic mobilization, and communication and collaboration.

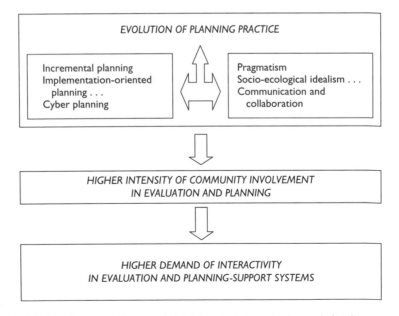

Figure 23.1 A basic assumption: the shift to interactivity in evaluation and planning

It should be noted that the differences between these approaches are usually semantic. In practice, planners often adopt mixed approaches and only partly implement many of the aforementioned styles. Moreover, the most recent approach to evaluation and planning should be added to the lists quoted by Khakee and Lawrence: the so-called 'digital planning', known also as 'cyber planning'. The failure of researchers to consider cyber planning as a 'style' of planning in the proper sense of the term may be due, in the first place, to the broadness of practices connected to it and, secondly, to the lack of real references. The following attempts to overcome this.

In a four set simple classification of interactive evaluation, planning processes may involve real working environments, such as traditional meeting points and councils, and virtual ones, such as tele-conferences and Web-based forums. They also may imply focussing on both real objects, such as a stone city and a concrete ecosystem, and virtual objects, such as computer-modelled cities and utopian settlements.

From this point on the said taxonomy will be termed real/virtual planning (*RVP*) classification, and the corresponding four sets will be called *RR*, *RV*, *VR* and *VV* domains (see Figure 23.2).

Many sceptical scholars warn that a digital divide still exists, which prevents an unlimited number of citizens participating in effective and deliberative decision-making by means of cyber planning. On the other hand, it seems that cyber planning may emphasize and enlarge most of the activities, which are now usually attributed to the communicative approach.

One of the major criticisms about rationalism is that it encourages practitioners to regard problems as 'obvious' and thus to choose mono-directional and

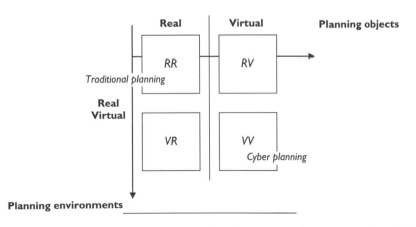

Figure 23.2 Scheme of the real/virtual planning (*RVP*) classification (Adapted from Batty, 2002)

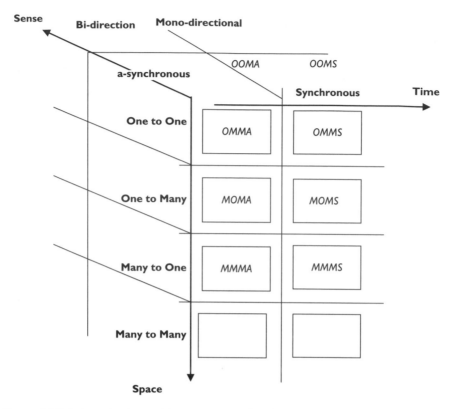

Figure 23.3 Scheme for the spatial-sense-temporal (SST) classification (Mitchell, 1999)

linear solutions. As for the reaction against rationalism, many approaches emphasize that questions, bottlenecks and problems first should be set and then solved.
In this sense, patterns of managing information definitely matter. Starting from a
four-box Table recently developed by Mitchell (1999), information exchange modalities can be classified into 16 different sets, with reference to space, sense, and
time. Here information flows may occur in one-to-one, one-to-many, many-to-one,
and many-to-many patterns. The permitted sense may be mono or bi-directional,
while temporal modalities may be synchronous or asynchronous.

From now on, this taxonomy will be termed the 'spatial-sense-temporal' (*SST*)
classification, and each domain will be indicated by the corresponding initial capital
letters. An example is sketched in Figure 23.3, with reference to eight mono-
directional domains.

INTERACTION AS A MEANS OF LEARNING IN COMMUNICATIVE AND CYBER STYLE PLANNING

During the past 30 years, practitioners and scholars have observed an explosion of applications aimed at interconnecting several points and allowing for interactivity among them. This is an evident phenomenon and parallels the diffusion of communicative and collaborative, as well as cyber styles of planning.

According to some authors (Forester, 1989, 2000; Sager, 1994; Innes, 1998a), interactive evaluation can be conceived as a complex process, with great emphasis on the way information is transmitted so that learning is facilitated among as wide a possible number of stakeholders. In these conditions, evaluation operates on an often non-systematic set of steps and involves consensus building, social mobilization, participation, and negotiation (Healey, 1997; Innes, 1998b). Here the argumentative capacity of planners becomes a central part of their activities when presenting the questions at stake, in discussing them, reflecting on different alternative scenarios and also, when necessary, in changing the main assumptions formulated at the beginning of the process (Forester, 1993; Healey, 1993, 1996).

Within this paradigm, decision-making is based on a deliberative attitude that implies continuous feedbacks through cyclical patterns along a route that usually cannot be predicted in advance (Healey, 1992; Innes and Booher, 1999). Thus there is particular interest in the development of methodological frameworks, operative strategies, and practical devices to encourage participation, involve communities, and allow for direct interaction throughout the process. In this sense, interactivity is always invoked, as a means of inducing learning by acting in a bi-directional and constructive environment.

In cyber planning and evaluation, the widespread diffusion of applications of the so-called 'information and communication technologies' (ICTs), both in an Internet and intranet pattern, means that interactive dialogue, learning, and evaluation processes can take place among agents situated in a virtually unlimited number of places (Castells, 1989, 2001; Levy, 1994, 1995a,b). One or more digital devices give shape to a cyber environment able to support bi-directional flows of information and, thus, interactivity. Planning and evaluation might occur also as deliberative processes based on public access with a degree of extension as large as that which net providers permit (Mitchell, 1995, 2000). The environments of these processes can occur both in physical settings, such as traditional meeting points, as well as in digital ones, such as virtual halls and laboratories.

This methodological shift seems to involve a change in practice. New demands require integration of the applications and produce a new generation of systems for the support of planning and evaluation. Hence one observes the diffusion of planning support systems (from now on called PSS), which embed interactive features,

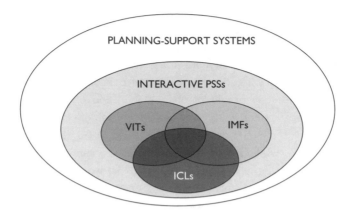

Figure 23.4 The relationships among PSSs, IPSSs, VITs, IMFs, and ICLs: a tentative classification

are accessible on-line by unlimited numbers of users, provide them with digital collaborative environments, and encourage the construction of shared contextual knowledge (see Bodum and Kjems, 2003; Moon, 2003; Shen *et al.*, 2003).

Incorrectly designed sophisticated systems, even though they allow advanced analysis, may discourage users from exchanging information or sometimes from any kind of interaction. Hence, the effectiveness of a PSS depends on its degree of interactivity, which is often proportional to the extent to which the visual devices used are suitable for constructing an intuitive language within the man–machine interface.

INTERACTIVITY IN THE DOMAIN OF PSS PRACTICE: LESSONS FROM A REVIEW OF CASE STUDIES

In a hard and information technology-driven sense, a PSS is defined as a computerized system, or an integration of many such systems, which is able to support judgement, evaluation and, thus, planning. In a softer sense of the word, and also for PSS designers, PSSs cannot be reduced to mere PC-programs. They have to be conceived as entire processes, as decisional environments, and as institutional settings, where planning activities are able to evolve successfully. Thus the technological aspect of a PSS, its computerized engine, is only useful functionally if the related planning process evolves properly. In government, PSSs can be used for processes where planning is supported and decision-making aided. Hence, a PSS can be defined as a system that embraces computer devices, institutions, procedures, officials, persons, citizens, and stakeholders, who wish to be involved and want to collaborate in attaining changing tasks in planning.

Interactive community learning scheme-based processes

Analysis of the scientific literature on environmental impact assessment shows that in many cases collaborative learning has been considered a successful strategy for involving communities in discovering new opportunities and developing innovative knowledge while participating in the activities.

Saarikoski (2000) describes the positive contribution of a task force for public involvement in a controversial debate on waste management in the region of Pirkanmaa, Finland. The main concern was the disagreement within the society about the policies directed at energy conversion. While a regional company responsible for waste management proposed incineration, non-governmental organizations claimed that the method chosen would be risky for the communities because of the increase of air pollution. The role of the task force was to follow each step of the impact evaluation process and to communicate and explain all the elements: its commitment, the policies of the stakeholders, feasible alternatives for waste management, possible impact, and criteria for decisions.

The task force developed traditional participatory instruments: seminars and meetings. The research effort was focussed on the degree of community involvement and pointed out that benefits were mainly obtained from full availability of documentation. Clear descriptions were given of the alternatives at stake, and everyone was aware that the ideas expressed by each party were included in a final report. Evidence was provided that some actors had changed their original opinions about the best alternative to endorse, while others had learned from the information and materials presented by their opponents and sometimes revised their original remarks.

Overall the exercise was deemed successful, because despite its shortcomings and legitimacy failures 'the process managed to produce a rather broad understanding among the parties and improve the communication among them' (Saarikoski, 2000: 699). With respect to the *RVP* classification, this case falls in the real-real (*RR*) domain, since it is based on face-to-face group meetings and on the use mostly of paper-based documents. According to the *SST* classification, this process belongs to the domain of one-to-many, bi-directional synchronous (*OMBS* domain) flow of information. It evolves along contemporaneous meetings based mostly on presentation of materials by a few speakers in a mono-directional pattern.

It should be noted that a great awareness exists of the need to involve as many public actors as possible in the evaluation procedure. Sometimes the focus of the process cannot be as clear as in the above-mentioned case of waste management policy. When long-term concerns are considered, strategies for regional involvement have to be developed (Wolfe *et al.*, 2001). In such cases, one should note the difficulty that the US National Assessment of Potential Consequences of Climate Variability and Change (NACC) has in finding strategies for constructing a collaborative public process for the evaluation of concerns that will only become urgent (hopefully) in the very long run.

While a huge effort has been made to distribute guidelines in 19 US regions and over several actors on the most effective participative strategies, the researchers did not understand clearly to what extent these documents were being adopted and used in practice. With respect to the *RVP* classification, this process belongs to the *RR* domain: working environment with mainly real workshops and assessment committees, although paper-based documents are utilized. In the *SST* classification, information has been managed in this process in a one-to-many, mono-directional, and asynchronous pattern (*OMMA* domain).

Sinclair and Diduck (2001) warn that the existence of an evaluative stage dedicated to public involvement does not ensure *per se* that final decisions will be made in a collaborative and multi-actor framework. Sinclair and Diduck (2001) observe that environmental evaluation, in its first stages, was applied using a rational-comprehensive approach. Participation was necessary, but only under the supervision of a technical leader and using top–down driven patterns. No change in direction of the original policy was conceived. There were no elaborated methodologies to cope with active and, thus, interactive public societies. In the last 20 years, there has been a shift to approaches based on a trans-active model of planning. This is mainly due to the evidence that impact evaluators must often cope with conflict, uncertainty, fuzziness, and change.

In view of this observation, it is argued impact evaluation should be 're-conceptualized as a form of trans-active, civic exploration reliant on mutual learning by all EA participants' (Sinclair and Diduck, 2001: 132). Here attention focuses on patterns of adult learning, pointing out relevant relationships and the need to adjust the learning process to the social context. On the basis that the theory of ideal conditions of learning can provide a good starting point for evaluation, Sinclair and Diduck (2001) attempt to define transformative learning as 'a process by which individuals improve their instrumental and communicative competence and develop more functional frames of reference' (Sinclair and Diduck, 2001: 114). The six rules of thumb of the transformative learner are accurate and complete information, freedom from coercion, openness to alternative perspectives, the ability to reflect critically upon presuppositions, equal opportunity to participate, and the ability to assess systematically and to accept a rational consensus as valid.

These rules have been used as reference criteria in evaluating 34 jurisdictional frameworks of impact assessment in Canada. Among the resulting proposals for policy reform, the following seem to be relevant: that government reclaim the responsibility for design and implementation of public involvement programmes; they enact fair and reasonable participant funding mechanisms; formalize public involvement at normative and strategic levels of planning; and availability via Internet guidance notes.

According to the *RVP* classification, the proposal of policy reform seems to suggest moving to the *RV* domain by adopting real working settings and digital Web-based documents for public involvement. Within the *SST* taxonomy, the proposed policy reform encourages the development of processes where information flows evolve in a many-to-many, bi-directional, and synchronous pattern (*MMBS* domain). With reference to a similar framework, Blatner *et al.* (2001) discuss the move Interactive evaluation from the rational approach to the collaborative learning approach. Here collaborative learning is believed to be based on a merger of three theories: soft system methodology, alternative dispute resolution, and learning theory. The result is 'a process designed to create a learning atmosphere, encourage systemic thinking about complex problems, discourage strategic (competitive) behaviour among stakeholders, and focus on desirable and feasible change rather than attempting to achieve absolute consensus on contentious land management issues' (Blatner *et al.*, 2001: 248). As in the previous case, classifications are referred to the proposed paradigm of community learning within land-use decision-making. According to *RVP* classification, this process seems to imply real working environments and real objects (*RR* domain), while the *SST* taxonomy indicates a tendency to incorporate many-to-many, mono-directional, and synchronous patterns of information flows (*MMMS* domain). Other authors present scientific evidence, which confirms that public participation, knowledge elaboration, and management and social learning are fundamental elements in successful evaluation activity in social domains (see Goma *et al.*, 2001; Sánchez-Triana and Ortolano, 2001; Deelstra *et al.*, 2003; Fagerström *et al.*, 2003).

In relation to social impact assessment, recent research emphasizes the role of the interactive community forum (ICF) (Becker *et al.*, 2003). This project was developed for the US Army Corps of Engineer's environmental impact study of alternatives for salmon recovery in the Snake River basin region of the United States. The ICF is a participatory approach to social impact assessment focussed on the assessment 'of citizen's judgement of the anticipated impacts of EIS alternatives' (Becker *et al.*, 2003: 368). The approach developed within the ICF is linked to the theories of small group interaction, since it facilitates open dialogue and discourse, promotes mutual learning, enhances the quality of individual judgement, and advances participatory democracy and empowerment. The main working framework was a cyclical process based on the following four steps: presentation of supplementary information; record of initial rating for each community dimension; facilitated group dialogue of individual rating and perspectives; and final rating and justification for rating.

Despite some shortcomings in the method, the ICF was found to enhance the community's understanding of each alternative in the impact assessment procedure and thus to increase its social deliberative capacity. According to the *RVP* taxonomy, this particular IPSS falls onto the *RR* domain, implying real working environments – a series of meetings – and real planning objectives – traditional documents. Along the *SST* classification, it belongs to the *OMMS* domain of the one-to-many, mono-directional, and synchronous patterns of information flows.

VISUAL INTERACTIVE TOOLS-BASED PROCESSES

According to recent studies, group learning among adults is an activity that can be encouraged by the adoption of suitable devices able to support collaboration and interaction. These tools, such as personal computer or Internet-based programs, are usually conceived and designed to allow for intuitive patterns of manipulation and use. There is no doubt that visual modelling still provides users with the most effective method of communicating in an intuitive and easy-to-grasp manner. Interactivity is thus directly dependent on a user-friendly visual interface between man and machine, available within the system.

A meta-analysis of 19 quantitative studies (Horton *et al.*, 1993) found that the collective learning tool of concept mapping enhanced knowledge attainment and attitudes. Concept mapping is a technique for representing knowledge in network graphs. It is often used successfully in planning support systems for several purposes, such as collective generation of scenarios, consensual building of master plan alternatives, and shared construction of criteria of environmental performances. In a recent study, Chiu *et al.* (2000) investigated the effectiveness of concept mapping on the interactions in a computer and Internet-based collaborative environment among 36 in-service teachers and pre-service student teachers in Taiwan. The system's visual interface, constructed on an Internet-based platform, allowed clients to access a chat room, construct a group concept map, obtain a feedback score of communicative performance online, and track the information about the process. The system also permitted the map of dialogues constructed by group members to be traced and the final resulting map shared. One of the main results was that the performance of the group was positively related to the amount and level of group interaction in network-supported concept mapping. Moreover, this result was directly linked to the presence of an adequate and attractive visual interface between groups and the Internet-based system. This visual interface encouraged a high degree of interaction among individuals and groups. According to the *RVP* classification, this system falls into the *VV* domain, since it implies digital working chat rooms and bits-based map files. Within the *SST* taxonomy, this process belongs in the *MMBS* domain, since it allows information to flow in many-to-many, bi-directional, and synchronous patterns.

Moving from the general field of education to planning, within an interactive participatory process on conservation planning in Loess Plateau, China (Fagerström *et al.*, 2003), several techniques were adopted to encourage interactions between farmers, as potential field researchers, and professionals. Three groups of methods were used to involve as many farmers as possible: sampling, interviewing and dialogue, and methods of visualizing and diagramming. Visual tools used included visual sketch models, timelines and seasonal calendars, ranking, and flows and diagrams. Visual models in particular 'were the main tools for studying current land resources in space and landscape' (Fagerström *et al.*, 2003: 8). They were constructed in two patterns: village sketch maps and village models. The first was based on a topographical map including all possible information on settlements, cropland, and other resources. The second model was constructed directly by the farmers as a 2×3 m three-dimensional rectangular model and with the heights sized at approximately the scale 1:600. Information was gathered by means of direct surveys and mapped with the use of materials such as stones for representing bedrock, soil/water mixture for topography, leaves for woodland, and crushed chalk of different colours for land use. The adoption of visual tools was found to be very effective especially because of language barriers caused by the complexity of the Chinese tongue for both the foreign researchers and the indigenous farmers themselves. The process is believed to be suitable for involving farmers in the whole planning process, so as to explore relevant alternatives for sustainable land use. According to the *RVP* taxonomy, this system belongs to the *RR* domain, as far as face-to-face real meetings and interviews support debates over very real visual models. According to the *SST* classification, this learning process falls into the *MMBA* domain of the many-to-many, bi-directional, and asynchronous patterns of information flow.

In ecosystem modelling, many studies focus on interactive visual tools in an attempt to favour the interpretation and manipulation of geographic information for learning and planning purposes by non-geographers. Chertov *et al.* (2002), for example, propose a combination of two spatial simulation software systems, EFIMOD 2 and DESCARTES, to construct spatial-temporal interactive maps to support Sustainable Forest Management (SFM). While the first system is constructed to manage simulations of environmental dynamics, the DESCARTES software system is a 'specially designed to support visual exploration of spatially reference data' (Chertov et al., 2002: 51). Special features of this system are: the automated presentations of data on maps and the ability to manipulate these maps interactively. Future developments of the system include the management of spatial-temporal maps and their integration in methods for multicriteria spatial decision-making. According to the *RVP* classification, this IPSS falls into the *VV* domain, since it provides the user with a digital working environment, enabling to manipulate virtual geographical maps. Within the *SST* classification, this system belongs to the *OOBS* domain, as far as it allows for one-to-one, bi-directional, and synchronous flows of information.

In planning, Al Kodmany (1999) discusses the beneficial contribution of the use of three visualization techniques in encouraging public participation in a planning of neighbourhoods in Pilsen, Chicago, IL, United States. These techniques are as follows: GIS manipulation of maps, sketching by an artist, and digital photo manipulation. While at the beginning of the process GIS provided a wealth of information about the geographical features of the places, which were the object of the future plan, the artist's sketches based on the ideas of each participant along with photo manipulation were fundamental in visualizing non-technical and psychological unfolded aspects of the proposed scenarios. Within this pattern, each participant had the opportunity to visualize directly the possible effects of the proposed plan, as he could see the most likely changes, first sketched as drafts and then reported in a photographically realistic reproduction of the area.

The main result of this study is that the combination of different visual techniques may well help in bridging the gap between planners, usually conceived as scenario-makers, and citizens, seen as scenario-takers. 'Freehand sketching and GIS were most effective for problem *identification* and brainstorming, while photo manipulation using computer imaging was most useful for exploring solutions to *previously-defined* issues' (Al Kodmany, 1999). With respect to the *RVP* classification, this IPSS falls into the *RV* domain, as far as it is grounded on face-to-face meetings and the use of virtual maps and geographic analysis. According to the *SST* taxonomy, it belongs to the *OMMS* domain, since information flows in a one-to-many, mono-directional, and synchronous way.

While in the above-mentioned case participation was encouraged by means of models – visual tools – in the sense they provide concrete reproductions of buildings and land cover – other pioneer researchers (see Shiffer, 1992) have attempted to foster participatory planning processes using virtual models (visual tools again) now considered as digital copies of physical entities. After more than a decade of experimentation, research still tries to combine the high performances of visual modelling provided by computer system-based virtual environment, with the ease of understanding and use offered by computerized, workbench-based physical relationships and commands. This system consists of a $36'' \times 48''$ horizontal touch-sensitive screen and allows manipulation either in direct ways, via human hands, or indirect ways, via pull-down command menus. This visually powerful interface can be accessed from all its four sides and encourages the participation of many users by direct actions on the screen and observation of the manipulative strategies of the other users. In this way, this system is believed to foster mutual adaptive learning by a continuous series of attempts towards collaborative sketch planning and design. Observation of the workbench in use demonstrates that users appreciate the opportunity to refer to a horizontal workspace and manipulate it directly. A process of quick adaptation has been recognized, while the round interface has provided a stimulating collaborative environment for planners. According to the *RVP* classification, this IPSS falls into the *RV* domain, as far as it involves the manipulation of virtual models within a real workshop. With respect to the *SST* taxonomy, it belongs to the *OMBS* as it allows the dialogue between one computer system and many (maximum four) users in a bi-directional and synchronous way.

Interactive multicriteria framework-based processes

Multicriteria analysis is grounded on almost 40 years of history in research efforts. Recently many studies have focussed on two directions: interoperability-based and interactivity-based multicriteria systems. These tools are likely to become part of the complex architecture of communicative planning-support systems, by interfacing with other computerized systems and by encouraging active participation of all the stakeholders involved. While there is an overwhelming mass of literature, three references, in particular, provide an adequate idea of these research efforts.

Bana e Costa and Vansnick apply multicriteria analysis to a real decision-making process, by means of a combination of several decision-support systems (Bana e Costa and Vansnick, 1999; Bana e Costa et al., 1999). The integration of different approaches was applied to a complex strategic problem faced by the Santa Caterina textile industry in southern Brazil. The construction of the whole process took place through a series of recursive cycles: there was a great need for interactivity to manage the flow of feedbacks to the beginning of the process. Four computer programs assisted the process in different stages: Graphics COPE (Banxia Software, 1995); MACHBETH (Bana e Costa and Vansnick, 1997); VISA (Visual Thinking International, 1995); and EQUITY (Krysalis, 1995). Graphics COPE was the main support for cognitive mapping, which in the first phase was dedicated to setting up the problem: this program allows digital maps to be constructed where fundamental and basic points of view are identified. Inter-criteria preference modelling was supported by MACHBETH, a multicriteria computer program with an interface that allows visual interactive learning through the construction of the judgement matrix, the choice of the type of the criteria measurement scale, etc. VISA was adopted to aid evaluation of the competing capacity of the textile firms, by visual sensitivity analysis of the final input, depending on the fundamental and basic points of view. The program EQUITY enabled directions for strategic action in each company to be generated and exploited, by means of intuitive representation of the results of the cost–benefit efficiency analysis. One of the main methodological findings of this process is that each computer program contributed, by means of its visual interactivity features, to the fostering of mutual learning between the actors and to construct common scenarios for the future strategies of the firms. According to the *RVP* classification, this IPSS seems to fall into the *RV* domain, as far as it involves the manipulation of virtual models within face-to-face workshops. In regard to the *SST* taxonomy, it belongs to the *OMBS*, since it allows for the dialogue between a computer system and group members in a bi-directional and synchronous way.

Group decision-making is believed to be a very complex activity, since group preferences cannot be inferred immediately from the simple 'sum' of the judgement scores of the group individuals. Mutual changes may induce uncertainty and groups may suddenly change their aggregate opinion to completely different kinds of concepts. Kim and Choi (2001) have recently developed a multicriteria interactive program, RINGS, able to interactively construct and manage group utility functions. The system adapts to situations of incomplete information, by 'modifying its information to be a concrete or a complete one' (Kim and Choi, 2001: 501). In this system, all the elements of a multi-criteria procedure, participants, alternatives, attributes and dominance relation information are stored in table form and can be processed using a linear programming model-base. RINGS presents a user-friendly visual interface, which helps group members to express preferences and compare them. According to the *RVP* classification, this IPSS falls into the *RV* domain, as far as it involves the manipulation of virtual models within a real workshop. In relation to *SST* taxonomy, it belongs to the *MMBS*, since it allows the dialogue among many actors in a bi-directional and synchronous way.

A feature often mentioned in a multi-criteria aid process is that algorithms may be able to offer results suitable to changing demands. A high degree of volatility, arising from the changing requests of different customers, occurs in the planning procedures of the sequence of shots to be taken from a satellite camera.

This has to be regarded as a day-by-day adaptive process. In a recent application, Gabrel and Vanderpoten (2002) have developed an interactive multicriteria device able to construct a shot-plan, which conforms daily to the requirements of the customers. The multi-criteria framework consists of two modules. The first is an algorithm able to analyse graphs in order to find the shortest path among the set of feasible ones. The second module helps to explore the set of candidate sequences in a flexible way. Two levels of interaction are allowed. The first one organizes the discussion of the criteria and their relevance, meant as 'aspiration level' (Gabrel and Vanderpoten, 2002: 541). The second level allows one to add further requirements even after criteria selection. According to the *RVP* classification, this IPSS falls into the *RV* domain, as far as it involves the manipulation of virtual models within a real working setting. In relation to *SST* taxonomy, it belongs to the *OOBS*, since it involves man–computer dialogues in a bi-directional and synchronous way.

CONCLUDING REMARKS

In this chapter, a tentative state of the art on the applications of interactive evaluation methodologies within decision-support systems has been elaborated. The case-study reviews set out provide the reader with a rich panorama of applications and confirms that widespread efforts are being made to promote forward-looking interactive participatory evaluation tools in planning. The case studies have been grouped for classification purposes into three groups: community learning (*ICL*), visual (*VIT*), and multi-criteria (*IMF*) IPSS. However, these sets are neither complete nor mutually exclusive. Even if each case study belongs to one set only, it may prove to be twofold or threefold and might belong to other sets. Since the introduction of interactivity in evaluation and planning-support systems is believed to be connected to the possibility of the increase in cyber planning and to the informational society, the examples described have also been analysed with respect to two other taxonomies called real/virtual planning (*RVP*) and spatial-sense-temporal information (*SST*) classifications.

To clarify the above, certain facts must be pointed out. First, the general assumption of the chapter seems to be confirmed by ongoing practices: the fundamental shift to collaborative and mutual learning in the practice of evaluation, policy, and planning has caused an increasing aggregate demand for interactivity. Secondly, according to negotiation, communicative and cyber planning, and their corresponding evaluative practices, an increasingly higher level of inter-active participation is required. Third, the panorama studied overall confirms that researchers are seeking visual intuition-based modelling both as a strategy for encouraging citizens' active participation and as a framework for shaping innovative man–computer interfaces. Fourth, the results of the *RVP* and *SST* taxonomies seem to indicate a shift in the design of the IPSS towards patterns that belong to the *RV* and *OMBS* domains. Radical movements of IPSS designers towards *VV* and *MMBS* domains still seem to be dominated by cautious behaviour. Fifth, with regard to the last point, information and communication technologies are sought to increase the level of interaction among different agents, rather than to substitute completely the concrete decisional settings with virtual screen-based remote environments. In other words, traditional physical debates still seem to be the indispensable basis for fair, transparent interactive evaluation.

REFERENCES

Al Kodmany, K. (1999), 'Using visualization techniques for enhancing public participation in planning and design: process, implementation, and evaluation'. *Landscape and Urban Planning*, 45: 37–45.

Bana e Costa, C.A. and Vansnick, J. (1997), 'Applications of the MACHBETH approach in the framework of an additive aggregation model'. *Journal of Multi-Criteria Decision Analysis*, 6(2): 107–114.

Bana e Costa, C.A. and Vansnick, J. (1999), 'The MACHBETH approach: basic ideas, software and an application'. In N. Meskens and M. Roubens (eds), *Advances in Decision Analysis*, Kluwer Academic Publishers, Dordrecht, Book Series: Mathematical Modelling: Theory and Applications, Vol. 4, pp. 131–157.

Bana e Costa, C.A., Ensslin, L., Correa, E.C. and Vansnick, J. (1999), 'Decision Support Systems in action: integrated application in a multicriteria decision aid process'. *European Journal of Operational Research*, 113: 315–335.

Banxia Software (1995), Graphics COPE User Guide.

Batty, M. (2002), Oral communication, *The Digital City: A Euroconference*, Granada, Spain, June 9–14, 2001.

Becker, D.R., Harris, C.C. and McLaughlin, W.J. (2003), 'A participatory approach to social impact assessment: the interactive community forum'. *Environmental Impact Assessment Review*, 23: 367–382.

Blatner, K.A., Matthew, S.C., Daniels, S.E. and Walker, G.B. (2001), 'Evaluation the application of collaborative learning to the Wanatchee fire recovery planning effort'. *Environmental Impact Assessment Review*, 21: 241–270.

Bodum, L. and Kjems, E. (2003), 'Using VR in Communicative Planning'. *Proceedings of the 8th International Conference on Computers in Urban Planning and Urban Management (CUPUM)*, Sendhai City, Japan, May 27–29, 2003.

Castells, M. (1989), *The Informational City: Information Technology, Economic Restructuring and the Urban-Regional Process.* Blackwell, Oxford, UK.

Castells, M. (2001), *The Internet Galaxy. Reflections on Internet, Business, and Society.* Oxford University Press, Oxford, UK.

Chertov, O., Komarov, A., Andrienko, G., Andrienko, N. and Gatalski, P. (2002), 'Integrating forest simulation and spatial-temporal interactive visualization for decision-making at landscape level'. *Ecological Modelling,* 148: 47–65.

Chiu, C.-H., Huang, C.-C. and Chang, W.-T. (2000), 'The evaluation and influence of interaction in network supported collaborative concept mapping'. *Computers & Education,* 34: 17–25.

Deelstra, Y., Nootboom, S.G., Kohlmann, H.R., van den Berg, J. and Innanen, S. (2003), 'Using knowledge for decision-making purposes in the context of large projects in The Netherlands'. *Environmental Impact Assessment Review,* 23: 517–541.

Fagerström, M.H.H., Messing, I. and Wen, Z.M. (2003), 'A participatory approach for integrated conservation planning in a small catchment in Loess Plateau, China'. Part I. Approach and Methods. *Catena,* 54: 255–269.

Forester, J. (1989), *Planning in the Face of Power.* University of California Press, Berkeley, CA, USA.

Forester, J. (1993), 'Learning from practice stories: the priority of practical judgements'. In F. Fisher and J. Forester (eds), *The Argumentative Turn in Policy Analysis and Planning,* Duke University Press, Durham, NC, USA.

Forester, J. (2000), *The Deliberative Practitioner: Encouraging Participatory Planning Processes.* The MIT Press, Cambridge, MA, USA, London, UK.

Gabrel, V. and Vanderpoten, D. (2002), 'Enumeration and interactive selection of efficient paths in a multiple criteria graph for scheduling an earth observing satellite'. *European Journal of Operational Research,* 139: 533–542.

Goma, H.C., Rahim, K., Nangendo, G., Riley, J. and Stein, A. (2001), 'Participatory studies for agro-ecosystem evaluation'. *Agriculture, Ecosystems and Environment,* 87: 179–190.

Healey, P. (1992), 'A planner's day-knowledge and action in communicative practice'. *Journal of the American Planning Association,* 68: 9–20.

Healey, P. (1993), 'Planning through debate: the communicative turn in planning theory'. In F. Fisher and J. Forester (eds), *The Argumentative Turn in Policy Analysis and Planning,* Duke University Press, Durham, NC, USA.

Healey, P. (1996), 'The communicative turn in spatial planning theory and its implications for spatial strategy formulation'. *Environment and Planning B,* 23: 217–234.

Healey, P. (1997), *Collaborative Planning. Shaping Places in Fragmented Societies.* Macmillan, London, UK.

Horton, P.B., McConney, A.A., Gallo, M., Woods, A.L., Senn, G.J. and Hamelin, D. (1993), 'An investigation of the effectiveness of concept mapping as an instructional tool'. *Science Education*, 77: 95–111.

Innes, J.E. (1998a), 'Information in communicative planning'. *Journal of the American Planning Association*, 64: 52–63.

Innes, J.E. (1998b), 'Planning through consensus building: a new view of the comprehensive planning ideal'. *Journal of the American Planning Association*, 62: 460–472.

Innes, J.E. and Booher, D.E. (1999), 'Consensus building and complex adaptive systems'. *Journal of the American Planning Association*, 65: 412–422.

Khakee, A. (1998), 'Evaluation and planning: inseparable concepts'. *Town Planning Review*, 69(4), 359–374.

Kim, J.K. and Choi, S.H. (2001), 'A utility range-based interactive group support system for multiattribute decision making'. *Computers & Operational Research*, 28: 485–503.

Krysalis (1995), EQUITY for Windows User Manual.

Lawrence, D.P. (2000), 'Planning theories and environmental impact assessment'. *Environmental Impact Assessment Review*, 20: 607–625.

Levy, P. (1994), *L'intelligence collective. Pour une anthropologie du cyberspace.* Éditions La Découverte, Paris.

Levy, P. (1995a), *Qu'est-ce que le virtuel?* Éditions La Découverte, Paris.

Levy, P. (1995b), *Cyberculture. Rapport au Conseil de l'Europe.* Éditions Odile Jacob, Paris.

Mitchell, W.J. (1995), *City of Bits, Space, Time and the Infobahn.* MIT University Press, Cambridge, MA, USA.

Mitchell, W.J. (1999), 'The City of Bits Hypothesis'. In D.A. Schön, B. Sanyal and W.J. Mitchell (eds), *High Technology and Low-Income Communities. Prospects for the Positive Use of Advanced Information Technology.* MIT Press, Cambridge, MA, USA, London, UK, pp. 105–130.

Mitchell, W.J. (2000), *E-topia. Urban Life, Jim – But Not As We Know It.* MIT University Press, Cambridge, MA, USA.

Moon, T. (2003), 'Development of Web-based Public Participation and Collaborative Planning System' (PPCPS). *Proceedings of the 8th International Conference on Computers in Urban Planning and Urban Management (CUPUM)*, Sendhai City, Japan, May 27–29.

Saarikoski, H. (2000), 'Environmental impact assessment (EIA) as collaborative learning process'. *Environmental Impact Assessment Review*, 20: 681–700.

Sager, T. (1994), *Communicative Planning Theory.* Averbury Press, Brookfield, VT, USA.

Sánchez-Triana, E. and Ortolano, L. (2001), 'Organizational learning and environmental impact assessment at Colombia's Cauca Valley Corporation'. *Environmental Impact Assessment Review*, 21: 223–239.

Secchi, B. (2000), *Prima lezione di urbanistica.* Laterza, Bari.

Shen, Z., Kawakami, M. and Kishimoto, K. (2003), 'Study on Development of On-line Coopera-tive Planning and Design System Using VRML and JAVA. A case study on a public park planning and design'. *Proceedings of the 8th International Conference on Computers in Urban Planning and Urban Management* (*CUPUM*), Sendhai City, Japan, May 27–29.

Shiffer, M. (1992), 'Towards a collaborative planning system'. *Environment and Planning B: Planning and Design*, 19: 709–722.

Sinclair, A.J. and Diduck, A.P. (2001), 'Public involvement in EA in Canada: a transformative learning perspective'. *Environmental Impact Assessment Review*, 21: 113–136.

Visual Thinking International (1995), V.I.S.A. for Windows User Manual.

Wolfe, A.K., Kerchner, N. and Wilbanks, T. (2001), 'Public involvement on a regional scale'. *Environmental Impact Assessment Review*, 21: 431–448.

24

Constructing Sustainable Urban Futures: From Models to Competing Pathways

Simon Guy and Simon Marvin

INTRODUCTION

How do policy-makers achieve the objective of building a sustainable urban future? This is the critical question that lies at the core of this book. We are not going to approach this question in a straightforward way. Instead we want to tackle a number of assumptions that, we argue, hinder thinking about how sustainable cities can be achieved. In particular, we want to enlarge the concept of a sustainable city by building a more complex and multi-layered understanding of what the city might become. While we cannot offer policy-makers a simple model or pathway towards a sustainable city, we do begin to build a conceptual framework that acknowledges the multiplicity of pathways towards different sustainable futures that often co-exist within a single city. There are three stages to our argument.

First, the shift from the concept of a singular towards multiple models of what the sustainable city might become. We question the emphasis that is placed on the achievement of sustainability through one model − compact urban form. It is not that we necessarily reject the notion that the physical re-ordering of the city can achieve environmental benefits, though even compact city advocates recognise that the evidence to support sustainability claims are complex and often contradictory. Rather, our concern is that the continued search for a simple and universal model of sustainable urban form can blind researchers and policy-makers to the multiplicity of innovations that could each make a quite distinctive contribution towards the development of more sustainable urban futures. Instead, we argue that the compact city debate is perhaps best understood as one amongst a number of different models of what might actually constitute a sustainable city.

Secondly, the rejection of the simplistic use of models and the development of competing pathways to sustainable cities. We are concerned that the notion of models is often used in an over-deterministic way. Models are often used as straightforward blueprints to be translated into reality through physical planning and design policies in a series of linear stages. Instead, we argue that models should be used in a much softer, more flexible fashion. Rather than view models as specifications for a city we argue that they are better employed as conceptual devices to sensitise us to different visions of what the sustainable city might become. We can for instance examine the extent to which the viewpoints and strategies of different urban actors, with often competing social, political and commercial interests, resonate or dissonate with the visions inscribed in particular models of development. In this sense we can then build an understanding of how the changing social organisation of urban development may promote particular pathways towards quite distinct urban futures.

Finally, the recognition that a wide diversity of sustainable urban futures are likely to co-exist within a single city. In this context we need to think quite differently about how the sustainable city could be achieved. Abandoning the search for a singular model, policy-makers would chart the multiplicity of pathways towards what might be quite different sustainable futures. The challenge here is to examine the tensions and similarities between these pathways, in particular focusing on the different social assumptions and biases built into them. We explore these competing strategies by reference to our own research into the management and development of electricity and water networks in the Newcastle Metropolitan region.

FROM SINGULAR TO MULTIPLE MODELS

Single model – the compact city discourse

We begin by highlighting a number of contradictions in the claims made for the compact city. A useful starting point here is the discussion and analysis of Jenks *et al.* (1996), which focuses the debate by posing the question whether the compact city can be considered a sustainable urban form. We do not need to rehearse the arguments made in support of the environmental benefits of the compact city. Instead we briefly develop an understanding of how Jenks *et al.* grapple with the contradictions of the sustainability claims made for the compact city.

Over the last decade a phenomenal effort has been expanded on the challenge represented by the shift towards more sustainable cities: three UK research council research programmes, international research and policy initiatives and at national and local level a high degree of activity and innovation. Jenks *et al.* (1996, p. 2) note that urban environmental problems 'are the most intractable and difficult to solve'. At the core of much of this research effort and policy development is the concept of the compact city. Reshaping the environmental profile of resource use in cities through the re-ordering of landuses, the layout of neighbourhoods and the design of buildings is perhaps the dominant discourse in urban sustainability debates. Consequently the compact city is 'today's visionary solution' hurriedly adopted by academics and politicians as an 'all-embracing panacea of urban ills' (Fulford, 1996, p. 122). The compact city is often presented as 'the big idea' with 'nothing less than the future of western lifestyles at stake' (Breheny, 1996, p. 13). The concept is so dominant that it 'seems inconceivable that anyone would oppose the current tide of opinion towards promoting greater sustainable development and the compact city in particular' (Smyth, 1996, p. 103). In this context it is not surprising that the 'move towards the compact city is now entrenched in policy through Europe' (Jenks et al. 1996, p. 275).

That the compact city discourse is extremely seductive is suggested by its popular support in the research community, and its rapid translation into the policy arena. However, even its proponents, and certainly the researchers cited above, recognise to differing degrees that there are considerable difficulties assessing the validity of the environmental claims made for the compact city. For example, Jenks et al. (1996, p. 12) argue that 'research has yet to find conclusively either in favour of, or against, the compact city', and consequently 'the battle between those in favour of the compact city and those against still rages' (ibid., p. 240). Detailed empirical analysis illustrates that the environmental benefits from urban compaction policies are likely to be small and the social and economic costs could be significant (Breheny, 1996, p. 25). Critically, there has been a tendency to focus on the lead role of planning in developing a blueprint of the compact city and rather less attention paid to the social, economic and technical processes involved in shaping the feasibility of the concept.

Recognising the complexity of much of the debate, the search for the 'ideal' land use pattern which is able to satisfy specific social, economic and environmental criteria is at risk of simplifying a complex and continually unfolding topic. Therefore discussion which focus only on the 'compact city' can only represent one facet of the debate as it stands 'today' (Thomas and Cousins, 1996). We would certainly agree with Jenks et al. (1996, p. 170) that 'an approach which addresses urban form alone is not enough'. How can the sustainable city debate move forward? Well there are a number of pointers. The research and policy community need to stop seeing the compact city as a singular model, a standardised pattern or a blanket solution that can be unproblematically implemented within an existing city. Instead we need to recognise that there may be a range of urban futures that may be called sustainable. The challenge for policy is to develop the most appropriate for a particular local context. Within this context the 'search for the ultimate sustainable urban form perhaps needs to be re-oriented to the search for a number of sustainable urban forms' that respond to a range of different settlement patterns and contexts (ibid., p. 345).

Multiple models of sustainable cities

In our own work we have attempted to link an analysis of new styles of infrastructure provision with their implications for the management of relations between users, buildings and territory in cities (Guy and Marvin, 1996a). We have found that utilities can actively shape resource flows of energy and water through the city using a range of economic, social and technological approaches to facilitate resource-saving action (Guy and Marvin, 1996b). These demand-oriented styles of network management do not necessarily rely on the construction of new buildings or the manipulation of landuses. Utilities can have powerful commercial and economic reasons for reshaping resource use within existing buildings on stressed parts of their networks (Marvin and Guy, 1997). While we recognise that the design and layout of buildings can have important implications for shaping infrastructure resource use (Guy, 1998), the very small level of new build means that we have to look at a much wider range of resource-saving strategies to reshape resource use in the existing rather than simply examining new configurations of urban form. Consequently, we need to develop an enlarged conception of the styles of sustainable urban management that can shape resource flows along existing infrastructure networks without solely relying on the re-ordering of the physical fabric of the city (Guy and Marvin, 1998).

In our work we have found Graham Haughton's work on models of sustainable urban development very useful in thinking through the connections between competing visions of the type of sustainable city that would support different styles of infrastructure management (Haughton, 1997). Each model represents a competing strategy through which urban form and functions are reconstituted to avoid or range environmental implications of resource use in the city. Figures 24.1–24.3 attempt to characterise the main elements of each model in diagrammatic form in relation to the water and sewage network.[1] What each model attempts to do is to link resource use in the city to its wider zone or 'sphere of influence'. Each model then examines how the extent and scope of the zone of influence could be reshaped through different styles of sustainability.

The Re-Designing Cities (RDC) model is based on the objective of 'planning for compact and energy efficient city regions' (Haughton, 1997, p. 191). Policies are designed to develop a city with a 'lowered urban metabolism' by reducing excessive resource flows and waste generation. The focus is within the city itself with little attempt to define or reduce the regional boundaries from which the city derives resources. The prime focus is on the development of a plan to re-design urban form and structure to reshape resource flows and human behaviour. These shifts link strongly to the strategic shift to higher densities in order to facilitate lower use of energy and other resources. In this sense the model clearly echoes many of the

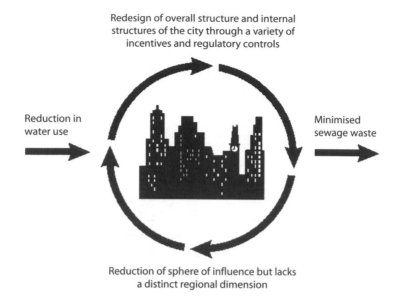

Redesign of overall structure and internal
structures of the city through a variety of
incentives and regulatory controls

Reduction in
water use

Minimised
sewage waste

Reduction of sphere of influence but lacks
a distinct regional dimension

Figure 24.1 Redesigning cities model

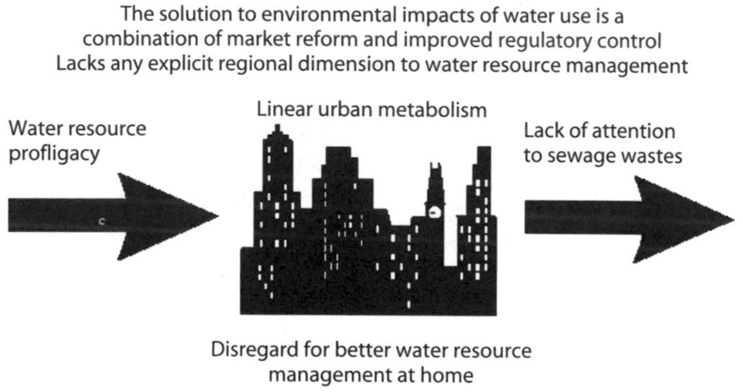

The solution to environmental impacts of water use is a
combination of market reform and improved regulatory control
Lacks any explicit regional dimension to water resource management

Linear urban metabolism

Water resource
profligacy

Lack of attention
to sewage wastes

Disregard for better water resource
management at home

Figure 24.2 Externally dependent city model

central assumptions embodied within the compact city debate. Haughton, however, develops other models of the sustainable city not simply based on the manipulation of urban form and densities.

A second model is the Externally Dependent City (EDC) based on the 'excessive externalisation of environmental costs, open systems, linear metabolism, and buying in additional "carrying capacity"' (Haughton, 1997: 192). This model

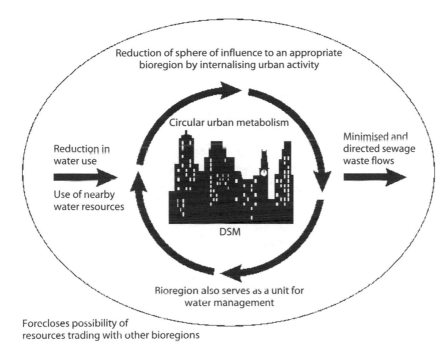

Reduction of sphere of influence to an appropriate bioregion by internalising urban activity

Circular urban metabolism

Reduction in water use

Use of nearby water resources

Minimised and directed sewage waste flows

DSM

Bioregion also serves as a unit for water management

Forecloses possibility of resources trading with other bioregions

Figure 24.3 Self-reliant city model

conceives the city as a node extracting resources from an increasing hinterland for urban consumption with little attention to the level of quality of wastes produced by the city. The metaphor for the city is of a 'linear urban metabolism' with a very open urban system that is resource profligate and ignores the benefits of more effective resource management. Instead resource managers invest in infrastructure supply tapping resources in hinterlands drawing them into the city, consuming resources and depositing wastes in the hinterland. In this context sustainable resource management would focus on more efficient market-pricing mechanisms that would internalise the costs of environmental damage. Rather than attempting to reduce the urban sphere of influence the objective would be to reshape it through market signals and cost compensation.

A third model is the Self-Reliant City (SRC) based on 'intensive internalisation of economic and environmental activities, circular metabolism, bio-regionalism and urban autarky' (Haughton, 1997, p. 190). This model takes as its starting point the objective of reducing the pattern of external dependence on resource use to restrict the urban sphere of influence. Central to this is the development of a 'circular urban metabolism' whereby the inputs of resources and outputs of waste are more closely linked. The sphere of influence is reduced to an appropriate bio-region within which resource flows, consumption and waste flows can be minimised and managed. This would place particular emphasis on use of small-scale technologies, recycling and demand management. Linked to this is a different type of social organisation which shifts from economic or technocratic styles of decision-making towards more localised and community-based forms of decision-making. The assumption being that users would need to be closely involved in a transition from centralised to decentralised technologies.

This shift from a singular to multiple model of the sustainable city is useful in a number of key respects. It helps shift the debate away from a relatively limited debate about the effectiveness of a policy based on physical reshaping of the form of the city to achieve compactness to a much enlarged range of policy options. We can start to develop an understanding that there may be alternative policy options not simply based on urban redesign but that could also contribute to the creation of sustainable cities. Acknowledging that there are multiple models, and there are likely to be more than those listed above, starts to present a more subtle and complex understanding of what the sustainable city might become. However, we need to be extremely careful to say precisely what work these models can and cannot do.

FROM MODELS TO COMPETING PATHWAYS

Transcending the constraints of models

At this stage it is important that we are clear about how these models should be used. First, it would be a mistake to employ these models as blueprints to implement within the context of the existing city. It is difficult to justify the claim that one model is any more or less sustainable than another. At the same time it would clearly be a mistake to view the models as representing sequential stages of development leading to a more sustainable city. Haughton is similarly drawn to the view that 'each model has its own value' and that 'the models lose value only when they inadvertently set in place professional and political blinkers that prevent consideration of a wider range of policy approaches' (Haughton, 1997, p. 194). Secondly, the models are not clearly connected to social processes and interests. Simply using them as end points does not adequately reflect the social, economic and technical complexity involved in re-ordering the city along the pathways implied within each model. Thirdly, although one model – RDC – is the most clearly based on physical changes this does not mean that other models exclude design policies. For instance, research could examine how pricing, regulatory and technological shifts envisaged in the other models could translate into different types of design and layout. Although the models are not explicitly attempting to define the precise form of the city, each model does provide a quite different social, economic and technological context within which landuse and buildings would be planned and managed.

Haughton's response to these issues is to construct a fourth model, entitled the 'Fair Share Cities' (FSC), which 'integrates the better aspects of the other three models, allied with greater concern for social justice and geographical equity concerns, provides one possible amalgam of approaches' (Haughton, 1997, p. 194). We, however, want to suggest a slightly different way of using the models that escapes seeing them as blueprints and therefore avoids the need for searching for the definitive model of sustainable urban development.

The emergence of pathways: Towards sustainable urban futures . . .

Rather than search for an ideal model we argue for the need to recognise that competing models represent multiple pathways towards a sustainable city. In this sense, the achievement of sustainable cities is a process and not the result of implementing a particular model. We argue that pathways do not exist as ideal types but are contested in particular local contexts as competing social actors grapple with the concept of sustainable development and its relation to wider practices of urban development. Here we are asking the models to do a bit more work that perhaps was originally intended in their formulation. We suggest the models are used as heuristic devices, or conceptual windows, through which we can map the contrasting visions of the sustainable city. We are not suggesting that the models should be applied in practice, that they represent the range of sustainable cities that might exist, or that they are mutually exclusive. Instead we argue their real analytical power is to act as a filter or lens through which we can start to see what the sustainable city might look like.[2]

In our own work on infrastructure provision we have attempted to develop an understanding of the emergence of new styles of sustainable infrastructure provision (Guy and Marvin, 1998). Within the context of comparative work on the shifts in infrastructure provision across energy, water, waste networks in Newcastle, Copenhagen, Berlin and the Greek island of Kos, we developed a research methodology that allowed us to understand the changing social organisation of infrastructure provision, the complex signals sent to infrastructure providers, the story lines and coalitions around sustainability, and the viewpoints that social actors developed (Guy et al., 2001). This process allowed us to link an understanding of what the sustainable city might become with particular pathways of development.

Figures 24.4 and 24.5 provide a diagrammatic representation of the application of this research methodology in the energy and water sectors of Newcastle. First, we focused on two key issues that have been closely linked to the sustainability agenda – energy efficiency and the issue of water transfers between Yorkshire and the North East. These were two of the most significant, but not only, sustainability issues being debated in the infrastructure sector when the fieldwork was

Energy efficiency (end-users)

Actors				
Central Government/ Regulators	National Power/ Northern Electric	Newcastle City Council	Environmental groups	Fuel poverty groups

Story lines and coalitions		
Need to use energy more efficiently		
Reliance on market forces	Stronger regulation and financial incentives to promote local initiatives	Focus on special needs of low-income groups
	inter-regional equity	eco-centrism

Models			
Externally dependent cities	(Fair shares cities)	Self-reliant cities	(Redesigned cities) (Self-reliant cities)

Figure 24.4 Views of energy efficiency in the north-east region

Water transfer

Actors			
Water companies (Lyonnaise des Eaux)	Economic regulators (DGWS and OFWAT)	Environmental regulators (EA)	Environmental groups (e.g. FoE)

Story lines and coalitions		
Realisation of water surplus in Newcastle and water deficit in Yorkshire		
Perceive no physical problem in transfer	Environmental implications	Against scheme
Compensation for water companies	Compensation for customers	Compensation for environmental improvements

Models		
Externally dependent city	Fair share city	Self-reliant city

Figure 24.5 Water transfer between the north-west and Yorkshire regions: competing views

undertaken. Secondly, we mapped the organisation of the social interests involved in each infrastructure sector – infrastructure managers, regulators and local government. In particular we paid special attention to the interactions between them and how they attempt to shape each other using a range of modes of interaction. Thirdly, we then traced the competing viewpoints emerging in debates around the sustainability issues. In particular we explored the interpretative flexibility of each issue in terms of the contrasting conceptualisations of both the problem and different types of response. Finally we linked actors' viewpoints to different models of the sustainable city. Here, we were particularly interested in how the models resonate and collide with actors' viewpoints to build a better understanding of the competing pathways towards a sustainable city. Boxes 24.1 and 24.2 provide short vignettes or case studies of the application of this research methodology.

BOX 24.1

Energy efficiency in Newcastle

The key environmental issue in the energy sector in Newcastle has been improving the efficiency of energy use within the city. But a number of competing pathways to sustainable energy efficiency and conservation measures can be identified. Figure 24.4 shows that a coalition of interest between the economic regulators and the energy providers argue that a competitive market in electricity supply will provide economic signals for energy conservation and efficiency measures. This pathway resonates strongly with the Externally Dependent City model with its focus on open markets and regulatory reform to improve the efficiency of local energy use. In contrast locally based actors are demanding more effective regulatory signals and financial support from central government and regulators to stimulate programmes of energy savings at the *local level*. The local authority, local environmental and fuel poverty groups all stress the longer-term environmental and social benefits of energy efficiency. Within these viewpoints there are strong resonances with the Self-Reliant Cities model as they seek to reduce the cities' sphere of influence not only through energy conservation measures but also including local energy production from photovoltaics and combined heat and power. However, within these local interests there are differences between these viewpoints with environmental groups arguing most strongly for Self-Reliance while in contrast fuel poverty groups argue for physical measures (building design and refurbishment) to reduce heat loss of low-income households – strongly echoing the urban Re-Designing model. An analysis of policy documents produced by the local authority produces a vision of an urban future that combines elements from all the three models – echoing one locally contingent form of the Fair Shares City model proposed by Haughton.

BOX 24.2

Water transfer between Yorkshire and the North East

The second case study focuses on competing views of the solution to the water shortage in Yorkshire between 1996 and 1997. All actors agreed that there was a problem with water shortage in Yorkshire but each had very different views about how the problem should be solved. The debate resolved around the evaluation of a water transfer scheme involving the construction of a pipe system for moving water between the resource surplus North East and dry Yorkshire to ensure security of supply. First, there was a high degree of overlap between the positions of the water companies and regulators who argued that the scheme should be constructed providing the water company and users in the North East were adequately compensated for the transfer. This position resonated strongly with the Externally Dependent Cities model with both actors viewing water as a commodity which can be traded between regions. Secondly, the Environment Agency were concerned to reduce the urban and regional sphere of influence through demand management options. Before considering supply augmentation the EA were concerned that water suppliers should exhaust demand management options – a position resonating strongly with the Self-Reliant and Re-Designing City models. However the EA recognised that in some circumstances water trading may be necessary and indeed desirable for consumers in Yorkshire but they argue that must take place in the least ecologically disruptive way. Therefore the EA argued for financial compensation from the scheme to speed environmental Improvements within the water and sewerage networks of the North East. In this sense the EA models appear to lean more closely towards the Fair Shares City with a form of autarky within limits rather than total autonomy. Finally, environmental groups were much more critical of the water transfer scheme and promoted options based on greater autonomy for the Yorkshire region. They proposed a range of social and technical options more closely linked to the Self-Reliant and Re-Designed City models to lower demand for water and reduce the urban sphere of influence without the need for water transfers.

Reaching closure?

Both case studies illustrate the wide diversity and contested understanding of what the sustainable city might become. There are a number of important points to make here. First, for a particular sustainability issue there are likely to be different strategies that co-exist together supported by particular coalitions of actors. The pathways resonate quite strongly with the different elements of the models proposed by Haughton. In this sense the models provide us with an understanding of what different types of sustainable city might look like particularly in terms of their connections with technologies, users and the management of place. They are not necessarily options or choices that can be selected from a menu – instead they provide a way of orienting our thinking about the potential for different types of sustainable city in particular local contexts. We need to develop an understanding of how the different notions of the sustainable city collide or resonate with one another. Secondly, the debate about the type of sustainable city that might be created can vary across different issues. In the case of energy efficiency, closure has not been reached around one particular option as a number of different pathways continue to co-exist together with relatively little interaction between them. But in the case of the water transfer, closure has been reached around the construction of the water transfer model. Yet even in this context with the Externally Dependent City as the dominant model other models still co-exist because the Environment Agency has also strengthened Yorkshire Waters demand management requirements simultaneously creating the potential for a more Self-Reliant Yorkshire. While multiple pathways towards sustainability can evidently co-exist alongside one another we still need a better understanding of how some pathways become more dominant than others. Finally, we need to problematise the notion of the Fair shares model. Again this does not exist as an independent construct of what a city might become – instead we should see it as relational, constructed out of a number of intersecting pathways towards sustainability. What is 'fair shares' in one context may not be in another. We need comparative research focusing on how pathways are constructed, how they can become dominant and marginalised, what interactions take place between them and how closure is reached around a particular solution.

MULTIPLE URBAN FUTURES

This chapter questions the use of a singular model to guide the achievement of sustainable cities. Instead, our research suggests that models should be used as heuristic windows through which we can identify how policy, regulatory and commercial strategies mesh or clash with the rather more messy world of urban development practices. We have not developed an argument for the rejection, acceptance or promotion of a particular model but argue that researchers and policy-makers employ them as conceptual devices for developing a more sensitive and richer understanding of the possible pathways towards the sustainable city. As ideal types they provide a lens through which we can begin to examine how different social interests involved in infrastructure provision envision the social, technical, institutional and spatial re-ordering of the city.

Critically, in our own research we did not start with the models. Instead we reviewed how different sets of social interests created quite different visions of how infrastructure can be restructured socially and technically. As we have seen these different forms of configuration tend to echo in varying degree the types of cities expressed in Graham Haughton's models. In this sense the model's power is not in their prescriptive vision, but in the ways in which we can link different social interests to views of the future sustainable city. But relatively little work has been undertaken that connects models of sustainability to the complexity of the social world within which infrastructure and other urban managers operate. In particular, we have shown how changing strategies of infrastructure management are quite clearly shaped by different ways of seeing the problem and the solution, and to competing visions of the future city. Models therefore need to be more closely related to the specific social organisation of infrastructure in a city, and more particularly to highlight how opportunities for environmental innovation link to the changing contexts of urban development. In this way models could help research and policy to more carefully trace the social interests linked to particular visions of the urban futures and the connections between competing viewpoints.

Used in this way the models can help us to understand the contested nature of shifts towards a sustainable urban future. Critical here is the recognition that there is not a singular future, vision or model, but rather many different futures that may coexist, supported by different sets of social interests. Here our approach differs slightly from Graham Haughton. Rather than attempt to combine the best elements of different models into an alternative vision or model based on a particular type of assessment of the optimum combination of strategies such as the Fair Shares City, we would argue for the need to identify how different social interests may connect to particular visions of the sustainable city. For instance our empirical findings have shown that particular social coalitions can emerge around a single vision. In other cases different sets of actors have quite different ideas about the type of city they are trying to create.

The central challenge for researchers is to more sensitively use models of sustainable cities as ideal types through which we can start to map the social and technical possibilities for different types of urban futures in specific cities. Rather than searching for a static notion of sustainable urban form we need to start identifying the complex pathways towards quite different urban futures that may all claim to be sustainable. We need to examine the social assumptions and biases built into different pathways, examine the resonances and dissonances between different pathways, review the relative dominance and weakness of different pathways and develop the potential for forging new coalitions of interest around particular development pathways. This agenda represents a significant challenge to a research and policy agenda that still seems to be searching for a singular definition of the sustainable city.

CONCLUSIONS

In highlighting the contested nature of debates around sustainable cities, our analysis raises significant questions about the positivistic scientific assumption underpinning the search for a consensual definition or model of sustainability. We suggest that environmental debates constitute sites of conflicting interpretations through which an often complex set of actors participate in a continuous process of defining and redefining the nature of the environmental problem itself. Debates about sustainable cities are shaped by different social interests, based on different interpretations of the problem and characterised by quite different pathways towards a range of sustainable futures. These competing environmental debates are the result, not of uncertainty, but are due to the existence of '*contradictory certainties:* Severely divergent and mutually irreconcilable sets of convictions both about the environmental problems we face and the solutions that are available to us' (Hannigan, 1995). The analytical framework of social constructivist theory developed here usefully demonstrates the contingent and contextual nature of technological innovation and building design. It further highlights arguably the most fundamental issue, understandably marginalised in the debate about consensus, that the environment is a contested terrain, and that implicit within alternative technological strategies are distinct philosophies of environmental place-making (Guy and Marvin, 1999). As we saw with Haughton's models, even the boundaries of the city-region are prefigured by the particular environmental problem presented. Seen this way, environmental concerns are both time- and space-specific and are governed by a specific modelling of nature. This same 'logic' can be applied to technology and to sustainable cities. In other words there is 'interpretative flexibility' attached to any artefact: it might be designed in another way (Moore, 1997, p. 25). This perspective points towards a multidirectional analytical model which recognises how certain technological development pathways fade away, while others are 'economically reinforced as members of a society come to share a set of meanings or benefits' attached to it (ibid).

Adopting a social constructivist perspective has critical implications for environmental practice, education and research. Rather than searching for a singular optimal technological pathway it is vital that we learn to recognise and listen to the number of voices striving to frame the debate, and the visions they express of alternative environmental places. The search for consensus that has hitherto characterised sustainable design and policy-making should be translated into the search for an enlarged context in which a more heterogeneous coalition of practices can be developed. In this sense, rather than viewing sustainable design practice as the 'implementation of a plan for action, it should be viewed as an on-going transformational process in which different actor interests and struggles are located' (Long and Long, 1992, p. 9).

In an educational context, there is an opportunity to encourage greater reflectivity in environmental students by challenging the search for a true or incontestable, consensual definition of green spaces. If the future direction and success of sustainable cities' strategies relies on the abilities of urban professionals to act as moral citizens, by engaging in an open process of negotiation, criticism and debate, then it is vital that students are encouraged to become more sensitive to the range of possible logics of innovation which may surface in design practice. This means searching for critical methods for understanding technological innovation that transcend both instrumental and deterministic interpretations and which can begin to open 'the discourse of technology to future designers in the hopes of engendering a more humane and multivocal world' (Allen, 1997, p. 2). Here, multiple opinions and perspectives are not only valid but highly desirable. Further, once a diversity of possible approaches have been exposed 'they might lead to a more reflective attitude towards certain environmental constructs and perhaps even the formulation of alternative scenarios' (Hajer, 1995, p. 258).

Finally, we cannot ignore the ways in which particular logics of environmental innovation take root in commercial development practices. This means accepting that the greening of cities is dependant on the contingent and dynamic strategies of those development actors, such as the privatised utilities, with the power to implement their chosen strategy (Guy et al., 1997). Social constructivist analysis could make an important contribution here through its ability to demonstrate how the power relations amongst competing development interests frame technological decision-making and subsequent design strategies. An analysis of the changing power relationships structuring this process suggests an important future direction in research (Guy, 1998). Such research may help to identify those societal actors with most influence over decision-making and enable practitioners and students to recognise their own position and role in the provision of more sustainable lifestyles. However, this may only be possible if, according to Hajer, 'ecological politics could shed its prevailing techno-corporatist format and create open structures to determine what sort of nature and society we really want' (Hajer, 1995, p. 294). In recognising the socially contested nature of environmental design, we might begin to engage in a very different dialogue about sustainable cities.

NOTES

1   We have had to simplify some of the complexity of Haughton's models and it is important to read the original paper.

2   While the models were originally intended to help develop an understanding of water flows through the city, the later write-up widened the remit to cover resource flows through the city. We are particularly interested in their application to infrastructure flows, widening the scope from water to other forms of infrastructure such as energy and waste.

REFERENCES

Allen, B.L. (1997) 'Rethinking Architectural Technology: History, Theory, and Practice', *Journal of Architectural Education*, 51(1): 2–4.

Breheny, M. (1996) 'Centerists, Decenterists and Compromisers: Views on the Future of Urban Form'. In Jenks, M., Burton, K. and Williams, K. (eds), *The Compact City: A Sustainable Urban Form?* Oxford: E&FN Spon, pp. 13–35.

Fulford, C. (1996) 'The Compact City and the Market: The Case of Residential Development'. In Jenks, M., Burton, K. and Williams, K. (eds), *The Compact City: A Sustainable Urban Form?* Oxford: E&FN Spon, pp. 122–133.

Guy, S. (1998) 'Developing Alternatives: Energy, Offices and the Environment', *International Journal of Urban and Regional Research*, 22(2): 264–282.

Guy, S. and Marvin, S. (1996a) 'Disconnected Policy: The Shaping of Local Energy Management', *Environment and Planning (C): Government and Policy*, 14(1): 145–158.

Guy, S. and Marvin, S. (1996b) 'Managing Water Stress: The Logic of Demand Side Infrastructure Planning', *Journal of Environmental Planning and Management*, 39(1): 125–131.

Guy, S. and Marvin, S. (1998) 'Electricity in the Marketplace: Reconfiguring the Consumption of Essential Resources', *Local Environment*, 3(3): 313–331.

Guy, S. and Marvin, S. (1999) 'Understanding Sustainable Cities: Competing Urban Futures', *European Urban and Regional Studies*, 6(3): 268–275.

Guy, S., Graham, S. and Marvin, S. (1997) 'Splintering Networks: Cities and Technical Networks in 1990's Britain', *Urban Studies*, February, 34(2): 191–216.

Guy, S., Marvin, S. and Moss, T. (2001) *Urban Infrastructure in Transition: Networks, Buildings, Plans*, London: Earthscan.

Hajer, M. (1995) *The Politics of Environmental Discourse*, Oxford: Oxford University Press.

Hannigan, J. (1995) *Environmental Sociology: A Social Constructivist Perspective*, London: Routledge.

Haughton, G. (1997) 'Developing Sustainable Urban Development Models', *Cities*, 14(4): 189–195.

Jenks, M., Burton, K. and Williams, K. (eds) (1996) *The Compact City: A Sustainable Urban Form?* Oxford: E&FN Spon.

Long, N. and Long, A. (1992) *Battlefields of Knowledge: The Interlocking of Theory and Practice in Social Research and Development*, London: Routledge, p. 9.

Marvin, S. and Guy, S. (1997) 'Infrastructure Provision, Development Processes and the Co-Production of Environmental Value', *Urban Studies*, 34(12): 2023–2036.

Moore, S.A. (1997) 'Technology and the Politics of Sustainability at Blueprint Demonstration Farm', *Journal of Architectural Education*, 51(1): 23–31.

Symth, H. (1996) 'Running the Gauntlet: A Compact City Within a Doughnut of Decay'. In Jenks, M., Burton, E. and Williams, K. (eds), *The Compact City: A Sustainable Urban Form?* Oxford: E&FN Spon.

Thomas, L. and Cousins, W. (1996) 'A New Compact City Form: Concepts in Practice'. In Jenks, M., Burton, K. and Williams, K. (eds), *The Compact City: A Sustainable Urban Form?* Oxford: E&FN Spon, pp. 328–338.

25

Conclusions
Mark Deakin, Gordon Mitchell, Peter Nijkamp and Ron Vreeker

Volume 1 of this book series outlined the principles, underlying concepts, models, vision and methodology of an integrated SUD (Curwell *et al.*, 2005). This drew attention to the framework BEQUEST has developed for gaining such an understanding of SUD and went on to set out the protocol(s) the network argued should be followed in carrying out an environmental assessment. Volume 1 then went on to set out the 'soft' and 'hard' gates of environmental assessment and develop the five (planning, property development, design, construction, operation and use) protocols for evaluating the sustainability of urban development. Having done this, it outlined the directory of environmental assessment methods available for such purposes and reported on how they are currently being used to evaluate the sustainability of urban development.

What this did not do, however, is provide a detailed examination of the environmental assessment methods, or how they are being used by the diverse range of stakeholders with interests in evaluating SUD. For while the examination drew attention to the legal instruments of environmental assessment and tense relationship emerging between the 'hard' certainties of the bio-physical sciences and the more uncertain and risky sphere of economic and social relations, it did not provide a detailed account of how the environmental assessment methods are being used. This has been the object of Volume 2 in this series on *Sustainable Urban Development*.

Volume 2 of this series on SUD has taken the BEQUEST framework and protocols as its point of departure and brought together a number of contributions from recognised experts in environmental assessment, many of them leading authorities in how the methods should be used. Part 1 has set out the statutory instruments put in place by the European Commission (EC) to assess the environmental impact of development proposals. It has sought to examine the development and use of SEA (strategic environmental assessment) and EIA (environmental impact assessment) to evaluate the sustainability of development programmes. Part 2 used these statutory instruments of environmental assessment as a platform to examine the systems thinking lying behind the methods, how their approach meets the challenge sustainable development poses and the role evaluation plays in this. Using this examination as a stage to account for further developments in environmental assessment,

Part 3 has set out the methods that can be used to evaluate the sustainability of urban development. This section provides an account of recent developments in the use of cost–benefit analysis (CBA), Multi-criteria analysis (MCA), Contingent Valuation Method (CVM) and the hedonic price method as environmental assessment methods. Part 4 examined the assessment methods that have emerged to meet the challenge SUD poses. Here, attention was drawn to the assessment methods that have recently developed in response to the call for environmental, economic and social evaluations of SUD.

Parts 3 and 4 have been taken from BEQUEST's survey of the environmental assessment methods currently available for evaluating SUD. The survey identified that 60 assessment methods are currently available to evaluate the sustainability of urban development. It also identified the said methods have been applied to the planning, property development, design, construction, operational and use activities of urban development and used to analyse the sustainability issues this raises at various scales of assessment. The list of methods were drawn from a survey of the scientific literature and unpublished technical reports, written by professional members of the community. The master list provides a survey of the methods that it is possible to select and deploy in Europe, North America and Canada and case-study reviews of how the assessment methods have been applied to evaluate the sustainability of urban development. Part 5 took the matter of SUD full circle. This was achieved by assessing the ecological integrity, equity and participation of the public in decisions taken about the futurity of urban development and on matters surrounding the sustainability of cities.

THE CO-EVOLUTIONARY APPROACH

The assessment methodology Volume 2 has adopted to cope with the uncertainty and risk related to the environment provides a new set of standards. Referred to as a 'co-evolutionary approach' to environmental assessment, this methodology manages to overcome the limitations of the past and focus attention on the so-called 'hard' certainties of the bio-physical science underlying the more uncertain, risky and 'softer' social relations of SUD. Set within the BEQUEST framework and protocols, Volume 2 provides a detailed account of the environmental assessment methods key to this transformation and examination of how those listed in the post-Bruntdland directory are currently being used to evaluate the sustainability of urban development. This has provided an account of the environmental assessment methods key in building the environmental capacity needed to qualify the ecological integrity of urban development and provide the techniques of analysis required to evaluate whether this brings about an equitable distribution of resources. Evaluate whether the ecological integrity of urban development brings about an equitable distribution of resources. An equitable distribution of resources in the sense which this distribution of resources is based on the participation of the public in decisions taken about the economic and social futures of cities.

This framework, set of protocols and assessment methods have gone a long way in enriching our understanding of SUD. Together they have provided the opportunity to both deepen and broaden our understanding of the subject. For while they take the statutory instruments of environmental assessment as the starting point, the framework and protocols have provided the opportunity to outline the systems-thinking underpinning this assessment methodology and draw particular attention to the multi-modal, human and cosmonomic complexity of the models underlying the evaluation of SUD. These contributions have served to underpin the principles set out in Volume 1 and are referred to as the four-dimensional model of SUD. The dimensions referred to in this volume as the ecological integrity and equity of resource distribution. The ecological integrity and equity of resource distribution represented here as the outcome of public participation in matters concerning the economic and social future of cities. The value of these principles rests with the standards of assessment they provide. The standard classes, types and scales of assessment these evaluations of urban development in turn provide as an index of sustainable cities.

ENVIRONMENTAL VALUATIONS

The three contributions on environmental valuations making up Part 3 have shown how it is possible to apply these standards. The chapters on CBA, MCA, contingent valuation and hedonic pricing illustrate how it is possible to evaluate the sustainability of urban development and show this in terms of urban green spaces and Dutch wetlands.

ENVIRONMENTAL, ECONOMIC AND SOCIAL ASSESSMENTS

The MCA basis of these evaluations have in turn been complemented with case studies on how to apply the spider, flag and regime analysis to assess the environmental, economic and social sustainability of urban developments relating to the green spaces and mixed land uses of European cities.

While the environmental, economic and social assessments have tended to focus on sectors of land use in the urban development process, many of them take this to offer evaluations of a city-wide landscape. The logic of this has been given extra weight in the case studies appearing in Part 4 of the volume. For here it is not so much the horizontal logic of the simple, complex, advanced and very advanced methods that have been developed, but the scale of the environmental, economic and social assessments which this calls for. Here the somewhat open-ended and ill-defined relationship between the development of urban land use and city-wide landscapes has been brought into sharp focus. The assessments here have been of urban green, mixed, multi-functional and compact urban developments, utility provision and transport services at the land use, building, estate, neighbourhood, district and city scales. Case-study examples of such assessments have been presented at each scale of SUD.

HIGHLY INTEGRATIVE AND MULTI-SCALAR ASSESSMENTS

The highly integrative and multi-scalar nature of these assessments are seen as of particular value because they highlight the significance of the BEQUEST framework in capturing the sustainability issues and representing them as matters of particular concern to the quality of life. They also expose the value of the protocols in dealing with the hard and soft issues of SUD. For while in Volume 1 the hard gates of the protocols were represented in statutory terms and therefore as rules of law – e.g. as the requirement of SEA and EIAs, Volume 2 has provided the opportunity to develop a harder edge to the bio-physical, economic and social science underlying the urban land-use planning, property development, design and construction of buildings. The buildings that make up the estates, neighbourhoods, districts of cities and whose environmental assessment methods support the rule of law. The rule of law that post-Brundtland has been brought into question because of the way buildings, estates and districts have tended to threaten ecological integrity and produce an inequitable distribution of resources. An inequitable distribution of resources that has been met with a call from the public for the development of environmental assessment methods able to restore ecological equity and produce a more equitable distribution of resources. An integrity and equity that is based on inclusive decision-making and which gives the public the power – entitlement, statutory right and opportunity – under the rule of law, to participate in matters concerning the future of urban development and surrounding the environmental, economic and social sustainability of cities.

In this way land use becomes the base standard for evaluating SUD. The base standard for building the environmental capacity – stock, transport, safety, security, health and well-being that are needed for cities to sustain a quality of life. The built stock, transport, safety, security, health and well-being that are needed for cities to institute a quality of life in the districts, neighbourhoods, estates and buildings which this process of urban development advances as sustainable communities.

The highly integrative and multi-scalar nature of these evaluations is considerable, for not only do they offer the opportunity to link sustainability issues to quality of life, but to be systematic, principled and disciplined about how these connections are made and related back to the statutory instruments of environmental assessment and stakeholders (planners, property developers, designers and contractors) responsible for such evaluations. This is useful not just for assessing how the environment impacts upon the quality of life, but for qualifying SUD in terms of the environmental, economic and social values this institutes. In this way it becomes possible to capture the complexity of the situation under examination, along with the critical nature of the sustainability issues being considered.

The wide range of methods that exist for the assessment of SUD can be divided into five types represented in terms of the complexity and completeness of the overall evaluation they provide. These being:

1 Environmental valuations to assess the sustainability (in this instance, ecological integrity) of urban development.

2 Simple base-line or benchmarking methods to assess the environmental, economic and social issues underlying the policy commitment to SUD.

3 More complex methods to assess whether the planning, property development programmes, design and construction of infrastructure projects (servicing energy, water and drainage, and transport) provide the environmental capacity (in this instance ecological integrity and equity) that is needed for urban development to carry the economic and social future of cities.

4 Advanced methods that assess the contribution of the construction sector to SUD. In particular how construction projects and installations − e.g. energy systems, waste management provisions, repair and maintenance technologies − operate and what effect they have upon the environmental sustainability of cities. This includes an assessment of whether they have levels of energy consumption and emissions that have an adverse effect, or an impact which is more environmentally friendly. Have an impact that is more environmentally friendly in the sense which the construction and operation of such installations augments, rather than diminishes, the environmental capacity (ecological integrity and equity) urban development has to carry the economic and social future of cities.

5 Very advanced models that assess the ecological integrity and equity of the alternative developments which it is possible for the public to participate in selecting as preferred options. The alternatives that it is possible for the public to participate in selecting and choose as those designs, constructions and operations which augment, rather than diminish, the environmental capacity of urban development to carry the economic and social future of cities.

THE TYPOLOGY OF ENVIRONMENTAL ASSESSMENT

Accepting this typology of environmental assessment, it then becomes possible to work out whether the evaluation is of SUD at the land use, building, estate, neighbourhood, district or city scale. The BEQUEST framework, protocols and directory of environmental assessment methods set out in Volume 1 provide the platform for this. The statutory instruments and systems-thinking underlying the assessment methods set out in Volume 2 provide well-principled, disciplined and firmly grounded case studies demonstrating how it is possible do this. Together the case studies illustrate the extent of the response from the assessment community to the public's call for SUD following publication of the Brundtland report and the Rio Earth Summit's statement on Agenda 21. The response that many of the contributions set out in this volume go a long way to demonstrate and are notable for the reason they have brought forward a number of significant methodological developments. The last decade has indeed been marked by a period of intense innovation and creativity in the development of environmental assessment methods, culminating in the vision and methodology of an highly integrated and increasingly multi-scalar SUD.

While it is noticeable the framework and protocols of this vision and methodology are based on the four-sided model of SUD (Symes *et al.*, 2005), it is also evident this is not explicitly multi-model, humanistic or cosmonomic in nature and, therefore, necessarily based on the type of systems-thinking recently set out by Brandon and Lombardi (2005). The systems-thinking of this multi-model, humanistic or cosmonomic model is a matter that has recently been examined by Deakin (2005) and Pearce (2005), raising questions about the nature of these modalities and exact purpose they serve. For Brandon and Lombardi (2005) the multi-modal model provides the opportunity to capture the high ground of systems-based thinking and apply the cosmology of this environmental assessment methodology to the land use of cities. While these high-level developments are most welcome, it should be noted that it has not been the object of BEQUEST's vision and methodology to tackle the 'philosophical' underpinnings of SUD.

BEQUEST's framework and vision does not attempt to take the high ground on such matters. What BEQUEST provides is a framework – a way of framing the issues and working with them – to try and make sense of SUD as a discourse on the protocols of environmental assessment. The territory it seeks to target, stake out and occupy is the middle ground between the 'high-level' issues and those found at the 'grass roots' level, where 'what it all means' gets 'bottomed out' as part of the emerging discourse on environmental assessment methods and represented as basic values (e.g. ecological integrity and equity) supporting the 'low-level' actions (urban planning, property development, design and construction, operation and use activities) promoted to deliver SUD.

This way SUD does not start with the cosmology of a given philosophical position, but a discourse on the ontology of the science and technology underlying the protocols supporting the evaluation of SUD. If we choose to approach the matter in this way, it subsequently becomes possible to run vertically, digging deep into the planning of the city's landscapes and use this as the basis to move horizontally, developing a platform of assessment methods for a much more extensive and far-reaching evaluation of SUD. The outcome of this is the development of an assessment methodology which manages to build bridges between the classes and the types and scales of evaluations that have previously been divided along the lines of: use and exchange value, singular and multi-criteria, cardinal and ordinal, deterministic and probabilistic, expert and lay, environmental and economic, cultural and social.

The kinds of divisions that have only served to frustrate the development of environmental valuations and undermine their transformation into environmental, economic and social assessments. Assessments capable of building the environ- mental capacity needed to qualify the ecological integrity of urban development and provide the techniques of analysis required to evaluate whether this brings about an equitable distribution of resources. An equitable distribution of resources that is the outcome of public participation, based on inclusive decisions which are taken about the economic and social future of cities. All of this captured in terms of the capacity which environmental assessment methods have to help stakeholders (plan- ners, property developers, architects and contractors) build the stock, transport, safety, security, health and well-being that is needed for cities to sustain a quality of life. The built stock, transport, safety, security, health and well-being that are needed for cities to institute a quality of life in the districts, neighbourhoods, estates and buildings which this process of urban development advances as sustainable communities.

While the aforesaid marks a significant achievement setting out the step- wise logic of a highly integrative and multi-scalar environmental assessment, it is also evident that most of the methods still fail to address the institutional issues which underlie the evaluation of SUD. This is because in their current form, the methods find it difficult to address issues relating to the governance, morality and ethics of SUD and while the reasons for this are not currently known, it may be because most attention has been focused on environmental, economic and social issues and this has resulted in relative under-development of the institutional considerations.

So it appears that if the assessment methods are to provide a fully comprehensive account of the evaluations, the governance, morality and ethics of urban development, shall also need to be integrated and scaled into assessments concerning the sustainability of cities. This is important because without an evaluation of the institutional basis of SUD, it will not be possible to throw light on the collaboration, consensus-building, commitment and leadership issues surrounding the actions taken to augment environmental capacity. Those actions and augmentations that are not only needed to build environmental capacity in such a step-wise fashion, but also required because they provide a stage upon which to 'reach-high', 'up-the-anti' and meet the challenge the search for ecological integrity and equity poses. The ecological integrity and equity of concern to the public and lying behind the call from them for a greater, more extensive and higher level of participation in decisions taken about the economic and social future of cities. Greater in the sense such participation is not just limited to urban land-use planning, but extends into the property development, design, construction, operation and use of buildings. More extensive in the sense this is not confined to the use of urban land, but is 'scaled-up', using the step-wise logic of the planning, property development, design and construction stages, to extend into and include the buildings, estates, neighbourhoods and districts of cities. The 'scaled-up', 'step-wise logic' that in turn takes us to a higher stage of public participation and which is not confined to the environment, but reaches out to include decisions taken about the economic and social future of cities. This shall be the object of Volume 3 in this series on *Sustainable Urban Development*.

REFERENCES

Brandon, P. and Lombardi, P. (2005) *Evaluating Sustainable Development in the Built Environment*, Blackwell Press, Oxford.

Curwell, S., Deakin, M. and Symes, M. (eds) (2005) *Sustainable Urban Development: The Framework and Protocols for Environmental Assessment*, Routledge, Oxford.

Deakin, M. (2005) 'Evaluating Sustainable Development: Is a Philosophical Framework Enough?' *Building Research and Information*, 33(5): 476–480.

Pearce, D. (2005) 'Do We Understand Sustainable Development?' *Building Research and Information*, 33(5): 481–483.

Symes, M., Deakin, M. and Curwell, S. (2005) 'Introduction', in Curwell, S., Deakin, M. and Symes, M. (eds) *Sustainable Urban Development: The Framework and Protocols for Environmental Assessment*, Routledge, Oxford.

Index